"For expository preachers and teachers of the Bible, this is truly a gold mine. Present and past members of the Reformed Theological Seminary faculty have produced a volume that is long overdue. Sound biblical-theological treatments of each book of the Old Testament, linked with good historical and literary comments, all conclude by pointing to the fulfillment of the texts in the person and work of Jesus. With this volume, no preacher should ever feel that preaching Christ from the Old Testament is too hard or too speculative."

Graeme Goldsworthy, Former Lecturer in Old Testament, Biblical Theology, and Hermeneutics, Moore Theological College

"For many Christians, the Old Testament is like a thousand pieces of a jigsaw puzzle. Where do you start? It helps to look at the box top and see how it all fits together. That's what these superb teachers of the church do in this insightful book."

Michael Horton, J. Gresham Machen Professor of Systematic Theology and Apologetics, Westminster Seminary California; author, *Core Christianity: Finding Yourself in God's Story*

"In this volume, a number of capable biblical scholars faithfully explore the Old Testament writings with sensitivity and sensibility. They do an admirable job not simply in describing the main themes and theology of each book but also in artfully showing that the Old Testament has a covenantal framework, a kingdom perspective, and Christ at its center. In brief, this is a superb volume, which provides an understandable and informative overview of the Old Testament. A great antidote to an embarrassing ignorance of the Old Testament by Christians."

Michael F. Bird, Lecturer in Theology, Ridley College, Melbourne, Australia; author, *Evangelical Theology*

"The purpose of this work, 'to show how the vast, eclectic diversity of the Scriptures has been woven together by a single, divine author over the course of a millennium as the covenantal testimony to the person and work of Jesus Christ by the power of the Holy Spirit according to the eternal decree of God the Father,' is grand in itself. Yet more noble still is the pursuit of that goal through the combined efforts of a great faculty who are honoring the fifty-year legacy of a blessed institution steadfastly committed to the inerrancy of God's Word and the historic distinctives of the Christian faith."

Bryan Chapell, President Emeritus, Covenant Theological Seminary; Senior Pastor, Grace Presbyterian Church, Peoria, Illinois

"A high regard for Scripture as the authoritative Word of God percolates through every chapter of this collection. Moreover, it repeatedly displays flashes of insight into the redemptive-historical outworking of God's salvation plan for his people. You may not agree with the position of every author, but you will be challenged to seriously consider each carefully crafted essay, all of which are written at a very accessible level. The book achieves an excellent tone in its awareness of the many difficult questions that an honest reading of the Old Testament introduces. These contributors are also sensitive to canonical and literary concerns. Finally, this volume even includes teaching on the 'prophetic idiom,' and if you don't know what that is, then take up and read! I'm so glad that Van Pelt has gathered such an able band of brothers to produce this fine book."

Bryan D. Estelle, Professor of Old Testament, Westminster Seminary California; author, *Salvation through Judgment and Mercy: The Gospel according to Jonah*

"Van Pelt and his colleagues offer every worshiper of Christ a means of drawing out the one story of the King and his kingdom as it runs through the Law and the Prophets. Their analyses of the individual books of the Old Testament reveal the beauty of the whole canon. *A Biblical-Theological Introduction to the Old Testament* is intellectually enriching and pastorally faithful, helping the church to grow in love for the Savior through reading the Hebrew Bible. Congregants and Bible students will find great joy in reading their Scriptures with the aid of this work!"

Eric C. Redmond, Assistant Professor of Bible, Moody Bible Institute; Pastor of Adult Ministries, Calvary Memorial Church, Oak Park, Illinois

A Biblical-Theological Introduction
to the Old Testament

A Biblical-Theological Introduction to the Old Testament

The Gospel Promised

Edited by Miles V. Van Pelt

FOREWORD BY J. LIGON DUNCAN III

WHEATON, ILLINOIS

Library of Congress Cataloging-in-Publication Data

A biblical-theological introduction to the Old Testament : the gospel promised
   / edited by Miles V. Van Pelt, PhD. : foreword by J. Ligon Duncan
     pages cm
   Includes bibliographical references and index.
   ISBN 978-1-4335-3346-4 (hc)
   1. Bible. Old Testament—Introductions. I. Van Pelt, Miles V., 1969– editor.
   II. Reformed Theological Seminary (Jackson, Miss.)
BS1140.3.B53   2016
221.06'1—dc23   2015027432

Contents

Foreword

As we approach the five hundredth anniversary of the beginning of the Protestant Reformation of the Christian church, Reformed Theological Seminary (RTS) is entering its fiftieth year. The seminary has existed for only a small fraction of the time of this important quarter of Christian history, but RTS has had and continues to have a significant role in this era in which Reformed theology has enjoyed a widely recognized renewal and influence in the global Christian world.

RTS came into being in a time when the mainline denominations and seminaries were administratively in the hands of theological moderates, neoorthodox, and liberals, but the growth curve was already with the evangelicals, both inside and outside the mainline. While denominational apparatchiks were trying to maintain a status quo that was already on the wane, growing numbers of Christians were becoming frustrated with theological educators who were indifferent to or hostile toward historic Christian confessional orthodoxy and unconcerned for the gospel work of the church. RTS was created to provide a robust, reverent, and rigorous theological education for pastors and church leaders, particularly in Presbyterian and Reformed churches yet also more broadly in the larger evangelical family, coming from the standpoint of a commitment to biblical inerrancy, Reformed theology, and the Great Commission.

Because RTS was confessionally defined but not denominationally controlled, the seminary could exercise influence in numerous denominational settings and in a variety of church traditions. Also, since the founders of RTS were connected to a global evangelical network, the seminary was able to have a worldwide reach from the beginning. Over the years, RTS has served over eleven thousand students from some fifty denominations: Presbyterian, Reformed, Baptist, Anglican, Congregational, and more. A seminary that began with fourteen students from one denomination in 1966 now has about two thousand students annually in eight cities in the United States, in its global distance education, and in a doctoral program in São Paulo, Brazil, with students from every continent representing dozens of denominations, and it is the largest Reformed evangelical seminary in the world.

During that time, the academic reputation and contributions of Reformed Theological Seminary faculty have grown. In biblical studies, the RTS faculty has established a pattern of widely appreciated excellence in the fields of the Old and New

Testaments. To give only a few examples, consider former RTS Old Testament professor O. Palmer Robertson, who played a significant role in the contemporary resurgence of covenant theology through his book *The Christ of the Covenants*. Former RTS-Jackson and current RTS-Charlotte Old Testament professor John Currid has produced a complete commentary on the Pentateuch and has done important work in archaeology and ancient Near Eastern studies. Longtime RTS-Orlando Old Testament professor Richard Pratt not only is a prolific author regarded for his excellent Old Testament scholarship, single-handedly producing topical articles for an entire study Bible, but also is known for his work on apologetics and prayer. Miles Van Pelt of RTS-Jackson may be the best biblical languages professor I have ever known, with an infectious passion for canonical, Christ-centered biblical theology. Former RTS-Jackson and current RTS-Orlando New Testament professor Simon Kistemaker served as the longtime secretary of the Evangelical Theology Society and completed the multivolume New Testament commentary begun by William Hendriksen. RTS-Orlando professor Charles Hill is not only an acclaimed New Testament specialist but also one of the world's top scholars in the eschatology of early Christianity. In addition, RTS-Charlotte president and professor of New Testament Michael Kruger is a recognized scholar of early Christianity and has made major contributions to recent discussions of the canon of Scripture. Indeed, Kruger and Hill, along with RTS-Orlando professor John Frame, were cited by D. A. Carson in a recent plenary address at the Evangelical Theology Society as having made outstanding contributions in the field of the doctrine of Scripture. RTS-Jackson New Testament scholar Guy Waters has published prolifically on various topics including ecclesiology and has helped reshape the current debates on the theology of Paul.

In an effort to pass along this world-class, faithful, consecrated scholarship to the next generation, the Old and New Testament professors at RTS—both past and present—have put together two new volumes: *A Biblical-Theological Introduction to the Old Testament: The Gospel Promised* (edited by Miles V. Van Pelt), and *A Biblical-Theological Introduction to the New Testament: The Gospel Realized* (edited by Michael J. Kruger). There are several unique features and aspirations of these volumes. First, they are aimed at pastors and interested Christian readers, rather than fellow scholars. We at RTS value and produce resources intended for a scholarly audience, but the aim of these volumes is churchly edification, hence they are designed for accessibility. Second, they are written by scholars of biblical studies who are unafraid of and indeed very much appreciative of dogmatics. In many seminaries, even evangelical seminaries, there exists an unhealthy relationship between biblical theology and systematic theology, but at RTS we value both and want our students to understand their necessary and complementary value. To understand the Bible, and the Christian faith, one needs both the insights of a redemptive-historical approach and those of topical-doctrinal study. Third, these volumes unashamedly come from the standpoint of biblical inerrancy and Reformed theology. A high view of Scripture and a warm embrace of confessional Reformed theology are hallmarks of RTS, and these ideals shine through these books. Fourth, these introductions are designed to be pastoral and helpful. Preachers, ministry leaders, Bible teachers, students, and others engaged in Christian discipleship are in view. We want to edify you and help you edify others.

May these volumes bless the church of Jesus Christ for generations to come as it seeks to know his Word better and to proclaim it to the nations.

J. Ligon Duncan III
Chancellor and CEO
John E. Richards Professor of Systematic and Historical Theology
Reformed Theological Seminary

Preface

Warning! This introduction to the Old Testament may not be what you expect. As the title for this book suggests, our work is intentionally and self-consciously nuanced. By producing a "biblical-theological" introduction, we have set out to provide a resource for pastors, teachers, and students of the Bible designed to articulate the message(s) of each individual Old Testament book in the context of the whole canon of Scripture. As such, we not only work to understand the meaning of each individual book in the larger context of the Old Testament, but we also recognize, affirm, and submit to the authoritative witness of the New Testament in establishing the full and final message of the Old Testament (e.g., John 5:39, 45–47; Luke 24:25–27, 44–45; Rom. 1:1–3; Heb. 12:1–3; 1 Pet. 1:11). In other words, our goal is not to dismantle the Scriptures into as many unrelated parts as possible but rather to show how the vast, eclectic diversity of the Scriptures has been woven together by a single, divine author over the course of a millennium as the covenantal testimony to the person and work of Jesus Christ by the power of the Holy Spirit according to the eternal decree of God the Father.

Because of the book's design and intended audience, we have minimized interaction with higher-critical models of analysis and devoted greater attention to issues that stem from an analysis of the final form of the text as represented by the Hebrew Masoretic text preserved in the Leningrad Codex (B19). We have kept textual-critical discussions to a minimum, except where they significantly affect larger questions of interpretation (e.g., the book of Jeremiah). Different books will require different degrees of interaction with different introductory matters. For example, the issue of human authorship does require at least some introductory attention in a volume like this for the book of Genesis but less so for a book like Ruth. In each case, we have allowed the text, the pedagogical context, and the good sense of the author to establish a sensible approach to the various books in the Old Testament canon.

It is also important to note that the contributors to this volume all have different areas of interest and specialty within Old Testament studies. Additionally, we do not always agree on how to interpret every single issue (e.g., the interpretation of the Song of Songs, the characterization of the judges in the book of Judges, or the significance of the arrangement of the twelve Minor Prophets). It would be a shame not to allow these distinctives to percolate through the pages of this work and to stimulate the interests of a variety of readers. However, in order to provide a measure of unity for the presentation of data by each author, we have chosen to organize the material in each chapter under the following six major headings: Introduction, Background Issues, Structure and Outline, Message and Theology, Approaching the New Testament, and Select Bibliography. By design, our intent is to provide readers with the preliminary information that will faithfully guide them through the biblical text in such a way as to understand the meaning of each biblical book in the context of the larger, overall message of Scripture. Those who labor as ministers of the Word of God are called to stand and proclaim, "Thus says the LORD." It is with this ultimate, practical goal in mind that we humbly offer our labor to the church.

When abbreviations are employed in the book, we have followed *The SBL Handbook of Style*, second edition. Also, unless otherwise noted, we have used the English Standard Version (ESV) for Bible translation.

Miles V. Van Pelt

Acknowledgments

Where there is collaboration, gratitude abounds. It is a profound gift to serve together with a group of men who love the Scriptures and labor to teach the Old Testament to the next generation of those who will serve the church through preaching and teaching that Word (2 Tim. 2:2). The fellowship of our calling has occasioned the production of this resource. We all belong (or have belonged) to an institution that is committed to teaching all the Scriptures to our students before graduation, even the Old Testament as the gospel promised beforehand, the faithful witness to the person and work of Jesus Christ (Rom. 1:1–3). For these reasons, I am thankful for each one of the contributors to this volume. In the midst of their already busy schedules, they have sacrificed much in order to share in this work.

What connects each of the contributors to this volume is our service at Reformed Theological Seminary, both past and present. It is a great privilege for us to serve in an institution committed to the authority of Scripture and the supremacy of Christ in all things. For this reason, we dedicate this work to Reformed Theological Seminary in honor of its fiftieth anniversary. As faculty members, our work would not be possible without all the institutional help and resources provided to us—from the accounting office to campus security, from academic administration to facility maintenance and IT, including every donor, trustee, administrator, and staff member. We all labor together happily in the service of the church (1 Corinthians 12).

Thank you, Justin Taylor and the whole Crossway team, for your partnership in the production of this volume and for the convictions that we share. It is always a delight to work with this group of men and women. I would also like to offer a special word of thanks to David Barshinger for his expert editorial work, as well as his kindness and patience with me. Additionally, thanks are due my teaching assistants, Joseph Habib and C. L. Pearce, who enable me to carve out time for publishing through their faithful work and encouragement as we serve together. And then there is my family. They are the delightful earthly context for all that I do. My wife, Laurie, is the perfect reflection of steadfast, sacrificial love, and my children happily (I hope!) endure the constant ridicularity of their father.

Miles V. Van Pelt

Abbreviations

BJSUCSD	Biblical and Judaic Studies from the University of California, San Diego
BLS	Bible and Literature Series
BMI	The Bible and Its Modern Interpreters
BRev	*Bible Review*
BSac	*Bibliotheca Sacra*
BTB	*Biblical Theology Bulletin*
BTCB	Brazos Theological Commentary on the Bible
BWA(N)T	Beiträge zur Wissenschaft vom Alten (und Neuen) Testament
BZ	*Biblische Zeitschrift*
BZAW	Beihefte zur Zeitschrift für die alttestamentliche Wissenschaft
CBC	Cambridge Bible Commentary
CBQ	*Catholic Biblical Quarterly*
CHANE	Culture and History of the Ancient Near East
CJT	*Canadian Journal of Theology*
ConcC	Concordia Commentary
COS	*The Context of Scripture*, ed. William W. Hallo, 3 vols. (Leiden: Brill, 1997–2002)
CTA	*Corpus des tablettes en cunéiformes alphabétiques decouvertes à Ras Shamra-Ugarit de 1929 à 1939*, ed. Andrée Herdner (Paris: Geuthner, 1963)
CTJ	*Calvin Theological Journal*
CurBS	*Currents in Research: Biblical Studies*
DCH	*Dictionary of Classical Hebrew*, ed. David J. A. Clines, 9 vols. (Sheffield: Sheffield Phoenix, 1993–2014)
DJD	Discoveries in the Judean Desert
EBS	Encountering Biblical Studies
ECC	Eerdmans Critical Commentary
FAT	Forschungen zum Alten Testament
FCI	Foundations of Contemporary Interpretation
FOTL	Forms of the Old Testament Literature
FRLANT	Forschungen zur Religion und Literatur des Alten und Neuen Testaments
HALOT	*The Hebrew and Aramaic Lexicon of the Old Testament*, by Ludwig Koehler, Walter Baumgartner, and Johann J. Stamm, trans. and ed. under the supervision of Mervyn E. J. Richardson, 4 vols. (Leiden: Brill, 1994–1999)
HAT	Handbuch zum Alten Testament

HOTE	Handbooks for Old Testament Exegesis
HS	*Hebrew Studies*
HSM	Harvard Semitic Monographs
HThKAT	Herders Theologischer Kommentar zum Alten Testament
HTR	*Harvard Theological Review*
HUCA	*Hebrew Union College Annual*
IBC	Interpretation: A Bible Commentary for Teaching and Preaching
IBT	Interpreting Biblical Texts
ICC	International Critical Commentary
IJST	*International Journal of Systematic Theology*
Int	*Interpretation*
ITC	International Theological Commentary
JAJ	*Journal of Ancient Judaism*
JAOS	*Journal of the American Oriental Society*
JBL	*Journal of Biblical Literature*
JBPR	*Journal of Biblical and Pneumatological Research*
JBR	*Journal of Bible and Religion*
JCS	*Journal of Cuneiform Studies*
JETS	*Journal of the Evangelical Theological Society*
JHebS	*Journal of Hebrew Scriptures*
JNES	*Journal of Near Eastern Studies*
JPS	Jewish Publication Society
JQR	*Jewish Quarterly Review*
JSOT	*Journal for the Study of the Old Testament*
JSOTSup	Journal for the Study of the Old Testament Supplement Series
JTS	*Journal of Theological Studies*
KEL	Kregel Exegetical Library
LB	*Linguistica Biblica*
LBC	Layman's Bible Commentary
LHBOTS	Library of Hebrew Bible / Old Testament Studies
LSAWS	Linguistic Studies in Ancient West Semitic
MAJT	*Mid-America Journal of Theology*
MC	Mesopotamian Civilizations
NAC	New American Commentary
NCB	New Century Bible

NIBCOT	New International Biblical Commentary on the Old Testament
NICOT	New International Commentary on the Old Testament
NIDOTTE	*New International Dictionary of Old Testament Theology and Exegesis*, ed. Willem A. VanGemeren, 5 vols. (Grand Rapids, MI: Zondervan, 1997)
NIVAC	NIV Application Commentary
NSBT	New Studies in Biblical Theology (InterVarsity Press)
NSBTE	New Studies in Biblical Theology (Eerdmans)
NTSI	New Testament and the Scriptures of Israel
Numen	*Numen: International Review for the History of Religions*
OBO	Orbis Biblicus et Orientalis
OBT	Overtures to Biblical Theology
OTG	Old Testament Guides
OTM	Oxford Theological Monographs
OTS	Old Testament Studies
OtSt	*Oudtestamentische Studiën*
RevQ	*Revue de Qumran*
RTR	*Reformed Theological Review*
SBAB	Stuttgarter biblische Aufsatzbände
SBJT	*The Southern Baptist Journal of Theology*
SBL	Society of Biblical Literature
SBLDS	Society of Biblical Literature Dissertation Series
SBLMS	Society of Biblical Literature Monograph Series
SBT	Studies in Biblical Theology
SBTS	Sources for Biblical and Theological Study
SCS	Septuagint and Cognate Studies
SHBC	Smyth & Helwys Bible Commentary
SHR	Studies in the History of Religions
SJOT	*Scandinavian Journal of the Old Testament*
SJT	*Scottish Journal of Theology*
SNTSMS	Society for New Testament Studies Monograph Series
SOTBT	Studies in Old Testament Biblical Theology
SR	*Studies in Religion*
SSU	Studia Semitica Upsaliensia
STI	Studies in Theological Interpretation

SubBi   Subsidia Biblica

SymS   Symposium Series

TAPA *Transactions of the American Philological Association*

TBC   Torch Bible Commentaries

TBS   Topics for Biblical Study

TDOT *Theological Dictionary of the Old Testament*, ed. G. Johannes Botter-
        weck and Helmer Ringgren, trans. John T. Willis et al., 8 vols. (Grand
        Rapids, MI: Eerdmans, 1974–2006)

TJ   *Trinity Journal*

TLOT *Theological Lexicon of the Old Testament*, ed. Ernst Jenni, with
        assistance from Claus Westermann, trans. Mark E. Biddle, 3 vols.
        (Peabody, MA: Hendrickson, 1997)

TLZ   *Theologische Literaturzeitung*

TOTC   Tyndale Old Testament Commentaries

TynBul *Tyndale Bulletin*

UCOP   University of Cambridge Oriental Publications

VT   *Vetus Testamentum*

VTSup   Supplements to Vetus Testamentum

WBC   Word Biblical Commentary

WTJ   *Westminster Theological Journal*

WUNT   Wissenschaftliche Untersuchungen zum Neuen Testament

YOSR   Yale Oriental Series, Researches

ZAW   *Zeitschrift für die alttestamentliche Wissenschaft*

Introduction

Miles V. Van Pelt

You have heard it said that our Bible contains sixty-six different books written by an unknown number of human authors in three different languages (Hebrew, Aramaic, and Greek) over a period of roughly fifteen hundred years with various and sometimes conflicting messages. But I say unto you that the Bible may also be understood as a single book by a single author containing both a unified message and a unified design (John 5:39, 45–47; Luke 24:25–27, 44–45; Acts 28:23, 31; Rom. 1:1–3; 2 Tim. 3:16; 1 Pet. 1:11). The Bible is like a large picture puzzle. Each puzzle piece (individual book) has its own unique shape and bears its own unique image. But these individual shapes were designed to fit together into something whole, and the image of the whole provides the context and makes sense of the smaller, individual images.

For this reason, it is helpful to understand that the Bible is *not* a love letter, a self-help guide, a history textbook, a story, a legal code, a collection of ancient letters, or a religious handbook, though these types of things certainly appear throughout the pages of the biblical text (diversity). Rather, altogether, the Bible is the record, the deposit, the testimony of God's good news in Jesus Christ (unity). It is a legal, objective, public document that describes and explains the covenantal relationship by which God has condescended and united himself first to this world and then to his people through Jesus Christ (function). And so, in order to understand the message of the Bible, we must labor to understand the *diversity* of its various parts, the *unity* of its overall message, and its *function* in the life of the people of God. It is vital that we work to understand this book, the whole of it, because the church is "built on the foundation of the apostles *and prophets*" (Eph. 2:20) and because this book is both living and life-giving (Ps. 119:25, 50; 2 Tim. 3:16; Heb. 4:12).

Because of its age, and the various foreign cultural contexts out of which the Bible emerged, it is often difficult to understand the message of the Bible and its significance for thinking and living in the twenty-first century. For example, what does it mean that Jesus is our High Priest (Gen. 14:18; Num. 35:9–34; Hebrews 7–9), and why does that matter in a context where high priests are no longer a part of everyday life? To complicate matters further, the Bible contains two different parts, the Old Testament and the New Testament, and at times these two parts appear to contradict each other. For example, which command should we follow, "an eye for an eye" (Ex. 21:24) or "turn the other cheek" (cf. Matt. 5:39)?

And so, before we turn to consider each of the individual books of the Old Testament in this introduction, it is important first to consider the message of the whole, which will ultimately make sense of the individual parts. When considering the whole, it is essential to begin with the entire Christian Bible, both the Old and New Testaments. It is especially important to understand how the apostolic testimony of the New Testament identifies and establishes the final meaning and design of the prophetic word contained in the Old Testament. This New Testament witness provides us with a unified conceptual framework by which we can comprehend the vast diversity presented to us in the pages of the the Old Testament.

The Old Testament is more complex, diverse, and removed from our modern contexts than the New Testament. Our English Bibles contain some thirty-nine books written by a number of different (identified and unidentified) authors between approximately 1400 and 400 BC. The Old Testament is also the larger of the two Testaments, constituting over three-quarters of the whole.[1] But we have not been left to our own devices when it comes to making sense of these ancient texts. The New Testament provides the final, authoritative context from which God's people can rightly understand the message and design of the Old Testament. But this relationship is not unidirectional. The Old Testament provides the background and conceptual categories for undertanding the message of the New Testament. These two Testaments, in all their diversity, are forever united as the Word of God, and what God has joined together, let not man separate.

What then does the New Testament teach us about the Old Testament, in terms of both its message and its design or function?[2] The answers to these questions are certainly debated, but a helpful place to begin appears in Acts 28. At the end of this chapter, Luke summarizes the apostle Paul's two-year teaching curriculum as follows: "From morning till evening he expounded to them, testifying to *the kingdom of God* and trying to convince them about *Jesus* both from *the Law of Moses* and from *the Prophets*" (Acts 28:23; see also 28:30–31). If we pay attention, we will come to understand that Luke, through Paul, has provided us with the answers to two fundamental questions. First, what is the Old Testament about? And second, what is the design or function of the Old Testament?

According to Acts 28, Paul spent two years in Rome using the Old Testament to teach about Jesus and the kingdom of God. To this end, we contend that the Old

---

[1] It is difficult to arrive at an exact percentage given the nature of counting Hebrew words. However, in the Hebrew Old Testament, there are approximately 473,020 words (including all prefixes with their own entry in the lexicon and pronominal suffixes) that appear in 23,213 verses. In the Greek New Testament, there are approximately 138,158 words that appear in 7,941 verses. By word count, therefore, the Hebrew Old Testament constitutes 77.3 percent of the Christian Bible. The Greek New Testament registers 22.7 percent. The word count in the Septuagint (the ancient Greek translation of the Old Testament) is higher than the original Hebrew and yields an even greater percentage for the Old Testament.

[2] A full answer to this question is well beyond the scope of this brief introductory chapter. The data provided here is limited to the scope and shape of this volume.

Testament—and the whole Bible, for that matter—is ultimately about Jesus and the kingdom of God. Jesus constitutes the sum and substance of the biblical message. He is God's gospel and the *theological center* for the whole of the Christian Bible. He is the source and the unifying force that makes sense of all the diversity found in the biblical record. With Jesus as the theological center of the biblical message, the kingdom of God functions as the *thematic framework* for that message. This is the theme within which all other themes exist and are united. It is the realm of the prophet, priest, and king; the place of wisdom and the scribe; the world of the apostles, elders, and deacons. Every biblical theme is a kingdom-of-God theme. If Jesus as the theological center gives meaning to the biblical message, then the kingdom of God as the thematic framework provides the context for that message.

In addition to the message of the Old Testament, we also catch a glimpse of its design in the abbreviated designation, "the Law of Moses and . . . the Prophets" (Acts 28:23). A longer description appears in Luke 24:44, where Jesus refers to the Old Testament as "the Law of Moses and the Prophets and the Psalms." Here Jesus is referring to the arrangement of the Old Testament in its original, threefold division: the Law, the Prophets, and the Writings. These divisions constitute the covenantal structure of the Old Testament in the categories of *covenant* (Law), *covenant history* (Prophets), and *covenant life* (Writings). This Old Testament covenantal design also serves as the pattern after which the New Testament was constructed. Seeing and understanding this comprehensive canonical design will provide us with important contextual clues for how to read, understand, and properly apply the Old Testament in the church today.

THE THEOLOGICAL CENTER: JESUS

Jesus is the theological center of the Old Testament. This means that the person and work of Jesus as presented in the New Testament (including his birth, life, teachings, death, resurrection, ascension, and return) constitute the singular reality that unifies and explains everything that appears in the Old Testament. It is perhaps clear to us that Jesus is the theological center of, or at least the central figure in, the New Testament. But both Jesus and the apostles also understood the theological center of the Old Testament to be the same as that of the New Testament.[3] The Old Testament is the shadow, and Jesus is the reality (Col. 2:16–17; Heb. 8:5; 10:1). Consider how the apostle Paul chose to begin his letter to the Romans:

> Paul, a servant of Christ Jesus, called to be an apostle, set apart for the gospel of God, which he promised beforehand through his prophets in the holy Scriptures, concerning his Son, who was descended from David according to the flesh. (Rom. 1:1–3)

---

[3] Contra Marshall, who is representative of a large portion of evangelicalism: "It follows that the OT can hardly be called 'a book about Jesus' as if he were the principal subject. Where there is a future hope, it is centered on God himself and in some places on a messianic figure who is not identified. Jesus is not explicitly present." I. Howard Marshall, "Jesus Christ," *The New Dictionary of Biblical Theology*, ed. T. Desmond Alexander and Brian S. Rosner (Downers Grove, IL: InterVarsity Press, 2000), 594.

In 1:1, Paul identifies himself as an apostle and states that he has been "set apart" for the good news or the "gospel of God." Then, in 1:2–3, Paul identifies the source and the content of this gospel. It is important to recognize that this gospel was not something new but something "promised beforehand." Following this statement about the gospel promised beforehand are three prepositional phrases that may change the way in which you think about the Old Testament. This gospel came (1) *through* his prophets, (2) *in* the holy Scriptures, and was (3) *concerning* his Son. The three prepositional phrases in 1:2–3 identify (1) the vehicle of gospel revelation, (2) the location of gospel revelation, and (3) the content of gospel revelation.

Paul states that the gospel promised beforehand came through the prophets, who functioned as the authorial instruments of God's Old Testament, covenantal revelation. Additionally, this revelation was deposited in, and constituted for Paul, the holy Scriptures. At this point it is important to remember that when someone like Paul mentions the Scriptures in the New Testament, he is referring back to the Old Testament. Thus, for Paul, the Old Testament is fundamentally the gospel promised beforehand. The last prepositional phrase in this series identifies the content of this Old Testament gospel revelation as Jesus Christ, the Son of God. In other words, the Old Testament, which came through the prophets, is the gospel promised beforehand because it has as its subject Jesus Christ, not only as the eternal Son of God but also as the offspring of David "according to the flesh" (1:3).

Paul's assertions concerning the nature and content of Old Testament revelation are supported by statements Jesus made that have been recorded in the Gospels. The first one appears in Luke 24:25–27 (see also 24:44–45). After rising from the dead, Jesus appeared on the road to Emmaus to instruct two very confused disciples:

> And he said to them, "O foolish ones, and slow of heart to believe all that the prophets have spoken! Was it not necessary that the Christ should suffer these things and enter into his glory?" And beginning with Moses and all the Prophets, he interpreted to them in all the Scriptures the things concerning himself.

Consider that these two disciples were rebuked as "foolish" and "slow of heart" because they did not believe that the Old Testament testified to the person and work of Jesus. Three times in these few verses the word "all" is used to describe the comprehensive nature of this reality—*all* that the prophets have spoken, *all* the Prophets, and *all* the Scriptures. And then, once again, we encounter a prepositional phrase that identifies the content of this prophetic revelation in "all the Scriptures": Jesus said that all the Scriptures contain "the things *concerning himself.*" In other words, Jesus tells us that he is the unifying principle, or theological center, of the Old Testament.

It is not difficult to understand what Jesus is saying here. However, for most of us, like the disciples to whom Jesus was speaking, it is difficult to believe and understand how this reality works throughout the whole of the Old Testament with all its various and diverse parts. Alec Motyer puts it this way:

The great Lord Jesus came from outside and voluntarily and deliberately attached himself to the Old Testament, affirmed it to be the word of God and set himself, at cost, to fulfill it (Mt. 26:51–54). This fact of facts cuts the ground from under any suspicion that the *doctrine* of biblical authority rests on a circular argument such as, "I believe the Bible to be authoritative because the Bible says it is authoritative." Not so! It was Jesus who came "from outside" as the incarnate Son of God, Jesus who was raised from the dead as the Son of God with power, who chose to validate the Old Testament in retrospect and the New Testament in prospect, and who himself is the grand theme of the "story-line" of both Testaments, the focal-point giving coherence to the total "picture" in all its complexities. . . . He is the climax as well as the substance and centre of the whole. In him all God's promises are yea and amen (2 Cor. 1:20).[4]

The encounter on the road to Emmaus was not the first time that Jesus had made such a bold and clear statement about the nature and content of the Old Testament. In a speech directed against those who opposed him before his death, Jesus said, "You search the Scriptures because you think that in them you have eternal life; and it is they that bear witness about me, yet you refuse to come to me that you may have life" (John 5:39–40). Once again, we are instructed by Jesus in the New Testament that those who "search" and study the Old Testament must understand that these Scriptures "bear witness" (μαρτυρέω) to Jesus. This is the very same thing that the author of the book of Hebrews states after a lengthy rehearsal of Old Testament history in Hebrews 11— including Abel, Abraham, Moses, the people of Israel, Rahab, Gideon, Barak, Samson, Jephthah, David, Samuel, and the prophets. These people are called "a great cloud of witnesses" (μαρτύρων) in Hebrews 12:1. Notice that these men and women are *not* called a "great cloud of examples" but rather witnesses, who testify or bear witness to the person and work of Jesus and who call us not to imitate them but rather to fix our eyes *with them* on "Jesus, the founder and perfecter of our faith" (12:2).

The testimony of Jesus and the New Testament is clear. Jesus is the theological center of the Old Testament. He is the unity that makes sense of all the diverse material encountered in the Old Testament Scriptures. We will discover that as "the first" and "the last" (Isa. 44:6) and as the Alpha and the Omega (Rev. 1:8; 21:6; 22:13), Jesus is the second Adam, the seed of the woman, the offspring of Abraham, the Ruler from Judah, faithful Israel, the Mediator of a better covenant, our eternal High Priest, the Judge who saves once and for all, the heir of David, the Prophet like Moses, the Wisdom of God, the incarnate Word of God. He was not joking when he declared of himself, "I am the way, and the truth, and the life" (John 14:6). We will never fully understand the Old Testament if we refuse to fix our eyes on Jesus when we read these Scriptures.

Goldsworthy is correct when he argues,

The hub of the church and of the life of the believer is Jesus Christ, the crucified and risen Lord. He is not only the hermeneutical center of the whole Bible, but, according to the biblical testimony, he gives ultimate meaning to every fact in the

---

[4] Alec Motyer, *Look to the Rock: An Old Testament Background to Our Understanding of Christ* (Grand Rapids, MI: Kregel, 1996), 21–22.

universe. He is thus the hermeneutical principle of all reality . . . providing the center that holds it all together.[5]

Goldsworthy moves beyond understanding Jesus as the theological center for just the Old Testament or for the Bible as a whole. He extends this principle to include all reality, including "every fact in the universe." In order to begin to understand the Old Testament, or the Bible, or life in general, we must first assess our view of the person and work of Jesus as presented in Scripture. Perhaps our inability to comprehend the fullness and unity of the inspired Word of God stems from our anemic estimation of the incarnate Word of God (John 1:1–3, 14).

THE THEMATIC FRAMEWORK: THE KINGDOM OF GOD

The kingdom of God (also construed as the kingdom of heaven) constitutes the thematic framework for the Bible, both Old and New Testaments. This is the theme that comprehends and encompasses every other theme encountered in the Scriptures, from creation to new creation—including covenant, law, prophet, priest, king, redemption, wisdom, war, the nations, inheritance, divine presence, idolatry, clothing, judgment, salvation, faith, hope, love, and any of the many other themes that cut across the pages of the Bible.[6] These are all kingdom-of-God themes. This framework extends to the outer limits of the canonical corpus. It unites, coheres, stabilizes, and shapes all other biblical themes and concepts.

The beginning of Jesus's preaching ministry in the Gospel of Mark is described in this way: "Jesus came into Galilee, proclaiming the gospel of God, and saying, 'The time is fulfilled, and *the kingdom of God is at hand*; repent and believe in the gospel'" (Mark 1:14–15). During the forty-day span between Jesus's resurrection and ascension, Luke summarizes the final days of Jesus's teaching ministry in the same way, "He presented himself alive to them after his suffering by many proofs, appearing to them during forty days and *speaking about the kingdom of God*" (Acts 1:3). From beginning to end, the message of Jesus about himself is described as the kingdom of God (heaven).[7] For three months, Paul taught in the synagogue at Ephesus, "reasoning and persuading them about *the kingdom of God*" (Acts 19:8). And later, for two whole years, Paul resided in Rome, "proclaiming *the kingdom of God* and teaching about the Lord Jesus Christ with all boldness and without hindrance" (Acts 28:31). Here we come to understand that Jesus and the apostles used the designation *kingdom of God* (or *heaven*) to summarize the content of their teaching and preaching ministries, and the book from which they taught was the Old Testament (cf. Acts 28:23).

John Bright captures the significance of this theme when he writes,

---

[5] Graeme L. Goldsworthy, "Biblical Theology as the Heartbeat of Effective Ministry," in *Biblical Theology: Retrospect and Prospect*, ed. Scott J. Hafemann (Downers Grove, IL: IVP Academic, 2002), 284.
[6] For a preliminary treatment of a vareity of biblical themes, see *New Dictionary of Biblical Theology*, ed. T. Desmond Alexander and Brian S. Rosner (Downers Grove, IL: InterVarsity Press, 2000), 365–863.
[7] This overarching theme for the Christian Bible is explicitly mentioned ninety-eight times in the New Testament. Of these ninety-eight occurrences, eighty-four (or 85 percent) occur in the Gospels.

For the concept of the Kingdom of God involves, in a real sense, the total message of the Bible. Not only does it loom large in the teaching of Jesus; it is to be found, in one form or another, through the length and breadth of the Bible—at least if we may view it through the eyes of the New Testament faith—from Abraham, who set out to seek "the city . . . whose builder and maker is God" (Heb. 11:10; cf. Gen. 12:1ff.), until the New Testament closes with "the holy city, new Jerusalem, coming down out of heaven from God" (Rev. 21:2). To grasp what is meant by the Kingdom of God is to come very close to the heart of the Bible's gospel of salvation.[8]

In the same way, Walther Eichrodt, in his two-volume *Old Testament Theology* from the 1960s, recognized the significance of this theme for understanding the relationship between the Old and New Testaments when he wrote, "that which binds together indivisibly the two realms of the Old and New Testaments . . . is the irruption of the Kingdom of God into this world and its establishment here."[9]

When it comes to understanding Jesus as the theological center of the Bible, we begin to recognize that the Old Testament makes sense only in light of his birth, life, teachings, death, resurrection, ascension, and return. And the theme of the kingdom of God gives the context for this theological center and comes to expression in the Old Testament through what is commonly called *redemptive history*.[10] This is the organic, progressive movement of God's covenantal activity across time, from the creation of the universe in Genesis 1–2 to the new creation in Revelation 21–22. God's kingdom unfolds throughout the pages of Scripture from age to age and from epoch to epoch. It begins with creation and the fall (Genesis 1–3), declines in judgment with the flood and Babel (Genesis 4–11), picks up with the patriarchs (Genesis 12–50), builds to the nation of Israel in the wilderness (Exodus–Deuteronomy), and then climaxes in the occupation of the land under Joshua, the judges, and the Davidic dynasty in the land of promise (Joshua–Kings). But just as soon as God had given David rest from his enemies and established his dynasty and the temple in Jerusalem was completed, the infidelity of Solomon (cf. 1 Kings 11) marked the beginning of Israel's decline into a divided kingdom and then into exile. Aspects of the exile are captured by some of the writing prophets and in books like Lamentations, Esther, Daniel, and Ezra–Nehemiah in the Writings. The Hebrew Old Testament concludes with unfulfilled expectations concerning the promised return from exile (Ezra 1:1–4; 2 Chron. 36:22–23; cf. Ezra 3:12; Hag. 2:6–9), causing us to wait for the arrival of the true King of the kingdom of God in the New Testament (cf. Mark 1:14–15).

---

[8] John Bright, *The Kingdom of God: The Biblical Concept and Its Meaning for the Church* (New York: Abingdon-Cokesbury, 1953), 7.

[9] Walther Eichrodt, *Theology of the Old Testament*, trans. J. A. Baker, OTL (Philadelphia: Westminster, 1961), 1:26.

[10] In addition to *redemptive history*, designations such as *salvation history*, *metanarrative*, or the German *Heilsgeschichte* are used to refer to the progressive, historical development and presentation of the biblical materials. However, it may be more accurate to employ the designation *covenantal history*, since this is the reality that motivates and shapes the presentation of history across the pages of Scripture, particularly in the categories of covenant prologue, covenant renewal, and covenant lawsuit (cf. the book of Genesis, esp. 15:7; Ex. 20:2; Deut. 1:9–3:29; Josh. 24:2–13; Judg. 6:7–10; 1 Sam. 12:6–12; Psalms 78; 105; 106; Neh. 9:5b–37; Acts 7; Hebrews 11).

THE COVENANTAL STRUCTURE: LAW, PROPHETS, AND WRITINGS

Having considered that the Old Testament is about Jesus and his kingdom, how then does the Bible work? One way to think about how to answer this important question relates to the shape or the final form of the Old Testament. Earlier we compared the Bible to a picture puzzle and indicated that the individual shapes and pieces of the puzzle find their ultimate meaning in their connection and contribution to the whole. An individual puzzle piece, by itself, has its own unique image and shape capable of description and analysis. But it is not until that individual piece is set into the context of the whole puzzle that we can understand its significance and contribution to the whole. The same can be said for the Old Testament. Each individual book in each individual section in each of the two Testaments maintains its own individual shape (structure) and image (meaning). But it is not until we understand the position of each book in the context of the whole Old Testament or Bible that we come to discover its full and final significance.[11]

The book of Ruth serves as a good example of this reality.[12] In our English Bibles, the book of Ruth follows the book of Judges. Its placement there is based on the chronological note that appears at the beginning of the book: "*In the days when the judges* ruled there was a famine in the land, and a man of Bethlehem in Judah went to sojourn in the country of Moab" (Ruth 1:1). According to the Babylonian Talmud,[13] however, the book of Ruth is located at the beginning of the Writings, the third section of the Hebrew Bible, just before the book of Psalms. Its position in this ordering appears to be based upon the genealogy at the end of the book (4:18–22), where Boaz (Ruth's husband) is listed as the great-grandfather of David, whom the Babylonian Talmud identifies as the author/collector of the Psalms. Yet in the final form of the Hebrew Bible, the one still in print today, the book of Ruth appears just after the book of Proverbs. Its position here is both theologically and pedagogically motivated. Proverbs 31 concludes with the famous oracle taught to King Lemuel by his mother, the oracle of the "excellent wife" (Prov. 31:10–31).[14] The designation "excellent wife" appears only three times in the Hebrew Bible, twice in Proverbs (12:4; 31:10) and once in Ruth (3:11). Ruth is the only actual (rather than ideal) woman in Scripture ever to receive this special designation. And so, based upon its position after Proverbs, it appears that Ruth is intended to function as the illustration of the ideal woman presented in Proverbs 31.

---

[11] For more on this topic see Rolf Rendtorff, *The Canonical Hebrew Bible: A Theology of the Old Testament*, TBS 7 (Leiden: Deo, 2005), 1–8, 717–39, and Stephen G. Dempster, *Dominion and Dynasty: A Theology of the Hebrew Bible*, NSBT 15 (Downers Grove, IL: InterVarsity Press, 2003), 15–43.

[12] For a superb treatment of this topic, see Stephen G. Dempster, "A Wandering Moabite: Ruth—A Book in Search of a Canonical Home," in *The Shape of the Writings*, ed. Julius Steinberg and Timothy J. Stone, with the assistance of Rachel Stone, Siphrut: Literature and Theology of the Hebrew Scriptures 16 (Winona Lake, IN: Eisenbrauns, 2015), 87–118.

[13] *Baba Bathra* 14b in the Babylonian Talmud represents the oldest known rabbinical order. It dates from between the third and sixth centuries AD. In this listing, the placement of books corresponds closely to the arrangement that appears in the current printed edition of the Hebrew Bible, with only two exceptions: Isaiah in the Latter Prophets and Ruth in the Writings. The position of the book of Ruth is described in *Baba Bathra* 14b, "The order of the Hagiographa is Ruth, the Book of Psalms, Job, Prophets, Ecclesiastes, Song of Songs, Lamentations, Daniel and the Scroll of Esther, Ezra and Chronicles. Now on the view that Job lived in the days of Moses, should not the book of Job come first?—We do not begin with a record of suffering. But Ruth also is a record of suffering?—It is a suffering with a sequel [of happiness], as R. Johanan said: Why was her name called Ruth?—Because there issued from her David who replenished the Holy One, blessed be He, with hymns and praises."

[14] The Hebrew expression אֵשֶׁת־חַיִל is translated in various ways, such as "excellent wife" (ESV, NASB), "wife of noble character" (NIV), and "virtuous woman" (KJV).

At this point we are not interested in defending one position against another. Rather, the point is to illustrate that the position of a book in the Bible can impact how we interpret it. Is the book of Ruth a chronological footnote to the book of Judges, a genealogical introduction to David—the sweet psalmist of Israel (2 Sam. 23:1)—or the narrative illustration of the excellent wife? The position of the puzzle piece matters. It shapes how we interact with both its message and its function. For this reason, it is worth taking a moment to briefly describe the final form of the Hebrew Old Testament and to defend our preference for treating the books of the Old Testament in this order, as they have been listed in the table of contents.

The arrangement of the books in our English Old Testament differs slightly from the arrangement of the books in our Hebrew Old Testament. It is important to note, however, that the English Old Testament and the Hebrew Old Testament contain the same books. They are simply grouped and arranged in different ways.

In the English Bible, the books of the Old Testament are arranged by genre, chronology, and authorship. As table 1 (p. 32) illustrates, the English Old Testament contains four main sections in which the books are grouped (more or less) accord-ing to their basic genre: law, history, poetry, and prophecy. The books in each of these sections are further positioned based on issues of chronology and authorship. For example, the five books of the Pentatuech were written by Moses (authorship) and appear in chronological order. The so-called Historical Books also appear in roughly chronological order. In the Poetical Books, those associated with Solomon are grouped together (Proverbs, Ecclesiastes, and the Song of Songs), and the placement of Lamentations after Jeremiah is motivated by the tradition that Jeremiah wrote Lamentations, even though the author is technically anonymous.

The arrangement of the books in the English Old Testament has come down to us from the Latin translation of the Bible called the Vulgate (ca. 400 AD). This Latin translation was used in the church prior to the emergence of English Bible transla-tions during the Reformation. The arrangement of the books in the Vulgate may have been adopted from an older Greek translation called the Septuagint, but this is difficult to determine with certainty.[15]

In contrast, the Hebrew Bible includes three major sections: Law, Prophets, and Writings. These divisions predate the time of Christ, and it appears that he was familiar with them in his own day when he referred to the Old Testament in Luke 24:44 as "the *Law of Moses* and the *Prophets* and the *Psalms*."[16] Another possible clue appears in Matthew 23:35 (cf. Luke 11:51), where Jesus refers to the blood of two martyrs, "from the blood of righteous Abel to the blood of Zechariah." It

---

[15] For more on the structure and design of the Old Testament, see Roger T. Beckwith, *The Old Testament Canon of the New Testament Church and Its Background in Early Judaism* (1985; repr., Eugene, OR: Wipf & Stock, 2008), Dempster, *Dominion and Dynasty*, 15–51; Andrew E. Steinmann, *The Oracles of God: The Old Testament Canon* (St. Louis, MO: Concordia, 2000); Greg Goswell, "The Order of the Books in the Hebrew Bible," *JETS* 51, no. 4 (2008): 673–88; and Goswell, "The Order of the Books in the Greek Old Testament," *JETS* 52, no. 3 (2009): 449–66.

[16] The designation *Psalms* for the third section represents the Jewish practice of naming the whole of something after what appears first in it. For example, the book of Exodus in Hebrew is called "these are the names" because those are the first words in the book. Today, we call this third section the "Writings." It is not uncommon in some circles to refer to the Hebrew Old Testament (or the English translations of it) as the "Tanak." This designation comes from putting together the first letters of each of the Hebrew names for these three sections: *torah*, *nevi'im*, and *kethuvim*.

English Bible Order	Hebrew Bible Order	
Pentateuch	**Law**	
Genesis	Genesis	
Exodus	Exodus	
Leviticus	Leviticus	
Numbers	Numbers	
Deuteronomy	Deuteronomy	
Historical Books	**Prophets**	
Joshua	Joshua	*Former Prophets*
Judges	Judges	
Ruth	Samuel	
1–2 Samuel	Kings	
1–2 Kings		
1–2 Chronicles	Isaiah	*Latter Prophets*
Ezra	Jeremiah	
Nehemiah	Ezekiel	
Esther	Book of the Twelve	
Poetry	**Writings**	
Job	Psalms	*Life in the Land*
Psalms	Job	
Proverbs	Proverbs	
Ecclesiastes	Ruth	
Song of Songs	Song of Songs	
	Ecclesiastes	
Prophets		
Isaiah	Lamentations	*Life in Exile*
Jeremiah	Esther	
Lamentations	Daniel	
Ezekiel	Ezra	
Daniel	Nehemiah	
The Twelve Minor Prophets	Chronicles	

Table 1

has been recognized that this is not a strictly chronological reference but rather a canonical reference. Abel is the martyr who appears in the first book of the Old Testament (Genesis 4), and Zechariah is the martyr who appears in the last book (2 Chronicles 24). Together, these two references by Jesus suggest that the Old Testament in his time contained three (not four) divisions, beginning with Genesis and ending with Chronicles (not Malachi). As indicated earlier, the way in which books are arranged can impact their interpretation. And so we must consider the implications for the arrangement of the Old Testament in the categories of Law, Prophets, and Writings and how that arrangement relates to the New Testament. Figure 1 attempts to illustrate that relationship by suggesting a covenantal arrangement for the Christian Bible.

	Law		Prophets		Writings		
Covenant Prologue	Exodus Leviticus Numbers Deuteronomy	Joshua Judges Samuel Kings	Isaiah Jeremiah Ezekiel The Twelve		Psalms Job Proverbs Ruth Song of Songs Ecclesiastes	Lamentations Esther Daniel Ezra Nehemiah Chronicles	**Covenant Epilogue**
Genesis							Revelation
	Matthew Mark Luke John		The Acts of the Apostles		Paul's Epistles Hebrews James	1, 2 Peter 1, 2, 3 John Jude	
	Covenant		**Covenant History**		**Covenant Life**		

Figure 1

Figure 1 endeavors to display the canonical construction of the Bible, both Old and New Testaments, in the categories of Law, Prophets, and Writings. The Old Testament is shaded in gray, signifying shadows of the realities (Col. 2:17; Heb. 8:5; 10:1), and the bulk of it appears in the upper register of blocks. The New Testament appears in white, with the bulk of it showing up in the lower register of blocks. Genesis and Revelation serve as bookends to the whole. The labels appearing with the descriptor *covenant* serve to explain the nature of each of the major divisions. The books of the Law are the *covenant* books. The Prophets contain what will later be described as *covenant history*, and the Writings cover issues related to *covenant life*. In other words, the categories of Law, Prophets, and Writings are covenantal in nature.[17] The Bible, as a covenantal document, is also covenantal in its construction and design.[18] The image of the picture puzzle that

---

[17] According to Rendtorff, "One might venture to say: in the first part of the canon *God acts*, in the second *God speaks*, and in the third part of the canon *people speak* to God and of God." *The Canonical Hebrew Bible*, 6. Dempster proposes that the arrangement of the Hebrew Bible grants readers a "comprehensive narrative framework" with poetic commentary. Dempster, *Dominion and Dynasty*, 22. The works of Rendtorff and Dempster are outstanding in their attempts to characterize the significance of the final form of the Hebrew Bible and its significance for interpretation (macrocanonical hermeneutics). However, the categories of acting and speaking (Rendtorff) and narrative and commentary (Dempster) are both comprehended by the covenantal arrangement proposed here.

[18] Horton rightly argues that the "particular architectural structure that we believe the Scriptures themselves to yield is the covenant. It is not simply the concept of the covenant, but the concrete existence of God's covenantal dealings in our

makes sense of the individual puzzle pieces, both in terms of placement and function, is *covenant*. The significance of the covenantal design for the Old Testament is reflected in the fact that the New Testament appears to have been arranged in the same way, as a mirror reflecting the Old Testament. And so the categories of *covenant* (Law), *covenant history* (Prophets), and *covenant life* (Writings) apply equally to the Old and New Testaments in each of their respective sections, as indicated in figure 1. It will be helpful to briefly consider how each of these sections work in both Testaments.

Covenant Prologue and Epilogue

The books of Genesis and Revelation are set apart in the Christian Bible as covenant prologue and covenant epilogue, the introduction and the conclusion to the whole. Though written at different times by different human authors from different cultures and in different languages, these two books were designed to fit together and shape the message of the Christian Bible. Every promise and covenant established in the book of Genesis (creation, redemption, Noah, Abraham) finds it fulfillment and consummation in the book of Revelation.

The close literary and theological relationship that these two books share (*protology* and eschatology) is demonstrated by the way in which Genesis begins and Revelation ends. This relationship is expressed through the literary device of chiasm, which also serves secondarily as a literary *inclusio* for the whole of the Bible. This chiasm is displayed in the following outline:

a   Creation of heaven and earth (Genesis 1–2)
   b   Marriage covenant: Adam and Eve—the bride comes to a garden-
      sanctuary from which rivers of water flow for the nations (Genesis 2)
      c   Satan's destruction promised (Genesis 3)
      c' Satan's destruction accomplished (Revelation 20)
   b' Marriage covenant: Lamb and bride—the bride comes to a city-sanctuary
      from which rivers of water flow for the nations (Revelation 21)
a' Creation of new heaven and earth (Revelation 21–22)

By beginning and ending in the same way (but in reverse!), the Bible exhibits a remarkable level of unity in both design and purpose. This reality illustrates the role of a single divine author working in conjunction with numerous human instruments who participated in the writing process. This chiasm also appears to function as a canonical *inclusio*,[19] providing internal evidence for a closed canon.

---

history that provides the context within which we recognize the unity of Scripture amid its remarkable diversity." Horton also contends that this "framework is largely hidden from view" but perhaps we are now beginning to recognize this grand covenantal framework. Michael Horton, *Introducing Covenant Theology* (Grand Rapids, MI: Baker, 2006), 13. Kline has argued that "biblical canonicity shows itself from its inception to be of the lineage of covenantal canonicity" and that "because Scripture is covenant, biblical canonicity, from beginning to end, belongs at the formal literary level to the more broadly attested category of authoritative treaty words. All Scripture is covenantal, and the canonicity of all Scripture is covenantal. Biblical canon is covenantal canon." Meredith G. Kline, *The Structure of Biblical Authority*, 2nd ed. (Eugene, OR: Wipf & Stock, 1989), 37, 75.

[19] *Inclusio* is a literary device used to mark the beginning and end of something by way of repetition. Examples appear in many of the so-called *hallelujah psalms* (e.g., Psalms 106; 113; 117:1–2; 135; 146–150).

Law: Covenant

There are four covenant books in the Old Testament (Exodus, Leviticus, Numbers, and Deuteronomy)[20] and four covenant books in the New Testament (Matthew, Mark, Luke, and John). In each Testament, the covenant books are framed by the birth and the death of the covenant mediator and contain the accounts of their lives and teachings in the context of covenant administration. In the Old Testament, the framing is comprehensive, beginning with the birth of Moses in Exodus 2 and concluding with his death in Deuteronomy 34. In the New Testament, the framing appears within each individual book (distributive). For example, in Matthew the birth of Jesus is recorded in chapter 1 and his death in chapter 27. This pattern is variously repeated in the other Gospels.

In addition to the larger, structural relationships that exist between the covenant books of the Old and New Testaments, numerous internal elements also connect these books. For example, both Moses and Jesus share a birth narrative where they are born under the threat of death by a foreign ruler and must flee into Egypt to escape (cf. Exodus 1; Matthew 2). Additionally, both men deliver the law from a mountain, experience transfigurations, perform miracles, and suffer under the constant rebellion of their people as covenant mediators. In many ways, the gospel narratives of the New Testament work to portray Jesus as a second Moses figure.[21]

In addition to these major features of correspondence, there are also important aspects of discontinuity. For example, in Exodus 32:30–34, Moses offers up to the Lord his life on behalf of the people of Israel because their sin had provoked the threat of death. However, this act of substitution is denied to Moses. But when it comes to Jesus under the new covenant, his request to circumvent this path to salvation is denied (cf. Matt. 26:39), and he becomes the ultimate substitute for the people of God, bearing the curse of their sin by his own death. Another example includes the way in which these covenant narratives end. In the old covenant, the narrative ends with the death of the covenant mediator, Moses. With Jesus in the new covenant, however, the death of the covenant mediator is not the final word. Each of the new covenant narratives climaxes in Jesus's victory over death by way of resurrection. It is important to understand that these instances of discontinuity do not sever the relationship between the covenant books in the Old and New Testaments. Rather, they were designed to highlight the person and work of Jesus by way of contrast as the Mediator of a better covenant (cf. Heb. 3:3; 7:22).

---

[20] Though a part of the Pentateuch with Exodus–Deuteronomy, the book of Genesis has been set apart from the other books in this canonical section (the Law). At the literary level, this division is achieved by means of poetic intrusion and type-scene. The book of Genesis ends with the poetic blessing of the twelve patriarchs by Jacob in Genesis 49 (poetic intrusion) and then the death of the blesser in Genesis 50 (type-scene). This literary combination is repeated at the end of Deuteronomy with the poetic blessing of the twelve tribes (patriarchs) by Moses in Deuteronomy 33 followed by the account of his death in Deuteronomy 34. In this way, the Law or Pentateuch is shown to have two parts: (1) Genesis and (2) Exodus–Deuteronomy. Thus, the identification of Genesis as a distinct covenant prologue is grounded in the literary construction of the Law.

[21] See Kline, "The Old Testament Origins of the Gospel Genre," in *The Structure of Biblical Authority*, 172–203, and Dale C. Allison Jr., *The New Moses: A Matthean Typology* (Minneapolis: Fortress, 1993), 137–290.

Prophets: Covenant History

The books of the Prophets contain the history of God's people living under his covenant administrations and the prophetic interpretation of that history. In the Old Testament, the Prophets appear in two sections, the Former and the Latter Prophets. The Former Prophets consist of Joshua, Judges, Samuel, and Kings. These books record the history of God's old covenant people and their tenure in the Land of Promise, from occupation in Joshua to exile in Kings. The material presented in this history is characterized by descriptions of God's faithfulness to his covenant promises and Israel's infidelity to that covenant. This aspect of God's faithfulness to the covenant functions as the literary frame for the Former Prophets and, as such, is programmatic for the interpretation of this material, as the following two texts from the first and last books of the Former Prophets demonstrate:

> Not one word of all the good promises that the LORD had made to the house of Israel had failed; all came to pass. (Josh. 21:45)

> Blessed be the LORD who has given rest to his people Israel, according to all that he promised. Not one word has failed of all his good promise, which he spoke by Moses his servant. (1 Kings 8:56)

The corresponding themes of God's faithfulness and Israel's infidelity already appear in Deuteronomy 29–31, which serves as the blueprint for the material presented in the Former Prophets. Here the pattern of occupation (Deut. 30:15–16; 31:13, 20), infidelity (29:25–26; 31:16, 20–21, 27–29), exile (29:27–28; 30:17–18; 31:17–18), and return (30:1–10) is established as the prophetic preword that shapes the characterization of Israel in the Former Prophets.

The so-called Latter Prophets consist of Isaiah, Jeremiah, Ezekiel, and the Book of the Twelve (i.e., what English Bibles often call the Minor Prophets).[22] At one level, this material constitutes the authorized, inspired, prophetic interpretation of Israel's history under the covenant. "Thus," as Rendtorff observes, "the prophetic word becomes a commentary on the history of Israel in the time of the kings."[23] Once again, this material shines a spotlight on God's faithfulness to his covenant, on Israel's infidelity that resulted in their expulsion from the land, and on the hope of a return from exile and the restoration of covenant blessing.

The latter prophets were called to serve as God's covenant officials, as covenant lawyers prosecuting the Lord's covenant lawsuit against his unfaithful people, Israel. In other words, the latter prophets function as the Lord's prosecuting attorneys. The Law (Exodus–Deuteronomy) contains the covenant regulations that stipulate and govern the life of the people of God. It represents the standard by which they were to live. The Former Prophets (Joshua–Kings) provide the historical evidence that documents the Lord's faithfulness to the covenant along with Israel's pervasive

---

[22] The Book of the Twelve is counted as a single book in the Hebrew Bible, much like Samuel, Kings, and Chronicles are each counted as a single book.

[23] Rendtorff, *The Canonical Hebrew Bible*, 7.

infidelity. These realities not only shape the content presented in those sections but aid in our understanding of how to use it in teaching and preaching.

Just as Deuteronomy 29–31 serves as the programmatic blueprint for the material that appears in the Former Prophets, so Deuteronomy 32 serves the same function for the Latter Prophets. Deuteronomy 32, the song of Yahweh, appears in the form of a covenant lawsuit[24] and represents the preliminary, prophetic witness against the people of God for their infidelity. It also establishes the literary and theological content of the Latter Prophets. In other words, Deuteronomy 32 represents the interpretive lens through which to understand and interpret Isaiah through Malachi. It is no accident that the song of Yahweh in Deuteronomy 32 and the entire corpus of prophetic literature both begin (cf. Isa. 1:2) with the call of heaven and earth to bear witness against Israel in the execution of Yahweh's lawsuit against his people. This song of witness includes a testimony of Yahweh's covenant faithfulness (Deut. 32:3–4, 7–14), Israel's infidelity (32:5, 15–18), judgment or the enactment of covenant curses (32:19–25), and then a surprising reversal where the lawsuit is "broken" and God's people are restored (32:36–43). This restoration takes place through an act of atonement by which the Lord "takes vengeance on his enemies" and "makes atonement for his land and people" (32:43, my trans.). It is this same pattern of judgment and restoration that the Latter Prophets exemplify in their anticipation of new covenant realities.

The New Testament includes a single book addressing *covenant history*, the book of Acts. This book also contains the account of the initial history of God's people under the new covenant, along with the prophetic-apostolic interpretation of that history.[25] If in the Former Prophets the goal of God's people was to occupy the land and establish God's name in Jerusalem (cf. Deut. 12:5, 11, 21; 14:23; 16:2, 6, 11; 26:2), then that goal is reversed in the book of Acts, where God's people are directed to move out from Jerusalem, to Judea, and then to the ends of the world in order to bear witness to God's name among all the nations.

Though not its own discrete unit like the Latter Prophets, the book of Acts contains within itself several programmatic speeches that function as the prophetic-apostolic interpretation of the history that is recorded in this book. Major examples include the speech of Peter in Acts 2, the speech of Stephen in Acts 7, and the speech of Paul in Acts 13. It is also worth mentioning that Stephen's speech functions as the final covenant lawsuit in the Bible. It was here that the Jewish religious leadership (the

---

[24] The form of the covenant lawsuit is derived from the covenant form itself: identification of the judge, testimony of innocence, indictments, witnesses, judgment, and call to repentance. For more on this topic, see Herbert B. Huffmon, "The Covenant Lawsuit in the Prophets," *JBL* 78, no. 4 (1959): 285–95; James Limburg, "The Root ריב and the Prophetic Lawsuit Speeches," *JBL* 88, no. 3 (1969): 291–304; G. E. Mendenhall, "Samuel's 'Broken Rib': Deuteronomy 32.1–43," in *No Famine in the Land: Studies in Honor of John L. McKenzie*, ed. James W. Flanagan and Anita Weisbrod Robinson (Missoula, MT: Scholars Press, 1975), 63–73; Kirsten Nielsen, *Yahweh as Prosecutor and Judge: An Investigation of the Prophetic Lawsuit (Rib-Pattern)*, trans. by F. Cryer, JSOTSup 9 (Sheffield: JSOT Press, 1978); G. Ernest Wright, "The Lawsuit of God: A Form-Critical Study of Deuteronomy 32," in *Israel's Prophetic Heritage: Essays in Honor of James Muilenberg*, ed. Bernhard W. Anderson and Walter J. Harrelson (New York: Harper, 1962), 26–46.

[25] In addition to the more general contours of covenantal function and content, additional elements may serve to connect this corpus of biblical literature. One such example may be the correspondence between the narrative account of Achan and his family in Joshua 7 and that of Ananias and Sapphira in Acts 5. In both instances, the covenant ethic of the kingdom is displayed in the deaths of the covenant violators.

Sanhedrin) received the same declaration of judgment that fell upon the wilderness generation after worshiping the golden calf: "stiff-necked" (cf. Ex. 32:9; 33:3, 5; 34:9; Acts 7:51). These were the people who failed to enter into God's rest and possess his promises because of their unbelief, and so they perished in the wilderness. Stephen pronounces the same judgment upon the Sanhedrin. Then, by way of martyrdom, Stephen is identified with the prophets whom their fathers persecuted in the very same way (Acts 7:51–53, 59–60). Though slightly different in design, the Former and Latter Prophets occupy the same category of *covenant history* and share the same function as the book of Acts, the *covenant history* book of the New Testament.

Writings: Covenant Life

The books in this third and final category of the covenantal Canon are those labeled as *covenant life*. These books teach us how to think and live by faith in light of the covenant to which we belong. These are the more "practical" books in the Bible, and they include some of the more popular books used for preaching and teaching in the church today.

There are twelve books in this final section of the Hebrew Old Testament, Psalms through Chronicles. These books appear to have been arranged in two subsections: those that pertain to life in the land (Psalms, Job, Proverbs, Ruth, Song of Songs, and Ecclesiastes) and those that pertain to life in exile (Lamentations, Esther, Daniel, Ezra–Nehemiah, and Chronicles). The sequence within which many of these books appear may be motivated by the pedagogical principle of exposition and illustration. For example, the most common type of psalm in the book of Psalms is the lament, and so Job follows as the illustration of what it looks like to experience suffering in life and to express that suffering through lamentation. Or consider the fact that the wisdom narrative of Ruth follows Proverbs 31, the exposition of the "excellent wife." The only historical woman in the Bible to receive this explicit designation is Ruth, the illustration of the "excellent wife." It may also be significant that the Song of Songs appears in conjunction with Proverbs 31 and the book of Ruth. In fact, it will be argued later that the Song of Songs functions as the counterpart to Proverbs 31 in terms of its basic function for training in wisdom. This subsection in the Writings concludes with Ecclesiastes, perhaps explaining the "vanity" or folly of a life without wisdom, a life lived "under the sun," meaning "without God."

The second subsection in the Writings (*covenant life*) begins with the book of Lamentations, which calls for God's people in exile to a life of faithfulness by waiting and hoping for the salvation of the Lord (cf. Lam. 3:25–31). Lamentations is then followed by the books of Esther and Daniel, containing the accounts of two people who lived faithfully in exile under the most difficult and challenging of circumstances. Esther and Daniel serve as examples for God's people, illustrating what it looks like to live a life of faith in exile, as aliens and strangers on the earth (cf. Heb. 11:13; 1 Pet. 2:11).

This section in the Old Testament concludes with Ezra–Nehemiah and Chronicles.

These books have been arranged in such a way as to characterize Israel's return from exile as falling short of the anticipated prophetic restoration (e.g., Ezra 3:12; Hag. 2:6–9). From the decree of Cyrus in Ezra 1:1–4 to the decree of Cyrus in 2 Chronicles 36:22–23, the promised return from exile did not exhibit the full restoration of the temple or the Davidic dynasty. And so the genealogies of Chronicles begin the search for the Davidic king from the tribe of Judah (1 Chronicles 2–4) and the Aaronic priest from the tribe of Levi (1 Chronicles 6). This book also highlights the work of planning and building the First Temple (1 Chronicles 22–2 Chronicles 7) and the celebration of the Passover that would anticipate a new exodus (2 Chronicles 30, 35), led by someone who would go up before God's people in a new conquest (2 Chron. 36:23).

It is not until we encounter the genealogies of the New Testament, in Matthew and Luke, that the genealogies of Chronicles find their expected fulfillment in the person of Jesus. He is the Davidic King from the tribe of Judah (e.g., Matt. 1:1; 12:23; Rom. 1:3; 2 Tim. 2:8), the eternal High Priest (e.g., Heb. 5:1–10), the Passover Lamb (John 1:29, 36), the new exodus (Luke 9:31), and the One who will lead God's people in the final battle of conquest (Revelation 19). In many ways, the book of Chronicles functions like the book of Revelation, bringing the whole of God's Old Testament Word into sharp focus by highlighting important people, institutions, and themes. It serves as the ideal canonical hinge connecting the Old and New Testaments. Like the book of Genesis, it begins with Adam and includes important genealogies. But it is the only other book in the Christian Bible besides Matthew to begin with a genealogy. There is little doubt that the book of Chronicles serves as the perfect conclusion to the Old Testament Scriptures (cf. Luke 11:51), anticipating that which would soon transpire in the opening Gospel accounts of the New Testament and beyond.

In the New Testament, the Epistles (Romans–Jude) serve the same basic covenantal function as the Old Testament Writings. They were designed to train God's people for life in the new covenant, both in terms of how we think (theology) and how we live (ethics). Paul's epistles serve as a good example. They are commonly divided into two main parts, the indicative and the imperative. In the first part (indicative), Paul describes the theological implications of the new covenant in light of the person and work of Christ (e.g., Romans 1–11). In the second part (imperative), Paul describes the practical or ethical implications of life in the new covenant. This method of presentation is not unfamiliar to Old Testament Wisdom Literature, a school of thought in which Paul was trained as a Pharisee. In the book of Proverbs, for example, the first section (Proverbs 1–9) presents readers with a theology of wisdom in opposition to folly. In the second section (Proverbs 10–31), readers encounter the practical or ethical implications of the life of wisdom. Based on the observations presented here, it seems reasonable to conclude that the correspondence between the *covenant life* books in the Old and New Testaments are intentional and provide readers with a macrocanonical hermeneutical lens through which to understand and apply this material appropriately in the life of the church.

CONCLUSION

We have come to understand that the Bible has (1) a theological center, (2) a thematic framework, and (3) a covenantal structure. This threefold perspective for biblical theology provides unity and comprehends diversity. When asked about the Bible's content, we can answer with confidence that it is about *Jesus and the kingdom of God*. When asked about the nature of the Bible, or how it works, our answer is simple: it works covenantally in the categories of *covenant* (Law), *covenant history* (Prophets), and *covenant life* (Writings), for both the Old and New Testaments.[26]

In this introductory chapter, we have labored to describe the larger biblical context that will help to make sense of each individual Old Testament book studied in the subsequent chapters, intentionally following the ordering of the books presented in the Hebrew Old Testament. This is the older tradition, and it is the tradition validated by Jesus and the authors of the New Testament. We have also seen that the New Testament books have been grouped and arranged after the pattern of the Hebrew arrangement for Old Testament books, *not* the English Bible arrangement! Thus, the construction of the Christian Bible in its macrocanonical structure exhibits an "intelligent design" that points to its ultimate, divine author and shapes the ultimate meaning or message of the one book.

This macrocanonical context helps us to understand the big picture, how the Old and New Testaments fit together and how the parts of each Testament relate to each other. It also shapes how we might interpret and apply each of the different books in each of the different sections in each of the different Testaments.[27]

We have also observed how Genesis and Chronicles fit together as the beginning and end of the Hebrew Old Testament. Both books begin with the figure of Adam and contain important genealogical lists that work to trace and identify the conquering, messianic seed of the woman that would fulfill all the covenantal promises of God and promote the consummation of the kingdom of God. But Chronicles also fits together with Matthew, the first book of the New Testament. These are the only two books in the Christian Bible that begin with genealogies, and the sought-after king and priest of Chronicles is found only in the arrival of the genealogical presentation of Jesus in the New Testament.

It may also be worth noting that the three sections of the Hebrew Old Testament—*covenant* (Law), *covenant history* (Prophets), and *covenant life* (Writings)—are glued together at the seams.[28] For example, the Old Testament Prophets and Writings begin with statements that express their dependence upon the Law by uniquely highlighting the protological importance of meditation on the "law of the LORD"

---

[26] So Rendtorff argues, "Thus the variety of voices within the Hebrew Bible gains its quite specific structure through the arrangement of the canon." *The Canonical Hebrew Bible*, 8.

[27] Dempster similarly explains that "canonization provides a literary context for all the texts, creating one Text from many. The fact that the Hebrew canon is structured in terms of a narrative sequence with commentary means that canonization does not 'flatten' the text into a one-dimensional uniformity; rather, it provides for evolution, diversity and growth within an overarching framework in which the various parts can be related to the literary whole." *Dominion and Dynasty*, 42–43.

[28] Dempster has noted, "Moreover, the final compilers of the biblical text ensured that the text was to be understood as a unity. There are not only major groupings of books, but editorial 'splices' that join the major groupings of the books with each other. Therefore, both theological and literary points are made simultaneously." *Dominion and Dynasty*, 32.

"day and night" (cf. Josh. 1:8; Ps. 1:2). Additionally, the Law and the Prophets also conclude with the expectation of a prophet like unto but greater than Moses and Elijah (cf. Deut 34:10–12; Mal. 4:4–6; Matt. 17:3–4; Mark 9:4–5; Luke 9:30–33). This covenantal-canonical glue provides evidence that this arrangement is not accidental but intentional, instructional, and hermeneutical. The Prophets and the Writings are grounded in the Law, or covenant documents, but this material is also eschataological in nature, striving to identify the ultimate Prophet who will usher in the day of the Lord.

Finally, it is important to understand that this arrangement is ultimately christological. Jesus is the seed of the woman who has come to crush the seed of the serpent, and he is the offspring of Abraham who fulfills every covenantal promise (Genesis; *covenant prologue*). Jesus is also the better covenant Mediator, the true and better Temple, and the true and better sacrifice. Jesus came to keep and fulfill the law of God (Exodus–Deuteronomy; *covenant*). Jesus Christ is the true and better Israel who was totally and completely obedient to the law of Moses, earning the righteousness that we could not earn for ourselves. He is the seed of David, according to the flesh, the King of the kingdom of God. Jesus Christ is also the true and better Prophet. Not only did he execute the ultimate prophetic lawsuit, but he bore its punishment for those who would receive his earned righteousness. He was not bound by the Old Testament prophetic messenger formula, "Thus says the Lord," but rather, spoke as Yahweh himself, "truly, truly I say to you" (Joshua–Malachi; *covenant history*). Jesus Christ is the true and better Wisdom, the ultimate praise of God, the very Wisdom of God (Psalms–Chronicles; *covenant life*). He is the way and the truth and the life (John 14:6). If you would understand the Old Testament, you must come to embrace Jesus, his kingdom, and the covenantal nature of his Word and work.

SELECT BIBLIOGRAPHY

Beckwith, Roger T. *The Old Testament Canon of the New Testament Church and Its Background in Early Judaism*. 1985. Reprint, Eugene, OR: Wipf & Stock, 2008.

Bright, John. *The Kingdom of God: The Biblical Concept and Its Meaning for the Church*. New York: Abingdon-Cokesbury, 1953.

Dempster, Stephen G. *Dominion and Dynasty: A Theology of the Hebrew Bible*. NSBT 15. Downers Grove, IL: InterVarsity Press, 2003.

Eichrodt, Walther. *Theology of the Old Testament*. Translated by J. A. Baker. 2 vols. OTL. Philadelphia: Westminster, 1961.

Goldsworthy, Graeme L. "Biblical Theology as the Heartbeat of Effective Ministry." In *Biblical Theology: Retrospect and Prospect*, edited by Scott J. Hafemann, 280–86. Downers Grove, IL: IVP Academic, 2002.

Goswell, Greg. "The Order of the Books in the Greek Old Testament." *JETS* 52, no. 3 (2009): 449–66.

———. "The Order of the Books in the Hebrew Bible." *JETS* 51, no. 4 (2008): 673–88.

Horton, Michael. *Introducing Covenant Theology*. Grand Rapids, MI: Baker, 2006.

Huffmon, Herbert B. "The Covenant Lawsuit in the Prophets." *JBL* 78, no. 4 (1959): 285–95.

Kline, Meredith G. *The Structure of Biblical Authority*. 2nd ed. Eugene, OR: Wipf & Stock, 1989.

Limburg, James. "The Root ריב and the Prophetic Lawsuit Speeches." *JBL* 88, no. 3 (1969): 291–304.

Mendenhall, G. E. "Samuel's 'Broken Rib': Deuteronomy 32.1–43." In *No Famine in the Land: Studies in Honor of John L. McKenzie*, edited by James Flanagan and Anita Weisbrod Robinson, 63–73. Missoula, MT: Scholars Press, 1975.

Motyer, Alec. *Look to the Rock: An Old Testament Background to Our Understanding of Christ*. Grand Rapids, MI: Kregel, 1996.

Nielsen, Kirsten. *Yahweh as Prosecutor and Judge: An Investigation of the Prophetic Lawsuit (Rîb-Pattern)*. Translated by F. Cryer. JSOTSup 9. Sheffield: JSOT Press, 1978.

Rendtorff, Rolf. *The Canonical Hebrew Bible: A Theology of the Old Testament*. TBS 7. Leiden: Deo, 2005.

Sailhamer, John. "Creation, Genesis 1–11, and the Canon." *BBR* 10, no. 1 (2000): 89–106.

Steinmann, Andrew E. *The Oracles of God: The Old Testament Canon*. St. Louis, MO: Concordia, 2000.

Wegner, Paul D. *The Journey from Texts to Translation: The Origin and Development of the Bible*. Grand Rapids, MI: Baker, 1999.

Wright, G. Ernest. "The Lawsuit of God: A Form-Critical Study of Deuteronomy 32." In *Israel's Prophetic Heritage: Essays in Honor of James Muilenberg*, edited by Bernhard W. Anderson and Walter J. Harrelson, 26–67. New York: Harper, 1962.

1

Genesis

John D. Currid

INTRODUCTION

The name of the first book of the Hebrew Bible derives from the opening word of the Hebrew text, בְּרֵאשִׁית. This word means "in the beginning," and it is an appropriate designation because the book is about beginnings: the beginning of the universe; the beginning of time, matter, and space; the beginning of humanity; the beginning of sin; the beginning of redemption; and the beginning of Israel. By deliberating over Genesis, then, we are essentially engaging in *protology*, the study of first things. That the cosmos has a beginning implies that it also has an end and that everything is moving toward a consummation (the study of these last things is called *eschatology*). The Scriptures, therefore, present a linear history, a movement from inception to completion.

Scholars have commonly tried to distinguish between this Hebraic view of history and that of other ancient Near Eastern cultures. Many have argued that the pagan cultures of the time believed in a cyclical history, teaching that nature is locked in an unending sequence of birth, life, death, and rebirth. And therefore, the world is heading nowhere; it is merely in a ceaseless, natural cycle. In reality, that contrast is too simplistic. The ancients were actually quite aware of history, which the great volume of historical records these peoples kept confirms. The ancient Egyptians, Assyrians, and Babylonians were skilled and proficient in preserving historical documents, annals, and chronologies.[1] The contrast between the two conceptions of the universe really boils down to the question of what is the foundation of history. The Hebrews had a worldview that centered on God as the Lord and overseer of history.

---

[1] See Pritchard, *ANET*; William K. Simpson, ed., *The Literature of Ancient Egypt: An Anthology of Stories, Instructions, Stelae, Autobiographies, and Poetry*, trans. Robert K. Ritner et al., 3rd ed. (New Haven: Yale University Press, 2003); D. Winton Thomas, *Documents from Old Testament Times*, Harper Torchbooks, TB 85 (New York: Harper & Row, 1958); and many others.

Everything that happens in the cosmos unfolds according to God's plan; he is the One who moves history from a beginning toward a final climax (Isa. 41:4; 43:1–15; 44:6; 48:12). He is sovereign and sits on the throne of history. The other cultures of the ancient Near East had no such theological conception.

BACKGROUND ISSUES
Authorship

For the past 150 years, the question of the formation and development of the book of Genesis, and the rest of the Pentateuch for that matter, has dominated Old Testament studies. Inquiries into authorship, date of writing, and place of writing have stood at the very forefront of Old Testament scholarship. Although people have asked such questions throughout the history of Judaism and Christianity, perhaps the first to struggle seriously with the issues was Jean Astruc (AD 1684–1766), a professor of medicine at the University of Paris. Astruc determined that someone brought together four original documents to make up the Pentateuch. He noticed that certain names for God dominated different parts of the literature, and this became one factor in determining what belonged to which source. He also believed that doublets—that is, a second telling of the same incident—demonstrated different sources. Although Astruc likely believed that Moses was the author of each of the four sources, his studies laid the foundation for the biblical criticism that would soon follow.

So what started the belief that Genesis was the writing of not one person but rather various authors whose sources redactors (i.e., editors) stitched together over time? Perhaps the most important impetus for this notion was the thinking not of a biblical scholar but of a philosopher. Georg Wilhelm Friedrich Hegel (1770–1831) formed an influential worldview that argued that all things in reality are changing or in process. Everything is developing from lower to higher degrees of perfection. This process occurs by means of the dialectic that moves things from one state (thesis) to its opposite (antithesis) and finally achieves a higher synthesis between the two. It repeats itself so that higher states of existence come into being. This is a natural process that affects all areas of life: culture, social systems, political systems, biology, economics, and religion. It is an evolutionary view of existence.

One of Hegel's colleagues, a biblical scholar named Wilhelm Vatke (1806–1882), took and applied Hegel's philosophy to the study of the Old Testament and, in particular, to the formation of the Pentateuch.[2] This marked a major turning point because "the application of Hegelian philosophy to the study of the Old Testament led to [Julius] Wellhausen's [1844–1918] establishment of the modern Documentary Hypothesis of the Pentateuch and eventually to the death of Old Testament theology."[3] Building upon these foundational presuppositions of Astruc, Hegel, and others, subsequent biblical scholars theorized that the Pentateuch was indeed a collation of numerous sources brought together by later editors. However, they did not

---

[2] Wilhelm Vatke, *Die Biblische Theologie* (Berlin: Bethke, 1835).
[3] Ralph L. Smith, *Old Testament Theology: Its History, Method, and Message* (Nashville: Broadman, 1993), 32.

agree on the sources and how they were collated. For example, those who adhere to the Supplementary Hypothesis argue that there was one core document of the Pentateuch to which redactors added numerous fragments over the centuries. On the other hand, others argue that the Pentateuch lacks a core document altogether and consists merely of a mass of fragments from numerous sources that have been collated and edited (this is called the Fragmentary Hypothesis).

The major source theory developed in the nineteenth century was the Graf-Wellhausen Theory, otherwise known as the Documentary Hypothesis. This theory proposed four basic sources for the Pentateuch, referred to as J, E, D, and P:

1. J is the **Jahwist** (or **Yahwist**) source. This is a source that primarily uses the name Jehovah (that is, Yahweh) to refer to God. The J source is considered the oldest source, and it can be viewed in Genesis 2:4–4:26, and in portions of Exodus and Numbers. The originators of the hypothesis thought that it had been derived from the period of the united monarchy during the reigns of David and Solomon.
2. E is the **Elohist** source. It employs the name Elohim for God, and it comes from a later period than the J source. A later redactor, referred to as R^{JE}, put the two sources together.
3. D refers to the **Deuteronomist**. This material was written even later than the first two, and it was commonly seen as coming from the time of King Josiah in the second half of the seventh century BC. Another redactor, called R^{D}, brought together this material with J and E to create one document.
4. P is the **Priestly** and final source. It includes much of the cultic, sacred, and sacrificial material and matters related to the priesthood. Scholars who adopt the Documentary Hypothesis believe the P source was written late and should be placed during the exilic and postexilic periods.

While these are the four main sources for the Pentateuch, this position also argues that numerous smaller fragments, such as Genesis 14, were inserted into these primary documents.

Very few scholars today accept the Documentary Hypothesis as originally formulated; the issue of authorship has become much more complex. There is, in reality, little consensus among scholars regarding who wrote what and when, even though they continue to use the acronym JEDP. Additionally, many scholars argue that each of those four major sources resulted from various editors and redactors bringing together many other sources. What is clear is that much Old Testament scholarship denies the historicity of the material of the Pentateuch and claims that the material we do have is a result of centuries of literary evolution.[4]

Literary Analysis

In the last three decades, scholars from a variety of perspectives have called for a focus on the final form of the text as a literary whole. Standing at the forefront of

---

[4] For further discussion, see Carl E. Amerding, *The Old Testament and Criticism* (Grand Rapids, MI: Eerdmans, 1983); Duane A. Garrett, *Rethinking Genesis: The Sources and Authorship of the First Book of the Pentateuch* (Grand Rapids, MI: Baker, 1991); Isaac M. Kikawada and Arthur Quinn, *Before Abraham Was: The Unity of Genesis 1–11* (Nashville: Abingdon, 1985); and Richard N. Soulen, *Handbook of Biblical Criticism*, 2nd ed. (Atlanta: John Knox, 1981).

this attention, Brevard Childs argued that exegesis should be based upon the final, canonical form of the biblical text.[5] This perspective has led many scholars to shift their focus away from merely working in source criticism to discovering the various levels of how the Pentateuch reached its final form. Leading this charge is Robert Alter, who wrote a truly groundbreaking work titled *The Art of Biblical Narrative*.[6] In this work, Alter defines a field of biblical study called literary analysis.

Literary analysis deals with what Alter calls "the artful use of language" in a particular literary genre.[7] This includes such conventions in Hebrew writing as structure, wordplay, imagery, sound, syntax, and many other devices that appear in the final form of the text. In Alter's own words, he defines it as follows:

> By literary analysis I mean the manifold varieties of minutely discriminating attention to the artful use of language, to the shifting play of ideas, conventions, tone, sound, imagery, syntax, narrative viewpoint, compositional units, and much else; the kind of disciplined attention, in other words, which through a whole spectrum of critical approaches has illuminated, for example, the poetry of Dante, the plays of Shakespeare, the novels of Tolstoy.[8]

This literary approach has yielded much fruit in biblical studies, and it has allowed scholars once again to see the literary qualities of the final form of a text.

For example, when source critics engage a text like Genesis 38, the account of Judah and Tamar, they understand it as a mixture of source documents dominated especially by J and E, and many see no connection between this story and the surrounding account of Joseph's life. For example, von Rad argues in his Genesis commentary that "every attentive reader can see the story of Judah and Tamar has no connection at all with the strictly organized Joseph story at whose beginning it is now inserted."[9] Speiser agrees when he says, "The narrative is a completely independent unit. It has no connection with the drama of Joseph, which it interrupts."[10] Genesis 38 is, therefore, a mere interpolation, probably inserted by the J or Yahwist author.

Literary analysis, however, demonstrates something different. It asks, why has the story been placed here? And it concludes, in this case, that the text of Genesis 38 has been masterfully and artistically woven into the context of the Joseph story. For example, Sprinkle, summarizing Alter, observes that the same motifs occur in chapter 38 as in chapter 37:

> As Joseph is separated from his brothers by "going down" to Egypt, so Judah separates from his brothers by "going down" to marry a Canaanite woman. Jacob is forced to mourn for a supposed death of his son, Judah is forced to mourn for the actual death of two of his sons. . . . Judah tricked Jacob, so Tamar (in poetic

---

[5] Brevard S. Childs, *Introduction to the Old Testament as Scripture* (Philadelphia: Fortress, 1979). Also at the forefront of this perspective is James Muilenburg, "Form Criticism and Beyond," *JBL* 88, no. 1 (1969): 1–18.
[6] Robert Alter, *The Art of Biblical Narrative* (New York: Basic Books, 1981).
[7] Alter, *The Art of Biblical Narrative*, 12.
[8] Alter, *The Art of Biblical Narrative*, 12–13.
[9] Gerhard von Rad, *Genesis: A Commentary*, trans. John H. Marks, OTL (Philadelphia: Westminster, 1961), 351.
[10] E. A. Speiser, *Genesis: A New Translation with Introduction and Commentary*, AB 1 (Garden City, NY: Doubleday, 1964), 299.

justice) tricks Judah. . . . Judah used a goat (its blood) in his deception of Jacob, so the promised harlot's price of a kid plays a role in his own deception.[11]

The story of Genesis 38 also has thematic ties to the subsequent account, serving as a foil to the story of Potiphar's wife. Judah marries a Canaanite, and after his wife's death, he has sexual relations with a woman he thinks is a prostitute. Joseph, on the contrary, does not fall victim to sexual temptation. Thus, whereas Judah succumbs to the allurements of the Canaanites, Joseph refuses to give in to the wiles of the Egyptian female.

Literary analysis is essential in studying the book of Genesis, for although Genesis includes numerous genres, such as genealogy, poetry, prayer, and so forth, the predominant genre is narrative. Yet because Hebrew narrative can exhibit the "artful" use of language in various stages, the literary analysis of Genesis can become quite complex. For the purpose of this introduction, we will consider three basic stages of analysis, moving from the simplest to the more complex, which will serve as a starting point for the reader.

Stage 1: Leitwort ("Lead or Guide Word")

Definition: "The German term *Leitwort* refers to a word or root-word that appears repeatedly throughout a pericope, and it is one of the most common components of narrative art in the OT. The role of a *Leitwort* is to highlight and to develop the principal theme of a narrative."[12]

Genesis example: In the account of Jacob's stealing the blessing from Esau in Genesis 27, two *Leitworter* (the German plural of *Leitwort*) define the narrative's thematic purpose. The words that occur repeatedly are צַיִד ("game," seven times as a noun and four times as its cognate verb, "hunt") and מַטְעַמִּים ("delicious food," six times). Waltke observes that "Isaac is said to 'love tasty food' by Rebekah, Isaac himself, and the narrator. This repetition makes clear the story's message: Isaac's cupidity has distorted his spiritual taste. He has given himself over to an indulgent sensuality."[13]

Stage 2: Leitphrase ("Lead or Guide Phrase")

Definition: The German word *Leitphrase* refers to the repetition of a phrase or clause, rather than a single word, that dominates a text.

Genesis example: In Genesis 1, the phrase "And there was evening and there was morning, the [numbered] day" appears six times (1:5, 8, 13, 19, 23, 31). That *Leitphrase* provides the temporal framework for the entire creation account.

Sometimes a pericope can be more complicated by including both stages of *Leitwort*

---

[11] Joe M. Sprinkle, "Literary Approaches to the Old Testament: A Survey of Recent Scholarship," *JETS* 32, no. 3 (1989): 302.
[12] John D. Currid and L. K. Larson, "Narrative Repetition in 1 Samuel 24 and 26: Saul's Descent and David's Ascent," in *From Creation to New Creation: Essays on Biblical Theology and Exegesis*, ed. Daniel M. Gurtner and Benjamin L. Gladd (Peabody, MA: Hendrickson, 2013), 51–62.
[13] Bruce K. Waltke, *An Old Testament Theology: An Exegetical, Canonical, and Thematic Approach*, with Charles Yu (Grand Rapids, MI: Zondervan, 2007), 116–17.

and *Leitphrase*. Genesis 39:1–6, for instance, gives the account of Joseph's servitude to Potiphar, his Egyptian master, and contains a number of *Leitworter*: כֹּל ("all," five times), בַּיִת ("house," five times), יד ("hand," four times), and מַצְלִיחַ ("success," two times). It also includes a *Leitphrase*: "the LORD was with Joseph" (two times). The complexity of these literary forms becomes apparent when one considers a story later in the chapter that describes Joseph's service to an Egyptian jailer (39:19–23). This account features the same leading words used in the earlier one: "all" (three times), "house" (four times), "hand" (two times), and "success" (one time). As well, the leading phrase "the LORD was with Joseph" appears twice. These repetitions highlight an echo (which reminds me of a great Mark Twain quote: "History doesn't repeat itself, but it does rhyme"); the recurring pattern demonstrates that Joseph is *successful* no matter what his earthly master places in his *hands* because *the Lord is with him*. This paradigm essentially repeats itself when Pharaoh later places *all* the *house* of Egypt into Joseph's *hands* (Gen. 41:37–45).

Stage 3: Leitmotif ("Leading Theme or Motif")

Definition: The German term *Leitmotif* identifies an account (which Alter also calls a *type-scene*) that is repeated, more or less, in different contexts.

Genesis example: In Genesis, the motif "she is my sister" appears three times (12:10–20; 20:1–18; 26:6–11). On the first two occasions, Abraham tells a foreign ruler that his wife, Sarah, is really his sister, and in the third instance, Isaac says the same thing about his wife, Rebekah. All three instances are examples of the patriarchs attempting to save themselves from possible danger posed by foreign rulers. Scholars commonly attribute this repetition of narrative to the duplication of sources. In other words, different authors employed the same story for different episodes and purposes. In reality, that reasoning is wanting because the *Leitmotif* is the very essence of biblical narrative. It is one of the primary ways the biblical writer relates his material. The recurrent stammer or echo of the "she is my sister" theme connects these narratives in a meaningful way through the use of similar deceptive tactics—it worked twice for Abraham and once for his son.

Another example of the *Leitmotif* in Genesis is one that begins there and echoes throughout the rest of the Bible. The "barren wife" scene pictures an Israelite woman unable to bear children, and then, by some extraordinary means, she conceives and bears a son. The male descendant then grows up to be a leader or deliverer of God's people. The motif first appears in Genesis 11:27–30, where Sarah, the wife of Abraham, is barren. Isaac, of course, is born supernaturally to the aged couple. This scene is repeated in Genesis 25:20–21 (Rebekah and Isaac) and in 29:31 (Rachel and Jacob). The "barren wife" motif continues throughout the Old Testament with the stories of other barren women, such as Samson's mother (Judg. 13:2) and Hannah, the mother of Samuel (1 Sam. 1:2). This type-scene reaches its climax in the virgin birth of Jesus to Mary in the New Testament: he, of course, is the climactic deliverer of God's people.

STRUCTURE AND OUTLINE

Literary Structure of Genesis

Genesis can be divided into three major sections: (1) the creation of the world (1:1–2:3); (2) the primeval history of the world from Adam to Abraham (2:4–11:26); and (3) the history of the patriarchs (11:27–50:26). After narrating the creation episode, the author provides a highly structured account that covers the history from Adam to Joseph, signaling new and significant sections of material with the recurring *toledoth* formula. This formula in Hebrew (תּוֹלְדוֹת) literally means "the generations of," and it stands behind the common heading "These are the generations of . . . ," which appears eleven times in Genesis (2:4; 5:1; 6:9; 10:1; 11:10, 27; 25:12, 19; 36:1, 9; 37:2).

The word תּוֹלְדוֹת is derived from the Hebrew root ילד, which means "to give birth, bear." Naturally, the formula often precedes a genealogy, which also generally includes narrative material. Its first appearance in 2:4 refers to the creation of the heavens and the earth and the subsequent objects or things that come forth from the subject named. The next occurrence of it relates to Adam and the subsequent people who descend from him. The book of Genesis is thus structured with a genealogical focus.

Theological Structure of Genesis

The basic message of the Bible has often been defined as creation, fall, and redemption. This is essentially correct. What often goes unrecognized is that these three distinctives are found in the book of Genesis and, in particular, in its first three chapters. Genesis 1–3, in reality, serves as a microcosm for the fundamental message of the whole Bible. We will consider each teaching in its order.

MESSAGE AND THEOLOGY

Creation

At the outset of the Old Testament, the reader is introduced at once to God in the essential fullness of his being. The author excludes all prefatory matter. To God and God alone is the reader brought: so Genesis declares, "In the beginning God . . ." (Gen. 1:1). The audience is to understand that the creation account is principally about God, not creation or humankind. It is theocentric and not anthropocentric. And in this passage in Genesis, God makes himself known through the works of his creative will, which the psalmist later recognized: "The heavens declare the glory of God, and the sky above proclaims his handiwork" (Ps. 19:1). It is also important to note that at the very beginning, the Old Testament provides no proofs for the existence of God. The Bible presupposes the very being of God; it does not need to be proven. Scripture stands on this very truth: God is.

God not only exists but also creates. Table 2 shows how the narrator recounts his creative work in Genesis 1 for each day according to a repeated structure.

1. Announcement	"And God said . . ." (1:3, 6, 9, 11, 14, 20, 24, 26)
2. Command	"Let there be . . ." (1:3, 6, 9, 11, 14, 20, 24, 26)
3. Report	"And it was so." (1:3, 7, 9, 11, 15, 24, 30)
4. Evaluation	"And God saw that it was good." (1:4, 10, 12, 18, 21, 25, 31)
5. Temporal Framework	"And there was evening and there was morning, the [first, second, etc.] day." (1:5, 8, 13, 19, 23, 31)

Table 2

This pattern has four theological implications. First, God's creative work was effortless; he spoke, and the universe came into existence. This mere verbal fiat displays God's awesome, crushing omnipotence (Ps. 33:6–9). Second, God's creative work was *ex nihilo*, that is, it came forth from nothing. All three dimensions of the universe—space, time, and matter—are brought into being at God's word (Heb. 11:3). Third, creation was an expression of God's will, and he instigated it and fulfilled it freely without any external compulsion (Rev. 4:11). Finally, the paradigm of creation underscores the doctrine of God's sovereignty. The Lord is Creator and King, and all things are subject to his rule because he made all things (Ps. 24:1–2).

Although the creation account of Genesis 1 centers on God and his work, it also defines the content of the creation. Verse 1 of the text designates it as "the heavens and the earth." The Hebrews had no single word to describe the universe in its totality, and so when they wanted to express the concept of all reality, they would use this phrase. It is a *merismus*, two opposites that are all-inclusive (cf. Ps. 139:8). The phrase is a totality of polarity, signifying that God created everything, including heaven and earth and all that is in them, on them, and between them (cf. Col. 1:16).

The narrator outlines the general content of God's work of creation in Genesis in a highly stylized structure (maybe even a "framework"), constructing three parallels within a seven-day design. Table 3 shows this structure.

Kingdoms/Domains	Kings/Rulers
Day 1 Light (1:3–5)	Day 4 Light bearers (1:14–19)
Day 2 Sea, sky (1:6–8)	Day 5 Fish, birds (1:20–23)
Day 3 Land (1:9–13)	Day 6 Land creatures (1:24–31)
Day 7 Sabbath (2:1–3)	

Table 3

The six days of creation include two sets of three days in parallel. The first triad (days 1–3) describes the kingdoms being created, and the second triad (days 4–6) portrays the creation of the rulers over those kingdoms. Days 1, 2, and 3 directly correspond with days 4, 5, and 6, respectively. Because of this detailed repetition and structure, some scholars have argued that the account is poetic.[14] Apart from its structure, though, Genesis 1 has very little in it that would classify it as Hebrew poetry. In fact, it has all the indicators that it is written as Hebrew narrative. However, it must be admitted that while it is not poetry, it is also not ordinary, common prose. It is narrative yet with an elevated style. Therefore, C. John Collins offers perhaps the best description of the genre of Genesis 1 when he calls it "exalted prose narrative."[15]

Theologians often describe the creation of mankind on day 6 as the "crown of creation" because humanity is the last thing created during the six days. In addition, mankind is the only entity created *imago dei*, that is, in the image of God (Gen. 1:26–27). The Hebrew word for "image" is צֶלֶם, and it appears sixteen times in the Old Testament. Originally the word meant "something cut from an object," as, for example, a piece of clay cut from a sculpture.[16] In such a case there exists a concrete resemblance between the object and the image. Thus, most of its occurrences in the Old Testament refer to idols that physically represent a god (e.g., 2 Kings 11:18). It is also used of a statue of a king that he sets up in a land he has conquered, symbolizing his sovereignty over that land (e.g., Dan. 3:1). This usage helps to demonstrate that, in regard to the creation of mankind, humanity is God's representative of God's rule over the earth.

Humans are not merely created in the image of God (*imago dei*) but are also to act like him (*imitatio dei*). It is a matter not merely of character but of function and activity. In Genesis 1–2, we see that mankind is to imitate God in three ways. To set the stage, Genesis 1:2 describes the state of the earth as תֹהוּ ("formless") and בֹהוּ ("emptiness"). In the first three days of creation (1:1–10), God subdues the formlessness and brings about an ordered world. He accomplishes this through the medium of the word by naming and separating different parts of the creation. In Genesis 2, man does the same thing, subduing and ruling over creation by cultivating the garden (2:15) and especially by naming the animals (2:19–20). His work is intelligent creativity, as was God's incipient labor. Secondly, in the final three days of creation, God fills the heavens with a starry host and fills the earth with animate life. Humankind follows that pattern by filling the earth with his progeny through reproduction (1:28) and also with produce through cultivation of the earth (2:15). Finally, on the last day of creation, God rests from his subduing and filling activity. It is certainly implied that mankind would do the same by working six days and resting on the Sabbath. This is later confirmed by the Sabbath laws (see Ex. 20:8–11, which ties the Sabbath to the creation).

---

[14] Meredith G. Kline says, "Exegesis indicates that the scheme of the creation week itself is a poetic figure and that the several pictures of creation history are set within the six-work day frames not chronologically but topically." "Genesis," in *The New Bible Commentary: Revised*, ed. Donald Guthrie, J. A. Motyer, and Francis Davidson, 3rd ed. (Downers Grove, IL: InterVarsity Press, 1970), 82. In later writings, Kline backed away from that claim by calling the genre of Genesis 1 "semi-poetic." Meredith G. Kline, "Because It Had Not Rained," *WTJ* 20, no. 2 (1958): 156. See, e.g., Meredith G. Kline, "Space and Time in the Genesis Cosmogony," *Perspectives on Science and Christian Faith* 48, no. 1 (1996): 2–15; Lee Irons and Meredith G. Kline, "The Framework View," in *The Genesis Debate: Three Views on the Days of Creation*, ed. David G. Hagopian (Mission Viejo, CA: Crux, 2000), 217–56, 279–303.

[15] C. John Collins, *Genesis 1–4: A Linguistic, Literary, and Theological Commentary* (Phillipsburg, NJ: P&R, 2006), 44.

[16] Ernest Klein, *A Comprehensive Etymological Dictionary of the Hebrew Language for Readers of English* (New York: Macmillan, 1987), 548.

Creation is a *Leitmotif* that echoes throughout the Bible. In Genesis 9, for example, we see God coming to Noah after the flood and essentially renewing the divine mandate given to Adam at creation. In other words, the divine commission and blessing that God gave to Adam is replayed with Noah, who is thus a second Adam. So in Genesis 9:1, God commands Noah to be fruitful and multiply, using the identical expression employed in Genesis 1:28. Significantly, humanity's relationship to the animals is a central point to both stories (1:26; 9:2). Both accounts also highlight the idea of man in the image of God, a concept that occurs only in these two places in the book of Genesis (1:27; 9:6). Finally, the provision of food for mankind is also an important aspect of the two narratives (1:29; 9:3), and the Noahic story makes direct reference back to Genesis 1:29. The fact of the matter is that Genesis 9 is a re-creation account, that is, a second mandate patterned after the original mandate given to humanity in the garden.

The creational mandate of Genesis 1 echoes again in Exodus 1. In verse 7 of the latter text, the author explains that the Hebrews have been very active in reproduction in Egypt: "But the people of Israel were fruitful and increased greatly; they multiplied and grew exceedingly strong, so that the land was filled with them." All five verbs in this verse mirror the language of creation. The writer is taking the audience back to the cultural mandate given in Genesis 1:28 and 9:7, demonstrating that the Hebrews are fulfilling the command to be fruitful, to multiply, and to fill the earth. Israel is, in a sense, another Adam attempting to keep the cultural mandate of Genesis 1.

Another example of creation as a *Leitmotif* in Scripture is the creation and preparation of a land for God's people to inhabit. We read in Genesis 1:9–10 how God divides the waters, brings forth land (אֶרֶץ, "earth, land"), and then abundantly supplies resources to sustain his people. The Old Testament repeats this pattern of water separation and land preparation two more times. Exodus 14:15–16 portrays God as dividing the waters of chaos, driving his people through the Red Sea on dry ground, and then taking his people to a new land where he will sufficiently supply all their needs. The echo underscores that land is a blessing to God's people: God creates it, prepares it, and leads his people into it. This pattern appears again in the book of Joshua, where God divides the waters of the Jordan River, drives his people through on dry ground, and places them in a land flowing with milk and honey (3:13–17). The repeated vocabulary in these accounts—"heap" (Josh. 3:13, 16; cf. Ex. 15:8) and "dry ground" (Josh. 3:17; cf. Ex. 14:21)—confirms that this is indeed a type-scene. Here again God has prepared a land for his people, a new garden of Eden, and he is placing them into that habitation by dividing the waters.

Fall

Genesis 3:1–7 is the description of mankind's fall into sin. Humanity's demise is a complex process involving a combination of factors: the temptation and lie of the Serpent, the twisted response of the woman, the human will to disobey, and the appeal of the tree to the physical senses that overwhelms the first humans.

First, the Serpent (that is, the Devil himself, or Satan; cf. Rev. 20:2) is described as "crafty," a word that reflects his deceptiveness and slyness (Gen. 3:1). This is immediately made evident when the Serpent approaches the woman in the garden and cunningly asks her about the commands of God. Second, when the woman answers the Serpent, she displays her ignorance of God's commands. The Lord's command to man was clear and direct in Genesis 2:16–17: mankind may freely eat from every tree of the garden except from the Tree of the Knowledge of Good and Evil. If they eat from that one tree, then they will certainly die. Third, the woman responds by twisting the word God had revealed. In her response to the Serpent (3:2–3), she exaggerates the prohibition ("neither shall you touch it"), she minimizes the privileges ("we may eat" rather than "you may eat freely"), and she minimizes the penalty ("lest you die" rather than "you will certainly die"). Fourth, the Serpent capitalizes on the woman's ignorance of God's word and pronounces a lie that "you will not surely die" (3:4; cf. John 8:44). And finally, once the prohibition is reasoned away, the practical and aesthetic appeal of the tree draws Eve. The first two humans then partake of the fruit that God had forbidden to them.

Man's disobedience to the command of God has far-reaching consequences, as the remainder of chapter 3 clearly demonstrates. The humans are, first of all, separated from God because of their sin. They have fear rather than fellowship with him, and thus they are alienated from God. They know, second of all, that they are naked, and so they cover themselves (3:7). They have shame rather than integrity and thus are alienated from one another. They are driven from the garden and thus alienated from it (3:17–19). They are alienated from eternal life (3:22).

The fall is also a *Leitmotif* that reverberates throughout Scripture. In particular, it generally prefigures the history of the nation of Israel. God called a people and delivered them from the land of Egypt through the Red Sea, and then he brought them into the land of Canaan by dividing the Jordan River. As we have already seen, these two episodes are considered re-creation events based upon Genesis 1. The land that he gives to his people is one that is "a good and broad land, a land flowing with milk and honey" (Ex. 3:8), a veritable garden of Eden (Gen. 13:10; Isa. 51:3; Ezek. 36:35; Joel 2:3). If Israel keeps the word of the Lord, then they will be blessed by him and remain in the Land of Promise (Deut. 28:1–14), but if they disobey, then God will drive them out of the land (Deut. 4:26–27). In the final outcome, Israel was expelled from the Promised Land because of their deep and repeated disobedience to the word of God.

Redemption

Genesis 3:14–19 is a prophecy spoken directly by the Lord, and it generally spells out the forthcoming history of humanity. God pronounces a postfall order to the universe that finds its essence in verse 15, where God proclaims that he will "put enmity between you and the woman." The noun "enmity" is the main topic of the verse because it appears as the first word in the Hebrew text. The term simply means "to be an enemy to." As a noun it occurs five times in the Old Testament, and in each instance it signifies hostile intent to the degree of killing another (cf. Num. 35:21–22; Ezek. 25:15; 35:5). The first part of the conflict is between the Serpent ("you") and the woman, and, of course, this discord began earlier in the chapter. A second stage of the conflict is then defined: "between your offspring and her offspring" (Gen. 3:15). The Hebrew term for "offspring" is commonly used for lineage, descent, or seed, and the Greek translation of the Old Testament (referred to as the Septuagint) normally renders this word as "sperm," which reflects the idea of posterity. Here we are introduced to the concept of two-seed theology, in which the theme of conflict can be traced through the history of mankind, all the way to the end of time (Rev. 12:13–17).

The conflict will reach its climax in a battle between two individuals: the Serpent ("you") and another figure ("he"). It is rightly concluded that this latter figure is the Messiah. The writer mentions the "he" first in the line perhaps to demonstrate his primacy and preeminence in the confrontation. And in the battle, the "he" strikes a blow to the Serpent's head, which is a mortal, deadly wound, while the "he" only receives a blow to his heel, one that is certainly not fatal. Thus, God promises in this verse that he will send a Redeemer to crush the enemy.[17] Readers can understand the remainder of Scripture as an unfolding of the prophecy of Genesis 3:15. Redemption is promised in this one verse, and the Bible traces the development of that redemptive theme to its very conclusion.

The theological structure of Genesis 1–3 as creation, fall, and redemption is mirrored in the eschatological conclusion of the Bible. The book of Revelation reverses the order of the sequence. The opening sections of John's vision center on the redemptive work of the Messiah (e.g., Rev. 5:5–6; 7:9–10). This is followed by the judgment and defeat of Satan (e.g., Rev. 12:13–17; 20:1–6) and his fall into the lake of fire and sulfur (Rev. 20:7–10). The final chapters of Revelation describe a new heavens and a new earth, a re-created order based upon the garden of Eden in Genesis 1–2.[18] Included in this eschatological picture is a lush garden-like existence with a river of life running through it and the Tree of Life in it (Rev. 22:1–5). In addition, whereas the institution of human marriage was established at the original creation, this re-creation scene contains the marriage feast of the Lamb and his people, they who constitute his bride (Rev. 19:6–9; 21:9).

---

[17] Certainly not all agree that this verse is messianic. Some argue that the word "he" actually refers to the seed earlier in the verse and thus that it could easily refer to Israel rather than the Messiah. See Claus Westermann, *Genesis 1–11: A Commentary* (Minneapolis: Augsburg, 1984), 355; von Rad, *Genesis*, 90; and Martin H. Wouldstra, "Recent Translations of Genesis 3:15," *CTJ* 6, no. 2 (1971):194–203. Other important works have been published that give great weight to the messianic interpretation. See T. Desmond Alexander, "Messianic Ideology in the Book of Genesis," in *The Lord's Anointed: Interpretation of Old Testament Messianic Texts*, ed. Philip E. Satterthwaite, Richard S. Hess, and Gordon J. Wenham (Carlisle, UK: Paternoster, 1995), 19–39, and C. John Collins, "A Syntactical Note (Genesis 3:15): Is the Woman's Seed Singular or Plural?," *TynBul* 48, no. 1 (1997):139–48.

[18] For a fascinating study of this idea and many other echoes, see G. K. Beale, *The Temple and the Church's Mission: A Biblical Theology of the Dwelling Place of God*, NSBT 17 (Downers Grove, IL: InterVarsity Press, 2004).

Excursus: Genesis 1–11 and Ancient Near Eastern Literature

One of the great dilemmas in the interpretation of the pre-Abrahamic literature of Genesis is its relationship to the writings of the surrounding cultures of the ancient Near East. The two great events of these early chapters of Genesis are the creation and the flood. Accounts of similar stories are found in the literary corpus of numerous nations, such as Egypt, Babylon, Assyria, and Ugarit. Simply put, the issue is that many of these pagan tales have numerous parallels, some that are quite detailed, with the biblical narratives. There is no doubt that a relationship exists between the Genesis writings and those of the surrounding cultures, but the question is, what is the nature and extent of that relationship?[19]

As an example, we will consider the deluge recorded in Genesis 6–9 and other ancient Near Eastern flood accounts.[20] Mythological stories of a great flood are found in many of the various cultures of the ancient Near East. The event of a massive deluge is so well known that in some cultures, such as at the city of Ugarit, the flood account became a paradigm for school texts and copyists. In addition, flood stories are not relegated to a particular time period but appear in a variety of cultures throughout the third to first millennia BC. The earliest reference to a great flood is perhaps the Sumerian King List, which dates to the twenty-second century BC.[21] Versions of the flood have been found in Sumer, Assyria, Babylon, Ugarit, and Egypt.

The flood story in the Epic of Gilgamesh from Mesopotamia, for example, is in some respects nearly identical to the biblical narrative.[22] It begins with a divine warning of a coming doom. The hero of the flood is then commanded to build a ship, which he does, and then he loads it with his relations and animals. The gods send torrential rains that destroy humanity. The flood subsides, and the ark lands on Mount Nisir. Utnapishtim, the hero, sends forth birds to see if the land has dried up. After everyone disembarks from the ship, Utnapishtim sacrifices to the gods, and they in turn bless him. "Not only are many of the details parallel (to the biblical account), but the structure and flow of the stories are the same. Such overwhelming similitude cannot be explained as a result of mere chance or simultaneous invention."[23] There is a clear relationship between these stories, but we must define the nature of that connection.

Many biblical historians simply assume that the biblical account of the flood is fundamentally no different from the pagan, mythic narratives. S. R. Driver comments, "There can be no doubt that the true origin of the Biblical narrative is to be found in the Babylonian story of the Flood."[24] According to this position,

---

[19] Recent literature on this issue includes Peter Enns, *Inspiration and Incarnation: Evangelicals and the Problem of the Old Testament* (Grand Rapids, MI: Baker, 2005); Jeffrey J. Niehaus, *Ancient Near Eastern Themes in Biblical Theology* (Grand Rapids, MI: Kregel, 2008); and John N. Oswalt, *The Bible among the Myths: Unique Revelation or Just Ancient Literature?* (Grand Rapids, MI: Zondervan, 2009).

[20] For a more detailed discussion, see John D. Currid, *Against the Gods: The Polemical Theology of the Old Testament* (Wheaton, IL: Crossway, 2013), 47–63.

[21] Thorkild Jacobsen, *The Sumerian King List* (Chicago: University of Chicago Press, 1939); and Pritchard, *ANET*, 265–66.

[22] See Alexander Heidel, *The Gilgamesh Epic and Old Testament Parallels*, 2nd ed. (Chicago: University of Chicago Press, 1949).

[23] Currid, *Against the Gods*, 55.

[24] Samuel R. Driver, *The Book of Genesis*, 6th ed. (London: Methuen, 1907), 103.

the Hebrew writers essentially borrowed the well-known flood myth from their neighbors and then "accommodated [it] to the spirit of Hebrew monotheism."[25] Thus, the Hebrew authors were, in the famous words of one historian, "guilty of crass plagiarism."[26]

As one considers the relationship between the flood account in the Bible and those in the surrounding nations, it is important to recognize that there are major differences between them. And these distinctions are not merely matters of detail; they exist at the deeper level of worldview, theology, and belief. For example, all the flood stories of the ancient Near East, except the Hebrew narrative, are polytheistic. And these many gods often act humanly, that is, with the same desires, faults, and needs as humans. There is a striking lack of morality among the gods: they often appear petty, self-absorbed, and depraved. To the contrary, the biblical account pictures one God who is in sovereign control of the entire flood episode from beginning to end. He is righteous and just.

Bruce Waltke concludes that the "most radical difference in the two accounts is the Bible's investing the story with a covenant concept."[27] The covenant is a binding contract and relationship between God and mankind, one that has been initiated and administered by him. The covenant highlights God's personal relationship with and commitment to his people (Gen. 9:8–17).

Still, how does one account for the many parallels that do exist between the biblical flood account and ancient Near Eastern myths of the deluge? One possibility is that the biblical tradition does not directly depend on the other accounts. Perhaps they are independent versions of a much earlier story and tradition. They are perhaps two separate traditions that stem from an actual, historical flood. I have written elsewhere:

> If the biblical stories are true, one would be surprised not to find some references to these truths in extra-biblical literature. And indeed in ancient Near Eastern myth we do see some kernels of historical truth. However, pagan authors vulgarized or bastardized those truths—they distorted fact by dressing it up with polytheism, magic, violence, and paganism. Fact became myth. From this angle the common references would appear to support rather than deny the historicity of the biblical story.[28]

Another distinct possibility is that the Hebrew writers, well aware of and familiar with pagan flood myths, were writing to dispute and impugn those other stories. In other words, they consciously and subversively used polemics against those other accounts in order to taunt them and to show that they are counterfeit. Polemics of this type serve to extol the Lord as the only true God and to expose the pagan gods as mere charlatans and pretenders.

---

[25] Driver, *The Book of Genesis*, 107.
[26] See Friedrich Delitzsch, *Babel and Bible: Two Lectures Delivered before the Members of the Deutsche Orient-Gesellschaft in the Presence of the German Emperor*, Crown Theological Library 1 (New York: Putnam, 1903).
[27] Waltke, *Old Testament Theology*, 291.
[28] John D. Currid, *Ancient Egypt and the Old Testament* (Grand Rapids, MI: Baker, 1997), 32.

Genesis 12–50 and the History of the Patriarchal Period

In Genesis 9–11, the biblical author stresses the wickedness of mankind, demonstrating that humanity acts the same as before the flood. The line of Ham is in great rebellion against God, and at Babel humans disobey the commands of God and attempt to establish themselves as sole rulers of the earth. It is the beginning of humanism. The Lord, however, begins to prepare a new nation to carry his word to mankind, and for this purpose he chooses Abraham to be the father of his chosen seed.

Many biblical historians place the patriarchal period in the first half of the second millennium BC.[29] However, certainly not all scholars agree with this chronology. For instance, Gosta Ahlstrom comments:

> It is quite clear that the narrator of the Genesis stories did not have accurate knowledge about the prehistory of the Israelites. That was not necessary either, because his purpose was not to write history. The social milieu and customs we meet in these texts, as well as the many peoples the patriarchs had contact with reflect a much later time.[30]

This statement reflects a dominant hermeneutic of suspicion that exists among many scholars. Benjamin Mazar, for example, accuses contemporary scholarship of going way too far in attempting to find "corroboration of the antiquity of the patriarchal accounts."[31] But the reality is, when all is said and done, that the narratives of the patriarchs best fit into the cultural environment of the Middle Bronze II period (2000–1550 BC) in ancient Palestine.[32] The excursus on "Archaeology and Genesis" explores a few of the areas of investigation that lend support to this chronology.

---

[29] See, for example, Kenneth A. Kitchen, *On the Reliability of the Old Testament* (Grand Rapids, MI: Eerdmans, 2003), 313–72.
[30] Gosta W. Ahlstrom, *The History of Ancient Palestine* (Minneapolis: Fortress, 1993), 186. See, as well, John Van Seters, *In Search of History: Historiography in the Ancient World and the Origins of Biblical History* (New Haven, CT: Yale University Press, 1983); and Benjamin Mazar, "The Historical Background of the Book of Genesis," *JNES* 28, no. 2 (1969): 73–83.
[31] Mazar, "Historical Background," 76.
[32] For a chart of the ages of antiquity, see John D. Currid, *Doing Archaeology in the Land of the Bible* (Grand Rapids, MI: Baker, 1999), 19.

Excursus: Archaeology and Genesis

The cities mentioned in the patriarchal stories of Genesis, such as Bethel, Hebron, Jerusalem, and Shechem, were occupied during the Middle Bronze II period. Hebron, for example, is located at Tel Hebron, approximately twenty miles south of Jerusalem. During the Middle Bronze II age, it was a major settlement covering some six to seven acres. It was fortified and contained some major building complexes. A cuneiform text from this period discovered at Hebron indicates that it was a major administrative center and perhaps a capital city for the region.

Shechem was founded during the Middle Bronze IIA period (2000–1800 BC). The site contained a large urban compound with a monumental building that some have identified as a temple. It was, however, probably not a religious structure but rather the residence or palace of a local chieftain. Like most of the settlements during this period, Shechem lacked walls and had no fortifications. By the Middle Bronze IIB–C period (1800–1550 BC), though, Shechem began to fortify. Excavations have uncovered a thriving urban center at the time.[33]

All the sites listed above are located on what is called the "spine" of the central hill country of Canaan, which goes from Shechem in the north to Hebron in the south. The patriarchs commonly used this route (Gen. 12:6; 13:18; 35:27).

The depiction of the lifestyle of the patriarchs in Genesis 12–50 is congruous with what we know about the Middle Bronze II period. This was a period of urbanization but also one of large migrations of people throughout the ancient Near East. The patriarchs were, first of all, pastoralists. "Pastoralism is a subsistence category, that is, it defines the means of their livelihood. They were keepers of herds and flocks. They were also *seminomadic*. They were not sedentary but made seasonal movements with their flocks and herds to find adequate water, sufficient forage, and good climate conditions. . . . They did not live in cities but normally camped outside them."[34]

Although the patriarchs, Abraham, Isaac, and Jacob, are never mentioned in any extrabiblical texts, their stories accurately reflect the time of the Middle Bronze II period.[35] So testify thousands of discovered tablets at the site of Mari in western Mesopotamia, which date to the first half of the eighteenth century BC, during the Middle Bronze II period. The Mari archive includes mainly economic, legal, and administrative texts. Yet these also reflect the cultural, political, and sociological manners of the time, and the setting described by the Mari tablets has many parallels with the narratives of the patriarchs found in Genesis.

We could cite many examples. For instance, both Mari and Genesis portray a dimorphic society, in which there is a social dichotomy between tribal chieftains, like Abraham, and powerful urban centers or city-states. Both literatures exhibit this dichotomy in the customs of economic exchanges between the city dwellers and the nomads, the concept of "resident aliens," and the nomads' common practice of camping in the vicinity of large cities. The social structure in both is organized in a three-tiered system: extended family, clan, and tribe. They also have other quite similar customs, such as census taking, inheritance laws, covenant oaths, and the prominence of genealogies. And the literatures of the two cultures even mention many of the same personal names and place names, such as the cities of Haran and Nahor.

Archaeologists made another important archival discovery at Nuzi, a site located near the Tigris River in Mesopotamia that was at its height in the mid-second millennium BC. To date, the archive contains some five thousand tablets.

---

[33] For a good study of the material remains from this time, see Amihai Mazar, *Archaeology of the Land of the Bible, 10,000–586 B.C.E.* (New York: Doubleday, 1990), 174–231.

[34] John D. Currid and David P. Barrett, *Crossway ESV Bible Atlas* (Wheaton, IL: Crossway, 2010), 69.

[35] Some have attempted to identify the name Abram on the triumphal relief of Shoshenk I at Karnak. Rings 71–72 appear to read "Fort of Abram" as a place name. To what "Abram" refers, however, is uncertain, and to tie it to the patriarch Abraham is a stretch. The identification of the place with the patriarch has a long history, and it first appears in Wilhelm Spiegelberg, *Aegyptologische Randglossen zum Alten Testament* (Strassburg: Schlessier und Schweikhardt, 1904), 14.

These texts, like the Mari documents, are devoted primarily to social, economic, and administrative matters. Many of them are routine business and legal texts. They do, however, shed considerable light on the customs of the patriarchal period in Genesis. For example, the Nuzi corpus includes an account of a man exchanging his inheritance rights for a sheep, not unlike Esau's selling of his birthright to Jacob in Genesis 25:29–34. In addition, the Nuzi texts consider a blessing binding and irrevocable, and that helps to explain why Isaac was unable to revoke the blessing he gave to Jacob even though it was given under false pretenses (Gen. 27:30–33). It was also a custom at Nuzi for a couple without a male offspring to adopt a son as an heir, and in exchange for the inheritance, the adopted son would care for the couple in their old age and make certain they received a proper burial. If a son was born to the couple after the adoption had taken place, much of the inheritance then reverted to the son by blood. These practices, of course, are reminiscent of Abraham's adoption of Eliezer of Damascus as the heir of his house because of Sarah's barrenness (Gen. 15:2–5).

According to the laws of Nuzi, the family gods (*teraphim*) played a vital role in the process of inheritance, for whoever possessed these images was considered the rightful heir. No wonder Laban was in a panic over the loss of his household gods when Jacob fled from him to Canaan (Gen. 31:33–35). Laban, in reality, was more concerned about the whereabouts of his gods than about his relatives and flocks.

We could consider other texts as well. The Execration Texts from Egypt, beginning in the reign of Senwosret III (1878–1841 BC), reflect a landscape in Canaan that is much in line with what we read in the patriarchal stories in Genesis. This is congruous with the Middle Bronze II period in Canaan.

Joseph in Egypt

The Middle Bronze II period was one of migration throughout the ancient Near East (see "Excursus: Archaeology and Genesis" on pp. 57–59). The Egyptians were so concerned about it that they constructed a huge canal running from Pelusium on the Mediterranean Sea to Lake Timseh just to the east of the Wadi Tumilat.[36] The canal measured 65 feet wide at the bottom and 230 feet wide at the surface level. The Egyptians used it to some extent for irrigation but primarily for defense and containment, that is, to keep Asiatics out and slaves in. In addition, Pharaoh Amenemhet I (1991–1962 BC) ordered that a series of Egyptian fortresses be built on the eastern border of Egypt to control Asiatic migration. Asiatic migration into Egypt was the setting of the Joseph story in Genesis 37–50.

The Joseph narrative fits well into the Egyptian cultural milieu of the early to midsecond millennium BC. At the beginning of the story, Joseph was brought to Egypt

---

[36] Amihai Sneh, Tuvia Weissbrod, and Itamar Perath, "Evidence for an Ancient Egyptian Frontier Canal: The Remnants of an Artificial Waterway Discovered in the Northeastern Nile Delta May Have Formed Part of the Barrier Called 'Shur of Egypt' in Ancient Texts," *American Scientist* 63, no. 5 (1975): 542–48; and William H. Shea, "A Date for the Recently Discovered Eastern Canal of Egypt," *BASOR* 226 (1977): 31–38.

and sold there by Midianites (Gen. 37:28). Egypt had a large caste of foreign slaves at any given period in its ancient history, and many arrived by way of a thriving slave trade. In fact, so many slaves came from Asia (i.e., Canaan, Hatti, and Mesopotamia) that the Egyptian word for "Asiatic" became synonymous with "slave." Joseph was sold for twenty shekels of silver, a common price for a male slave between five and twenty years of age during the first half of the second millennium BC.[37]

After Joseph was falsely accused of molesting Potiphar's wife, he was placed in prison. Imprisonment was a punishment unknown in the law codes of the ancient Near East, including in biblical legislation. However, it is well attested in Egyptian documents, and therefore, the story accurately echoes the culture of ancient Egypt. The story line of the episode regarding Potiphar's wife is not unique in the literature of the ancient Near East. This "spurned seductress" motif, in fact, occurs in ancient Egypt in a text called "The Tale of the Two Brothers."[38] One brother accuses the other of forcing a sexual relationship on his wife. The wife, in reality, is the deceitful one, and she blames the situation on her brother-in-law, who, like Joseph, refused her advances. The story ends differently, however, as the husband kills both his brother and, after discovering the truth, his wife.[39]

After a long term of imprisonment, Joseph is freed and elevated to a high position in the Egyptian government through his God-given ability to interpret dreams, most importantly the dreams of Pharaoh. Through interpreting Pharaoh's dreams, Joseph prophesied a coming time of great famine in Egypt, which allowed the Egyptians to prepare for the disaster. As I note elsewhere, "At least as early as the Middle Kingdom the Egyptians believed that dreams were a means used by the gods to reveal the future to humans. In fact, the Egyptians collected written dream omens. The structure and content of these dream omens are quite similar to the dream accounts in the story of Joseph. It is tempting to think that Joseph was really defeating the Egyptians on their own ground."[40]

Pharaoh then places Joseph "over the land of Egypt" (Gen. 41:41). He was likely the vizier in Egypt, whose duties are spelled out in a document from the Tomb of Rekhmire from the mid-second millennium BC. The vizier was the "grand steward of all Egypt," and all the activities of the nation were under his purview. Rekhmire was vizier under Thutmosis III, and he served as overseer of the treasury, chief justice, police chief, war minister, secretary of agriculture, secretary of the interior, and other positions. Aside from Pharaoh, the vizier was often the most powerful leader in Egypt.

The author of Genesis spends an extraordinary amount of time discussing the life of Joseph. It can properly be described as a novella, a "short long story" or a "long short story." Why does the writer give so much space (Genesis 37, 39–50) to it? His overarching purpose seems to be to demonstrate how all Israel ended up in the land

---

[37] This is the same price as in the Code of Hammurabi, laws 116, 214, and 252. It was written in the eighteenth century BC.
[38] John A. Wilson, "The Story of the Two Brothers," in Pritchard, *ANET*, 23–25.
[39] See Currid, *Against the Gods*, 65–73.
[40] Currid and Barrett, *Crossway ESV Bible Atlas*, 75. The most important collection of dream omens from Egypt is the Chester Beatty Papyrus III, which may date as early as the nineteenth century BC. See Alan H. Gardiner, *Hieratic Papyri in the British Museum*, 3rd series, Chester Beatty Gift (London: British Museum, 1935).

of Egypt. This, then, lays the groundwork for God's greatest redemptive act of the Old Testament, the Lord's deliverance of Israel out of the land of darkness and his bringing the people to the Land of Promise.

When all is said and done, it should be clear that the vast majority of the patriarchal narrative material fits nicely into the first half of the second millennium BC. The details appearing in these narratives that perhaps reflect a later date—such as the mentioning of the Philistines (e.g., Gen. 21:32)—are, in the grand scheme of things, very few in number and merely represent an updating of the material by the biblical author.[41]

Centrality of the Covenant

The relationship that God has with his people in the book of Genesis is defined by a covenant or treaty concept. In the ancient Near East, people, leaders, and nations formalized relationships using an oath that followed a particular structure and was commonly written down.[42] Those in the ancient Near East employed two types of covenant forms: those governing relationships between *equal* parties and those specifying relationships between *unequal* parties. The second type of covenant was between an overlord or suzerain (the superior party) and a vassal (the inferior party). Many of the extant treaties were between a king and his subjects. Well over half the suzerain/vassal treaties uncovered through archaeology come from the Hittite Empire of the second millennium BC, while others survive from the first millennium BC, including the Hittites, Assyrians, Egyptians, and others.

In Genesis, the suzerain/vassal covenant form determines the relationship between God and his people. Within this structure, the suzerain, as the more powerful party, takes on most of the responsibility for the stipulations of the treaty. Although the vassal also has certain obligations, because of his limited capabilities and resources he is not held accountable to the same extent and degree as the suzerain. The suzerain or sovereign, because of his position, is also the one who initiates the covenant agreement. The oath between the two parties is predominantly to the point of life and death. Because of all these common elements, this type of covenant has been appropriately defined as "a bond in blood sovereignly administered."[43]

The covenant is a pact that God makes with his people throughout history in which he will be their God and they will be his people (called the "Immanuel Principle," that is, "God is with us"). The church today is in covenant with God, as Jesus secured a new covenant with his people through his life, death, and resurrection (Matt. 26:28). The new covenant, however, is the final manifestation of the covenant concept in Scripture. This concept begins with the covenant that was in operation in the garden

---

[41] For further development of this idea, see Kitchen, *On the Reliability of the Old Testament*, 368–72.

[42] For an introduction to this study, see Meredith G. Kline, *Treaty of the Great King: The Covenant Structure of Deuteronomy: Studies and Commentary* (Grand Rapids, MI: Eerdmans, 1963); Meredith G. Kline, *The Structure of Biblical Authority* (Grand Rapids, MI: Eerdmans, 1972); Kenneth A. Kitchen, *Ancient Orient and Old Testament* (Chicago: InterVarsity Press, 1966); Dennis J. McCarthy, *Treaty and Covenant: A Study in Form in the Ancient Oriental Documents and in the Old Testament* (Rome: Pontifical Biblical Institute, 1978); George E. Mendenhall, "Covenant Forms in Israelite Tradition," *BA* 17, no. 3 (1954): 50–76.

[43] O. Palmer Robertson, *The Christ of the Covenants* (Grand Rapids, MI: Baker, 1980), 4.

of Eden prior to the fall of mankind into sin, which we call the covenant of works (Hos. 6:7). After the fall, in the book of Genesis, God renews and reestablishes the covenant (the covenant of grace) with Noah, with Abraham, with Isaac, and with Jacob. Later in biblical history, the Lord renews the covenant with Moses, with Joshua, and with David as the covenant mediators between Israel and God. It is important for the church today to understand that the covenant originates in Genesis, develops through the Old Testament, and then finds its ultimate fulfillment in the coming of the final covenant mediator, Jesus Christ.[44] In that way, the church can see that the very promises that God made to Abraham and to the other patriarchs are the very ones that he has made to his people today.

Covenant with Noah

In Genesis 6:18, the Lord says to Noah, "I will establish my covenant with you." God's grace comes to Noah in covenantal form. This is the first time that the word "covenant" (בְּרִית) is used in the Bible, although as we already mentioned, such a covenant relationship between God and mankind was in effect in the garden. In fact, the language of the covenant with Noah closely reflects that of the covenant that existed in Eden. It should be noted that this covenant with Noah was initiated and established by God prior to the flood coming on the earth.

After the flood, God reaffirms the covenant with Noah (Gen. 9:8–17). A common element of any ancient Near Eastern treaty between a suzerain and a vassal is that the royal party must initiate and establish the binding agreement.[45] That is the case here, as God says, "Behold, I establish my covenant with you and your offspring after you" (9:8). The covenant established is ongoing, as reflected in verse 11, where the verb "establish" (קוּם) signifies the maintaining and renewing of the initial activity.[46] As with many covenants in the ancient Near East, the suzerain provides a physical sign for the vassal that symbolizes the reality of the covenant relationship. Such signs as exchanging sandals (cf. Ruth 4:7), dividing animals (Gen. 15:9–10), and signing pledges are well known from the literature. The sign here is a "bow in the cloud" (Gen. 9:13) which is likely a reference to a rainbow.

The Hebrew term for "bow" normally refers to a commonly used weapon in the ancient Near East. Pagan mythologies often employed the weapon to portray gods taking up the bow to engage in battle against other gods or humans. In the Mesopotamian creation legend, after Marduk destroys Tiamat and the gods of chaos using a bow, the gods hang his bow in the sky, and it becomes a constellation.[47] A parallel may be at work here. In the story of Noah, God hangs his bow in the sky perhaps to signify the end of hostility, the beginning of peace, and the renewal of the covenant with mankind.[48]

---

[44] William J. Dumbrell, *Covenant and Creation: An Old Testament Covenant Theology* (Exeter, UK: Paternoster, 1984).
[45] William J. Dumbrell, "The Covenant with Noah," *RTR* 38, no. 1 (1979): 1–9.
[46] Speiser, *Genesis*, 58–9.
[47] Pritchard, *ANET*, 69.
[48] Bernard F. Batto, "The Covenant of Peace: A Neglected Ancient Near Eastern Motif," *CBQ* 49, no. 2 (1987): 187–211.

Covenant with Abraham

In Genesis 15, after Abraham has settled in the land of Canaan, the Lord appears to him in a vision in order to establish the covenant with him. The formal inauguration of the treaty begins with God making a declaration of self-identification: "I am the LORD" (15:7). In many covenant documents of the second millennium BC, kings similarly commence treaties with a statement of self-identification.[49] God then briefly reviews the history of the relationship between Abraham and himself, and he promises to him the land of Canaan as a possession. A covenant ceremony follows in which the Lord orders Abraham to gather some animals, sever them, and place them in two separate but parallel rows. Abraham is arranging a typical ancient Near Eastern ritual for the ratification of a covenant (cf. Jer. 34:15–20).

The purpose of the ritual is to invoke a curse. The parties are, in effect, inviting God to cut them in two, like the animals, if they do not keep their covenant promises. In the ancient Near East, "Animals are an obvious substitute for human beings in ceremonial curses."[50] So the fate of the animals points to what would befall mankind if they violated the covenant.

In the midst of the ceremony, God issues a promise regarding the future of Abraham's posterity. They will enter bondage for four hundred years, be redeemed, and then eventually gain possession of the land of Canaan. This prophecy essentially establishes the nation of Israel, giving them national identity in the context of covenant making.

Finally, in ancient Near Eastern covenants like this one, both parties to the covenant would walk through the midst of the severed animal parts. We witness here, however, that only God, in a fire theophany (or visible manifestation of God), passes through the pieces (Gen. 15:17). He is taking on full responsibility for the promises of blessings and curses in the covenant. However, it "is not right to say that Gen. 15:18 contains only a promise, but no obligations (for Abram). The obligations were built into the making of the covenant, and without obligation to loyalty there would have been no promise."[51] Thus, Abraham is required to be a loyal covenant keeper, and God, by passing through the animals alone, is ensuring that Abraham will be compliant.

Whereas Genesis 15 describes the inauguration of the Abrahamic covenant, Genesis 17 declares the institution of the covenant seal, one that Abraham and his posterity would wear on their very flesh. This chapter also adds details to the earlier agreement: for instance, it highlights to a greater degree the eternal, binding nature of the covenant and the possession of a land. It also specifies Abraham's obligations in the treaty; in particular, all the male members of his household are to be circumcised.

Circumcision is not a Hebrew invention, nor did the people of God uniquely use it. For example, the Egyptians from their earliest periods used circumcision; a number

---

[49] For an example, see Pritchard, *ANET*, 203.
[50] George E. Mendenhall, "Puppy and Lettuce in Northwest-Semitic Covenant Making," *BASOR* 133 (1954): 29.
[51] Arvid S. Kapelrud, "The Covenant as Agreement," *SJOT* 1 (1988): 33.

of tomb scenes from the Old Kingdom (ca. 2575–2134 BC) depict the practice. In Egypt, it appears to have been a sign of ritual purity and was a requirement "for men who were going to serve in the temples."[52] The uniqueness of circumcision for the Israelites is that it symbolizes inclusion in the covenant community established by the Lord.

Covenant with Isaac

After Abraham dies, the Lord appears to Isaac in a theophany (Gen. 26:1–6), as he had done with Abraham. In this short section, the promises of the covenant that God had given to Abraham are now repeated for Isaac. He receives the promise of an innumerable posterity (cf. 15:5; 22:17), as many as the stars of heaven; the promise of a land to inherit (cf. 15:7, 18–21); and the promise that nations will be blessed through him (cf. 12:3; 18:18). At the very heart of this covenant declaration is the Immanuel Principle, that is, God's promise that "I will be with you" (26:3; cf. 17:8). This episode, therefore, constitutes a covenant renewal: the covenant God made with Abraham is now applied to the promised seed of Abraham, his son Isaac.

Covenant with Jacob

After Jacob flees for his life from Esau to the land of Haran, the Lord appears to him on the way in a dream theophany. The text describes the picture that he sees as "behold, there was a ladder set up on the earth, and the top of it reached to heaven. And behold, the angels of God were ascending and descending on it! And, behold, the Lord stood above it." (Gen. 28:12–13a). The Hebrew word for "ladder" (סֻלָּם) occurs only here in the Old Testament, and it stems from the noun סֹלְלָה, which means "mound."[53] It is perhaps related to the Akkadian word *simmiltu*, which means "steps." The dream picture is one of a series of steps that lead up to an entrance or gate into the heavenly city.

 This theophany in a dream confirms Jacob as the true heir of Abraham and the recipient of the covenant. God speaks to Jacob, and he gives him promises that are quite similar to the ones he made to Abraham in Genesis 13:14–17. In fact, much of the wording of the two exchanges is exactly alike.[54] God pledges that he will make Jacob's posterity numerous like the dust of the earth, that he has given to them the land of Canaan, that all the families of the earth will be blessed through Jacob and his descendants, and that God is with Jacob and his seed (28:13–15). Jacob names the place Bethel, which means "house of God" (28:19).

 Later in the Jacob pericope, the Lord commands Jacob to move back to Bethel, and there he reveals himself to the patriarch in another theophany (Gen. 35:9). He again speaks to Jacob and says essentially the same thing he had spoken to Abraham in Genesis 17:1–8. Table 4 shows the similarities.

---

[52] Jack M. Sasson, ed., *Civilizations of the Ancient Near East* (New York: Scribner, 1995), 1:378.
[53] Francis Brown, Samuel Rolles Driver, and Charles Augustus Briggs, *A Hebrew and English Lexicon of the Old Testament* (Oxford: Clarendon, 1906), 700.
[54] Zeev Weisman, "National Consciousness in the Patriarchal Promises," *JSOT* 31 (1985): 55–73.

Element in Genesis 35	Parallel in Genesis 17
1. Introduction: "I am God Almighty" (35:11)	17:1
2. "be fruitful and multiply" (35:11)	17:2, 6
3. "nations shall come from you" (35:11)	17:4–6
4. "kings shall come from your own body" (35:11)	17:6
5. "the land" (35:12)	17:8
6. "to your offspring" (35:12)	17:8

Table 4

As I say elsewhere, the "conclusion to be drawn here is that the covenant promises to Abraham are renewed in their totality to Jacob. Jacob's change of name (Gen. 35:10) to Israel further signifies that the promises of God are to come to pass through the person of Jacob: he is the promised seed through whom the people of God are to come, a descent that finds its climax in the person of the Messiah."[55]

The reality is that the covenant concept defines the relationship of God and his people not merely in the book of Genesis but throughout the entirety of Scripture. The unfolding nature of the covenant and its promises throughout the remainder of the Bible is one of the great unifying theological themes in Scripture. It truly highlights the homogeneity of the Bible's message.

APPROACHING THE NEW TESTAMENT

The book of Genesis lays the foundation for a proper understanding and interpretation of all Scripture. If the church is to have a good and full view of basic biblical doctrines with regard to such topics as sin, judgment, salvation, the character of God, the Messiah, and a myriad of other relevant and central subjects, it must begin with the study of Genesis. Many of these doctrines are found in seed form in Genesis, and they need to be traced throughout the rest of the Bible as they develop and unfold.

Although this idea is simple, in reality it receives little attention today in biblical studies.[56] For example, when one reads about ecclesiology—and, in particular, eldership—it is surprising how infrequently authors pay attention to the office of elder in the Old Testament. It is important that one does the work of *protology* when considering biblical ideas and themes. Thus, if one wanted to discern the proper role of labor in the believer's life, one ought to study that mandate for work given by God to Adam in the garden of Eden. That cultural mandate is as relevant today as it was in the first human environment.

---

[55] John D. Currid, *Genesis*, vol. 2, *Genesis 25:19–50:26*, EP Study Commentary (Darlington, UK: Evangelical Press, 2003), 165.
[56] Consider the following important works by Graeme Goldsworthy: *According to Plan: The Unfolding Revelation of God in the Bible* (Leicester: Inter-Varsity Press, 1991); *Gospel and Kingdom: A Christian Interpretation of the Old Testament*, new ed. (Carlisle, UK: Paternoster, 1994); and, for an application of this methodology in preaching, *Preaching the Whole Bible as Christian Scripture: The Application of Biblical Theology to Expository Preaching* (Grand Rapids, MI: Eerdmans, 2000). On preaching from the Old Testament, see also Dale Ralph Davis, *The Word Became Fresh: How to Preach from Old Testament Narrative Texts* (Fearn, Ross-shire, Scotland: Mentor, 2006).

The New Testament, in its history, its theology, and its doctrine, does not appear in a vacuum; it developed out of the teachings of the Old Testament. This method of interpretation mirrors that of Jesus, who, for example, when he was asked about the nature of marriage, responded by quoting Genesis 2.

In addition to establishing a foundation for understanding the rest of the Bible, Genesis also foreshadows the central event of Scripture: the life, death, and resurrection of Christ. We've already mentioned the prophetic word given in Genesis 3:15, which speaks of a coming seed of the woman who will crush the Serpent's head and redeem humanity. The New Testament itself often refers or alludes to Genesis in explaining the way of the gospel. From the showcase of patriarchs who modeled faith in God's promises in Hebrews 11 to Christ explicitly connecting God's preservation of Noah in the flood with God's preservation of his people when judgment comes (Matt. 24:36–44), Genesis includes many images that prefigure the gospel. One of the most significant is the picture of Adam sinning in the garden and thus bringing death upon all people. The apostle Paul comments that Adam was a type of the One who was to come (Rom. 5:14). This second Adam, Jesus Christ, brings life for his people and not death. As Paul further comments, "But the free gift is not like the trespass. For if many died through one man's trespass, much more have the grace of God and the free gift by the grace of that one man Jesus Christ abounded for many" (Rom. 5:15).

We could explore many such parallels, but the point is clear: Genesis lays the groundwork for the whole of the Bible, both as a historical and theological prologue and as a shadow of the gospel that would be made visible in the person and work of Jesus Christ.

SELECT BIBLIOGRAPHY

Aalders, G. Charles. *Genesis*. Grand Rapids, MI: Zondervan, 1981.

Arnold, Bill T. *Encountering the Book of Genesis*. EBS. Grand Rapids, MI: Baker, 1998.

Belcher, Richard P., Jr. *Genesis: The Beginning of God's Plan of Salvation*. Fearn, Ross-shire, Scotland: Christian Focus, 2012.

Cassuto, Umberto. *A Commentary on the Book of Genesis*. Jerusalem: Magnes, 1961.

Coats, George W. *Genesis, with an Introduction to Narrative Literature*. FOTL 1. Grand Rapids, MI: Eerdmans, 1983.

Collins, C. John. *Genesis 1–4: A Linguistic, Literary, and Theological Commentary*. Phillipsburg, NJ: P&R, 2006.

Currid, John D. *Genesis*. 2 vols. EP Study Commentary. Darlington, UK: Evangelical Press, 2003–2004.

Hamilton, Victor P. *The Book of Genesis: Chapters 18–50*. NICOT. Grand Rapids, MI: Eerdmans, 1995.

Heidel, Alexander. *The Babylonian Genesis: The Story of the Creation*. 2nd ed. Chicago: University of Chicago Press, 1951.

———. *The Gilgamesh Epic and Old Testament Parallels*. 2nd ed. Chicago: University of Chicago Press, 1949.

Kline, Meredith G. "Because It Had Not Rained." *WTJ* 20, no. 2 (1958): 146–57.

———. *Kingdom Prologue*. South Hamilton, MA: M. G. Kline, 1993.

Lambert, W. G. "A New Look at the Babylonian Background of Genesis," *JTS* 16, no. 2 (1965): 287–300.

Mathews, Kenneth A. *Genesis 1–11:26*. NAC 1A. Nashville: Broadman, 1996.

Redford, Donald B. *A Study of the Biblical Story of Joseph (Genesis 37–50)*. VTSup 20. Leiden: Brill, 1970.

Robertson, O. Palmer. *The Christ of the Covenants*. Grand Rapids, MI: Baker, 1980.

Ross, Allen P. *Creation and Blessing: A Guide to the Study and Exposition of the Book of Genesis*. Grand Rapids, MI: Baker, 1988.

Sailhamer, John H. *The Pentateuch as Narrative: A Biblical-Theological Commentary*. Grand Rapids, MI: Zondervan, 1992.

Sarna, Nahum M. *Genesis: The Traditional Hebrew Text with the New JPS Translation*. JPS Torah Commentary. Philadelphia: Jewish Publication Society, 1989.

Speiser, E. A. *Genesis: A New Translation with Introduction and Commentary*. AB 1. Garden City, NY: Doubleday, 1964.

von Rad, Gerhard. *Genesis: A Commentary*. Translated by John H. Marks. OTL. Philadelphia: Westminster, 1961.

Wenham, Gordon J. *Genesis 1–15*. WBC 1. Waco, TX: Word, 1987.

2

Exodus

John D. Currid

INTRODUCTION

The book of Genesis ends with the Hebrew word בְּמִצְרָיִם, which literally means "in Egypt." This, of course, provides the setting for the book of Exodus, and in reality, it is a foreboding comment because the Hebrews at the beginning of Exodus have been enslaved in Egypt for over four hundred years since the ending of Genesis. This slavery fulfills the prophecy God gave to Abraham in Genesis 15, in which he says, "Know for certain that your offspring will be sojourners in a land that is not theirs and will be servants there, and they will be afflicted for four hundred years" (15:13). However, in the midst of that covenantal ceremony, God makes another promise to Abraham: "But I will bring judgment on the nation that they serve, and afterward they shall come out with great possessions" (15:14). The central message of the book of Exodus is God's keeping of that promise by delivering Abraham's offspring from slavery in the land of Egypt.

The Hebrew title of the book (ואלה שמות) comes from the first two Hebrew words in the text, which are translated, "And these are the names of . . ." Note that the text begins with the word "and" (the conjunctive *waw* in Hebrew), a word that many modern translations omit. This conjunction, however, ties the exodus story to the preceding material of Genesis. It demonstrates a natural flow of the narrative and highlights that this is a story in development. The phrase "And these are the names of . . ." is also a common introductory formula for a genealogy in the book of Genesis (25:13; 36:10, 40). This repetitive phrase ties the two books together and demonstrates that the author of Exodus has a deep and remarkable familiarity with Genesis—a truth repeatedly driven home throughout the book of Exodus.

The title Exodus is derived from a Greek word that means "going out," which the New Testament uses to refer to Israel's departure from Egypt. Hebrews 11:22 says, "By faith Joseph, at the end of his life, made mention of the exodus of the Israelites and gave directions concerning his bones." This title is derived from the ancient Greek translation of the Hebrew Bible (the Septuagint), which employed this leading word from the text as the focus of the book's message. Indeed, a large portion of the book recounts Israel's departure or "going out" from the land of Egypt by the hand of the Lord.

BACKGROUND ISSUES

Scholars often question how much the writer of the book of Exodus understood about Egypt. Donald Redford, for instance, concludes that "there is little Egyptian coloring in the Exodus account, almost wholly homonymic in nature; but the Egyptologist would soon sense that it is anachronistic."[1] This perspective is hardly new. Writing in the 1920s, the English Egyptologist T. Eric Peet commented, "The main fact which strikes the Egyptologist is that there is nothing whatsoever in [the biblical accounts with Egyptian colorings] which suggests the Hyksos period, or indeed any particular period at all. It is all the sort of vague general knowledge."[2] Such suspicion has been a dominant hermeneutic in both biblical studies and Egyptology.

Recent works have attempted to demonstrate that the writer of Exodus was, in fact, quite familiar with Egyptian practices and beliefs.[3] For example, the episode of the serpent confrontation in Exodus 7:8–13 is "saturated with elements of Egyptian religious and cultural background. Only an author well versed in Egyptian tradition could have composed this poignant piece that reeks of Egypt."[4] Numerous stories in the book of Exodus subtly criticize Egyptian manners, customs, and beliefs. For example, episodes like the dividing of the Red Sea are ironic critiques of similar accounts in Egyptian literature.

The biblical author often employs parallel idiomatic expressions in order to disparage Egypt. For instance, the Bible describes the Lord as humiliating and destroying Pharaoh and Egypt with "a strong arm" (Ex. 3:19–20; 6:1; 7:4; 15:16; etc.). This is ironic because ancient Egyptian texts characteristically explain pharaonic power in terms of Pharaoh's "strong hand"; he was the "possessor of a strong arm" and "the one who destroys enemies with his arm."[5] In the midst of the plague account, the Lord prophesies that an intense hailstorm will strike Egypt "such as never has been in Egypt from the day it was founded until now" (9:18). This announcement reflects a common Egyptian expression of the time. Pharaohs, such as Thutmosis III, would pronounce that they had done something greater "than all the things that were in the

---

[1] Donald B. Redford, "An Egyptological Perspective on the Exodus Narrative," in *Egypt, Israel, Sinai: Archaeological and Historical Relationships in the Biblical Period*, ed. Anson F. Rainey (Tel Aviv: Tel Aviv University Press, 1987), 138.
[2] T. Eric Peet, *Egypt and the Old Testament* (Liverpool: University Press of Liverpool, 1922), 93.
[3] See, in particular, John D. Currid, *Ancient Egypt and the Old Testament* (Grand Rapids, MI: Baker, 1997), and James K. Hoffmeier, *Israel in Egypt: The Evidence for the Authenticity of the Exodus Tradition* (New York: Oxford University Press, 1997).
[4] Currid, *Ancient Egypt*, 103. See, in addition, John D. Currid, "The Egyptian Setting of the 'Serpent' Confrontation in Exodus 7,8–13," *BZ*, n.s., 39, no. 2 (1995): 203–24.
[5] See James K. Hoffmeier, "The Arm of God versus the Arm of Pharaoh in the Exodus Narratives," *Bib* 67, no. 3 (1986): 378–87; and David R. Seely, "The Image of the Hand of God in the Exodus Traditions" (PhD diss., University of Michigan, 1990).

country since it was founded."[6] The Lord employs the same idiom to demonstrate his power over Pharaoh, Egypt, and natural phenomena.

The biblical author also employs Egyptian vocabulary in the book of Exodus.[7] Sometimes he uses Egyptian terms as wordplays. For example, there is the obvious wordplay on the name of the Egyptian god Ra and the Hebrew concept of רַע (*ra*) in Hebrew ("evil"); apparent allusions are found in Exodus 5:19; 10:10; 32:12, 22, and elsewhere in the Pentateuch. The author used these double entendres to taunt the main god of Egypt.[8] Another interesting pun involves the naming of Moses by the daughter of Pharaoh. At some point in his youth, Moses was brought to Pharaoh's daughter, and he was considered "her son" (2:10). She then names him "Moses," which is derived from a Hebrew verb that means "to draw out." That word, however, is also an Egyptian word that means "son of." Egyptian names often employ it in compound with other words; for example, the name of the Egyptian Pharaoh Thutmosis is literally "son of Thut," and the king Ahmosis is "son of Ah." The name Moses has no object and therefore simply means "son of." This is perhaps a pun by the writer to emphasize the point that Moses is not a son of Egypt or her gods but rather a son of Israel and the Lord. He later disowned allegiance to Egypt (see Heb. 11:24–25).

STRUCTURE AND OUTLINE

There is little scholarly consensus regarding the structure of the book.[9] However, it appears to be a diptych, that is, two panels or basic parts hinged together. Chapters 1–18 deal with Israel in Egypt and then the escape to Mount Sinai in the wilderness; chapters 19–40 describe the giving of the law at Mount Sinai. While the two sections are hinged historically and chronologically, they are distinct in many ways. In the first place, chapters 1–18 are, for the most part, historical narrative, while chapters 19–40 are principally legislative. Although the second section clearly includes narrative, God's revealing of legal matters dominates. Second, a great theological shift takes place from one section to the other. As Douglas Stuart says, "In Egypt, Israel was the servant of Pharaoh; at Sinai they became God's servants."[10] Thus, the structure of the book is simple: the first section explains how Israel got to Sinai, and the second section tells what happened at Sinai.

The opening section of the diptych has its own structure, and this structure demonstrates that this section is a coherent, unified literary piece. The structure casts the early life of Moses as a prototype and microcosm for the exodus event. In other words, the episodes of the life of Moses in Egypt, Midian, and Sinai model

---

[6] Umberto Cassuto, *A Commentary on the Book of Exodus* (Jerusalem: Magnes, 1967), 117.
[7] See Thomas O. Lambdin, "Egyptian Loan Words in the Old Testament," *JAOS* 73, no. 3 (1953): 145–55; Lambdin, *Loan Words and Transcriptions in the Ancient Semitic Languages* (PhD diss., Johns Hopkins University Press, 1952); and Ronald J. Williams, "Egypt and Israel," in *The Legacy of Egypt*, ed. J. R. Harris, 2nd ed. (Oxford: Clarendon, 1971), 257–90.
[8] Gary A. Rendsburg, "The Egyptian Sun-God Ra in the Pentateuch," *Henoch* 10, no. 1 (1988): 3–15.
[9] The issues regarding the writing of the entire Torah are complex. See, for example, Duane A. Garrett, *Rethinking Genesis: The Sources and Authorship of the First Book of the Pentateuch* (Grand Rapids, MI: Baker, 1991); Isaac M. Kikiwada and Arthur Quinn, *Before Abraham Was: The Unity of Genesis 1–11* (Nashville: Abingdon, 1985); Gordon J. Wenham, *Genesis 1–15*, WBC 1 (Waco, TX: Word, 1987); and R. N. Whybray, *The Making of the Pentateuch: A Methodological Study*, JSOTSup 53 (Sheffield: JSOT Press, 1987).
[10] Douglas K. Stuart, *Exodus*, NAC 2 (Nashville: B&H, 2006), 20.

and prefigure the salient events in the life of the emerging nation of Israel. Consider the parallels in table 5.

Moses	Israel
1. Exodus 2:1–2. Moses is born a slave in Egypt; he is born under oppression and persecution; and Pharaoh attempts to murder him (Ex. 1:15–22).	**1. Exodus 1:8–22.** The Israelites are born slaves in Egypt; they live under cruel bondage; and Pharaoh attempts to murder the male infants.
2. Exodus 2:3–10. Moses undergoes a water ordeal and is delivered.	**2. Exodus 14:1–15:21.** Israel undergoes a water ordeal at the Red Sea and is delivered.
3. Exodus 2:11–22. Moses escapes to Midian/Sinai.	**3. Exodus 16:1–18:27.** Israel escapes to Midian/Sinai.
4. Exodus 3:1–22. God appears to Moses in a theophany on Mount Sinai.	**4. Exodus 19:1–40:38.** God appears in a theophany on Mount Sinai.
5. Exodus 4:1–17. Moses hesitates and doubts, but God is faithful.	**5. Remainder of Torah.** Israel responds by being unfaithful, but God is faithful.

Table 5[11]

Not only do the two accounts correspond in major ways, but they also flow in the same pattern. Even the words and phrasing in the two narratives resemble one another to a great degree. For instance, in parallel 3 of the Moses column in table 5 (Ex. 2:11–22), the daughters of Jethro are being oppressed by shepherds who drive them away from watering their father's flock. In response, Moses intercedes as deliverer and rescues them from cruel maltreatment. The Hebrew word for "rescue" in verse 17 (יֹשִׁעַ) is one of the primary terms used for the deliverance of Israel out of Egypt (e.g., 14:30). In Exodus 2:19, the women declare that "an Egyptian delivered us out of the hand of the shepherds." That clause repeats almost word for word what Jethro later says, "Blessed be the Lord, who has delivered you out of the hand of the Egyptians" (18:10). Such linguistic affinities demonstrate that the episode of Moses rescuing Jethro's daughters is paradigmatic for the Lord (through Moses) delivering Israel out of Egypt.

MESSAGE AND THEOLOGY
The Exodus as a Leitmotif

The exodus represents a defining moment for Israel for its own import not only in their history but also in their future. Thus some of the later prophets in the Old Testament picture the exodus event as paradigmatic of a second redemptive act, the return from the exile in Babylon. For example, the eighth-century prophet Isaiah foretells that Israel and Judah will be destroyed but that one day "the Lord will extend his hand yet a second time to recover the remnant that remains of his people, from Assyria, from

---

[11] This chart is adapted from John D. Currid, *Exodus*, vol. 1, *Exodus 1–18*, EP Study Commentary (Darlington, UK: Evangelical Press, 2000), 23.

Egypt, from Pathros, from Cush, from Elam, from Shinar, from Hamath, and from the coastlands of the sea" (Isa. 11:11; cf. Zech. 10:9–11). Israel will escape from bondage and return to the Land of Promise, just like they did in the first exodus: "And there will be a highway from Assyria for the remnant that remains of his people, as there was for Israel when they came up from the land of Egypt" (Isa. 11:16).

The book of Ezra likewise parallels the return of God's people from Babylon with the exodus out of Egypt. In other words, the two returns narrated in Ezra are modeled on the Egyptian exodus; they are echoes of the original escape and return. The book begins with a first return (538 BC), in which the people occupy and settle in the Land of Promise (Ezra 2:70). After they settle, the first thing the people do is build the altar of burnt offering and begin to offer the daily sacrifices, morning and evening, that Moses had commanded Israel to do at Sinai (Ezra 3:2–3; cf. Ex. 29:38–39). The people then celebrate their first feast in the land, the Feast of Booths, or Tabernacles (Ezra 3:4). This national festival called Sukkot commemorates God's sustaining of Israel during the perils of their escape from Egypt (Lev. 23:42–43). It highlights God's care for his people as they returned to the Promised Land, and it is quite fitting that the Babylonian exiles would now celebrate it upon their return. Beginning with Ezra 3, the Israelites are rebuilding the temple to God in Jerusalem, just as the Hebrews did after the Egyptian exodus and the securing of the land of Canaan. At its completion, they dedicate the house of God in a manner quite similar to Solomon's dedication of the First Temple in 1 Kings 8. Finally, the people celebrate the Passover, which commemorates the deliverance of the Israelites from Egypt, and now they apply it to the returnees from Babylon (Ezra 6:19–22).

Other writings recognize the relationship between these two exodus events. Second Esdras (or 2 Ezra) of the Apocrypha determines that the priest Ezra is a second Moses. It declares that Ezra is the new lawgiver (14:19–48) and that he rewrote or edited the Scriptures in forty days (cf. Moses on Sinai for forty days). Although this writing is extracanonical, its interpretation of Ezra in relation to Moses is insightful. Ezra 7:10 says, "For Ezra had set his heart to study the Law of the LORD, and to do it and to teach his statutes and rules in Israel," and this statement appears to be based on Deuteronomy 4:5–6, in which Moses is described as one who does the same thing. Similarly, in Ezra 7:25, Ezra appoints judges to oversee the application of the law in the land, just as Moses had done at Midian (Ex. 18:21–22).

The return from Babylon is to be understood as a second exodus, and Ezra as a second Moses. Yet it is an echo without heightening and intensification. It is a second exodus but not a greater exodus. It simply lacks the redemptive punch of the first exodus. Later in Scripture, however, the exodus does serve the purpose of pointing to a greater deliverance. In the New Testament, Matthew structures his Gospel on the paradigm of the exodus event.[12] Consider the parallels in table 6.

---

[12] See Dale C. Allison, *The New Moses: A Matthean Typology* (Minneapolis: Fortress, 1993); Wayne S. Baxter, "Mosaic Imagery in the Gospel of Matthew," *TJ* 20, no. 1 (1999): 69–83; John Dominic Crossan, "From Moses to Jesus: Parallel Themes," *BRev* 2, no. 2 (1986): 18–27; and Barnabas Lindars, "The Image of Moses in the Synoptic Gospels," *Theology* 58 (1955): 78–83.

Exodus	Matthew
1. Begins with genealogy (1:1–5)	1. Begins with genealogy (1:1–17)
2. Birth of deliverer (2:1–10)	2. Birth of deliverer (1:18–25)
3. Pharaoh persecutes Israel (1:8–14; 2:11)	3. Herod oppresses the Jews (2:1–12)
4. Moses flees from Egypt (2:15)	4. Jesus flees to Egypt (2:13–15)
5. Pharaoh kills male children (1:15–22)	5. Herod kills male children (2:16–18)
6. Israel goes through the Red Sea (14:1–31)	6. Jesus is baptized (3:13–17)
7. Israel is tempted in the wilderness for forty years (Numbers)	7. Jesus is tempted in the wilderness for forty days (4:1–11)
8. Giving of law at Mount Sinai (Ex. 20:1ff.)	8. Sermon on the Mount (5:1–7:29)

Table 6

The climax of the escape from Egypt is the institution of the Passover, in which God judges Egypt and delivers Israel (Ex. 11:1–12:51). This climactic act points to the culminating event in the life of Christ in the New Testament: like the Passover lamb in the Old Testament, Jesus shed his blood to cover the sins of his people and to stay God's hand of wrath from coming upon them (John 1:29; 1 Pet. 1:19). As the apostle Paul declares, "Christ, our Passover lamb, has been sacrificed" (1 Cor. 5:7). Jesus is the Passover Lamb, who by the shedding of his blood is a substitute for his people, protecting them from the wrath and judgment of God. In other words, "as Israel is covered by the blood of the Passover lamb, so the new Israel is covered by the blood of the Messiah."[13]

Ancient Near Eastern Literature and the Exodus Narrative

Many of the incidents in the book of Exodus and in the life of Moses, in particular, reflect common plot-motifs in the ancient Near East.[14] For example, one of those motifs found in various cultures of the area, including Egypt, is a birth narrative in which a baby faces threat of destruction but survives and grows up to become a leader/deliverer of his people. In the ancient Near East, this plot line is old and familiar. It appears in Mesopotamia, Egypt, and Hatti, and its first appearance occurs at the end of the third millennium BC. As we will see, these stories contain striking parallels with the birth narrative of Moses recorded in Exodus 2:1–10. The question is, how do we understand the relationship of the two? "Is there dependence between them? Is the biblical author merely borrowing well-known literature from the surrounding cultures and employing it for his own purposes? Is the biblical material legend, myth, or history?"[15]

---

[13] Currid, *Exodus*, 1:253.
[14] The term "plot-motif" is taken from Thomas L. Thompson and Dorothy Irvin, "The Joseph and Moses Narratives," in *Israelite and Judaean History*, ed. John H. Hayes and J. Maxwell Miller (Philadelphia: Westminster, 1977), 183; they define it as "a plot element which moves the story forward a step."
[15] John D. Currid, *Against the Gods: The Polemical Theology of the Old Testament* (Wheaton, IL: Crossway, 2013), 75.

Many scholars believe the birth account of Moses is clearly related to the Legend of Sargon from Mesopotamia.[16] While the two accounts share some parallels, these actually appear to be quite general and weak. Instead, one should look for connections with the literature of Egypt because the biblical birth narrative of Moses takes place there. Gary Rendsburg correctly remarks, "the nature of biblical literature suggests that we should look not to Mesopotamia to explain a feature in a story set in Egypt, but rather to Egypt."[17] In fact, archaeologists have discovered a text in Egypt, commonly known as the Myth of Horus, that contains the plot-motif of the "exposed infant."[18]

The story tells a tale that occurs in the realm of the gods. The god Seth, the deity of chaos and war, murders Osiris, the ruling god of the underworld. Isis, the wife of Osiris, responds by raising Osiris from the dead and then becoming impregnated by him. She gives birth to a son named Horus "in the marshlands of Chemmis." This is a dangerous situation because if Seth hears of Horus's birth, he will kill the child. Isis and the child are able to elude Seth, and they hide out in the marshlands of the Delta. There Isis conceals Horus in thickets of papyrus by placing him in a papyrus basket.[19] Seth attempts to kill the child, but Horus survives, and by the end of the text he has aged and is ready to fight Seth and to become a leader of the gods.

The biblical account of the birth of Moses echoes the narrative of the Horus birth story. The general parallels are shown in table 7.

Birth of Horus	Birth of Moses
1. The newborn is in great danger: Seth is attempting to kill him.	1. The newborn is in great danger: Pharaoh is attempting to kill him (Ex. 1:15–22).
2. The role of the mother is highlighted: Isis protects the newborn.	2. The role of the mother is highlighted: Jochebed protects the newborn (Ex. 2:2).
3. Isis places the child in a papyrus basket and hides him in papyrus reeds.	3. Jochebed places Moses in a papyrus basket and hides him in the reeds by the banks of the Nile (Ex. 2:3).
4. A second female from the family guards the child: Horus's aunt, Nephthys.	4. A second female from the family guards the child: Moses's sister, Miriam (Ex. 2:4).
5. Isis nurses the child.	5. Jochebed nurses the child (Ex. 2:7–9).
6. The god Thoth gives aid to Isis and Horus.	6. The Lord comes to the aid of all Israel (Ex. 2:23–25).
7. Horus rises to become the first state god of Egypt, incarnated in Pharaoh.	7. Moses rises to be leader of the deliverance of Israel from Pharaoh's hand.

Table 7[20]

---

[16] The literature on this connection is vast. See, e.g., Brevard S. Childs, "The Birth of Moses," *JBL* 84, no. 2 (1965): 109–22; and Benjamin R. Foster, "The Birth Legend of Sargon of Akkad," in *COS*, 1:461.
[17] Gary A. Rendsburg, "Moses as Equal to Pharaoh," in *Text, Artifact, and Image: Revealing Ancient Israelite Religion*, ed. Gary M. Beckman and Theodore J. Lewis, BJS 346 (Providence, RI: Brown Judaic Studies, 2006), 201–19.
[18] Donald B. Redford, "The Literary Motif of the Exposed Child," *Numen* 14, no. 3 (1967): 209–28.
[19] Daniel S. Richter, "Plutarch on Isis and Osiris: Text, Cult, and Cultural Appropriation," *TAPA* 131 (2001): 191–216. Plutarch's account is quite late, dating to about the end of the first century AD, yet it probably reflects much earlier material.
[20] Adapted from Currid, *Against the Gods*, 81–82.

The birth account of Moses reflects Egyptian customs and beliefs. It even includes Egyptian vocabulary. For example, Jochebed places Moses in "a basket made of bulrushes" (Ex. 2:3), an Egyptian designation that identifies the papyrus vessel. The account simply has Egypt written all over it.

Gary Rendsburg rightly says that "the sum of the evidence is clear: not surprisingly, a biblical story set in Egypt echoes a well-known and popular myth from Egypt."[21] The connection between the two stories is undeniable, but the question is, how do the two accounts relate to each other? Why would the biblical writer purposefully draw a parallel between the two? He may have been consciously employing this echo from a well-known Egyptian myth for polemical reasons. What was no more than a myth in Egypt truly came to pass for Israel in Egypt. In other words, the author takes a famous pagan myth and turns it on its head in order to ridicule and taunt Egypt and then to highlight the truth of the biblical story.

Another example is the dividing of the waters of the Red Sea narrated in Exodus 14:13–31. The ancient Egyptians had their own story of how a priest separated a large body of water. The tale is part of the Westcar Papyrus, which describes a series of miracles by various magicians during the Third and Fourth Dynasties of ancient Egypt (ca. 2649–2465 BC).[22] The text was written later, however, and perhaps dates as early as the twentieth century BC. In any event, it precedes the exodus event by hundreds of years. The papyrus tells the story of a bored Pharaoh Snofru who summons one of his chief priests named Djadjaemonkh in order to get some advice on how to find some pleasure. Djadjaemonkh suggests that the king go for a boat ride on a lake with many pretty, naked women rowing the boat. Pharaoh agrees and is happy with the expedition until one of the women drops her fish-shaped charm into the lake. The woman will take no replacement, so Pharaoh calls for Djadjaemonkh to solve the problem with his secret arts. The priest pronounces some spells and thus divides the lake, placing one side on top of the other. He finds the charm lying on top of a potsherd, and retrieves it for the woman. Finally, he conjures more spells and brings the water of the lake back to its original position.

The biblical narrative of the dividing of the Red Sea is reminiscent of this Egyptian story. But for what purpose would the biblical writer draw a parallel between the two tales? He may have been critiquing Egyptian magic and its spells. While the chief lector priest of Egypt may have separated the waters of a lake in order to retrieve a valuable charm, God through Moses parts the entire Red Sea in order to deliver his people from slavery in Egypt. Who displays the greater power?

The Plague Account

The Plagues as Ridicule

The judgment that God brings upon Egypt and the means of escape for the Hebrews is structured according to ten plagues in Exodus 7:8–12:51. At the center of the plague

---

[21] Rendsburg, "Moses as Equal to Pharaoh," 207.
[22] See Aylward Manley Blackman, *The Story of King Kheops and the Magicians* (Reading, UK: J. V. Books, 1988); and Miriam Lichtheim, ed. and trans., *The Old and Middle Kingdoms*, vol. 1 of *Ancient Egyptian Literature* (Berkeley: University of California Press, 1975), 215–22.

narrative is a contest, but it is not primarily a contest between Moses and Pharaoh or between Moses and the Egyptian magicians or, for that matter, between Israel and Egypt. This is heavenly combat, that is, a war between the God of the Hebrews and the deities of Egypt. The biblical writer accurately sees that the matter at hand is theological. It is a question of who is the one true God, who is sovereign over the operation of the universe, and whose will is going to come to pass in heaven and on earth.

In support of this proposition is the teaching that each of the ten plagues is directed by the Lord against particular Egyptian deities.[23] One can account for each of the plagues in this manner. For example, the opening plague (Ex. 7:15–25) is clearly aimed against the Nile River. The Egyptians believed that the Nile, when inundated, became a deity, personified as the god Hapi. In artistic renderings, the Egyptians pictured Hapi as a bearded man with female breasts and a hanging stomach (perhaps a sign of pregnancy). This hermaphroditic portrayal reflects the concept of fertility. The ancient Egyptians truly believed that the Nile in its inundation sustained Egypt, a belief that many surviving texts confirm.[24] Therefore, when the Lord turns the Nile River to blood, he is directly attacking this deity; the fertility god Hapi is no longer able to supply for the needs of the Egyptian people. This disaster taunts the Egyptian god because true sustenance comes only from the hand of the sovereign Lord of the universe and not from a false deity.

We can cite a second example at this point. The ancient Egyptians regarded Amon-Ra, who is personified in the sun, as the chief deity. They believed that when Amon-Ra rises in the east, he symbolizes new life and resurrection. In fact, many texts picture Amon-Ra as the creator-god.[25] However, when that god goes down in the west, he becomes an antithesis representing death and the underworld. Thus, when the Lord so wills it, as in the ninth plague, the sun is darkened (Ex. 10:21–29), and Amon-Ra is unable to shine on his people as a symbol of life. To the contrary, he symbolizes judgment, death, and hopelessness.

To the point, the plagues that the Lord brings upon Egypt to deliver his people are a direct attack upon the gods of Egypt. The Old Testament understands it that way: "On the day after the Passover, the people of Israel went out triumphantly in the sight of all the Egyptians, while the Egyptians were burying all their firstborn, whom the Lord had struck down among them. On their gods also the Lord executed judgments" (Num. 33:3b–4). Mockery of Egyptian polytheism is a central focus of the plague account (cf. Jer. 46:25).

The Plagues as De-creation (Protology)

When considering an account like the ten plagues, it is important that the reader look at the context of the episode in light of the unfolding nature of God's revelation. As

---

[23] See, e.g., Charles F. Aling, *Egypt and Bible History: From Earliest Times to 1000 B.C.*, Baker Studies in Biblical Archaeology (Grand Rapids, MI: Baker, 1981), 103–10; John James Davis, *Moses and the Gods of Egypt: Studies in the Book of Exodus*, 2nd ed. (Grand Rapids, MI: Baker, 1986), 98–153; George A. F. Knight, *Theology as Narration: A Commentary on the Book of Exodus* (Grand Rapids, MI: Eerdmans, 1976), 62–79; and Nahum M. Sarna, *Exploring Exodus: The Heritage of Biblical Israel* (New York: Schocken, 1986), 78–80.

[24] See, e.g., "The Hymn to the Nile," in Adolf Erman, *The Literature of the Ancient Egyptians: Poems, Narratives, and Manuals of Instruction, from the Third and Second Millennia B.C.*, trans. Aylward M. Blackman (New York: Dutton, 1927), 146–49.

[25] See, for example, Pritchard, *ANET*, 365.

mentioned in the chapter on Genesis, we must give attention to the work of *protology* ("the study of first things"). The author of Exodus is familiar with the book of Genesis, and he structures his account of Exodus 1–15 on the theology and language of the Genesis creation account.[26] That is to say, the narrative of Israel's deliverance out of Egypt and the crossing of the Red Sea reflects the account of the original creation. We can see this connection in a number of ways. First, in the opening paragraph of the book of Exodus, the writer declares that "the people of Israel were fruitful and increased greatly; they multiplied and grew exceedingly strong, so that the land was filled with them" (1:7). This statement, which lays the setting for the book, uses five verbs that mirror the language of creation and particularly the creation mandate of Genesis 1:28. The author purposefully echoes Genesis in order to underscore that the Hebrews, while in Egypt, were fulfilling this mandate and that Israel is a second Adam. Thus, the writer of the book of Exodus is casting the narrative as a re-creation account.

Second, the episode of Moses undergoing a water ordeal in the Nile River echoes the Noahic flood account in Genesis 6–8. After Moses was born and his mother could no longer hide him from the authorities, she placed him in a "basket" (תֵּבָה, Ex. 2:3). That Hebrew word is used twenty-four times in the Noah account to refer to the "ark." In addition, Moses's mother covers the basket with "bitumen and pitch" (Ex. 2:3), as did Noah with the ark (Gen. 6:14). As we saw in our study of the book of Genesis, the Noah account is a re-creation event in which God reiterates the cultural mandate to Noah, who is cast as a second Adam figure (Gen. 9:1). That decree is the same one that the Hebrews are in the process of fulfilling in Exodus 1, as they multiply their number in Egypt. The biblical author is presenting the deliverance of Israel out of Egypt as a re-creation.

Third, the great saving event at the Red Sea is shaped according to the paradigm of the Genesis creation account. As Warren Gage comments, "the redemptive creation of Israel at the sea is cast in the same narrative style of original creation as the pillar of divine presence brings light into darkness (Ex. 13:21, cf. the first creative day), the waters are divided (Ex. 14:21, cf. the second creative day), and the dry land emerges (Ex. 14:29, cf. the third creative day)."[27] The biblical narrative teaches that the dividing of the Red Sea—and the entire exodus event, for that matter—is a second creation. It is a new conquest of chaos, another prevailing over the waters of the deep, and the creation of Israel as God's covenant people.

These protological elements are widely recognized in the literature of biblical studies. What is rarely seen is that the plague account ironically reverses the creation account as it pertains to the land of Egypt.[28] In other words, the main elements of the creation account as related in Genesis 1 are being assaulted and thrown into confusion in Egypt by God's onslaught of the plagues, as visible in table 8.

---

[26] Meredith G. Kline, *Images of the Spirit* (Grand Rapids, MI: Baker, 1980), 13–42.
[27] Warren Austin Gage, *The Gospel of Genesis: Studies in Protology and Eschatology* (Winona Lake, IN: Carpenter, 1984), 20–21.
[28] The groundbreaking study in this regard is Ziony Zevit, "Three Ways to Look at the Ten Plagues," *BRev* 6, no. 3 (1990): 16–23, 42, 44.

Creation Day	Description	Plague on Egypt	Description
Day 1: Gen. 1:3–5	Light created out of darkness	Plague 9: Ex. 10:21–29	Darkness prevailing over the light
Day 2: Gen. 1:6–8	Waters ordered and separated	Plague 1: Ex. 7:15–25	Chaos by changing water to blood
Day 3: Gen. 1:9–13	Dry land and vegetation appear	Plagues 7–8: Ex. 9:13–10:20	Destruction of vegetation
Day 4: Gen. 1:14–19	Creation of the luminaries	Plague 9: Ex. 10:21–29	Darkening of the luminaries
Day 5: Gen. 1:20–23	Creation of birds, fish, and sea life	Plagues 1–2: Ex. 7:15–8:15	Death of fish and frogs
Day 6: Gen. 1:24–31	Creation of animals and humans	Plagues 3–6: Ex. 8:16–9:12 Plague 10: Ex. 11:1–12:51	Plague of insects, anthrax, boils on beasts and humans; killing of firstborn

Table 8[29]

This connection demonstrates that the Lord, the Creator of heaven and earth, is using the plagues to throw the natural order into chaos in Egypt.

Echoes of the Plagues (Eschatology)

The plague account in the book of Exodus begins a theme that appears repeatedly throughout the Scriptures. For example, the plague model is obviously visible in the ark narrative of 1 Samuel 4–7.[30] In this account, the Philistines defeat Israel and capture the ark of the covenant. The ark, therefore, lies in subjection in a foreign land. One of the consequences of this event is that God brings a plague upon the Philistines in the same way he inflicted plagues on Egypt in order to secure the release of the ark from oppression (see 1 Sam. 6:4 in which the word "plague" appears). A definite correspondence exists between the two accounts.

The affinities between the two events are evident on both the linguistic level and the thematic level. Linguistically speaking, much of the prominent vocabulary used in the two stories is the same. This is particularly striking in 1 Samuel 5:6–6:4. For example, when God brings the plague of tumors on the Philistines, the text uses the word "afflicted/struck" (נכה in 1 Sam. 5:6, 9, 12), a verb frequently used in the exodus account (e.g., Ex. 9:15). The term used for "plague" in 1 Samuel 6:4, while not a very common word in the Hebrew lexicon, appears in Exodus 9:14 as a summary term for all the plagues brought on Egypt. The Hebrew word for "panic" is also not a commonly used term in the Old Testament, but it appears twice in the ark episode (1 Sam. 5:9, 11) and in Exodus 14:24, when God throws the army of Egypt into great confusion. In 1 Samuel 5:7, the Ashdodites declare that the Lord's

---

[29] This chart is adapted from Currid, *Ancient Egypt*, 115.
[30] For an in-depth look at this paradigm, see David Daube, *The Exodus Pattern in the Bible*, All Souls Studies 2 (London: Faber & Faber, 1963), 73–82.

hand is "hard" (קשה) against them. This, too, is an important word in the exodus narratives (Ex. 6:9; 13:15), and it is used as one of the standard terms to denote the hardening of Pharaoh's heart (e.g., Ex. 7:3).

A curious expression occurs twice in 1 Samuel 5:10–11, where the Ekronites respond to the plague coming upon them. The Hebrew text is translated literally as "to kill me and my people." What makes the statement odd is its use of the singular pronouns "me" and "my" when in fact the Ekronites (plural) are speaking. Some argue that perhaps a spokesman is talking on behalf of the Ekronites, or perhaps the singular carries a collective sense. It should be observed, however, that the expressions "me and my people" or "Pharaoh and his people" appear over twenty times in the exodus story. Exodus 8:8, for example, quotes Pharaoh as saying, "Plead with the LORD to take away the frogs *from me and from my people*, and I will let the people go to sacrifice to the LORD." Consequently, the text of 1 Samuel 5:10–11 appears to refer to the exodus account and demonstrates that the plague model undergirds the ark episode.

The writer of 1 Samuel recognizes this pattern, and he quotes the Philistines to establish it. The Philistine priests and diviners say to their people, "Why should you harden your hearts as the Egyptians and Pharaoh hardened their hearts? After he had dealt severely with them, did they not send the people away, and they departed?" (6:6). Even in the midst of the plague, the Philistines acknowledge the echo, as they lament, "Woe to us! Who can deliver us from the power of these mighty gods? These are the gods who struck the Egyptians with every sort of plague in the wilderness" (4:8). Although the Philistines are confused about Hebrew monotheism, they rightly see the paradigm of the Egyptian plagues playing out in their situation.

The theme of the Exodus plague account reaches a crescendo in the book of Revelation, in which the plagues will strike the followers of Satan at the end of time (cf. Revelation 16). In other words, the plague narrative serves as a paradigm of the judgment that will come upon all unbelievers one day. For example, Revelation repeats the first plague in Egypt through the second and third bowls of wrath, which are described as follows: "The second angel poured out his bowl into the sea, and it became like the blood of a corpse, and every living thing died that was in the sea. The third angel poured out his bowl into the rivers and the springs of water, and they became blood" (Rev. 16:3–4). The similarities between these descriptions and the narratives in Exodus are obvious. The apostle John cites other plagues as well, such as the seventh plague of hail: "And great hailstones, about one hundred pounds each, fell from heaven on people; and they cursed God for the plague of the hail, because the plague was so severe" (Rev. 16:21). The size of the hailstones in Revelation underscores the intensity and severity of the plague in the eschaton; it is so much greater than the plague in Egypt. In reality, the disaster that falls on the Egyptians is a mere foretaste of the final judgment at the end of time. In other words, the plagues of Exodus echo into the book of Revelation, and they foreshadow what will come upon God's enemies in the final days.

Universal Order: Ma'at

The ancient Egyptians believed in a universal order they called *ma'at*. It may be defined as the "cosmic force of harmony, order, stability, and security . . . and the organizing quality of created phenomena."[31] In their view, this force was a result of the first creation and was the opposite of chaos; it was what holds the universe together. In Egypt, it was the pharaoh's responsibility to maintain *ma'at* because he was considered the very essence and being of *ma'at*. In fact, when a new king ascended the throne, it was his duty and obligation to reestablish and reaffirm *ma'at*. He was to maintain the order of creation throughout his reign and his land. According to Cyril Aldred, the "means by which the king established *ma'at* were his 'Authoritative Utterance' and his 'Understanding.'"[32] As I have noted elsewhere, "restoring and maintaining this harmony were imperatives for the Egyptian king, expectations that befit his office as the son of Re and the god-king."[33]

When the Lord assaulted Egypt with the plagues, he was sending Egypt into chaos. Not only was he reversing the creation, but he was also de-creating Egypt. He was casting the universal order (*ma'at*) into wild disorder or pandemonium. It was ultimately an attack on Pharaoh and his vaunted power and sovereignty. Was Pharaoh able to withstand the invasion of his sphere of control? That he could not highlights a major theme of the book of Exodus and the plague accounts in particular: "to challenge this basic concept [*ma'at*] by showing that Pharaoh was powerless before the God of the covenant, Yahweh (Ex. 12:12)."[34] The destruction of the Egyptian concept of *ma'at* demonstrates that the Lord alone is in control of the universe; he alone is sovereign.

Hardening of Pharaoh's Heart

Another theme in the book of Exodus that underscores the sovereignty of God is the hardening of Pharaoh's heart. This central motif is found throughout the first half of the *diptych*, chapters 1–18. It is a leading theme that underscores the entire conflict in Egypt between God and Pharaoh. The first instance of the concept appears in Exodus 4:21, where God says about Pharaoh, "I will harden his heart, so that he will not let the people go." Throughout the narrative the author frequently specifies that the Lord is the One who hardens Pharaoh's heart (7:3; 9:12; 10:1, 20, 27; 14:4, 8). Three different Hebrew terms are used throughout the text to indicate the hardened state of Pharaoh's heart; the one used in 4:21 for "harden" bears the idea of Pharaoh maintaining a strong, determined will not to give in to the demands of the Lord to let the people go.[35] God is the cause of that hardening.

Egyptian background illuminates how deeply meaningful this theme is. Ancient

---

[31] John A. Wilson, *The Burden of Egypt: An Interpretation of Ancient Egyptian Culture* (Chicago: University of Chicago Press, 1951), 48.

[32] Cyril Aldred, *The Egyptians*, Ancient Peoples and Places 18 (London: Thames and Hudson, 1961), 161.

[33] Currid, *Ancient Egypt*, 119.

[34] John H. Sailhamer, *The Pentateuch as Narrative: A Biblical-Theological Commentary*, Library of Biblical Interpretation (Grand Rapids, MI: Zondervan, 1992), 252.

[35] For an in-depth study of these three terms, see G. K. Beale, "An Exegetical and Theological Consideration of the Hardening of Pharaoh's Heart in Exodus 4–14 and Romans 9," *TJ*, n.s., 5, no. 2 (1984): 129–54.

Egyptian texts teach that the heart is the very essence of a person, the inner spiritual center of the self. It is arguably the most important part of the human being in ancient Egyptian religion. Pharaoh's heart was especially important because the Egyptians believed his heart to be the sovereign, all-controlling force in both history and society. The Egyptians further taught that the hearts of the gods Ra and Horus are ultimately sovereign over everything.[36] And because they understood Pharaoh to be the incarnation of those two gods, they viewed his heart as equally sovereign over everything that exists. This motif that the Lord hardens Pharaoh's heart thus demonstrates that only the Hebrew God is the true sovereign of the universe. The Lord even controls the heart of Pharaoh, a central truth to the entire book of Exodus. This account illustrates well what the writer of Proverbs says: "The king's heart is a stream of water in the hand of the LORD; he turns it wherever he will" (21:1).

In Exodus 7:14 the Lord declares that "Pharaoh's heart is hardened." The term used for "hardened" here means, in its most basic sense, "to be heavy." Again, ancient Egyptian beliefs shed light on the idea that Pharaoh's heart is heavy.[37] During the Egyptian New Kingdom period, when the exodus took place, Egyptians believed that after death, a person would face judgment in the underworld. The heart of the deceased, the very essence of the person, would be weighed on the scales of truth. On one side of the scale was the heart and on the other was the feather of truth and righteousness. If the heart weighed heavy with misdeeds, the person was deemed unjust and unrighteous and would be banned entrance into the Field of Reeds, the Egyptian afterlife.

In the exodus narrative, the verdict that Pharaoh's heart is heavy indicates that he is in essence unjust and full of iniquity. This is especially striking in light of the ancient Egyptian view that Pharaoh is sinless. The Lord's assault on Pharaoh directly attacks the prevailing notion that the Egyptian king's character is pure and untainted.

It should also be noted that at other times in the account, the text declares that Pharaoh hardened his own heart (e.g., Ex. 8:15, 32). This alternative cause perhaps teaches that Pharaoh is responsible for his own sin, while at the same time he is under the sovereign hand of the Lord. This appears to be the conclusion that the apostle Paul draws in this matter (Rom. 9:14–24).

The Law

At the very beginning of Exodus 19, the Hebrews arrive at Mount Sinai, and there God calls Moses up the mountain to establish a covenant with Israel and to reveal his law to them. This second half of the *diptych* (Exodus 19–40) is presented primarily in the genre of a legislative text. It does include a variety of literary forms, such as narrative (32:1–35), promise (23:20–33), and intercession (33:12–23), but the overwhelming and dominant literary style is jurisprudence. We will begin our study of Hebrew law with a consideration of the Decalogue or Ten Commandments.

---

[36] Pritchard, *ANET*, 54.
[37] For much greater detail to this argument, see John D. Currid, "Why Did God Harden Pharaoh's Heart?" *BRev* 9, no. 6 (1993): 46–51; Currid, "Egyptian Setting of the 'Serpent' Confrontation," 18–40; Currid, *Ancient Egypt*, 96–103.

Before we consider Hebrew law, it is important that we also comment on ancient Egyptian law because it provides the setting for the revelation at Mount Sinai. Of all the tens of thousands of texts that survive from ancient Egypt, there has not been discovered a single legislative code. Documents like the Demotic Legal Code of Hermopolis West are not codified law but mere guidelines for how to live and act.[38] The reality was that the pharaohs were the definers and executors of justice and law. They enacted new laws and changed old laws by their own prerogatives. It was the pharaoh who pronounced, "Thus says" (Ex. 5:10), and he could change or alter a law capriciously, which explains why there is no known codified law in ancient Egypt. The Lord, to the contrary, is not capricious, but he reveals his law, which stands forever.

The Ten Commandments (Ex. 20:1–17)

God's revelation of law to Israel through Moses at Mount Sinai begins with the Decalogue because that is the foundational and principial law upon which all the law of Israel stands. The structure and content of the Ten Commandments highlight the peculiarly binding nature of the Decalogue upon the congregation of Israel. First, it should be noted that the Lord reveals these laws directly to the people without any mediation of Moses or another prophet (Ex. 20:1). God does not merely speak the commandments themselves but also inscribes them with his very finger on stone tablets (31:18; 32:15–16). Second, God gives *ten* commandments (or "words"), and this number appears to symbolize in Hebrew culture the idea of completeness—no additions are allowed. The text further reveals that the tablets are written on both sides and completely filled, leaving no room for additions (32:15). Finally, these commands are written in stone, never to be erased.[39]

The Decalogue is divided into two parts. The first four commandments pronounce and describe our duty to God, and the next six describe our duty to man. When Jesus is asked by a lawyer to name the greatest commandment, he answers by summarizing the Ten Commandments in the following way: "You shall love the Lord your God with all your heart and with all your soul and with all your mind. This is the great and first commandment. And a second is like it: You shall love your neighbor as yourself. On these two commandments depend all the Law and the Prophets" (Matt. 22:37–40). Jesus thus clearly supports and advocates the continued application and relevance of the Decalogue for the church.

Throughout church history, many have argued that Jesus actually abrogates some of the Ten Commandments in the Sermon on the Mount in Matthew 5–7. In reality, his purpose there is not to revoke the Decalogue but to strengthen it by teaching its proper interpretation. So, for example, Jesus explains, "You have heard that it was said to those of old, 'You shall not murder; and whoever murders will be liable to judgment.' But I say to you that everyone who is angry with his brother will be

---

[38] That particular text is quite late, appearing in the Ptolemaic period. For a translation, see K. Donker van Heel, ed. and trans., *The Legal Manual of Hermopolis: [P. Mattha]: Text and Translation* (Leiden: Papyrologisch Instituut, 1990).

[39] It is likely that each tablet contains the Decalogue and that one copy belongs to the suzerain and the other to the vassal. Israel's copy is to be housed in the ark of the covenant (Deut. 10:5). See the discussion in Meredith G. Kline, *Treaty of the Great King: The Covenant Structure of Deuteronomy: Studies and Commentary* (Grand Rapids, MI: Eerdmans, 1963).

liable to judgment; whoever insults his brother will be liable to the council; and whoever says, 'You fool!' will be liable to the hell of fire" (Matt. 5:21–22). Here, Jesus is interpreting the sixth commandment (Ex. 20:13). Many of the Jews of his day, including the Pharisees, believed that if they had never murdered anyone, then they had wholly kept this law. But Jesus argued, to the contrary, that not only do our actions condemn us but our hearts do as well. Thus, Jesus understood the Ten Commandments to be much more strict and condemning in their application than the Pharisees and others did. The Westminster Confession of Faith (1646) summarizes this point when it says, "Neither doth Christ in the gospel any way dissolve [the Ten Commandments], but much strengthen, this obligation" (19.5).

The Book of the Covenant (Ex. 21:1–23:33)

The laws contained in the Book of the Covenant are different from the commandments given by the Lord in the Decalogue. These laws were written down by the hand of Moses and not by the hand of the Lord (Ex. 24:4). This underscores Moses's mediatorial role in giving this law to the people (21:1), whereas the Lord spoke directly to the people in revealing the Decalogue. In the opening verse of the Book of the Covenant (21:1), the laws are specifically called "rules" (מִשְׁפָּטִים), a term referring to case decisions that rest upon prior precedent. In other words, the laws of the Decalogue are principial, foundational, permanent, and eternal, whereas the laws of the Book of the Covenant deal with the specific social and economic contexts of the people of Israel.

For instance, Exodus 22:1 states, "If a man steals an ox or a sheep, and kills it or sells it, he shall repay five oxen for an ox, and four sheep for a sheep." This is a legal case decision applying the principle of the eighth commandment, "You shall not steal" (20:15), to the needs of the emerging nation of Israel. Again, the Decalogue reveals the fundamental legal principles that need to be applied to society at any time and in any place. The Book of the Covenant is derivative, applying the principles of the Decalogue to the specific social contexts of Israel as a nation, and it was valid only in that particular era.

Construction of the Tabernacle

Much of the remainder of the book of Exodus describes the Lord's command to the people to build a tabernacle as central to the worship of Israel. Exodus 25:1–31:11 contains the specific instructions and directions God gives for this building project, and Exodus 35:1–40:38 narrates the Israelites obeying and making the tabernacle. The tabernacle is a portable temple that the Israelites carry throughout the wilderness wanderings, and it serves as their central shrine until the Hebrews build the temple in Jerusalem during Solomon's reign. As such, the design, style, and materials of the tabernacle reflect the nomadic conditions of Israel's existence.[40] The Hebrew word

---

[40] Menahem Haran, *Temples and Temple-Service in Ancient Israel: An Inquiry into Biblical Cult Phenomena and the Historical Setting of the Priestly School* (Winona Lake, IN: Eisenbrauns, 1985), 195–96.

for "tabernacle" is related to an Akkadian term meaning "tent," and it is also used in the Old Testament in relation to shepherding.[41]

Tent-shrines were common in antiquity. They appear over a long period, from ancient Phoenicia to modern Islam.[42] Portable shrines in Egypt date to as early as the third millennium BC and are attested to in written sources from the time of Rameses II (1290–1224 BC). The construction methods used by the Israelites, in fact, reflect "well-established Egyptian techniques."[43]

The Golden Calf Incident

Although the Israelites ratify the covenant at Sinai (Ex. 24:3–8), they soon turn away from it. In Exodus 32, the people ask Aaron to fashion gods that might lead them (32:1). Aaron complies and casts a golden calf out of the people's jewelry (32:2–3). When the people see it, they thunder, "These are your gods, O Israel, who brought you up out of the land of Egypt!" (32:4). This expression echoes what Yahweh claimed that he had done for Israel (see Ex. 20:2; cf. Lev. 26:13; Ps. 81:10). Aaron responds to the frenzy of the crowd by announcing that "Tomorrow shall be a feast to the LORD [Yahweh]" (Ex. 32:5). What we are witnessing is an episode of syncretism—that is, Aaron is creating a common ancient Near Eastern metal idol and declaring that it represents Yahweh, the God of Israel. The incident's syncretistic nature is evident in that the people ask for a plurality of gods (the verb "who will go" in verse 1 is a third person plural), yet Aaron only manufactures one idol. A central tenet of the worship of Yahweh is monotheism, and thus Aaron appears to be holding the line there.

Aaron and the people were breaking the second commandment by creating a physical image of the Lord for worship. Aaron even employed a graving tool to make the idol. The Lord had earlier disallowed Israel from using such a tool even to build an altar for him (Ex. 20:25); the temptation to fashion a physical representation of God would be too great.

This incident served as a historical precedent for Jeroboam setting up golden-calf worship at Dan and Bethel (1 Kings 12:25–33). Note, in particular, that Jeroboam directly quotes the rebellious people at Sinai; after making the two calves, the king proclaims, "Behold, your gods, O Israel, who brought you up out of the land of Egypt" (12:28). This event highlights the tragic apostasy of the people at Sinai and of the people of Israel in Jeroboam's day.

Ancient Near Eastern Law Codes

The Mosaic law code—first revealed in the book of Exodus and then expanded throughout the rest of the Pentateuch—is clearly not the earliest law code found in the ancient Near East. Some of the law codes of Mesopotamia precede the Mosaic law by centuries. Important written codes appear around the beginning of the second

---

[41] Sarna, *Exploring Exodus*, 197.
[42] Frank M. Cross, "The Tabernacle: A Study from an Archaeological and Historical Approach," *BA* 10, no. 3 (1947): 45–68.
[43] Sarna, *Exploring Exodus*, 196–200.

millennium BC, such as the Code of Lipit-Ishtar and the Laws of Shauna.[44] The best-known Mesopotamian legislation is the Code of Hammurabi, named after its author, who was king of Babylon (1792–1750 BC).

It has often been argued that the law of Moses depends directly on these Mesopotamian law codes. However, no direct, concrete evidence proves such borrowing. There is no question that the law codes exhibit similarities, but "that can be explained by the limitation in the variety of crimes and in the possible forms of punishment."[45] It also needs to be noted that there are vast differences between the Hebrew law and the codes of Mesopotamia. For instance, in the Code of Hammurabi, class distinctions often determine how they apply the law, but the Mosaic law code has no such differences—each individual is equal under the law. In addition, the Mesopotamian codes exhibit far less value on human life in general; the Old Testament law, for example, places a stress on one's duty to care for the widow, orphan, and sojourner that is not evident in the laws of Mesopotamia. The absence of spiritual and ethical principles in the Mesopotamian laws contrasts with the Mosaic law code, in which they are foundational. Finally, the Mosaic law is revealed by God as part and parcel of the covenant relationship between himself and the people; no such idea is even hinted at in other ancient Near Eastern codes of jurisprudence. These major differences clearly indicate that Hebrew law is different from—not to mention a vast improvement upon—Mesopotamian law.

APPROACHING THE NEW TESTAMENT

The book of Exodus narrates the episode of God's deliverance of Israel out of Egypt. This is by far the greatest salvific event in the Old Testament. It is a monumental act in itself, but it is even greater as it foreshadows the heightened redeeming work of Jesus Christ. As pointed out earlier in the chapter, Christ is the ultimate Passover Lamb who shed his blood to deliver his people from death and darkness. As Paul says in 1 Corinthians 5:7, "For Christ, our Passover lamb, has been sacrificed."

In addition to this central idea of salvation, Exodus points to Christ in other ways. For example, the tabernacle, which is constructed in Exodus 25–40, is a foreshadowing of Christ. John 1:14 declares that "the Word became flesh and tabernacled among us" (my trans.); the Word itself is Jesus Christ (see John 1:1–5; Rev. 21:1–3). In fact, the act of the high priest sprinkling blood on the mercy seat within the tabernacle on the Day of Atonement typified Christ's atoning blood on behalf of his people. For instance, in Romans 3:24–25, the word often translated as "propitiation" in fact means "mercy seat." And thus, the text may correctly read, "in Christ Jesus, whom God put forward as a mercy seat by his blood, to be received by faith" (my trans.). Christ, therefore, is the ultimate fulfillment not only of the tabernacle itself but of the very event of the Day of Atonement.

We could easily consider many other parallels and types, such as Moses as a

---

[44] Pritchard, *ANET*, 159–163.
[45] John D. Currid and David P. Barrett, *Crossway ESV Bible Atlas* (Wheaton, IL: Crossway, 2010), 67.

pointer to Christ and the manna as a foreshadowing of him, but the message stands: Exodus contains many shadows of the coming Messiah that became full reality in the appearance, person, and work of Jesus Christ.

In Exodus 15, immediately after the great deliverance of Israel by God through the Red Sea, Moses leads the people in singing a hymn of praise to the Lord. It is a doxology. The opening verse of the song highlights one of the primary themes of the book of Exodus: "I will sing to the LORD, for he has triumphed gloriously; the horse and his rider he has thrown into the sea" (15:1). After the song is finished, Miriam leads the women of Israel in response by singing the same words antiphonally (15:20–21). These words serve as the refrain for the larger hymn, and the purpose of a refrain is to underscore the hymn's most important teaching: the Lord is triumphant and sovereign. He alone is King of kings and Lord of lords.

The second verse of the song in chapter 15 underscores a second great theme of the book of Exodus. The people sing, "The LORD is my strength and my song, and he has become my salvation." The Lord is the Deliverer and Savior of his people. He had promised Abraham that though his descendants would be slaves in a foreign land, he would deliver them from bondage after four hundred years (Gen. 15:13–14). This he did in the book of Exodus: he is a God who keeps his word by delivering his people from oppression.

Finally, the Lord does not merely deliver his people from slavery, but he also solidifies an ongoing relationship with them. The hymn of Moses in Exodus 15 accentuates that reality: "You have led in your steadfast love the people whom you have redeemed; you have guided them by your strength to your holy abode" (15:13). This truth is displayed in what has come to be known as the Immanuel Principle: "I will take you to be my people, and I will be your God" (Ex. 6:7). This relationship between God and Israel is formalized on Mount Sinai, where God establishes his covenant with the Hebrews.

SELECT BIBLIOGRAPHY

Baines, John, and Jaromír Málek. *Atlas of Ancient Egypt.* New York: Facts on File, 1980.

Cassuto, Umberto. *A Commentary on the Book of Exodus.* Jerusalem: Magnes, 1967.

Childs, Brevard S. *The Book of Exodus: A Critical, Theological Commentary.* OTL. Louisville: Westminster, 1974.

Currid, John D. *Ancient Egypt and the Old Testament.* Grand Rapids, MI: Baker, 1997.

———. *Exodus.* 2 vols. EP Study Commentary. Darlington, UK: Evangelical Press, 2000–2001.

Currid, John D., and David P. Barrett. *Crossway ESV Bible Atlas.* Wheaton, IL: Crossway, 2010.

Edelman, Diana. "The Nile in Biblical Memory." In *Thinking of Water in the Early Second Temple Period*, edited by Ehud Ben Zvi and Christoph Levin, 77–102. Berlin: de Gruyter, 2014.

Enns, Peter. *Exodus*. NIVAC. Grand Rapids, MI: Zondervan, 2000.

Hoffmeier, James K. *Israel in Egypt: The Evidence for the Authenticity of the Exodus Tradition*. New York: Oxford University Press, 1997.

Lichtheim, Miriam. *Ancient Egyptian Literature*. 3 vols. Berkeley: University of California Press, 1975–1980.

Motyer, J. A. *The Message of Exodus: The Days of Our Pilgrimage*. The Bible Speaks Today. Downers Grove, IL: InterVarsity Press, 2005.

Propp, William H. C. *Exodus 1–18: A New Translation with Introduction and Commentary*. AB 2. New Haven, CT: Yale University Press, 1999.

Rainey, Anson F., ed. *Egypt, Israel, Sinai: Archaeological and Historical Relationships in the Biblical Period*. Tel Aviv: Tel Aviv University, 1987.

Redford, Donald B. *Egypt, Canaan, and Israel in Ancient Times*. Princeton, NJ: Princeton University Press, 1992.

Sarna, Nahum M. *Exodus: The Traditional Hebrew Text with the New JPS Translation*. JPS Torah Commentary. Philadelphia: Jewish Publication Society, 1991.

———. *Exploring Exodus: The Heritage of Biblical Israel*. New York: Schocken, 1986.

Stuart, Douglas K. *Exodus*. NAC 2. Nashville: B&H, 2006.

Walton, John H. *Israelite Literature in Its Cultural Context: A Survey of Parallels between Biblical and Ancient Near Eastern Texts*. Library of Biblical Literature. Grand Rapids, MI: Zondervan, 1989.

3

Leviticus

Michael G. McKelvey

INTRODUCTION

Today, common opinions about the book of Leviticus often reflect attitudes of indifference and confusion. The book predominantly pertains to sacrifice and ceremonial acts, which are no longer in force for the New Testament people of God. It is often asked, "Why should we study dietary laws since God has declared all foods clean?" Or, "Since Christ abolished the need for sacrifices, why read about the various kinds of Old Testament offerings?" Again, "The priesthood is no longer functioning, so these legislations are irrelevant for today." While many in the contemporary church seem to ignore the book, Leviticus remains extremely relevant to the New Testament and its message. In fact, it may be argued, with qualifications, that no book is more relevant for understanding certain aspects of the New Testament.

"Why?" someone may ask. First, it lays a foundation for understanding the necessity of salvation and the manner in which it comes to sinful human beings. How can sinful man be forgiven and reconciled to the holy God he has offended? How can this God dwell with his sinful people, which is his ancient promise to a fallen race (Gen. 26:3; 31:3; 48:21; Ex. 3:12)? How is God able to redeem mankind? How will it be known that God's people truly are his people as they live among the nations of the earth? Leviticus begins to answer these very questions and lays the groundwork for what will be progressively revealed regarding the mystery of God's saving purposes. Therefore, studying this ancient work will not only provide an appreciation for the historical practices of Israelite religion but will also impart a greater understanding of the whole counsel of God.

BACKGROUND ISSUES

Authorship

Traditionally, Moses, the man of God, has been considered the author of Leviticus along with the other four books of the Pentateuch. With the rise of higher criticism and Julius Wellhausen's Documentary Hypothesis,[1] scholars throughout the past century began to theorize that the book predominately comes from the so-called P source, which many believed to have originated in postexilic times. In the last half of the twentieth century, however, scholars seem to have reversed the tide of opinion by arguing for a preexilic origin for much of the Priestly material.[2]

With that said, it is more productive to investigate the book itself in order to discover its purpose and meaning. Notably, the book of Leviticus clearly indicates from whom the words came and to whom the words were given. No other book in all Scripture (except perhaps Jeremiah) plainly states more than Leviticus that it is derived from the mouth of God. Over and over again the work asserts, "And [Yahweh] spoke to Moses . . ." (Lev. 1:1; 4:1; 5:14; 6:1, 8, 19, 24; 7:22, 28; 8:1; 11:1; 12:1; 13:1; 14:1, 33; 15:1; 16:1; 17:1; 18:1; 19:1; 20:1; 21:16; 22:1, 17, 26; 23:1, 9, 23, 26, 33; 24:1, 13; 25:1; 27:1).[3] So Yahweh stands as the originator of the words and Moses as their recipient. It is, therefore, not unreasonable to argue that Moses is the original author of the book, in that he received and repeated the words of Yahweh for the purpose of recording and setting down the statutes of Israel's God. As Rooker states, "Mosaic authorship is clearly affirmed by a straightforward reading of the biblical text."[4] In other words, Leviticus is God's word given through Moses for his people.

Title

The book's title, Leviticus, comes from the Latin *leuitikon* via the Septuagint (the ancient Greek translation of the Hebrew Bible), while the Talmud refers to the book as "The Law of the Priests." Similarly, the Peshitta calls it "The Book of the Priests." The Masoretic text, however, uses the title "And he [i.e., Yahweh] called."[5] Some question the appropriateness of the title Leviticus in our English Bibles. In fact, the Levites are mentioned only four times in the book, and those occurrences are in two consecutive verses. Leviticus 25:32–33 states, "As for the cities of the Levites, the Levites may redeem at any time the houses in the cities they possess. And if one of the Levites exercises his right of redemption, then the house that was sold in a city they possess shall be released in the jubilee. For the houses in the cities of the Levites are their possession among the people of Israel." Nevertheless, since the book centers around the cultic world of the priests, the title is not altogether unfitting. All

---

[1] See Julius Wellhausen, *Prolegomena to the History of Israel* (Edinburgh: Adam & Charles Black, 1885).
[2] E.g., Yehezkel Kaufmann, *The Religion of Israel, from Its Beginnings to the Babylonian Exile* (London: Allen and Unwin, 1961). See also John Currid's discussion on the authorship of the Pentateuch and the history of Old Testemant studies in his chapter on Genesis in this volume.
[3] Gordon J. Wenham appropriately comments, "At the beginning of nearly every chapter, and often several times within a chapter, it says, 'The Lord spoke to Moses.'" *The Book of Leviticus*, NICOT (Grand Rapids, MI: Eerdmans, 1979), 5.
[4] Mark F. Rooker, *Leviticus*, NAC 3A (Nashville: B&H, 2000), 39.
[5] It was common in the Hebrew Bible to use the first word(s) as a title for the work—e.g., בראשית, "in the beginning," for Genesis, and ואלה שמות, "and these are the names of," for Exodus.

priests were Levites, though not all Levites were priests. With that said, the content does not apply only to the priests. These laws were for the whole nation, even as the priests were charged with teaching the law to the people: "and you are to teach the people of Israel all the statutes that the Lord has spoken to them by Moses" (10:11).

Historical Context and Audience

The narrative context for the book of Leviticus is Exodus and Numbers.[6] These three books are to be read as consecutive works, beginning with the giving of the law on Mount Sinai in Exodus 20. Later, in Exodus 34, God makes the new tablets and gives instructions to Moses for the building of the tabernacle (Ex. 35–40). In the final verses of Exodus (40:34–38), the "glory of the LORD" fills the tabernacle, and Leviticus picks up right were Exodus ends: "And he called to Moses and spoke to him from the tent of meeting" (Lev. 1:1). The form of the verb "called" (with the *waw*-consecutive) at the beginning of the book indicates a continuation of narrative, not a new beginning.[7] Thus, the content of Leviticus exists as a part of the revelation that God gave to Moses at Sinai. Consequently, after Leviticus, Numbers 1:1 continues the account: "The LORD spoke to Moses in the wilderness of Sinai, in the tent of meeting, on the first day of the second month, in the second year after they had come out of the land of Egypt." While the book of Leviticus consists predominantly of instructions on religious requirements, it is set within the "narrative framework"[8] of the exodus, the wilderness wanderings, and the eventual conquest of Canaan. As Wenham puts it, "it is essential to recognize that all the laws are set within this historical frame if their arrangement is to be appreciated."[9]

The content of Leviticus came to Moses not long after the Israelite exodus from Egypt.[10] Israel was a new political entity. Previously, they were slaves under the tyranny of a pharaoh who did not know their ancestor Joseph (Exodus 1), and they cried out for help and rescue. The Lord heard them, and they witnessed the miraculous power of the sovereign God of their forefathers. He crushed Egypt and its so-called gods in order to deliver them from "the house of slavery" (Exodus 4–12; quotation from Ex. 20:2). On their way out of Egypt, Yahweh wondrously rescued them from the Egyptian army by parting the Red Sea (Exodus 14). They later entered into covenant with God as he thundered his law from Mount Sinai (Exodus 20). God chastised them for their idolatry with the golden calf (Exodus 32), and yet they also experienced his mercy in remaining with them, thanks to Moses's intercession (Exodus 33).

Much has taken place in a relatively short period of time. Israel now receives God's instruction for how they are to live and worship as his chosen people. Thus, the

---

[6] James L. Mays highlights, "The reader must think constantly about what has gone before and what comes after, as he studies Leviticus and Numbers. Their concerns and characters and movement are of a piece with the other four books." *The Book of Leviticus; The Book of Numbers*, LBC 4 (Richmond, VA: John Knox, 1971), 8.

[7] See John Currid's discussion on the title of Exodus earlier in this volume.

[8] Wenham, *Leviticus*, 5.

[9] Wenham, *Leviticus*, 6.

[10] The traditional view for the date of the exodus is 1446 BC. For a discussion of both this traditional date and the mid-thirteenth-century BC date, see John D. Currid, *A Study Commentary on Leviticus*, EP Study Commentary (Darlington, UK: Evangelical Press, 2004), 27–32.

audience of this work is first the exodus generation. However, this group of Israelites is not the only audience in view. Each successive generation will receive God's law as binding upon them. God has entered into covenant with Abraham, Isaac, Jacob, and their descendants. This implies that the book of Leviticus would be handed down to subsequent generations.

With its historical context in view, it is also important to consider the book in light of the future of Israel. The outworking of Israel's history in the conquest provides a record for how Israel failed to implement these laws. What transpires in Scripture is a picture of inconsistency, neglect, and rebellion. The failure of Israel to keep God's covenant led to repetitive chastisement (cf. the book of Judges) and eventually exile—the dissolution of the nation (cf. 2 Kings). On the one hand, reading Leviticus provides a clear picture of what God required of his people. On the other hand, reading Leviticus brings a dread of what awaits the Israelites, who are unable (and even unwilling) to keep God's covenant.

STRUCTURE AND OUTLINE

The book of Leviticus has two main parts: (1) worshiping God (chapters 1–10) and (2) living in relationship with God (chapters 11–27). In chapters 1–10, God sets forth his expectations for the corporate worship of God through various sacrifices and priestly regulations. Chapters 11–27 reveal how the covenant community must live with the presence of the holy God in their midst. The outline below fleshes out the details of this bipartite structure.

    I. Part 1: Worship of the Holy God (1:1–10:20)
        A. Laws about sacrifices (1:1–7:38)
            1. Instruction about sacrifices (1:1–6:7)
            2. Instruction for priests (6:8–7:38)
        B. A narrative (8:1–10:20)
            1. Aaron and his sons consecrated (8:1–9:24)
            2. Nadab and Abihu dishonor Yahweh (10:1–20)
    II. Part 2: Living with the Holy God (11:1–27:34)
        A. Laws pertaining to ritual cleanness (11:1–15:33)
        B. The Day of Atonement (16:1–34)
        C. Laws about holiness (17:1–25:55)
        D. Blessing for obedience and cursing for disobedience (26:1–46)
        E. Vows and gifts to the Lord (27:1–34)

This structure exhibits a pattern that begins with the worship of God and then moves to the implications of belonging to God. The various sacrifices (five in particular) are described in Leviticus 1:1–6:7, detailing when and how the offerer and the priests will perform these religious acts. More detailed instruction is then provided for the priests in Leviticus 6:8–7:38 regarding their roles in the sacrificial system. Chapters 8–10 follow with a narrative account of Moses consecrating Aaron and his sons to the office of priest. Of particular note, Leviticus 10 contains the account of

Nadab and Abihu's offering of "strange fire" before the Lord. God responds to this act with his own fire coming forth and consuming Nadab and Abihu. This account illustrates how serious it is to worship God properly, as detailed in Leviticus 1:1–6:7.

Part two of the book provides direction for how Israel is to live as the covenant community with God in their midst. Leviticus 11–15 pertains primarily to ritual cleanness (e.g., dietary laws [clean and unclean animals], postbirth purification laws, laws about skin diseases, laws about bodily discharges). Leviticus 16 appears to be the pivotal text of the entire book. This passage provides instruction for the Day of Atonement, on which the once-a-year sacrifice was offered on behalf of the whole nation. Only on this day could the high priest enter the Most Holy Place and sprinkle blood on the mercy seat. Then, the high priest would lay his hands on the live goat, symbolizing the transfer of guilt from Israel to the goat, and the goat would be set free into the wilderness.[11] This act highlights the expiation (i.e., removal) of Israel's sin.

From this point, the remainder of the book details the laws for holiness (e.g., prohibition from blood, child sacrifice, idolatry, and sexual immorality; civil and ceremonial laws; laws for priests; feasts and festivals [sacred time]; rights of redemption). In this way, Leviticus 17–25 provides what has been called the "Holiness Code" for the nation of Israel. A curious narrative regarding the stoning of a blasphemer occurs in Leviticus 24:10–16. Apart from the Nadab and Abihu event, this passage is the only other narrative in the book. Its presence appears to illustrate the Holiness Code at work—unholy speech about Yahweh is punishable by death!

According to the instructions in this book, adherence to these laws will bring blessing to the people, but failure to obey will bring cursing (Leviticus 26). So the Lord warns the nation one final time regarding the obligation of covenantal faithfulness and the consequences for failure. Leviticus 27 concludes the book and has been called an appendix[12] by some, as it pertains to laws about vows and gifts to the Lord. However, this final chapter should not be viewed as out of place in terms of the tenor of the book or, in particular, of Leviticus 17–25, since it concerns covenantal ethics.

With this structure in view, the book of Leviticus also appears to contain a series of manuals for worship. Currid provides a helpful outline of these manuals or directories within the book:[13]

1. Manual of sacrifice for all Israel (1:1–6:7)
2. Manual of sacrifice for priests (6:8–7:38)
3. Cleanness Code (11:1–15:33)
4. Day of Atonement—for the high priest (16:1–34)
5. Holiness Code (17:1–26:46)
6. Manual for funding the temple (27:1–34)

This outline demonstrates the purpose of the book regarding the worship and ethics of God's covenant people. Awareness of these directives enables the reader to

---

[11] See the discussion on "scape-goat" in *NIDOTTE*, 3:360–63.
[12] Rooker states, "The book is marked by a beginning (1:1–2) and a conclusion (26:45), with the last chapter functioning as an appendix that contains a closing formula for the entire Mosaic legislation (27:34)." *Leviticus*, 42.
[13] Currid, *Leviticus*, 18.

appreciate Leviticus as instruction for both community life and cultic (i.e., worship) functions.

MESSAGE AND THEOLOGY

Holiness

The holiness of God constitutes the central theme in the book of Leviticus, which, in turn, demands the holiness of Israel. Leviticus 19:1–2 contains the thesis statement for the work: "And the LORD spoke to Moses, saying, 'Speak to all the congregation of the people of Israel and say to them, You shall be holy, for I the LORD your God am holy.'"[14] In fact, the holiness motif permeates the book. Notably, the Hebrew root for holy, holiness, or consecrate (קדשׁ) occurs some 143 times throughout the book—by far the most of any Old Testament book.[15] Thus, it is appropriate to designate Leviticus as the "Book of Holiness."

Significantly, God's holiness provides the starting point and foundation for the concept of holiness in general. To be holy means to be "set apart, not common, devoted, pure." The word actually has a very rich semantic range,[16] but at its heart remains the idea of something uncommonly special and distinct. Gentry states, "The basic meaning of the word is 'consecrated' or 'devoted.'"[17] This definition begins to construct a concept of holiness that helps us better understand the holiness of God. Yahweh is set apart from man, he is not common, and he is distinctly special. And as one reads Leviticus, it becomes clear that "clean and unclean" run parallel to the ideas of "holy and unholy." So holiness also takes on a sense of purity—both morally and ceremonially—a theme with which Leviticus is plainly concerned.

Moreover, holiness in the book occurs in degrees: in the camp, within the tabernacle court, in the Holy Place, and in the Most Holy Place. Whatever is deemed unholy and unclean must be removed from the camp of Israel, taken outside its boundaries and discarded. In this way, as one moves closer to the dwelling place of God (which is above the mercy seat in the Holy of Holies), the degree of holiness increases. Also, the access of the people narrows with one's proximity to the presence of God. Only clean Israelites may come inside the camp. The worshiper may enter into the court of the tabernacle to make his offering with the priests. Only the priests are allowed in the Holy Place. Notably, the high priest alone may enter into the Most Holy Place and then only once a year, following the proper procedures. So the closer one came to the place where God dwelt, the more sacred was the space.

With that said, God's holiness must be understood in view of humanity's unholiness. In other words, the two realities enlighten each other, and they cannot really be understood separately. We better appreciate and grasp God's holiness in the light

---

[14] See similar statements in Lev. 11:44–45; 20:7; and, applied to the priests, 21:6–8.

[15] The book of Exodus takes second place with one hundred occurrences of the Hebrew root for "holy" (קדשׁ).

[16] See *HALOT*, 1072–1078, for more discussion of the semantic scope of the term. See also *NIDOTTE*, 3:874–85; *DCH*, 7:180–84, 190–95, 196–204.

[17] Peter J. Gentry, "Sizemore Lectures Part II: No One *Holy* Like the Lord," *Midwestern Journal of Theology* 12, no. 1 (2013): 37. See the full article for Gentry's discussion of the definition of *holy*.

of man's lack of holiness, and we better comprehend man's lack of holiness in the light of God's holiness. Leviticus—really, the whole Bible—declares that Yahweh is holy in his being, morality, and character.[18] This implies that he is good, pure, righteous, faithful, and truthful. Indeed, holiness *is* his nature, and the possibility for God to be unholy is nonexistent. Thus, he is the epitome of holiness—the standard of holiness—and as a consequence, nothing unholy or unclean may exist in his presence. So what about men and women? They have sinned and are unholy and unclean. However, God has chosen to take a people for himself and make them holy in order that they might dwell together in covenant relationship with him. Hence, the purpose of Leviticus comes into view.

Leviticus is a book concerned primarily with sanctifying (i.e., making holy) the people of Israel because God has chosen them to be his people.[19] Therefore, they need to be sanctified (i.e., made holy) and made clean so that they may dwell before the holy God of all the earth. The laws given in Leviticus facilitate this relationship between Yahweh and his people. God outlines rules for sacrifice so that the people may be forgiven and atonement might be made for their iniquity. This reason for sacrifices clearly contrasts with the practice of sacrifice among other ancient Near Eastern societies. Many polytheistic and henotheistic (i.e., worshiping one god while not denying the existence of other gods) groups gave offerings, instead, to feed the deities. As the gods were fed, it was believed that they would bless and provide for their worshipers. In other words, human beings existed to serve the gods[20] in order to make the gods stronger among the other deities in the pantheon of gods.[21] Sacrifice in Israel suggests nothing of the sort. It existed to enable worshipers to draw near to the presence of the one and only holy God.

Additionally, laws denoting what is clean and unclean (i.e., dietary [Kosher] laws, relationship laws, priesthood laws, household laws, laws about diseases) provide the criteria for the people to remain undefiled before God (see Leviticus 11–15 and 17–25). Requirements for worship also clarify how Israel may approach God for praise and thanksgiving. In the end, the laws of Leviticus are to be viewed as good; they make it possible for sinful man to know and commune with the holy God.[22]

Many have viewed Leviticus as tedious, unnecessary, and even boring. However, the book actually reveals the majesty of the Most High God. He is high and exalted, and not a God with which to trifle. He is to be revered and respected, and those who draw near to him must do so with fear and reverence, knowing their need to be cleansed of their sin. So the book is not merely a collection of cultic

---

[18] Wenham notes that the book "tells us about God's character and will." *Leviticus*, 16.

[19] Currid writes, "The entire Holiness Code (Lev. 17–26) deals with the issue of *sanctification*, that is, how one is to live as a member of the covenant people." *Leviticus*, 25.

[20] See, e.g., Pritchard, *ANET*, 68, 69, 117.

[21] See Merrill C. Tenney, ed., *The Zondervan Pictorial Encyclopedia of the Bible* (Grand Rapids, MI: Zondervan, 1976), 5:195–99.

[22] Allen P. Ross states that Leviticus reveals "how the covenant people were supposed to approach this holy Lord, how they were supposed to regulate their lives in light of his presence, and how they were supposed to follow holiness in every aspect of their lives so that they might realize their priestly calling." *Holiness to the Lord: A Guide to the Exposition of the Book of Leviticus* (Grand Rapids, MI: Baker, 2002), 21.

rules but a powerful statement of the glory and holiness of Yahweh. It saves man from approaching him flippantly lest he be destroyed (e.g., Nadab and Abihu). It also shows God's love for his people and his desire to make it possible to dwell in their midst.

In addition, the laws of Leviticus were meant to "set apart" Israel from the other nations. So Deuteronomy 26:18–19 says, "And the LORD has declared today that you are a people for his treasured possession, as he has promised you, and that you are to keep all his commandments, and that he will set you in praise and in fame and in honor high above all nations that he has made, and that you shall be a people holy to the LORD your God, as he promised." They were no ordinary people but a chosen race and a royal priesthood, called out of the world to be a distinct people group—i.e., one that belongs to Yahweh. The Levitical code demonstrates to the world God's ownership of them. Their holiness would reveal God's holiness and would show the world Yahweh's glory. The statement "Be holy for I am holy" encapsulates this union between God and his people. It is the principle of *imitatio dei*, the "imitation of God."

Sacrifice

In order to sanctify (make holy) what is unsanctified (unholy) and cleanse what is unclean, sacrifice must be offered. As Wenham states, "According to Leviticus, . . . sacrificial blood is necessary to cleanse and sanctify. Sacrifice can undo the effects of sin and human infirmity. Sin and disease lead to profanation of the holy and pollution of the clean. Sacrifice can reverse this process."[23] The sacrificial system of Leviticus served to rectify the problem of Israel's sin and uncleanness by providing a positive manner in which to bring God and man together (see table 9 on pp. 98–99).

Interestingly, the sacrificial system showed the various ways in which Israel could be reconciled to God. Leviticus 1:1–6:7 recounts five different sacrifices/offerings that were to be employed in the worship of Yahweh: (1) the whole burnt offering, (2) the grain offering, (3) the peace offering, (4) the sin offering, and (5) the guilt offering. Mooney and DeRouchie highlight their importance:

> The text describes each offering twice. The first descriptions appear in Leviticus 1:1–6:7 and detail the procedures and purposes of the offerings, with special emphasis given to the responsibilities of the laity. The second appear in 6:8–7:10 and clarify the handling, eating, and disposal of the offerings, with special focus given to the work of the priest. The severity of the sacrificial act, namely the destruction of life, conveys the chasm between God's holiness and Israel's natural state. Yet, sacrifice resulted in God's pleasure in and forgiveness or purification of an individual, group, or object.[24]

So the act of sacrifice brought both parties together that they might live in unity.

---

[23] Wenham, *Leviticus*, 26.
[24] D. Jeffrey Mooney and Jason S. DeRouchie, "Leviticus," in *What the Old Testament Authors Really Cared About: A Survey of Jesus' Bible*, ed. Jason S. DeRouchie (Grand Rapids, MI: Kregel, 2013), 106.

In the burnt offering, the entire animal was consumed by fire, and it was considered the most important sacrifice because it made atonement for the worshiper's sin. It was "a pleasing aroma to the LORD" (Lev. 1:9, 13, 17), in which the animal provided a death-penalty substitute on behalf of the offerer due to his or her sin. Secondly, the sin offering focuses on the blood of the sacrifice being used to cleanse items in the tabernacle. Some prefer to call this sacrifice the "purification" offering since it purified whatever was unclean or impure. The guilt offering, a third offering, was given to make restitution for the wrong committed against God. The animal's blood was sprinkled upon the altar, and its fat, kidneys, and liver were burnt with fire. Only the priests were allowed to partake of the remainder of the sacrifice. Next, the grain offering consisted of harvested grain with part of it burnt upon the altar and part given to the priests for food. Alexander notes that "the cereal offering was possibly viewed as a gift or tribute paid to God in recognition of his divine sovereignty."[25] Finally, the peace offering is distinct in that the worshiper kept most of the animal for a meal. Certain portions belonged to the Lord and the priests, but the remainder was used in a feast.

The sacrifices and offerings in Leviticus reveal humanity's need for substitution and atonement. Since God's first warning about disobedience, he made clear that the penalty for sin is death: "And the LORD God commanded the man, saying, 'You may surely eat of every tree of the garden, but of the tree of the knowledge of good and evil you shall not eat, for in the day that you eat of it you shall surely die'" (Gen. 2:16–17). Thus something must die (i.e., blood must be shed) in order to atone (or make amends) for the wrong that has occurred. The animal would be slaughtered in the place of the worshiper, receiving the penalty for sin, and its blood would make amends for guilt incurred. So Leviticus 17:11 states, "For the life of the flesh is in the blood, and I have given it for you on the altar to make atonement for your souls, for it is the blood that makes atonement by the life." Young comments, "The thought seems to be that the blood which was shed and applied to the altar blotted out or obliterated sin from the sight of God by being smeared over the altar. Man and his sin is that which needs covering, and this covering is procured by God, not by man."[26] The grain offering was different in that no animal was killed, but it was still a sacrifice by giving the best parts (i.e., "first fruits") of the harvest to Yahweh and his servants the priests. Each offering reminded worshipers that they needed to make amends in order to relate to the holy God because, by themselves, they were unable to draw near to him in their sinfulness.[27]

Lest someone think this sacrificial system was merely religious ritual, the language of Leviticus makes clear that worshipers were to offer sacrifices from a sincere heart. Leviticus 4–6 describes worshipers as "realizing" their guilt and then making an offering. This process entails a conscious understanding of

---

[25] T. Desmond Alexander, *From Paradise to the Promised Land: An Introduction to the Pentateuch*, 2nd ed. (Grand Rapids, MI: Baker Academic, 2002), 221.

[26] Edward J. Young, *An Introduction to the Old Testament*, rev. ed. (Grand Rapids, MI: Eerdmans, 1970), 82.

[27] For a more extensive discussion on these offerings, see Alexander, *Paradise*, 219–23.

violating God's law and a desire to make amends. There are "unintentional" and "intentional" sins, but as the covenant member realizes them in this life, he is to humbly offer to God a substitution in order to be reconciled. The ritual itself does not bring reconciliation, but the offerer's desire for forgiveness and trust in God does so as he engages in the act. David illustrates this principle well in his confession in Psalm 51:16–19: "For you will not delight in sacrifice, or I would give it; you will not be pleased with a burnt offering. The sacrifices of God are a broken spirit; a broken and contrite heart, O God, you will not despise. . . . [T]hen will you delight in right sacrifices, in burnt offerings and whole burnt offerings; then bulls will be offered on your altar."

Offerings in Leviticus[28]

Offering	Occasion	Sacrifice	Stipulations	Burnt Portion	Sacrifice-Specific References	General Offering References
Burnt	*Regular*	Bull	No blemish; male	All	1:3–9	6:9–13
		Sheep/goat			1:10–13	
		Pigeon/dove		All but crop	1:14–17	
Sin	*Priest*	Bull	No blemish; male	Fat portions	4:3–12	4:1–2; 6:24–30
	Congregation				4:13–21	
	Ruler	Goat	No blemish; male		4:22–26	
	Individual	Goat/sheep	No blemish; female		4:27–5:6	
		Two pigeons/doves		First bird, all; second bird, all but crop	5:7–10	
		1/10 ephah of choice flour	No oil/frankincense	Handful	5:11–13	
Guilt	*Holy things*	Ram/monetary equivalent	No blemish	Fat portions	5:14–16	7:1–7
	Transgression				5:17–19	
	Deceit				6:1–7	

[28] Special thanks to Jason E. Weimar for creating this table.

Offering	Occasion	Sacrifice	Stipulations	Burnt Portion	Sacrifice-Specific References	General Offering References
Grain	*Regular*	Flour/wafers with oil	No leaven	Handful	6:14–18	2:1–16
	Ordination			All	6:19–23	
Peace	*Regular*	Bull/cow	No blemish; the offerers themselves bring forward the sacrifice	Fat portions	3:1–5	7:19–36
		Goat/sheep			3:6–16	
	Thank	Bull/cow	Brought with three types of cakes		7:11–15; 22:29	
		Goat/sheep				
	Votive	Bull/cow	No blemish		7:16–18 22:17–25; 27:9–13	
		Goat/sheep				
	Freewill	Bull/cow	Can have irregular limb		7:16–18; 22:17–25	
		Goat/sheep				

Table 9

Time

For the covenant people of God, even their time belonged to the Lord. Leviticus yields a picture of God's requirements for Israel's religious calendar. There was the weekly Sabbath after six days of labor: "Six days shall work be done, but on the seventh day is a Sabbath of solemn rest, a holy convocation. You shall do no work. It is a Sabbath to the LORD in all your dwelling places" (Lev. 23:3). Yet the Israelites were to honor and celebrate other periods of significance during the year (the Feast of Booths, Passover, etc.). These patterns reveal that just as God gave holy laws for sacrifice, diet, ceremonial matters, and daily living, he also gave laws pertaining to sacred time (see table 10 on pp. 101–2).

The zenith of sacred time in the life of Israel was the Day of Atonement, which appears first in Leviticus 16 and then again in Leviticus 23:26–32. The Day of Atonement took place on the tenth day of the seventh month, and it was to be a Sabbath in the sense that no work would be done that day. During this holy convocation, the high priest would prepare himself and offer a bull as a sin offering for him and his family. He would then sprinkle some of the blood on the mercy seat within the Most Holy Place. Likewise, the high priest would take one of two goats and offer it as a sin offering, and then he would bring its blood inside the Most Holy Place and sprinkle it on the mercy seat. This would "make atonement for the Holy Place, because of the uncleannesses of Israel and because of their transgression, all their sins" (16:16). Only the high priest could enter the Holy of Holies—once a year on this day—to make this offering on behalf of himself and all the people. After making this sacrifice, the high priest would then place his hands upon the second goat's head, confess Israel's iniquity over it, and set it free into the wilderness. This act of the high priest signified the transfer of the people's guilt to the goat and the removal of the people's sin as it was let go into the wilderness. This symbolic act pointed to the expiation (i.e., removal) of Israel's sin. This holy time of observance was a central act of Israel's worship of Yahweh that made Israel "clean before the LORD from all [their] sins" (16:30).

The placement of the Day of Atonement within the book of Leviticus highlights its centrality to Israel's year:

> The Day of Atonement regulations in Lev 16 are well placed within the book since they provide the literary and theological conclusion to the consecration and purification procedures in Lev 8–15 as well as the cultic link between the two halves of the book, chs. 1–15 and chs. 17–27. On that day the holiness and purity of both the tabernacle and the nation were in view. There were actually five offerings presented according to Lev 16 . . . the blood atonement sin offerings for the priests and the people (16:3, 5, and esp. vv. 11–19), the single scapegoat sin offering for the whole congregation (including the priests and the people, 16:20–22) and, finally, the two burnt offerings for the priests and the people (16:23–24). All of them are specifically said to have made atonement (vv. 6, 10, 11, 16, 17, 18, 20, 24, 27, 30, 32, 33, 34).[29]

There were other calendar observances vital to the community's relationship with God. Feasts and festivals were plenteous, and each represented something important from Israel's past that the nation would continue to remember throughout its existence. One of these was the Passover. This appointed feast began on the fourteenth day of the first month in remembrance of the Lord's Passover in Egypt (see Exodus 12). Leviticus 23:6–8 describes what follows after that day: "And on the fifteenth day of the same month is the Feast of Unleavened Bread to the LORD; for seven days you shall eat unleavened bread. On the first day you shall have a holy convocation; you shall not do any ordinary work. But you shall present a food offering to the LORD for seven days. On the seventh day is a holy convocation; you shall not do any ordinary work." Thus, this feast was a time of remembering what God had done for his people and thanking him for it. The other appointed feasts function in a similar manner: the Feast of Firstfruits (23:9–14),

---

[29] *NIDOTTE*, 2:691–92.

the Feast of Weeks (23:15–22), the Feast of Trumpets (23:23–25), and the Feast of Booths (23:33–43).

Perhaps one of the most curious celebrations was the Sabbath Year and the Year of Jubilee. In Leviticus 25:1–7, the Lord commanded that after six years of working the land, the people were to cease from working the land for the whole seventh year. In giving the land rest, God said, "The Sabbath of the land shall provide food for you, for yourself and for your male and female slaves and for your hired worker and the sojourner who lives with you, and for your cattle and for the wild animals that are in your land: all its yield shall be for food" (25:6–7). In addition, after seven of these Sabbath Years, there would be a Year of Jubilee (25:8–55). In the fiftieth year, no one would work the land, and liberty would be declared. All the land would go back to the original clans, and debts would be forgiven, property returned, and slaves set free. It was a time of renewal and a fresh start for the people. These Sabbath Years and Jubilees provided the people with rest and hope of a restoration to come, echoing the crucial theme of redemption that permeates the Scriptures.

Sacred Dates in Leviticus[30]

Occasion	Time Frame	Details	Verses
Sabbath	Seventh day of every week	A holy convocation is held, and no work is to be done.	23:3
Passover	Fourteenth day of first month	At twilight, the Passover offering is made. The following day commences the Feast of Unleavened Bread.	23:5–8
Feast of Unleavened Bread	Week of fifteenth day of first month	Throughout the week, all Israel eats unleavened bread and presents offerings to the Lord. On the first and seventh days, holy convocations are held, and no work is to be done.	23:5–8
Feast of First Fruits	Day after Sabbath following harvest	The sheaf of the first fruits of harvest is brought to the priest, and he raises it to the Lord. With it a burnt offering of a year-old lamb is made, along with drink and grain offerings. Until this offering is made, no one is allowed to eat of the harvest.	23:9–14
Feast of Weeks	The day that is seven weeks after the Feast of First Fruits	A holy convocation is held, and no work is to be done. The people present an elevation offering of two loaves; burnt offerings of seven lambs, one bull, and two rams; a sin offering of one goat; a peace offering of two lambs; a grain offering; and drink offerings. The priest raises the elevation offering and the two lambs alongside the bread of First Fruits.	23:15–21

---

[30] Special thanks to Jason E. Weimar for creating this table.

Occasion	Time Frame	Details	Verses
Feast of Trumpets	First day of seventh month	A holy convocation is held, and no work is to be done. The people present offerings to the Lord and commemorate the day with trumpet blasts.	23:23–25
Day of Atonement	Tenth day of seventh month	A holy convocation is held, and no work is to be done. The people present offerings to the Lord, and everyone is to deny themselves. The high priest enters the Holy Place to make atonement for himself and the people.	16:1–34; 23:26–32
Feast of Booths	Week of fifteenth day of seventh month	Offerings are presented throughout the week. On the first and eighth days, holy convocations are held and no work is to be done. During the week, all Israel is to live in booths and rejoice before God with the fruits, branches, and boughs of trees.	23:33–43
Sabbath Year	Every seventh year	The land is given complete rest for the year; no seed is to be sown, and no vineyard is to be pruned.	25:1–7
Year of Jubilee	Every fiftieth year, starting on the Day of Atonement	The trumpet is sounded throughout the land. Everyone returns to his land and family. All land, except for houses in walled towns, reverts back to its original owners. All Israelite slaves are set free.	25:8–55

Table 10

Approaching the New Testament

As I stated at the beginning of the chapter, one can argue that no book is more relevant for understanding the New Testament than the book of Leviticus. As such, it is worth considering some pertinent themes, motifs, and connections between this Old Testament book and the message of the New Testament.

First, when considering the sacrifices and what they foreshadowed, it becomes clear that Christ's substitutionary atonement on behalf of his people fulfills that entire system. God required a sacrifice to atone for humanity's sin. Blood must be shed to atone for iniquity, and something must take the place of the sinner in order for him or her to come before the holy God. Jesus Christ is that once-for-all sacrifice for sins. As John the Baptist so wondrously declared about Jesus, "Behold, the Lamb of God, who takes away the sin of the world!" (John 1:29). God himself has provided the perfect sacrifice for sin in his Son. Notably, the themes of sacrifice, the priesthood, and the ceremonial law permeate the book of Hebrews. The writer highlights the essential nature of sacrifice: "Indeed, under the law almost everything is purified with blood, and without the shedding of blood there is no forgiveness of sins" (9:22). He also notes that "it is impossible for the blood of bulls and goats to take away sins" (10:4). The whole argument of the book of Hebrews states that Christ is the better sacrifice: "But when Christ had offered for all time a single sacrifice for sins, he sat down at the right hand of God, waiting from that time until his enemies should be made a footstool for his feet. For by a single offering he has perfected for all time those who are being sanctified" (Heb. 10:12–14). Jesus was the perfect sacrifice for sin because he was holy, that is, without sin, as Hebrews 4:15 explains: "For we do not have a high priest who is unable to sympathize with our weaknesses, but one who in every respect has been tempted as we are, yet without sin." The apostle Paul writes, "For our sake he made him to be sin who knew no sin, so that in him we might become the righteousness of God" (2 Cor. 5:21). As a whole, the New Testament gloriously proclaims Christ as the sufficient Savior who has taken his people's place in judgment, received the curse of death (Gal. 3:13), and rose from the grave so that all his people would be saved (Rom. 4:25). In this way, the sacrifices of Leviticus point forward to Jesus, the great sacrifice for sin!

Married to this motif of the sacrificial system is the theme of priesthood. The priesthood highlights the need of a mediator to go between the people and Yahweh and to offer sacrifices on their behalf. The people could not approach God without a priest, and even on the Day of Atonement, the high priest alone could make the offering—and then only after he made a sacrifice for his own and his family's sins (Lev. 16:11). So what God's people ultimately needed was a high priest who was without sin and was able to bring the people before God. Once again, the book of Hebrews emphasizes Christ's role as that Great High Priest: "Since then we have a great high priest who has passed through the heavens, Jesus, the Son of God, let us hold fast our confession" (4:14). Jesus is not of the Levitical priesthood, through which perfection was unattainable (Heb. 7:11), but he is of the order of Melchizedek (Hebrews 5 and 7): "The former priests were many in number, because they were prevented by death from continuing in office, but he holds his priesthood permanently, because he continues forever" (Heb. 7:23–24). So Christ remains both the perfect priest and the perfect sacrifice for the people of God.

Now that Jesus has fulfilled the law of God and inaugurated the new covenant, the ceremonial laws of sacrifice and the Holiness Code no longer continue for believers. Thus Hebrews 8:13 says, "In speaking of a new covenant, he makes the first one obsolete. And what is becoming obsolete and growing old is ready to vanish away." With Christ's sacrifice, the sacrificial system becomes unnecessary (Hebrews 9). And with Christ cleansing the unclean once for all, the Holiness Code and dietary laws are abrogated (see Acts 10:9–48). Jesus has procured all that is necessary for sinners to come to God. Those who come to God through Christ will live with him forever; they have eternal life!

While Christ has made the ceremonial and sacrificial codes obsolete, the moral and ethical commands of God remain obligatory for the believer. Christ, by his holiness and obedience, has procured all that is needed for a believer to enter into the presence of God, and he represents the believer before his Father (2 Cor. 5:2; Heb. 4:14–16; 1 John 1:9–2:1). Therefore, the essentials of holiness must mark the Christian because he has been saved to become like Christ, who *is* holy! Thus Peter quotes Leviticus 19:2 in 1 Peter 1:14–16: "As obedient children, do not be conformed to the passions of your former ignorance, but as he who called you is holy, you also be holy in all your conduct, since it is written, 'You shall be holy, for I am holy.'" Christ calls the believer—who has been justified by faith alone to be sanctified through the power of the Holy Spirit—to die to sin and live to righteousness. In other words, the goal of Christ's sacrificial and priestly work is the complete transformation of the Christian from unholy to holy, from sinner to saint, and from being unlike Christ to being just like him. This is the redemption that Yahweh has promised and foreshadowed in the Old Testament, particularly in the book of Leviticus.

While Leviticus may offend our modern notions of worship with its graphic portrayals of sacrifice and its meticulous laws, the overall presentation of the book makes a glorious statement about God's work in redemptive history. The people of Israel have been brought into covenant with Yahweh, the Creator of heaven and earth, and he has set them apart for himself (i.e., made them holy). Therefore, their lives must now be lives of holiness. However, the laws of Leviticus were not an end unto themselves but a pointer and tutor (παιδαγωγὸς, "pedagogue" [Gal. 3:24]) to Christ. Where Israel failed to obey, the Son of God has come and fulfilled the law of God. Jesus stands as both the perfect, once-for-all sacrifice for sin and the perfect High Priest for his people. So while the reader finds himself at times wondering about the application and relevance of the book of Leviticus, he need only look to the New Testament and see that the gospel reveals the book's *telos*. In other words, Leviticus provides the foundation for understanding the gospel—the penal substitutionary atonement of Christ, the work of Christ as Priest, and the purpose of Christ to sanctify (i.e., make holy) his people. In the end, the book of Leviticus teaches us the nature and extent of God's holiness and the cost of making holy for himself an unholy people.

SELECT BIBLIOGRAPHY

Alexander, T. Desmond. *From Paradise to the Promised Land: An Introduction to the Pentateuch*. 2nd ed. Grand Rapids, MI: Baker Academic, 2002.

Bonar, Andrew A. *A Commentary on Leviticus*. 5th ed. Carlisle, PA: Banner of Truth, 1972.

Currid, John D. *A Study Commentary on Leviticus*. EP Study Commentary. Darlington, UK: Evangelical Press, 2004.

DeRouchie, Jason S., ed. *What the Old Testament Authors Really Cared About: A Survey of Jesus' Bible*. Grand Rapids, MI: Kregel, 2013.

Gane, Roy. *Leviticus, Numbers*. NIVAC. Grand Rapids, MI: Zondervan, 2004.

Goldberg, Louis. *Leviticus: A Study Guide Commentary*. Grand Rapids, MI: Zondervan, 1980.

Gorman, Frank H., Jr. *Divine Presence and Community: A Commentary on the Book of Leviticus*. ITC. Grand Rapids, MI: Eerdmans, 1997.

Harrison, R. K. *Leviticus: An Introduction and Commentary.* TOTC. Downers Grove, IL: InterVarsity Press, 1980.

Hill, Andrew E., and John H. Walton. *A Survey of the Old Testament.* 2nd ed. Grand Rapids, MI: Zondervan, 2000.

Kaufmann, Yehezkel. *The Religion of Israel: From Its Beginnings to the Babylonian Exile.* Chicago: University of Chicago Press, 1960.

Kiuchi, Nobuyoshi. *Leviticus.* ApOTC 3. Downers Grove, IL: InterVarsity Press, 2007.

Longman, Tremper, III, and Raymond B. Dillard. *An Introduction to the Old Testament.* 2nd ed. Grand Rapids, MI: Zondervan, 2006.

Mays, James L. *The Book of Leviticus; The Book of Numbers.* LBC 4. Richmond, VA: John Knox, 1971.

Rooker, Mark F. *Leviticus.* NAC 3A. Nashville: B&H, 2000.

Ross, Allen P. *Holiness to the Lord: A Guide to the Exposition of the Book of Leviticus.* Grand Rapids, MI: Baker, 2002.

Wellhausen, Julius. *Prolegomena to the History of Israel.* Edinburgh: Adam & Charles Black, 1885.

Wenham, Gordon J. *The Book of Leviticus.* NICOT. Grand Rapids, MI: Eerdmans, 1979.

Young, Edward J. *An Introduction to the Old Testament.* Rev. ed. Grand Rapids, MI: Eerdmans, 1970.

4

Numbers

Michael J. Glodo

INTRODUCTION

The English title of the fourth book of Moses, Numbers (derived from the Septuagint ἀριθμοὶ [*arithmoi*] and echoed by the Vulgate *Numeri*), draws attention to its most prominent literary feature: the two censuses that occur at the beginning and near the end of the book (1:1–4:49; 26:1–65).[1] This, perhaps more than any other feature in the Old Testament, suggests something less than excitement. Yet nothing could be further from the truth, for these censuses mark preparations for war. Even so, the drama of prospective war is surmounted by the more imminent conflict of testing the relationship between God and his people, meaning that Numbers would be among the leading candidates for drama among all the Old Testament books.

The Hebrew title, בְּמִדְבַּר ("in the wilderness," 1:1), draws the reader's attention to the setting of the book's events, and just as setting is crucial to all great drama, the wilderness setting of Numbers provides the context in which this great drama occurs. In this setting, God's people will have to rely utterly upon God's provision and protection—for the wilderness is a place of barrenness and chaos. They will experience want in the form of hunger and thirst. They will experience heat, cold, and weariness. They will meet hostility from the likes of Arad, the Amorites, Bashan, and Moab. They will encounter sedition from within the congregation and even from the ranks of leadership in the persons of Korah, Aaron, and Miriam. And on the verge of the Promised Land, a tense interfraternal standoff will play out with the tribes of Reuben, Gad, and a portion of Manasseh. Will God be willing and able to keep the promise that he made to Abraham, their father, to bring them to the land? Will they be willing to trust in God alone to provide for them and to protect them

---

[1] While 1:1–46 is the census of all tribes except Levi, I include 1:47–4:49 for reasons given in the following analysis.

in the wilderness and to give them victory over the inhabitants of the land—to be the "shield" and great "reward" promised to Abraham (Gen. 15:1)? Establishing a theme spanning the whole of Scripture, Numbers shows that the wilderness is a place of testing and trials, even as God tests Israel's faithfulness and Israel tests his.[2]

This drama began with great promise. After being redeemed from slavery in Egypt four hundred years after Jacob's clan went down to the land of the Nile (Gen. 15:13), Israel moved from Mount Sinai toward the Land of Promise, a land occupied by the Canaanites with great cities "fortified up to heaven" (Deut. 1:28). God had acted powerfully, putting on display the powerlessness of Egypt's gods before him (Ex. 12:12), yet his people had acted faithlessly by doubting God's faithfulness and power (Ex. 16:1–17:7) and by worshiping other gods at the foot of Mount Sinai, even while the mountain was enshrouded in God's glory (Ex. 32:1–10). Would that first generation trust the Lord by continuing to trust his servant Moses? Would God forebear with his people in order to vindicate his own power and promises (Num. 14:15) by bringing them into the land he had promised their father Abraham (Ex. 32:12–14)? This is the drama played out on the wilderness stage of Numbers. And while the first generation proved faithless and rebellious, God proved faithful in preserving his people in the wilderness and bringing the second generation to the "verge of Jordan" to land them "safely on Canaan's side." But it would not happen until after a trial of forty years in which the unbelieving exodus generation would fail to enter into the promise of God's rest (see Psalm 95).

This drama introduces one of the most discussed and nuanced theological questions of the Christian faith. How can a redeemed people fall short of receiving God's promises? What is the relationship of initial salvation to ultimate outcomes? These are not questions that can be relegated only to Numbers or to the inefficiency of the old covenant, because the New Testament writers themselves refer to the experiences of the exodus generation when they raise this same conundrum regarding the Christian life (1 Cor. 10:1–13; Heb. 3:7–4:13). Hence, neither in the Old Testament nor in the New does the covenant of grace preclude the challenge to "work out your own salvation with fear and trembling" (Phil. 2:12).

Background Issues

Numbers and Higher Criticism

Traditionally the book of Numbers was accepted, along with the Pentateuch as a whole, as the substantial product of Moses. But with the rise of the historical-critical method and source criticism, scholars increasingly regarded Numbers as predominantly the product of the hypothetical P (Priestly) source, given its prominent treatment of such subjects as the duties of the Levites and priests, the Tent of Meeting, the consecration of the tabernacle, Aaron's authority, and numerous cultic provisions regarding such matters as ritual cleansing and sacrifices. How this source theory plays

---

[2] For more, see David W. Baker, "Wilderness, Desert," in *Dictionary of the Old Testament: Pentateuch: A Compendium of Contemporary Biblical Scholarship*, ed. T. Desmond Alexander and David W. Baker, IVP Bible Dictionary Series 1 (Downers Grove, IL: InterVarsity Press, 2003), 893–97; *NIDOTTE*, 4:520–28.

out in the details depends on the scholar. Critical scholars have debated whether P is exilic or postexilic, while a minority have argued for a preexilic origin that places P before D (Deuteronomist). Several view chapters 11–12 and 21–24 as the preexilic JE, that is, the integrated J (Yahwist) and E (Elohist) sources that, according to Budd, are now read largely as one; in this view, chapters 10, 13–14, 16, 20, and 25–32 are regarded as JE with Priestly-source influence.[3] According to higher critics, the final form of Numbers with its Priestly redaction would place the historical origin of most of its material during or after the Babylonian exile and the final form of the book after the return.[4]

The details of these proposals and recent trends in biblical studies render this reconstruction less than convincing. For example, while a postexilic setting might be compatible with Numbers' considerable attention to priestly concerns and virtual silence on the monarchy, the same is no less true of the actual historical situation in the book, which describes Israel as having full possession of the law of Sinai and the tabernacle with the monarchy yet over three centuries away. Israel in the wilderness was even less influenced by a monarchy than postexilic Israel.

In addition, the trend toward canonical interpretation raises new questions about the higher-critical approach. Critical scholars should account for how the literary approach of recent decades affects the foundational assumptions of higher criticism. In other words, critical scholars more and more take a synchronic approach to the text (i.e., looking at the present state of the text as a whole) without questioning their tradition's diachronic analysis (i.e., attempting to reconstruct the development of the text).[5] For example, Budd, like many scholars, affirms that "there remains a very wide measure of agreement as to the identity and extent of the priestly material (P)," attributing directly to P or the heavy influence of P all but chapters 11–12 and 21–24.[6] But then he proceeds to analyze the book in such a way as to show greater coherence and purpose than that generally recognized by earlier source critics. This reflects a broader trend in recent scholarship that assumes the general results of source criticism but then, counterintuitively, sets about to demonstrate the coherence of the present form of the text.[7]

As Budd's analysis shows, the shift in mainstream scholarship from a primarily diachronic to a primarily synchronic approach to the Old Testament has done little to cause critical scholars to question the philosophical and methodological foundations

---

[3] Philip J. Budd, *Numbers*, WBC 5 (Waco, TX: Word, 1984), xxii–xxv.
[4] For an overview and summary of the history of and present state of critical approaches to Numbers, see Brevard S. Childs, *Introduction to the Old Testament as Scripture* (Philadelphia: Fortress, 1979), 192–94; Dennis T. Olson, "The Book of Numbers," in *Dictionary of the Old Testament: Pentateuch*, ed. Alexander and Baker, 613–14; Dennis T. Olson, *The Death of the Old and the Birth of the New: The Framework of the Book of Numbers and the Pentateuch*, BJS 71 (Chico, CA: Scholars Press, 1985), 9–30; Budd, *Numbers*, xxi–xxv.
[5] Diachronic approaches include source criticism, the Documentary Hypothesis, form criticism, redaction criticism, and sociological criticism.
[6] Budd, *Numbers*, xviii–xix.
[7] For two other examples, see Richard Hess's discussion of doublets as a literary feature of Genesis and John Ronning's type-scene analysis of the wife/sister episodes in Genesis. Richard S. Hess, "Genesis 1–2 in Its Literary Context," *TynBul* 41, no. 1 (1990): 143–53; Hess, "The Genealogies of Genesis 1–11 and Comparative Literature," *Bib* 70, no. 2 (1989): 241–54, esp. 249n25; John L. Ronning, "The Naming of Isaac: The Role of the Wife/Sister Episodes in the Redaction of Genesis," *WTJ* 53, no. 1 (1991): 1–27. On the doublets, see also Isaac M. Kikawada, "The Double Creation of Mankind in *Enki and Ninmah, Atrahasis I 1–351* and *Genesis 1–2*," *Iraq* 45, no. 1 (1983): 43–45.

on which the Documentary Hypothesis developed. While the increasingly perceived coherence in the canonical form undermines the very criteria used to establish historical-critical conclusions, at best we find some who assume the higher-critical reconstructions as generally valid (often disagreeing widely on the details of said reconstructions) yet who, in spite of this, attempt to understand the text as it stands on its own terms.[8]

Put simply, the more coherent the canonical form is seen to be under the new literary analysis, the more dubious the foundations of the higher-critical method become. This is what has been termed the problem of the "disappearing redactor."[9] Well-developed arguments have elsewhere defended the literary coherence of the Pentateuch as a whole, and these further strengthen the present approach of seeing Numbers as a work of literary integrity and skill.[10]

Authorship

Numbers bears witness to the writing activity of Moses (33:2). Further, Moses is described in Numbers as the recipient of the divine revelation that became part of the content of Numbers. On no less than forty-one occasions, Numbers reports the contents of divine speech to Moses with the phrase "the Lord spoke to Moses."[11]

There was an already-developing scribal class, or group of official historians, in the days of Moses. The instructions of Numbers 1:5, 16 describe the appointment of scribe-like record keepers long before the days of Ezra. Harrison notes that since the rise of higher criticism, archaeologists have discovered a considerable amount of written records in the ancient Near East dating from the era of Moses. Thus "it is now possible to entertain a properly-accredited process of compilation by recognizing the intrinsic historical worth of the various records emerging from the wilderness period" as opposed to the "delineation of hypothetical literary sources as practiced by liberal scholars."[12] With the rise of that class of persons responsible for the broad range of official writing activities, "their function, under the supervision of Moses, was to assist in recording and administering judicial decisions" (Num. 1:16–18; 5:23; 17:3; Deut. 16:18).[13]

The rest of the Old Testament and the New Testament regard the Pentateuch as a whole, of which Numbers is an essential part, as the substantial product of Moses.[14] Numbers is cited as part of "the Book of Moses" (Ezra 6:18). No other authorship tradition is known within Scripture or for the nearly three millennia of history leading up to the rise of higher criticism.

These references and conditions provide significant support for the traditional

---

[8] Thus the canonical approach of Childs, *Introduction to the Old Testament as Scripture.* For an assessment along these lines, see John N. Oswalt, "Canonical Criticism: A Review from a Conservative Viewpoint," *JETS* 30, no. 3 (1987): 317–25.

[9] John Barton, *Reading the Old Testament: Method in Biblical Study* (Philadelphia: Westminster, 1996), 56.

[10] John H. Sailhamer, *The Pentateuch as Narrative: A Biblical-Theological Commentary* (Grand Rapids, MI: Zondervan, 1995); Thomas W. Mann, *The Book of the Torah: The Narrative Integrity of the Pentateuch* (Atlanta: John Knox, 1988); David J. A. Clines, *The Theme of the Pentateuch,* 2nd ed., JSOTSup 10 (Sheffield: Sheffield Academic Press, 2001).

[11] 1:1; 2:1; 3:5, 11, 14, 44; 4:1, 17, 21; 5:1, 5, 11; 6:1, 22; 8:1, 5, 23; 9:1, 9; 10:1; 13:1; 14:26; 15:1, 17; 16:20, 23, 36, 44; 17:1; 18:25; 19:1; 20:7; 25:16; 26:52; 28:1; 31:1; 33:50; 34:1, 16; 35:1, 9.

[12] R. K. Harrison, *Numbers,* Wycliffe Exegetical Commentary (Chicago: Moody Press, 1990), 15.

[13] Harrison, *Numbers,* 16.

[14] See Edward J. Young, *An Introduction to the Old Testament,* rev. ed. (Grand Rapids, MI: Eerdmans, 1964), 45–46.

view that Numbers is the substantial product of Moses. Therefore, this treatment will proceed on the basis of Moses as the fundamental author. While there is evidence of a limited number of post-Mosaic additions or elaborations (e.g., Num. 12:3; 21:14–15; 32:34–42), none have any substantial effect on meaning.

Because the book of Numbers concludes with a reminder of its setting on the plains of Moab, it is intended to be read from that standpoint. While it might be said in more nuanced terms that account for continued scholarship since it was first written, Edward J. Young's formulation remains sufficiently clear and relevant:

> When we affirm that Moses wrote, or that he was the author of, the Pentateuch, we do not mean that he himself necessarily wrote every word. To insist upon this would be unreasonable. Hammurabi was the author of his famous code, but he certainly did not engrave it himself upon the stele. Our Lord was the author of the Sermon upon the Mount, but He did not write it Himself. Milton was the author of *Paradise Lost*, but he did not write it all out by hand.
>
> The witness of sacred Scripture leads us to believe that Moses was the fundamental or real author of the Pentateuch. In composing it, he may indeed, as Astruc suggested, have employed parts of previously existing written documents. Also, under divine inspiration, there may have been later minor additions and even revisions. Substantially and essentially, however, it is the product of Moses. The position for which conservatives contend has been well expressed by [Robert Dick] Wilson: "That the Pentateuch as it stands is historical and from the time of Moses; and that Moses was its real author, though it may have been revised and edited by later redactors, the additions being just as much inspired and as true as the rest."[15]

Date and Audience

With the assumption, then, of fundamental Mosaic authorship, the date and occasion of Numbers are fairly concrete. Given the account of the passing of the first generation and the concluding setting on the plains of Moab, at its earliest Numbers would have been written to the second generation on the plains of Moab in anticipation of the conquest. "Repeated references to Jericho suggest that the book may have been written very near the end of Moses's life as Israel looked ahead to the conquest of the land."[16] Given that Deuteronomy recounts these wilderness journeys in summary form, anticipates life in the land as yet future, and relates the death of Moses, Numbers would have been written prior to Deuteronomy. Therefore, we will treat the original audience as the second generation of Israel on the plains of Moab prior to the covenant renewal of Deuteronomy (Num. 22:1; 36:13).[17]

---

[15] Young, *Introduction to the Old Testament*, 45–46, citing Robert Dick Wilson, *A Scientific Investigation of the Old Testament* (1926; repr., Chicago: Moody Press, 1959), 11.
[16] Richard L. Pratt Jr., *He Gave Us Stories: The Bible Student's Guide to Interpreting Old Testament Narratives* (Phillipsburg, NJ: P&R, 1993), 284.
[17] Approximately 1405 BC, which I calculate by beginning at 1446, the traditional early date for the exodus, and adding one year and one month at Sinai plus forty years of wandering. Other scholars include the year at Sinai in the forty-year total, thus arriving at an approximate date of 1406 BC.

STRUCTURE AND OUTLINE

Childs has observed that "the book of Numbers has generally been regarded as the least unified composition within the Pentateuch."[18] On the other hand, Budd argues that "the book is by no means as disordered and incoherent as is sometimes claimed."[19] One of the most prominent features of the book as a whole is the censuses that occur at the beginning and at a strategic point toward the end. These censuses mark the beginnings of the stories of both the first and second generations, but they also bracket off a narrative that has "a certain unified progression which no critical analysis can destroy."[20] Despite the book's variety of genres (narrative, prophecy, civil laws, cultic laws, oracles), this variety, as Longman and Dillard note, occurs fundamentally "within the broader contexts of narrative and law."[21] Thus they categorize the book as "instructional history writing," favoring Olson's twofold outline of Numbers, which consists of "the end of the old generation" (Numbers 1–25) and the "birth of the new" (Numbers 26–36).[22]

While scholars have yet to reach a consensus on a comprehensive structure of Numbers, Olson's outline highlights a recognized two-phase progression marked by the three prominent locations of Sinai, Kadesh, and Moab. These two phases between the three stops exhibit extensive parallels between the first and second generations but with dramatically different responses and outcomes.[23]

The story begins with Israel at the foot of Mount Sinai thirteen months after the exodus from Egypt (1:1). This location provides not only geographical and chronological context but also literary continuity with Leviticus, for in Leviticus the nation was given the means by which they could be a holy people (Lev. 11:45), such that God could fulfill his promise to dwell in their midst (Ex. 25:8).

Numbers goes on to unfold in three major stages (it is helpful to split the first-generation phase in Olson's outline into two stages): the census and preparation of the first generation at Sinai (1:1–10:10); the first generation's march to Canaan, the bad report of the land's inhabitants, and the failed invasion (10:11–25:18); and the census and preparation of the second generation to enter the land (26:1–36:13). When the military significance of the censuses and the numerous requirements for consecration and holiness are perceived, the shadow of holy war is cast over the whole book. In that light, Numbers may be outlined as follows:[24]

I. Consecration of the First-Generation Army (1:1–10:36)
   A. Census of all men of fighting age (1:1–46)
   B. Exemption of Levites as priest-soldiers (1:47–54)

---

[18] Childs, *Introduction to the Old Testament as Scripture*, 192.
[19] Budd, *Numbers*, xx.
[20] Young, *Introduction to the Old Testament*, 86.
[21] Tremper Longman III and Raymond B. Dillard, *An Introduction to the Old Testament*, 2nd ed. (Grand Rapids, MI: Zondervan, 2006), 95.
[22] Longman and Dillard, *Introduction to the Old Testament*, 97, referring to Olson, *The Death of the Old and the Birth of the New*, 118–20.
[23] For more, see Gordon J. Wenham, *Numbers: An Introduction and Commentary*, TOTC 4 (Downers Grove, IL: InterVarsity Press, 1981), and the outline in this section.
[24] Pratt follows a similar schema. *He Gave Us Stories*, 284.

The first generation had witnessed the mighty acts of God in the plagues, the exodus, the glorious lawgiving at Sinai, and the miraculous wilderness provisions, and yet they failed to trust in God's goodness and power to bring them into the land he had promised their father Abraham. They had been an idolatrous people in Egypt (Josh. 24:14) and even at the foot of Mount Sinai (Exodus 32), desiring the provision and predictability of slavery in Egypt to the challenge of utter dependency upon God in the wilderness (Num. 11:5; 14:1–4). In spite of their resistance, God continued to demonstrate his faithfulness, vindicate his appointed leaders, and even provide means to atone for their rebelliousness and cleanse their guilt. But as the people among whom God dwelt and as his holy army preparing to enter into holy war against the Canaanites, they were to trust God fully, obey his appointed leaders, and purify themselves. For holy war is a war of the righteous God against sin. Only warriors who are consecrated and holy can be assured of victory and freedom from the defeat of God's judgment. For holy war is ultimately a war against sin and unbelief, be it against the idolatrous Canaanites or unbelieving Israel.[25]

But so that God could be faithful to his promises, he began again with a remnant. The second generation led by Joshua and Caleb would understand the reasons for the first generation's fate and, most importantly, would strive to avoid its mistakes. By the proofs of God's faithfulness, recorded in Numbers, they could be confident that if they trusted in God's power and provision, they would enter into the Land of Promise. But if they did not trust God, they would suffer the same fate as their parents' generation. The purpose of Numbers is well summarized by Walton and

---

[25] For more on God as the divine warrior, see Tremper Longman III and Daniel G. Reid, *God Is a Warrior*, SOTBT (Grand Rapids, MI: Zondervan, 1995), especially chap. 3, "God Is an Enemy: The Wars against Unfaithful Israel."

Hill: "to contrast the faithfulness of God with the faithlessness and rebellion of the Israelites."[26] And yet, to narrow in on the purpose of the censuses and the great challenge that lay across the Jordan, the book of Numbers also aimed "to call the second generation of Israel to arms as the holy army of God."[27]

Contrasting and comparing the generations points to two overarching patterns of parallels, as Wenham observes. He notes both literary/historical parallels comparing the three journeys of Israel—from the Red Sea to Sinai, from Sinai to Kadesh-Barnea, and from Kadesh-Barnea to Moab (see table 11)—and the parallels associated with the three major venues themselves (see table 12).[28]

Element of Journey	Red Sea to Sinai	Sinai to Kadesh	Kadesh to Moab
Led by cloud	Ex. 13:21	Num. 10:11ff.	——
Victory over Egypt	Ex. 14:1–31	——	cf. Num. 21:21–35
Victory song	Ex. 15:1–18	cf. Num.10:35–36	Num. 21:14–15
Miriam	Ex. 15:20–21	Num. 12	Num. 20:1
People's complaint	Ex. 15:23–24	Num. 11:1	Num. 21:5
Moses's intercession	Ex. 15:25	Num. 11:2	Num. 21:7
Well	Ex. 15:27	——	Num. 21:16
Manna and quail	Ex. 16:1–36	Num. 11:4–35	——
Water from rock	Ex. 17:1–7	——	Num. 20:2–13
Victory over Amalek	Ex. 17:8–16	——	cf. Num. 21:1–3
Jethro	Ex. 18:1–12	cf. Num. 10:29–32	——

Table 11

Topic	Sinai	Kadesh	Moab
Divine promises	Ex. 19:5–6; 23:23–31	Num. 13:2	Num. 22:1–24:25
Forty days	Ex. 24:18	Num. 13:25	——
Rebellion	Ex. 32:1–8	Num. 14:1–12	Num. 25:1–3
Moses's intercession	Ex. 32:11–13	Num. 14:13–19	——
Judgment	Ex. 32:34	Num. 14:20–35	Num. 25:4
Plague	Ex. 32:35	Num. 14:37	Num. 25:8–9
Laws of sacrifice	Ex. 34:18–26; Lev. 1:1–7:38; etc.	Num. 15:1–31	Num. 28:1–31

---

[26] John H. Walton and Andrew E. Hill, *Old Testament Today: The Journey from Ancient Context to Contemporary Relevance*, 2nd ed. (Grand Rapids, MI: Zondervan, 2013), 105.
[27] Pratt, *He Gave Us Stories*, 284.
[28] Wenham, *Numbers*, 16.

Topic	Sinai	Kadesh	Moab
Trial	Lev. 24:10–23	Num. 15:32–36	Num. 27:1–11
Rebellion against priests	Lev. 10:1–3	Num. 16:1–35	——
Atonement through priests or Levites	Ex. 32:26–29	Num. 16:36–50	Num. 25:7–13
Priestly prerogatives	Lev. 6:1–7:38; 22:1–33	Num. 17:1–18:32	Num. 31:28–30; 35:1–8
Impurity rules	Lev. 11:1–16:34; Num. 9:6–14	Num. 19:1–22	Num. 35:9–34
Census	Num. 1:1–4:49	——	Num. 26:1–65

Table 12

These parallels serve to heighten the comparison of the two generations, all while God remains constant and faithful.

MESSAGE AND THEOLOGY

Consecration of the First-Generation Army (Num. 1:1–10:36)

Census of All Men of Fighting Age (Num. 1:1–46)

Numbers begins with a census of the first generation but only of fighting-age males (1:2–3). This makes it clear that its purpose was military. Knowing troop strength wasn't necessary from God's point of view. His army consisted principally of the hosts of heavenly angels. This is why at certain junctures Israel is commanded to stand by and watch God accomplish victory unaided by man (Ex. 14:13; Josh. 6:1–27; 2 Sam. 5:23–24; 2 Kings 6:17; 19:32–37; cf. Ps. 48:4–8). It is necessary, however, for Israel to know their numbers by tribes in order to deploy themselves tactically on the battlefield and at camp in guarding the tabernacle.[29]

There is a similar census in 2 Samuel 24 that God condemns. How is this to be reconciled with the fact that twice in Numbers God commands troop counts? The explanation emerges from a wide-ranging motif grounded in Deuteronomy 17:14–20. When Israel chose a king, it was not to choose a king "like all the nations" (17:14). Such a king would have the propensity to create political alliances through marrying foreign wives (as well as adulterating the cultus) and to build up a large standing army (17:16–17). Rather, he was to trust in Yahweh as Israel's sovereign Lord who would protect and give victory to his loyal servant king. That was, after all, what Yahweh's name connoted in light of the parallelism of Exodus 15:3—"Yahweh is a warrior, Yahweh is his name" (my trans.). This is why the psalmist sings, "Some trust in chariots and some in horses, but we trust in the name of [Yahweh] our God" (Ps. 20:7).

The particular incident of 2 Samuel 24 came near the end of David's reign when

---

[29] While it was principally the Levites' responsibility to guard the tabernacle, Israel as a kingdom of priests (Ex. 19:6) was to protect the priestly venue of the camp and later the Holy Land itself from unholiness and injustice. See the discussion of "priest-soldiers" later in this chapter.

he was aged and weak. In numbering Israel's army, he was acting in the tradition of a king "like all the nations," not trusting in Yahweh as Israel's sovereign King to defend it. David had once understood this principle, as he declared in the Valley of Elah before Goliath, "the battle is the LORD's" (1 Sam. 17:47). But as his own strength waned, he failed to retain full confidence in Yahweh's strength.

In the case of the Numbers censuses, Israel had not yet learned to trust the Lord by following him into battle. The first generation, then, was to prepare itself to be God's army on the march through the wilderness into the land that God had promised them. And they were to do so by numbering all who could fight.

Exemption of Levites as Priest-Soldiers (Num. 1:47–54)

The Levites were not to be numbered among the fighting men (1:47). Yet this did not mean that the Levites were exempt from military service. They were charged with war not against the Canaanites and Israel's harassers along the way but against those who would encroach upon the tabernacle in an unauthorized way (1:50–51). Faithful priestly duty meant, for them, to be guardians of the sanctuary. Their warfare was guarding God's presence from the offense of sin (1:51; 3:38).

This is consistent with the office of priest in the larger cultural context. "Every priest was chosen and installed to serve in a sanctuary. The ruling was universally acknowledged particularly by the Arabs in the days before Islam. The priest was for them essentially a *sadin*, a 'guardian' of the temple; he looked after the sanctuary, received visitors and took charge of their gifts."[30] In fact, the Levites' general duties here as well as the particular ones in 3:1–4:49 are set forth by the Hebrew verb שָׁמַר, which can mean "keep" but in these instances means "guard."[31]

Camp Formation of Israel (Num. 2:1–34)

The order and manner in which Israel was to encamp around the tabernacle reflected this priestly guardianship, with the Levites stationed adjacent to the tabernacle to the north, west, and east. Aaron's family was stationed immediately to the east at the entrance.

The priestly guardianship of all the tribes is exhibited in their positions of encampment as well. In his paternal blessing, Jacob had anticipated Judah's lead role in the defeat of Israel's enemies: "Judah, your brothers shall praise you; your hand shall be on the neck of your enemies" (Gen. 49:8). Joshua, from the tribe of Judah, would lead Israel into Canaan, and Judah would take the initiative in the days of the judges (Judg. 1:2; 20:18). Thus Judah would camp to the east, the direction in which the tabernacle faced, and toward which it would head when moving out. This organization would also preserve the identity of the tribes and clans, which would

---

[30] Roland de Vaux, *Ancient Israel: Its Life and Institutions* (New York: McGraw-Hill, 1965), 348.

[31] The Levites' priestly duties are prescribed using the verb שָׁמַר, "to guard," and the cultic sense of עָבַד, "to serve," the same two verbs used to describe Adam's responsibility in Eden (Gen. 2:15), thus establishing that Adam's role, too, was that of priestly guardian of God's sanctuary. For more on this, see Meredith G. Kline, *Kingdom Prologue: Genesis Foundations for a Covenantal Worldview* (Eugene, OR: Wipf & Stock, 2006), 54ff.

prove important when the second generation entered the land and the land was apportioned (and preserved going forward into the future) by those allotments.[32]

Census and Duties of the Priest-Soldiers (Num. 3:1–4:49)

To Aaron and his sons, God had given the service of the tabernacle, especially the inner sanctuary (Ex. 28:1–29:46; 40:9–15). The general service of the tabernacle, including its assembly and reassembly, were assigned to the tribe of Levi as a whole (Num. 3:6). Each clan within the tribe held specific responsibilities.

The Levites' special service stemmed from the Passover, during which God required every firstborn male in Israel to be set apart as holy to the Lord, belonging to him (Ex. 13:2, 15). There had been a death in every house in Egypt on that first Passover night, but in the Israelites' houses there had been the substitutionary death of a spotless lamb.[33] Every firstborn had been redeemed by this substitute, thus every firstborn son in Israel belonged to the Lord. God provided, however, that he would claim the whole tribe of Levi in substitute for each firstborn male (Num. 3:40–51).

Here we find a numerical difficulty in the text. Numbers 3:43 indicates that there were 22,273 firstborn among the other eleven tribes, requiring a redemption price for the 273 differential with 22,000 Levites reported in 3:39 (see 3:46). The problem is that, according to the Hebrew text, there were actually 22,300 Levites (7,500 Gershonites in 3:22; 8,600 Kohathites in 3:28; and 6,200 Merarites in 3:34). However, an important textual witness in the Septuagint (the Greek translation of the Hebrew Bible) indicates that the Kohathites numbered 8,300.[34] Since the difference between 300 and 600 in the Hebrew is the omission of one letter, it is likely that the original was 8,300 and a copying omission resulted in 8,600.[35] If this is the case, which seems likely, then the numbers cohere precisely.

Consecration for Holy War (Num. 5:1–9:14)

Because Israel was preparing itself for holy war, it had to be holy itself. Otherwise it would be subject to the same outcome as the idolatrous Canaanites.[36] Thus, the essence of cleanness and uncleanness under the Levitical laws are fronted in summary form in 5:1–4.

Holy war is a consequence of God's imminence. When God becomes present, sin is judged and righteousness vindicated. God's promise to Israel was that he would dwell among them, but he could only do so through the sacrificial and atoning provisions of the tabernacle and its worship (Ex. 25:8). While Israel would enjoy God's immediate presence in the camp and as they went in to take the land, they had to be consecrated properly to avoid the same fate as the Canaanites. Numbers 5:1–9:14

---

[32] On preservation through tribal allotments, see the discussion in this chapter concerning the widows of Zelophehad in Numbers 36.

[33] For an insightful and profound development of this theme, see Meredith G. Kline, "The Feast of Cover-Over," *JETS* 37, no. 4 (1994): 497–510.

[34] Τριακόσιοι, 300, instead of ἑξακόσιοι, 600, per the so-called Lucianic Recension of the Septuagint.

[35] The Hebrew for *300* is שְׁלֹשׁ while for *600* is שֵׁשׁ.

[36] For a comprehensive treatment of the dynamics of holy war, see Longman and Reid, *God Is a Warrior*, and Vern S. Poythress, *The Shadow of Christ in the Law of Moses* (Phillipsburg, NJ: P&R, 1995), esp. chaps. 5 and 10.

can be seen as various provisions, in addition to those in Leviticus, for how they were to achieve the holiness required for God to dwell in their midst.

Some of these provisions may seem obscure, arbitrary, or even objectionable to the modern mind. A few even appear to leave people subject to mere chance (e.g., 3:16–31). But bear in mind that they are administered by the God of providence. Though his ways are inscrutable to us, and human hearts inscrutable to men, God is the One to whom every thought is laid bare (Heb. 4:13). While these ceremonial laws are no longer binding on us in the same form today, they were an efficient means at the time for God to speak.

While Numbers 5:1–31 provides remedies for the presence of sin in the camp, 6:1–9:14 relates acts of consecration—of the individual Nazirite in 6:1–27 and of the tabernacle and Levites in 7:1–9:14. Numbers 7 recapitulates what was related previously in Exodus 40 and Leviticus 8. This account provides a clear example of the biblical narrator's willingness to break with a strict chronology when it suits his purpose and to do so without in any way misleading the reader. Many modern critical readers fault the biblical record for not conforming to modernist expectations of precision—a subtle form of hermeneutical colonialism. Additionally, many evangelical readers have unnecessarily contrived explanations of strict chronology when none was required.

After the priests consecrated the tabernacle through ritual offerings (Num. 7:1–88), God would make himself present in the Tent of Meeting and make known his will to his servant Moses as he spoke to him from between the cherubim over the ark (7:89; cf. Ex. 25:22). Relatedly, the lampstand rituals were to be followed, its light being the anticipated consequence of the divine presence.[37] The Levites as a whole were to be consecrated (Num. 8:5–22), and a relevant digression explored the limits of Levitical service (8:23–26), given that its work was strenuous as well as dangerous (8:26).

These successive acts of consecration climaxed in the first celebration of the Passover following the exodus from Egypt. As such, it too reminded Israel that they belonged to the Lord by virtue of their redemption from slavery.

Divine Acceptance and Assurance (Num. 9:15–23)

Once the people had completed the consecration, the glory cloud descended upon the tabernacle (Num. 9:15; cf. Ex. 40:34–38). This divine act not only fulfilled God's stated intent to dwell among his people in the tabernacle (Ex. 25:8) but also affirmed God's response to Moses's intercession following the golden calf incident. God initially agreed to see Israel to the Promised Land but refused to be present with them (Ex. 33:3). Moses pleaded that it was God's presence that made them a "distinct" people, prevailing upon God to guarantee his presence (Ex. 33:16–17). The account in Numbers adds greater detail about the characteristic, day-to-day manifestation of God's glory. It emphasizes that Israel's movements, to camp or to

---

[37] For more on the significance of the lampstand and all the tabernacle furnishings, see Poythress, *Shadow of Christ*, especially chap. 2, and Richard E. Averbeck, "Tabernacle," in *Dictionary of the Old Testament: Pentateuch*, ed. Alexander and Baker, 807–27.

march, were completely contingent on whether the glory cloud was stationary or on the move, and that their responsiveness was in full obedience to Moses (Num. 9:22–23).

Departure in Battle Array (Num. 10:1–36)

The use of the two silver trumpets explicitly connected this movement to obedience to Moses. When played in various combinations, the two trumpets signaled either the assembling of the congregation, the breaking of camp, the assembling of the tribal leaders, or an alarm at some threat (10:1–10). These trumpets continued to have use in worship after Israel settled in the land. In battle in the wilderness and beyond, the trumpets would also summon God's help, a reminder that Israel depended upon him for victory and had to call upon him in times of trouble (10:9).

Israel's departure in formation from Sinai served not just an organizational purpose but also a military purpose, providing defensive as well as tactical advantages. This is consistent with the censuses having a military purpose and is confirmed by Moses's formulaic invocation to carry the ark forward whenever the glory cloud moved: "Arise, O Lord, and let your enemies be scattered" (10:35). This formula called for God to fight on behalf of his people, but it was particularly associated with the ark, because the ark, as a multivalent symbol, represented God's battle chariot as well as the footstool of his throne (1 Chron. 28:2). As the ark would be carried forward, God was seen as leading his heavenly army in battle.

Craig Broyles captures this concept well:

> In the wilderness the ark served to *lead* the people (Num. 10:33). At the beginning of each stage of the journey Moses invoked what is commonly called "the song of the ark": "*Arise [qûmâ]*, O Lord, let your enemies be scattered and your foes flee before you" (v. 35). Similarly, whenever the ark "came to rest" (*nwḥ*), Yahweh is implored to "return" (*šûbâ*). The scattering of enemies and flight of foes associates the ark with *battle*. This is confirmed later in Num. 14:44, which presupposes that the ark must precede the people in the conquest of the land. Also related to the ark is the "cloud of the Lord," which led them on their journey.[38]

This is why the prayers for rescue in the Psalms are in some instances couched in this imagery; "Arise, O Lord, and go to your resting place, you and the ark of your might" (Ps. 132:8). This allusion is immediately preceded by a call to worship God "at his footstool" (132:7). Broyles goes on to argue that the Psalter's use of key terms associated elsewhere with the ark indicates a role for the ark in the cult long after David brought it to its resting place in Jerusalem. For our purposes, it is enough to see that the psalmist's frequent prayer "Arise, O Lord" draws upon the background of Numbers. The use and misuse of the ark in the battles of the so-called "ark narrative" of 1 Samuel 4:1–7:1 also rely on this context.

---

[38] Craig C. Broyles, "The Psalms and Cult Symbolism: The Case of the Cherubim-Ark," in *Interpreting the Psalms: Issues and Approaches*, ed. David G. Firth and Philip S. Johnston (Downers Grove, IL: IVP Academic, 2006), 141.

Failure of the First-Generation Army (Num. 11:1–25:18)
Rebellion and Its Consequences (Num. 11:1–20:29)

Immediately after the census, consecration, glorious indwelling, and setting out of the camp, the first generation displayed their unbelief and rebellion. These episodes both foreshadow and reveal the root of why the attempted conquest would fail and the first generation would perish in the wilderness. In this respect, it would serve as a warning to the second generation. As they themselves prepared to enter the Promised Land, why should they trust the Lord, trust in the ordinances he gave through Moses, trust Joshua, Moses's successor, and trust in the priesthood of Aaron's descendants? The answer comes in three parts. First, because of their repeated and deep rebellion, the people merited their fate. Second, Moses and Aaron often prevailed upon God to relent. Finally, God vindicated Moses and Aaron, and thus Moses's decrees and the priestly ministry can be seen as clearly God's will.

Table 13 provides a summary of the episodes of rebellion in this section. Although we can detect no precise pattern, we can identify general elements that occur variously in the different episodes. They always begin with a complaint, usually attributed to some specific condition. The initial response may come directly from God or Moses, and this initial response can generate additional actions and reactions before the final result. Presented in the format of a table, one can quickly observe the cumulative weight of the various rebellions.

As table 13 shows, Moses often proved, as he did at Sinai, to be an effective intercessor for a sinful people. Yet he exhibited a growing intemperance that brought hefty consequences. It is first detected in the initial complaint in 11:11–15 when Moses suggested that God had left him with too much to bear and was not sufficiently attentive to those he had redeemed. Thus, he gave God an ultimatum to kill him or to help him (11:15). This intemperance grew into rebellion itself in 20:2–13, the second incident of God providing water from the rock. Unlike the first episode in Exodus 17:1–7, in which God instructed Moses to strike the rock, in Numbers God only told Moses to speak to the rock. Moses, in apparent anger, struck it twice (or a second time). As he did so, he said to the people, "Hear now, you rebels: shall we bring water for you out of this rock?" Whether the "we" is Moses and Aaron, Moses and God, or the "royal we" of Moses alone, Moses attributed the outcome at least partially to himself. His words and his action brought upon him the same divine sentence declared previously on the first generation as a whole: "Because you did not believe in me, to uphold me as holy in the eyes of the people of Israel, therefore you shall not bring this assembly into the land that I have given them" (20:12).

This episode informs how one reads not only Numbers but also Exodus. With both being written to the second generation, they address the question of Moses's authority. The second generation might well wonder why it should observe the laws given through Moses when Moses himself failed to enter the land. God's frequent

Numbers	Complaint	Response	Result
11:1–3	The people grumble about general misfortunes	• God's anger is kindled • Outer camp is burned	• People cry out to Moses • Moses prays • Fire dies down • Place is named Taberah
11:4–35	The rabble complain of no meat or fresh vegetables	• God's anger "blazed hotly" (11:10) • Moses complains to God, not able to "carry all this people alone" (11:14)	• Elders are appointed to share Moses's burden • God gives Israel a month of meat to chastise them • God strikes the camp with a plague • Place is named Kibroth-hattaavah
12:1–16	Miriam complains about Moses's Cushite wife and questions Moses's unique authority	• God vindicates Moses's unique authority • Miriam is afflicted with leprosy	• Moses intercedes for Miriam • Miriam is cleansed
13:1–14:38	The people lament the spies' report, their departure from Egypt, and Moses's leadership; they threaten to stone Caleb and Joshua	• God appears at Tent of Meeting and threatens pestilence, disinheritance, and a remnant nation • Moses intercedes, appealing to God's glory	• God relents • But God decrees that the people will wander for forty years in the wilderness • God bans the whole first generation from entering the land, Caleb and Joshua excepted
16:1–40	Korah, Dathan, Abiram, and On rebel against Moses and Aaron	• Moses rebukes rebels, announces contest of incense offerings • God declares intent to punish all • Moses intercedes • God calls all Israel to separate from the rebels	• The ground opens and swallows the rebels and their households • Rebel fire pans are made into altar plates
16:41–17:13	The people grumble about the judgment upon the rebels	• God threatens to consume the people and commences a plague • Moses instructs Aaron to hastily make an atonement offering • Plague is arrested	• Aaron's rod blossoms
20:2–13	The people complain of no water	• Moses intercedes angrily toward God	• God provides water from the rock (again) • Moses is rebuked and sentenced to the fate of the first generation
21:4–9	The people question God's benevolence	• God sends a plague of fiery serpents • God provides the bronze serpent as a remedy	• Moses fashions the bronze serpent • All who look to the bronze serpent are healed

Table 13

endorsements of Moses's leadership (and Aaron's) in both books provide the answer to any doubts. Moses was chosen by God to lead Israel. He was an effective
intercessor at several critical moments. He bore much in leading and ruling over
the people on the Lord's behalf. Yet his actions constituted a failure to trust God
sufficiently and to treat him as holy (Num. 20:12). He was faithful in God's house,
as God himself said (12:7), but he was *of* the first generation, perhaps providing a
lesson in covenantal solidarity.

The catalog of complaints concludes with the transfer of high priestly authority
to Eleazar, Aaron's son, and the death of Aaron, for he too was complicit in Moses's
failure at Meribah (Num. 20:24), as well as in Miriam's rebellion (12:11).

Hope for a Remnant (Num. 21:1–35)

Like the other ten spies, Caleb and Joshua had given a good report about the abundance in the Promised Land. Unlike the others, only they had believed that God
would give them victory over its intimidating inhabitants. Therefore, they alone of
the first generation would enter the land (14:30, 38). Thus, the turning of generations marked by the deaths of Miriam and Aaron produce a dramatic change of
fortunes for Israel, which 21:1–3 highlights. While 21:1 marks an apparently minor
defeat, 21:3 reports a total victory. From this point on in Numbers, Israel would
encounter only victory. In between these two episodes stands the second generation's vow of full obedience (21:2). As such, 21:1–3 can be viewed as the turning
point of the entire book.[39]

When the Canaanite king of Arad came out against Israel in a preemptive strike,
God gave Israel victory (21:1–3). They also defeated Sihon, king of the Amorites,
when he refused Israel unharassed transit through his territory (21:21–30). Likewise,
Israel enjoyed victory against Og, king of Bashan (21:31–35). Within the book of
Numbers, these represent tastes of victory for the second generation, since the first
generation had already sealed its fate. These victories proved that God could do what
the ten spies and the first generation did not believe he could or would.

The final complaint episode comes in the curious incident of the bronze serpent.
The complaint itself is nondescript. The particular cause is not mentioned, but Israel's sentiment echoes a past grievance—they preferred the bread of slavery in Egypt
over the bread of heaven in the wilderness. God's chastisement comes in the form
of "fiery serpents" (21:6). While it has been debated whether "fiery" refers to their
appearance, the pain of their bites, or both, the bites were proving fatal to some and
of sufficient agony to produce a plea for forgiveness (21:7).

What is curious is the form of the cure. God instructed Moses to cast a serpent
out of bronze and to fasten it to a pole long enough for all to see it (21:8–9). Why
would God use a symbol associated with entities such as Satan and Pharaoh as an

---

[39] For more on the importance of this passage for the book, see Iain M. Duguid, *Numbers: God's Presence in the Wilderness*,
Preaching the Word (Wheaton, IL: Crossway, 2006), 259; Won W. Lee, *Punishment and Forgiveness in Israel's Migratory
Campaign* (Grand Rapids, MI: Eerdmans, 2003), 266–68; and David L. Stubbs, *Numbers*, BTCB (Grand Rapids, MI:
Brazos, 2009), 164. My thanks to former student Peter Goodrich for this insight and these sources.

object to elicit faith? Some have speculated that God intended not these negative associations but different associations with healing, such as the staff of Aesculapius from Greek mythology, still used today as a symbol for the healing arts. This argument is implausible given the distance of that association and the nearness of these other associations so central to the narrative of the Hebrew Scriptures. It is, in fact, the negative association with Pharaoh (and secondarily Satan) on which its meaning depends, but the key in this situation is the form of its display.

Moses was to display the bronze serpent, which represented all the fiery serpents in the act of biting the Israelites, not merely on a pole but on a pike. It was hoisted up not as a sign of living hope but as a symbol of the dead Pharaoh and the powerlessness of his serpentine god(s). It was God's reminder of the status of the powers of Egypt, those powers to which the complainants wished to return. The gods of Egypt were dead, and those who worshiped them would become like them (Ps. 115:8). The bites of the serpents were likely reminders of the sting of slavery, perhaps even the sting of the Egyptian whips. In contrast, the God of Israel was the living God who demonstrated his superiority over Pharaoh and the gods of Egypt (Ex. 12:12) and had sustained them in the wilderness for forty years.

Balak and Balaam: Future Threat and Promise (Num. 22:1–25:18)

The Balaam story presents many curiosities as well. The Moabite king Balak had heard of Israel's victories and the great number of its people, and he feared that Israel would decimate Moab. Instead of employing the previous kings' failed strategy of direct engagement, he retained the services of a famed Mesopotamian diviner named Balaam. Balaam claimed to be a worshiper of Israel's God and was initially unwilling to help Balak (22:13, 18). After a second embassy from Moab, Balaam went but with apparent evil intent (22:22). In the highly ironic, even satirical, scene that followed, the all-seeing prophet was unable to see the threatening Angel of the Lord, but his dumb animal, a donkey, not only saw the threat but also spoke to his master (22:30). The "crooked" (22:32, my trans.) way of Balaam was straightened out, and he was given divine permission to proceed as long as he was willing to obey the Lord.

In the threefold cycle of sacrifices (23:1, 14, 29–30), encounters with God (22:12, 20, 22–35), and oracles (23:7–10; 18–24; 24:3–9) that follow, Balaam is unable to perform the curses commissioned by Balak. In the spirit of the story's irony, he is unable to gain a physical vantage point from where he can see the whole of Israel in order to administer the curses (23:13, 27). This dramatic element confirms the vast number of Israel. In fact, it touches on the essence of why Balaam in the end can only do what God wills him to do. He cannot number Israel because its population is so great (23:10). God has blessed Israel and is present among them (23:20–21). Israel will prosper and be numerous (24:5–7). "Blessed are those who bless you, and cursed are those who curse you" (24:9). These are all elements of God's covenant promises to Abraham. Balaam cannot speak a contrary word because God's promise to bless Abraham has been fulfilled.

Was Balaam a saint or a sinner?[40] On the one hand, he is characterized as a believer ("the LORD my God," 22:18). He resolutely refused to curse Israel, and in the end, he blessed Israel and foretold Moab's doom at their hands (24:14–25). Yet Deuteronomy 23:3–6 indicates that he was culpable. He was treated as an enemy in the conquest (Josh. 13:22). Later passages confirm his mercenary intent, which prompted God's opposition and the donkey episode (Num. 22:22; cf. Josh. 24:9–10). The New Testament's condemnation is even more unequivocal (2 Pet. 2:15–16; Jude 11). George Coats concludes that the question must be answered not on the basis of Balaam's character or intent but on his repeated insistence that he would only speak what God allowed him to speak. Yet that evidence must be considered alongside his mercenary status. Most importantly, Balaam's counsel to Balak—not divulged until the ensuing narrative—revealed his true colors.

In the account that follows, the intermingling between Israel and Moab, both in idol worship and in male-female relations, prove to be more of a threat to Israel than Balaam's oracles (Num. 25:1–9). Only subsequently is it indicated that this was Balaam's counsel to Balak: "Behold, these [women of Midian], on Balaam's advice, caused the people of Israel to act treacherously against the LORD in the incident of Peor, and so the plague came among the congregation of the LORD" (31:16). The proximity of Balaam's conclusion and the sin of Baal-Peor might have suggested it, but this passage confirms that Balaam did not leave Balak without a strategy against Israel. While Balaam may have stuck to the "letter of the law" concerning his oracles—to pronounce only what God permitted—he provided Balak counsel that did lead to Israel being cursed, at least cursed to the extent that twenty-four thousand people died, until the zeal of faithful Phinehas turned away God's anger (25:10–13).

This narrative highlights the great unlearned lesson of much of Israel's history. The enemy without could never prevail. But the enemy within would never fail. Israel, with God as their Protector, was unassailable by any nation. The greatest threat to Israel was its covenant Lord when it harbored sin within the camp. Just like the serial victories of 21:1–3, the zeal of Phinehas prompted a new hope. The second generation had learned from the failure of the first. Idolatry and immorality would still occur, but Israel's new leaders and the second generation would be decisive in confronting it.

Consecration of the Second-Generation Army (Num. 26:1–36:13)

Census of All Men of Fighting Age (Num. 26:1–56)

The second census of men of fighting age is worded nearly identically to the first (cf. 1:2–3; 26:2). It does not conclude the book but marks a new beginning in which God's people will trust him fully. They had seen the first generation fall short because of unbelief, and they stood on the plains of Moab overlooking the Promised Land, knowing that God had been faithful in spite of their parents' failure. The narrative

---

[40] So George W. Coats poses the question in "Balaam: Sinner or Saint?," *Biblical Research* 18 (1973): 21–29.

draws attention to the fact that not one of those numbered at Sinai were numbered on the plains of Moab save Caleb and Joshua (26:63–65).

Census of Levites as Priest-Soldiers (Num. 26:57–65)

Similarly, the Levites were numbered for the same purpose as in 3:1–54. They were not exempt from soldierly duty but instead were to conduct their holy war in the precincts of the tabernacle and the camp of Israel. Phinehas had already turned aside the anger of God against syncretism, and those numbered here were to continue in that role for the nation.

Preservation of the Bereft (Num. 27:1–11)

From 27:1 through the end of Numbers, various situations arise that may not lend themselves to an explicit literary structure but which do have a natural logic. In the case of the daughters of Zelophehad, we encounter the first of several situations that anticipate occupation of the land. These women, fatherless and without brothers, would be bereft in the Promised Land because land inheritance followed the custom of male inheritance rights.

The Promised Land was a gift of inheritance from God to his people. Title was not to be regarded as a commodity that could pass from any person to another. Such a commoditized system would lead to impoverishment for those who experienced calamity or tragedy or whose ancestors made sinful or foolish decisions.

The allotment of the land by tribe and clan was a social system that, working in conjunction with the Sabbath Year and the Year of Jubilee, would preserve families in perpetuity. It would not spare them all hardship, but it would prevent them from becoming chronically bereft for generations. This system was grounded in the fact that God never relinquished title to the land, and thus it was God's grant of steward-ship to his vassal lords (Lev. 25:23). As Christopher Wright has pointed out, "If the exodus was God's idea of *redemption*, the jubilee was God's idea of *restoration*."[41]

The ruling that God gave Moses in the case of the daughters of Zelophehad provided for one such circumstance in which the vulnerable could have been cut off not only from land but from tribe and clan. As such, it anticipated life in the land, which was premised upon the success that God would give the second generation as they were willing to believe the Lord.

Joshua to Succeed Moses (Num. 27:12–23)

Moses had one final opportunity to intercede for God's people. As he neared the end of his life, gazing from the heights across the Jordan into the Land of Promise (27:12), his true character as Israel's shepherd shone through once again. The resentment and bitterness of his previous complaints, issued albeit amid the unrelenting unbelief of the first generation, gave way to the heart of one to whom God would speak as to

---

[41] Christopher J. H. Wright, *The Mission of God: Unlocking the Bible's Grand Narrative* (Downers Grove, IL: IVP Academic, 2006). Emphasis original.

a friend. He pleaded for a shepherd to succeed him so that "the congregation of the LORD may not be as sheep that have no shepherd" (27:17). While God had been Israel's shepherd since the days of the patriarchs (Gen. 48:15), during the days of the exodus he had administered his shepherd care through human undershepherds of his own choosing. The second generation would have witnessed the divinely authorized transfer of authority from Moses to Joshua, as verified by the ministry of their new high priest, Eleazar, so that they would have trusted in Joshua as God's provision for leadership.

Consecration and Renewal (Num. 28:1–30:16)

Learning from the example of the first generation, the second generation would have known the critical importance of consecrating God's holy army. The sacrifices in this section serve this strategic purpose in the flow of the Numbers narrative, recapitulating and elaborating on the offerings of Leviticus. Likewise the provisions on vows for men and women would have reinforced the importance of integrity.

A Taste of Victory (Num. 31:1–54)

God narrowly defined the venue and objects of holy war in the Old Testament as within the confines of the Promised Land because it was fundamentally a matter of worship, necessitated by the imminent presence of God within those confines. Where God's special presence dwells, holiness and righteousness must prevail as a consequence. For this same reason, God's people—whether the camp of Israel in the wilderness or the Land of Promise after settlement—must also maintain holiness and righteousness.

The only exceptions to this principle of holy war were those people who harassed Israel along their route to the Promised Land. This was not simply because of national or security concerns but because their harassment threatened to cut off God's people from God's inheritance. This was particularly the case with Moab and Midian, which together engaged in a strategy to disaffect Israel from the Lord by adulterating Israel's worship (25:1–9). Therefore the Moabites and Midianites merited the status of the Canaanites and became the object of this new generation's first full-scale engagement (31:1–2).

In this way this first major engagement portended success in the land, a success that ten of the twelve spies believed was impossible but which the two faithful ones—Caleb and Joshua—believed God would give them.

The Transjordan Tribes Compromise (Num. 32:1–42)

Before full-scale entry into the land, the tribes of Reuben and Gad, as well as a portion of Manasseh, saw that the land east of the Jordan was desirable. They sought permission from Moses to choose that territory as their allotment. Moses granted permission but only after challenging their motive: "Shall your brothers go to the war while you sit here?" (32:6). Moses either discerned or questioned that their motive mirrored that of the ten unfaithful spies (32:7). Their request would be granted only after they first showed their full trust in the Lord by supporting the other ten tribes in the conquest.

Moses's condition had a twofold purpose. One was to prove their faith. No unbeliever would have an inheritance with the Lord. They could not come short of full faith and still receive God's gracious provision. The second purpose was to preserve the covenantal solidarity of the nation. God's people are not a confederation of spiritual opportunists but are one people. There is no "each tribe for himself," much less "each man for himself." The covenantal community that trusts and obeys him is the prime venue through which God displays his power and attributes (Deut. 4:32–40). Fraternal fractures are symptoms of unbelief. After what may have been a tense standoff of undetermined duration, the so-called "Transjordan tribes" consented to participate in the conquest in support of their fellow Israelites (Num. 32:17).

The Journey Recapitulated (Num. 33:1–49)

As the dramatic time for conquest approached, Numbers recounted for the second generation all that the nation had experienced. Hardship and God's faithfulness had marked the journey from place to place. This retrospective reaches back to the foundations of Israel's provision—redemption from slavery in Egypt. Throughout the Old Testament, as here, Israel will look back upon the exodus as a principal means of engendering and strengthening faith (cf. Ps. 77:11–20).

Moses's Final Exhortation (Num. 33:50–56)

Moses issued a final exhortation to the second generation, outlining principles for allotting the land in anticipation of success. Besides implicitly anticipating success, he explicitly warned of the consequences of coming short of full obedience. Just as the Moabites' infiltration of Israel's worship and tents proved a threat to Israel's existence, even more so would the inhabitants of the land (33:55). If Israel accommodated the idolatrous Canaanites, they would become as Canaanites themselves. This warning is ominous, both here and as it is echoed in the books of Joshua and Judges (Josh. 23:6, 12–13; Judg. 2:3, 14–15, 20–23).

Final Provisions for Allotment of the Land (Num. 34:1–36:13)

Numbers concludes with additional anticipations of success. God delineated the boundaries of the land for the nine and a half tribes that would dwell there (34:1–15). And Moses empowered tribal chiefs to allocate the land (34:16–29).

As God's inheritance, the Levites did not receive a specific area of allotted land. Further, they were to perform functions for all the tribes throughout the land. Therefore, certain cities were designated as Levitical cities along with adjacent pasture lands to sustain their cultic and life needs (35:1–34). These cities would also serve a unique cultic function. As cities of refuge, they would provide sanctuary for anyone guilty of manslaughter who fled an avenging relative of the deceased. This provision reminds us that there was no absolute distinction between the cultic and the civil elements of the nation. The whole land had a cultic character because God had made it a sanctuary by his very presence. Therefore every civil crime was cultic as well (35:33).

The closing chapter of Numbers revisits the matter of the daughters of Zelophehad. In a model of jurisprudence, this case corrected the inequity or unintended consequences of the previous ruling (27:1–11). The previous ruling was not overturned but qualified so that the land that the daughters of Zelophehad might have received would not unintentionally pass out of the tribe of Manasseh if any of them married men of other tribes. This is the nature of casuistry—or case law—as an ongoing process of interpreting and applying the norms of prescriptive law. Life is complicated, and both moral reasoning and moral norms are necessary to faithful living.

Numbers concludes on the plains of Moab by the Jordan across from Jericho (36:13). The future is before the second generation, with every hopeful prospect if they will trust the Lord and act faithfully. Graciously, the past is also before them—the past of the first generation with its failings. Never were the words of William Faulkner more apt: for the second generation, "the past is never dead. It's not even past."[42] It looms behind them as a reminder even as success lies on the horizon before them.

APPROACHING THE NEW TESTAMENT

The book of Numbers fulfills an essential role in the foundations of the Old Testament. Along with Exodus and Deuteronomy, it recounts the history of God's faithful acts toward his covenant people, whom he redeemed from slavery in Egypt according to the promises made to the patriarchs. It gave Israel its shape both as a congregation ordered around the divine presence and as a holy army on the march with its divine Warrior-King in the lead. Both in the camp and on the march they were to be a holy people, consecrated to Yahweh. His gracious provision and protection even included the means of serving his sanctuary presence and of atoning for their sins.

Numbers also provides a grand object lesson on unbelief and its consequences. The first exodus generation did not trust in God's provision and protection in spite of unmerited favor. This account teaches us that unconditional grace is not without the condition of receiving and resting upon that favor. At its core, the disobedience of the first generation was a failure to believe the word of God. As Deuteronomy 1:30–32 recapitulates (cf. Deut. 9:23),

> The LORD your God who goes before you will himself fight for you, just as he did for you in Egypt before your eyes, and in the wilderness, where you have seen how the LORD your God carried you, as a man carries his son, all the way that you went until you came to this place. Yet in spite of this word you did not believe the LORD your God, who went before you in the way to seek you out a place to pitch your tents, in fire by night and in the cloud by day, to show you by what way you should go.

---

[42] William Faulkner, *Requiem for a Nun*, in *William Faulkner: Novels 1942–1954*, ed. Joseph Blotner and Noel Polk, Library of America 73 (New York: Library of America, 1994), 535.

It was not the promises of God that failed but the first generation who failed to believe those promises (Josh. 21:45).

Yet the promises of God were not in vain. God preserved a faithful remnant in Caleb, Joshua, and the second generation. After the passing of the first generation, God provided tokens of victory as they moved toward the land and anticipatory provisions for life in the land. The only enemy they truly had to fear was unbelief, especially that arising out of adulterated life and worship as recorded in the events of Baal-Peor. While the fate of the first generation was tragic, it became a means of grace to the second generation, displaying the life-and-death consequences of trusting their faithful Lord.

Even before the time of the New Testament, the lessons of Numbers played a prominent role in Israel's worship. Psalm 78 labors to review the history in Numbers:

> that the next generation might know them,
>   the children yet unborn,
> and arise and tell them to their children,
>   so that they should set their hope in God
> and not forget the works of God,
>   but keep his commandments;
> and that they should not be like their fathers,
>   a stubborn and rebellious generation,
> a generation whose heart was not steadfast,
>   whose spirit was not faithful to God. (Ps. 78:6–8)

Likewise, Psalm 95:7b–9 says,

> Today, if you hear his voice,
>   do not harden your hearts, as at Meribah,
>   as on the day at Massah in the wilderness,
> when your fathers put me to the test
>   and put me to the proof, though they had seen my work.

This lesson is not abrogated by the new covenant, contriving opposition between faith and faithful obedience. Rather it emphasizes the role that the wilderness period of redemptive history is to play in the lives of believers today: "Now these things took place as examples [τύποι] *for us*, that we might not desire evil as they did" (1 Cor. 10:6). Even as both the first and second generations in Numbers experienced God's grace, so also does everyone in the church. Yet just as with the first generation, when his grace is not met with genuine faith, it is of no benefit. Paul continues:

> Now these things happened to them as an example, but they were written down for our instruction, on whom the end of the ages has come. Therefore let anyone who thinks that he stands take heed lest he fall. (1 Cor. 10:11–12)

Quoting Psalm 95, the writer of Hebrews makes the same application and concludes, "Take care, brothers [and sisters], lest there be in any of you an evil, unbelieving heart, leading you to fall away from the living God" (Heb. 3:12).

Herein lies the critical distinction in doctrine between so-called "eternal security" and "perseverance of the saints." The former is associated with the view that there is nothing the believer can do to lose his salvation and to fall away from God's favor. "Once saved, always saved." While this may be true in itself, it is precarious by itself. For the Scriptures also teach that there is something that every believer will do in order not to fall away from God's favor—he will persevere in faith. While the ultimate cause of the believer's security is found in God and his decree, the instrumental means of his perseverance is a faith that obeys.[43] So when we encounter the New Testament's elaboration on this doctrine, we must not blunt the warnings with false assurance. Rather, we should make full use of the warnings as a means of grace so that the Spirit-awakened conscience will "examine [himself], to see whether [he is] in the faith" (2 Cor. 13:5).

The other principal way in which Numbers is meaningful to the Christian is in how it situates the church in precisely the same kind of circumstance as Israel in the wilderness. While those who are Gentiles are no longer alienated from God (Eph. 2:12, 19), Christians do live as "sojourners" and "exiles" on the earth (1 Pet. 1:17; 2:11). We are in a better position in terms of the clarity and efficacy of God's promises than those Old Testament saints who "died in faith, not having received the things promised, but having seen them and greeted them from afar" (Heb. 11:13). Through the victory of Jesus Christ, we have "come to Mount Zion and to the city of the living God, the heavenly Jerusalem" (Heb. 12:22). Nevertheless, this should not lead us into presumption, as the earlier discussion would warn us, so that we "do not refuse him who is speaking" (12:25). Our citizenship is in heaven, from which we await the appearing of our great God and Savior Jesus Christ (Phil. 3:20; Titus 2:13). Thus, as Stephen reminded the Sanhedrin, "the Most High does not dwell in houses made by hands" (Acts 7:48). So we, like the wilderness generations, await our full inheritance in the new heavens and new earth, when "the kingdom of the world has become the kingdom of our Lord and of his Christ" (Rev. 11:15). Yet, like the wilderness generations, the most important and blessed aspects of life in the Promised Land have come to us in the wilderness. For the glory descended upon the new Israel at Pentecost, and we have the living water of the Spirit and the true bread that has come down out of heaven and given life to the world (Acts 2; John 4:1–45; 6:22–59). We are not sheep without a shepherd, because the Good Shepherd has laid down his life for us and taken it up again, and he has appointed undershepherds over us so that we will know the provision and protection of God until we enter into our final rest (John 10:1–18; Acts 20:28; 1 Pet. 5:1–4). All this is because, just as the serpent was lifted up in the wilderness, Jesus Christ was lifted up on the cross to become the cursed one and to overthrow the ruler of this world (John 3:14–15; 12:31–32).

Embracing the wilderness setting of the church in exile has empowered the church throughout the ages, as embodied in one of its greatest hymns:

---

[43] For more, see the Westminster Confession of Faith, chap. 17; the Heidelberg Catechism, questions 86 and 87; Herman Bavinck, *Reformed Dogmatics*, vol. 4, *Holy Spirit, Church, and New Creation*, ed. John Bolt, trans. John Vriend (Grand Rapids, MI: Baker Academic, 2008), 269–70.

Guide me, O Thou great Jehovah,
Pilgrim through this barren land.
I am weak, but Thou art mighty;
Hold me with Thy powerful hand.
Bread of heaven, Bread of heaven,
Feed me now and evermore;
Feed me now and evermore.[44]

SELECT BIBLIOGRAPHY

Allen, Ronald B. "Numbers." In *Numbers–Ruth*. Vol. 2 of *The Expositors Bible Commentary*, edited by Tremper Longman III and David E. Garland, 23–456. Rev. ed. Grand Rapids, MI: Zondervan, 2012.

Ashley, Timothy R. *The Book of Numbers*. NICOT. Grand Rapids, MI: Eerdmans, 1993.

Baker, David W. "Wilderness, Desert." In *Dictionary of the Old Testament: Pentateuch: A Compendium of Contemporary Biblical Scholarship*, edited by T. Desmond Alexander and David W. Baker, 893–97. IVP Bible Dictionary Series 1. Downers Grove, IL: InterVarsity Press, 2003.

Brown, Raymond. *The Message of Numbers: Journey to the Promised Land*. The Bible Speaks Today. Downers Grove, IL: InterVarsity Press, 2002.

Cole, R. Dennis. *Numbers*. NAC 3B. Nashville: Broadman, 2000.

Currid, John D. *A Study Commentary on Numbers*. EP Study Commentary. Darlington, UK: Evangelical Press, 2009.

Duguid, Iain M. *Numbers: God's Presence in the Wilderness*. Preaching the Word. Wheaton, IL: Crossway, 2006.

Gillespie, George. *Aaron's Rod Blossoming, or the Divine Ordinance of Church Government Vindicated*. Harrisonburg, VA: Sprinkle, 1985.

Harrison, R. K. *Numbers*. Wycliffe Exegetical Commentary. Chicago: Moody Press, 1990.

Longman Tremper, III, and Daniel G. Reid. *God Is a Warrior*. SOTBT. Grand Rapids, MI: Zondervan, 1995.

Milgrom, Jacob. *Numbers: The Traditional Hebrew Text with the New JPS Translation*. JPS Torah Commentary. Philadelphia: The Jewish Publication Society, 1990.

Olson, D. T. "Numbers, Book of." In *Dictionary of the Old Testament: Pentateuch: A Compendium of Contemporary Biblical Scholarship*, edited by T. Desmond Alexander and David W. Baker, 611–18. IVP Bible Dictionary Series 1. Downers Grove, IL: InterVarsity Press, 2003.

Origen. *Homilies on Numbers*. Edited by Christopher A. Hall. Translated by Thomas P. Scheck. Ancient Christian Texts. Downers Grove, IL: IVP Academic, 2009.

Poythress, Vern S. *The Shadow of Christ in the Law of Moses*. Phillipsburg, NJ: P&R, 1995.

Pratt, Richard L., Jr. *He Gave Us Stories: The Bible Student's Guide to Interpreting Old Testament Narratives*. Phillipsburg, NJ: P&R, 1993.

Stubbs, David L. *Numbers*. BTCB. Grand Rapids, MI: Brazos, 2009.

Wenham, Gordon J. *Numbers: An Introduction and Commentary*. TOTC 4. Downers Grove, IL: InterVarsity Press, 1981.

---

[44] Lyrics written by William Williams in 1745 and translated from Welsh into English by Peter Williams in 1771.

5

Deuteronomy

John Scott Redd

INTRODUCTION

The book of Deuteronomy constitutes the theological core of the Old Testament. Situated at the end of the Pentateuch, this book provides a theological summation of Genesis through Numbers by way of a covenant renewal. Its position also prepares readers to encounter the Former Prophets (Joshua, Judges, Samuel, and Kings), laying the theological foundation for how God will evaluate the people in their subsequent history and outlining the covenantal principles that the prophets will evoke throughout the rest of the Old Testament.

Deuteronomy is often referred to as the hub around which the entire Old Testament revolves. Perhaps a better metaphor is that of the engine, one that is ignited and fueled by the stories of the Pentateuch and whose motion drives the subsequent histories, prophecies, and teachings that come after it. The book of Deuteronomy is a powerhouse of the Old Testament, a distillation not only of covenant theology but also of covenant history in the past and the future. For example, the so-called Shema of Deuteronomy 6:4–9 makes sense only after the creative and redemptive wonders of the Lord have been retold in detail. Yet it is the theology of the heart articulated in the Shema that returns later in Scripture, not only to evaluate the faithfulness of the king (1 Sam. 13:14; Acts 13:22; cf. 1 Sam. 10:9; 12:24; 1 Kings 2:4; 14:8; 2 Kings 10:31; 23:3, 25) but also to evaluate the faithfulness of the people (1 Kings 8:23; Jeremiah).

Readers of the New Testament should not be surprised to find that, given its central role in the Old Testament, the book of Deuteronomy is quoted at length in the teachings of Jesus and his apostles.[1] Likewise, it is no wonder that archaeologists

---

[1] Richard N. Longenecker, *Biblical Exegesis in the Apostolic Period* (Grand Rapids, MI: Eerdmans, 1975), 57–59, 108–11, 164–66, 196–97. See also N. T. Wright's assertion that Deuteronomy 27–34 forms the structural rationale for the Gospel of Matthew. N. T. Wright, *The New Testament and the People of God* (Minneapolis: Fortress, 1992), 387–90.

have collected from Qumran more manuscripts of Deuteronomy—thirty-two in all—than any other book of the Bible except the Psalms.[2]

BACKGROUND ISSUES

Title

The English name for the book derives from the Greek term δευτερονόμιον (Deut. 17:18 Septuagint), meaning "second law," a problematic translation of the Hebrew expression מִשְׁנֵה הַתּוֹרָה, which means "copy of the law." That phrase referred to the teaching that the king is called to write a copy of the law when he first ascends the throne. The Hebrew name for the book follows the ancient custom of naming a work after its initial word or group of words, which in this case is the verbless clause of Deuteronomy 1:1, אֵלֶּה הַדְּבָרִים, translated "these are the words," leading to the name (by way of transliteration) *Devarim*.

Authorship

Questions about the authorship and composition of Deuteronomy have become a complicated topic. Traditional readings of the text recognize that the book itself purports to include several public discourses by Moses, which either Moses or an anonymous narrator bound together into a cogent treatise on Israelite law and history. According to the book itself, the Israelites receive the discourses on the desert plateau of the rift valley, along the western border of Moab (Deut. 1:5; 29:1; 34:1, 8).

Many, though not all, conservative scholars today speak of the "essential Mosaic authorship" of the book (and the Pentateuch for that matter), leaving room for various positions on who compiled the speeches into a canonical text and when. Some conservative scholars recognize a narrator other than Moses who was nevertheless inspired. This narrator compiled the discourses, referred to Moses in the third person, and gave an account of Moses's death. Certain other aspects of the book's language seem to have been updated later, such as references to the Transjordan region (e.g., Deut. 1:1), which presuppose a speech situation within the land. It is quite possible that these features reflect natural updates to the text for the sake of future audiences. In Joshua 24:26, for example, Joshua appears to be adding words to the "Book of the Law of God" following the covenantal ceremony at Shechem, indicating that certain additions were made following Moses's death.

Date and Setting

Anyone familiar with critical studies of Pentateuchal composition will not be surprised to learn that much of modern critical scholarship has questioned the traditional date and setting of the first five books of the Bible.[3] Deuteronomy, however, poses several unique problems related to these questions.

---

[2] The Psalms manuscripts number thirty-seven, and the Isaiah manuscripts twenty-two. Eugene Ulrich, "The Bible in the Making: The Scriptures Found at Qumran," in *The Bible at Qumran: Text, Shape, and Interpretation*, ed. by Peter W. Flint, with the assistance of Tae Hun Kim, Studies in the Dead Sea Scrolls and Related Literature (Grand Rapids, MI: Eerdmans, 2001), 53.

[3] See Currid's treatment of Genesis authorship on p. 44 of this volume.

For one, the book of Deuteronomy, as a whole or in parts, bears many similarities to ancient Hittite treaties (particularly *Catalogues des Textes Hittites* [CTH] 113) and to neo-Assyrian documents (particularly the Vassal Treaty of Esarhaddon [VTE]), and this question has some bearing on dating.[4] If the text of Deuteronomy shares features with Hittite documents, then such a connection would corroborate a dating of the text in the second millennium BC (in the time of Moses). If, however, the text shares features with neo-Assyrian documents, then it would fit more with a seventh-century dating. Many scholars in recent decades have supported the theory of neo-Assyrian influence, though some have made efforts to revive the theory of Hittite influence.[5]

The discussion is no insignificant matter. If the Hittite connection can be proved, then the seventh-century dating falls, thereby abolishing "an Archimedian point [that critical] scholars use to date other biblical texts."[6] The reverse, however, is not true, since any connection between Deuteronomy and the neo-Assyrian VTE (especially in Deuteronomy 28) might be construed as an editorial change or update of an older document. In fact, scholars like Levinson and Stackert contend that Deuteronomy may likely contain "*multiple treaty influences* that themselves differ in significant ways."[7] As a result, the discussion of treaty type will not by itself settle the matter of date for us.

Due largely to the testimony in Deuteronomy itself (1:1; 4:44–45; 5:1; 29:1; 31:1; especially 31:9), and to the Old and the New Testament attribution of the book to Moses (2 Chron. 35:12; Ezra 3:2; 6:18; Neh. 8:1; 13:1; Mark 7:10; Luke 24:44; John 5:46; 7:19; Rom. 10:5; 1 Cor. 9:9), this chapter will assume a second-millennium dating (from the time of Moses). This position is corroborated by the book's theme that the audience ought to prepare themselves for life in the land as a *future* reality. It is further supported by the unique similarities between Deuteronomy and second-millennium Hittite treaties, such as the emphasis on the love of the vassal king (Israel) in response to the faithfulness and benevolence of the suzerain (Yahweh), as well as the requirement that the vassal and the suzerain both retain copies of the treaty. Such features are not common to the later neo-Assyrian documents.

Bearing on this discussion of date and setting is Martin Noth's proposal that Deuteronomy–Kings (excepting Ruth) constitutes a unified historical account, called

---

[4] See George E. Mendenhall, *Law and Covenant in Israel and the Ancient Near East* (Pittsburgh: Biblical Colloquium, 1955); Meredith G. Kline, *The Treaty of the Great King: The Covenant Structure of Deuteronomy: Studies and Commentary* (Grand Rapids, MI: Eerdmans, 1963); Kline, *The Structure of Biblical Authority* (Grand Rapids, MI: Eerdmans 1972); Dennis J. McCarthy, *Treaty and Covenant*, AnBib 21 (Rome: Pontifical Biblical Institute, 1963); Klaus Baltzer, *The Covenant Formulary in Old Testament, Jewish, and Early Christian Writings*, trans. David E. Green (Philadelphia: Fortress, 1971). See also Donald J. Wiseman, ed. and trans., *The Vassal-Treaties of Esarhaddon*, (London: British School of Archaeology in Iraq, 1958).

[5] See Joshua Berman, "CTH 133 and the Hittite Provenance of Deuteronomy 13," *JBL* 130, no. 1 (2011): 25–44; Berman, "Histories Twice Told: Deuteronomy 1–3 and the Hittite Treaty Prologue Tradition," *JBL* 132, no. 2 (2013): 229–50; Ada Taggar-Cohen, "Biblical *Covenant* and Hittite *išḫiul* Reexamined," *VT* 61, no. 3 (2011): 461–88. For a discussion with Berman, see Bernard M. Levinson and Jeffrey Stackert, "Between the Covenant Code and Esarhaddon's Succession Treaty: Deuteronomy 13 and the Composition of Deuteronomy," *JAJ* 3, no. 2 (2012): 133–36; Joshua Berman, "Historicism and Its Limits: A Response to Bernard M. Levinson and Jeffrey Stackert," *JAJ* 4, no. 3 (2013): 297–309; Bernard M. Levinson and Jeffrey Stackert, "The Limitations of 'Resonance': A Response to Joshua Berman on Historical and Comparative Method," *JAJ* 4 (2013): 310–33.

[6] Levinson and Stackert, "Limitations," 310.

[7] Levinson and Stackert, "Between the Covenant Code," 136 (emphasis original).

the Deuteronomistic History, most of which was organized by one anonymous voice, the so-called deuteronomistic historian.[8] In the decades since Noth published this theory in the mid-twentieth century, many aspects have been revised or debunked—in part because of its "tireless hair-splitting and verse-splitting techniques."[9] Nevertheless, Noth's theory rightly highlights at least one point, namely, that the perspective of the book of Deuteronomy provides a clear theological foundation for the historiography of Joshua–Kings. The distribution of the land, the reigns of the judges, the emergence of the kings, and the faith of the people all seem to be evaluated according to the teaching of the book of Deuteronomy. Since it appears that Moses is the author, allowing for minimal editorial additions by a later hand, then the text should be read in light of the historical circumstances immediately preceding the conquest of the land.

Audience

The authority and echoes of Deuteronomy in the Bible support the text's own witness that Moses is speaking not merely to his immediate audience on the plains of Moab but also to the faithful generations who will descend from them (Deut. 5:2–3; 31:9–13, 24–26). Depending on one's dating of the conquest, this would put the addresses of Deuteronomy at either the late fifteenth or late thirteenth century BC. The speeches would have been compiled slightly later, if one avoids the ditch on either side of the ideological road: the conservative one (Moses wrote prophetically of his own death) and the critical one (Deuteronomy is, like the histories that follow it, an exilic or postexilic literary creation).[10]

The audience, therefore, in our reading is the second generation of Israelites to come out of Egypt. With the exception of Joshua and Caleb, this generation is composed of the children of the unfaithful Israelites who rejected the Lord at the base of Mount Sinai even before the Lord ratified his covenant with them (Exodus 32–34). In doing so, this first generation rejected the gift of deliverance that the Lord had bestowed on them in the exodus, and so God gave the eschatological promise of land to their children instead. In Deuteronomy, this promise is offered to the second generation of the exodus, the audience awaiting instructions on the steppes of Moab, as well as to those future generations who would inherit and live in the land (Deut. 31:9–13).

Taken as a whole, the internal logic of the book assumes a conquest-era audience, and it addresses the concerns of this audience explicitly and implicitly. In doing so, it answers questions like these:

- Will the Lord go with them in conquest?
- Can they rely on him to deliver the land to them?

[8] Martin Noth, *Schriften der Königsberger Gelehrten Gesellschaft* (1943; 2nd ed. *Überlieferungsgeschichtliche Studien* [Tübingen: Max Niemeyer Verlag, 1957]; 3rd ed. 1967).
[9] Antony F. Campbell and Mark A. O'Brien, *Unfolding the Deuteronomistic History: Origins, Upgrades, Present Text* (Minneapolis: Fortress, 2000), 2–3. See especially Gerhard von Rad, *Studies in Deuteronomy*, SBT 9 (London: SCM, 1953); Frank M. Cross, *Canaanite Myth and Hebrew Epic: Essays in the History of the Religion of Israel* (Cambridge, MA: Harvard University Press, 1973), 287–89; Linda S. Schearing and Steven L. McKenzie, eds., *Those Elusive Deuteronomists: The Phenomenon of Pan-Deuteronomism*, JSOTSup 268 (Sheffield: Sheffield Academic Press, 1999).
[10] Bruce K. Waltke, "The Date of the Conquest," *WTJ* 52, no. 2 (1990): 181–200.

- How should they treat nations in the land?
- What about nations outside the land?
- How might they live productive lives in the land, avoiding the discipline their parents experienced in the desert?
- What can they expect from this covenant with the Lord in the future?

Such concerns were imminently practical for the generation of the conquest and for the lives that awaited them in the land.

The book also assumes a timelessness in application as well. To use the common metaphor for biblical interpretation, the modern reader is clearly overhearing a conversation between God and a historic community, but it is a conversation that is meant to be overheard. The modern audience ought to pay heed to the addresses of Moses. They ought to feel acknowledged in the text through its references to the covenant community of the future. Again and again, the book implicitly addresses them as the children mentioned in the Shema (Deut. 6:4–9; cf. 6:2), the recipients of the law held secure by the priests and elders (Deut. 31:9), and those who might attest to Moses's standing as a singular prophet in Israelite history (34:10–12).

Moses enjoyed unequaled access to Yahweh himself (Num. 12:6–8), and he held authority as the covenant mediator who articulates and administers the law of God for the people of God. He was unlike any other prophet known to the implied audience of the book, and his stature shows that the book is presented as covenantal literature for the kingdom of God for all time.

STRUCTURE AND OUTLINE

The discovery of ancient Hittite and Assyrian treaty documents had profound effects on the study of Deuteronomy's structure. By the 1950s, scholars like George Mendenhall had already presented helpful observations about similarities between the elements of ancient Near Eastern treaties and the structure of this biblical book. Later scholars such as Kline, McCarthy, and Baltzer developed this structure, adding detail and noting similarities with other treaty formats.[11] While the elements differ slightly, the basic format of such treaties emerges as follows:

    I. Historical Prologue (cf. Deut. 1:1–4:43)
   II. Stipulations (cf. Deut. 4:44–26:19)
  III. Provisions for Storing the Covenant and Reading It Periodically (cf. Deut. 31:9–13)
  IV. List of Witnesses (no clear parallel in Deuteronomy, though witnesses are mentioned in ceremonial summons [cf. Deut. 30:19–20] and the song of Moses [cf. Deut. 32:1, 43])
   V. Blessings and Curses (cf. Deut. 27:1–28:68)

In a treaty or covenant document, these elements can be varied in their placement, as visible in the similarities identified above. The outline of the book appears

---

[11] See note 4 on p. 135.

to loosely follow the format of an ancient treaty while maintaining its own unique elements. For instance, the book traces several public addresses given by Moses, whose personal passion often comes out in the oration. As a result, some describe the book's genre as "preached law," and McConville is certainly correct in noting that the format of treaty, as it is currently understood, seems to be employed rather "freely."[12] Deuteronomy is both political and pedagogical, legislative and homiletic. While the book has national implications (which are applied in Israel's history), it also serves the purpose of instructing the individual in the ways of the Lord—how they ought to love him and what that means for their life in the land.

Some scholars have argued for an outline that highlights certain literary features, and these approaches can be highly illuminating. Christensen makes one of the most compelling proposals, mapping the text as a concentric pattern:

a   The Outer Frame: A Look Backward (Deuteronomy 1–3)
  b   The Inner Frame: The Great Peroration (Summary) (4–11)
    c   The Central Core: Covenant Stipulations (12–26)
  b' The Inner Frame: The Covenant Ceremony (27–30)
a' The Outer Frame: A Look Forward (31–34)[13]

This format has much to commend it, and its divisions follow the broad categories of the covenantal format. It could be taken as a corollary to the general covenantal understanding of the book's order. Perhaps most convincing about this arrangement of the text is the centrality of the covenant stipulations and the clear continuity between the "outer frames," which exhibit observable repetition from chapter 3 to chapter 31.

In this work, we will use an outline of Deuteronomy that is framed largely by covenantal concerns.

  I. Historical Prologue (1:1–4:43)
  II. Stipulations (4:44–26:19)
    A. Ten Commandments (4:44–5:33)
    B. First commandment: Monotheism (6:1–11:32)
    C. Second commandment: Worship (12:1–32)
    D. Third commandment: Honoring the name (13:1–14:21)
    E. Fourth commandment: Sabbath (14:22–16:17)
    F. Fifth commandment: Honoring authority (16:18–18:22)
    G. Sixth commandment: Human dignity (19:1–22:12)
    H. Seventh commandment: Sexual fidelity (22:13–23:18)
    I. Eighth commandment: Personal property (23:19–24:22)
    J. Ninth commandment: Truthfulness (25:1–19)
    K. Tenth commandment: Contentment (26:1–15)
    L. Formal conclusion (26:16–19)
  III. Ratification Ceremony (27:1–28:68)
  IV. Redemptive-Historical Prospectus: Blessings and Curses (29:1–30:20)
  V. Historical Epilogue (31:1–34:12)

---

[12] J. Gordon McConville, *Deuteronomy*, ApOTC 5 (Downers Grove, IL: InterVarsity Press, 2002), 24.
[13] Duane L. Christensen, *Deuteronomy 1–21:9*, rev. ed., WBC 6A (Dallas: Word, 2001), lviii.

MESSAGE AND THEOLOGY

Historical Prologue (Deut. 1:1–4:43)

The greater part of the first four chapters deals with the redemptive-historical background for the theological treatise to follow. The first five verses of chapter 1 establish the time, place, and speaker of the discourses that follow. Moses delivered the discourses on the east side of the Jordan, an eleven-day march from Horeb (Sinai). Despite the relatively short distance, the disobedient generation had languished in the wilderness for more than thirty-eight years, traversing the region before arriving at the Jordan (Deut. 2:14; cf. Numbers 13–14). After alluding to Israel's disobedience, the narrator points to the Lord's care for them in the defeat of Sihon the Amorite and Og of Bashan (Deut. 1:4). This description of God's favor in spite of Israel's disobedience sets the agenda for the travelogue of Israel in the wilderness found in Deuteronomy 1:6–4:43.

The travelogue begins with Moses receiving the word from the Lord at Mount Horeb, after the exodus from Egypt has taken place. Though the account mentions the confrontation between Moses and Pharaoh only generally (cf. Deut. 1:30; 4:34), the exodus looms large in the theology of the book of Deuteronomy, standing as the redemptive foundation for the covenant that God is establishing with his people (1:27, 30; 4:20, 34, 37, 45–46; 5:6, 15; 6:21; 9:26; 16:1, 6, 12; 23:4; 24:9; 25:17; 26:8). The law that Moses reiterates here for the people of God is not a means by which they are to earn either their redemption from slavery or the presence of the Lord in their midst. These blessings belong to them as God's people. The instruction of Deuteronomy explains theologically what these events mean for Israel as God's people, and it offers a faithful, inspired guide for how Israel ought to respond to their singular, holy, and loving covenant Lord.

Moses recounts how, following their departure from Horeb (1:6–8), he established a system of judges who would help him govern the people as they traveled in the wilderness (1:9–18). He then relates how the exodus generation disobeyed at Kadesh-Barnea (1:19–33) and how the Lord subsequently judged them (1:34–46). The following section describes the wilderness wandering, including several historical asides about the mighty people groups who lived in the region and about the Lord's distribution of land to other nations (2:1–25). Near the end of the wilderness years, Israel is confronted with two stubborn kings, Sihon and Og, both of whom are defeated and whose land in the Transjordan is allotted to Israel since they treated God's people inhospitably (2:26–3:22; cf. Gen. 12:3; Num. 24:9). This travelogue section ends with Moses's personal account of desiring to enter the land and the Lord refusing to grant his request because of Moses's disobedience (3:28–29). Deuteronomy makes no mention of the offending event, but the account of Numbers 27:12–14 describes Moses as failing to venerate the Lord properly at the spring of Meribah.

This section (4:1–43) moves to a theological summary of the covenant. In response to his divine favor, the Lord requires faithfulness from his people (4:1–14) and singularity of worship (4:15–31) that acknowledges his claim as covenant Lord (4:31). The purpose of recounting the Lord's past benevolence is to strengthen the faithful response of his people in the present that they "might know that the LORD is God; there is no other besides him" (4:35). This pattern of past blessings as the foundation for present faith is distinctly covenantal in nature and is present throughout Scripture (e.g., Deut. 6:20–25; 1 Sam. 17:34–37; Isa. 5:1–4; Mic. 6:3–8; Acts 7:1–53; Rom. 1:1–6).

The final passage of this section (Deut. 4:41–43) reveals God's concern for mercy expressed in the establishment of three cities of refuge in the Transjordan region. The notion of established refuges is found in Exodus 21:13, while the number of six cities of refuge is set out in Numbers 35:6—three in the Transjordan and three to be established in Canaan (Deut. 19:1–13).

Stipulations (Deut. 4:44–26:19)

The longest section of Deuteronomy deals with the stipulations of the covenant. Stephen Kaufman argues convincingly that the order and content of the Ten Commandments set the structural agenda for this section, though scholars have widely disagreed about how the commandments should be organized.[14] In this chapter, the outline of the commandments and the corresponding sections of Deuteronomy follow the divisions proposed by John Walton with minor modifications.[15]

Ten Commandments (Deut. 4:44–5:33)

Deuteronomy 4:44–49 introduces the section on the laws that are to follow, first in the Ten Commandments and then in their exposition. This passage forms an *inclusio* with the headnote (1:1–5) due to the elements that are repeated in both passages. For instance, both 1:1–5 and 4:44–49 mention that Moses gave "this law" (זֹאת הַתּוֹרָה; 1:5; 4:44) to Israel in the Transjordan (1:1; 4:46). Both mention Sihon whom Moses "defeated" (1:4; 4:46), as well as Og (1:4; 4:47) and the Arabah (1:1; 4:49). While Kline included this section with the prologue in his outline, he admits that it is "transitional" in nature, both concluding the prologue and introducing the stipulations.[16] Because of the multiplicity of terms related to covenantal stipulations—e.g., "the testimonies, the statutes, and the rules," הָעֵדֹת וְהַחֻקִּים וְהַמִּשְׁפָּטִים (4:45; cf. 5:31; 6:20; 2 Chron. 33:8)—as well as the need for a headnote for Moses's second discourse, there is a benefit to reading Deuteronomy 4:44–49 with the following section of stipulations, as is done in this chapter.

The next passage (5:1–33) reminds God's people about the covenant he made with them at Horeb (Sinai), which is here summarized in the Ten Commandments.[17]

---

[14] Stephen A. Kaufman, "The Structure of the Deuteronomic Law," *Maarav* 1, no. 2 (1979): 105–58.

[15] John H. Walton, "Deuteronomy: An Exposition of the Spirit of the Law," *Grace Theological Journal* 8, no. 2 (1987): 213–25; Andrew E. Hill and John H. Walton, *A Survey of the Old Testament* (Grand Rapids, MI: Zondervan, 2009), 169; Jack R. Lundbom, *Deuteronomy: A Commentary* (Grand Rapids, MI: Eerdmans, 2013), 77–78; Walton, "The Decalogue Structure of the Deuteronomic Law," *Interpreting Deuteronomy: Issues and Approaches*, ed. David G. Firth and Philip S. Johnston (Downers Grove, IL: IVP Academic, 2012), 93–117.

[16] Kline, *Treaty of the Great King*, 61.

[17] There are several small but not insignificant differences between the stipulations found in Deuteronomy and those found in Ex. 20:1–17, including the rationale for Sabbath observance (creation in Exodus vs. slavery and redemption in Deuteronomy) and the extent of the application of the tenth commandment. For a more thorough comparison, see John D. Currid, *Deuteronomy*, EP Study Commentary (Darlington, UK: Evangelical Press, 2006), 121–54.

Moses himself introduces this section, reminding his audience about his role as covenant mediator because they were afraid of the Lord (5:4–5; Ex. 20:18–19). The people can be confident that the Lord has not abandoned them in the wilderness. He has been faithful, and consequently they ought to respond by hearing, learning, and keeping the Lord's commands (Deut. 5:1).

The commandments are presented as a direct quotation of the Lord, who follows the covenantal structure by citing past blessings as grounds for present faith. The proclamation "I am the LORD your God, who brought you out of the land of Egypt" (5:6) creates the context in which God requires covenant faithfulness. We should note that the Ten Commandments are annunciated first and foremost *in response* to divine benevolence, not *as the grounds* of divine benevolence. The Lord first identifies himself as Israel's Redeemer and then gives the commandments. Table 14 lists them with their respective expositions later in the book.

Commandment	Declaration	Exposition
First commandment: Monotheism	Ex. 20:3; Deut. 5:7	Deut. 6:1–11:32
Second commandment: Worship	Ex. 20:4–6; Deut. 5:8–10	Deut. 12:1–32
Third commandment: Honoring the name	Ex. 20:7; Deut. 5:11	Deut. 13:1–14:21
Fourth commandment: Sabbath	Ex. 20:8–11; Deut. 5:12–15	Deut. 14:22–16:17
Fifth commandment: Honoring authority	Ex. 20:12; Deut. 5:16	Deut. 16:18–18:22
Sixth commandment: Human dignity	Ex. 20:13; Deut. 5:17	Deut. 19:1–22:12
Seventh commandment: Sexual fidelity	Ex. 20:14; Deut. 5:18	Deut. 22:13–23:18
Eighth commandment: Personal property	Ex. 20:15; Deut. 5:19	Deut. 23:19–24:22
Ninth commandment: Truthfulness	Ex. 20:16; Deut. 5:20	Deut. 25:1–19
Tenth commandment: Contentment	Ex. 20:17; Deut. 5:21	Deut. 26:1–15

Table 14

Organizing the commandments into categories can help clarify their logic. The division that appears immediately is between those commandments dealing with God's character (first–fourth) and those dealing with human interaction (fifth–tenth). The Ten Commandments are theocentric (i.e., God-centered) in the sense that they show how humans relate best with each other when they first understand how to relate to God. We will explore this aspect of the commandments further when we discuss Deuteronomy 6:4–9.

John Walton has proposed a twofold table of laws, each referring to particular aspects of divine and human character (see table 15).[18]

Divine	Category	Human
Commandment 1	**Authority**	Commandment 5
Commandment 2	**Dignity**	Commandments 6–8
Commandment 3	**Commitment**	Commandment 9
Commandment 4	**Rights and Privileges**	Commandment 10

Table 15

Longman and Dillard are correct to note that Walton's proposed organization (including the idea that the Ten Commandments set the agenda for the rest of the stipulations) is not altogether clear from the divisions of the book.[19] Still, this way of organizing the commandments does provide a useful paradigm for studying and teaching the book of Deuteronomy. This sort of approach also highlights an important aspect of the Ten Commandments and, in fact, the whole book of Deuteronomy. The commandments are not to be read as merely precise, discrete rules for particular relationships and situations, but rather, they introduce categories and principles meant to be applied to all life: "when you sit in your house, and when you walk by the way, and when you lie down, and when you rise" (Deut. 6:7).[20]

First Commandment: Monotheism (Deut. 6:1–11:32)

The exposition of the first commandment sets the theological foundation for the commandments that follow. It bears covenantal priority because it is the fundamental principle for faith and wisdom. It is not surprising that one of the great confessional statements of the Old Testament, the Shema, appears at the outset of this section (6:4–9). After all, if God is "their LORD" and if he is "one," then their response should be commensurate with his character, one of singular love throughout the whole person, including "heart," "soul," and "might." The Shema emphasizes love that begins within the person and extends to all aspects of life. This inner-to-outer movement is further described in the passage that follows (6:6–9). God's instructions are to be on the heart, bound to the body, discussed in the household and in every sphere of life, and evident in the use of property and in commerce. These commands are repeated in Deuteronomy 11:18–20 and thus provide a frame for this entire section. According to Moses, God desires not merely a cognitive assent to his lordship but the whole of his people.

In the following discussion, Moses describes the victories that Israel will experience in Canaan, emphasizing the Lord's complete control of the upcoming conquest

---

[18] Walton, "The Decalogue Structure of the Deuteronomic Law," 94.
[19] Tremper Longman III and Raymond B. Dillard, *An Introduction to the Old Testament*, 2nd ed. (Grand Rapids, MI: Zondervan, 2006), 113.
[20] Currid, *Deuteronomy*, 20–21.

lest the Israelites seek aid from the false gods of the Canaanites. The chapter closes with a call to pass down the theological tradition from generation to generation (6:20–25). Here Moses includes the inheritance of the land along with the exodus as a key part of God's benevolence in the past. God's faithfulness and sovereignty are so indisputable that the upcoming conquest can be treated as an accomplished reality.

Moses continues by describing Israel's status as chosen by God, warning against rebellion, and reminding the people of their past faithlessness. Then he makes a second declaration of God's unique lordship: "the LORD [Yahweh] your God is God of gods and Lord of lords, the great, the mighty, and the awesome God, who is not partial and takes no bribe" (Deut. 10:17). The emphasis on social justice in this passage provides an opportunity to introduce the plight of the stranger, the widow, and the orphan. This threefold category represents the disenfranchised of Israel's society, and the Lord reveals that, unlike many pagan deities, he will not show favoritism based on social status. This combination occurs elsewhere in Deuteronomy (10:18; 14:29; 16:11, 14; 24:17, 19–21; 26:12–13; 27:19) and in the prophets (Jer. 7:6; Ezek. 22:7; Zech. 7:10; Mal. 3:5). His people are called to take up the cause of the disenfranchised. If they do not, then the Lord will take up their cause to the detriment of their oppressors. The divine relationship is meant to influence human relationships. God's people are to relate to one another in a way that reflects how he relates to them as individuals and as a community (see fig. 2).

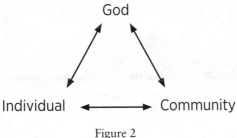

Figure 2

This dynamic between God, the individual, and the community provides a paradigm for biblical ethics as a whole. God's redemptive aims for the community offer inspiration, modeling, and purpose for interpersonal relations between individuals and the community. Because God showed mercy to his people when they were in Egypt, their relationships ought likewise to be marked by mercy and justice (Deut. 10:18–19; Mic. 6:8). The covenant makes claims on all their relationships: how they relate to individuals, how they relate to the community, and how they relate to the Lord.

Second Commandment: Worship (Deut. 12:1–32)

Once Israel enters the land of Canaan, they will be confronted with the idolatry of its former inhabitants. The message of this section is clear: Israel is to have nothing to do with idol collection or practice. Two key elements arise from this exposition of the second commandment. First, Israel must completely destroy all idols and pagan paraphernalia because the Lord has banned them from his worship. Second, the Lord will choose a location where he will place his name and make his dwelling (12:5, 11, 21; 14:23–24; 16:2, 6, 11; 26:2). The correlation between God's name and his presence is important; it will become a common refrain used to describe the center of worship in the land. The presence of the Lord requires holy worship. This worship must not draw from the practices of those in the land (12:4, 30, 31) but must follow the Lord's instructions.

We should also note that the Lord encourages his people to enjoy the abundant resources they will encounter in the land (12:15), but they must do it according to his instructions. In that way, they will exhibit the special relationship they have with their covenantal Lord. These instructions also display the Lord's mercy as he makes concessions for those who live too far from the worship center (12:21–23).

Third Commandment: Honoring the Name (Deut. 13:1–14:21)

The commandment to honor the name of the Lord involves more than merely honoring the Lord with one's speech, even if this is the primary application heard in the church today. The name of the Lord represents his presence, a presence that renders his people holy and set apart from the nations. The Lord does not merely require monotheistic faith and rejection of idol worship; he requires faithfulness that touches every aspect of the Israelites' lives. They must not take him lightly, nor should they mistake him for the local pagan deities who could be manipulated in order to give the people the object of their desire (usually related to the agricultural cycle).

This section evokes commitment to the Lord, whose name (presence) is in their midst. It opens by denouncing false prophets, whom God uses as a divine test to see if the Israelites' hearts are wholly committed to him (13:3). False prophets must be purged, as must be family members and friends who attempt to draw one away from the Lord. And when someone makes a charge of syncretism or idolatry, the Israelites must investigate carefully and put to death the guilty parties as if they were Canaanites subject to the ban (13:12–17).

The people's covenantal relationship with God, which calls for their holiness, also carries implications for the way they deal with animals. Covenant making in the ancient Near East is often depicted in familial terms, describing the two parties as father and son or as husband and wife[21]—a parallel that sheds light on the use of sonship language in 14:1. Having been set apart from the other nations by their divine father, Israel is called to distinguish between clean and unclean animals (see also the Holiness Code in Leviticus 17–26). The categories of clean and unclean physically reinforce the spiritual categories of holy and profane, a practical applica-

---

[21] Frank M. Cross, "Kinship and Covenant in Ancient Israel," in *From Epic to Canon: History and Literature in Ancient Israel* (Baltimore: Johns Hopkins University Press, 1998), 3–21.

tion that places a premium on discerning between the two and disciplining oneself to remain holy and clean.[22]

Fourth Commandment: Sabbath (Deut. 14:22–16:17)

Sabbath observance implied more than merely setting aside the end of the workweek as holy to the Lord. This section begins with a mandate to return to the Lord a tenth of one's produce, a practice that finds precedence going back to the patriarchs (Gen. 14:20; 28:22; cf. Lev. 27:30–32; Num. 18:21–28). God offers a concession to those who must travel a long distance to the central sanctuary; they may exchange their livestock and goods for silver to be exchanged back after the journey. Every third year a tenth is to be set aside for the care of the Levites, who have no inheritance in the land (Num. 18:20) and for the disenfranchised who depend on such gifts for sustenance (Deut. 14:29).

The Lord set aside every seventh year as a year of "release," when the Israelites were to cancel debts. Some scholars have argued that this year of release refers to a year of reprieve after which the debt is reinstated, but such a view seems implausible.[23] More likely, the loans and repayment schedule would be calculated based on the time until the year of release to protect both the lender and borrower. Foreigners in the land do not receive the blessing of release (15:3), perhaps in an effort to entice them toward covenant membership.

Servants should be treated fairly and should also be offered release from service in the seventh year, unless they choose to stay and serve in perpetuity. Again, Moses justifies this kind of fair treatment on the basis of Israel's identity as a nation that was redeemed from slavery (15:15).[24]

The apparent contradiction between 15:4, "there will be no poor among you," and 15:11, "there will never cease to be poor in the land," can be clarified by the nuances of Hebrew grammar. The verb used in verse 4 should be understood as having obligatory force ("ought") rather than predictive force ("will"), since Moses is making a point about the ideal situation that should obtain in the land. Moses, however, recognizes the tragic reality of the poor and the ample opportunity that God's people will have to serve them with generosity.

Firstborn male animals are to be dedicated to the Lord, which itself is an act of faith, expressing a reliance on the Lord to provide again in the future. The Israelites are to eat these animals yearly in the sanctuary that the Lord chooses. Firstborn animals that are deformed or have any blemish may be eaten in the hometown without any of the ritual reserved for sacrifices as long as the cleanness rules described previously are followed (12:16, 23–24; cf. Acts 15:29).

---

[22] T. Desmond Alexander, *From Paradise to Promised Land: An Introduction to the Pentateuch*, 2nd ed. (Grand Rapids, MI: Baker Academic, 2002), 110–22; Patrick D. Miller, *The Religion of Ancient Israel* (Louisville: Westminster John Knox, 2000), 149–55; 158–61.

[23] For this position, see Peter C. Craigie, *The Book of Deuteronomy*, NICOT (Grand Rapids, MI: Eerdmans, 1976), 236–37. For the contrary, see Eugene H. Merrill, *Deuteronomy*, NAC 4 (Nashville: B&H, 1994), 243–44, following A. D. H. Mayes, *Deuteronomy: Based on the Revised Standard Version*, NCB (Grand Rapids, MI: Eerdmans, 1981), 247–48.

[24] The legislation regarding manumission of slaves in Deuteronomy may be more generous than the corresponding instructions in Ex. 21:1–11, which does not include female slaves and their children. Lundbom, *Deuteronomy*, 49–50. Or possibly the latter case assumes that the year of liberation does not apply to the female slave.

Finally, all males are required to participate in the three pilgrimage feasts of the liturgical calendar: the Feast of Unleavened Bread (Passover), the Feast of Weeks (Pentecost), and the Feast of Booths (or Tabernacles). These three feasts mark key moments in the agricultural cycle, and during these feasts every male of the family is called to appear "as he is able" in the sanctuary before the Lord in response to the blessings received from him (Deut. 16:16–17; cf. Ex. 23:17; 34:23). The explicit mention of females in Deuteronomy 16:11 and 16:14 indicates that they were encouraged but not required to participate.

Fifth Commandment: Honoring Authority (Deut. 16:18–18:22)

The commandment to honor parental authority also relates to authority structures outside the family unit. The people are to appoint judges whose jurisdiction will be composed of the tribe out of which they were called. This justice system will depend on the impartiality of the judges and the honesty of all who participate in the system, and the prosperity of the people in the land will depend on the integrity of the system (16:20). God sets certain limitations in place; for example, in capital offenses, the alleged perpetrator may not be put to death on the testimony of one witness. The justice system must be above reproach because anyone who openly rejects its judgment may be put to death (17:12–13).

God had long before promised that his people would produce kings (Gen. 17:6, 20), but the Mosaic covenant set limitations on this royal office and warned the people that human kingship could produce unintended consequences. The king of Israel must be chosen by the Lord and must descend from an Israelite tribe (Deut. 17:15). He must not accrue many horses or acquire many wives, whose competing commitments would draw his heart from the Lord, nor should he build up excessive wealth. Upon ascending the throne, he must write a copy of the law by his own hand and read it regularly throughout his reign. Each of these stipulations was meant to ensure the king remained committed to God as he guided the people of Israel. It is not extraneous to point out that King Solomon's failure in these areas indicated that his reign would not usher in the prosperity for which many had hoped (1 Kings 10:14–11:8).

The last category of authority to be described in this section is the special purpose and place of the tribe of Levi in the Mosaic administration. Moses and Aaron were Levites, and the Lord had set apart their tribe for special cultic purposes. The tribe's lack of inheritance in the land indicates their special service to the Lord. Priests are to hail from Aaron's line, but the entirety of the tribe receives certain privileges and performs certain responsibilities. In this passage, God reveals more details concerning how Israel is to provide for the needs of the Levites (cf. Lev. 7:32–34; Num. 18:11–12), lays out rules for accommodating Levites serving in the sanctuary, and identifies Canaanite practices that Israel is to rigorously reject.

As covenant mediator, Moses represented the highest authority as the prophet who spoke the words of the covenant Lord to the people. The future prophet described in Deuteronomy 18:15 would perform the role of mediator between the people and the

Lord, seeing God face-to-face in order to receive the divine revelation for the people. A true prophet makes verifiable statements about the future because he is speaking for a sovereign, unchanging God who brings his will to bear in human history (Isa. 46:8–11). The same cannot be said of false or pagan prophets, because they cannot gain access to the divine assembly (Jer. 23:16–22).

Sixth Commandment: Human Dignity (Deut. 19:1–22:12)

God bestowed a great measure of dignity on humanity when he made them in his image (Gen. 1:27), so any perversion or dishonoring of that image must be taken seriously. That means grave consequences for those who take human life. But in cases of unintentional homicide, the dignity of the perpetrator must also be honored through cities of refuge. Just as three cities of refuge were set aside in the Transjordan (Deut. 4:41–43), so must three cities be appointed in Canaan, where these individuals may be safe from reprisal while their case is considered. If a person is found to be guilty of murder, it falls to the community to turn him over for punishment.

The implications of human dignity extend beyond the taking of life and overlap in some ways with the seventh and eighth commandments. Personal property is founded upon the distribution of the land following the conquest, and the people are to honor such distribution as marked by boundary stones. Likewise, the whole system of justice that upholds these safeguards depends on fair trials and honest witnesses. The famous *lex talionis* ("an eye for an eye . . . ," 19:21) ensures that sentences should be rigorous but commensurate with the degree and kind of crime committed.

Honoring life also has implications for the way in which Israelite armies fight the nation's wars. Unlike the exodus generation, they must trust in the Lord as their Warrior who fights for them. He will confound the superior technology or numbers they will face on the field of battle. Because the Lord wants his people to enjoy the blessings of the land, those who are recently married or have newly acquired crops are exempt from military service (20:1–9). They will face two kinds of people groups as a nation: those situated outside the land and those living in the land. The simple fact that the Lord gives rules for engagement outside the land indicates his desire for the nation to expand outside the borders of Canaan. This engagement is to be marked by diplomacy and alliances. Those living in the land, however, are to be devoted to destruction, as a result of their widespread sin (Gen. 15:16). We should note that the Canaanite Rahab repents and joins with the Israelite army under Joshua, and not only is her life spared but she also receives an honored position in the lineage of David and Jesus (Matt. 1:5; cf. Heb. 11:31; James 2:25), suggesting that faithful repentance may have been an acceptable way of escaping destruction.

The concern for human dignity informs recompense in unsolved murder cases (Deut. 21:1–9), the protection of female captives in war (21:10–14), and the inheritance rights of firstborn sons (21:15–17). This latter passage reveals that the Mosaic system tolerated the ancient practice of polygamy, though the Old Testament rarely describes it in a positive light. But what is most striking is the protection afforded the unfavored wife in such arrangements. Fathers are required to recognize the rights of primogeniture even when doing so conflicts with their personal affections.

In a system of government that relies upon stable family dynamics in order to protect the stability of the nation, sustained rebellion against parents is tantamount to treason against the state. Furthermore, rejecting parental authority perhaps betrays a deeper inclination to reject the Lord's authority, an offense taken very seriously. As a result, such sustained rebellion is a capital offense under the Mosaic administration (21:18–21). It should be noted that the verb forms in this passage (as well as several other passages) may be read as permissive in modality (e.g., "*may* stone him to death," 21:21), instead of merely commissive (e.g., "*shall* stone him to death"), identifying a maximum instead of a mandatory sentence.

The final section (22:1–12) is transitional. It introduces miscellaneous legislation related to the dignity of life (pertaining to negligence, 22:8) and private property (22:1–4), as well as issues concerning sexuality and procreation (22:5, 6–7) and mixing of types (22:9–11). The diversity of topics handled resists classification for those seeking to map out the logic of the legal collection.

Seventh Commandment: Sexual Fidelity (Deut. 22:13–23:18)

God calls his people to a holistic covenantal faithfulness that transforms every aspect of life, including physical relationships. In the theology of Deuteronomy, the physical realm and the human body matter, so we should not be surprised to find that the Lord requires faithfulness in the area of human sexuality. The seventh commandment prohibits sexual intercourse outside marriage, thereby establishing loving covenantal marriage as the proper relational sphere within which humans exercise their sexuality. Marriage provides the relational plumb line by which all sexual freedoms and prohibitions are understood. The laws prescribed in Deuteronomy 22:13–30 each deal with sexuality inside and outside the marriage covenant. While not exhaustive, these laws do establish certain principles for the protection of sexual wholeness within marriage.[25]

At a time when women depended on men for safety and well-being, as seen in the dilemma presented in the book of Ruth, these laws gave advantages to women. Such stipulations provide them with protections from abandonment (22:13–21), from encounters outside the community (22:25–27), and from sexual exploitation before they were married (22:28–29). Many of these laws may seem insensitive to the modern Western reader, but they were meant to safeguard the marriage covenant as the foundation of family and community structures. We should note that, later in this passage, Israelite men and women are also strictly prohibited from being consigned to cultic prostitution, a significant protection of their sexual dignity and the honor of the Lord (23:17–18).

---

[25] Old Testament sexual ethics tolerates polygamy while never presenting it as a goal (Deut. 21:15–17), much like it tolerates divorce in certain cases due to "hardness of heart," a point Jesus notes in Matt. 19:8. Jesus, however, affirms that the model for biblical marriage is one man and one wife. Similarly, the New Testament bars polygamists from service as church elders, listing polygamy in a list of other attributes like drunkenness, inhospitality, greed, and a propensity for violence, all of which are considered sins for all Christians, not merely candidates for church leadership (1 Tim. 3:2–3).

As in the case of the animal divisions (14:3–21), the Israelites are to observe divisions related to human sexuality. Those whose sexual organs are deformed or mutilated are prevented from entering the holy assembly, as are the descendants of couplings forbidden by the law (23:1–2). This is not to say that such individuals were barred from covenant membership but that certain restrictions reminded the Israelites of the Lord's holiness. Cleanness laws also relate to bodily emissions and uncleanness, and certain procedures are necessary in order to restore the individual to the community (23:9–14).

Providing protection for runaway slaves, the laws of Deuteronomy 23:15–16 anticipate the eighth commandment regarding matters of personal property and the intention of the slave who seeks relief. The law regarding prostitution (23:17–18), however, again addresses the issue of sexual integrity and as such belongs with the section related to the seventh commandment.

Eighth Commandment: Personal Property (Deut. 23:19–24:22)

The commandment not to steal touches upon a range of issues related to personal property. God forbids interest-based loan arrangements as a form of exploiting members of the community, though embedded in this directive is the incentive for foreigners to join the covenant community in order to enjoy the same protection (23:19–20). Solemn vows are to be kept as moral commitments (23:21–23). The Israelites are to honor the produce of a neighbor's field—one might take a meal's worth, but the unauthorized harvest of another's crop is outlawed (23:24–25). The community is to protect dignity and social status as well; thus, after an authorized divorce, a woman is free to remarry and cannot be exploited by her previous husband (24:1–4).

The laws prohibiting the newly married from serving in the military (24:5) and the use of a millstone as surety for a pledge (24:6) reveal a concern for the right of the individual to work and provide for a family. Holding a millstone for a debt affords the creditor nothing of value but merely prevents the debtor from working to pay back the debt and further support himself and his family. Likewise, any sort of servitude based on kidnapping is considered unjust and qualifies as a capital offense (Deut. 24:7; cf. Ex. 21:16). As in Exodus 22:25–26, surety like a cloak must be treated in a way that favors the debtor (Deut. 24:10–13). Social equity ought to be pursued at all levels of business: workers ought to be paid in a timely manner (24:14–15), the disenfranchised protected from predatory lending (24:17–18), and the basic needs of the marginalized provided for by the community (24:19–22).

Ninth Commandment: Truthfulness (Deut. 25:1–19)

The next section deals with dishonest slander and other obstructions of the justice system. All Israelites must submit to the system of jurisprudence, as well as the implications for punishment and acquittal (25:1–3). The widow receives special protection from poverty through the responsibilities of her husband's family, and she can bring her claim before the elders if her husband's brother fails to fulfill his duty (25:5–10).

Crooked business practices, like false weights that skew trade, receive harsh condemnation as an abomination to the Lord (25:13–16), because they especially exploit the poor and disadvantaged. The Amalekites had similarly exploited the weak stragglers during the exodus, and they would receive judgment as a result (25:17–19; cf. 1 Samuel 15).

Tenth Commandment: Contentment (Deut. 26:1–15)

The call for contentment stems from the divine source of all blessings in the land. Because the Lord has delivered Israel from slavery in Egypt and provided an inheritance of land for them, all that they enjoy is ultimately the provision of their Redeemer Lord (26:1–10). The title "wandering Aramean" (26:5) refers to the lowly and oppressed state of the nation's lineage, most likely to Jacob himself.

Formal Conclusion (Deut. 26:16–19)

The formal declaration of this final section ("This day," 26:16) establishes the covenantal commitments contained in the collection and evokes the faithful response required of the people. Because the Lord has entered into covenant with Israel, they are to respond with obedience. For his part, the Lord promises them global renown, honor, and holy identification with their God (26:19).

Ratification Ceremony (Deut. 27:1–28:68)

Somewhat fitting after the declaration of covenantal intent in 26:16–19, the next section transitions to a third address by Moses. It includes instructions for a ceremony ratifying the covenant at Mount Ebal once Israel has entered and taken the land. Hill has argued that the ceremony described here comports with the unique land-grant ceremony of the ancient Near East, which is certainly appropriate to this occasion.[26] The altar for this ceremony reflects the consuming holiness of the Lord, marked by the uncut stones, which may also represent the "wilderness" (Ex. 5:1; see also the uncut hair of those dedicated to service in the sanctuary, Num. 6:5).

The mention of Mount Ebal and Mount Gerizim (Deut. 27:4, 13; see also 11:29) points to the vicinity of Shechem as an early cultic center for covenant renewal. The large monument stones mark two significant events: the immediate entrance into the land by fording the Jordan ("on the day," 27:2–3) and the later ratification ceremony in which the stones play a prominent role (Josh. 8:30–35). The elements of the covenant are repeated in the ceremony's liturgy, which includes the parties to the arrangement (Israel and God), as well as the terms (laws) and sanctions (blessings and curses in the land).

The ceremony instruction is divided into three speeches, each delineated by three opening statements (Deut. 27:1, 9, 11). The first and second opening statements attribute the speech to "Moses and the elders" and then to "Moses and the Levitical priests," suggesting that the ceremony required civic and cultic participation. For the ceremony in the land, the Levites are charged with declaring the curses on various

---

[26] Andrew E. Hill, "The Ebal Ceremony as Hebrew Land Grant?," *JETS* 31, no. 4 (1988): 399–406.

transgressors of the law, and the people are to respond antiphonally with "Amen." The next section describes the blessings that come with covenant faithfulness (28:1–14) and the curses that will befall the nation if it persists in covenant breaking (28:15–68).

Redemptive-Historical Prospectus: Blessings and Curses (Deut. 29:1–30:20)

In this section Moses provides a covenantal summary and calls for immediate commitment to the Lord (29:14–15). The section follows a covenantal structure: historical prologue (29:2–8), stipulations (29:9–15), curses (29:16–29), blessings (30:1–10), summary (30:11–18), and witnesses (30:19–20). The covenant foreshadows Israel's future in and out of the land, giving expression to what might be called basic Mosaic eschatology. The conquest would be followed by a time in the land of the Lord showing patience toward his people despite their failures. Finally, a precipitous sin, or period of sinfulness, would trigger the Lord's judgment, resulting in their loss of the land. Having been disciplined, the repentant Israel would return to the Lord and would then be gathered from the nations to again enjoy the provision and protection of the Lord (cf. Leviticus 26).[27]

Historical Epilogue (Deut. 31:1–34:12)

This last section (31:1–34:12) can be read with chapters 1–3 as the "outer frame" of the book, together presenting the historical context within which the stipulations were situated. This final section deals with the covenantal posterity, particularly with the investiture of Joshua as successor to Moses (31:1–30), Yahweh's song of witness (32:1–52), Moses's blessing of the nation (33:1–29), and Moses's obituary (34:1–12). To ensure covenant faithfulness in the future, the Lord provides a faithful covenant leader after Moses's impending death. Here also, Moses is described as transmitting his oral law into a written law, which is to be canonized and read regularly at communal gatherings (31:9–13).

Yahweh's song of witness (32:1–43) and Moses's blessing of the nation (33:1–29) exhibit typical features of biblical Hebrew poetry. In both songs, Israel is referred to by the name Jeshurun (32:15; 33:26), a title that emphasizes Israel's "uprightness." The title is clearly ironic in the former case, which draws attention to Israel's wickedness. In Deuteronomy 33, it celebrates the nation as the recipient of the Lord's instruction and majesty.

Yahweh's song follows the form of a covenant lawsuit, which is reflected in covenant lawsuits found in the Latter Prophets (Isa. 1:1–20; Jer. 2:4–13; Hos. 4:1–6; Mic. 6:1–5).[28] The song begins with a summons to the cosmos as witness, a common feature in lawsuit poetry (cf. Isa. 1:2; 49:13; Jer. 2:12; summoning mountains, Mic. 6:1–2). The imagery is richly agrarian and pastoral: his words are like "rain," "dew," and "showers" (Deut. 32:2), and Israel is fed by "the produce of the field,"

---

[27] While both Deuteronomy 29–30 and Leviticus 26 propose the basic futures of Israel, the latter text includes the provision for a sevenfold increase in judgment if repentance is not forthcoming (Lev. 26:18, 21, 24, 28), a detail that may serve as the basis for the sevenfold increase in the exilic years in Dan. 9:24.

[28] Isaiah 1, for instance, includes echoes of the lawsuit in Deuteronomy 32 (Isa. 1:3 < Deut. 32:28; Isa. 1:10 < Deut. 32:32).

the "honey out of the rock," and the "milk from the flock" (32:13). If the nation turns away from the Lord, the people will suffer curses both in nature (famine, drought, pestilence, 32:23–24) and warfare (subjugation, defeat, and exile, 32:25–27). In memorizing and reciting this song, the people speak their judgment with their own lips, if they should fail in the covenant.

Moses's final blessing (33:1–29) on the tribes puts him in the place of Jacob, who offered his own blessings at the end of the book of Genesis (49:1–27). In true covenantal fashion, the blessings follow a brief restatement of the benevolence and glory of God that has been revealed in the past (33:2–5). The song itself presents some problems and has been described as "enigmatic and difficult to translate,"[29] but the purpose of the song, to bestow blessings for each of the tribes as they settle in their respective territories, is readily accessible.

Finally, the obituary of Moses in chapter 34 describes the somewhat mysterious circumstances of Moses's death and burial (34:6), the people's period of mourning, and the confirmation of Joshua as Moses's successor, who had received the unction of "the spirit of wisdom" appropriate for his vocation (34:9). The book—and the Pentateuch, for that matter—ends with a final superlative about Moses as a unique prophet of the Lord due to his immediate interaction with the Lord and the grandeur of his mighty works in the service of the Lord.

There is a notable literary link between Genesis 49–50 and Deuteronomy 33–34. The two sections both involve a poetic blessing of the Israelite tribes followed by a narrative of the covenant head's death. In the case of Genesis 49–50, Jacob blesses the tribes individually, after which we have an account of his death and that of Joseph. This sort of "tail linkage" at the end of the first and last books of the Pentateuch demarcates them and the three books between them as a literary whole. The end of Malachi makes a link to the Pentateuch in general and to Deuteronomy in particular that is different in type but similarly explicit. The call to "remember the law of my servant Moses" (Mal. 4:4) draws the prophetic corpus to an end by returning to the covenantal foundations upon which the prophetic office is established.

Approaching the New Testament

It is difficult to overstate the influence of Deuteronomy on the theology of the Bible. Its presence is felt throughout the Scriptures, not merely in the Old Testament, where it provides the summary and foundation of covenant life, but also in the New Testament, where it is shown to speak of the character of the Redeemer, the true Israel, and the people of God.

Deuteronomy and the Pentateuch

As the theological capstone of the Torah, Deuteronomy is more than a mere epilogue.[30] The book contains an expansive theological and ethical application of the events and

---

[29] Patrick D. Miller, *Deuteronomy*, IBC (Louisville: John Knox, 1990), 239.
[30] David N. Freedman, "Pentateuch," in *Divine Commitment and Human Obligation: Selected Writings of David Noel Freedman*, vol. 1, *Ancient Israelite History and Religion*, ed. John R. Huddlestun (Grand Rapids, MI: Eerdmans, 1997), 123.

teachings of Genesis through Numbers.[31] Much of the Pentateuch narrates Israel's history while interspersing segments of verse, covenant, and instruction throughout, but Deuteronomy moves from the story to the imperative, from the identity of Israel and the people of God to the claims that God makes on them as his people.

This shift becomes apparent in the opening chapters of the book, which recount a series of defining events from Israel's sojourn. The account ends with Joshua's commissioning (3:28) and then shifts to instruction (4:1). At first, the transition from travelogue to teaching can seem jarring, as if a section of this first discourse was left out. But in Deuteronomy—and in all Scripture, for that matter—historical accounts are told in order to teach the audience about theological and ethical truths relevant to their contemporary lives.[32] Redemptive history should find expression in redemptive living.

Given the context of the book at the end of a collection structured around historical narrative, we can understand how the relationship between Deuteronomy and the previous four books is analogous to the relationship between Deuteronomy 4 and the previous three chapters. Israel's future conquest is given meaning and motivation from the story of God and humanity, beginning with creation, the fall, the flood, Babel, the identification of Abraham and his descendants as a covenant people, the Joseph cycles, and the exodus account. This history of the world and God's people in it constitutes the mine from which the theological ore of Deuteronomy is excavated and forged into a community ethic. Why internalize the law? Because the Lord promised this land to us through our forefathers (6:10, 23), he has already secured our liberation from Egypt by mighty works (6:12; 20–22), he does not suffer unfaithfulness (6:15), and he does not tolerate presumption, as Israel exhibited in the wilderness (6:16). The instruction is not arbitrary but flows directly from divine revelation and activity in the past.

Deuteronomy and the Former Prophets

The text of Deuteronomy is also intricately sewn into the fabric of the books that follow it in the canon, which is why scholars have contended that it should be understood as the beginning of a historical account that continues into Joshua, Judges, Samuel, and Kings. Clear textual threads stitch the books together, such as the accounts of the death of Moses and the announcement of the succession of Joshua, both of which are present at the end of Deuteronomy and at the beginning of Joshua (Deut. 34:1–9; Josh. 1:1–9).

Furthermore, as Waltke has pointed out, the divine speech of Joshua 1:2–9 contains a sampling of the teaching of Deuteronomy (Deut. 5:32–33; 7:24; 10:11; 11:23–24; 30:10; 31:2, 6–8).[33] The book of Joshua's use of Deuteronomy highlights

---

Reprint of "Pentateuch," *Interpreter's Dictionary of the Bible*, ed. George A. Buttrick (New York: Abingdon, 1962), 3:711–27.

[31] J. Gordon McConville writes, "Deuteronomy is the capstone of the Pentateuch; it gives the climactic and consummate form of the Old Covenant." *Grace in the End: A Study in Deuteronomic Theology* (Grand Rapids, MI: Zondervan, 1993), 9.

[32] Samuel R. Driver, *Deuteronomy*, 3rd ed., ICC 3 (1902; repr., Edinburgh: T&T Clark, 1996), 62.

[33] Bruce K. Waltke, *An Old Testament Theology: An Exegetical, Canonical, and Thematic Approach*, with Charles Yu (Grand Rapids, MI: Zondervan, 2007), 514n10.

the authority of Moses's voice in the rest of the Old Testament. Deuteronomy presents the teaching as Moses's commands, while Joshua 1:2–9 presents them as God's words, highlighting the continuity between the voice of the prophet and the voice of the Lord. Wenham draws out five themes which bind the two books together: the holy war of conquest, the distribution of the land, the unity of all Israel, Joshua as the successor of Moses, and the covenant.[34]

Additional reasons for reading Joshua–Kings as a single, coherent narrative must be presented elsewhere, but the theological features of this history depend heavily upon the teaching of Deuteronomy. Both Deuteronomy and the later Historical Books prominently feature God's self-revelation, God's universal authority and power over all creation, Israel's election by God to bless the nations, God's personal presence, the dynamics of the covenant, and God's inexhaustible grace. Deuteronomy provides the theological framework through which the history of Israel is retold and evaluated in Joshua–Kings. If we take this in light of its place as the capstone of the Pentateuch, it becomes clear that Deuteronomy is the prevailing historiographical grid through which the primary history of Genesis–Kings is conveyed.

Deuteronomy and the Latter Prophets

The teaching of Deuteronomy is present in much of the teaching found in the prophetic writings. As advocates of the covenant, the Hebrew prophets confronted the threat, reality, or memory of the exile, as well as the hope for restoration, by calling the people of Israel to return to the Lord of the covenant.

Deuteronomic themes thus play central roles in many of the prophetic writings. For example, prophetic oracles against the nations—such as Isaiah 14–23, Jeremiah, Amos 1–3, Obadiah, Jonah, and Nahum—all assume the Lord's universal authority, power, and presence as described in Deuteronomy (cf. Deut. 4:38; 7:1, 22; 8:20; 9:4–5; 28:1). We could explore many other examples, but the case of Jeremiah will sufficiently illustrate Deuteronomy's pervasive presence in the prophets.

The life and prophecies of Jeremiah might be described as an extended exploration of the theology of Deuteronomy in the late preexilic period (627–586 BC). Due to the rediscovery of the Book of the Covenant in 620 BC and King Josiah's subsequent reforms (2 Kings 22–23), the covenant looms large in the oracles of Jeremiah. Deuteronomistic language saturates the prophet's sermons and prayers, including his call narrative (Jer. 1:5–12), which borrows language from Deuteronomy 18:15–19.[35] The temple sermon of Jeremiah 7 shows his concern for "the sojourner, the fatherless, [and] the widow" (Jer. 7:6; cf. Deut. 10:18; 14:29; 16:11, 14; 24:19–21; 26:12–13; 27:19), the purity of the central sanctuary that bears the Lord's name (Jer. 7:12, 14; cf. Deut. 12:5, 11, 21; 14:23–24; 16:2, 6, 11; 26:2), and Israel's lack of singular obedience to the voice of the Lord (Jer. 7:28; cf. Deut. 8:20; 13:18; 15:5; 27:10; 28:1, 2, 15, 45, 62; 30:8, 10).

---

[34] Gordon J. Wenham, "Deuteronomic Theology of the Book of Joshua," *JBL* 90, no. 2 (1971): 140–48.

[35] Lundbom provides a useful list of the exact wording from Deuteronomy appearing in Jeremiah. Lundbom, *Deuteronomy*, 41–42. See also Driver, *Deuteronomy*, xcii.

Jeremiah's theology of the heart is evocative of the same in Deuteronomy, particularly as it is expressed in the Shema (Deut. 6:4–9). Since the covenant requires wholehearted devotion, Jeremiah draws the people's attention to their great deficit of heart. Their hearts are "deceitful above all things, and desperately sick" (Jer. 17:9). Jeremiah borrows the image of a circumcised heart (Jer. 4:4; 9:26; cf. Deut. 10:16; 30:6) to explain how covenantal faithfulness must be a matter of the person's inner parts and not merely the outer body. Unless they repent sincerely and "wash [their] heart from evil" (Jer. 4:14), they will suffer judgment.

The heart problem facing Judah can only be remedied by the Lord's provision of a new heart, a heart of faithfulness. After the righteous remnant have suffered in exile, the Lord will restore them through repentance. This repentance will not be insincere but will be derived from a new heart given to them by the Lord (24:7). With this new heart, they will be equipped to seek him with "all [their] heart[s]" (29:13), and this new heart will have the law of the Lord written upon it that they might never forget it (31:31–34). For Jeremiah, this new heart, the one the people need to worship the Lord, is a blessing of the new covenant (32:38–39)—a theme given prominence in the New Testament (e.g., Luke 22:20; 2 Cor. 3:1–6; Heb. 8:1–10:25; 12:24).

Deuteronomy and the New Testament

The book of Deuteronomy is one of the most cited Old Testament books in the New Testament, along with Genesis, Isaiah, and the Psalms. The Synoptic Gospels depict Jesus as employing and interpreting the book throughout his ministry. When tempted in the desert, he quotes Deuteronomy each time he is tested (Deut. 8:3; 6:13, 16; Matt. 4:4–10; Luke 4:4–12). The Sermon on the Mount (Matthew 5–7) includes several explicit references to Deuteronomy, including an expansion on the requirements of particular laws like divorce laws (Matt. 5:31–32) and the *lex talionis* (Matt. 5:38–42). Other discussions of Deuteronomy appear in Mark 10:4; 12:19; Matt. 19:7; 22:24–25; and Luke 20:28, showing the lasting authority it had in Jesus's life and ministry.

One cannot help but wonder if there are echoes of the Shema in Mark 2:7 ("Who can forgive sins but God alone?") and 10:18 ("Why do you call me good? No one is good except God alone"). Jesus clearly cites the Shema elsewhere as the greatest commandment (Mark 12:29–30; Luke 10:27), and its language seems to guide a section of his High Priestly Prayer (John 17:20–26). Peter's reference to Jesus as "Lord of all" (Acts 10:36) is not merely an affront to Caesar but a clear identification with the one Lord of the Shema.[36] Paul picks up this important liturgical passage of the Mosaic covenant and updates it to account for the revelation of the Son in 1 Corinthians 8:6 ("yet for us there is one God, the Father, from whom are all things and for whom we exist, and one Lord, Jesus Christ, through whom are all things and through whom we exist").

---

[36] Richard B. Hays, *Reading Backwards: Figural Christology and the Fourfold Gospel Witness* (Waco, TX: Baylor University Press, 2014), 65.

Paul also shows a strong grasp of the book of Deuteronomy elsewhere and cites it often as a formative influence on his theology. As in Deuteronomy, the church in Corinth should purge unrepentant people from their community, though in this case through excommunication, not execution (1 Cor. 5:13). In church trials, the rules regarding multiple witnesses still apply (2 Cor. 13:1; cf. Deut. 19:15), and wages ought to be fair and timely (1 Cor. 9:9). It has been argued convincingly that the end of Deuteronomy, particularly chapters 27–30 and 32, play a unique role in Paul's understanding of his own apostolic ministry and the place of Gentiles in the developing church.[37]

Going beyond direct references, the themes of Deuteronomy are worked out thoroughly in the writings of the apostles, who saw the incarnation and redemptive work of Jesus as the fulfillment of the law's requirements and promises (Matt. 5:17). For instance, Moses promises a faithful Israel, restored from exile and circumcised of heart (Deut. 30:1–8), while Jesus is identified with true, righteous Israel (Matt. 2:15; 3:17; and "true vine," John 15:1–17), who proclaims the restoration from exile (Matt. 4:13–17; Luke 4:17–20) and whose Spirit indwells his people, giving them new, circumcised hearts of faith (Rom. 2:29; 5:5; 2 Cor. 3:3; 4:6; Eph. 3:14–17; Col. 3:15) and uniting them with him (John 17:20–23). The restoration of the people to a loving relationship with God is complete. Christ calls his people to pray to God as if he were their covenant Father (Matt. 6:9; cf. Deut. 1:31; 8:5; 32:6), and Paul teaches that their union with Christ means that they too are sons and heirs with him in the kingdom (Gal. 4:6–7).

Because the guilt of sin is poured out on Christ and the righteousness of Christ is poured out on his people, his people no longer have to fear the condemnation that comes from the law (Rom. 7:5–6; 8:2–3). For them, the teaching of Deuteronomy is useful for personal growth in righteousness (2 Tim. 3:16), but it does not condemn them. Rather, the obligation to the law is fulfilled, and they are set free by the Spirit of Christ (Rom. 8:2–4). Like the Israelites in Moses's day, followers of Christ are called to love the Lord their God with every aspect of their lives (Deut. 6:4–5), and they can be confident that the Holy Spirit is at work in them filling them with the love of God (Rom. 5:5; 2 Tim. 1:7).

In ancient Israel, the temple in Jerusalem would become the central sanctuary where the Lord would place his name (Deut. 12:11, 21; 14:23; 16:2, 6, 11; 26:2), but Christ claims that he is the true temple, the earthly representation of God (John 2:21). As a result, his followers become temples of his presence through the indwelling of the Spirit at Pentecost (1 Cor. 6:19; cf. Acts 2:17). Because of this shift in sanctuary, the geographical city of Jerusalem is no longer the earthly location of God's presence, nor is it the capital city of God's people, whose citizenship is in heaven with the risen and glorified Christ (Phil. 3:20; Gal. 4:25–26). As the dwelling place of the Spirit of the Lord, the church is called to proclaim the good news about Jesus Christ to the nations, discipling them according to his Word (Matt. 28:18–20).

---

[37] Guy Waters, *The End of Deuteronomy and the Epistles of Paul*, WUNT, 2nd ser., 221 (Tübingen: Mohr Siebeck, 2006).

The book of Deuteronomy is a textual force whose influence is felt throughout the whole of Scripture, and it continues to be felt today. It distills the events of the exodus and conquest into a practical theology that touches just about every sphere of daily life. It makes bold claims on the individual, but it sees the individual as a part of a broader community whose responsibility it is to worship the Lord, enjoy the land, and care for each member as the Lord has cared for them. Those who would disregard Deuteronomy's teaching as mere legalism or arbitrary ancient legislation neglect a book that has been the source of great strength and encouragement for the people of God throughout history, even for the Lord Jesus Christ himself.

SELECT BIBLIOGRAPHY

Block, Daniel I. *Deuteronomy*. NIVAC. Grand Rapids, MI: Zondervan, 2012.

Christensen, Duane L. *Deuteronomy 1:1–21:9*. Rev. ed. WBC 6A. Dallas: Word, 2001.

Craigie, Peter C. *The Book of Deuteronomy*. NICOT. Grand Rapids, MI: Eerdmans, 1976.

Currid, John D. *Deuteronomy*. EP Study Commentary. Darlington, UK: Evangelical Press, 2006.

Driver, Samuel R. *Deuteronomy*. 3rd ed. ICC 3. 1902. Reprint, Edinburgh: T&T Clark, 1996.

Kaufman, Stephen A. "The Structure of the Deuteronomic Law." *Maarav* 1, no. 2 (1979): 105–58.

Kline, Meredith G. *Treaty of the Great King: The Covenant Structure of Deuteronomy: Studies and Commentary*. Grand Rapids, MI: Eerdmans, 1963.

Lundbom, Jack R. *Deuteronomy: A Commentary*. Grand Rapids, MI: Eerdmans, 2013.

Mayes, A. D. H. *Deuteronomy: Based on the Revised Standard Version*. NCB. Grand Rapids, MI: Eerdmans, 1981.

McConville, J. Gordon. *Deuteronomy*. ApOTC 5. Downers Grove, IL: InterVarsity Press, 2002.

Merrill, Eugene H. *Deuteronomy*. NAC 4. Nashville: B&H, 1994.

Miller, Patrick D. *Deuteronomy*. IBC. Louisville: John Knox, 1990.

Thompson, John A. *Deuteronomy: An Introduction and Commentary*. TOTC 5. Downers Grove, IL: InterVarsity Press, 1974.

Tigay, Jeffrey H. *Deuteronomy: The Traditional Hebrew Text with the New JPS Translation*. JPS Torah Commentary. Philadelphia: Jewish Publication Society, 1996.

von Rad, Gerhard. *Deuteronomy*. OTL. Philadelphia: Westminster, 1966.

Walton, John H. "The Decalogue Structure of the Deuteronomic Law." In *Interpreting Deuteronomy: Issues and Approaches*, edited by David G. Firth and Philip S. Johnston, 93–117. Downers Grove, IL: InterVarsity Press, 2012.

Wright, Christopher J. H. *Deuteronomy*. Peabody, MA: Hendrickson, 1996.

6

Joshua

Daniel C. Timmer

INTRODUCTION

The book of Joshua recounts the fulfillment of God's promise to Abram that he would give him and his descendants a land (Gen. 12:1–3). The elaboration of that promise in Genesis 15 includes an important detail as to the timing and manner of Yahweh's gift of the land: the sin of the "Amorites" will at a certain point be "complete," and then Abram's descendants will possess the land (Gen. 15:16). This detail implies that the entry into Canaan will involve punishment for the Canaanites' sin, although the nature of that punishment, and especially Israel's role in it, are left unclear. Accordingly, the book of Joshua goes out of its way to articulate how Israel can play a role in what is essentially a divine judgment on sin. This accounts for various features like the book's use of חרם (meaning "ban"), the nearly exclusive divine agency in the taking and destruction of Jericho, and the partial explanation that Yahweh hardened the hearts of the Canaanites (Josh. 11:16–20).[1]

The book is not a simple "conquest account," however.[2] Once the Israelite leaders complete allocating the Canaanite territory to Israel's tribes, the tone of the book changes from accomplishment and rest to probation and warning. This shift can be explained at least partially by the importance of the Abrahamic covenant for the

---

[1] Here and throughout this chapter I take for granted the historical veracity of Israel's entry of Canaan from outside, without suggesting that no significant questions remain or that the biblical books involved were even intended to provide a relatively complete historical picture of the era. See esp. Iain W. Provan, V. Philips Long, and Tremper Longman III, *A Biblical History of Israel* (Louisville: Westminster John Knox, 2003), and for a contrasting viewpoint, Israel Finkelstein and Amihay Mazar, *The Quest for the Historical Israel: Debating Archaeology and the History of Early Israel*, ed. Brian B. Schmidt, ABS 17 (Atlanta: Society of Biblical Literature, 2007).

[2] See K. Lawson Younger Jr.'s very helpful interpretation of Joshua 9–12 in light of "ancient conquest accounts" in *Ancient Conquest Accounts: A Study in Ancient Near Eastern and Biblical History Writing*, JSOTSup 98 (Sheffield: JSOT Press, 1990), and James K. Hoffmeier's helpful study of Joshua 1–11 in light of the annals of Thutmose III in "The Structure of Joshua 1–11 and the Annals of Thutmose III," in *Faith, Tradition, and History: Old Testament Historiography in Its Near Eastern Context*, ed. A. R. Millard, James K. Hoffmeier, and David W. Baker (Winona Lake, IN: Eisenbrauns, 1994), 165–80.

granting of the land on the one hand and of the Mosaic covenant for keeping it on the other. As we will see, the speeches of chapters 23–24 go back in complex ways to Abrahamic *and* Mosaic elements as a way to prepare Israel for retaining the land. As the New Testament's occasional references to the taking and tenure of the land show, the Joshua account is theologically rich and remains relevant to Christian readers today despite the thorny issues and complex theological questions it raises.[3]

Background Issues

Date and Authorship

The book of Joshua is anonymous. The only explicit clue to its author appears in the "we/us" that some translations include in 5:1, 6, which could locate the author's perspective in the time frame of Israel's entry into Canaan. However, both references are textually somewhat uncertain, and 5:6 ("the land that the Lord had sworn to their fathers to give to us"), which is textually more reliable, could reflect the perspective of an author living after the time of Joshua who embraced the perpetual nature of Yahweh's gift of the land.[4]

This lack of data has not stopped many scholars from trying to find clues of authorship in rather dubious ways, such as insisting that an author's vocabulary, interests, and theology are monochromatic and very limited. For example, Nelson proposes five distinct sources for material in Joshua: (1) a scattering of elements similar to Deuteronomy throughout the book; (2) organizational patterns using language that differs from Deuteronomy; (3) the land allotment in chapters 13–19; (4) the material from chapter 24, which constitutes a second "farewell" speech, distinct from the speech in chapter 23; and (5) "Priestly" material with an interest in divine presence, the tabernacle, and cultic matters.[5] Not only do such readings attribute various parts of the book to separate and often contradictory authors on tenuous grounds (isolated vocabulary, unique perspective), but they are connected to an equally dubious reconstruction of Israel's religious history that most notably dates the law after the prophets. They therefore offer no more solid information on authorship than do 5:1, 6.[6]

In terms of date, much of the information in Joshua evidently goes back to second-millennium BC sources (e.g., the land allotment in chapters 13–19),[7] and a number of elements likely reflect composition in the second half of the second millennium. These include the prominence of Sidon (not Tyre) as Phoenicia's leading city (11:8; 19:28), something that was the case only until about 1200 BC, and references to the Jebusites and "the Jebusite city" (i.e., Jerusalem), which imply that it had not yet

---

[3] See esp. Oren R. Martin, *Bound for the Promised Land: The Land Promise in God's Redemptive Plan*, NSBT 34 (Downers Grove, IL: InterVarsity Press, 2015).
[4] Cf. David M. Howard Jr., *Joshua*, NAC 5 (Nashville: Broadman, 2002), 151.
[5] See Richard D. Nelson, *Joshua: A Commentary*, OTL (Louisville: Westminster John Knox, 1997), 5–9.
[6] See Gene M. Tucker, "The Law in the Eighth-Century Prophets," in *Canon, Theology, and Old Testament Interpretation: Essays in Honor of Brevard S. Childs*, ed. Gene M. Tucker, David L. Peterson, and Robert R. Wilson (Minneapolis: Fortress, 1988), 201–16.
[7] This case can be made, for example, regarding Joshua 1–11. Hoffmeier, "Structure of Joshua 1–11," 165–80.

been conquered (cf. Judg. 1:8, 21; 2 Sam. 5:6–9).[8] However, the book also contains many "until this day" statements that show the author's perspective to be to one degree or another later than the events narrated (cf. also 24:31, which describes the generation after Joshua's).[9] These and other data allow us to affirm that the book, although composed after Joshua, contains and faithfully preserves sources that go back to his time.

Historical Context

Although the book gives almost no indication of who might have written it and little indication of when, information that bears on its historical setting is both abundant and clear. The collection of some 350 Amarna letters, mostly written by Egyptian vassals in Syria-Palestine to the pharaoh, gives incidental descriptions of the state of affairs across much of the Levant in the mid-fourteenth century BC.[10] These vassals were responsible for making regular vassal payments to Egypt and for supporting Egyptian military and diplomatic personnel in Canaan. The letters bear witness to more or less constant disorder caused by conflicts between Canaanite towns or between towns and the marauding *apiru* (groups of nomadic raiders of uncertain ethnicity). As an example, in letter 288 Abdi-Heba, the mayor of Jerusalem, states that he is at war with neighboring cities and that "now the Apiru have taken the very cities of the king. Not a single mayor remains to the king, my lord; all are lost."[11]

A stela set up by the Egyptian king Merenptah is an important extrabiblical confirmation of the presence of a group of "Israelites" in Canaan not later than ca. 1208 BC.[12] The stela recounts that Merenptah's forces entered Canaan, confronted various Canaanite groups, "and knocked off a few of them, by way of warning."[13] The stela is largely dedicated to a campaign against Lybian enemies about the same time, and the mention of Israel occurs in a short, final section that lists "Israel" (with a determinative indication that the reference is to a people group and not to a territory) alongside five other Palestinian opponents, asserting that "Israel is wasted, its seed is not."[14]

The book of Joshua presents the Late Bronze situation in very similar terms.[15] Cities in Canaan sometimes cooperate militarily (as in Josh. 10:1–6) and sometimes stand alone (Jericho); Israel destroys only a few cities (Jericho, Ai, Hazor) so that no widespread destruction occurs; Israel's population often melds with the indigenous

---

[8] See a list of nine such elements in Richard S. Hess, *Joshua*, TOTC 6 (Downers Grove, IL: InterVarsity Press, 1996), 27–33.

[9] The phrase "to this day" appears in Josh. 4:9 (stones in Jordan); 5:9 (place named Gilgal); 6:25 (Rahab and her family still members of Israel); 7:26 (heap of stones in the Valley of Achor); 8:28 (Ai in ruins); 8:29 (the heap of stones at Ai); 9:27 (the Gibeonites' status in Israel); 10:27 (the stones that close the cave at Makkedah); 13:13 (Geshur and Maacath living in Israel); 14:14 (Hebron as Caleb's inheritance); 15:63 (Jebusites living in Jerusalem); 16:10 (Canaanites living in Ephraim).

[10] See Raymond Cohen and Raymond Westbrook, eds., *Amarna Diplomacy: The Beginnings of International Relations* (Baltimore: Johns Hopkins University Press, 2000).

[11] Bill T. Arnold and Bryan E. Beyer, *Readings from the Ancient Near East: Primary Source Readings for Old Testament Study*, EBS (Grand Rapids, MI: Baker Academic, 2002), 168.

[12] James K. Hoffmeier, trans., "The (Israel) Stela of Merneptah (2.6)," in *COS*, 2:40–41.

[13] Kenneth A. Kitchen, *On the Reliability of the Old Testament* (Grand Rapids, MI: Eerdmans, 2003), 229.

[14] Hoffmeier, trans., "The (Israel) Stela of Merneptah (2.6)," 41.

[15] The biblical date of Israel's entry into Canaan depends on the date of Israel's exodus from Egypt and therefore can be dated to either the late fifteenth or late thirteenth century. Cf. Lawson G. Stone, "Early Israel and Its Appearance in Canaan," in *Ancient Israel's History: An Introduction to Issues and Sources*, ed. Bill T. Arnold and Richard S. Hess (Grand Rapids, MI: Baker Academic, 2014), 127–64.

Canaanite population so that cultural and archaeological traces are often indistinct (Josh. 13:13; 15:63; 17:13; 23:7, 12); Israel is not centralized, with its tribes eventually spread over the land and relatively independent; and despite the success of the first stages of the conquest, at the end of Joshua's life the majority of the land remains unconquered (Josh. 13:1; 15:63; 16:10; 17:13; 18:1–3; 23:4–5).

STRUCTURE AND OUTLINE
Outline
Although the book of Joshua manifests various structures, a very useful one can be derived from the work of Koorevaar (see table 16).[16] It captures the main lines of the book's message and is tied to a key word in each section.

Joshua 1–5	Preparation for entry, "cross," עבר
Joshua 6–12	Entry into Canaan, "take," לקח
Joshua 13–21	Allocating Canaan, "divide," חלק
Joshua 22–24	Keeping Canaan/covenant, "serve," עבד

Table 16

Explanation
The verb to "cross over" (עבר) appears six times in Joshua 1–5, always with the Jordan River as its object. It is used first in a divine command to Joshua (1:2), then in three commands of Joshua to the people (1:11, 14; 3:6), followed by one anticipatory use (3:14) and a final command to the priests at the moment of the crossing (4:5). This "crossing" brings Israel into the Promised Land, but at that point none of it is under their control.

The "taking" of Canaan in chapters 6–12 involves various terms, but the summary section in 10:29–11:23 uses the verb לקח, "take," at key points (11:16, 19, 23). A series of military victories gives Israel an initial yet tenuous hold on some of its inheritance, although much remains unconquered. Once Israel has broken the initial Canaanite resistance, the allocation of each tribe's territory follows in chapters 13–21, being described with the verb חלק, "divide," which appears some fourteen times in that section.

Finally, once each tribe's inheritance has been allocated, the questions of possessing it (by dispossessing the Canaanites) and keeping it arise. Both possessing and keeping can be achieved only by living in complete trust and obedience toward Yahweh (cf. Josh. 22:5), and the book's final chapter repeatedly summarizes this relationship in terms of "serving" (עבד) him (e.g., Josh. 24:15).

This structure captures both the achievements that the book records and the

---

[16] Hendrik Jacob Koorevaar, *De opbouw van het boek Jozua* (Heverlee: Centrum voor bijbelse vorming België, 1990), cited in *NIDOTTE*, 4:813–14. Koorevaar proposes a more complex chiastic structure centered on Josh. 18:1–10, but the four units he identifies create a simple and equally meaningful structure.

open-ended nature of Israel's relationship with God at the end, with the land as a key barometer of that relationship. Despite all that God has already done for Israel during Joshua's lifetime in fulfillment of his promises to Abraham, Israel's covenant life with Yahweh requires ongoing trust, dedication, fidelity, and obedience.

MESSAGE AND THEOLOGY

Historically, the conquest was in the first place *for* Israel and *against* the Canaanites. Theologically, Yahweh's gift of the land to Israel presents that process as an important precursor to God's ultimate, eschatological salvation and judgment in and through the work of his Son.

Israel and the Land

The book of Joshua opens with a divine speech calling Joshua to lead Israel forward in order to receive the land "that I swore to their fathers to give them" (1:6). In the same breath, as it were, God also exhorts Joshua to embrace holistic fidelity to the law of Moses, establishing an important connection between faith and obedience that continues throughout the book.

Here our focus is on the Abrahamic basis for the giving of the land. It is preferable to speak of "giving" rather than "taking" because the former emphasizes God's decisive role in every aspect of the process, while "taking" introduces a focus on Israel's agency—something the book goes to great lengths to minimize. The term *conquest* should also be used carefully, mainly because the word implies a completed process, whereas the book of Joshua shows that during this period Israel possessed only *part* of the land.

Abrahamic Basis

As just suggested, Israel's settlement in Canaan has two primary facets: the "giving" of the land to Israel and the punishment of the Canaanites on account of their sin. The land is one of several gifts or blessings that God had promised to give to Abraham and his descendants in Genesis 12, later ratified as a covenant in Genesis 15 and 17. Apart from the land (12:1), Yahweh promised descendants, blessing, the role of globally transmitting blessing, and protection from those who would lightly esteem Abraham and his line (12:2–3). Among other things, the prominence of "seed" and "blessing" in the covenant with Abraham suggests that it will move forward God's plan to overcome both the line of the Serpent (3:15) and the multifaceted curse that human sin has elicited.

In order to understand the theological function of the land, we first have to look backward.[17] Israel's forced servitude in Egypt is the primary (and contrasting) antecedent, chronologically speaking, to Israel's rest in the land. "Egypt" was to be

---

[17] See Philip Johnston and Peter Walker, eds., *The Land of Promise: Biblical, Theological, and Contemporary Perspectives* (Downers Grove, IL: InterVarsity Press, 2001), and Norman C. Habel, *The Land Is Mine: Six Biblical Land Ideologies*, OBT (Minneapolis: Fortress, 1993).

banished from Israel's experience so that she might serve Yahweh freely (note the plays on "serve" language in the exodus narrative). The wilderness thus transitions Israel both geographically and conceptually. God's allotment of the land to individual tribes also guarded against the main vehicle of internal financial oppression, the power of abused land rights and acquisition.[18]

Israel and Rest in the Land

"Rest" is the term most often used in Joshua to describe Israel's experience once she has gained initial control of the land (not total displacement of the Canaanites, something the Old Testament never affirms).[19] By definition, rest does not exist and cannot be enjoyed outside the land, whether before entering Canaan (when Israel was in Egypt) or when the covenant curses have reached their apogee in exile (Deut. 28:65). Deuteronomy foresees the granting of rest from Israel's enemies upon completion of the conquest, followed by God's designation of a centralized location at which Israel is to worship him (12:10–14). The book of Joshua makes clear that both took place: Israel had rest from her enemies, and the cult was centralized, first in Shiloh and later (apparently) in Shechem. Even then, once a central cult location had been chosen, much of the land had yet to be fully subdued (Josh. 23:7, 12; Judg. 1:1). After Joshua's death, things did not improve, and several centuries elapsed before Israel's rest in the land came to its fullest realization in the reign of the Davidic monarchs and the construction of the temple at Jerusalem (2 Sam. 7:1, 11; 1 Kings 5:4; 8:56).[20]

What Is "Rest" in Joshua?

In the book of Joshua, "rest" is a precondition to obedient life in the land, expressed especially through exclusive worship of Yahweh at his designated cult site. This reality suggests that "rest" in Joshua does not possess the ultimate character that some other biblical presentations of the motif have,[21] which is simply due to the different things from which one can have rest. In Joshua and books whose theology is similar, it is particularly rest from warfare,[22] while in the Priestly world of thought it is rest from one's own works or is simply equated with God's own rest.[23]

---

[18] So Paul R. House, "The God Who Gives Rest in the Land: Joshua," *SBJT* 2 (1998): 27.

[19] A nuanced summary of the biblical presentation of the "conquest" comes from Alan Millard: "Israel entered Canaan from the east under Joshua, who led a series of lightning raids to break the back of local opposition, then following generations gradually spread across the land, taking over some places, mostly settling alongside the Canaanites in existing towns and colonizing the countryside. It is in that process that we learn of particular tribes in particular areas, which were called by their names, while they were known collectively as Israel. The tribes are portrayed as warring with the indigenous peoples and, occasionally, with each other, under leaders who arose in different tribes and acted for some or all of the tribal grouping." Alan R. Millard, "Amorites and Israelites: Invisible Invaders—Modern Expectations and Ancient Reality," in *The Future of Biblical Archaeology: Reassessing Methodologies and Assumptions*, ed. James K. Hoffmeier and Alan R. Millard (Grand Rapids, MI: Baker, 2004), 153.

[20] "In the story that unfolds from Deuteronomy to Samuel, the expected 'rest' is postponed until the greater victories of David, who subdues the Philistines and takes Jerusalem (2 Sam 7.1)." J. Gordon McConville, *God and Earthly Power: An Old Testament Political Theology, Genesis–Kings*, LHBOTS 454 (London: T&T Clark, 2006), 105.

[21] See Patrick D. Miller, "The Story of the First Commandment: Joshua," in *Covenant or Context: Essays in Honour of E. W. Nicholson*, ed. A. D. H. Mayes and Robert B. Salters (Oxford: Oxford University Press, 2003), 80–90.

[22] See Georg Braulik, "Zur deuteronomistichen Konzeption von Freiheit und Frieden," in *Studien zur Theologie des Deuteronomiums*, ed. Georg Braulik, SBAB 2 (Stuttgart: Katholisches Bibelwerk, 1988), 219–30.

[23] The Deuteronomic concept of rest is conceived of especially in spatial and national terms, specifically as the divinely procured absence of military opposition within Canaan (Deut. 3:20; 12:9–10; 25:19). The Priestly concept is mapped especially with time and spiritual disposition (trust in divine provision obviates the need for human exertion one day in

This point is important enough to merit further exploration. In Joshua "rest," usually based on the root נוח, is a precondition for life in the land (1:13) rather than the goal itself, and it will be given to Israel by God. It is first promised in terms of taking possession of the land (1:15; cf. 22:4) and is given to Israel by God (21:44; 22:4; 23:1) once they have gained initial control over some of the land (cf. 18:1–2; 20:1–9). This rest is explicitly defined as the absence of war ("on every side," 21:44; "from all their surrounding enemies," 23:1).[24] It is not a question of Israel's obedience producing rest but of God giving it in fulfillment of his promises, essentially regardless of Israel's behavior.[25]

The most important intrabiblical connection of this "rest from enemies in the land" theme is probably to Eden, which is itself *not* the same as the eschatological rest held out in Genesis 2:1–3.[26] Eschatological rest is, rather, the promised reward for obedience on the part of the first couple living in Eden. Accordingly, we cannot equate the possession of the land in Joshua with eschatological rest; the appropriate connection is Eden-land. Both Eden and Canaan have the same theological function as the place in which God's people are to demonstrate their fidelity to him and, after successfully completing that probation, to enter into the full possession of the promised good—eternal life in the case of Edenic obedience, holistic blessing in the land in the case of the Sinai covenant. Tragically, in both cases human disobedience led to the expulsion of the party concerned from its place of residence and to the forfeit of the promised blessing.

Other biblical books confirm that Joshua's presentation of rest as the absence of conflict with other nations is distinct from an eschatological rest that is verbally identical but semantically different (e.g., Pss. 81:13–16; 95:1–11). Although distinct, these two conceptions of rest are complementary and connected. The connection between the two appears in Joshua's stress on *serving Yahweh*. Rest in the land is a precondition for obedient life there, and obedience leads to the soteriological rest that ultimately connects with God's own rest in Genesis 2. The two kinds of rest therefore move in the same direction but should remain distinct in our biblical theology.[27]

Joshua's Theology of Rest and Biblical Theology

In light of the preceding discussion, we can say that rest in Joshua is significant not by virtue of an organic relation to divine rest but rather because of its place in both

---

seven). Both concepts express a common dependence upon Yahweh to provide prominent covenant blessings, but this does not mean that they are theologically equivalent.

[24] So also Ronald L. Hubbard, *Joshua*, NIVAC (Grand Rapids, MI: Zondervan, 2009), 86: "finally to settle in peace and security—truly to be serenely 'home' at last—after years of migration, struggle, and war."

[25] Patrick D. Miller, "The Gift of God: The Deuteronomic Theology of the Land," *Interpretation* 23, no. 4 (1969): 461.

[26] McConville, *God and Earthly Power*, 113 and passim, sees the conquest as an "earnest" of humanity's creation mandate to subdue the land in light of Josh. 18:1 but does not confuse that with eschatological rest or with the obedience necessary to it.

[27] See especially Jon Laansma, *"I Will Give You Rest": The "Rest" Motif in the New Testament with Special Reference to Mt 11 and Heb 3–4*, WUNT, 2nd ser., 98 (Tübingen: Mohr Siebeck, 1997), and Daniel C. Timmer, *Creation, Tabernacle, and Sabbath: The Sabbath Frame of Exodus 31:12–17; 35:1–3 in Exegetical and Theological Perspective*, FRLANT 227 (Göttingen: Vandenhoeck & Ruprecht, 2009). Note, by contrast, the connection between rest in the land and soteriology proposed by J. Gary Millar, "Land," in *New Dictionary of Biblical Theology*, ed. T. Desmond Alexander and Brian S. Rosner (Downers Grove, IL: InterVarsity Press, 2000), 623–27.

the obedience-justification-life triad and the sin-condemnation-death triad.[28] These triads are quite well suited to Joshua's theology since they present Israel's rest in the land, free from the presence of the nations as a source of temptation, as the *context* for obedient service of Yahweh. Scripture correlates not the rest in the land, which is the context for obedience, but the obedience itself with soteriological rest, which overlaps with God's own rest in Genesis 2 (cf. Numbers 14; Psalm 95). To develop a point mentioned earlier, it is notable that both Eden and the land of Israel were in some way sanctified by God's presence, whether occasional in the garden or more constant in Canaan; that obedience is a condition for continued residence in both; and that obedience leads either to eternal life (in the case of Eden) or to blessings that symbolize it (in the case of Canaan).[29]

The biblical-theological changes that attend the coming of a "better," new covenant are clearly seen in the New Testament's replacement of the land with something closer to its eschatological antitype. Goldsworthy puts it succinctly: "By being the place where God meets his people, [Jesus] fulfills the meaning of the land."[30] Vos thus states that the Christian's "center of gravity" now lies outside this world in Christ, and the new heavens and new earth, with Christ at their center, will one day constitute the full realization of the land motif that is so important in the book of Joshua.[31]

The Non-Israelite Nations and the Giving of the Land

The second facet of the giving of Canaan to Israel brings us to what is probably the most difficult facet of the book, both theologically and ethically—the destruction of a significant fraction of the Canaanite population by Israelite arms.[32] The most thorny aspect of this facet is probably the idea of a people group dispossessing another and sometimes personally killing the populations of whole cities on the basis of a divine command.[33] Here we will first develop a theological understanding of the expulsion and destruction of the Canaanites by Israel and then more briefly discuss the ethical problems the book of Joshua poses.

Canaanites and Death in Joshua

First, with respect to the Canaanites, the idea of death as a punishment for sin originates not with the book of Joshua. As early as Genesis 15:16, God states that the "iniquity of the Amorites" is the catalyst for Abraham's descendants to "come back" to the land (cf. Lev. 20:23; Deut. 9:4–5). Further, Noah's curse upon Ham's descendants set the stage for one people group dominating another; to the best of our knowledge, the Amorites, Canaanites, Philistines, Egyptians, and Hittites are

---

[28] See Chris Alex Vlachos, "Law, Sin, and Death: An Edenic Triad? An Examination with Reference to 1 Corinthians 15:56," *JETS* 47, no. 2 (2004): 277–98.

[29] On the place of the Sinai covenant, see Cornelis P. Venema, "The Mosaic Covenant: A 'Republication' of the Covenant of Works?," *MAJT* 21 (2010): 35–101.

[30] Graeme Goldsworthy, *Gospel-Centered Hermeneutics: Foundations and Principles of Evangelical Biblical Interpretation* (Downers Grove, IL: IVP Academic, 2006), 255.

[31] Geerhardus Vos, "The Structure of the Pauline Eschatology," *Princeton Theological Review* 27, no. 3 (1929): 439.

[32] Here I use *Canaanites* as a collective for the various ethnic groups mentioned in the biblical sources and do so only for simplicity.

[33] See the criticisms leveled by John J. Collins, *Introduction to the Hebrew Bible* (Minneapolis: Fortress, 2004), 193–95.

Hammitic (Gen. 10:6–20). And God's promise to punish the Serpent committed him to fatally wounding the Serpent's lineage while preserving that of Eve.

Israelites and Death in Joshua

Second, while the dour theme of death is common to the conquest and the חרם (*herem*, meaning "ban, complete destruction") that governs how the conquest applies to the inhabitants of the land on account of their sin, it is extremely significant that sinful *Israelites* can be and are put to death in Joshua for the same reason. This appears in three contexts: (1) when the Transjordanian tribes commit to enforcing capital punishment for anyone who rebels against Joshua (Josh. 1:18); (2) when Achan and his household are executed for violating the ban (7:25); and (3) when the Cisjordanian tribes intend to go to war with the Transjordanian tribes for apparently violating the single-altar law (22:10–34). There are also statements scattered throughout Joshua that identify a wide variety of activities that would lead to the death of Israelites, including unfaithfulness to Yahweh (22:16 [bis], 22); rebellion against Yahweh (22:16, 19, 22, 29); turning away from Yahweh (22:18, 23, 29); serving gods other than Yahweh (23:16; cf. Deut. 4:25–26; 11:16–17; 28:20); committing iniquity (with reference to Achan, Josh. 22:20); following the ways of the nations (23:13); and transgressing the covenant (23:16).

Firm Ethnic Categories, Porous Covenantal Categories
Defining Israel

This brings us to what may seem to be a surprising question: Who are the "Canaanites" or "nations" in Joshua? On one level, the answer is obvious: they are those who are not part of Israel. But there are at least two important qualifications to such an ethnic or national definition of "Canaanite." First, the integration of Rahab's family and the Gibeonites into Israel (particularly the former) shows that the distinction between Israel and the nations is porous, so that ethnicity is not the only and absolute criterion. In the same vein, it is noteworthy that the covenant renewal of Joshua 8:33, 35 includes not only the genetic descendants of Abraham but also "the sojourners who lived among them" (8:35).[34]

Second, while the integration of Canaanites into Israel and their being spared the punishment of death shows that Canaanite ethnicity is not a sufficient condition for *death* or *exclusion* from God's people in Joshua, the capital punishment exercised against Achan and his family for his sin shows that physical descent from Abraham is likewise no guarantee of *inclusion* in God's people nor of being *spared* from death as a punishment for sin. The Achan episode demonstrates in practice, much as the threats of death against disobedient Israelites in 1:18 and chapter 22 contemplated in theory, that the book of Joshua does not express a mechanical mode of being received into or denied membership in the people of God due to ethnicity. This is also

---

[34] McConville similarly observes, "The equation of nationhood with ethnicity, which we found to be negated by the political vision of Deuteronomy, is precluded [in Joshua] too." *God and Earthly Power*, 104.

clear from the passing mention of the death of the entire unbelieving generation of Israelites in the wilderness (Josh. 5:4).

Canaanites outside Israel

Israel's porous limits as a people group allow us to distinguish between those ethnic Canaanites who are part of Israel and those who are not. Having considered the first group, we now turn to consider those Canaanites who do *not* recognize Yahweh's uniqueness or join his people during the events described in Joshua. Typically, the Canaanites actively or passively resist Israel during its campaigns to take Canaan. In the cases of Jericho and Ai, the Caananites adopt a defensive posture, but in all subsequent military action, they are on the offensive, proactively taking up arms against Israel. Both the southern (after Jericho and Ai-Bethel) and northern campaigns are thus Israel's response to the Canaanites' aggression against itself or its covenanted allies (9:1–2; 10:1–6), something God promotes by hardening their hearts (11:19–20; cf. Pharaoh). Interestingly, however, despite the passive nature of its opposition, even Jericho (and perhaps Ai) is said in 24:11 to have "fought against" Israel.[35] Not opening their gates to Israel probably indicates the inhabitants' commitment to their gods and a refusal to reckon with what they already know about Yahweh.[36]

Behind this rather phenomenological description lies a theological explanation. Given the theological nature of warfare in the ancient Near East, Yahweh's supremacy over the nations of Canaan is nothing less than a demonstration of his supremacy over their gods.[37] "The LORD is king forever and ever; the nations perish from his land" (Ps. 10:16). This theme appears in the language of his military supremacy (and consequently his incomparable divinity) in the accounts of the Jericho campaign (2:9–11; 5:1), Gibeonite campaign (9:1–2, 9–10), southern campaign (10:1–5), and northern campaign (11:1–5). Yahweh's fame comes to include his actions in the progressive punishment and expulsion of the Canaanites, which is connected with the exodus and God's victory over Egypt (note, for example, the parallels between the crossing of the Jordan and the crossing of the Red [or Reed] Sea; cf. Josh. 4:19, 23 with Ex. 12:2–3; 14:21–22).

Alongside punishing the Canaanites for their sins, Yahweh hardens the Canaanites' hearts with the result that they resist the Israelites. This allows Yahweh to destroy them (Josh. 11:20). But similarly to the hardening of the Egyptian Pharaoh's heart in Exodus, the hardening of the Canaanites' hearts is preceded (in narrative and chronology) by their own hostility toward Israel. In the Canaanites' case, they both hear of Israel's initial victories and decide to take up arms against Israel *before* God hardens their hearts (9:1–2). The Canaanites who resist the evident supremacy of Israel's God are contrasted with the Gibeonites (9:3–27; 11:19), who, despite their

---

[35] The expression involves various kinds of opposition, including Balak's sending of Balaam in Num. 24:9.

[36] Hess states this point well but unnecessarily omits the Canaanites' previous sin from the picture: Josh. 11:19–20 "demonstrates how for Joshua the reason for the destruction of the Canaanites was neither their wickedness nor their cursed origins (Gen. 9). Instead, it was their rebellion against the will of God for Israel, a rebellion that led to armed resistance." Hess, *Joshua*, 240.

[37] See J. Michael Thigpen, "Lord of All the Earth: Yahweh and Baal in Joshua 3," *TJ*, n.s., 27, no. 2 (2006): 245–54.

size and prowess (10:2), recognize God's unparalleled power and avoid conflict with him by submitting to Israel (albeit deceitfully).

The Ethical Problems Raised by the "Conquest"

This discussion has raised a few considerations that are helpful in addressing the ethical questions that Joshua raises.[38] Here we will pursue some of these threads a little further, without claiming to fully resolve the complex issues involved.

1. God is the owner of the land (Josh. 1:3–4; 22:19). This explains why the conquest's spoils are consecrated to him and not to the Israelites. This also means that he has the right to give the land to whomever he chooses.
2. Similarly, it is not the Israelites' military prowess or expertise that allows them to take control of parts of Canaan. That too is due to God's miraculous intervention (24:12–13). As Habel puts it, "Yahweh is the all-sufficient divine warrior who dispossesses the land for the chosen people."[39] It is thus *impossible* that Israel would successfully pursue a conquest on her own (note the failed entry of Canaan in Numbers 14); Yahweh takes ultimate responsibility for the conquest.
3. As already noted, most of the Canaanite city-states choose preemptive aggression against Israel over submission or repatriation. Conversely, Israel defends the Gibeonites, with whom they have made a covenant, though they are not ethnic Israelites!
4. On rare occasions, Canaanites (Rahab, 2:10; the Gibeonites, 9:9–10) do avoid military conflict with Israel because of what they have heard about God's mighty acts on her behalf. Habel states, "Those Canaanites who survive do so by their own initiative and their total acknowledgement of YHWH as the God of the conquest."[40]
5. The primary reason for Yahweh's actions against the Canaanites is their "iniquity." In this respect the conquest closely resembles the flood, the language of which it echoes in 10:40; 11:11, 14 by stating that "all that breathed" died (cf. Gen. 7:22).
6. Even though Israel is in a covenant relationship with Yahweh, if she is unfaithful to him, he will treat her as he did the Canaanites (Josh. 24:20). The case of Achan shows that Yahweh's commitment to punish sin is not subject to ethnic prejudice and that it includes a strong corporate aspect.
7. Removing the Canaanites with their gods is part of God's plan for purifying Israel and preserving her from corrupting religious and cultural influences so that she might remain faithful to him (Deut. 20:16–18).
8. Finally, as with the flood and the overthrow of Sodom and Gomorrah, the conquest uniquely foreshadows God's perfect and just judgment on those who oppose him and pursue life autonomously. The different rules of engagement

---

[38] See Walter Brueggemann, *Divine Presence Amid Violence: Contextualizing the Book of Joshua* (Eugene, OR: Cascade, 2009); Lawson G. Stone, "Ethical and Apologetic Tendencies in the Redaction of the Book of Joshua," *CBQ* 53, no. 1 (1991): 25–35; J. Gary Millar, *Now Choose Life: Theology and Ethics in Deuteronomy*, NSBT (Downers Grove, IL: InterVarsity Press, 1998), 155–60; J. P. U. Lilley, "The Judgment of God: The Problem of the Canaanites," *Themelios*, n.s., 22 (1997): 3–12; Paul Copan, *Is God a Moral Monster? Making Sense of the Old Testament God* (Grand Rapids, MI: Baker, 2011); and Heath Thomas, Jeremy A. Evans, and Paul Copan, eds., *Holy War in the Bible: Christian Morality and an Old Testament Problem* (Downers Grove, IL: InterVarsity Press, 2013).

[39] Habel, *The Land Is Mine*, 60.

[40] Habel, *The Land Is Mine*, 61.

for the conquest on the one hand and for normal warfare in Deuteronomy 20 on the other make clear that Israel's treatment of the Canaanites in Joshua is exceptional and is not to be repeated.[41]

In sum, these factors remove Israelite autonomy in initiating the conquest, make it clear that only divine help would make the conquest possible (there is no Israelite "military might"), and so remove it from the sphere of humanly conceived and executed imperialism. There is even an aspect of self-defense in response to the proactive, unilateral action of the Canaanites in the southern and northern campaigns.[42] The question of who has rights to the land is cast in terms of Yahweh as landowner; Yahweh gives residence to those who revere and obey him and removes from the earth those who rebel against him regardless of their ethnicity. This accounts for the prominence of the "ban" in the account and why it is applied not only to the Canaanites but also to Israel when she sins (Joshua 6–7). Seen in light of the whole Canon, the conquest is "anticipated eschatology,"[43] and Joshua's "rhetoric of violence is used in such a way that it is clear that the aggression could only be applied then and there to a selection of peoples."[44]

In Revelation, God's judgment against sinful humanity evokes praise and worship (Rev. 18:6–8, 19–20), and even in the Old Testament, the nations are told to rejoice in the conquest (Ps. 47:3–4). As long as we recognize that the "ethic" of the taking of the land is unique and cannot be replicated, there is no tension between it and either Jesus's ethical directives or those attributed to Moses that cover normal situations apart from the conquest. Indeed, Jesus's teaching on the topic of interpersonal ethics in large part repeats what God had already said through Moses (Lev. 19:18, cf. Matt. 5:43).

Israel and Yahweh

As hinted earlier, the theology of Joshua is dynamic, as the book's narrative flow clearly shows. While we have seen it play out in terms of the Israelite-Canaanite contrast, here we will explore its Israelite side. Our main reason for doing so is that this contrast early in the book forms the basis for the book's closing speeches (Josh. 23:1–24:28). These speeches then draw the book's account of the land's possession to a close in a hortatory manner (24:14–15). Despite having received the land as a free gift from Yahweh, is Israel even willing to continue as his people?

Israel's Unity

This question may seem radically pessimistic, for the book of Joshua presents Israel as essentially unified on the religious front. At the outset of the book, and for a good while afterward, Israel's unity is a prominent theme in Joshua. Israel is habitually

---

[41] As Hubbard puts it, "The Old Testament rarely recalls the violent conquest, never glories in its goriness, and never promotes it as policy for the future." *Joshua*, 47.
[42] These details undermine Collins's protest that "the unprovoked conquest of one people by another is an act of injustice." *Introduction to the Hebrew Bible*, 195.
[43] Meredith G. Kline, *The Structure of Biblical Authority* (Grand Rapids, MI: Eerdmans, 1972), 162–64.
[44] Koert van Bekkum, *From Conquest to Coexistence: Ideology and Antiquarian Intent in the Historiography of Israel's Settlement in Canaan*, CHANE 45 (Leiden: Brill, 2011), 581.

referred to as "the whole congregation," which implies their unity (cf. Joshua 22) and makes possible a contrast with the Canaanites. This unity also demands corporate responsibility, as is visible in Achan's case (Joshua 7; cf. also 22:18, 20). All in all, the nation remains unified throughout the book.

Israel's Obedience

Moreover, Israel displays a consistent record of obedience, at least until chapters 23 and 24. The absence of any large-scale disobedience in Joshua is all the more striking given the dark outlook of Deuteronomy. In this way, Vannoy is right to say that in the book of Joshua, "Israel has arrived at a high point in its history."[45] Consider the following list of positive aspects of Israel's actions and attitudes in Joshua:

- Israel's positive view of its present-tense obedience to Moses (1:17)
- The Transjordanian tribes' threat to execute Israelites who do not obey Joshua (1:18)
- Israel's collective execution of judgment on sinful Israelites who are identified corporately (7:24–26)
- Israel's victory over the Anakim, whom an earlier generation failed to dislodge from the land because they lacked faith in God (11:21–22; cf. Numbers 14)
- The fulfillment of the obligation of the Reubenites, Gadites, and half tribe of Manassehites to help the rest of Israel take Canaan (Josh. 22:1–4)
- The Cisjordanian tribes' readiness to enter a full-scale war against Reuben, Gad, and half of Manasseh for apparently violating the one-altar law (22:16; cf. Deut. 12:13–32)
- All Israel's "serving" God during the time of Joshua and his elders (Josh. 24:31)
- The burial of Joseph's bones at Shechem (24:32)

This list surely furnishes enough data to establish a trend! Yet apart from the last two items, all Israelite obedience appears *prior to* Joshua's closing speeches, which even in terms of literary order must be taken as the guide to interpreting the book as a whole. We thus need to determine what motivated Joshua to ask the radical question he did in those speeches. Before turning to the last chapter of the book, however, we must return briefly to the porous nature of Israel's boundaries as a people group and to the book's priority on fidelity to Yahweh rather than on ethnicity as the basis for being included in the people of God.

Inclusion in the People of God

We have already seen that Rahab's family and the Gibeonites both gained entry into Israel, the one on the basis of faith and the other for more pragmatic reasons. These two methods of entry into Israel receive different evaluations from the author of Joshua, who affirms that Rahab "has lived in Israel to this day, because she hid the messengers whom Joshua sent to spy out Jericho" (Josh. 6:25). The Gibeonites, however, are said to have been made "cutters of wood and drawers of water for the

---

[45] Vannoy, "Joshua: Theology of," 810.

congregation and for the altar of the LORD" (9:27). This difference underlines the legitimacy of entering Israel by faith and the illegitimacy of entering it without faith and by deception, and while Rahab attracts the positive attention of later biblical authors, the same cannot be said for the Gibeonites.

What makes Rahab's entry into Israel legitimate? While the book describes in some detail how she acts toward the spies and keeps her promise to them, it gives extensive attention to what she says to the spies in Joshua 2:9–13. This passage mentions a number of epistemological and spiritual commitments that Rahab has made in light of Israel's approach, and these clearly explain her behavior in this context.

Rahab begins her confession by affirming fundamentally that Yahweh is giving Israel the land on which she and the other Canaanites have lived until now. She continues by admitting that fear has seized the entire population because of what Yahweh did at the Red (or Reed) Sea and to Sihon and Og. Her closing statement crystallizes her belief in Yahweh as "God in the heavens above and on the earth beneath" (2:11; arguably an echo of Deut. 4:39, where it is part and parcel of an affirmation of Yahwistic monotheism; cf. Josh. 3:11; 1 Kings 8:23). That Rahab clearly recognizes Yahweh's supremacy and acts consistently with such a confession led later biblical authors to speak of her faith in contrast to that of the other Canaanites (Heb. 11:31), and James finds evidence in the narrative that her faith preceded her works (James 2:25).

Joshua's Final Speech and Israel's Identity

As we now turn to Joshua's closing speech, we do so with the example of Rahab especially in mind. Until Joshua 24 the evidence suggests that Israel's belief and behavior have been acceptable, if not above reproach, but in chapter 24 Joshua claims that there are fundamental problems with Israel's heart and life. The distinction that Joshua makes in his speech between those who are truly part of Israel and those who are not has been introduced in earlier episodes in the book, especially those concerning Rahab and Achan, but Joshua develops it further at this point.

Israel's Disobedience

We begin with Israel's obedience, or lack thereof. It seems that the book has intentionally withheld information from the reader until chapter 24 (a common literary technique), although there have been hints that not all is well with Israel. The following points, admittedly few in number, cast into doubt the absoluteness of Israel's obedience prior to Joshua's closing speech, which itself mentions other factors. These earlier hints include the following:

- Manasseh could not, and then did not, "utterly drive out" the Canaanites (17:13; similarly 15:63; cf. 17:18, which commands dispossession despite the Canaanites' strength).
- Ephraim did not drive out "the Canaanites who lived in Gezer" (16:10; similarly 13:13).

- This failure becomes descriptive of the majority of Israel by Joshua 18, as seven tribes have neglected "going in to take possession" of their inheritance (18:3).

Joshua's Final Command

To these veiled critiques of Israel's faith and practice we now add Joshua's accusations, which his audience does not refute and which occur in the very significant context of a covenant renewal (24:25; cf. the relation of 24:1b to Ex. 19:17).[46] These accusations include in particular the paired commands to "put away the foreign gods that are among you, and incline your heart to the LORD, the God of Israel" (Josh. 24:23). Throughout this speech the idea of "serving" Yahweh predominates, and in the dialogue between Joshua and Israel, those speaking for the community seem to discount entirely Joshua's increasingly sharp accusation that Israel is not presently "serving" Yahweh. When called to choose whom they will serve, a question that implies the absence of a clear choice to date, the speakers distance themselves from the accusation (24:14–18). When Joshua then states that Israel cannot serve Yahweh faithfully *as she is* but will inevitably forsake him and so deprive herself of the possibility of forgiveness, Israel reiterates her intention to serve Yahweh *as she is* (24:19–21).

After a warning, Joshua makes a last call for Israel to change, using the sharpest accusation in the speech and indeed in the book: "put away the foreign gods that are among you, and incline your heart to the LORD, the God of Israel" (24:23). Joshua tells the nation that if they intend to continue their covenant relationship with Yahweh, they must jettison the foreign gods that, by definition, are in their possession—at the present!—and turn their hearts to Yahweh. The audience's response to this last command is telling: Israel *does nothing* with respect to either jettisoning foreign gods or inclining her heart to Yahweh but merely reiterates her apparently superficial intention to do Yahweh's will (24:23–24).

Israel's Bifurcated Identity

Joshua 24 brings the book to a surprising close. Joshua and his household, defined as those who "serve Yahweh," are set over against the majority of the nation, which misunderstands true "service" of Yahweh by making it so superficial that idolatry is swept under the rug. Rahab's example of faithful obedience also leaves the reader to ponder how most of Israel as described in Joshua 24 would compare with her.

Perhaps most striking is the fact that in Joshua's closing speech, Israel remains one entity on the national level while clearly being divided into two on the religious level. Her identity, and thus her fate, seem to hang in the balance, and one must read the book of Judges to see how this question is resolved.[47]

---

[46] Hess, *Joshua*, 330.
[47] Given the polysemy of the term "serve" in Joshua 24, I am hesitant to affirm much as to the sense of 24:31 (cf. Judg. 2:7–10).

Approaching the New Testament

Despite the book's focus on the land, the main poles around which the theology of Joshua turns are the extermination of those who resist God and the granting of rest and partial enjoyment of the covenantal inheritance to those who believe and obey. Such trust and obedience are drawn into the future as the condition for Israel to retain the land already given and are constitutive of the covenant that Israel renews several times (Joshua 5; 8; 24). The conditionality that characterizes Israel's covenantal experience is complemented by the permeability of Israel's ethnic definition. Since birth in Israel is no guarantee of remaining in the land or avoiding the punishment that sin deserves (Achan), being born outside Israel or its territory poses no obstacle to the non-Israelite who submits to Yahweh and trusts him for deliverance from sin's punishment.

In covenantal terms, the book of Joshua shows that the Sinai covenant does not inevitably change the human condition. Death as a punishment for sin threatens all, and Joshua repeatedly asserts that faith and obedience are the way to life. The centralization of the cult in Joshua completes the picture of a life fully dedicated to Yahweh, allowing faithful Israelites to properly deal with sin's guilt and opening the way toward retention of the land and, ultimately, the covenant's fullest blessings.

All these themes find their fulfillment in the incarnation, life, death, resurrection, and rule of Jesus Christ. Taking these points in reverse order, Jesus's perfect obedience and substitutionary death are imputed to sinners of any ethnicity who place their trust in him as the only One who can deliver them from the wrath of God that threatens sinners. Union with Christ in his death and resurrection entails the most profound internal change, making those united with him alive to God and dead to sin (Rom. 6:11) and sealing them with the Spirit who is given as the ultimate blessing of the Abrahamic covenant (Gal. 3:2–9). Accordingly, there is neither Jew nor Gentile in the new covenant (Gal. 3:28), and the gospel is offered to all alike and without restriction. Union with Christ is also the fulfillment of what settled life and rest in the land prefigured, since by virtue of his perfect life and atoning death, believers have constant, unhindered access to God (Hebrews 9–10). Finally, Christ as Judge will one day apply the ultimate sanction of eternal death to those who persist in sinful rebellion against him.

By transforming the "nations" into a largely spiritual enemy (2 Cor. 10:3–6; Eph. 6:10–18), the New Testament recasts how God exercises his justice, having demonstrated it especially in the cross. Only in the eschaton (cf., e.g., Rev. 19:11–21) does God's wrath once again come to bear fully against guilty humanity, and in that case God's people are not his instrument. In the meantime, Israel's divinely enabled expulsion and destruction of the Canaanites must be seen as an analogy to the spread of the gospel over the globe in Acts, as King Jesus gradually extends his reign through the preaching of his Word and people's willful acceptance of it by faith and repentance. The New Testament's nonethnic, nonterritorial, spiritual paradigm provides clear boundaries for legitimate applications of the theology of Joshua to the church in the present age.

SELECT BIBLIOGRAPHY

Bekkum, Koert van. *From Conquest to Coexistence: Ideology and Antiquarian Intent in the Historiography of Israel's Settlement in Canaan*. CHANE 45. Leiden: Brill, 2011.

Brueggemann, Walter. *Divine Presence Amid Violence: Contextualizing the Book of Joshua*. Eugene, OR: Cascade, 2009.

Copan, Paul. *Is God a Moral Monster? Making Sense of the Old Testament God*. Grand Rapids, MI: Baker, 2011.

Finkelstein, Israel, and Amihay Mazar. *The Quest for the Historical Israel: Debating Archaeology and the History of Early Israel*. Edited by Brian B. Schmidt. ABS 17. Atlanta: Society of Biblical Literature, 2007.

Goldsworthy, Graeme. *Gospel-Centered Hermeneutics: Foundations and Principles of Evangelical Biblical Interpretation*. Downers Grove, IL: IVP Academic, 2006.

Habel, Norman C. *The Land Is Mine: Six Biblical Land Ideologies*. OBT. Minneapolis: Fortress, 1993.

Hess, Richard S. *Joshua*. TOTC 6. Downers Grove, IL: InterVarsity Press, 1996.

Hoffmeier, James K. "The Structure of Joshua 1–11 and the Annals of Thutmose III." In *Faith, Tradition, and History*, edited by A. R. Millard, James K. Hoffmeier, and David W. Baker, 165–80. Winona Lake, IN: Eisenbrauns, 1994.

House, Paul R. "The God Who Gives Rest in the Land: Joshua." *SBJT* 2 (1998): 23–33.

Howard, David M., Jr. *Joshua*. NAC 5. Nashville: Broadman, 2002.

Hubbard, Ronald L. *Joshua*. NIVAC. Grand Rapids, MI: Zondervan, 2009.

Johnston, Philip, and Peter Walker, eds. *The Land of Promise: Biblical, Theological, and Contemporary Perspectives*. Downers Grove, IL: InterVarsity Press, 2001.

Laansma, Jon. *"I Will Give You Rest": The "Rest" Motif in the New Testament with Special Reference to Mt 11 and Heb 3–4*. WUNT, 2nd ser., 98. Tübingen: Mohr Siebeck, 1997.

Lilley, J. P. U. "The Judgment of God: The Problem of the Canaanites." *Themelios*, n.s., 22 (1997): 3–12.

Martin, Oren R. *Bound for the Promised Land: The Land Promise in God's Redemptive Plan*. NSBT 34. Downers Grove, IL: InterVarsity Press, 2015.

McConville, J. Gordon. *God and Earthly Power: An Old Testament Political Theology, Genesis–Kings*. LHBOTS 454. London: T&T Clark, 2006.

Millar, J. Gary. "Land." In *New Dictionary of Biblical Theology*, edited by T. Desmond Alexander and Brian S. Rosner, 623–27. Downers Grove, IL: InterVarsity Press, 2000.

———. *Now Choose Life: Theology and Ethics in Deuteronomy*. NSBT. Downers Grove, IL: InterVarsity Press, 1998.

Miller, Patrick D. "The Gift of God: The Deuteronomic Theology of the Land." *Interpretation* 23, no. 4 (1969): 461–65.

———. "The Story of the First Commandment: Joshua." In *Covenant or Context: Essays in Honour of E. W. Nicholson*, edited by A. D. H. Mayes and Robert B. Salters, 80–90. Oxford: Oxford University Press, 2003.

Nelson, Richard D. *Joshua: A Commentary*. OTL. Louisville: Westminster John Knox, 1997.

Provan, Iain W., V. Philips Long, and Tremper Longman III. *A Biblical History of Israel*. Louisville: Westminster John Knox, 2003.

Stone, Lawson G. "Early Israel and Its Appearance in Canaan." In *Ancient Israel's History: An Introduction to Issues and Sources*, edited by Bill T. Arnold and Richard S. Hess, 127–64. Grand Rapids, MI: Baker Academic, 2014.

———. "Ethical and Apologetic Tendencies in the Redaction of the Book of Joshua." *CBQ* 53, no. 1 (1991): 25–35.

Thigpen, J. Michael. "Lord of All the Earth: Yahweh and Baal in Joshua 3." *TJ*, n.s., 27, no. 2 (2006): 245–54.

Thomas, Heath, Jeremy A. Evans, and Paul Copan, eds. *Holy War in the Bible: Christian Morality and an Old Testament Problem*. Downers Grove, IL: InterVarsity Press, 2013.

Timmer, Daniel C. *Creation, Tabernacle, and Sabbath: The Sabbath Frame of Exodus 31:12–17; 35:1–3 in Exegetical and Theological Perspective*. FRLANT 227. Göttingen: Vandenhoeck & Ruprecht, 2009.

Vannoy, J. Robert. "Joshua, Theology of." In *New International Dictionary of Old Testament Theology and Exegesis*, edited by Willem A. VanGemeren, 4:810–19. Grand Rapids, MI: Zondervan, 1997.

Younger, K. Lawson, Jr. *Ancient Conquest Accounts: A Study in Ancient Near Eastern and Biblical History Writing*. JSOTSup 98. Sheffield: JSOT Press, 1990.

7

Judges

Michael J. Glodo

INTRODUCTION

The book of Judges records the history of Israel's unfaithfulness and their repeated deliverance through heroic figures raised up by their faithful covenant God. It is the second of the Historical Books, or Former Prophets, a term reminding us that biblical history is not merely a catalog of "brute facts" but the "preaching" of history with its divine meaning.

In Judges this proclamation indicts the people of Israel living between the times of Joshua and the monarchy, not only with the fourfold refrain found in its epilogue—"In those days there was no king in Israel" (Judg. 17:6; 18:1; 19:1; 21:25), with the first and fourth occurrences adding, "Everyone did what was right in his own eyes"—but also in its characterization of the judges themselves. Even though the judges were courageous and successful, representative actions reveal flaws either in themselves or in those associated with them. The judges were, after all, called out from among the very people who went after other gods.

Yet the book of Judges also proclaims the Lord as Israel's long-suffering and powerful deliverer (2:18) who raised up the judges to relieve the oppression of his people (2:16). Israel was to understand these oppressive times as the chastening hand of their faithful covenant Lord aiming to turn them back to himself (2:22).

These judges were nothing like the black-robed figures of modern courts; they were military and tribal leaders. Waltke proposes the more descriptive term "warlords," highlighting their military and ruling roles.[1] While the book of Judges at least once refers to a judge exercising a judicial role (4:5), the focus of their activity was bringing

---

[1] Bruce K. Waltke, *An Old Testament Theology: An Exegetical, Canonical, and Thematic Approach*, with Charles Yu (Grand Rapids, MI: Zondervan, 2007), 588–89.

salvation through military action as an agent of God. And so the work of the judges is often described as "saving" or "salvation" (3:9, 31; 10:1; 13:5). The introduction to the book (1:1–3:6) refers to the judges collectively as "judges," though none are referred to individually as a "judge." However, their actions are often described by the verb "to judge" (שָׁפַט, e.g., 3:10; 4:4; 10:2–3). Perhaps this was intended to reinforce the notion that the Lord was Israel's true Judge (11:27).

BACKGROUND ISSUES

Based on the traditional date for the exodus (1446 BC), the period of history covered by Judges is approximately 1375–1092 BC. If Joshua was forty years old when the spies were sent into the land (Josh. 14:7) and a forty-year gap separated the exodus from the conquest, then Joshua would have been eighty at the start of the conquest, around 1406 BC. Therefore, at 110 years old (Judg. 2:8), Joshua would have died around 1376 BC. If David's reign began in 1010 BC and Saul reigned thirty-two years prior to that, and if we estimate eighty years for the combined rules of the last two judges, Eli and Samuel (treated in 1 Samuel), the events in the book of Judges would end around 1122 BC.[2] A linear reconstruction of the chronological references within the book totals 410 years, but because the reigns of various judges in different regions could have overlapped, such a reconstruction is tenuous.[3]

The authorship of Judges is anonymous. However, the author presents and evaluates the events of the book through a consistent theological perspective, the perspective of Deuteronomy. The fact that the book of Judges reflects the theology of Deuteronomy simply means that the author of Judges understood the covenant of Deuteronomy as the basis on which to evaluate Israel's unfaithfulness and God's faithfulness. This reality affirms that "Deuteronomy is both the capstone of the Pentateuch and the foundation stone of the Deuteronomistic History [i.e., Former Prophets]."[4]

The canonical version of Judges was likely completed some time after the monarchy began, as indicated by the refrain, "in those days there was no king in Israel" (17:6; 18:1; 19:1; 21:25). The expression "the day of the captivity of the land" in 18:30 holds several possibilities for dating, ranging from the Babylonian captivity to an early, premonarchic situation, such as a local incursion of the Philistines (e.g., when the ark was seized in 1 Sam. 4:1–11).[5] The unfaithfulness and idolatry of the northern tribes (e.g., Judg. 1:27–36) and Benjamin (19:1–20:48) suggest a pro-Judah and Davidic perspective.[6] Pratt suggests a date for completion that coincides with

---

[2] So Barry G. Webb, *The Book of Judges*, NICOT (Grand Rapids, MI: Eerdmans, 2012), 10.

[3] The proposal of 410 years with some overlapping is more plausible than the approximately 120-year span of the judges necessitated by a late date for the exodus in 1267 BC, which most critical and some evangelical scholars hold. Also, the early date for the exodus would put Jephthah's statement regarding three hundred years of occupation around 1105 BC (Judg. 11:26). Late-date proponents must take his statement as hyperbole or else it would have happened around the time of Solomon's dedication of the temple in 966 BC. See the table in Lawson G. Stone, "Judges, Book of," in *Dictionary of the Old Testament: Historical Books: A Compendium of Contemporary Biblical Scholarship*, ed. Bill T. Arnold and Hugh G. M. Williamson, IVP Bible Dictionary Series 2 (Downers Grove, IL: InterVarsity Press, 2005), 601.

[4] Waltke with Yu, *Old Testament Theology*, 57.

[5] For a brief but thorough discussion of these and several options, see Tremper Longman III and Raymond B. Dillard, *An Introduction to the Old Testament*, 2nd ed. (Grand Rapids, MI: Zondervan, 2006), 135.

[6] Dale Ralph Davis, *Judges: Such a Great Salvation*, Focus on the Bible: Expositor's Guide to the Historical Books (Fearn, Ross-shire, Scotland: Christian Focus, 2007), 24, 80–82, 130–31.

the completion of 1–2 Samuel because the account of Samuel's birth parallels that of Samson's birth.[7]

The accounts of the individual judges likely developed as they happened, moving from oral to fixed literary forms. These narratives, due to their similar subject matter, would have been gathered by official historians.[8] The prologue(s) and epilogue(s), with their interpretive agendas, could have been added at any point within the range of possible dates discussed earlier. Because the author and the original audience are not indicated by the text or any subsequent tradition, we must make sure that our interpretive approach accommodates the range of possibilities while adhering to the historical integrity of the events.

STRUCTURE AND OUTLINE

Literary Composition

Judges features a prologue (introduction) and an epilogue (conclusion) with a main body containing the storied accounts of Israel's twelve judge-deliverers. Davis has provided a helpful threefold outline: (1) the failure of the second generation (1:1–3:6); (2) the salvation of a long-suffering God (3:7–16:31); and (3) the confusion of a depraved people (17:1–21:25).[9] The prologue and the epilogue each reveal a twofold or double structure. The prologue is marked by the twofold mention of Joshua's death (1:1; 2:8), and the epilogue is identified by two lengthy but related narratives of the Levite (17:1–18:31; 19:1–21:25).

Scholars frequently suggest that Judges has a chiastic structure centering on "the personal story of flawed Gideon" with contrasting pairs of women that provide a dramatic contrast between the first and second halves of Judges.[10] At the center stands either Gideon—with his struggle to believe, his casting of an idolatrous ephod, and his establishment of false worship in Ophrah—or Abimelech—as a self appointed anti-judge.[11] There is little question, however, that after the Gideon-Abimelech sequence, a decline occurs in Israel's spiritual state and the national conditions marked by increasing intrafraternal strife. As Waltke summarizes, "From Gideon onward, the behavior of Israel's tribal leaders . . . progressively becomes more questionable."[12]

Proposed Outline

Enclosed by dual prologues and epilogues, the main body contains six major judges, six minor judges, and one anti-judge (Abimelech). The first prologue relates Israel's history after the death of Joshua from the standpoint of Israel's experience. The second prologue presents the same events from God's point of view, revealing the

---

[7] Richard L. Pratt Jr., *He Gave Us Stories: The Bible Student's Guide to Interpreting Old Testament Narratives* (Phillipsburg, NJ: P&R, 1993), 290.

[8] See the discussion of official historians, or the scribal class, in the "Authorship" section of the chapter on Numbers (p. 110).

[9] Davis, *Judges*, 12. That said, the term "confusion" does not go far enough to describe the cause and conditions of the prologue(s).

[10] Waltke with Yu, *Old Testament Theology*, 592–93.

[11] See "Abimelech (Judg. 9:1–57)" on p. 190. The term "anti-judge," while broadly used, I received from my colleague Miles Van Pelt.

[12] Waltke with Yu, *Old Testament Theology*, 593n16.

cause-and-effect relationship between Israel's disobedience and the resulting national strife. The main body of Judges recounts the individual cycles of apostasy, servitude, supplication, and salvation summarized in the second prologue. The two-part epilogue concludes by demonstrating the depth of Israel's idolatry through the setting up of the idolatrous shrine in Ephraim and through Israel's fraternal fractiousness, where Benjaminites act like Sodomites, provoking the whole nation into holy war against Benjamin.

I. Prologues (1:1–3:6)
   A. Prologue 1: Conquest after Joshua—Israel's perspective (1:1–2:5)
      1. Initial success behind Judah (1:1–26)
      2. The conquest falters and fails (1:27–36)
      3. Covenant reminder and warning (2:1–5)
   B. Prologue 2: Conquest after Joshua—divine perspective (2:6–3:6)
      1. The death of Joshua and loss of covenant memory (2:6–10)
      2. The descent into apostasy and its consequence (2:11–15)
      3. Summary of judgment cycles (2:16–3:6)
II. Israel's Judges: Cycles of Apostasy, Servitude, Supplication, and Salvation (3:7–16:31) *(see table 17 for an analysis of the judges)*
III. Epilogues: The Depths of Israel's "Canaanization"[13] (17:1–21:25)
   A. Epilogue 1: Apostasy in Dan (17:1–18:31)
   B. Epilogue 2: Strife with Benjamin (19:1–21:25)

MESSAGE AND THEOLOGY

The message of Judges is summed up well in 2:11–23. Though experiencing limited success after the death of Joshua and under the leadership of Judah, the conquest of the Promised Land stalled because of unbelief and idolatry. Contrary to the warnings of Exodus (23:23–33), Numbers (33:55–56), and Deuteronomy (7:1–5), Israel permitted the Canaanites to coexist with God's people. Even where the tribes of Israel had the advantage, they placed Canaanites into forced labor rather than devoting them to destruction. As their zeal for the covenant flagged, Israel grew more and more vulnerable to idolatry. They eventually began to worship and serve the gods of the Canaanites. Consequently, God subjected his people to oppression by these peoples as a way of humbling them. When they cried out to the Lord, he sent deliverers to save them. However, after each deliverance, Israel relapsed into accommodation and idolatry and repeated the cycle, degenerating further each time. Judges contrasts these tendencies with the covenant faithfulness of God.

Judges must be read against the background of Joshua, which describes a more positive beginning for God's people in the land (Josh. 1:16–18). With the death of Joshua, Israel was left without the necessary leadership to keep them from idolatry. Judges vindicates God's chastening, for though he chastened, he did not abandon his people. He was faithful to preserve, hear, deliver, and provide for them, but the temporary judges were insufficient to prevent the cycle from recurring. Israel would

---

[13] The term *Canaanization* was coined by Daniel I. Block, *Judges, Ruth*, NAC 6 (Nashville: Broadman, 1999), 473.

Major judge	Minor judge	Judges passage	Israel does evil in the eyes of the Lord	The Lord's anger is provoked; an enemy oppresses them	Israel cries out to the Lord	The Lord hears their cry and provides a savior	The Lord chooses and empowers the savior by the Spirit	The oppressor submits, followed by a period of peace under the judge	The deliverer dies	Years of oppression / peace
Summary		2:11–23	✓	✓	✓	✓			✓	
Othniel		3:7–11	✓	✓	✓	✓	✓	✓	✓	8 / 40
Ehud		3:12–30	✓	✓	✓	✓			✓	18 / 80
	Shamgar	3:31								
Deborah and Barak		4:1–5:31	✓	✓	✓	✓				20 / 40
Gideon		6:1–8:35	✓	✓	✓	✓	✓	✓	✓	7 / 40
[Abimelech]*		9:1–57					†		✓	3‡ / 23
	Tola	10:1–2							✓	
	Jair	10:3–5							✓	0 / 22
Jephthah		10:6–12:7	✓	✓	✓	✓	✓		✓	18 / 6
	Ibzan	12:8–10						✓	✓	0 / 7
	Elon	12:11–12							✓	0 / 10
	Abdon	12:13–15							✓	0 / 8
Samson		13:1–16:31	✓			✓	✓ (4x)		✓	40 / 20

Table 17

* Not truly a judge.
† The Spirit of God doesn't empower Abimelech, but God does send an "evil spirit" to bring disharmony between Abimelech and the leaders of Shechem (Judg. 9:23).
‡ The 3 here refers to the unusual mention in 9:22 that Abimelech "ruled over" (שׂרר) Israel three years, the only time this verb is used in Judges and a term that differs from the verb "to judge" (שׁפט). Given the overall negative characterization of Abimelech, this reference may reveal the author's intentionally ambivalent assessment of those three years.

have to look to God to do what Deuteronomy 17 anticipated: appoint a king who would rule according to God's covenant. But not a king from the northern tribes, which so easily acceded to the Canaanites, and not one from Benjamin, which was unable to drive out the Jebusites from Jerusalem and acted wickedly toward their own countryman (Judges 19). The king must come from Judah—"Judah shall go up" (Judg. 1:1)—just as the patriarch Jacob had anticipated over five centuries earlier (Gen. 49:8–10).

Judges must also be read against the backdrop of past warnings (Ex. 23:23–33; Josh. 23:11–13, 15), as summarized in Numbers 33:55.

> But if you do not drive out the inhabitants of the land from before you, then those of them whom you let remain shall be as barbs in your eyes and thorns in your sides, and they shall trouble you in the land where you dwell. (Num. 33:55)

Judges echoes the verity of those warnings: "So now I say, I will not drive them out before you, but they shall become thorns in your sides, and their gods shall be a snare to you" (Judg. 2:3).

In Wilcock's analogy, Judges is like a "precarious bridge" suspended between the exodus and the monarchy, but only apparently precarious because God upholds his people even in precarious times: "God's people are as secure on it as the cliffs at either end of it."[14]

Prologues (Judg. 1:1–3:6)

The first prologue (1:1–2:5) describes initial but limited success. The arrival of the angel of the Lord (2:1) marks a shift in perspective, and the second prologue (2:6–3:6) presents this other, divine perspective. Both mention Joshua's death (1:1; 2:6–8) and cover the same series of events, but the first is a sheer statement of events with hints for the perceptive reader, while the second makes explicit the true nature of the events. As Gros Louis and Van Antwerpen explain,

> Judges 1–3 provides a thematic link with Joshua, and the description of 2:12–21 underlines for us the changed order. The pattern described here is imitated through the accounts of the greater judges . . . There is a certain futility about the alternation of glory and misery in Judges that, while not overwhelming in Joshua, certainly is presaged. There is not, however, anything aimless or meaningless about this futility . . . since here God comes repeatedly to Israel's aid, and his actions indicate a profound concern and affection for Israel.[15]

Prologue 1: Conquest after Joshua—Israel's Perspective (Judg. 1:1–2:5)

The first prologue relates the progress of conquest from the death of Joshua to the unfortunate equilibrium that characterizes Israel's situation under the judges. Under

---

[14] Michael Wilcock, *The Message of Judges: Grace Abounding*, The Bible Speaks Today (Downers Grove, IL: InterVarsity Press, 1992), 15.

[15] Kenneth R. R. Gros Louis and Willard Van Antwerpen Jr., "Joshua and Judges," in *A Complete Literary Guide to the Bible*, ed. Leland Ryken and Tremper Longman III (Grand Rapids, MI: Zondervan, 1993), 144.

Joshua, the key cities were subdued, but the subsequent, full securing of the territories proved to be anything but easy. With Judah in the lead, Israel experienced initial success, but as the movement progressed from south to north, their success waned. Unlike the victories chronicled in Joshua 12, the tribes were not able to completely drive out the Canaanites (Judg. 1:19, 21) and resorted to placing them under forced labor (1:28, 30, 33), as those partially vanquished were permitted to live among the Israelites (1:32, 33).

The conquest itself was to have been characterized by a complete ban (i.e., holy war), not subjugation and enrichment. To devote the Canaanites to absolute destruction (חֵרֶם) was not simply to annihilate but to make a burnt offering of the offending presence of sin and idolatry. This is also what the law required of an idolatrous Israelite city that must be "devot[ed] to destruction" and made "a whole burnt offering" (Deut. 13:14–16).[16] No plunder was to be retained and no combatants preserved, unlike normal state war in which "to the victor go the spoils."

The partial victories here may have ended hostilities and gained a labor force, but that labor force would eventually become the "snare and trap" about which Moses and Joshua had warned (Num. 33:55; Josh. 23:13; cf. Judg. 2:3).[17] Since these dire consequences seem to have been forgotten by the first generation in Judges (2:10b), the angel of the Lord had to visit Israel again to remind them. The "remaining Canaanites would not be so much a military threat as a spiritual cancer."[18]

As Waltke points out, covenant fidelity was the condition for taking the land, possessing it, and retaining it. In order to be faithful to the Lord and remain in the land, "Israel must possess the Land by dispossessing its contagious inhabitants. . . . Unless they drive out the Serpent/the Canaanites out of the Garden/Land, the Serpent/Canaanite defilement will drive them out. Peaceful coexistence with this spiritual enemy is not an option."[19]

Prologue 1 provides the historical material upon which the theological characterization of prologue 2 depends. "Indeed, it builds its first stage in its pattern of divine help on the fact of Israel's disobedience. . . . The point is thus made that in spite of the repeated intervention of divine aid, the period is correctly characterized by the state of the nation in the introduction."[20]

Prologue 2: Conquest after Joshua—Divine Perspective (Judg. 2:6–3:6)

The second prologue reviews the same events but from the divine perspective, delineating the true cause-and-effect relationship. Failure to take the land had constituted a breach of the covenant. While the second generation had witnessed God's faithfulness,

---

[16] Vern S. Poythress, *The Shadow of Christ in the Law of Moses* (Phillipsburg, NJ: P&R, 1995), 139–42.
[17] This is the heart of the problem in 1 Samuel 15, when Saul punished the Amalekites. He spared Agag and the best of the spoils, purportedly to make a burnt offering of the latter and perhaps to subjugate Agag as a vassal king. In attempting to elevate himself as both a priestly and a kingly figure, he sinned in the manner of Achan (Joshua 7) and of the compromised conquest. This is partly why a Saulite king would not do. For more on understanding holy war in its Old Testament context and under the progress of redemption, see Tremper Longman III and Daniel G. Reid, *God Is a Warrior*, SOTBT (Grand Rapids, MI: Zondervan, 1995), 31–60.
[18] Davis, *Judges*, 24.
[19] Waltke with Yu, *Old Testament Theology*, 544.
[20] Brevard S. Childs, *Introduction to the Old Testament as Scripture* (Philadelphia: Fortress, 1979), 259.

this generation had "covenant amnesia" (cf. 2:10b). They had failed to preserve the lesson of Balaam's stratagem that threats from within were more lethal than those from without (Num. 31:6). Consequently, God would allow Israel to be oppressed by the Canaanites in the land so that his people would turn back to him. If they did, God would raise up a judge through whom he would bring salvation (Judg. 2:18). Even though God would deliver his people, the lessons were not learned, hearts were not changed, and the results did not last. So the cycle would begin again, and Israel would experience what Davis terms "generation degeneration."[21]

Webb detects a progression in this process, much like what we see of Lot in relation to Sodom. Lot lived in the vicinity of Sodom, then outside Sodom, and finally within the city. The Canaanites first lived at a distance, then they lived among the Israelites, and eventually Israel dwelt among the Canaanites.[22]

Israel's Judges: Cycles of Apostasy, Servitude, Supplication, and Salvation (Judg. 3:7–16:31)

Following the dual prologue, the individual accounts of the twelve judges proceed. The perceptive eye will not only decipher each individual story on its own but also detect a deterioration as he or she passes from one judge to the next. For example, as table 17 (p. 181) shows, the years of oppression under each judge increase while the years of peace decrease. So not only will each individual judge account show the need for a king, so will the trajectory of all the accounts taken together. These accounts remain distinctive yet have been woven into a quilt, if you will, under the hand of a skilled *litterateur*. "This editor provided a uniform pattern into which he fitted a collection of very disparate events . . . [with] one common purpose of illustrating a recurring pattern within history" such that "the pattern did not seriously alter the original shape of the stories."[23]

Othniel (Judg. 3:7–11)

Othniel, the son-in-law of Caleb (1:13–15; cf. Josh. 15:13–19), is the first of the major judges. This account constitutes the standard from which the rest of the judges may be judged. The plot contains the basic elements of the judgment cycles: Israel sinned by turning away from God and toward the Canaanite gods; God became angry; Israel fell into oppression by a foreign people group and was subjugated for a time; they cried out to God; and then he saved them by raising up a deliverer. The first deliverer, Othniel, was empowered by the Spirit of God, fought against the dominating power, and was given victory by God such that Israel was free for a specified period of time.[24]

Freedom from oppression is expressed in terms of the land having "rest" (שָׁקַט,

---

[21] Davis, *Judges*, 29.

[22] Barry G. Webb, *The Book of the Judges: An Integrated Reading*, JSOTSup 46 (Sheffield: JSOT Press, 1987), 99.

[23] Childs, *Introduction to the Old Testament as Scripture*, 260.

[24] The contemporary reader should not misconstrue endowment with the Spirit of God to correlate with personal holiness. In Judges this expression denotes divine agency and empowerment without necessarily referring to the spiritual fitness, or "sanctification," of the person. For a treatment of the role of the Holy Spirit in the Old Testament, see B. B. Warfield, "The Spirit of God in the Old Testament," in *The Person and Work of the Holy Spirit*, ed. Samuel G. Craig (Phillipsburg, NJ: P&R, 1968), 127–57.

Judg. 3:11, 30; 5:31; 8:28). The sense of "rest" here is freedom from enemies, language associated with God's promise to David (2 Sam. 7:1, 11) and the success of Solomon (1 Kings 5:4). Othniel is the window through which we look at all the other judges. Of the seven elements characteristic of the judge cycles (see table 17 on p. 181), all are present here. As the cycles progress, devolution is reflected in the decreasing number of elements that appear in each cycle.

With Othniel we see the central function of a "judge" in Judges—to go to war (Judg. 3:10). The term for "deliverer," מוֹשִׁיעַ, is derived from the verb "to save," יָשַׁע. In a very genuine sense, then, "deliverer" means "savior." The description of how Othniel saved is almost nondescript, especially when compared to the other judges. However, as a member of the tribe of Judah, as the first judge mentioned and as one who lacks the glaring faults of most of the other judges, Othniel feeds the pro-Judah agenda of Judges.

Ehud (Judg. 3:12–30)

The story of Ehud is, by contrast, bursting with vivid detail. It is a viable candidate for the most intentionally ironic tale in Scripture. The occasion for the rise of tension is not the characteristic statement that God was angry with Israel because of its idolatry but the mention that God "strengthened" or "hardened" Eglon against Israel (3:12)—the same term used to describe God's hardening of Pharaoh in Exodus (e.g., Ex. 7:3, 22; 8:19).

Israel "served" (Judg. 3:14) the Moabite king, Eglon, whose name means "calf"—eerily reminiscent of idolatrous Israel at the foot of Mount Sinai worshiping the golden calf. Eglon's league with Ammon and Amalek constituted a coalition of non-Canaanites, all of whom had harassed Israel needlessly as it passed through the wilderness (Ex. 17:8–16; Num. 21:21; 22:1–24:25). The combination of these factors creates a setting that resembles the wilderness testing that the first generation had failed.

Ehud's father is Gera, a son of Benjamin, which translates "a son of the right hand" (cf. Judg. 3:15). Yet he is also described as left-handed or literally "bound in the right hand."[25] The term used here for "left" is not the common Hebrew term for "left." The Bible uses this expression only here and in Judges 20:16, where it refers to the Benjaminites in the conflict following the scandalous events of chapter 19. So even though he will deliver Israel, he is a Benjaminite—and a left-handed one at that. The Benjaminites among David's mighty men were renowned for being ambidextrous in battle, according to 1 Chronicles 12:2, but that passage uses the common term for "left-handed." Being "bound in the right hand" likely means Ehud had limited usage of that hand, a sometimes desired quality in those chosen for diplomacy because of its disarming effect—he would not have been perceived as a threat. And it was in this role of ambassador for God that Ehud solicited Eglon to hear a "secret message" from the Lord (Judg. 3:19).

---

25 Wilhelm Gesenius and Samuel Prideaux Tregelles, *Gesenius's Hebrew and Chaldee Lexicon to the Old Testament Scriptures* (New York: John Wiley & Sons, 1893), 35.

As Alter points out, the detailed description of the preparation of the sword is "rather uncharacteristic" in the Old Testament.[26] The sword's length is more suitable for close quarters or an assassination, not battle. It had two edges, or literally "two mouths," and it was made especially for this task (3:16). Ehud's "word" for the king is expressed in the Hebrew noun דָּבָר, which can mean "word," "message," or "thing." The irony becomes clear when Ehud's embrace reveals that this "word" from the Lord was a custom-tailored sword thrust into his abdomen.

We know that Eglon was obese, not a quality normally associated with a warrior-king. His name, which means "calf," thus has a dual connotation. He turns out to be a fatted calf ready for slaughter.[27] He is unmistakably gluttonous and gullible, a dumb animal ready for the slaughter he deserves. In the final irony of the story, the murder weapon is subsumed into the victim and the odor of his defecation provides a cover for the assassin's escape.

Shamgar (Judg. 3:31)

While Ehud used a custom dagger, Shamgar employed an ox goad, or cattle prod, to defeat Israel's enemies. The armory of the judges ranges widely—Jael assassinated Sisera with a mallet and tent peg, Abimelech's skull was crushed by a millstone, and Samson slew his thousands with a donkey's jawbone. A complete inventory would include trumpets, clay pots, torches, burning foxes, and pillars. Most are weapons of opportunity, and they all reflect unconventional warfare. Though the description of Shamgar's exploits is brief, he is memorialized in Deborah's song (5:6).

Deborah and Barak (Judg. 4:1–5:31)

The Deborah and Barak cycle reaches back to the rule of Ehud as a reference point (4:1). The nemesis this time is Sisera, proxy general of the Canaanite king, Jabin, in Hazor, within the territory of the northern tribe Naphtali. In this instance, God "sold" (4:2) Israel into their hands because of their evil, as he would in the days preceding Jephthah (10:7). Sisera, like the foes of Judah in 1:19, had "chariots of iron" (4:3), perhaps meaning armored wooden chariots.

Deborah is presented as a prophetess who presided as a judge or arbiter (4:4–5), perhaps explaining why she expected that Barak should rise to the occasion as deliverer (4:6). Barak's reticence and Deborah's response (4:9)—along with her dual role with Jael in achieving success—highlights the important role of women in the book of Judges.

Barak, in response to Deborah's rebuke and her prophetic announcement of assured victory, attacked and prevailed, but Sisera escaped. He sought shelter in the tent of Jael, a Kenite (Kenites were non-Israelites descended from Jethro, Moses's father-in-law, who had chosen to remain with Israel and were allied with Judah, 1:16). Her alluring invitation and nonthreatening ethnicity lured Sisera into a false confidence

---

[26] Robert Alter, *The Art of Biblical Narrative* (New York: Basic Books, 1981), 38.
[27] Waltke with Yu, *Old Testament Theology*, 598.

and into her tent. Sated from the milk she provided and wearied by battle, Sisera fell asleep, whereupon Jael quietly but efficiently drove a tent peg into his skull. Her tent was no sanctuary after all.

Was Barak a coward? Deborah's chide invites the question (4:6). Webb thinks Barak's faith was present but not exemplary.[28] After all, he did lead Israel to overwhelming victory. His name means "lightning," suggesting that he was a fitting instrument of judgment against those who worshiped the storm god Baal. He fought on behalf of the true God of the storm (5:4–5; cf. Psalm 104). Yet his hesitation cost him the glory of felling Sisera (Judg. 4:9).

Jael is the first of three renowned heroines in Jewish history who bested powerful men in scenes involving sleeping chambers and satiation, the other two being Esther and Judith.[29] However, as the conclusion of Deborah and Barak's song reminds us, God is the real hero who scatters his enemies and returns to his covenant people with salvation (Judg. 5:31; Num. 10:35–36). The crushing of Sisera's head reminds us of God's promise in Genesis 3:15 that the seed of the woman will crush the head of the seed of the Serpent.

Gideon (Judg. 6:1–8:35)

The Gideon narrative (including Abimelech) fills four chapters. The story begins with the refrain of Israel doing evil in God's sight (6:1) and Midian becoming the oppressor. Midian descended from Abraham and his second wife, Keturah (Gen. 25:1–2). Midian's descendants purchased Joseph and took him to Egypt as a slave (Gen. 37:28, 36). Thus the Midianites along with the Amalekites were, as with the oppressors in the Deborah cycle, from beyond the borders of Canaan. Israel was living in "dens," "caves," and "strongholds" because the Midianites and others would come from the east and sweep across southern Israel plundering everything in their path (6:2). Israel also feared the gods of the Amorites, Baal worshipers in Canaan (6:10). Israel's cries to God were heeded when he sent a prophet to remind Israel of God's great acts of deliverance from Egypt (6:7–9). The mighty acts of God in Egypt and the conquest were to be the source of Israel's confidence in the present (cf. Ps. 77:11–20). Like a modern-day evangelist, the prophet came declaring that the great act of salvation had already occurred in the past, and thus God could be trusted to provide salvation in the present.

The well-known call sequence of Gideon follows. He was called by the angel of the Lord in a way reminiscent of Moses (Judg. 6:11–32); he struggled to accept that call (6:36–7:18); and he finally responded by leading his downsized army to victory in a manner echoing Joshua at Jericho (7:19–8:21; cf. Joshua 6). When he was called, Gideon was treading grain in a winepress, which he hoped would hide him (Judg. 6:11), like Moses who fled in fear of Pharaoh. Also like Moses, the angel of the Lord appeared to Gideon and announced that God had heard the cry of his people, had

28 Barry G. Webb, "The Wars of Judges as Christian Scripture," *RTR* 67, no. 1 (2008): 27.
29 Nicole Duran, "Having Men for Dinner: Deadly Banquets and Biblical Women," *BTB* 35, no. 4 (2005): 117–24.

called the deliverer, and had promised his divine presence (6:12; cf. Exodus 3). And as with Moses, Gideon disputed with God about his call (Judg. 6:13–16). Whereas Barak had the witness of a prophetess, Gideon had the witness of the Lord himself that he would succeed. God's response to Gideon's hospitality (6:19–24) brought Gideon a full realization that his guest was the Lord himself whose personal message to Gideon was "Peace be to you. Do not fear" (6:23).

Following this calling episode, Gideon obeyed God's command to tear down the altar of Baal—with no response from Baal. Baal and the Asherim had proven powerless—or disinterested—so Gideon should have been emboldened. But instead, he asked for a sign. In the persuasion sequence that followed, Gideon specified what proof of his calling he wanted God to give: the fleece (6:36–40). And God condescended to grant him the sign.

Was the fleece request an act of faith or unbelief? Waltke is unequivocal when he says, "His request for a wet fleece in a dry field and then a dry fleece in a wet field reveals his lack of faith in God's word from none other than the awesome angel of I AM."[30] Wilcock first takes a middle position—"the important thing about guidance is not the method but the fact"—but then tilts toward the negative: "Here the Lord is coaxing along a reluctant leader who really is 'diffident, modest and shy', and who needs to have his confidence built up step-by-step by a patient, loving, but determined God."[31] Davis sees Gideon as "hesitant, but not unbelieving."[32] Webb states, "Gideon's fleece is hardly exemplary. It certainly doesn't show him at his best, and the common practice of taking it as a model for seeking and obtaining divine guidance is highly questionable, to say the least."[33] Gideon himself seemingly admitted the same by saying, "Let not your anger burn against me" (6:39).

However, the criteria for Gideon's test weren't arbitrary. As Chisholm notes, they involved a test between Israel's God and Baal, the Canaanite god of rain and dew. "In one Ugaritic legend Baal's weakness results in the disappearance of rain and dew. . . . One of Baal's daughters is even named 'Dew.'"[34] Gideon was asking God to show his sovereignty over Baal by showing his sovereignty over the dew. Gideon clearly understood what God had commanded. The fleece was a request for God to confirm his power, not merely for Gideon to discover his will. Again, recalling Moses is helpful. Like Gideon, Moses doubted God's power to do what he had announced. In response, God gave Moses the sign of the rod turned into a serpent, which prefigured God's conquest over the serpentine god of Egypt (Ex. 4:1–9; cf. 12:12). These more nuanced associations of the fleece make it clear that the sign involved the power of the Lord over that of the gods of Israel's oppressor.

God provided further reassurance in the "reduction of force" sequence (Judg. 7:1–8). God would create a situation in which he would get full credit for the victory. The scene took place as Israel was camped by "the spring of Harod (7:1)," a

---

[30] Waltke with Yu, *Old Testament Theology*, 602.
[31] Wilcock, *Message of Judges*, 82.
[32] Davis, *Judges*, 99.
[33] Webb, *Judges*, NICOT, 239.
[34] Robert B. Chisholm Jr., *A Commentary on Judges and Ruth*, KEL (Grand Rapids, MI: Kregel, 2013), 279.

name that means "trembling" (7:3). The reduction of forces took place in two stages. Those who were afraid and "trembling" were sent home first. Those who remained were invited to drink; some lapped the water like a dog, while others kneeled and scooped water with their hands.

Why were the lappers kept? Were the lappers more cautious? It would seem the opposite. Was it because, as more doglike, they were more likely to be fierce? No, the purpose of the exercise was to achieve the smallest number, i.e., the least likely way to drink water. As Chisholm notes, "It is unlikely that their drinking posture implies anything about the character of the men. The test is simply designed to reduce the army to a mere remnant."[35] Similarly, Block says that "the means by which Yahweh identifies the men through whom he will achieve the victory over Midian may have been purely arbitrary."[36] Fear was the pressing issue. The lappers might possibly have been less fearful than the kneelers. But as Wolff points out, the expression in 7:8 that Gideon "retained" the three hundred is the same Hebrew expression used in 19:4 and Exodus 9:2, where it has the sense of compulsion. So even those who were retained had to be compelled to stay.[37]

The Midianites and Amalekites had been described twice as locustlike (Judg. 6:5; 7:12). Yet it is of Gideon's army that God says "you are too many" (7:2). The two scenes of give-and-take between God and Gideon reflect Gideon's twofold fears—fear of Baal and fear of the enemy's great number. The first scene established that God was greater than Baal, the second that numbers didn't matter to God. The dream Gideon overheard in the camp of the Midianite coalition shows that the balance of fear shifted to the enemy (7:11–14). When Gideon's men charged, the enemy was so terrified that they attacked one another in confusion.

Gideon's victory gives way to three stories of fraternal tension, showing that Israel continued to suffer from tribal factionalism. Ephraim had participated in the Deborah/Barak victory and was praised (5:14). Gad had not and thus made it on Deborah's list of shamed tribes (see "Gilead," 5:17). As a parallel, under Joshua the other ten tribes had been willing to make war against Reuben and Gad for the sake of tribal unity but, more importantly, of success in conquest (Numbers 32, esp. 32:6–7). Even in Gideon's day, Gad (where Succoth and Penuel lay) still held to the "every tribe for itself" philosophy. However, Chisholm highlights two considerations indicating that Gideon was unjustified in exacting revenge. First, God is barely mentioned in the narrative. Second, "Gideon seemed more willing to show mercy to Zebah and Zalmunna than he did to his own countrymen. He executed the Midianite kings only when he discovered they had murdered his brothers. In fact, one can see a desire for personal vengeance as the primary motive in each of the violent actions attributed to Gideon in this chapter (Judg. 8:16–17, 21)."[38] As Webb observes, Gideon was the

---

[35] Chisholm, *Judges and Ruth*, 282.
[36] Block, *Judges, Ruth*, 277.
[37] Herbert Wolf, *Judges*, in *The Expositor's Bible Commentary*, ed. Frank E. Gaebelein (Grand Rapids, MI: Zondervan, 1992), 3:425.
[38] Chisholm, *Judges and Ruth*, 289–91.

first judge to attack a fellow Israelite.[39] These postbattle incidents highlight both the deepening fractures within the nation and the character of Gideon.

The final phase in the Gideon story is his refusal of kingship and his death (notwithstanding that the whole Abimelech story is in a certain respect a continuation of the Gideon story). In light of his victory, the people of Israel called upon Gideon to "rule over" them (8:22). The Hebrew verb מָשַׁל, "to rule over," is not used in relation to any of the judges except with Gideon's refusal (8:23) and Abimelech's ultimatum (9:2). The verb מָלַךְ, "to reign as king," is likewise avoided. Judges are only described as "judging" (שָׁפַט). Israel was united under the desire not for God to reign over them but for the security Gideon and his army provided. Gideon's verbal subtlety in refusing kingship did not prevent him from acting in a very kingly way by gathering a large harem (8:30), accumulating a substantial fortune (8:26), and acquiring a royal wardrobe (8:27; cf. Deut. 17:16–17).

While Gideon declined the title of king, he embraced the function of priest. The effect of this action was as direct as the immediacy of the report in the same verse—Israel "whored" (Judg. 8:27), providing a specific instance of the general summary appearing in 2:17. This verb, which can mean "to be unfaithful" or "to fornicate," is used again in 8:33. While Gideon may have restrained Israel from full-fledged idolatry, his influence was limited. "As soon as Gideon died" (8:33), Israel's idolatry returned.

Gideon was dogged by fear of the Midianites and their gods, but with sufficient proofs and assurances, he acted to accomplish God's purposes. Yet his subsequent actions revealed his vengeful spirit, and his refusal of the kingship was at least partly insincere—after all, he did name his son "Abimelech," which means "my father is king." Additionally, when the Midianite princes referred to his brothers, they observed, "Every one of them resembled the son of a king" (8:18). Gideon is most certainly "ambiguity embodied."[40]

Abimelech (Judg. 9:1–57)

The next account begins with the rise of Abimelech to power. This narrative is legitimately read in continuity with Gideon's narrative because (1) Abimelech is the son of Gideon; (2) both stories entail a level of ascendency to kingship; and (3) fraternal strife appears in both accounts.

Abimelech's move for power was sudden and decisive. He appealed for support from his mother's relatives, and after taking funds out of the treasury of the temple of Baal at Ophrah—which apparently is what had become of Gideon's shrine, returning to the state of things under Gideon's father (6:24–27)—Abimelech and an unscrupulous troop (9:4) slaughtered seventy brothers who were potential rivals to his power.[41] Only Jotham, by fleeing, survived, and from the top of Mount Gerizim,

---

[39] Webb, *Judges*, NICOT, 258.
[40] Stone, "Judges, Book of," 592.
[41] As Webb suggests, the seventy shekels of silver is equal to the number of Abimelech's doomed brothers, which "hints, in a particularly sinister way, at what he might do with it." Webb, *Judges*, NICOT, 271.

he told a cautionary parable to the leaders of Shechem. Perhaps playing off the detail that Abimelech had been made king by a sacred oak at Shechem (9:6), the parable of the trees illustrated the consequences of choosing as king either a fruit-bearing tree, which needed nothing from the people but instead provided for them, or a bramble bush, which can only offer fire and thorns (9:7–15). The fruit of Abimelech had already been seen in the murder of his seventy brothers. Jotham raised an ethical challenge to Abimelech's selection in the words, "if you acted in good faith and integrity" (9:16, 19), apparently mocking a phrase Abimelech had used to persuade the people to anoint him king (9:15). Jotham's challenge was not whether it was a "free and fair" election but whether it was an act of faith and integrity toward the late Gideon and all that he had done.

Abimelech "ruled over" (שָׂרַר) Israel three years, a rare verb used of no other judge and elsewhere associated only with royal power (e.g., Prov. 8:16; Isa. 32:1). God intervened by sending an evil spirit to provoke strife between Abimelech and the leaders of Shechem (Judg. 9:23), an accomplishment that surely was not difficult given the character of the king and the people. Personal security—one of the prime things expected of a king—was not forthcoming, as the bandits of 9:25 indicate. When Gaal, their leader, began to openly undermine Abimelech, we begin to see the insecure nature of his popular support. Yet through the intelligence of Abimelech's commander, Zebul, Abimelech was able to launch an ambush (9:34) against the ambush bandits (9:25) and to subdue the uprising. This action ironically led Abimelech to attack those who had first chosen him as king. In prophetic fulfillment of Jotham's warning (9:20), Abimelech set fire to the fortified tower at Shechem (9:48). Motivated by his success, he moved on to nearby Thebez, which may indicate that Abimelech's bloodlust had exceeded his strategic thinking. His overzealous nature became apparent when, attempting to set fire to a second defensive tower, he was felled by a millstone dropped from above by a woman (9:52–57). This incident eventually became a cautionary tale in Israel's military lore (2 Sam. 11:21).

In ironic similarity with Sisera, a fellow Israelite had his skull crushed by a female noncombatant using a weapon of opportunity. The blow was fatal but not immediate. This compelled Abimelech to call for his servant to kill him in order to keep his name from becoming infamous for the manner of his death (Judg. 9:54). Although this move succeeded in hastening his death, it did not keep Abimelech from becoming a proverb for what wise warriors should never do. Abimelech's call for his servant to kill him anticipates King Saul attempting the same (1 Sam. 31:1–7). The point for both narratives is the same: Israel is not to have a king like Abimelech or Saul.

Tola and Jair (Judg. 10:1–5)

At the end of the Abimelech narrative, we are not told that the land had rest as in earlier instances (3:11, 30; 5:31; 8:28). Tola is nondescript. Jair's sons are described in terms similar to Gideon's sons. They were numerous (cf. 8:30) and princelike, riding on donkeys (cf. 2 Sam. 13:29; 16:2), which suggests "a dynastic tendency and a consolidation of power that could prove detrimental to the Israelite social order."[42] Neither is described explicitly as being raised up by God. As table 17 (on p. 181) indicates, none of the characteristic elements of the judges are found in either except their deaths. Although the same is true of Shamgar, it was said of him that he "saved" Israel, whereas these two only "judged." As table 17 further shows, it appears that they had more in common with Abimelech.

Jephthah (Judg. 10:6–12:7)

The Jephthah cycle begins with Israel deep in idolatry (10:6). As a result, God sent the Ammonites and Philistines to oppress Israel. The Ammonites, whose appearance is limited to the Jephthah cycle, were descended from Lot and his younger daughter (Gen. 19:36–38). They occupied a territory to the east of Gad (Num. 21:24), and they were not regarded as combatants during the conquest because the Lord had given them their land as descendants of Lot (Deut. 2:19). The Philistines lived along the coastal plain of Judah, and their descent is listed in the table of nations (Gen. 10:14). While they shared civil relations with Abraham, after he died that peace deteriorated (Gen. 26:15). Their occupation of the coastal plain was a prime reason God led Israel to Canaan by the east (Ex. 13:17). Philistia, with its five city-states, was among those territories not yet conquered as Joshua entered old age (Josh. 3:2–3; Judg. 3:3).

There are several distinctives of Jephthah's rise.[43] First, the narrative describes the return of Israel to its evil ways in more detail than in any other cycle (10:6–18). Second, Jephthah is presented not as having been raised up by God but as having been recruited by his desperate kinsman (11:1–12). Third, although Jephthah is described as being empowered by the Spirit, he makes a rash vow (11:29–40). Fourth, the account of his victory is very brief, only three sentences (11:32–33). Finally, the account makes no mention of a period of peace and rest.

As military confrontation was imminent, the leaders of Gilead searched for someone who would serve as their "head" (10:18; cf. 11:8–11 [three times]), a term not applied to any other judge but which is used of Saul (1 Sam. 15:17). Jephthah, a "mighty warrior" (Judg. 11:1) who had previously been spurned by his kinsmen and had taken up with "worthless fellows" (11:3; the same term used of Abimelech's entourage in 9:4), was offered this "headship" if he would lead Gilead against the Ammonites. Once deprived of citizenship among them, Jephthah was now offered governorship. Having accepted, Jephthah disputed the Ammonite claim that Israel had taken its land on its way to Canaan (11:12–28), and he declared his confidence that God would judge between them (11:27).

The central interpretive issue of the Jephthah cycle is his so-called "rash vow," which, according to the majority of modern interpreters, resulted in the sacrifice of his only child, a daughter, as a burnt offering. There is no piece of evidence in the narrative that characterizes Jephthah positively. Perhaps our only hesitation might

---

[42] Chisholm, *Judges and Ruth*, 325.
[43] The last three of these are derived from Block, *Judges, Ruth*, 342.

come from Hebrews 11:32, which includes Jephthah among those commended for their faith. He did defeat Israel's enemy, yet the narrative tells us not that he saved or judged Israel but that God was the One who gave the victory (Judg. 11:32).

In his vow, Jephthah was doing with God precisely what he had done with the elders of Gilead and with the Amorite king—he was negotiating. But unlike the elders of Gilead, God was silent.[44] "Though cautious bargaining was perhaps necessary when dealing with the Gileadites" and most certainly so with the Ammonites, if he was a man of virtue, "Jephthah did not need to bargain with the Lord, for he was the champion of a just cause (vv. 12–28) and was already energized by the divine spirit (v. 29)."[45]

What precisely did Jephthah vow? Like Barak and Gideon (4:8; 6:17, 36–37), he began with "if," perhaps indicating his own uncertainty of victory. Olson suggests that the vow functions something like a bribe, which was prohibited in the covenant law (Deut. 10:17; 16:19).[46] He vowed that, upon his return from victory, he would make a "whole burnt offering" of whatever or whoever came out of his house to meet him. The Hebrew participle allows for some flexibility. It is literally "the thing or one that comes out." The moral difficulty appears when imagining that Jephthah intended to include a person among the possibilities (Judg. 11:34), because the old covenant law condemned human sacrifice (Lev. 18:21; 20:2–5; Deut. 12:31; 18:9–10). Chisholm points out that "the one going out who goes out" is used elsewhere to refer to inanimate objects (Num. 21:13; 32:24 [cf. the KJV rendering of the Hebrew]) and that the infinitive "to meet me" can be used of animals as well as persons, but "it was far more likely that a woman would greet him."[47]

In a footnote, Chisholm notes several sources that see Jephthah as promising to devote this person or thing to the Lord *or* make it a burnt offering. In this view, his subsequent action was not actually to sacrifice his daughter but to dedicate her to God such that she would never marry, as indicated by how her friends "wept for her virginity" (Judg. 11:38).[48] However, this doesn't seem to account for the deep grief of Jephthah, the mourning sequence preceding the implementation of the vow, or its institutionalization among the daughters of Israel (11:39–40). That the daughter was grieved but willing to comply doesn't support this lesser option any more than Isaac's willingness to be put under the knife (Genesis 22). If anything, it portrays her incipient faith of the kind her father should have had.

Human sacrifice was prevalent enough in the surrounding cultural environment that the covenant law had explicitly prohibited it. Israel, at its deepest syncretistic point between Moses and the monarchy, may well have tolerated or practiced it in spite of the law's prohibitions. Jephthah, who would have had every reason to expect God to give him victory, rashly offered a price beyond his own reckoning. In

---

[44] Webb, *Judges*, NICOT, 365.
[45] Chisholm, *Judges and Ruth*, 351.
[46] Dennis T. Olson, *The Book of Judges*, in *The New Interpreter's Bible*, ed. David L. Peterson (Nashville: Abingdon, 1998), 2:832.
[47] Chisholm, *Judges and Ruth*, 353.
[48] Chisholm, *Judges and Ruth*, 355.

addition to the parallel with Saul suggested earlier, this vow parallels Saul's vow in 1 Samuel 14:24–30, who for the sake of victory over his enemies placed his son Jonathan under a death sentence.

The Jephthah cycle ends with conflict, including the well-known "Shibboleth" episode (Judg. 12:5–6). Israel, it seems, was not one people under their covenant Lord but was divided by speech like the nations scattered from Babel (Genesis 11).

Ibzan, Elon, and Abdon (Judg.12:8–15)

The three minor judges who follow Jephthah hail from the south, north, and center of Israel, respectively. Ibzan and Abdon are described similarly to Jair (10:3–4). The number of their children suggests polygamous and dynastic tendencies as did Gideon's and Abimelech's children. The short tenure of their judgeships suggests that the spiral continued downward. This same reality persists as we encounter Samson, the last of the judges.

Samson (Judg. 13:1–16:31)

The final and climactic judge is Samson. He was born to deliver God's people from the oppression of the infamous Philistines. Unlike any of the other judges, his account begins with a birth narrative. He was to be a Nazirite from birth (13:4–5). However, his actions reveal him to be an impetuous and passionate character with great strength but little self-control. The account of Samson may be divided into five parts:

1. Samson's birth (13:1–25)[49]
2. Samson's marriage to a Philistine woman from Timnah (14:1–20)
3. Samson's destruction of the Philistines (15:1–20)
4. Samson's betrayal by Delilah (16:1–22)
5. Samson's death and the deliverance of Israel (16:23–31)

The narrative of Samson's birth sets him apart from the other judges, placing him in a category with the likes of Isaac, Jacob, Moses, Samuel, John the Baptist, and Jesus. In Samson's birth narrative, the angel of the Lord declared that he would be a Nazirite for life (cf. Num. 6:1–21), a designation in Scripture shared only with John the Baptist. Samson and John the Baptist also shared a similar type of death. Both were betrayed by women into the hand of the enemy where they died at the hand of their captors.

Four times the text states that the Spirit of God empowered Samson (Judg. 13:25; 14:6, 19; 15:14). The Spirit also came upon Othniel (3:10) and Jephthah (11:29), and the Spirit "clothed" or was "put on" Gideon (6:34). A similar expression is used for Saul when God empowered him to deliver Israel and for David after Samuel anointed him to be king (1 Sam. 16:13). However, Samson's unpredictable and violent actions

---

[49] For more on the biblical motif of barrenness, see "Barrenness," in *Dictionary of Biblical Imagery*, ed. Leland Ryken, James C. Wilhoit, and Tremper Longman III (Downers Grove, IL: InterVarsity Press, 2000), 75. For other examples of this type-scene, see 1 Samuel 1–2 (Hannah); Luke 1:5–25 (Elizabeth).

appear to characterize him as someone who "inhabits the borderlands between the civilized and the wild."[50]

Upon seeing a particular Philistine woman from Timnah, Samson desired her for a wife (Judg. 14:1) and requested that his parents secure her for him (14:2, 7). That God had a greater purpose in the marriage—"seeking an opportunity against the Philistines" (14:4)—was not disclosed to Samson and as such did not justify his desire to have a wife from among Israel's idolatrous oppressors. Whereas Samson sinfully meant it for himself, God meant it for good. When he went on to eat honey from the carcass of a dead lion, he committed a threefold act of defilement—lions were unclean animals and dead animals were unclean, which twice rendered Samson defiled, but then he defiled his parents by giving them some of the honey without telling them its source.

In the wedding account of Judges 14–16, the image of fire appears, an image that will further characterize Samson. It occurs no less than six times, leading to the conclusion that "fire has become a metonymic image of Samson himself: a blind, uncontrolled force, leaving a terrible swath of destruction behind it, finally consuming itself together with whatever stands in its way."[51] Samson displayed his impetuousness further when he visited the Philistine prostitute in Gaza (16:1–3) and allowed himself to be seduced by the Philistine Delilah (16:4–22). Although attempts have been made to vindicate Samson from sexual relations with the prostitute, the Hebrew verbiage of 16:1 is commonly used to describe sexual encounters (Gen. 38:18; 2 Sam. 12:24; Ezek. 23:44). This prostitute served as the middle step in Samson's decline. He went from wife to prostitute to mistress, each presenting greater threat and risk to him, emblematic of Israel's adultery with the gods of the surrounding peoples.

In misleading Delilah on the source of his strength, Samson reflected a hubris that may have arisen from the awareness of his birth account. It is a reminder that God's calling is not to be the basis for presumption, something the nation of Israel failed to heed. Having been deprived of the source of his strength and then bound and blinded, Samson became calculating. His loss of sight finally made him perceptive rather than impulsive. Even though his prayer for final strength was more vengeful than self-sacrificing (Judg. 16:28), as Samson brought final destruction down on himself, he finally brought relief for his people: "So the dead whom he killed at his death were more than those whom he had killed during his life" (16:30). Even so, as Block notes, the Samson cycle does not end with a "tranquility formula" describing Israel's rest from enemies.[52] The downward spiral had almost reached the bottom, and there could be no rest for Israel under those conditions. Samson was Israel personified—set apart from the womb by the electing grace of God, destined for holiness, but prone to seduction by the *femme fatale* of other gods, which ended in slavery and death.

---

[50] Webb, *Judges*, NICOT, 368.
[51] Alter, *Art of Biblical Narrative*, 94–95. Emphasis added.
[52] Block, *Judges, Ruth*, 343.

Epilogues: The Depths of Israel's "Canaanization" (Judg. 17:1–21:25)

Judges ends like it begins, with a double epilogue in the reverse order of its prologues. The first epilogue highlights the vertical, divine-human problem epitomized by the idolatrous shrine in Ephraim. The second epilogue highlights the horizontal, fraternal disorder of Israel represented by sodomitic sin and war against Benjamin. As Childs explains, the two epilogues

> perform an analogous role and together complete the framework about the Deuteronomic pattern of the judges. The final stories do not provide a chronological perspective, but describe a quality of life which picks up the elements of the introduction. . . . The two stories [in the epilogue] portray Israel's growing idolatry and the scandal which threatens the unity of the nation. However, the major difference in perspective between the introduction [prologue] and the appendix [epilogue] lies in the latter's looking forward to the future kingdom rather than back to the earlier period.[53]

Thus it is in these epilogues that we find the fourfold refrain "there was no king in Israel" (17:6; 18:1; 19:1; 21:25).

Epilogue 1: Apostasy in Dan (Judg. 17:1–18:31)

In the first epilogue, we are twice told that "there was a man" (17:1; 7), the first being the man Micah of Ephraim and the other an itinerant Levite. The phrase appears to join them in moral equivalency. The Ephraimite Micah was a thieving son whose mother unknowingly cursed him when she cursed the thief who stole her silver. He was rewarded by his mother for returning her stolen silver—which, unbeknownst to her, he himself had stolen. She then took a portion to have an idol made in her son's honor. Micah established a shrine in his house, installed his idols, self-commissioned a golden ephod, and ordained one of his own sons as priest. This unauthorized ordination violated the exclusive endorsement of Aaron's priesthood and God's vindications of it in the wilderness (Leviticus 10; Numbers 17).

In Judges 17:7–13 Micah hired an enterprising young Levite to serve at his idolatrous shrine. As one who should have been zealous for authorized worship (Ex. 32:28), he was an accessory to false worship. The sequence ends with Micah ordaining the Levite and making the ironic statement, "Now I know that the LORD will prosper me, because I have a Levite as priest" (Judg. 17:13).

The second part of this first epilogue introduces the tribe of Dan. Members of Dan, driven off their inheritance by the Ammonites (Josh. 19:40, 47; Judg. 1:34), received intelligence of an unsuspecting people in Laish in the northern extremes of the Promised Land. Happening upon Micah's unauthorized priest, they requested an oracle regarding their prospects. The priest's assurance was both ambiguous and ominous—God would be watching them (18:6). The positive report of the five spies back to their fellow tribesmen is reminiscent of what should have been the report of

---

[53] Childs, *Introduction to the Old Testament as Scripture*, 259.

the twelve spies in Numbers 14. Had Dan been zealous for the inheritance God had given them, they would not have been seeking land elsewhere. After the war party of Dan surreptitiously took Micah's ephod, images, and priest, Micah's complaint ironically spoke truth when he described them as "my gods *that I made* and the priest" (Judg. 18:24).

The people of Dan destroyed the unsuspecting city of Laish and renamed it Dan (18:27–29), eschewing their divine inheritance adjacent to Judah because they could not drive out the land's inhabitants there. They also established a false worship center as the northern tribes were wont to do (18:30–31). Dan couldn't conquer and hold its tribal allotment, so it ended up plundering a fellow Israelite and establishing itself in a territory other than what God gave them.

Epilogue 2: Strife with Benjamin (Judg. 19:1–21:25)

The second epilogue also involves a Levite in the hill country of Ephraim. Rather than being from Bethlehem, as the Levite in the preceding story, he took a wife from Bethlehem who had been a concubine. His pursuit of her after her unfaithfulness ("harlotry," 19:2–3) characterizes him positively ("to speak kindly"), in contrast to Micah's Levite. Achieving success, he attempted to leave but was compelled by his father-in-law's lavish hospitality to stay in Bethlehem for five days (19:4–9). The narrative depicts a blissful and abundant family occasion. Bethlehem is a place of hospitality, setting an ominous foil for the following scene.

The Levite was determined to leave on the fifth day, but due to the lateness of the hour could only travel as far as Jerusalem, called "Jebus (that is, the city of the Jebusites)" (19:10, my trans.), reminding us what we had been previously told— Benjamin had not been able to conquer and hold Jerusalem (1:21; cf. 19:12). Given those conditions, the Levite decided they should lodge in Gibeah, a Benjaminite city (19:14). In Gibeah they experienced events reminiscent of the divine contingent's visit to Sodom in Genesis 19. A fellow Ephraimite who now lived in Gibeah invited them in with the assurance that "there is no lack of anything" in his house (19:19), and the ominous warning against a night in the open public square (19:20).

What followed is almost unspeakable. A group of men from the city gathered outside the Ephraimite's house and demanded he send out the Levite so they could rape him. The Ephraimite refused but offered his virgin daughter and the Levite's concubine instead. They clamored for the man, and finally the Levite "seized" his concubine (19:25) and shoved her out the door, where she was subjected to gang rape all night. The next morning, for the second time, the Levite "seized" (19:29) his concubine, although this time her lifeless body. The joining of his two actions by the same verb confirms his complicity in handing her over in the first place. Dismembering her remains into twelve pieces, he sent one to each of the other eleven tribes to report the horror of Gibeah's inhospitality as a gruesome call to arms against

Benjamin (19:30; cf. 1 Sam. 11:7).[54] The scene ends ominously, declaring that this was the worst evil ever to happen since the exodus from Egypt.

Echoes of Sodom reverberate throughout the narrative (Judg. 19:22–26) but without divine rescue. Yet these aren't the men of Sodom; these are brother Israelites of Benjamin. Sodom was the epitome of depravity, representing the worst kind of evil and the highest expression of divine wrath (Jer. 23:14; Jude 7; 2 Pet. 2:6). Now Benjamin had earned that status. The tribe of Benjamin had become fully Canaanite.

The second part of this epilogue recounts the war of the tribes against Benjamin. Ironically, Israel had not been so united since the days of Joshua. "Then all the people of Israel . . . and the congregation assembled as one man to the LORD at Mizpah" (Judg. 20:1). "And all the people arose as one man" (20:8). Instead of handing over the perpetrators, Benjamin chose to go to battle (20:13–14). The cry went up from Israel for the first time since the start of this decline, "Who shall go up first for us to fight . . . ? And the LORD said, 'Judah shall go up first'" (20:18).

After initial defeats, the eleven tribes went to the Lord's dwelling place in Bethel (20:26–27) and consulted him through his authorized Aaronic priest, Phinehas, the grandson of Aaron (20:28). Perhaps this action marked a hopeful sign of God's people once again seeking him at his chosen dwelling place through his authorized means, for it resulted in a stratagem leading to victory. The rout, however, ended with the decimation not only of the warriors but also of all the men and beasts of Benjamin (20:48) and apparently the women and children as well since wives for the survivors had to be found. The final chapter recounts how the tribal coalition compassionately preserved the tribe of Benjamin (21:6). To the remnant of the warriors of Benjamin besieged at the rock of Rimmon (20:47; 21:13) they gave the virgin daughters of those who did not go up to fight Benjamin (21:8–12). These were the men of Jabesh-gilead, the city that Saul would later defend in his first battle as king (1 Sam. 11:1). These Benjaminite warriors were given leave to supplement that number with the daughters of those in Shiloh, who also had not gone to war.

Taken together, these dual epilogues suggest that the ruling influence of the Levites was in disarray. This is confirmed by the moral decrepitude of Micah's Levite and the complicity of the Levite in the abuse at Gibeah. As Waltke has suggested, "Lacking a king, and having only the apostate house of Levi as their spiritual shepherds, the nation falls into moral anarchy. In fact, the book's epilogue, as we shall see, fingers the tribe of Levite [*sic*] as the villain during the dark age when warlords ruled."[55]

APPROACHING THE NEW TESTAMENT

The book of Judges testifies to God's faithfulness in spite of Israel's unfaithfulness. He upheld the covenant with warnings from the angel of the Lord and allowed the Canaanites to periodically oppress his people in order to turn their hearts back to him. God raised up judges to rally the nation, and he gave them victory over their

---

[54] Presumably one piece went to each of the half tribes of Manasseh and Ephraim.
[55] Waltke with Yu, *Old Testament Theology*, 588.

oppressors. Yet these victories were temporary. The limited, short-lived success of the judges pointed to the need for a greater, more effective, and abiding solution to Israel's idolatrous heart. Judges confirms what the Balaam narrative should have taught Israel—that the real threat was not external but internal (Numbers 25).

Old Testament Israel is universal human nature writ large. Moses had set before Israel the choice of life and death, to trust in the Lord wholeheartedly or to turn away after other gods (Deut. 30:15–20). But in spite of all that God had done *for* his people and *before* their eyes, they lacked the thing necessary for that trust—"But to this day the LORD has not given you a heart to understand or eyes to see or ears to hear" (Deut. 29:4). This is the dilemma of all humanity: witnessing the glory of our Creator (Rom. 1:18–32) and experiencing his benevolence (Matt. 5:45; Rom. 2:4), yet trusting in the idols of our hearts instead of him. Even as his covenant people, we often share our affections with the gods of this world and are conformed to it (Rom. 12:2). Just as God allowed the nations to afflict his people so that they might turn back to him, in Christ we have a loving Father who will discipline us for our good (Heb. 12:5–11). We must watch for the leaven within the camp and its corrupting power (1 Cor. 5:6–7).

To the extent that the judges saved God's people, we see the saving work of God in and through Jesus Christ. He is the divinely appointed Savior who defeated sin and death and freed us from the powers of this fallen world (John 12:31; Col. 1:13; 2:15; 1 Cor. 15:57). He is the "one man," fewer than Gideon's three hundred, who was qualified. While one must remember the vast gap separating the imperfect judges from the perfect Son of God, Christ may nonetheless be preached from every judge since each one anticipates what Christ would do in the ultimate deliverance of his people.

Just as the book of Judges proved the need for God's king, so we too are defenseless and unruly apart from Christ's rule over us individually and as the people of God. As the Westminster Shorter Catechism teaches us, "Christ executeth the office of a king, in subduing us to himself, in ruling and defending us, and in restraining and conquering all his and our enemies."[56] While we live on the victorious side of the cross and resurrection, we still live in this fallen world where idols abound and syncretism and oppression press in constantly against us. In this respect, we live in a time similar to Israel in the book of Judges. John Bunyan's *Holy War* concludes with the citizens of Mansoul in this same situation. Even though the great victory of King Shaddai has been won by his son Emmanuel over Diabolus, the enemy's minions continue to live within city Mansoul's gates. In response to their question why, Emmanuel replies in words that well sum up the purpose of Judges for us today:

> It is to keep thee waking, to try thy love, to make thee watchful, and to cause thee yet to prize my noble captains, their soldiers and my mercy.
>
> It is also that yet thou mayest be made to remember what a deplorable condition thou once wast in, I mean when, not some, but all did dwell, not in thy wall, but in thy castle, and in thy stronghold, O Mansoul.

---

[56] Westminster Shorter Catechism, question 26.

O my Mansoul, should I slay all them within, many there be without that would bring thee into bondage; for were all there within cut off, those without would find thee sleeping, and then as in a moment they would swallow up my Mansoul. I therefore left them in thee, not to do thee hurt (the which they yet will, if thou hearken to them, and serve them) but to do thee good, the which they must, if thou watch and fight against them. Know therefore that whatever they shall tempt thee to, my design is that they should drive thee, not further off, but nearer to my Father, to learn thee war, to make petitioning desirable to thee, and to make thee little in thine own eyes. Hearken diligently to this my Mansoul.[57]

SELECT BIBLIOGRAPHY

Block, Daniel I. *Judges, Ruth*. NAC 6. Nashville: Broadman, 1999.

Boda, Mark J. "Judges." In *Numbers–Ruth*. Vol. 2 of *The Expositors Bible Commentary*, edited by Tremper Longman III and David E. Garland, 1043–1288. Rev. ed. Grand Rapids, MI: Zondervan, 2012.

Chisholm, Robert B., Jr. *A Commentary on Judges and Ruth*. KEL. Grand Rapids, MI: Kregel, 2013.

Davis, Dale Ralph. *Judges: Such a Great Salvation*. Focus on the Bible: Expositor's Guide to the Historical Books. Fearn, Ross-Shire, Scotland: Christian Focus, 2007.

Gros Louis, Kenneth R. R. "The Book of Judges." In *Literary Interpretations of Biblical Narratives*, edited by Kenneth R. R. Gros Louis, James S. Ackerman, and Thayer S. Warshaw, 141–62. Bible in Literature Courses. Nashville: Abingdon, 1974.

Gros Louis, Kenneth R. R., and Willard Van Antwerpen Jr. "Joshua and Judges." In *A Complete Literary Guide to the Bible*, edited by Leland Ryken and Tremper Longman III, 137–50. Grand Rapids, MI: Zondervan, 1993.

Klein, Lillian R. *The Triumph of Irony in the Book of Judges*. JSOTSup 68. Sheffield: Almond, 1989.

Longman, Tremper, III, and Raymond B. Dillard. *An Introduction to the Old Testament*. 2nd ed. Grand Rapids, MI: Zondervan, 2006.

Longman, Tremper, III, and Daniel G. Reid. *God Is a Warrior*. SOTBT. Grand Rapids, MI: Zondervan, 1995.

Ortlund, Raymond C., Jr. *God's Unfaithful Wife: A Biblical Theology of Spiritual Adultery*. NSBT 2. Downers Grove, IL: InterVarsity Press, 2003.

Satterthwaite, Philip E., and J. Gordon McConville. "Judges." In *Exploring the Old Testament*. Vol. 2, *A Guide to the Historical Books*. Downers Grove, IL: InterVarsity Press, 2012.

Schwab, George M. *Right in Their Own Eyes: The Gospel According to Judges*. The Gospel according to the Old Testament. Phillipsburg, NJ: P&R, 2011.

Stone, Lawson G. "Judges, Book of." In *Dictionary of the Old Testament: Historical Books: A Compendium of Contemporary Biblical Scholarship*, edited by Bill T. Arnold

---

[57] John Bunyan, *The Holy War*, in *Allegorical, Figurative and Symbolical*, vol. 3 of *The Works of John Bunyan*, ed. George Offor (Glasgow: Blackie and Son, 1853), 372.

and H. G. M. Williamson, 592–606. IVP Bible Dictionary Series 2. Downers Grove, IL: InterVarsity Press, 2005.

Webb, Barry G. *The Book of Judges*. NICOT. Grand Rapids, MI: Eerdmans, 2012.

———. *The Book of the Judges: An Integrated Reading*. JSOTSup 46. Sheffield: JSOT Press, 1987.

———. "The Theme of the Jephthah Story (Judges 10:6–12:7)." *RTR* 45, no. 2 (1986): 34–43.

———. "The Wars of Judges as Christian Scripture." *RTR* 67, no. 1 (2008): 18–28.

Wilcock, Michael. *The Message of Judges: Grace Abounding*. The Bible Speaks Today. Downers Grove, IL: InterVarsity Press, 1992.

Younger, K. Lawson, Jr. *Judges and Ruth*. NIVAC. Grand Rapids, MI: Zondervan, 2002.

8

1–2 Samuel

Michael G. McKelvey

INTRODUCTION

How did kingship emerge in Israel? Who were the major players during the transition from the period of the judges to the rule of the monarchy? What was God's purpose in this tremendous shift in leadership within the nation? These issues and more are addressed in the book of Samuel. This work traces the political history of Israel from a fledgling nation with seemingly weak tribal connections to a unified kingdom under the rule of a single monarch. The accounts reveal a tumultuous period in which the descendants of Jacob were oppressed and assailed by the surrounding nations. Additionally, Israel had failed in the conquest of Canaan to depose all the inhabitants of the land, which added to their overall adversity and idolatry. Nevertheless, the monarchy arose, bringing unity to a realm of chaos.

While the book was written in narrative form, it is not merely a historical account. It is theologically driven, and it highlights the purposes of God in the unfolding of redemptive history. The book focuses upon Yahweh's relationship with Israel following a period dominated by the maxim, "In those days there was no king in Israel. Everyone did what was right in his own eyes" (Judg. 17:6; 18:1; 19:1; 21:25). Samuel must be read in the light of its scriptural context. There was great need for order and rule, but the people of the land were not looking to the one true Ruler, the One who entered into covenant with them at Sinai; they wanted a man to govern them like the nations. As Yahweh gave the people the desire of their hearts, he revealed his own purposes through the events of that time. In this way, the books of 1–2 Samuel provide not only the history of the nation but also the history of redemption, and they progressively point the reader to the necessity of a messiah.

BACKGROUND ISSUES

Composition and Authorship

Originally, 1–2 Samuel existed as a single book in the Hebrew Bible, but the Septuagint divided it into two sections called 1–2 Kingdoms. The Septuagint connected these two books with the book of Kings, which was also divided and named 3–4 Kingdoms. The Latin tradition continued to employ these divisions, which led to the present Western/English arrangement. While the divisional history of Samuel can be traced, its authorship remains unknown. The Hebrew text refers to the work as Samuel in view of the prophet's prominence at its beginning, but Samuel's death in 1 Samuel 25:1 precludes his involvement in the completed volume. Arnold notes, "The Talmud preserves the rabbinic tradition that these books were written by prophets who lived contemporaneously with the events described."[1] In the end, the book makes no mention of the author, and it remains an anonymous work.

With this said, the text gives potential indicators regarding the date of 1–2 Samuel's completion. The reference to Ziklag in 1 Samuel 27:6 seems to offer some evidence: "So that day Achish gave him Ziklag. Therefore Ziklag has belonged to the kings of Judah to this day." Tsumura suggests that this allusion indicates a final form of the book occurring likely no later than the late tenth century BC.[2] With the book of 1–2 Kings focusing on the monarchy post-David, it seems reasonable to hold to an early compositional view for 1–2 Samuel. Nonetheless, "it is all but impossible to recover the compositional history of the book."[3]

Historical Background

The book of Joshua describes the Israelite conquest of the land of Canaan (ca. 1406 BC). From the crossing of the Jordan River (Joshua 3–4) to the destruction of Jericho (Joshua 6) and Ai (Joshua 7–8) to the allocation of the land to the tribes (Joshua 13–21; ca. 1400 BC), the writer highlights the movements and decisions of the nation as it settles into the land. As Joshua prepares for his death, he charges the leaders of Israel to continue to push out the nations that remain:

> And you have seen all that the LORD your God has done to all these nations for your sake, for it is the LORD your God who has fought for you. Behold, I have allotted to you as an inheritance for your tribes those nations that remain, along with all the nations that I have already cut off, from the Jordan to the Great Sea in the west. The LORD your God will push them back before you and drive them out of your sight. And you shall possess their land, just as the LORD your God promised you. Therefore, be very strong to keep and to do all that is written in the Book of the Law of Moses, turning aside from it neither to the right hand nor to the left, that you may not mix with these nations remaining among you or make mention of the names of their gods or swear by them or serve them or bow down

---

[1] Bill T. Arnold, *1 & 2 Samuel*, NIVAC (Grand Rapids, MI: Zondervan, 2003), 25.
[2] David Toshio Tsumura, *The First Book of Samuel*, NICOT (Grand Rapids, MI: Eerdmans, 2007), 11.
[3] Tremper Longman III and Raymond B. Dillard, *An Introduction to the Old Testament*, 2nd ed. (Grand Rapids, MI: Zondervan, 2006), 153.

to them, but you shall cling to the LORD your God just as you have done to this day. . . . Be very careful, therefore, to love the LORD your God. For if you turn back and cling to the remnant of these nations remaining among you and make marriages with them, so that you associate with them and they with you, know for certain that the LORD your God will no longer drive out these nations before you, but they shall be a snare and a trap for you, a whip on your sides and thorns in your eyes, until you perish from off this good ground that the LORD your God has given you. (Josh. 23:3–8, 11–13)

Israel's failure to carry out this commission led the Lord to chastise the nation in the succeeding generations.

The book of Judges chronicles God's punishment of his people for their disobedience by causing foreign nations to oppress portions of the land. As the people would cry to the Lord for mercy, Yahweh would raise up judges to deliver them and to bring a temporary period of peace, until they would eventually revert to their rebellious ways. This cycle highlighted the need for the people to have a single ruler over them to protect, defend, and lead them in the law of the Lord. That ruler was supposed to be Yahweh himself and his Messiah (cf. the provision of kingship law in Deut. 17:4–20), but the people rejected God as their King (see 1 Samuel 8).

One of the primary enemies of the Israelites during the time of 1–2 Samuel was a people called the Philistines. They were apparently one of the "Sea Peoples," likely immigrating from the Aegean Sea area or Crete, who eventually settled the eastern part of the Mediterranean coast.[4] The Philistines caused the nation significant trouble during the time of the judges (e.g., Judges 13–16), as well as during the reigns of Saul and David. They eventually captured the ark of the covenant (1 Samuel 4), which devastated the nation.[5] God soon judged the Philistines for this act, and they sent the ark back to Israel (1 Sam. 5:1–7:2). While the Philistines were not the only adversaries of Israel during this period, they do play a prominent role in the book of Samuel. It is in this light that the people asked Samuel for a king: "But the people refused to obey the voice of Samuel. And they said, 'No! But there shall be a king over us, that we also may be like all the nations, and that our king may judge us and go out before us and *fight our battles*'" (1 Sam. 8:19–20). Saul and David would battle the Philistine kings for decades, and this group would prove to be Israel's proverbial "thorn in the flesh."

Audience

This book was written for the coming generations of Israelites. It has many purposes for this audience. The book reveals Israel's past. It stands within the progressive narrative (primary history) that began with the book of Genesis and explains Israel's origin and purpose. The rise and significance of Israelite kingship is also displayed in the book's pages. In addition, God's work in history through Israel and the nations

---

[4] For a fuller discussion of the uncertain history of the Philistines, see *NIDOTTE*, 3:628–32, and John D. Currid and David P. Barrett, *Crossway ESV Bible Atlas* (Wheaton, IL: Crossway, 2010), 113.
[5] See 1 Sam. 4:21–22, "And she named the child Ichabod, saying, 'The glory has departed from Israel!' because the ark of God had been captured and because of her father-in-law and her husband. And she said, 'The glory has departed from Israel, for the ark of God has been captured.'"

takes center stage. These things ultimately highlight the progressive outworking of God's promises, first to Abraham and then to David (2 Samuel 7). By the end of the book, the audience knows that God reigns and that he has chosen David's line to reign forever through a coming messiah. Moreover, the reader becomes acutely aware that human kingship thus far has not been sufficient to fulfill the task of reigning as God's vicegerent. So at the conclusion of the book, there remains an anticipation regarding how God will bring about his gracious promises.

STRUCTURE AND OUTLINE

Many structures have been put forth for 1–2 Samuel, and they can be very detailed. For the sake of simplicity, it seems best to divide the book as follows:

I. Focus on Samuel (1 Sam. 1:1–7:17)
  A. Birth narrative and dedication of Samuel (1 Sam. 1:1–2:11)
  B. Eli's household rejected (1 Sam. 2:12–36)
  C. Samuel in the tabernacle (1 Sam. 3:1–21)
  D. The Philistines and the ark (1 Sam. 4:1–5:12)
  E. The ark returned (1 Sam. 6:1–7:2)
  F. Samuel the judge (1 Sam. 7:3–17)
II. Focus on Saul (1 Sam. 8:1–15:35)
  A. Israel desires a human king (1 Sam. 8:1–22)
  B. Saul chosen and anointed (1 Sam. 9:1–10:27)
  C. Saul's victory (1 Sam. 11:1–15)
  D. Samuel's farewell speech (1 Sam. 12:1–25)
  E. Saul's foolishness (1 Sam. 13:1–14:52)
  F. Saul rejected by the Lord (1 Sam. 15:1–35)
III. Focus on David (1 Sam. 16:1–31:13; 2 Sam. 1:1–24:25)
  A. David anointed as king (1 Sam. 16:1–23)
  B. David and Goliath (1 Sam. 17:1–58)
  C. David's troubles with Saul (1 Sam. 18:1–26:25)
  D. David with the Philistines (1 Sam. 27:1–12)
  E. Saul and the necromancer (1 Sam. 28:1–25)
  F. David rejected by the Philistines (1 Sam. 29:1–11)
  G. David's wives captured (1 Sam. 30:1–31)
  H. Death of Saul and David's response (1 Sam. 31:1–13; 2 Sam. 1:1–27)
  I. David and Saul's house (2 Sam. 2:1–4:12)
  J. David's united kingdom (2 Sam. 5:1–25)
  K. David and the ark (2 Sam. 6:1–23)
  L. The Davidic covenant (2 Sam. 7:1–29)
  M. Victories of David (2 Sam. 8:1–10:19)
  N. Adultery, conspiracy, and consequences (2 Sam. 11:1–12:31)
  O. David's family woes (2 Sam. 13:1–19:43)
  P. More challenges (2 Sam. 20:1–21:22)
  Q. David's song (2 Sam. 22:1–51)
  R. David's last words and mighty men (2 Sam. 23:1–39)
  S. Census and consequences (2 Sam. 24:1–25)

This general division reveals the purpose of the book in recounting the transition of leadership from the period of the judges to the monarchy—from Samuel to Saul to David. The major figures and events in each of these periods are discussed in what follows.[6]

MESSAGE AND THEOLOGY
Samuel (1 Samuel 1–7)

As the book begins, the reader is introduced to Hannah, the mother of Samuel. In chapter 1, the writer notes that Hannah was a barren woman who yearned for a son, to the extent that she vowed in prayer to give the boy to the Lord "all the days of his life" (1:11). Yahweh answered her prayer, and when Samuel was weaned, Hannah presented him to the house of the Lord for service (1:28).[7] Eventually, Samuel became the final judge of the nation, as well as the replacement for the priestly house of Eli, since God had rejected his evil sons (2:12–4:22). Samuel judged the nation into his old age, yet his sons did not follow in their father's footsteps: "They took bribes and perverted justice" (8:3). This led the elders of Israel to ask Samuel to appoint a king for Israel "to judge us like all the nations" (8:5).

The book records very little regarding the ministry of Samuel as a judge before the institution of the monarchy (see 7:3–17). What is recorded relates the deliverance of Israel from the hands of the Philistines and a military victory for the people of God. As a memorial, Samuel erected a stone commemorating the Lord's help in the battle. He called it "Ebenezer" saying, "Till now the LORD has helped us" (7:12). This event was momentous for Israel since it brought a time of relative peace to the nation, as God's hand "was against the Philistines all the days of Samuel" (7:13). There was also peace with the Ammorites (7:14). So while the portion of the book that documents Samuel's days as a judge is brief, its significance must not be over-looked. In a sense, it was the calm before the storm!

Notably, Samuel was "judge," "priest," and "prophet" in Israel,[8] but as the nation transitioned to the monarchy, his prophetic role took on an advisory nature. He anointed the king whom God chose and then counseled him according to the word he received from God. Thus, his function shifted from political leadership as a judge to that of a divinely appointed consultant to the king. In this way, as VanGermen states, "Samuel became the role model for the prophets as the guardian of the theocracy."[9]

After Saul was anointed king, Samuel gave a farewell address in 1 Samuel 12 in which he chastised Israel for their rejection of God's kingship in order to have a

---

[6] Additionally, Dale Ralph Davis has noted four apparent summary sections positioned throughout the book that may add further insight into the book's construction: 1 Sam. 7:15–17; 14:47–52; 2 Sam. 8:15–18; 20:23–26. *2 Samuel: Out of Every Adversity*, Focus on the Bible (Fearn, Ross-shire, Scotland: Christian Focus, 2007), 10. These segments may very well function in a transitional manner, either highlighting a shift from one concern to another or from one chronological stage to the next, or perhaps signaling both thematic and chronological shifts. Regardless, the presence of these summaries in the book are noteworthy and may furnish greater insight into the book's structure and purpose.

[7] Birth narratives are rare in the Bible (only seven), and they always introduce important redemptive-historical figures (Isaac, Jacob, Joseph, Samson, Samuel, John the Baptist, and Jesus).

[8] Willem A. VanGemeren, *Interpreting the Prophetic Word: An Introduction to the Prophetic Literature of the Old Testament* (Grand Rapids, MI: Zondervan, 1990), 35.

[9] VanGemeren, *Interpreting the Prophetic Word*, 35. See also VanGemeren's discussion on "The Development of Prophetism" in Israel. *Interpreting the Prophetic Word*, 18–40.

human king. He also challenged them to fear the Lord and obey him, threatening punishment if they broke the covenant. Even though he was dissatisfied with Israel's actions, Samuel remained loyal to God and to God's people. He said, "Moreover, as for me, far be it from me that I should sin against the LORD by ceasing to pray for you, and I will instruct you in the good and the right way. Only fear the LORD and serve him faithfully with all your heart. For consider what great things he has done for you" (12:23–24). Thus, Samuel's love for God and the people undergirded this final speech. However, as he made very clear in his last statement, "But if you still do wickedly, you shall be swept away, both you and your king" (12:25).

The speech in 1 Samuel 12 is not Samuel's final appearance. The prophet later condemned Saul for his unlawful sacrifice and declared that his kingdom would not continue (13:8–14). Samuel again declared the Lord's rejection of Saul when he failed to annihilate everything belonging to the Amalekites (15:10–29). After this, he did not see Saul "until the day of his death," and he grieved over Saul (15:35). In the next chapter, the Lord called Samuel to anoint David as the king of Israel (16:1–13). Samuel's death is recorded in 1 Samuel 25:1, but a curious event takes place in 1 Samuel 28. King Saul was at war with the Philistines, and God no longer answered him. So he visited a necromancer in En-dor and had her conjure up the spirit of Samuel. Samuel appeared (28:14) and declared that God had taken the kingdom away from him and given it to David because he did not obey God's command to destroy all the Amalekites (28:16–17). Even in death, Samuel's loyalty to Yahweh, and to Yahweh's word, remained steadfast.

Kingship

A major theme in the book of Samuel is kingship, both God's and man's. Israel was officially constituted as a nation at Sinai (Exodus 19–20) with a theocratic political system. A theocracy is a system of government whereby God rules over a people group as King, and the leadership is carried out by priests and other divinely chosen authority figures such as judges and prophets. For Israel, God reigned over the nation, and they were to look to him as their King (see Ex. 15:18, "The Lord will reign [i.e., is king] forever and ever"). The implications of God's kingship for the people meant that he would care for them and they would serve him. However, they often failed to serve him by not keeping his commands and by committing idolatry (e.g., Exodus 32). Nevertheless, the Lord remained faithful in his rule over the people.

Toward the end of Samuel's judgeship, the people apparently grew tired of the political arrangement, and since Samuel's sons were corrupt, they asked him to anoint a king over the house of Israel: "Now appoint for us a king to judge us like all the nations" (1 Sam. 8:5). The request revealed their discontentment with God's kingship over them. As the Lord stated later,

> Obey the voice of the people in all that they say to you, for they have not rejected you, *but they have rejected me from being king over them.* According to all the deeds that they have done, from the day I brought them up out of Egypt even

to this day, forsaking me and serving other gods, so they are also doing to you. Now then, obey their voice; only you shall solemnly warn them and show them the ways of the king who shall reign over them. (8:7–9)

Samuel obeyed God's word and warned the people of what their request would entail:

These will be the ways of the king who will reign over you: he will take your sons and appoint them to his chariots and to be his horsemen and to run before his chariots. And he will appoint for himself commanders of thousands and commanders of fifties, and some to plow his ground and to reap his harvest, and to make his implements of war and the equipment of his chariots. He will take your daughters to be perfumers and cooks and bakers. He will take the best of your fields and vineyards and olive orchards and give them to his servants. He will take the tenth of your grain and of your vineyards and give it to his officers and to his servants. He will take your male servants and female servants and the best of your young men and your donkeys, and put them to his work. He will take the tenth of your flocks, and you shall be his slaves. And in that day you will cry out because of your king, whom you have chosen for yourselves, but the LORD will not answer you in that day. (8:11–18)

With this warning against human kingship, one would have thought that the people would reconsider their petition. However, there was apparently no wavering, even in the light of the words of God's faithful servant. Israel "refused to obey the voice of Samuel. And they said, 'No! But there shall be a king over us, that we also may be like all the nations, and that our king may judge us and go out before us and fight our battles'" (8:19–20). Interestingly, Scripture states that *Yahweh* fought Israel's battles (see Ex. 14:14; Deut. 1:30; 3:22; 20:4; Josh. 10:14; 10:42; 23:3; Neh. 4:20). After the Red Sea crossing, Moses and Israel sang of *God*, the divine Warrior-King, defeating the Egyptian armies (Ex. 15:1–21). The song even stated that Yahweh would establish Israel in the land of Canaan by his power:

Terror and dread fall upon them [i.e., the inhabitants of Canaan];
    because of the greatness of your arm, they are still as a stone,
till your people, O LORD, pass by,
    till the people pass by whom you have purchased.
You will bring them in and plant them on your own mountain,
    the place, O LORD, which you have made for your abode,
    the sanctuary, O LORD, which your hands have established. (Ex. 15:16–17)

In 1 Samuel 17, David also affirmed that God fights for Israel when he faced Goliath: "For the battle is the LORD's, and he will give you into our hand" (17:47).

There remains the question of whether it was wrong for Israel to have a king at all. In the book of Deuteronomy, God gave laws that the king must follow as the ruler of his people (see 17:14–20). Deuteronomy 17:14–15 states,

When you come to the land that the LORD your God is giving you, and you possess it and dwell in it and then say, "I will set a king over me, like all the nations that are around me," you may indeed set a king over you whom the LORD your God will choose. One from among your brothers you shall set as king over you. You may not put a foreigner over you, who is not your brother.

This may indicate that having a human king was not inherently wrong according to the law. Thus the problem in 1 Samuel may be not human kingship but rather the state of the people's heart in requesting a king. God said that they were *rejecting him* as their king. So the issue was not kingship itself but that Israel's heart was inclined away from Yahweh as their king. This reveals that the state of the heart toward the Lord is the primary concern.[10] In the end, the Lord gave the people what they desired, and immediately, in 1 Samuel 9, the reader is introduced to Saul, the son of Kish.

Saul (1 Samuel 8–15)

Human kingship in Israel began with Saul, a Benjaminite from Gibeah. The people asked for a king like all the other nations, and the Lord gave them exactly what they asked for (Saul's name in Hebrew means, "what was asked for"). Given how the book of Judges ends, with the Benjaminites from Gibeah acting like Sodomites and nearly going extinct (Judges 19–21), the selection of a king from this tribe and city is shocking and foreshadows the disappointment of Saul's reign and the termination of his dynasty.

While Saul was shy at first (1 Sam. 10:21–22), he appeared to fit the mold regarding the look of a king: "Then they ran and took him from there. And when he stood among the people, he was taller than any of the people from his shoulders upward. And Samuel said to all the people, 'Do you see him whom the LORD has chosen? There is none like him among all the people.' And all the people shouted, 'Long live the king!'" (10:23–24). The Lord told Samuel to anoint Saul as king over Israel, and the new king eventually rallied the troops to defeat the Ammonites, thereby establishing his kingdom (1 Samuel 11). His favor before Lord was short lived, however, for he soon lost the kingdom by disobeying God's commands. Saul offered unlawful sacrifices when Samuel was delayed (13:8–15), and he did not destroy everything belonging to the Amalekites, nor did he kill their king, Agag, as Yahweh commanded (15:8–11). Even though God's favor toward Saul was brief, his reign over Israel would continue for forty years.

King Saul was a complex man. Early on, the Spirit of God would come upon him and he would prophesy, but when the Lord sought another man for the kingship (13:14; chaps. 15–16), Saul's life and reign took a turn for the worse. He made foolish vows that jeopardized his soldiers' welfare and his own son's life (14:24–46), a harmful spirit sent from Yahweh tormented him (16:14–23), and war with the Philistines plagued him throughout his reign (14:52). The first king of the Israelite monarchy showed how leadership apart from God would never succeed and only made matters worse for the nation.

---

[10] For the theme of the "heart" in 1–2 Samuel, see "The Heart" on p. 218.

While Saul spent much time at war with the surrounding nations, especially the Philistines, his life soon became consumed with destroying David the son of Jesse. Initially, Saul favored young David because he was skilled at playing the lyre, a stringed musical instrument. Whenever a harmful spirit tormented Saul, David played music that would calm him, and the spirit eventually departed (16:14–23). David also became Saul's armor bearer, a trusted companion in battle. Additionally, young David slayed the formidable Philistine Goliath when every Israelite warrior cowered before the giant man's presence (1 Samuel 17). However, when they returned from David's defeat of Goliath, the women of Israel sang, "Saul has struck down his thousands, and David his ten thousands" (18:7). This provoked Saul to jealousy: "And Saul was very angry, and this saying displeased him. He said, 'They have ascribed to David ten thousands, and to me they have ascribed thousands, and what more can he have but the kingdom?' And Saul eyed David from that day on" (18:8–9). The writer continues,

> The next day a harmful spirit from God rushed upon Saul, and he raved within his house while David was playing the lyre, as he did day by day. Saul had his spear in his hand. And Saul hurled the spear, for he thought, "I will pin David to the wall." But David evaded him twice.
>
> Saul was afraid of David because the LORD was with him but had departed from Saul. (18:10–12)

Saul made David an officer in his army to get him out of his presence, but the Lord blessed David's endeavors, and the people of Israel grew in their love for him.

Interestingly, and even ironically, David had extremely close ties with the house of Saul. Jonathan, Saul's son, loved David and made a covenant with him (18:1–5), and Jonathan never turned against David, notably warning him when Saul was seeking to kill him (1 Samuel 20). Jonathan even swore his allegiance to David before David became king (20:12–17, 42; 23:17–18). Additionally, David married Michal, Saul's daughter (18:17–30). Saul gave her to David hoping that she would be a snare to him, but Michal loved David. This marriage arrangement actually worked against King Saul: "But when Saul saw and knew that the LORD was with David, and that Michal, Saul's daughter, loved him, Saul was even more afraid of David. So Saul was David's enemy continually" (18:28–29). David may have had one of the worst fathers-in-law of all time!

When Saul was not chasing David around the wilderness, he was battling the enemies of the nation, and it was in the midst of war with the Philistines that Saul died along with three of his sons, Jonathan, Abinadab, and Malchi-shua (1 Samuel 31). His sons were struck down by the Philistines on Mount Gilboa, and he was wounded by the archers. On the surface, there appears to be some discrepancy between the accounts of Saul's death in 1 Samuel 31 and 2 Samuel 1. At the end of 1 Samuel, the writer describes Saul's death as finally occurring when he intentionally fell on his own sword (1 Sam. 31:4; see 1 Chron. 10:1–7). In 2 Samuel 1:1–16, an Amalekite came to David reporting that he found Saul leaning upon his spear still alive. Saul apparently told the Amalekite to kill him because of his pain and because his life was lingering. So the Amalekite killed him and brought Saul's crown and armlet to David. It seems best to view 2 Samuel 1 as the Amalekite seeking to impress David and expecting to be rewarded. Ironically, instead of being rewarded, David had the man executed for not being afraid to lift his hand against "the LORD's anointed" (2 Sam. 1:14–16). The house of Saul eventually terminated with the death of Ish-bosheth (4:1–3). The only descendant of Saul who remained was Jonathan's crippled son, Mephibosheth (4:4), and because of the covenant with Jonathan, David showed him kindness (2 Samuel 9).

Saul's legacy is one of tragic failure. Even though he reigned for forty years, he did so without the favor and presence of Yahweh. His kingship represented kingship apart from God, a king like all the other nations had. While he was technically "the LORD's anointed" (*messiah*), he was not a king who represented the Lord or the Lord's kingship. A better king was needed—one who loved Yahweh and would seek to rule in a manner that honored him.

David (1 Samuel 16–2 Samuel 24)

After God's rejection of Saul, Yahweh called Samuel to go to Bethlehem to anoint a new king from among the sons of Jesse (1 Samuel 16). As Jesse's eldest son, Eliab, came before Samuel, he thought, "Surely the LORD's anointed is before him" (16:6). However, God's response reveals something crucial for understanding both kingship and the book of Samuel. He says to Samuel, "Do not look on his appearance or on the height of his stature, because I have rejected him. For the LORD sees not as man sees: man looks on the outward appearance, but the LORD looks on the heart" (16:7).[11] The remainder of Jesse's sons came before Samuel, and the Lord chose none of them to be king. It was not until the youngest son, David, was called in from pasturing the sheep that the new king was revealed to the prophet. God commanded Samuel to anoint David (16:12–13), and the Spirit of the Lord "rushed" upon him "from that day forward." Notably, the following verse states, "Now the Spirit of the LORD departed from Saul, and a harmful spirit from the LORD tormented him" (16:14).

David's service to King Saul was marked by success and loyalty. He defeated Goliath (1 Samuel 17) and prospered in his military endeavors (18:14, "And David had success in all his undertakings, for the LORD was with him"). David noted his faithfulness to Saul while being pursued by the king:

> Behold, this day your eyes have seen how the LORD gave you today into my hand in the cave. And some told me to kill you, but I spared you. I said, "I will not put out my hand against my lord, for he is the LORD's anointed." See, my father, see the corner of your robe in my hand. For by the fact that I cut off the corner of your robe and did not kill you, you may know and see that there is no wrong or treason in my hands. I have not sinned against you, though you hunt my life

---

[11] This verse is difficult to translate. In Hebrew, it literally reads, "for I have rejected him, for not as man sees/looks, for man sees/looks to/for/at the eyes, but Yahweh sees/looks to/for/at the heart." See "The Heart" on p. 218.

to take it. May the LORD judge between me and you, may the LORD avenge me against you, but my hand shall not be against you. (24:10–12; see also 1 Samuel 26)

In his relationship to Saul, David sought to honor the king as "the LORD's anointed" and never turned against him.

Nevertheless, Saul's jealousy provoked him to persecute David. For much of Saul's reign, David fled from the king in order to stay alive. He had to flee to Gath (1 Samuel 21), hide in the cave of Adullam (1 Samuel 22), hide in a cave near Wildgoats' Rock (1 Samuel 24), dwell in the wilderness of Ziph (1 Samuel 26), and even dwell among the Philistines (1 Samuel 27). However, the Lord's faithfulness to David continued as he escaped the hand of Saul on numerous occasions. God also blessed David by progressively adding faithful warriors to his entourage, giving him victory against his enemies while on the run and giving him favor with Achish, the Philistine king of Gath. So Yahweh's kindness to David prevailed, and when Saul died (1 Samuel 31), David's life as a refugee came to an end, and his reign began (2 Samuel 2).

However, war continued between the house of Saul and the house of David (2 Sam. 3:1) until the death of Ish-bosheth (4:1–2). So David ruled over Judah at Hebron for seven years and six months initially and then over both Israel and Judah for thirty-three years, making David's total reign about forty years (5:4–5). During this time, David established his capital in Jerusalem by conquering the Jebusites (5:6–10). His kingdom prospered and expanded as he defeated the Philistines (2 Samuel 5, 8, 10), the Moabites, the king of Zobah, the Edomites, the Amalekites (2 Samuel 8), the Ammonites (2 Samuel 10), and the Syrians (2 Samuel 8, 10).

King David displayed a fierce loyalty to Yahweh his God, and the author of Samuel highlights his efforts to honor the Lord. Many of the events recorded reveal that David trusted in God (e.g., the battle with Goliath, his relationship with Jonathan, fleeing from Saul). Some events further underline his zeal for the Lord, particularly his attempts to bring the ark of the covenant back to the tabernacle at Jerusalem. Even though his first attempt failed and cost Uzzah his life (since the ark was not moved according to God's law, 6:1–11), it showed the king's desire to have the presence of Yahweh in the midst of Jerusalem. When the second attempt succeeded (6:12–15), Israel celebrated, and "David danced before the LORD with all his might" (6:14).

David even desired to build God a house in which the ark of the covenant would dwell, and while at first Nathan the prophet approved of the king's plans, Yahweh vetoed the project. Instead, God intended to build a house for David, and he commanded Nathan to say,

> Thus says the LORD of hosts, I took you from the pasture, from following the sheep, that you should be prince over my people Israel. And I have been with you wherever you went and have cut off all your enemies from before you. And I will make for you a great name, like the name of the great ones of the earth. And I will appoint a place for my people Israel and will plant them, so that they may dwell in their own place and be disturbed no more. And violent men shall afflict them no more, as formerly, from the time that I appointed judges over my

people Israel. And I will give you rest from all your enemies. Moreover, the LORD declares to you that the LORD will make you a house. When your days are fulfilled and you lie down with your fathers, I will raise up your offspring after you, who shall come from your body, and I will establish his kingdom. He shall build a house for my name, and I will establish the throne of his kingdom forever. I will be to him a father, and he shall be to me a son. When he commits iniquity, I will discipline him with the rod of men, with the stripes of the sons of men, but my steadfast love will not depart from him, as I took it from Saul, whom I put away from before you. And your house and your kingdom shall be made sure forever before me. Your throne shall be established forever. (7:8–16)

This special display of God's favor to the king (the so-called Davidic covenant) would provide the basis for how God related to the Davidic kings who followed, and it anticipated a coming king (i.e., the Messiah) who would reign forever. David's response to this covenant revealed his gratefulness and amazement that the Lord would bless him in this way (7:18–29).[12]

While David expressed a vibrant faith in Yahweh, his personal life revealed that he was still a fallen man. The writer of 1–2 Samuel did not hide David's faults or sinful actions. The main incident revealing his weakness is his act of adultery and conspiracy to commit murder (2 Samuel 11). The king lusted after Uriah the Hittite's wife, Bathsheba, and committed adultery with her while Uriah was faithfully fighting the king's battles. When Bathsheba made her unexpected pregnancy known to David, he tried to conceal his actions by calling Uriah back to Jerusalem and encouraging him to go home to his wife, likely hoping that he would have sexual relations with her. The pregnancy could then be linked to Uriah instead of David. However, Uriah showed a greater sense of honor than the king. Uriah refused to enjoy the comforts of home while his men were at war. When his initial cover-up proved unsuccessful, David then sent Uriah back to the battlefront with a note to Joab, the general, that contained a plan to ensure Uriah's death. Joab followed the king's orders, and Uriah was killed in battle. David then took Bathsheba to be his wife, but his conspiracy did not go unnoticed. God knew what David had done and so sent Nathan the prophet to confront him for his sin (12:1–15). David repented, but as a consequence, he lost the child that Bathsheba carried (12:14–23). Later, Bathsheba gave birth to another child, Solomon, who would become David's heir.

David's sin brought about hardship for himself and for his family. The Lord said to David, "Behold, I will raise up evil against you out of your own house. And I will take your wives before your eyes and give them to your neighbor, and he shall lie with your wives in the sight of this sun. For you did it secretly, but I will do this thing before all Israel and before the sun" (12:11–12). Trouble came to David in the form of his son Amnon raping his half-sister Tamar (13:1–22). Though David became angry, he apparently rendered little, if any, punishment against Amnon.[13]

---

[12] See "The Davidic Covenant" on p. 216.

[13] The Septuagint and Dead Sea Scrolls add to 2 Sam. 13:21, "But he would not punish his son Amnon, because he loved him, since he was his firstborn."

Consequently, Tamar's brother Absalom became enraged, but he held his peace until he was able to create a plot to kill Amnon. After assassinating Amnon, Absalom fled to Geshur and later returned to Jerusalem (2 Samuel 13–14). However, like his father, Absalom engaged in his own conspiracy, in this case to take the kingdom away from David (2 Samuel 15). His treachery was successful, and David, along with those loyal to him, fled from Jerusalem (2 Samuel 15–16). After Joab killed Absalom (2 Samuel 18), David returned to Jerusalem. He eventually faced another rebellion led by a Benjaminite named Sheba, but the revolt was quelled by the act of a wise woman (2 Samuel 20). David's last recorded sin was his ordering of a census, for which the Lord sent a pestilence upon the people (2 Samuel 24). The writer states, "And there died of the people from Dan to Beersheba 70,000 men" (24:15). Needless to say, David's sinfulness brought great heartache to himself, his family, and his people.

In view of David's sins, one might wonder why Yahweh rejected Saul for his sin and not David as well. The answer is found in God's election. The Lord chose Saul as king for Israel in accord with their desire (i.e., a king like the nations), but God chose David according to his purposes. While the book of Samuel emphasizes David's faith in contrast to Saul's foolishness, the fundamental distinction between the two kings pertains to God's choice of David and his house (1 Samuel 16; 2 Samuel 7). Both were unworthy of God's kindness, but the Lord granted his everlasting favor to one and not the other.

Excursus: David and the Psalms

Many psalms reflect upon David's experiences as the king of Israel. These psalms also play an important role in revealing the nature of human kingship as it relates to God's kingship.[14] Multiple psalms contain superscriptions (i.e., titles) that signify Davidic authorship,[15] giving the reader a glimpse into the spiritual, emotional, and inner life of the king as a believer in Yahweh. Notably, some superscriptions identify specific events in David's life as the background or reason for the psalm's composition. For example, Psalm 3 was written "when he fled from Absalom his son." David penned Psalm 18 "when the LORD rescued him from the hand of all his enemies, and from the hand of Saul." Psalm 51 was composed when "Nathan the prophet went to him, after he had gone in to

---

[14] See Michael G. McKelvey, *Moses, David and the High Kingship of Yahweh: A Canonical Study of Book IV of the Psalter*, Gorgias Dissertations in Biblical Studies 55 (Piscataway, NJ: Gorgias, 2014), 309–22, for a discussion on the relationship between Yahweh's kingship and Davidic kingship in the Psalter. See also James L. Mays, *The Lord Reigns: A Theological Handbook to the Psalms* (Louisville: Westminster John Knox, 1994).

[15] Of the 150 psalms in the Psalter, all but 34 have titles. Of the 116 with titles, 100 signify an author, and 73 are attributed to David. Are these reliable or original titles? The oldest manuscripts contain the titles, but they are not formally part of the compositions. It is difficult to prove one way or the other, but since they are attested in the manuscripts, it seems best to take them as original and reliable. Apparently, the compilers of the Psalter intended the superscriptions to be read as authentic. Relatedly, scholarly debate surrounds the issue of authorship. For example, the Hebrew title לְדָוִד can be translated "of/to/for David." Does this title mean that a psalm was penned by David or about him or for him? While the phrase can be variously translated, in its most natural sense the title appears to signify origination, i.e., that the psalm comes from the person signified.

Bathsheba." Much of the Psalter highlights the experiential nature of David's life, or in other words, it shows us his heart as the events of his life unfolded. Additionally, the psalms are written in such a manner that even though they may provide an author's identity and a historical context, any believer may employ the psalms in his or her own Christian walk. Because of this connection, it is helpful to read the Psalms in light of 1–2 Samuel and vice versa.

The Davidic Covenant

Before moving on in the book of Samuel, the importance of the Davidic covenant within the Old Testament must be understood in order to appreciate God's overall covenantal purposes throughout redemptive history. To begin, the Davidic promises overlap significantly with the Abrahamic promises. The matter of kingship is particularly noteworthy. As the Lord chose to enter into covenant with Abraham and his seed, the book of Genesis reveals that God's redemption, as well as kings, would come through a particular family. Within the context of the Abrahamic covenant (see Genesis 12; 15; 17), the Lord says,

> I will make you exceedingly fruitful, and I will make you into nations, and *kings shall come from you.* And I will establish my covenant between me and you and your offspring after you throughout their generations for an everlasting covenant, to be God to you and to your offspring after you. And I will give to you and to your offspring after you the land of your sojournings, all the land of Canaan, for an everlasting possession, and I will be their God. (Gen. 17:6–8)

Also, Genesis 17:15–16 reads, "As for Sarai your wife, you shall not call her name Sarai, but Sarah shall be her name. I will bless her, and moreover, I will give you a son by her. I will bless her, and she shall become nations; *kings of peoples shall come from her.*" Not only does the promise of kings coming from Abraham and Sarah find fulfillment in David, but also God's promise to David regarding his descendants and kingdom carries God's covenantal purposes further along (2 Sam. 7:8–16).[16] Gentry and Wellum also note that the promise to Abraham regarding the land finds fulfillment in David's line:

> The borders of the land as envisioned in Genesis 15:18–21 are defined in Deuteronomy 11:24 as Israel's "place." First Kings 4:20–21 indicates that the geographical "place" belonged to Israel during the time of Solomon, David's son. So the covenant with David was a means to fulfill the promises in the Abrahamic Covenant.[17]

---

[16] Note also Jacob's blessing upon David's ancestor Judah: "The scepter shall not depart from Judah, nor the ruler's staff from between his feet, until tribute comes to him; and to him shall be the obedience of the peoples" (Gen. 49:10). The "scepter" and "ruler's staff" are emblems of kingship.

[17] Peter J. Gentry and Stephen J. Wellum, *Kingdom through Covenant: A Biblical-Theological Understanding of the Covenants* (Wheaton, IL: Crossway, 2012), 423–24.

These two covenants exhibit significant connections, especially when considering God's goal of bringing salvation and restoration through the means of a king.

The Psalter contains a restatement of the Davidic covenant in Psalm 89 after the nation had gone into exile. In 89:3–4 he proclaimed, "You have said, 'I have made a covenant with my chosen one; I have sworn to David my servant: "I will establish your offspring forever, and build your throne for all generations."'" In poetical fashion, the psalmist then summarized the Davidic covenant (2 Sam. 7:8–16) in Psalm 89:20–37. However, the fall of Davidic kingship and the experience of exile moved the psalmist to lament God's apparent rejection of his "anointed": "But now you have cast off and rejected; you are full of wrath against your anointed. You have renounced the covenant with your servant; you have defiled his crown in the dust" (89:38–39). The Babylonian exile challenged Israel's understanding of their status and future. Exile marked the end of human kingship in the land, and their nationhood was terminated. Nevertheless, this question still remained: What about God's promise to David? The psalmist concluded his lament, crying, "Lord, where is your steadfast love of old, which by your faithfulness you swore to David? Remember, O Lord, how your servants are mocked, and how I bear in my heart the insults of all the many nations with which your enemies mock, O Lord, with which they mock the footsteps of your anointed" (89:49–51). Even with the monarchy destroyed, God's covenant with David was still valid, and the psalmist called upon Yahweh to remember that covenant. Psalm 89 provides a vivid example of the profound connection between the Davidic covenant and God's redemptive purposes.

The recurring mention of a coming Davidic king in the Prophets also highlights the central role of the Davidic covenant in redemptive history. For example, Isaiah 55:3 said to a future people in Babylonian exile, "Incline your ear, and come to me; hear, that your soul may live; and I will make with you an everlasting covenant, my steadfast, sure love for David."[18] Isaiah revealed that the exiles' hope for redemption was tied to the Davidic promise. The prophet Jeremiah disclosed this idea as well:

> Behold, the days are coming, declares the Lord, when I will raise up for David a righteous Branch, and he shall reign as king and deal wisely, and shall execute justice and righteousness in the land. In his days Judah will be saved, and Israel will dwell securely. And this is the name by which he will be called: "The Lord is our righteousness." (Jer. 23:5–6)

While in Babylon, Ezekiel foretold of God's coming restoration for his people:

> My servant David shall be king over them, and they shall all have one shepherd. They shall walk in my rules and be careful to obey my statutes. They shall dwell in the land that I gave to my servant Jacob, where your fathers lived. They and their children and their children's children shall dwell there forever, and David my servant shall be their prince forever. I will make a covenant of peace with them. It shall be an everlasting covenant with them. And I will set them in their land and

---

[18] See Gentry and Wellum, *Kingdom through Covenant*, 410–21, for an extensive discussion of this passage. Isaiah 55:3 is cited by the apostle Paul in Acts 13:34.

multiply them, and will set my sanctuary in their midst forevermore. My dwelling place shall be with them, and I will be their God, and they shall be my people. Then the nations will know that I am the LORD who sanctifies Israel, when my sanctuary is in their midst forevermore. (Ezek. 37:24–28)

In the postexilic period, Zechariah prophesied,

And the LORD will give salvation to the tents of Judah first, that the glory of the house of David and the glory of the inhabitants of Jerusalem may not surpass that of Judah. On that day the LORD will protect the inhabitants of Jerusalem, so that the feeblest among them on that day shall be like David, and the house of David shall be like God, like the angel of the LORD, going before them. (Zech. 12:7–8)

These examples underscore the prominent place of the Davidic covenant in God's redemptive scheme. As history unfolded, the coming messianic Davidic king became the anticipated figure who would usher in God's kingdom and procure salvation for God's people. The New Testament confirms that this Davidic covenant is ultimately fulfilled in Jesus Christ. He has secured salvation, has established the everlasting new covenant, and will reign as King forever.

The Heart

The topic of the "heart" occurs in many books of the Old Testament. The book of Samuel especially highlights the issue of the heart in several of its main characters, as well as in the people of Israel. In 1 Samuel 1–2, the writer refers to Hannah's heart multiple times. Her husband, Elkanah, asked her, "Why is your heart sad?" (1:8). As Hannah spoke to the Lord at the tabernacle, she spoke "in her heart; only her lips moved, and her voice was not heard" (1:13). After she gave birth to Samuel, she prayed, "My heart exults in the LORD" (2:1). These opening chapters emphasize the condition of the heart in the experience of faith and life.

After the Lord announced his rejection of Eli's house and its coming destruction, Eli's sons, Hophni and Phinehas, were killed in battle, and the ark of the covenant was captured by the Philistines (1 Samuel 3). As an old man, Eli awaited news of the battle, and when a messenger arrived, "Eli was sitting on his seat by the road watching, for his heart trembled for the ark of God" (4:13). Once again, the writer highlights the inner nature of the character.

Samuel addressed the heart of the people of Israel in 1 Samuel 7:3: "If you are returning to the LORD with all your heart, then put away the foreign gods and the Ashtaroth from among you and direct your heart to the LORD and serve him only, and he will deliver you out of the hand of the Philistines." After Samuel anointed Saul as king, "God gave him [i.e., Saul] another heart" (10:9). In his farewell address, Samuel responded to the people's acknowledgment that they wrongly asked for a king: "Do not be afraid; you have done all this evil. Yet do not turn aside from following the LORD, but serve the LORD with all your heart. . . . Only fear the LORD and serve him faithfully with all your heart. For consider what great things he has done for you" (12:20–24).

When God chose a king to replace Saul, Samuel stated, "The LORD has sought out a man after his own heart, and the LORD has commanded him to be prince over his people, because you have not kept what the LORD commanded you" (13:14).[19] Later, as we saw earlier, Samuel went to Jesse in Bethlehem and thought that Eliab was the clear choice as the new king. However, God said to Samuel, "Do not look on his appearance or on the height of his stature, because I have rejected him. For the LORD sees not as man sees: man looks on the outward appearance, but the LORD looks on the heart" (16:7). God chose David instead. Johnson notes that "the right heart of David will become a motif in the books of Kings, and he will be the benchmark against whom future kings will be compared" (see 1 Kings 11:4–6, 33, 38; 14:8; 15:3–5, 11; 2 Kings 14:3; 16:2; 18:3; 22:2).[20]

There are many more examples in 1–2 Samuel, but suffice it to say that this emphasis on the heart ties into the overall emphasis of Scripture that all matters of life flow from the heart (Prov. 4:23). We can understand the significance of the heart for the book of Samuel by looking to Deuteronomy, which describes the circumcised heart (Deut. 10:16; 30:6). God is not merely concerned with outward matters because human beings are not simply creatures with outward lives. God created man and woman with both body and soul, and the inward life affects and determines the outward actions. Readers are to look not merely at what these characters do but also at what is going on in their inner persons. This is humanity—complex creatures, living in a fallen world, with significant heart issues. Jesus explained, "But what comes out of the mouth proceeds from the heart, and this defiles a person. For out of the heart come evil thoughts, murder, adultery, sexual immorality, theft, false witness, slander" (Matt. 15:18–19). Ultimately, God shows the reader of 1–2 Samuel that what people need most is a new heart. Yahweh is the only one who can provide it, and he has thankfully promised to give it: "And I will give you a new heart, and a new spirit I will put within you. And I will remove the heart of stone from your flesh and give you a heart of flesh" (Ezek. 36:26).

APPROACHING THE NEW TESTAMENT

Along with the Old Testament, the New Testament portrays God's kingdom as a prominent theme. When reading through the Gospels, the reader quickly observes that the kingdom of God/heaven takes center stage in Jesus's ministry. For example, Matthew 4:17 states, "From that time [i.e., after his baptism] Jesus began to preach, saying, 'Repent for the kingdom of heaven is at hand.'" Jesus said in Mark 1:15, "The time is fulfilled, and the kingdom of God is at hand; repent and believe in the gospel." Luke recorded Jesus declaring, "I must preach the good news of the kingdom

---

[19] The interpretation of the phrase "after his own heart" is highly debated. Traditionally, the phrase "as/like/according to his [i.e., Yahweh's] heart" has been viewed as referring to David's heart reflecting God's heart. However, modern scholarship favors the position that this phrase refers to God's choice or election; see P. Kyle McCarter Jr., *I Samuel: A New Translation with Introduction and Commentary*, AB 8 (Garden City, NY: Doubleday, 1980), 229; Tsumura, *The First Book of Samuel*, 349; David G. Firth, *1 & 2 Samuel*, ApOTC (Downers Grove, IL: InterVarsity Press, 2009), 156. For a recent work supporting the traditional interpretation, see Benjamin J. M. Johnson, "The Heart of YHWH's Chosen One in 1 Samuel," *JBL* 131, no. 3 (2012): 455–66.

[20] Johnson, "Heart of YHWH's Chosen One," 459.

of God to the other towns as well; for I was sent for this purpose" (4:43). Finally, Jesus said to Nicodemus, "Truly, truly, I say to you, unless one is born again he cannot see the kingdom of God" (John 3:3). The kingdom of God points to the rule or kingship of Yahweh, which is realized in the kingship of Christ.

Notably, the New Testament writers also connect human kingship with divine kingship in the person of Jesus. As the Davidic king, Jesus fulfills the promises of God to David since he is the Son of David who will reign forever (see 2 Sam. 7:16), and in Christ, the reign of God is identified with the reign of David. For instance, both Matthew and Luke's genealogies highlight Jesus as the descendant of David (Matt. 1:1–17; Luke 3:23–38). Peter declared in Acts 2:34–36, "For David did not ascend into the heavens, but he himself says, 'The Lord said to my Lord, "Sit at my right hand, until I make your enemies your footstool."' Let all the house of Israel therefore know for certain that God has made him both Lord and Christ, this Jesus whom you crucified" (see also Acts 15:16–18; 2 Tim. 2:8–13). Christ himself connected God's reign with David's reign. Speaking to the Pharisees, Jesus said,

> "What do you think about the Christ? Whose son is he?" They said to him, "The son of David." He said to them, "How is it then that David, in the Spirit, calls him Lord, saying, 'The Lord said to my Lord, "Sit at my right hand, until I put your enemies under your feet"'? If then David calls him Lord, how is he his son?" And no one was able to answer him a word, nor from that day did anyone dare to ask him any more questions. (Matt. 22:42–46)

Through this questioning, Jesus reveals that he is both David's Son and David's Lord; he is both man and God, reigning over God's kingdom forever (cf. Rom. 1:1–3).

In the history of Israel, every Davidic king failed to achieve perfection in his reign, and they all experienced God's chastisement (cf. 2 Samuel 7; see Psalm 89). However, with the coming of David's greater Son, Davidic success was realized in the fullest possible way. Jesus stands as the perfect King of Israel, who rules over his people in righteousness, equity, justice, compassion, and grace. He reigns over the kingdom of God, and his reign will never end. Paul writes in Philippians 2:5–11,

> Have this mind among yourselves, which is yours in Christ Jesus, who, though he was in the form of God, did not count equality with God a thing to be grasped, but emptied himself, by taking the form of a servant, being born in the likeness of men. And being found in human form, he humbled himself by becoming obedient to the point of death, even death on a cross. Therefore God has highly exalted him and bestowed on him the name that is above every name, so that at the name of Jesus every knee should bow, in heaven and on earth and under the earth, and every tongue confess that Jesus Christ is Lord, to the glory of God the Father.

Thus, Christ's kingship fully displays God's kingship, and he will reign forever as both God and man in one person.

The New Testament also sheds light on the matter of the heart. The Old Testament—and specifically 1–2 Samuel—reveals that human beings need a new heart, that only God can give a new heart, and that he has promised to do so. The New Testament confirms these realities and shows that Jesus has accomplished this promise. Through Peter's preaching at Pentecost, his hearers were "cut to the heart" (Acts 2:37). Speaking of the Gentiles in Acts 15:8–9, Peter said, "And God, who knows the heart, bore witness to them, by giving them the Holy Spirit just as he did to us, and he made no distinction between us and them, having cleansed their hearts by faith." Acts 16:14 states, "The Lord opened [Lydia's] heart to pay attention to what was said by Paul." Paul writes, "For God, who said, 'Let light shine out of darkness,' has shone in our hearts to give the light of the knowledge of the glory of God in the face of Jesus Christ" (2 Cor. 4:6). He also notes that God "has sent the Spirit of his Son into our hearts, crying, 'Abba! Father!'" (Gal. 4:6); he explains that believers have had "the eyes of [their] hearts enlightened" (Eph. 1:18); and he prays that "Christ may dwell in your hearts through faith" (Eph. 3:17). The book of Hebrews encourages Christians to "draw near with a true heart in full assurance of faith, with [their] hearts sprinkled clean from an evil conscience and [their] bodies washed with pure water" (10:22). This heart change occurs by the work of the Holy Spirit, whom Christ has poured out upon his people (see John 14:15–31; 16:5–15; Acts 1:5; 2:1–21). Jesus's work of salvation has fulfilled God's promise to circumcise the hearts of God's people (Deut. 30:6) and to conform their hearts to his likeness as he reigns within them.

What is the point of the book of Samuel? It records a crucial part of Israel's history, when it transitioned to the monarchy. It also focuses on the first two kings by contrasting them and the outcome of their reigns. However, 1–2 Samuel reveals much more than facts about an ancient nation. The message of the book is primarily that God is King. When his people looked to human kings, it did not turn out well, and the consequences were severe. However, the sovereign God used these events to work out his ultimate purpose, which was to bring about the seed of the woman (Gen. 3:15)—through Abraham (Genesis 12, 15, 17), through Israel, through David—to reign forever over his everlasting kingdom. As the reader sees the place of the book of Samuel within the canon of Scripture and redemptive history, the hand of the Most High King becomes visible as he orchestrates his eternal purpose of redemption. God is always faithful, even when his people continue to reject him (cf. Deut. 32:4–5, 10–18). So it is not the human actions and failures of a nation that are preeminent but the hand of God, which is able to usher in his eternal kingdom in spite of weak and broken human vessels. This book points everyone to Christ the King, and this is the main purpose of all Scripture (cf. John 5:39–40).

SELECT BIBLIOGRAPHY

Ackroyd, Peter R. *The First Book of Samuel*. CBC. Cambridge: Cambridge University Press, 1971.

———. *The Second Book of Samuel*. CBC. Cambridge: Cambridge University Press, 1977.

Anderson, A. A. *2 Samuel*. WBC 11. Waco, TX: Word, 1989.

Arnold, Bill T. *1 & 2 Samuel*. NIVAC. Grand Rapids, MI: Zondervan, 2003.

Baldwin, Joyce G. *1 and 2 Samuel: An Introduction and Commentary*. TOTC 8. Downers Grove, IL: InterVarsity Press, 1988.

Bergen, Robert D. *1, 2 Samuel*. NAC 7. Nashville: Broadman, 1996.

Brueggemann, Walter. *First and Second Samuel*. IBC. Louisville: John Knox, 1990.

Currid, John D., and David P. Barrett. *Crossway ESV Bible Atlas*. Wheaton, IL: Crossway, 2010.

Davis, Dale Ralph. *2 Samuel: Out of Every Adversity*. Focus on the Bible. Fearn, Rossshire, Scotland: Christian Focus, 2007.

Eslinger, Lyle M. *Kingship of God in Crisis: A Close Reading of 1 Samuel 1–12*. BLS 10. Decatur, GA: Almond, 1985.

Evans, Mary J. *1 and 2 Samuel*. NIBCOT 6. Peabody, MA: Hendrickson, 2000.

Firth, David G. *1 & 2 Samuel*. ApOTC 8. Downers Grove, IL: InterVarsity Press, 2009.

Gentry, Peter J., and Stephen J. Wellum. *Kingdom through Covenant: A Biblical-Theological Understanding of the Covenants*. Wheaton, IL: Crossway, 2012.

George, Mark K. "Yhwh's Own Heart." *CBQ* 64, no. 3 (2002): 442–59.

Gordon, Robert P. *1 & 2 Samuel: A Commentary*. Exeter: Paternoster, 1986.

Hays, J. Daniel. "1–2 Samuel." In *What the Old Testament Authors Really Cared About: A Survey of Jesus' Bible*, edited by Jason S. DeRouchie, 200–17. Grand Rapids, MI: Kregel, 2013.

Hill, Andrew E., and John H. Walton. *A Survey of the Old Testament*. 2nd ed. Grand Rapids, MI: Zondervan, 2000.

Johnson, Benjamin J. M. "The Heart of YHWH's Chosen One in 1 Samuel." *JBL* 131, no. 3 (2012): 455–66.

Klein, Ralph W. *1 Samuel*. WBC 10. Waco, TX: Word, 1983.

Longman, Tremper, III, and Raymond B. Dillard. *An Introduction to the Old Testament*. 2nd ed. Grand Rapids, MI: Zondervan, 2006.

Mauchline, John. *1 and 2 Samuel*. NCB. London: Oliphants, 1971.

Mays, James L. *The Lord Reigns: A Theological Handbook to the Psalms*. Louisville: Westminster John Knox, 1994.

McCarter, P. Kyle, Jr. *I Samuel: A New Translation with Introduction and Commentary*. AB 8. Garden City, NY: Doubleday, 1980.

———. *II Samuel: A New Translation with Introduction and Commentary*. AB 9. Garden City, NY: Doubleday, 1984.

McKelvey, Michael G. *Moses, David and the High Kingship of Yahweh: A Canonical Study of Book IV of the Psalter*. Gorgias Dissertations in Biblical Studies 55. Piscataway, NJ: Gorgias, 2014.

Smith, Henry Preserved. *A Critical and Exegetical Commentary on the Books of Samuel*. ICC. New York: Charles Scribner's Sons, 1904.

Tsumura, David Toshio. *The First Book of Samuel*. NICOT. Grand Rapids, MI: Eerdmans, 2007.

VanGemeren, Willem A. *Interpreting the Prophetic Word: An Introduction to the Prophetic Literature of the Old Testament*. Grand Rapids, MI: Zondervan, 1990.

9

1–2 Kings

William B. Fullilove

INTRODUCTION

The book of Kings (1–2 Kings together) is the last book of the Former Prophets, completing the narrative of God's people in the land of Canaan that began in the books of Deuteronomy and Joshua.[1] In another sense, Kings provides the conclusion to an even more extensive narrative arc, one that began much earlier, before the exodus of Israel from Egypt with the calling of Abraham in the book of Genesis. As part of this ongoing narrative, Kings traces the history of God's people from the beginning of Solomon's reign until the destruction and exile of the nation of Judah. As such, Kings is not only theologically rich in its own right, with messages about God's justice and God's covenant, but it also gives a historical context in which to read many of the Latter Prophets (Isaiah, Jeremiah, Ezekiel, and the Twelve).

Key areas of discussion about Kings include its authorship and compositional history, its genre, the trustworthiness of the historical information it reports, its chronology, and its theological message and rhetorical point. Further, Kings connects in multiple ways to the New Testament and to Jesus Christ. Most obvious among these is the kingship itself. The kingship, intended to be the answer to the debacle of leadership by the judges, instead became its sad recapitulation. Just as rule by judge failed because of the sinfulness of human judges, so also rule by king failed because of the sinfulness of human kings. The book of Kings highlights the need for a true leader of Israel, a true king after God's own heart. The evident need is for a seed of David who will be more than David (who was a man after God's own heart but

---

[1] The books of 1–2 Kings in the English Bible correspond to 1–2 Kings in the Masoretic text of the Hebrew Bible, though their verse numbering differs in the following locations: 1 Kings 4:21–34 [Masoretic text: 5:1–14], 1 Kings 22:43–53 [Masoretic text: 22:44–54], and 2 Kings 11:21–12:21 [Masoretic text: 11:22–12:22]. Also, the books of 1–2 Kings correspond to 3–4 Kingdoms in the Septuagint but with noticeable differences between the Masoretic text and the Septuagint, for which see "Compositional History" on p. 226.

deeply sinful), not less than him (which is what his successors proved to be). Further connections to the New Testament include the motifs of city and temple, links to the Elijah and Elisha stories, and the interaction of prophets and kings.

BACKGROUND ISSUES

The books of 1–2 Kings provide a single, continuous narrative that covers events beginning with the accession of Solomon, extending through the division of the northern and southern kingdoms (Israel and Judah, respectively) and culminating in the destruction of both kingdoms. The period covered by this narrative is quite extensive. Scholars conventionally date the accession of Solomon to the throne in 970 BC, the first wave of the exile of Judah to 597 BC, and the ultimate destruction of Jerusalem and final phase of the exile of Judah to 586 BC. This chronology would make the last time reference in the book—the thirty-seventh year of the exile, counting from 597 BC (2 Kings 25:27)—to be approximately 561 BC. Accordingly, the narrative encompasses over four hundred years of time. Kings was most likely split into the two books of 1–2 Kings because of its length, not because of a particular theological or compositional rationale, as the break between the two occurs in the midst of the narratives concerning Ahaziah's reign and Elijah.

Author and Date

Kings is an anonymous work, most likely produced by a Judean author or compiler, given the greater attention it shows to Judah and the fact that it continues past the end of the northern kingdom of Israel. A curiosity about the book is the complete absence of the character of Jeremiah, which led some Jewish traditions to surmise that he himself was the author, though modern scholars generally view this approach as speculation. The composition of Kings in its canonical form must be dated after the destruction of Jerusalem in 586 BC, since 2 Kings 25 records events that occurred during the exile of Judah, especially the Judean king Jehoiachin being given special favor in Babylon during the thirty-seventh year of the exile of Judah (2 Kings 25:27–30).[2] Given that the book makes no mention of the return from exile in 539/38 BC (see Ezra–Nehemiah), one can narrow down the possible dates when the canonical book of Kings was produced to a tight range of years—between 560 and 538 BC.[3]

While the author or compiler never explicitly states his purpose, the content and shape of the book allow the reader to infer its goal: to justify that Yahweh's exile of his people was, in fact, a just punishment since they broke the Mosaic law. Most telling in this regard is that the unknown author or compiler of Kings expressed his full agreement with the theology of the book of Deuteronomy. Regarding the northern kingdom, for instance, 2 Kings 17:7–8 makes this theological position relatively explicit:

---

[2] Some argue that most of Kings was written earlier, based on the claim that the last four verses of the book were added later. For this, see "Compositional History" on p. 226.

[3] Many posit that passages in the current canonical books of 1–2 Kings were added later by prophets after this period. These arguments are discussed briefly in "Compositional History" on p. 226.

And this occurred because the people of Israel had sinned against the LORD their God, who had brought them up out of the land of Egypt from under the hand of Pharaoh king of Egypt, and had feared other gods and walked in the customs of the nations whom the LORD drove out before the people of Israel, and in the customs that the kings of Israel had practiced. (2 Kings 17:7–8)

Though specifically about only the northern kingdom, these verses reflect the theology of the entire work—the author or compiler of the book is a theological historian writing during the exile who wants to explain that Yahweh has been just.

Genre

Kings may be described as selective and theological history writing—in other words, historical writing with a theological purpose. On its face, the narrative gives evidence of an attempt to be historical with appeals to dates and sources. The book aims to provide an ordered account of the history of Israel and Judah from the beginning of Solomon's reign to the end of the independent existence of each kingdom. Like any attempt at historical writing, however, Kings is both selective and ideological.[4] It hardly tells all details—even all major events—of each nation, but only includes items picked to make the case for the author or compiler's interpretation of that history. This selectivity is visible simply enough in the disproportionate space given to certain kings, as the book mentions many kings with barely more than an introduction and summary evaluation (e.g., 2 Kings 15 covers Zechariah, king of Israel; Shallum, king of Israel; Menahem, king of Israel; Pekahiah, king of Israel; and Pekah, king of Israel), yet dwells at length on the reigns and lives of other kings (e.g., Hezekiah). Even in the cases of the kings treated in depth, the text of Kings records only a tiny fraction of the events of that king's life and reign.

The author or compiler of the book, then, is giving—under the inspiration of God—an accurate theological take on events in the history of God's people. That theological take is that God was justly judging his people for sin. Such a viewpoint would have competed with other potential, inferable explanations for the fall of Israel and Judah: that they had made poor alliances or simply had not won the geopolitical contest (a modern approach), that Yahweh had lost a battle against other gods in the heavenlies (an ancient approach), or even possibly that the people had failed to be sufficiently devoted to Baal (which some in Israel and Judah might well have suggested). Instead, the author is arguing that God's people were in exile because God had willed it as a judgment for their disobedience to the law, especially as presented in Deuteronomy. This theological viewpoint, as detailed in what follows, is seen in

---

[4] The same is necessarily true of modern historians, and of historians of any generation, including those who wish to argue for an alternative interpretation of the history given in Kings. Historical writing is of necessity selective and of necessity imposes an order and a theme (or themes) upon its material. This observation implies that the modern historical writer is ideological, just as the author or compiler of Kings would have been. No author, modern or ancient, gives an unmediated take on events, but instead, all are ideological in some way or ways. The implication of this point is important: if in favor of an alternative take on the history of Israel and Judah, one cannot simply dismiss the claims of Kings as "ideologically biased" without further argument, for the modern historian is also ideologically biased, just possibly in a different way.

the clear influence of the theology of Deuteronomy, the evaluations of each king, and the doctrine of delayed retribution.

Compositional History

This chapter's repeated reference to the "author or compiler" of Kings is necessitated by the complex debates over the compositional history of the book. These debates result not simply from critical theories but from the text itself, as the text shows clearly unifying elements but also testifies to the use of sources. Such debates are intensified by the disparities in the Septuagint and Qumran manuscripts of Kings and by the larger debate over the composition of the books from Deuteronomy through Kings (commonly called the Deuteronomistic History).

The text of Kings exhibits several unifying elements. First, the plot line of the book itself focuses consistently on the broad moral decline of Israel and Judah and their resulting military and political troubles. Second, the chronological structure gives it a consistently unifying flow. Third, the regnal formulas that introduce and conclude the account of each king in the divided kingdom period unify those episodes of the book. The author or compiler uses a standard form to present the dates of a king's rule, its length, his death and burial, and further sources of information about that king's reign. Further, the accession report of each king typically synchronizes his reign with that of the king reigning in the other kingdom and in the case of Judah also includes the name of the king's mother. Fourth, the consistent presence of the Deuteronomic law as an evaluative standard provides possibly the most striking unifying characteristic of the book. If kings act in accordance with the words of Deuteronomy, they receive a positive evaluation, whereas if they do not, the narrator's evaluation is negative.

These unifying themes of the text, however, do not imply that the author worked from first-person knowledge or created his text in one fell swoop. The text of Kings itself is clear that the author or compiler used sources. Those include at a minimum three stated sources: the annals of the kings of Judah, the annals of the kings of Israel, and the book of the annals of Solomon. They may well include other, uncited sources. This use of sources is particularly evident in the "to this day" passages (1 Kings 8:8; 9:13, 21; 10:12; 12:19; 2 Kings 2:22; 8:22; 10:27; 14:7; 16:6; 17:34, 41). A few of these passages, such as 1 Kings 10:12, could potentially be explained as still true during the exile, but most of these are, at first blush, problematic because they would not have been true at the time the canonical book of Kings was completed.

First Kings 8:8 is illustrative: "And the poles [of the ark of the covenant] were so long that the ends of the poles were seen from the Holy Place before the inner sanctuary; but they could not be seen from outside. And they are there to this day" (1 Kings 8:8). At the time of the exile, when the text that includes 2 Kings 25 was set down as a single narrative, the temple had been destroyed, and the poles of the ark of the covenant were quite obviously no longer visible. The author or compiler of the book, then, must have been using sources for which the "to this day" statements had been true at the time of the source's composition, but the author or compiler chose not to edit the text of those unnamed sources when he included it in Kings.

The Septuagint and Qumran versions provide further evidence for the compositional history of Kings. The Greek and Hebrew texts of Kings show different chronological data. While some passages are probably the result of added commentary (e.g., 3 Kingdoms 2:35a–o), the dating-system differences are not so easily explained because they seem to rely on different textual traditions.[5] The upshot of these observations is that the line between text criticism and redaction criticism is quite blurry regarding the text of Kings.

Further, in the Masoretic text, Kings reflects much of the same theology and style as Joshua, Judges, and Samuel. For this reason, the issues of the date, author, and location of the writing of Kings are all tied up in the question of the compositional history of the larger complex of books from Genesis to Kings, and especially Deuteronomy to Kings. At the theoretical level, Kings could be anything from a separate book written to dovetail with already existing books, to a piece of a larger, integrated composition, or anywhere in between.[6]

STRUCTURE AND OUTLINE

Arrangement

The basic arrangement of Kings is undoubtedly chronological. The author or compiler aims for precision by including an explicit statement of the length of each king's reign in each nation. Further, he seeks to correlate and coordinate the timing of the reigns of the kings of Israel and Judah during the divided kingdom. In the divided kingdom section, Kings tells two parallel (and often intersecting) stories as it traces the downfall of Israel and then Judah. To do so, the author could have tried to tell the story in a straight chronological line. Doing so, however, would have meant jumping incessantly back and forth from Judah to Israel—much like the filming style of a

---

[5] James Donald Shenkel, *Chronology and Recensional Development in the Greek Text of Kings*, HSM 1 (Cambridge, MA: Harvard University Press, 1968), 5–42.

[6] The history of scholarly views on the compositional history of Kings shows an ebb and flow between multiple-author theories and single-author theories. Alternately put, the proposed compositional history of Kings was quite complex up until the time of Martin Noth, who then simplified the theory. After Noth the complexity of these theories gradually increased. But again, more recently, scholars have shown renewed interest in more streamlined theories regarding the book's composition.

In the decades prior to the publication of Noth's *The Deuteronomistic History* (1943), scholars commonly argued that the hypothesized Pentateuchal sources (JEDP in shorthand) extended past Deuteronomy into Joshua and Judges, and even into Samuel and Kings. Against such theories, Noth argued that there was an underlying unity in both language and theology that extended from the book of Deuteronomy through 2 Kings (excluding Ruth) and that this entire section of Scripture was the work of one individual. Noth named this individual "the Deuteronomist" and argued that this Deuteronomist was an individual writing sometime during the exile. Noth's novel contribution, and quite possibly his largest, was to argue that the author of Kings was not an editor of a text that was already basically in shape but instead a creative author and assembler. Martin Noth, *The Deuteronomistic History*, 2nd ed., JSOTSup 15 (Sheffield: Sheffield Academic Press, 2001), 110–48. Noth's theory gradually won wide acceptance by the late 1960s, but reactions did develop, both in American and German scholarship, and reintroduced complexity into the proposed compositional history of Kings. Since about 1970, scholars have modified Noth's thesis in various ways.

Certainly, the text of Kings shows clear markers of a compositional history—markers such as the text's references to sources and the "to this day" passages that the author or editor chose not to smooth out. Beyond those markers, however, the compositional history debate becomes one of judgment calls. Given the continuing, and even increasing, divergence of scholarly opinions on the issue, it is becoming increasingly common for commentaries to focus on the final form of the inspired text.

modern sitcom. Such an arrangement would be quite difficult in a text, and instead, the author follows an alternating pattern, once the kingdom divides, between the history of the northern and southern kingdoms. The alternation is not strict but is driven by the length of the kings' reigns—once the narrative begins to tell the story of a particular king, it continues with that king until his death, only then switching to report the parallel kingship in the other nation.

Upon the division of Israel and Judah, then, Kings begins with Israel and then traces the story of the king or kings of Israel until the end of his or their lives. Once that narrative has outdistanced the ruler in Judah, the narrative goes back in time and tells the story of the king of Judah who reigned concurrently. It then continues reporting successive Judean kings until it passes the point where it last left Israel. At that point, the narrative switches back to tracing the next Israelite king or kings until the Israelite history passes the death of the last Judean king to be covered, and so forth. In such a way, the text achieves an alternating pattern while keeping the reign of each king in a contiguous narrative section.

Relative and Absolute Chronology in Kings

This chronological structure raises questions of both relative and absolute chronology in Kings. The question of *relative chronology* concerns how the events within the text relate to each other according to the chronological markers stated inside the text. The question of *absolute chronology* revolves around whether the relative chronology of the text can be coordinated with dates outside the narrative to enable us to date its events in relation to a modern calendar.

The relative chronology of Kings can be determined generally to within a year or two, but exact precision is elusive in some places. For example, 2 Kings 8:25 indicates that Ahaziah the king of Judah began to reign in the twelfth year of Joram the king of Israel, but 2 Kings 9:29 indicates that Ahaziah's reign began in the eleventh year of Joram king of Israel. At least three factors may contribute to such difficulties. First, Kings gives evidence of coregencies, such as David and Solomon in 1 Kings 1–2 and Jotham and Uzziah in 2 Kings 15, yet it is not clear how these coregencies are reckoned when counting the length of each king's reign. Second, there may have been two different dating systems in play when measuring the length of a king's reign: an antedating system in which a partial year of a king's reign was counted as his first year and a postdating system in which only the first full year of a king's reign was considered his first regnal year. The text is not clear whether one or both dating systems are in play at any given time, and the earlier-mentioned sources may not be consistent. Third, some scholars also argue that there was a calendar reform or a dual-calendar system in use in Israel and Judah with the text not always specifying which calendar is in view. Thiele, for instance, in an extensive attempt to solve the relative chronological problems of Kings, argues that the kingdoms switched back and forth between antedating and postdating systems and also posits a large number of coregencies.[7] While all acknowledge the amount of effort and ingenuity in Thiele's work, many question whether he has forced the text to fit his goal.[8] Similarly, many caution that ancient numerical systems allowed significant approximation and did not entail the exacting precision (even by the fairly precise author of Kings!) that would be expected in a modern history.[9]

Relating the relative chronology of Kings to an absolute chronology is possible because of various common events reported in both Kings and either Egyptian, Assyrian, or Babylonian records. Particularly helpful are the Assyrian *limmu* lists, written in Akkadian. The *limmu* was a high official who would preside over a yearly festival in the Assyrian capital, such that the year could be referenced by his name. Preserved overlapping lists enable modern historians to name the *limmu* for each year from 892–648 BC. These lists are particularly helpful because they often mention significant events that happened during the year of a particular *limmu*. For example, one list mentions an eclipse in relation to the year of the *limmu* Bur-Segal, and astronomical calculations enable us to date that eclipse to 763 BC, therefore allowing us to date any other events mentioned in that list. Such calculations make possible the absolute dating of biblical events with relative precision, such as dating the fall of Samaria to 722 BC. The net effect is that the precise internal chronology of Kings is difficult to sort out, complicated by the relative chronology of the book, but most events of the narrative can be dated in relation to a modern calendar within a year or two.

Historical Accuracy

The intersection of events in the biblical narrative of Kings with real-world dates and events raises the question of the historical reliability and accuracy of Kings. Many modern historians have increasingly—and skeptically—questioned whether the biblical text helps us discern actual historical events at all.[10] The trend has become, in many sectors, to distinguish "biblical Israel" from "historical Israel" and to imply that they are completely distinct entities. Others, however, defend the historical accuracy of Kings either methodologically[11] or archaeologically.[12]

Kings clearly portrays itself as speaking about actual events of the past, so it cannot be read under the rubric of being "just a literary story." Further, Kings recounts events from an era in which extrabiblical sources exist that report information corresponding to biblical events. It would be methodologically too much to say those extrabiblical sources "prove" Kings to be true, as Kings is making *theological* claims

---

[7] Edwin R. Thiele, *Mysterious Numbers of the Hebrew Kings*, 3rd ed. (Grand Rapids, MI: Zondervan, 1983), 165–69.
[8] Raymond Dillard, "The Reign of Asa (2 Chronicles 14–16): An Example of the Chronicler's Theological Method," *JETS* 23, no. 3 (1980): 207–18.
[9] Iain W. Provan, *1 and 2 Kings*, NIBCOT 7 (Peabody, MA: Hendrickson, 1995), 19n21.
[10] Thomas L. Thompson, *The Mythic Past: Biblical Archaeology and the Myth of Israel* (New York: Basic Books, 1999), 319–21.
[11] Iain W. Provan, V. Philips Long, and Tremper Longman III, *A Biblical History of Israel*, 1st ed. (Louisville: Westminster John Knox, 2003), 1–104.
[12] Kenneth A. Kitchen, *On the Reliability of the Old Testament* (Grand Rapids, MI: Eerdmans, 2006), 7–64.

about events. Nonetheless, archaeological discoveries such as the Mesha Stela, which depicts a Moabite take on the rebellion of Moab against Israel (cf. 2 Kings 3), provide extrabiblical verification of some events in Kings.[13] Similarly, the Black Obelisk of Shalmaneser III, now housed in the British Museum, depicts Jehu, king of Israel, bringing tribute to Shalmaneser III.[14] Various histories of Israel and other related works detail more examples like these.[15] Kings is most certainly shaped in both theological and literary ways, but the acknowledgement of literary shaping need not imply (though it is often made to do so) that Kings is unreliable in reporting events that it claims occurred.

Structure

This chronological arrangement of Kings should not be considered an attempt to give "equal time" to each king or even to each kingdom. The author or compiler clearly prioritizes certain kings in terms of text allocated to their reigns and certain other characters such as Elijah and Elisha. The content of the book, then, is best handled by looking at the major sections of this historical narrative—where it spends its time and where the narrative "slows down" to dwell more heavily.

Outline

    I. The Solomon Narratives (1 Kings 1:1–11:43)
   II. The Divided Kingdom (1 Kings 12:1–2 Kings 17:41)
       A. Various kings prior to Elijah's time (1 Kings 12:1–16:28)
       B. The Elijah narratives (1 Kings 16:29–2 Kings 2:14)
       C. The Elisha narratives (2 Kings 2:15–10:36)
       D. Various kings after Elisha's time (2 Kings 11:1–17:41)
  III. Judah Alone (2 Kings 18:1–25:30)

MESSAGE AND THEOLOGY

As history, but history with a theological message, Kings traces the story of the decline of the kingship after the end of David's life and rule. The Solomon narratives are a story of lost promise, and both the northern and southern kingdoms show a slide farther and farther from God's ways into a deserved judgment of destruction. In the midst of these declines are the conspicuously different Elijah and Elisha narratives. Common to all these accounts are theological emphases on the Mosaic covenant, the Davidic covenant, and the authority of the prophetic word.

---

[13] Note that Lemaire's reconstructed line 31 of the Mesha Stela includes a reference to the "house of David." His reconstruction is not universally accepted but if correct represents the earliest extrabiblical reference to David's house. See Andre Lemaire "'House of David': Restored in Moabite Inscription," *BAR* 20, no. 3 (1994): 30–37.

[14] Note that some have questioned the identification of the Black Obelisk's reading of ʾia-ú-a DUMU ḫu-um-ri-i as Jehu, though this identification as Jehu, king of Israel, is still generally accepted. For an example of the minority position, see P. Kyle McCarter, "'Yaw, Son of Omri': A Philological Note on Israelite Chronology," *BASOR* 216 (1974): 5–6. For an example of a reaffirmation of the generally accepted position, see Baruch Halpern, "Yaua, Son of Omri, yet Again," *BASOR* 265 (1987): 81–85.

[15] See, for instance, Kitchen, *On the Reliability of the Old Testament*, 239–41; Provan, Long, and Longman, *A Biblical History of Israel*, 64–68, 361.

Theological Emphases

The Mosaic Covenant as Expressed in Deuteronomy

The story of Kings is, fundamentally, a story of broken covenant, as God's people repeatedly break the terms of his covenant with them. The covenant in question is the Mosaic covenant, especially as enunciated in Deuteronomy. Kings evidences a deep reliance on the theology of Deuteronomy as the evaluative standard for the kings of Israel and Judah, and it assumes the dynamics of covenantal administration from Deuteronomy. As the evaluative standard for the reigns of kings, then, Deuteronomy provides necessary background reading for any study of Kings. Particularly important are the commands for the centralization of worship at the Jerusalem temple in Deuteronomy 12 and the dynamics of covenant in Deuteronomy 28.

In Deuteronomy 12, God commands the centralization of worship at the temple in Jerusalem and the destruction of all high places, since those high places will prove an irresistible temptation to idolatry:

> These are the statutes and rules that you shall be careful to do in the land that the Lord, the God of your fathers, has given you to possess, all the days that you live on the earth. You shall surely destroy all the places where the nations whom you shall dispossess served their gods, on the high mountains and on the hills and under every green tree. You shall tear down their altars and dash in pieces their pillars and burn their Asherim with fire. You shall chop down the carved images of their gods and destroy their name out of that place. You shall not worship the Lord your God in that way. But you shall seek the place that the Lord your God will choose out of all your tribes to put his name and make his habitation there. There you shall go, and there you shall bring your burnt offerings and your sacrifices, your tithes and the contribution that you present, your vow offerings, your freewill offerings, and the firstborn of your herd and of your flock. And there you shall eat before the Lord your God, and you shall rejoice, you and your households, in all that you undertake, in which the Lord your God has blessed you. . . . Take care that you do not offer your burnt offerings at any place that you see, but at the place that the Lord will choose in one of your tribes, there you shall offer your burnt offerings, and there you shall do all that I am commanding you. (Deut. 12:1–7, 13–14)

One must distinguish two uses of high places for sacrifice in Kings, a high place for sacrifice to Yahweh and a high place for sacrifice to pagan deities. The second is always wrong in the eyes of the narrator because it is blatant idolatry. The first is tolerated by the narrator until the building of the temple, though with great distaste. With the building of the temple, however, sacrifice of any kind is, according to Deuteronomy 12, to be centralized under the eyes of the priests at the temple, mainly to protect God's people from drifting into idolatry. The existence of high places, even where the people worship Yahweh, is seen to be a risk, a temptation to splinter off into worshiping Yahweh in unsanctioned ways and eventually to become disloyal to God by worshiping pagan deities at the high place.

This background from Deuteronomy explains the heavy emphasis in Kings on the construction and indwelling of the temple (1 Kings 5–8). Further, the kings of Israel and Judah are consistently evaluated by their fidelity (or lack thereof) to this command. Israel is indicted for its consistent idolatry, beginning with the golden calves that Jeroboam sets up as an alternative to the worship of Yahweh at the temple complex in Jerusalem (12:25–33). Judean kings who walk in similar ways are condemned (e.g., Manasseh in 2 Kings 21:3), and Judean kings who support the temple are praised. Particularly important in this regard are Hezekiah, praised for removing the high places in Judah (18:5), and Josiah, praised for refurbishing the temple and reforming worship (23:25).

In Deuteronomy 28, God lays out the dynamics of covenantal administration in Israel, especially the blessings (28:1–14) and the curses (28:15–68) that will come to Israel from respectively keeping or breaking her covenant with Yahweh. Kings emphasizes the fulfillment of these dynamics in the decline of Israel. Agricultural disaster and resulting famine are threatened in Deuteronomy 28:15–19 and inflicted in 1 Kings 18, 2 Kings 4–8, and 2 Kings 25. Disease is threatened in Deuteronomy 28:21–22 and inflicted in 2 Kings 15:5. Military defeat is threatened in Deuteronomy 28:25–26 and inflicted in 2 Kings 10:32. Most of all, exile is threatened in Deuteronomy 28:36–37 and inflicted in 2 Kings 17 and 2 Kings 24–25. Kings repeatedly emphasizes that God's people have broken covenant and have deserved the punishments that correspond to their covenant unfaithfulness.

The Davidic Covenant

The Davidic covenant is also operative in Kings. The Davidic covenant had been presented in Samuel as ultimately unconditional in God's love and promise to David but with blessing for David's heirs explicitly conditioned upon faithfulness to the law:

> When your days are fulfilled and you lie down with your fathers, I will raise up your offspring after you, who shall come from your body, and I will establish his kingdom. He shall build a house for my name, and I will establish the throne of his kingdom forever. I will be to him a father, and he shall be to me a son. When he commits iniquity, I will discipline him with the rod of men, with the stripes of the sons of men, but my steadfast love will not depart from him, as I took it from Saul, whom I put away from before you. And your house and your kingdom shall be made sure forever before me. Your throne shall be established forever. (2 Sam. 7:12–16)

This faithfulness of God to David is reported in 1 Kings 15:4, when the narrator reports:

> Nevertheless, for David's sake the LORD his God gave him a lamp in Jerusalem, setting up his son after him, and establishing Jerusalem, because David did what was right in the eyes of the LORD and did not turn aside from anything that he commanded him all the days of his life, except in the matter of Uriah the Hittite. (1 Kings 15:4–5)

The emphasis on the Davidic kingship explains the Judean focus of the book of Kings, since the Davidic kings reigned in Judah and since God's love of David caused God to show such great patience and longsuffering during the long downward spiral of the house of David.

These covenants imply both an unconditionality and a conditionality. Unconditionally, God has instituted his covenant with his people and has made sure promises from which he will not turn (cf. 2 Samuel 15–16). In the expression of life under the covenant, however, immediately after issuing such sure promises, God makes a conditionality clear. The presence of covenant curses—applied based on the behavior of the kings and the people in following their kings—means that neither the temple nor the kingship will protect against the consequences of prolonged disobedience to the covenant. This note is repeatedly sounded throughout Kings. For example, consider the Lord's words to Solomon after the dedication of the temple:

> And the LORD said to him, "I have heard your prayer and your plea, which you have made before me. I have consecrated this house that you have built, by putting my name there forever. My eyes and my heart will be there for all time. And as for you, if you will walk before me, as David your father walked, with integrity of heart and uprightness, doing according to all that I have commanded you, and keeping my statutes and my rules, then I will establish your royal throne over Israel forever, as I promised David your father, saying, "You shall not lack a man on the throne of Israel." But if you turn aside from following me, you or your children, and do not keep my commandments and my statutes that I have set before you, but go and serve other gods and worship them, then I will cut off Israel from the land that I have given them, and the house that I have consecrated for my name I will cast out of my sight, and Israel will become a proverb and a byword among all peoples. And this house will become a heap of ruins. (1 Kings 9:3–8a)

Similar statements are made in 1 Kings 2:2–4; 6:11–13; and 8:25, as well as in 2 Samuel 7:12–14 and Jeremiah 7:1–15.

In Deuteronomy 17, God had emphasized the role of the law in nurturing the king's faithfulness:

> When you come to the land that the LORD your God is giving you, and you possess it and dwell in it and then say, "I will set a king over me, like all the nations that are around me," you may indeed set a king over you whom the LORD your God will choose. One from among your brothers you shall set as king over you. You may not put a foreigner over you, who is not your brother. Only he must not acquire many horses for himself or cause the people to return to Egypt in order to acquire many horses, since the LORD has said to you, "You shall never return that way again." And he shall not acquire many wives for himself, lest his heart turn away, nor shall he acquire for himself excessive silver and gold.
>
> And when he sits on the throne of his kingdom, he shall write for himself in a book a copy of this law, approved by the Levitical priests. And it shall be with him, and he shall read in it all the days of his life, that he may learn to fear the LORD his God by keeping all the words of this law and these statutes, and doing them, that his heart may not be lifted up above his brothers, and that he may not turn

aside from the commandment, either to the right hand or to the left, so that he may continue long in his kingdom, he and his children, in Israel. (Deut. 17:14–20)

Should the king turn aside from the law, the very nature of a covenant arrangement meant that God would judge that disobedience. The text of Kings echoes these words of Deuteronomy 17 in its indictment of Solomon (1 Kings 10:14–28; 11:3). Conversely, it praises Josiah's obedience to and passion for the law of God, for which he is rewarded (22:8–20).

The Prophetic Word and Delayed Retribution

Deuteronomy 18:21–22 indicates that the Deuteronomic test of a true prophet is whether his words come to pass. Unsurprisingly, then, Kings emphasizes the fulfillment of prophecy. This emphasis would have been particularly necessary because the prophets often stood against the kings, insisting that they must follow the Lord's ways, not those of the surrounding kingdoms or those that seemed most politically expedient (e.g., Isaiah advising Ahaz in 2 Kings 16; cf. Isaiah 7–8). The emphasis on fulfilled prophecy in Kings is most prominently visible in the Elijah and Elisha narratives, but other instances of fulfilled prophecy include the prophecy against Eli (1 Sam. 2:30–36; 1 Kings 2:27), Ahijah's prophecy of the divided kingdom (1 Kings 11:29–39; 12:20), the word against Jeroboam by the man of God from Judah (1 Kings 13), Ahijah's pronouncement of judgment on Jeroboam (1 Kings 14:6–18; 15:29), and the prophecy that Naboth's blood would be avenged (2 Kings 9:24–26).

This emphasis on the fulfillment of the prophetic word is particularly important because the book of Kings simultaneously shows a doctrine of delayed retribution. The book details the longsuffering and patient God of Judah who, for David's sake, delays retribution for the sins of the people for decades and even centuries. While Judah has some good kings (eight out of twenty receive praise from the narrative), her sins and broken covenant could have led to judgment far more quickly than they did. Even Manasseh's exceptional level of sin (2 Kings 21:1–18) results in eventual, not immediate, judgment.[16] The majority of the writing prophets of the Old Testament would have been active during the time reported by Kings, continually warning of the judgments and exile to come if the people would not repent. The people, in fact, would not repent (cf. Isa. 6:9–13), and delayed judgment might have seemed like proof that the prophetic word did not come true. Writing from the perspective of the exile, however, the author of Kings insisted that the prophetic word was, in fact, reliable—retribution was delayed, but it had come, and justly so.

Hope in Exile?

One ongoing point of debate about Kings is the question of whether the narrative was meant to convey any hope to the Israelites in exile. Noth viewed the whole of his proposed Deuteronomistic History as displaying only judgment, no hope—that it was

---

[16] Compare the 2 Kings account with the portrayal of Manasseh in 2 Chronicles 33:1–20, which evidences the Chronicler's doctrine of immediate retribution.

a story only of a deserved catastrophe.[17] The ending of 2 Kings 25, however, as von Rad pointed out shortly after Noth's work was published, does provide—though in muted tones—exactly that: hope, indicating that the promise to David had not been completely forgotten.[18] Certainly the main purpose of Kings was to show that God had been faithful to the covenant and that the disaster of exile was, in fact, the fault of the people, not their Lord. Nonetheless, the curious ending with the elevation of Jehoiachin provides a small glimmer of hope, a sense that God might not yet be done with the house of David, that the Lord had not abandoned his promise to David of a descendant reigning upon the throne forever.[19]

Solomon's Kingdom

The force of the Solomon narrative in 1 Kings 1–11 is to show something that starts well but ends badly. Solomon is responsible for establishing true worship in Israel via the temple and then for desecrating that worship via his idolatry, resulting in God's judgment via the division of the nation. The narrative begins by establishing Solomon as the rightful heir to David's throne, both in his claim to succession—seen in his rebuttal of Adonijah, who attempts to be the new Absalom (1:1–53)—and in his removal of the major threats to his rule: Joab, Shimei, and Adonijah (2:1–46). David's charge in 2:1–9 is likely included to show that Solomon was not simply bloodthirsty but was righting wrongs that for various reasons had not been punished under his father, David.

The majority of the Solomon narrative is then devoted to Solomon's establishment of the temple, the institution that will finally fulfill the command of Deuteronomy 12 and usher in true worship in Israel. This section encompasses 1 Kings 3–9, which is marked off as a section by the mention of Pharaoh's daughter as a literary frame (3:1–3; 9:24–25). Chapter 3 focuses on Solomon's idealized wisdom as a prelude to the positive work of building the temple. The narrative of Solomon's wisdom is framed by God giving him that wisdom (3:4–15) and by mankind recognizing that gift (4:29–34). Inside that frame, Solomon demonstrates his wisdom judicially (3:16–28) and politically (4:1–28).

Once Solomon's divinely given wisdom has been established, the narrative moves to the building of the temple itself, recounted in 1 Kings 5–6 and 7:13–51. The ark of the covenant is brought, and the temple is dedicated in chapter 8. As an important contrast to pagan temples with their plethora of idols, the only material item present is the ark of God, which contains his law: "There was nothing in the ark except the two tablets of stone that Moses put there at Horeb, where the LORD made a covenant with the people of Israel, when they came out of the land of Egypt" (8:9).

---

[17] Noth, *The Deuteronomistic History*, 97.

[18] Gerhard von Rad, "The Deuteronomistic Theology of History in the Books of Kings," chap. 7 in *Studies in Deuteronomy*, trans. Davis Stalker, SBT 9 (London: SCM, 1953).

[19] Though Noth felt that the final verses of 2 Kings 25 were the product of the Deuteronomist, others who view Kings as providing no hope argue that this ending is a later addition. Instead, one might note that it connects perfectly to one of the book's struggles—that God had promised a Davidic dynasty, yet that those Davidic kings had sinned. Would God still honor his promise to David? The view taken here, then, is that 25:27–30 are a real glimmer of hope, though one should justly note that it was a faint glimmer. After all, it was a dark time.

God clearly blesses the endeavor by indwelling the temple in the glory cloud (8:10), and Solomon responds with a model theological prayer from 8:22–53, at which point the dedication by sacrifice occurs (8:62–66). God then responds by appearing to Solomon and emphasizing the continued responsibility to keep covenant so that Israel will remain in the land and flourish under God's blessing (9:1–9).

For all the initial promise of Solomon's reign and the blessing of the building of the temple, the ultimate story of Solomon's reign is that of rot underneath the impressive exterior. First Kings 3:1–3 had already sounded a disquieting note at the beginning of the narrative of Solomon's wisdom and temple building:

> Solomon made a marriage alliance with Pharaoh king of Egypt. He took Pharaoh's daughter and brought her into the city of David until he had finished building his own house and the house of the LORD and the wall around Jerusalem. The people were sacrificing at the high places, however, because no house had yet been built for the name of the LORD. Solomon loved the LORD, walking in the statutes of David his father, only he sacrificed and made offerings at the high places.

Solomon's alliance with Egypt and taking a foreign wife to seal that alliance violated Deuteronomy 17:17. Further, at the beginning of the narrative of building the temple, the institution that was to finally allow the removal of the high places, the narrator indicates that Solomon himself never even left behind the temptation of such worship. The tragic tale is that such worship ultimately consumed him and destroyed the kingdom.

Starting in 1 Kings 10, the rot begins to show through. Chapter 10 begins with what seem to be continued positive notes: Solomon's international renown (10:1–13) and his vast wealth (10:14–29). It must be emphasized that Solomon's wealth was not the problem per se, as God delights to bless his people and as wealth was a sign of the nation's ascendant geopolitical fortunes. But one can note, with Matthew 6:19–21, that wealth entails spiritual danger, and as the descriptions of Solomon's wealth continue through chapter 10, more and more they bring the warnings in Deuteronomy 17:16–17 back to mind. For example, 1 Kings 10:26 shows that Solomon broke the prohibition of acquiring many horses: "And Solomon gathered together chariots and horsemen. He had 1,400 chariots and 12,000 horsemen, whom he stationed in the chariot cities and with the king in Jerusalem."

In this regard, hints of Solomon's spiritual decay due to the distractions of wealth may appear as early as the temple building account. The story of Solomon building his palace curiously interrupts the temple narrative reported in 1 Kings 7:1–12. Note that David had indicated concern at building his palace before the temple (2 Sam. 7:2) and that in Exodus the construction of the tabernacle was immediately followed by its furnishing (Exodus 38–40). For all his efforts in building the temple, Solomon does not seem to share this concern and urgency but instead shows a somewhat divided heart. The Hebrew text subtly hints at this contrast. Provan explains:

A translation that better brings out the relationship between [the two houses], and particularly the significance of the word order, runs as follows: "He completed (*klh*) the temple (*bayit*) . . . he spent seven years building it (*bnh*). But his own house (*bêtô*) Solomon spent 13 years building (*bnh*), and he completed (*klh*) the whole of his house (*kol-bêtô*)." There are two "houses" in view, and an emphatic contrast is made between them.[20]

The key point is that the temple could not begin its role until it was both built and furnished, and in these duties Solomon delayed, tolerating the continued worship of the Lord at the high places, where he himself eventually would be drawn into apostasy.

Wherever exactly the narration turns from approving to disapproving Solomon's behavior, this turn is complete by 1 Kings 11. There the narrative revisits the initially disquieting themes of 3:1–3, this time explicitly criticizing Solomon for marrying foreign women. Solomon's love of those wives "turned away his heart after other gods" (11:4) and led him into full-blown idolatry (11:5–8). As a result, the Lord declares judgment, that the kingdom will be divided, with only one tribe left to Solomon's son—and that only for the sake of David (11:9–12). The Solomon narrative therefore ends with Solomon's increasing trouble on all sides, a marked counterpart to the "rest on every side" he had enjoyed in 5:4. Solomon begins to experience covenant curses. Hadad of Edom becomes a threat from the south, Rezon of Damascus a threat from the north and—most tellingly—Jeroboam son of Nebat a threat from within. Instead of kingly rest and peace, Solomon begins to face danger on all sides. The narrative is one of lost promise, because it moves from the prophet Nathan securing the kingship for Solomon to the prophet Abijah ripping it away. Solomon's kingship rules at the height of the nation's influence but with a spiritual rot that eventually emerges. The wisest man of all time was no match for a divided heart that made him, biblically, a fool.

The Northern Kingdom of Israel

First Kings 12 begins the chronology of the divided kingdom, with the northern kingdom of Israel rebelling against Rehoboam, Solomon's son, who in the end rules only the southern kingdom of Judah. Jeroboam returns from Egypt, where he had fled from Solomon, and he quickly becomes the leader and spokesman for the northern tribes. In the ensuing interactions, God's words to Solomon (11:9–13) and Ahijah's prophecy (11:29–39) come to pass via the poor judgment and harsh rule of Rehoboam. The ten northern tribes rebel, and the united kingdom that David had created is no more.

In the new situation, the prophets call for religious unity despite political diversity, but Jeroboam rejects such an endeavor, convinced that if the religious loyalty of the people remains in Jerusalem, their political loyalty will soon return there as well (12:26–27). Jeroboam's concern is for religion in the service of the state, and thus he immediately leads Israel into an idolatry from which it never recovers. Jeroboam fashions two golden calves and says to the people, "You have gone up to Jerusalem

<hr>

[20] Provan, *1 and 2 Kings*, 69.

long enough. Behold your gods, O Israel, who brought you up out of the land of Egypt" (12:28). Jeroboam's move is quite sophisticated, as he effectively appeals to an alternate Exodus tradition (Exodus 32), one that he can insinuate has been unfairly stamped out by the priests in Jerusalem but represents a true Israelite faith. Of course, the author of Kings takes no such perspective, stating, "this thing became a sin," considering them idols, not an alternatively acceptable means of worshiping Yahweh (1 Kings 12:30). In fact, the false worship that Jeroboam established (12:31–33) was a sin that was never removed from Israel (1 Kings 14:16; 15:30; 2 Kings 3:3; 10:29, 31; 13:2, 11; 14:24; 15:9, 18, 24, 28; 17:22).

Following the approximately twenty-year reign of Jeroboam, the text of Kings moves with little comment through four Israelite kings (Nadab, Baasha, Elah, and Zimri). The next major focus in recounting the history of the northern kingdom is on the kings of the Omride dynasty: Omri, his son Ahab, and Ahab's sons Ahaziah and Joram (also spelled as Jehoram). While a group of four rulers may seem less than worthy of the term *dynasty*, in the prevailing political instability of the northern kingdom, the term can be applied, even with its ironic connotation fully noted. The text focuses mainly on the reigns of Ahab, Ahaziah, and Joram, as their rules form the backdrop for the Elijah and Elisha narratives. Ahab and his wife, Jezebel, made Baalism the state religion. The narrator notes, "And as if it had been a light thing for him to walk in the sins of Jeroboam the son of Nebat, he took for his wife Jezebel the daughter of Ethbaal king of the Sidonians, and went and served Baal and worshiped him. He erected an altar for Baal in the house of Baal, which he built in Samaria. And Ahab made an Asherah. Ahab did more to provoke the LORD, the God of Israel, to anger than all the kings of Israel who were before him" (1 Kings 16:31–33).

The Omride dynasty occupies the physical center of the narrative of Kings as a book. Such a center may seem odd at first, but one must recall that for much of the divided kingdom period, Israel, not Judah, was the stronger nation militarily, economically, and politically. Israel was able to invade Judah and threaten Jerusalem (2 Kings 16:5–6; cf. Isa. 7:1), not the reverse. Further, Israel under Omri's son Ahab was part of the coalition that fought the Assyrian king Shalmaneser III at Qarqar.[21] And while the Assyrians won that battle, they had to return again in short order for another military action, meaning that their victory must have been less than complete. Accordingly, the time of the Omride dynasty represents the collision of the strongest kings with Elijah and Elisha, the strongest prophetic voices in the book.

After four Omride kings, Jehu is anointed by Elisha to eliminate the house of Omri from its rule and role in Israel (2 Kings 9:6–10), which he does with remarkable bloodlust. The text treats Jehu's dynasty differently than the other northern kings in that it is the only case where a northern king is divinely appointed and in that it represents the only dynasty with any real staying power, lasting over a century. Jehu does destroy Baal worship in Israel (10:28), and in response, the Lord grants him a

---

[21] William W. Hallo, "From Qarqar to Carchemish: Assyria and Israel in the Light of New Discoveries," *BA* 23, no. 2 (1960): 34–61.

dynasty of four generations. However Jehu does not return to the true worship of Yahweh, instead continuing in the sins of Jeroboam son of Nebat (10:29, 31), and the text indicates that as a result, God brings covenant curses in warfare (10:32–33).

After four generations of Jehu's dynasty, the northern kingdom enters a swift decline, with a series of short-lived rulers. The backdrop to this period is the rejuvenated and expanding Assyrian empire pushing west into Syria and Palestine. The eighth-century Assyrian invasions of Palestine were among the most pivotal (and brutal) events in the entire history of Israel or Judah, forming the backdrop to the ministries of many of the writing prophets. The Assyrians were adept not only at warfare but also at terror, with particularly brutal treatment of conquered populations. In the 730s the Assyrian emperor Tiglath-pileser III campaigned in Palestine and not only imposed tribute on Israel but also annexed many of its regions. This situation explains the political instability in Israel, which had become a tiny and weak nation, splintered by coups and disunity caused by political factions trying to determine how to address the looming and continuing Assyrian threat.

After the death of Tiglath-pileser III, Pekah king of Israel joined in alliance with the Syrian states to attempt to resist the Assyrians, pressuring Judah to join their alliance and invading it when Judah's king declined the offer. Nonetheless, this Syrio-Israelite coalition was short lived, falling to the Assyrian war machine in less than a decade. In 722 BC, Samaria was destroyed after a three-year siege begun by the Assyrian emperor Shalmaneser V, and the northern kingdom of Israel ceased to exist, with the people taken into exile and scattered throughout the Assyrian empire (2 Kings 17:1–6).

As far as Kings is concerned, the focus is not so much on the events themselves but instead on the theological explanation for those events. The author or compiler reports the siege and destruction of Samaria in the first six verses of 2 Kings 17 but then gives the theological reason much more space (17:7–23). Kings insists that the ultimate cause of the exile was neither politics nor military strength but sin: "And this occurred because the people of Israel had sinned against the LORD their God, who had brought them up out of the land of Egypt from under the hand of Pharaoh king of Egypt, and had feared other gods" (17:7).

The Southern Kingdom of Judah

Whereas the religious situation in the northern kingdom is completely negative, with the only bright spot being the return to "only" the sins of Jeroboam, the situation in the south is more mixed. Without question, the southern kingdom takes the same ultimate trajectory as Israel, a descent away from the worship of the Lord into idolatry, covenant curses, and eventual exile, this time at the hand of the resurgent Babylonian empire. Unlike the north, however, Judah's history includes some good kings who interrupt and occasionally delay or temporarily reverse the downward trend.

During much of the time of the divided kingdom, the sins of the northern kingdom also seep into Judah. For example, Athaliah, the daughter of Ahab, marries into the

Davidic royal family in Judah (2 Kings 8:25–27) and devotes herself to establishing Baal worship in Judah, just as it had been established in Israel. Her attempt to destroy the royal family (11:1) almost extinguishes the line of David. Even in the case of kings who resist Israelite influence, such as Ahaz king of Judah, the moral situation is bad, as he allies with the Assyrians against Israel (16:7–9) and adopts their idolatrous worship (16:10–18). And even for the eight southern kings whom the narrative praises, 2 Kings 12:2–3 is emblematic: "And Jehoash did what was right in the eyes of the LORD all his days, because Jehoiada the priest instructed him. Nevertheless, the high places were not taken away; the people continued to sacrifice and make offerings on the high places."

Two kings, however, receive particularly positive treatments in the narrative of 2 Kings: Hezekiah for his trust and Josiah for his obedience. Hezekiah is praised in Kings for his trust in the Lord. He removes the high places, purifies worship, and follows the law (18:1–4). The summary note at the beginning of his narrative is exceptionally positive: "He trusted in the LORD, the God of Israel, so that there was none like him among all the kings of Judah after him, nor among those who were before him. For he held fast to the LORD. He did not depart from following him, but kept the commandments that the LORD commanded Moses" (18:5–6).

Hezekiah even rebels against the king of Assyria (18:7b). While the text does not explicitly say that Hezekiah's rebellion is at the Lord's urging, it is strongly slanted toward such an impression: "And the LORD was with him; wherever he went out, he prospered. He rebelled against the king of Assyria and would not serve him. He struck down the Philistines as far as Gaza and its territory, from watchtower to fortified city" (18:7–8).

Hezekiah's rebellion, however, invites a vigorous response from Sennacherib, the Assyrian emperor who in Hezekiah's fourteenth year invades and defeats him, exacting a huge tribute that requires Hezekiah to empty the temple and palace treasuries and to strip the gold off the temple doors and doorposts in order to buy off the Assyrians (18:14–16). Sennacherib's siege of Jerusalem, which is recounted starting in verse 17, is thought by some to represent a second invasion but is more likely from this same invasion in 701 BC. The text is merely giving more specific information about the events recounted generally in 2 Kings 18:1–16, focusing specifically on Hezekiah and his need to trust Yahweh in the face of overwhelming odds. With Jerusalem surrounded by the most effective, efficient, and terrifying army the ancient Near East had ever known, Hezekiah's response is to mourn (19:1a), to go to the temple (19:1b), and to call for the prophet Isaiah (19:2–4), who prophesies hope and deliverance for Jerusalem (19:5–7). After a partial withdrawal by the Assyrian army to fight an Egyptian force (19:8), the siege of Jerusalem continues (19:9–13). Hezekiah's response to the Assyrian threat results in one of the model prayers of Scripture in 19:14–19, and his repentance and trust are rewarded: Isaiah prophesies deliverance (19:20–34), and the angel of the Lord provides that deliverance, decimating the Assyrian camp and fulfilling Isaiah's prophecy (19:35–37).

Second Kings 20:12–21 is clearly a flashback, as it reports Hezekiah showing envoys from Babylon all his treasures in the temple, which were given away in chapter 18. Accordingly, the events recorded in 20:12–21 must have occurred before the Sennacherib invasion in 701 BC. Merodach-Baladan, the king of Babylon, led his revolt against the Assyrians in 704 BC, and the gift mentioned in 20:12 is most likely his attempt to encourage Hezekiah to join him in revolt against Assyria. Hezekiah's response of showing his treasury to the Babylonian envoys then would likely have been an attempt to show them his own strength, that he was a worthy partner in the rebellion. The prophet Isaiah rebukes this action (20:16–19), probably viewing it as naïve; indeed, that same potential to create wealth would one day induce Babylon itself to invade Judah. For all his good as a king, which is exceptional, Hezekiah's response to the prophecy of a future invasion can only leave one wanting: "Then Hezekiah said to Isaiah, 'The word of the LORD that you have spoken is good.' For he thought, 'Why not, if there will be peace and security in my days?'" (20:19). While this narrative occurs chronologically earlier than that of 18:17–19:37, the author or compiler has moved it to the end of Hezekiah's life, either to prepare the reader for the evil reign of Manasseh that will follow or to indicate that, for all his good, even Hezekiah contributes to the eventual exile of Judah in Babylon.

The other outstanding king of the period is Josiah, praised for his obedience. Like Hezekiah, the text notes that Josiah walks "in all the way of David his father" (2 Kings 22:2). Josiah becomes king at age eight, doubtlessly with significant oversight by others until he comes of age. At age twenty-six, he initiates work to repair the temple, which presumably had fallen into disrepair during his grandfather Manasseh's fifty-five-year idolatrous reign (22:3–7). In the process the Book of the Covenant is rediscovered and given to the king, who repents and embarks on religious reform to return the nation to a life under God's law (22:8–13).[22] These efforts include both a cleansing from idolatry (23:1–20) and restoration of the Passover (23:21–23). The summary account of Josiah's life is remarkable for its positive tone: "Before him there was no king like him, who turned to the LORD with all his heart and with all his soul and with all his might, according to all the Law of Moses, nor did any like him arise after him" (23:25).

Nonetheless, in the end, Josiah's efforts are, according to Kings, too little and too late. The prophetess Huldah—whom Josiah consulted after finding the Book of the Covenant and repenting—had indicated that Josiah's repentance would forestall the judgment on Judah but not eliminate it (22:18–20). Second Kings 23:26–27 indicates the same conclusion, that God's wrath was now set against Judah:

---

[22] It is worth noting that critical scholarship uniformly rejects this narrative as a fiction composed by Josiah to cover the religious reforms he wished to create. (One can see the echoes of this approach in the "Compositional History" section on p. 226.) The wholesale rejection of this narrative creates the curious situation of Josiah basing an entire religious reform on a single, fundamental lie. One cannot doubt that there have been many religious leaders, both ancient and modern, who have based huge constructs of teaching on, fundamentally, a lie. Nonetheless, if Josiah were simply a utilitarian powerbroker, one is hard pressed to understand the payoff he would have seen in converting the country to Deuteronomistic worship. It ought to be considered possible that this narrative exists because the Book of the Covenant really was rediscovered, perhaps after it had been relegated to obscurity during the fifty-five-year reign of Manasseh.

> Still the LORD did not turn from the burning of his great wrath, by which his anger was kindled against Judah, because of all the provocations with which Manasseh had provoked him. And the LORD said, "I will remove Judah also out of my sight, as I have removed Israel, and I will cast off this city that I have chosen, Jerusalem, and the house of which I said, My name shall be there."

As good as Josiah was as a king—and he was good—the lot had already been cast.

The remainder of 2 Kings moves quickly from the death of Josiah to the exile of Judah. The initial power over Judah is not the Babylonians but Pharaoh Neco of Egypt, who defeats and kills Josiah in battle (23:29) and then appoints a puppet king. The main backdrop to these events, however, is the campaigning of the resurgent Babylonian Empire in the western half of the ancient Near East. Babylon had begun to rise in the mid-600s, conquering Nineveh, the capital of Assyria, just before the turn of the century. By 605 BC the Babylonians were projecting their power into Palestine. After initially paying tribute to Babylon, the Judean king Jehoiakim rebelled in 602 BC (24:1). In 597 BC the Babylonian army sacked Jerusalem and exiled the next king, Jehoiachin, in the third month of his reign. Judah continued as a vassal kingdom until the reigning king of the time, Zedekiah, revolted against Babylon again (24:20), bringing the final destruction of Jerusalem in 586 BC.

Just as with the northern kingdom of Israel, the author or compiler of Kings is not merely interested in recounting the facts but instead aims to give a theological take on events. The narrative of the final years of Judah is peppered with references to the ultimate cause of Judah's destruction and exile: its unfaithfulness to the Lord. Second Kings 24:2 makes it clear that the origin of the Babylonian, Aramean, Moabite, and Ammonite raiders who preceded the main Babylonian attack was, ultimately, the Lord: "Surely this came upon Judah at the command of the LORD, to remove them out of his sight, for the sins of Manasseh, according to all that he had done, and also for the innocent blood that he had shed. For he filled Jerusalem with innocent blood, and the LORD would not pardon" (24:3–4). Similarly, the verdict on Zedekiah, who certainly made an idiotic decision to revolt against Nebuchadnezzar (see Jeremiah 37–39), is still, in the end, theological:

> And he did what was evil in the sight of the LORD, according to all that Jehoiakim had done. For because of the anger of the LORD it came to the point in Jerusalem and Judah that he cast them out from his presence. And Zedekiah rebelled against the king of Babylon. (2 Kings 24:19–20)

Judah had taken longer to get there, but it had ended up in the same place as Israel, under the ultimate curse of God for disobedience to the covenant—exile from the land.

The Elijah and Elisha Narratives

As mentioned earlier, the Elijah and Elisha narratives occupy the central portion of Kings (1 Kings 16–2 Kings 10), standing distinct from the surrounding accounts in that they largely interrupt the chronological pattern of the divided kingdom narratives.[23] The pace of the story slows down, and the characterization changes, focusing less on the kings and more on the activities and emotions of these two prophets. Further, the emphasis on miracles goes up considerably. How is this to be explained, and what is the function of this section of Kings?

First, the Elijah and Elisha narratives are set against the backdrop of the dynasty of Omri in Israel, and the prophets' direct condemnation of kings becomes the rule in much of this section of the book. These narratives preserve the clash of the most powerful kings with God's most powerful prophets, and these clashes are emblematic of the question of the entire book: will the kings of Israel and Judah be faithful to the Lord according to his word given through the law and the prophets, or will they seek after their own ways to their destruction? These narratives have a central place in the book because they highlight this central challenge. In that challenge, Kings leaves no doubt who has power—Yahweh, not Baal. Elijah defeats the prophets of Baal on Mount Carmel (1 Kings 18:20–46), Ahaziah's attempts to take Elijah by force are defeated by fire from heaven (2 Kings 1:1–18), and Elisha traps the Arameans (2 Kings 6:8–23).

Second, the miracles recounted in the Elijah and Elisha stories are not as haphazard as they may seem upon a casual reading. Instead, these miracles form a polemic against Baal worship. The Omride dynasty was marked by Ahab and Jezebel's effort to cement Baal worship as the religion of Israel (1 Kings 16:30–31). The Ugaritic literature, though substantially older than the time Kings would have been written, gives a relatively comprehensive picture of Baal, who had just begun to rise to prominence in the Ugaritic pantheon. Though Baal worship had many local manifestations, the basic outlines from Ugarit likely still apply. Baal was the storm god, more specifically with lightning as his weapon and rain as his blessing. Therefore it is no accident that fire from heaven is a key component of the miracles in Kings (1 Kings 18:38; 2 Kings 1:9–16; 2:11; 6:17). Nor is it likely an accident that control of rain and provision of water feature prominently in the miracles of Kings (1 Kings 17:1; 18:41–46; 2 Kings 3:16–17). As the supposed giver of rain, Baal would have been considered the ultimate source of food, and not surprisingly, many of the miracles in Kings relate to the provision of food (1 Kings 17:1–6, 8–16; 19:1–6; 2 Kings 4:1–7). Ugaritic literature even discusses Baal's conquering of Judge River, his rival, while both Elijah and Elisha can strike the Jordan and command it to part (2 Kings 2:7–8, 14). The Ugaritic Baal myth includes Baal rising from the dead in an annual cycle, yet both Elijah and Elisha even raise the dead (1 Kings 17:17–23; 2 Kings 4:18–37; 13:20–21). In the Elijah and Elisha narratives, then, God and his prophets are victorious not just over wayward kings but even over the

---

[23] This distinction is strong enough that scholars often hypothesize that these narratives constitute a preexisting source used by the compiler of the final book of Kings. Such a position is viable (see "Compositional History" on p. 226), but one should note that these sections represent not thematic uniqueness but a thematic climax—the power of the prophets—as the emphasis on fulfilled prophecy in Kings extends beyond the Elijah and Elisha narratives.

other gods those kings follow. Anything Baal is said to do is actually instead done by Yahweh's prophets.[24]

APPROACHING THE NEW TESTAMENT

The first and most obvious connection between Kings and the New Testament is the institution of the kingship itself, as Jesus is the Son of David (Matt. 1:6–17). Continuing the theme of Samuel, the book of Kings stresses the line of David as the rightful kings of the nation of Judah. But on balance, what a terrible line! The kings of Israel and Judah largely serve as antimodels (e.g., Zedekiah, Manasseh), proof that a merely human king will fail. The people were in exile because of the disobedience of David's heirs. They needed a king from David's line who would follow the law perfectly (like Josiah) and trust the Lord completely (like Hezekiah). Matthew 1 and Acts 2 teach that Christ is that great Son of David through whom God fulfilled the promises he made to David and his sons. Beyond simply giving models and antimodels, the Davidic covenant reaches its climax in Christ because the implicit question of the book of Kings is finally answered—how can God have a son of David reign forever when the sons of David are so wayward? In fact, even Solomon, the wisest king ever, had been a disaster when it came to faithfulness to the law. But as Matthew 12:42 and Luke 11:31 report, "something greater than Solomon is here." No merely human king—even a Josiah or Hezekiah—could truly fulfill the covenant, so God came incarnate as the Son of David to do so himself. Christ is the ideal king to whom the kingship points.

Second, the theme of God's just judgment for sin highlights the common spiritual situation of all mankind apart from Christ. The emphasis of the book of Kings is that God's judgment on the sin of the nation is aptly deserved, having been repeatedly justified. Through the centuries of moral decline in Israel and Judah, it would have been easy for one to believe that God would not actually climactically judge sin, that such was not his nature (e.g., the implicit argument of Jeremiah's opponents in Jer. 7:1–4). The book of Kings, however, encourages the opposite viewpoint, that God's immediate and final judgment is just and that any delay of that judgment is his mercy. The long period during which retribution for sin was delayed was a chance to repent, and the prophets continually called the people to turn back to God instead of continuing in their sin. Such is the situation of all in advance of the second coming of Christ, and the time while this world awaits Christ's return is the opportunity for repentance (2 Pet. 3:9).

Third, the book of Kings ends in the captivity of exile. The people stand under just judgment for sin, unable to free themselves from captivity and awaiting deliverance by a true king, one who would restore them from exile. They long for what Isaiah 40–66 envisions, a return from this exile, a restoration to their place as God's chosen

---

[24] Note that this polemic against Baalism also limits modern attempts to argue for a single postexilic redactor, some even suggesting dates in the Greek period. By 200 BC, the Jews in Palestine were not dealing with Baalism as the threat to their national existence and way of life. The content of these books, opposing Baalism as the mortal (and highly successful) enemy of Yahwism, would make much less sense if Kings were composed in the Greek era.

people living in blessing, not slavery. God's people are captives needing to be freed. Luke 4:18–21 indicates that Jesus is that true King who ended exile by bringing out the captives. Exile is the true spiritual state of all humanity absent the sacrifice and resurrection of Christ.

Fourth, the New Testament echoes the Elijah and Elisha narratives. John the Baptist is the Elijah to come from Malachi 4:5–6 (not literally, but figuratively; cf. Matt. 11:14; 17:12; John 1:21), wearing the same dress and interacting with much the same bite. Elijah is also present at the transfiguration of Jesus (Matthew 17; Mark 9; Luke 9), and while the significance of Elijah's presence is much debated, the passage clearly shows Jesus as greater.[25] Further, Matthew intriguingly parallels John the Baptist with Elijah and Christ with Elisha, the former coming with a ministry of judgment and the latter a ministry of mercy. While this last parallel is evident, Matthew does not exploit it as strongly as he might have, most likely because he wants to avoid any sense that Jesus is John's less-famous successor in a way similar to Elisha succeeding Elijah.[26]

Fifth, the temple focus of Kings has obvious connections throughout the New Testament. As detailed earlier, Kings itself is intent on highlighting the importance of the temple stipulations in Deuteronomy 12. In John 2:19–22 Christ indicates that he embodies the temple. In 1 Corinthians 3:16–17 the church is considered the temple, and in Revelation 21–22 there will be no temple because the Lord himself will be the light of the city—or, alternately put, because the whole city will be a Holy of Holies (cf. the shape of the city in Rev. 21:16).

Sixth and finally, the deepest connection to Christ from the book of Kings may be the idea of prophet, priest, and king in harmony. As stated earlier, Christ is the ideal King. Yet kingship and temple stand together in the book of Kings—or at least they are supposed to. The ideal king was the one loyal to the worship of God in the temple alone, supporting the priesthood in its role. The New Testament shows Christ ministering as Priest for believers in the heavenly palace of God (Hebrews 6), and it identifies his body as the temple destroyed and rebuilt in three days (John 2). Christ, then, is the ideal Priest. And the ideal king heeded the word of God's prophets. The kings of Israel and Judah were always throwing off God's word, ignoring the prophets. The central contest of the book as noted previously was that of prophet versus king. And Christ is the Prophet who brings God's Word fully to humanity, face to face (Heb. 1:1–2), and Christ, the true Son of David, is the ultimate King of Israel. Kings points to the need for prophet, priest, and king to work in harmony, something that was almost never even approached, much less achieved. Yet in Christ, all those roles are achieved simultaneously and perfectly. While Kings treats these three roles in a different order, the book nonetheless points to Christ as the fulfillment of this ideal, as the one true Prophet, Priest, and King.

---

[25] Elijah's presence at the transfiguration also indicates that Christ's statement in Matt. 11:14 about John is figurative, focusing on the mission and power of Elijah, not a bodily reincarnation.

[26] Provan, 1 and 2 Kings, 234.

SELECT BIBLIOGRAPHY

Auld, A. Graeme. *Kings without Privilege: David and Moses in the Story of the Bible's Kings*. Edinburgh: T&T Clark, 1994.

Campbell, Antony F., and Mark A. O'Brien. *Unfolding the Deuteronomistic History: Origins, Upgrades, Present Text*. Minneapolis: Fortress, 2000.

Cogan, Mordechai. *I Kings: A New Translation with Introduction and Commentary*. AB 10. New Haven, CT: Yale University Press, 2008.

Cohn, Robert L. *2 Kings*. Berit Olam: Studies in Hebrew Narrative and Poetry, edited by David W. Cotter. Collegeville, MN: Liturgical Press, 2000.

Cross, Frank M. *Canaanite Myth and Hebrew Epic: Essays in the History of the Religion of Israel*. Cambridge, MA: Harvard University Press, 1997.

Dillard, Raymond. "The Reign of Asa (2 Chronicles 14–16): An Example of the Chronicler's Theological Method." *JETS* 23, no. 3 (1980): 207–18.

Gerbrandt, Gerald Eddie. *Kingship according to the Deuteronomistic History*. Dissertation Series 87. Atlanta: Scholars Press, 1986.

Gray, John. *I and II Kings: A Commentary*. 2nd ed. OTL. Philadelphia: Westminster, 1970.

Hobbs, T. R. *2 Kings*. WBC 13. Waco, TX: Word, 1986.

House, Paul R. *1, 2 Kings*. NAC 8. Nashville: Broadman, 1995.

Kitchen, Kenneth A. *On the Reliability of the Old Testament*. Grand Rapids, MI: Eerdmans, 2006.

Knoppers, Gary N., and J. Gordon McConville, eds. *Reconsidering Israel and Judah: Recent Studies on the Deuteronomistic History*. SBTS 8. Winona Lake, IN: Eisenbrauns, 2000.

Long, Burke O. *1 Kings: With an Introduction to Historical Literature*. FOTL 9. Grand Rapids, MI: Eerdmans, 1984.

McKenzie, Steven L. *The Trouble with Kings: The Composition of the Book of Kings in the Deuteronomistic History*. VTSup 42. Leiden: Brill, 1991.

Nelson, Richard D. *First and Second Kings*. IBC. 1987. Reprint, Louisville: Westminster John Knox, 2012.

Provan, Iain W. *Hezekiah and the Books of Kings: A Contribution to the Debate about the Composition of the Deuteronomistic History*. BZAW 172. Berlin: de Gruyter, 1988.

———. *1 and 2 Kings*. NIBCOT 7. Peabody, MA: Hendrickson, 1995.

Rost, Leonhard. *Die Überlieferung von der Thronnachfolge Davids*. BWA(N)T 42 (=Folge 3, Heft 6). 1926. Reprint, Stuttgart: Kohlhammer, 2011.

Shenkel, James Donald. *Chronology and Recensional Development in the Greek Text of Kings*. HSM 1. Cambridge, MA: Harvard University Press, 1968.

Tetley, M. Christine. *The Reconstructed Chronology of the Divided Kingdom*. Winona Lake, IN: Eisenbrauns, 2004.

Thiele, Edwin R. *Mysterious Numbers of the Hebrew Kings*. 3rd ed. Grand Rapids, MI: Zondervan, 1983.

Van Seters, John. *In Search of History: Historiography in the Ancient World and the Origins of Biblical History*. Winona Lake, IN: Eisenbrauns, 1997.

von Rad, Gerhard. "The Deuteronomistic Theology of History in the Books of Kings." Chap. 7 in *Studies in Deuteronomy*. Translated by Davis Stalker. SBT 9. London: SCM, 1953.

10

Isaiah[1]

Willem A. VanGemeren

INTRODUCTION

The book of Isaiah was well loved in the early church as the fifth Gospel.[2] The church fathers discovered patterns of interpretation by studying how the Lord Jesus and his apostles read Isaiah[3] and by apprehending how they lived out and modeled the message of Isaiah in their ministries, lives, preaching, teaching, and witnessing.[4] Throughout the history of the church, Christians have had a special relationship with the book, though often complicated by the difficulty of understanding its far-reaching message.[5] Several passages of the book are well worn in our Bibles—such as the naming of Immanuel (7:14), the promise of the Davidic child (9:6–7), the suffering of the servant (52:13–53:12), and the proclamation of comfort (61:1–3)—because of their use in the New Testament.

John Calvin wisely understood that while Isaiah addressed issues within the context of his ministry, his message extended the meaning of the text to the postexilic era, the coming of Jesus, the apostolic mission, the story of the church, and the consummation of Christ's kingdom. He did not restrict fulfillment to a particular event. He wrote,

---

[1] This chapter is dedicated to my wife, Evona, for her support, understanding, and love as we celebrate fifty years of marriage and the fifty-year anniversary of Reformed Theological Seminary, with which we were deeply involved from 1978–1992.
[2] John F. A. Sawyer, *The Fifth Gospel* (New York: Cambridge University Press, 1996).
[3] The New Testament has more than six hundred citations of, allusions to, and echoes of Isaiah.
[4] See Rikk E. Watts, "Isaiah in the New Testament," in *Interpreting Isaiah: Issues and Approaches*, ed. David G. Firth and H. G. M. Williamson (Downers Grove, IL: IVP Academic, 2009), 213–34; Steve Moyise and Maarten J. J. Menken, eds., *Isaiah in the New Testament*, NTSI (London: T&T Clark, 2005). For a general approach of the fathers to the Old Testament, see Ronald E. Heine, *Reading the Old Testament with the Ancient Church: Exploring the Formation of Early Christian Thought*, Evangelical Ressourcement (Grand Rapids, MI: Baker Academic, 2007). Heine writes about the church fathers "dwelling" in the text: "Living in the text means living in the story of the text, not trying to live in the ancient history of the text," because "the biblical text, in both its vision and vocabulary, shaped the vision, discourse, and the life of the fathers." *Reading the Old Testament*, 176, 179.
[5] See Brevard S. Childs, *The Struggle to Understand Isaiah as Christian Scripture* (Grand Rapids, MI: Eerdmans, 2004).

> They [the prophecies] must undoubtedly be referred [*sic*] to the universal kingdom
> of Christ;—universal, I say, because we must look not only at the beginning, but
> also at the accomplishment at the end; and thus it must be extended even to the
> second coming of Christ. . . . This prediction relates, no doubt, to the deliver-
> ance from Babylon, but as that deliverance might be regarded as the earnest and
> foretaste of another, this promise must undoubtedly be extended to the last day.[6]

Calvin's use of the term *predictive* is more generic than our usage. He speaks of
human expectations of salvation that God sovereignly and providentially works out
over time according to his plan. The study of Isaiah suggests many figurations[7] that
intersect with God's work before, in, and after Jesus Christ.

BACKGROUND ISSUES
Unity of the Book

In the last century, students of Isaiah have been chiefly concerned with the history
of the composition of the book. The critical approach to Isaiah has separated the
modern student of Isaiah from the Reformation, the ancient church, and our Lord
and his apostles by creating reconstructions and hypotheses as to how the book
came into being. The modern, critical approach was shaped by Bernard Duhm's
commentary on Isaiah (1892). He argued that the message of the prophet Isaiah
(Isaiah 1–66) underwent significant developments resulting in three collections.[8] First
Isaiah (1–39) was largely, but not wholly, the work of the eighth-century prophet.
Second Isaiah (40–55) was written during the Babylonian exile by an Isaianic writer.
Third Isaiah (56–66) came about after the Babylonian exile, suggesting a Palestinian
(Jerusalem) context of writing. Duhm also treated the four servant songs (42:1–4;
49:1–6; 50:4–9; 52:13–53:12) as separate from the servant texts in Isaiah. Over
time scholars have divided the book into increasingly smaller form-critical units,
separated the parts from the whole, and reconstructed the historical context of each
individual text. Because they occupied themselves with dating and reconstructing
the literary units, it was not uncommon to assume that the book's final form hailed
from a late postexilic period. Historically separating the oracles of salvation (late)
from the judgment oracles (early) became axiomatic.

A major change took place when scholars discovered the thematic unity of the
book,[9] especially when viewed as a result of redactors stitching together layers in a
late scripturalization process.[10] They posed that the Isaianic text underwent many

---

[6] John Calvin, *Commentary on the Book of the Prophet Isaiah*, trans. William Pringle (Grand Rapids, MI: Eerdmans, 1948), comment on Isa. 25:8.

[7] For the nature and significance of figuration, see "Literary Factors" on p. 252.

[8] For a brief survey of critical approaches to Isaiah, see H. G. M. Williamson, "Isaiah, Book of," in *Dictionary of the Old Testament: Prophets*, ed. Mark J. Boda and J. Gordon McConville, IVP Bible Dictionary Series 4 (Downers Grove, IL: IVP Academic, 2012), 366–71. See also Marvin A. Sweeney, "On the Road to Duhm: Isaiah in Nineteenth-Century Critical Scholarship," in *Society of Biblical Literature: Seminar Papers 2002* (Atlanta: Society of Biblical Literature, 2002), 191–211.

[9] Christopher R. Seitz, "Isaiah 1–66: Making Sense of the Whole," in *Reading and Preaching the Book of Isaiah*, ed. Christopher R. Seitz (Philadelphia: Fortress, 1988), 105–26; Ronald E. Clements, "The Unity of the Book of Isaiah," *Int* 36, no. 2 (1982): 117–29; Richard J. Clifford, "The Unity of the Book of Isaiah and its Cosmogonic Language," *CBQ* 55, no. 1 (1993): 1–17.

[10] For a discussion on scripturalization and canon formation, see Jake Stromberg, "Formation of the Prophetic Books," in Boda and McConville, *Dictionary of the Old Testament: Prophets*, 271–9.

redactions over time whereby "scribes" added comments (glosses) that were incorporated into the book. They created a sense of unity. Others saw a redactional unity at a much earlier stage encouraging a reading of First and Second Isaiah in relation to each other.[11] But this left the question of how Third Isaiah fit in with the process of scripturalization.[12] Williamson's warning applies to all approaches that seek to read the parts of the book in the light of the whole: "Thus, one's understanding of the growth of the earlier parts of the book is likely to affect how one envisages the process in these closing chapters."[13]

Rhetorical, poetical, canonical, and intertextual analyses have become productive tools suggesting integrative ways of reading the parts of Isaiah in relation to the whole and of explaining the thematic variety in Isaiah diachronically.[14] The rediscovery of the many literary and thematic connections between the three "books" of Isaiah has also encouraged a more holistic reading of so-called Second and Third Isaiah in the context of First Isaiah. In their search for understanding how Isaiah was composed, scholars are discovering how multilayered the book is.[15]

Where do evangelicals stand? They do not reject critical attention to Isaiah but are cautiously pessimistic of abandoning the witness of Scripture and the long legacy of the interpretation of Isaiah in the history of the church. Instead, they hold to a critical "realism" that permits exploration in order to find out if the investigation leads to reality. They hold to a believing criticism[16] that anchors their thoughts in the Word of God. Richard Schultz persuasively argues for the authorial unity of Isaiah.[17] He reminds evangelicals that they need to "conserve" the ancient connection between book and author, to reject what he calls "scholarly dogmatism," and to affirm "believing criticism."[18] He rightly argues against the temptation to give in to popular critical assumptions, because "the history of biblical study is marked by an ongoing revision and replacement of various explanatory theories, often owing to new approaches to the same observed textual phenomena."[19] The following discussion will highlight the canonical, literary, and theological integrity of the book, while remaining fully cognizant of the complex shape, perceived or real, of the book of Isaiah.

---

[11] H. G. M. Williamson, *The Book Called Isaiah: Deutero-Isaiah's Role in Composition and Redaction* (Oxford: Clarendon, 1994); Williamson, "Recent Issues in the Study of Isaiah," in Firth and Williamson, *Interpreting Isaiah*, 21–40; Williamson, "Isaiah, Book of," 366–71; Rolf Rendtorff, "The Composition of the Book of Isaiah," in *Canon and Theology: Overtures to an Old Testament Theology*, trans. Margaret Kohl (Minneapolis: Fortress, 1993), 146–69.

[12] Jake Stromberg, *An Introduction to the Study of Isaiah*, T&T Clark Approaches to Biblical Studies (London: T&T Clark, 2011); Stromberg, *Isaiah after Exile: The Author of Third Isaiah as Reader and Redactor of the Book*, OTM (Oxford: Oxford University Press, 2011).

[13] Williamson, "Isaiah, Book of," 369.

[14] See L. Wray Beal, "Literary Approaches," in Boda and McConville, *Dictionary of the Old Testament: Prophets*, 506–13.

[15] See especially H. G. M. Williamson, *The Book Called Isaiah*; Williamson, *Variations on a Theme: King, Messiah, and Servant in the Book of Isaiah* (Carlisle, UK: Paternoster, 1998); Williamson, "Isaiah: Book of," 366–71.

[16] On believing criticism, see Mark A. Noll, *Between Faith and Criticism: Evangelicals, Scholarship, and the Bible in America* (Vancouver: Regent College Publishing, 2004), 156–60.

[17] Richard L. Schultz, "How Many Isaiahs Were There and What Does It Matter? Prophetic Inspiration in Recent Evangelical Scholarship," in *Evangelicals and Scripture: Tradition, Authority, and Hermeneutics*, ed. Vincent Bacote, Laura C. Miguélez, and Dennis L. Okholm (Downers Grove, IL: InterVarsity Press, 2004), 150–70; "Isaiah, Isaiahs, and Current Scholarship," in *Do Historical Matters Matter to Faith? A Critical Appraisal of Modern and Postmodern Approaches to Scripture*, ed. James K. Hoffmeier and Dennis R. Magary (Wheaton, IL: Crossway, 2012), 243–61.

[18] Schultz, "Isaiah, Isaiahs," 260–61.

[19] Schultz, "Isaiah, Isaiahs," 259.

STRUCTURE AND OUTLINE

Both evangelical and critical scholars are amazed at the complexity of Isaiah. The canonical shape of Isaiah is multilayered. In reading Isaiah, one is continually reading backward and forward while connecting expressions, themes, motifs, and patterns (figurations).[20] The text is like a mirror as it reflects on what has been read and anticipates what lies ahead. A prospective and retrospective reading connects aspects of the text into an ever-growing web.[21] Williamson insightfully encourages the reader of Isaiah "to consider each individual part of the book in the light of the whole."[22] Schultz observes, "A close analysis of Isaiah as a whole reveals a carefully edited composition."[23] Blenkinsopp notes that the book has undergone "successive restructurings . . . in the course of a long history" and that it still reveals a unity, such as that found in Isaiah 1–12: "[these chapters] achieve a kind of unity by coalescing into an overview of the triumph and eventual collapse of the Assyrian imperial power . . . , a theme that dominates the entire first section of the book [Isaiah 1–39]."[24] The book of Isaiah is shaped by theological, literary, and historical forces.

Theological Factors

The *theological* thrust of the book flows out of Isaiah's vision of the Holy One of Israel (Isa. 6:3) and the expectation that his manifest presence (glory) will fill the whole earth (6:3). Isaiah's vision of Yahweh's holiness and glory (Isaiah 6) is a mirror text that shapes the message of the whole book with its motifs of Yahweh's kingship, God's cleansing of Isaiah, Israel's defilement and hardening, Isaiah's proclamation of judgment and salvation, the desolation and decimation of Zion, and the small remnant ("holy seed").

The opening (1:2–2:22) and closing chapters (63:7–66:24) constitute bookends[25] by common themes (the desolation [1:7–8; 2:6–22; 64:10–12] and restoration of Zion [1:26–27; 2:2–4; 65:19–25]);[26] by common vocabulary (heaven and earth [1:2; 65:17; 66:1, 22]; rebellion [1:2; 66:24]); by images of Israel (the father-child relationship [1:2; 63:16; 64:8; 66:7–12], the city of God [1:21; 66:8–14], and the people of God [1:3–4; 63:16; 64:8, 10, 11; 65:2]); and by concepts (such as the reversal of

---

[20] See Willem A. VanGemeren, "Our Missional God: Redemptive-Historical Preaching and the Missio Dei" in *Living Waters from Ancient Springs: Essays in Honor of Cornelis Van Dam*, ed. Jason Van Vliet (Eugene, OR: Pickwick, 2011), 198–217; Frances Young, "Typology," in *Crossing the Boundaries: Essays in Biblical Interpretation in Honour of Michael D. Goulder*, ed. Stanley E. Porter, Paul Joyce, David E. Orton, BibInt 8 (Leiden: Brill, 1994), 29–48; James M. Hamilton Jr. *What Is Biblical Theology: A Guide to the Bible's Story, Symbolism, and Patterns* (Wheaton: Crossway, 2014); Hans W. Frei, *The Eclipse of Biblical Narrative: A Study in Eighteenth and Nineteenth Century Hermeneutics* (New Haven, CT: Yale University Press, 1974), 28–29.

[21] Brevard S. Childs, "Retrospective Reading of the Old Testament Prophets," *ZAW* 108, no. 3 (1996): 362–77.

[22] Williamson, "Isaiah, Book of," 373. He further observes that the variety in Isaiah "will always bring balancing features into play that need also be included." "Isaiah, Book of," 371.

[23] Richard S. Schultz, "Isaiah, Book of," in *Dictionary for Theological Interpretation of the Bible*, ed. Kevin J. Vanhoozer (Grand Rapids, MI: Baker Academic, 2005), 341.

[24] Joseph Blenkinsopp, *Isaiah 1–39: A New Translation with Introduction and Commentary*, AB 19 (New York: Doubleday, 2000), 172.

[25] See Anthony J. Tomasino, "Isaiah 1:1–2:4 and 63–66, and the Composition of the Isaianic Corpus," *JSOT* 57 (1993): 81–98.

[26] See Roy F. Melugin's reading of the book of Isaiah in the light of chap. 1 in "Figurative Speech and the Reading of Isaiah 1," in *New Visions of Isaiah*, ed. Roy F. Melugin and Marvin A. Sweeney, JSOTSup 214 (Sheffield: Sheffield Academic Press, 1996), 282–305.

fortunes—from temporal desolation and shame [1:7–8; 63:18–19; 64:10–11] to the manifestation of Yahweh's everlasting glory [66:18]).

Isaiah's vision displays "the other world" of God's blessed presence with a new community made up with representatives from all nations and a new heaven and earth (66:22; 65:8–25). It presents a grand view of God's kingdom in holiness and glory. The Creator-God, the holy God of Mount Sinai, is the God who dwells in Zion, whose kingdom extends to all the nations. Though the creation is defiled, he will restore it to himself.

Isaiah contrastively speaks of God's exaltation and human abasement, of God's faithfulness and freedom, of God's hiddenness and nearness, of human rebelliousness and God's forgiveness, of defilement and purification, of a cut-down oak tree and "a holy and blessed stump" (6:13b, my trans.), of judgment and salvation, of curse and blessing, of the desolation and inclusion of all nations, of vengeance and vindication, and of shame and glory. We will highlight these various theological themes in the treatment of Isaiah's message, which together give us a "window into Isaiah."

Historical Factors

The theological perspective is set within the stage of the *historical* context of the Assyrian rise to power (1:7–9; 36:1–37:38), the 734 BC Syro-Ephraimite crisis (6:1–9:7), the exile of the northern tribes in 722 BC, the Assyrian desolation of Judah in 701 BC, and the prospect of both Judah's exile by the Babylonians and her restoration (Isaiah 39–66). The book opens with the portrayal of Judah having undergone a massive desolation by the Assyrians and Jerusalem barely surviving (1:7–9; cf. 36:1–37:38), and it anticipates the further humiliation of Jerusalem, realized in the Babylonian captivity (Isaiah 39–48; 586–537 BC). The book closes on the hope of the restoration of Zion (Isaiah 40–66). At the center of the book is the Hezekiah narrative (Isaiah 36–39) with its message of Yahweh's deliverance (Isaiah 36–38) and judgment (Isaiah 39).

The exilic experience shaped the literary structure of the book,[27] but a late redaction does not suggest that the oracles were of exilic or postexilic provenance. Childs notes the lack of a concrete historical context in the book.[28] The specificity in the naming of Cyrus is not matched by any specifics of his activities. This ambiguity leads Schultz to conclude that "most of Isaiah 40–55 . . . has no clear links to the sixth century."[29] Similarly Sweeney comments that Isaiah "never actually portrays a ruined or destroyed Jerusalem."[30] Seitz observes that "the fall of the temple and its restoration . . . are not meaningful literary, historical or theological indexes in Isaiah."[31] The eighth-century prophet Isaiah applies God's word to his generation, but his message spans the history of God's people from his day into the new creation. He closes an era of God's favor,

---

[27] Craig A. Evans, "On the Unity and Parallel Structure of Isaiah," *VT* 38, no. 2 (1988): 129–47.
[28] Brevard S. Childs, *Introduction to the Old Testament as Scripture* (Philadelphia: Fortress, 1979), 325–26.
[29] Schultz, "Isaiah, Isaiahs," 251.
[30] Marvin A. Sweeney, *Tanak: A Theological and Critical Introduction to the Jewish Bible* (Minneapolis: Fortress, 2012), 276.
[31] Christopher R. Seitz, "Isaiah, Book of (Third Isaiah)," in *ABD*, 3:502–3.

grace, and patience with Israel and Judah and opens up an era of the coming of the kingdom of God and the purification and glory of Zion, the mother of all nations.

Literary Factors

In addition to theological and historical factors, *literary* considerations helpfully explain the shaping of the book, which has come to us in two distinct parts:

Part 1 – Isaiah's Vision concerning Judah and Jerusalem (Isaiah 1–39)
Part 2 – The Book of Zion's Comfort (Isaiah 40–66)

The traditional Jewish division of Isaiah is twofold: 1–39 and 40–66.[32] In the discussion of the prophet's message for part 1 (Isaiah 1–39), we will highlight five windows: (1) the exaltation of the Holy One of Israel in judgment and in salvation, (2) the hardening of Israel, (3) the promise of the "holy seed," (4) messianic expectations, and (5) God's exclusion and inclusion of Israel and the nations.

Part 2 (Isaiah 40–66) is continuous with the first while creating another theological and literary world. First, Israel is no longer rebellious but is slow to respond to the good news of their election, future, and the new exodus. The prophet confronts unbelief (Isaiah 40–48), while affirming God's election. Second, Israel's future is contingent on the ministry of the *faithful servant of the Lord* (Isaiah 49–55). This shift in focus creates a sense of dissonance. Instead of focusing on the future of the Davidic dynasty (Isaiah 1–39), Isaiah turns his attention to the future of Zion (Isaiah 40–66). The suffering servant is God's instrument to extend the good news of the kingdom to Israel and to the nations (Isaiah 49–55). He models God's expectations and teaching to all who will listen. His followers are called to be *"servants" of the Lord*. They constitute a new community that will inherit the new creation and the new Zion (Isaiah 56–66). They endure persecution (57:1), humiliation (57:15), and divine alienation (57:16). They are encouraged to excel in their service (Isaiah 58) but lament their inability to succeed (59:1–15). In the end, the Lord himself responds with a series of salvific acts: (1) he comes as the divine Warrior to redeem his servants (59:16–21); (2) he glorifies Zion (60:1–22); (3) he endows his servants with his Spirit to proclaim the good news of his coming and of Zion's glory (Isaiah 61–62); and (4) he executes his vengeance against the opposition (63:1–6). A final lament asks the Lord to vindicate his servants (63:7–64:11), to which the last two chapters sound a ringing response (Isaiah 65–66).

Poetical Features

The poetry of the book is exquisite. The author's style, parallelism, vocabulary, terseness, ambiguity, and imagery invite the reader to get lost in the text. It is difficult to catch this richness in English translations. Commentaries will help but cannot fully capture the complex ways in which Isaiah uses the Hebrew language. He wants to

---

[32] Abraham Ibn Ezra, Shaddal, and more recently, Shalom M. Paul, *Isaiah 40–66: Translation and Commentary*, ECC (Grand Rapids, MI: Eerdmans, 2012).

be understood, but he uses language in such a manner that readers may perceive that they have only partially understood him. Each text can be understood by itself, but like any composite plot, new insights are gained by dwelling on Isaiah and by reading the parts in relationship to the whole.

When we pay attention to the theological, historical, and literary dimensions of Isaiah, the text comes to life.[33] The prophet presents the readers with a view of God that transcends time and space. Instead of being driven by events, such as creation and redemption, Isaiah presents us with the Creator, Redeemer, and King. The *Maker* of heaven and earth also "created" Israel (בָּרָא; see 41:20; 42:5; 43:1) as an agent in working out his providential purposes.

Figuration

Figuration takes place when we read any text in Isaiah in connection with the whole book. For example, Isaiah's play on the word *righteousness* in 56:1 has two senses: "Keep justice, and do *righteousness*, for my salvation will come, and my *righteousness* be revealed." In the first line, righteousness is connected with justice, and in the second line, righteousness is parallel with salvation. The double sense of righteousness as justice and as salvation connects Isaiah 56–66 with Isaiah 1–39 and 40–55. This variation in the meaning may best be explained diachronically.

First, the exhortation to maintain justice and righteousness harkens back to Isaiah's usage in Isaiah 1–39. The Davidic monarchs and Zion were called to be agents of divine justice on earth. The prophet charges Judah/Jerusalem with injustice. Though they followed Mosaic regulations (1:10–15), they failed in their mutual concern for each other (1:21–23). Using Mosaic images, Isaiah portrays them as corrupt and foolish children (Isa. 1:2–4; see Deut. 32:5), as a harlot (Isa. 1:21; cf. Deut. 31:16; Hos. 2:2), as an unproductive vine(yard) (Isa. 5:2b; cf. Deut. 32:32), and as Sodom and Gomorrah (Isa. 1:9, 10; cf. Deut. 32:32). Yahweh had expected them to live as true children of Abraham by living wisely and righteously. After all, righteousness and justice were the foundation of God's expectation of Abraham and his children (Gen. 18:18; cf. 17:1), and the Mosaic law exemplifies and codifies in great detail the practices of justice, mercy, and faithfulness (Deut. 16:20; cf. Matt. 23:23). Instead, God's children spurned Yahweh and his instruction (Isa. 1:4; 5:24; cf. 1:15b–17; 5:8–24) by failing to observe the qualities of justice and righteousness. Throughout chapters 1–39, Isaiah details Judah's offenses, especially in the twofold listing of "woes" (see Isaiah 5; 28–33).[34] Isaiah also prefigures the new world in which God's righteousness and justice will be established by his Spirit (11:1–9; 32:15–20; cf. 32:1–3). Then the whole of society will be blessed and at peace (32:15–20; cf. 32:1–2).

Second, the collocation of righteousness with salvation occurs in the second half of the book (against the backdrop of the Babylonian exile). The conjunction of righteousness with salvation is found repeatedly in Isaiah 40–66 (45:8; 46:13; 51:5,

---

[33] See Hamilton, *What Is Biblical Theology?*, 61–91.
[34] Two more woes are found in Isa. 10:1–7.

6, 8; 56:1b; 62:1), where it carries the sense of triumph or victory.[35] It signifies the whole process of the coming of God's victorious kingdom on earth, including his acts in history (Cyrus and the fall of Babylon, Isaiah 45–47), the new exodus, the entry into Zion (62:1), and the new creation. Righteousness includes a judicial aspect but is largely associated with the victorious, triumphant, and glorious coming of God's kingdom, which the Jewish Publication Society translation of 62:1b captures well: "Till her victory [righteousness] emerge resplendent, And her triumph [salvation] like a flaming torch."

Third, the combination of these two senses in one verse opens the reader to a new perspective. On the one hand, the ethical requirements of the kingdom are continuous with God's expectations of Israel and of the Davidic dynasty before the exile, but on the other, they are also contingent on the benefits of God's righteousness promised to a people in exile. God's people must walk in the way of the Lord (cf. Gen. 18:18), but Isaiah denies them the possibility of ever attaining a righteousness apart from God's "righteousness," because history has shown that all people fall short of God's expectations (Isa. 59:9–15; 64:5–6; cf. Rom. 3:20). Salvation is the decisive victory, and triumph is Yahweh's alone (Isa. 59:16–17). As this example shows, the message of Isaiah is textual, and the textual web created gives rise to *figuration*, i.e., a way of figuring out Isaiah's message.

MESSAGE AND THEOLOGY

The heading (Isa. 1:1) claims that this prophecy is a vision (חֲזוֹן) of Isaiah, and this claim is repeated in 2:1 (concerning Judah and Jerusalem) and in 13:1 (concerning the nations). Unlike Moses, with whom Yahweh had spoken "face to face" (Num. 12:8 NIV), this prophecy comes in the form of a vision. Isaiah's message contextualizes the Mosaic revelation. It demands "theological exegesis,"[36] that is, an integration and appreciation of God's distinct revelation to Isaiah in association with Moses, the Prophets, the Writings, and the New Testament (Heb. 1:1–3).

The Message of Isaiah 1–39

This first section may be divided into six subsections: (1) the vision concerning Judah and Jerusalem (Isaiah 1–12); (2) oracles concerning the nations (Isaiah 13–23); (3) the world aflame and Zion's fame (Isaiah 24–27); (4) six oracles of woe (Isaiah 28–33); (5) visions of vengeance and vindication (Isaiah 34–35); and (6) the Hezekiah narrative (Isaiah 36–39).

The Vision concerning Judah and Jerusalem (Isaiah 1–12)

Isaiah's prophecy is a vision (1:1; cf. 2:1) concerning Judah and Jerusalem "in the days of Uzziah, Jotham, Ahaz, and Hezekiah, kings of Judah" (1:1) which, together

---

[35] See Rolf Rendtorff, *The Old Testament: An Introduction* (Philadelphia: Fortress, 1983), 199–200.
[36] Mark Gignilliat, "Theological Exegesis as Exegetical Showing: A Case of Isaiah's Figural Potentiality," *IJST* 12, no. 2 (2010): 217.

with the call narrative (Isaiah 6), frames the unfolding and complex message of the book.[37] Isaiah 1–12 opens and closes in a surprising manner. It opens with the charge that Israel has spurned "the Holy One of Israel" (1:4; cf. 5:24). They are guilty of folly and rebelliousness (1:2–4), insensitive to punishment (1:5–9), selective in their obedience of God's instructions (1:10–15), and guilty of judgment (1:24–25). Shockingly, the concluding chapter of this section closes with a song of praise when the Holy One of Israel turns his wrath to comfort and saves his people (12:1–3). The highlight of God's comfort is the assurance that the Holy One of Israel will dwell in the midst of the people of Zion (12:6). The opening and closing frames get at the heart of Isaiah's message: the Holy One of Israel is the author of both judgment and salvation.

In the middle of these chapters, we find Isaiah's narrative of his vision of the holy, glorious, exalted, almighty King (Isaiah 6). He narrates a theophanic experience (6:1–4) in which he saw "the Lord seated on a throne, high and exalted" (6:1), heard the seraphim proclaiming Yahweh's holiness and glory, and experienced the phenomena of smoke and an earthquake. When he became aware that he had seen "the King, the LORD of hosts" (6:5), he confessed his defilement and that of his people. The book of Isaiah presents the reader with Yahweh's exaltation in holiness and glory. He is the King over all creation.

As rebellious as Judah is, the Lord's love and commitment are much greater. Yahweh invites Judah's leaders and people to turn to him and learn from him lest they perish (1:10–20). Though sinners will suffer judgment (1:28–31), Zion, faithless and filthy like a prostitute, will be brought down only to be cleansed and renewed in righteousness and faithfulness (1:21–27; cf. Hos. 2:19–20). Zion will even become a light to the nations as they come to receive instruction from the Lord, submit to his rule, and participate in peace on earth (2:2–4).

The picture of Zion as the center of the nations stands in stark contrast to Judah's rebelliousness and dependency on human beings. Isaiah portrays the exaltation of the Lord over against the ultimate judgment and humiliation of human beings (2:6–22). The Lord will decimate the leadership and shame their wives (3:1–4:1). He also promises to cleanse and consecrate to himself a remnant (4:2–6) and to reveal his glory and presence to them, as he did in the days of the first exodus. The prophet returns to the reasons for Judah's judgment in the parable of the vineyard and the six woes, explaining the reasons for the Lord's anger with his people (5:1–29).[38] The deep darkness that God's people experience (5:29; cf. 8:22) stands in stark contrast to the light that the nations will experience through the Lord's teaching (2:2–4; cf. 49:7; 51:4). This contrast explains Isaiah's exhortation to Israel to return and walk in the light of the Lord (2:5). The prophet's vision, call, and commission further amplify Judah's desperate situation (Isaiah 6). Her people are blind and deaf. They are hardened, and they harden themselves against the Holy One of Israel.

---

[37] W. A. M. Beuken, "The Manifestation of Yahweh and the Commission of Isaiah: Isaiah 6 Read against the Background of Isaiah 1." *CTJ* 39, no. 1 (2004): 72–87.

[38] The refrain "his anger is not turned back" occurs in 5:25; 9:11, 16, 20; 10:4.

The prophet saw "the Lord sitting upon a throne, high and lifted up" (6:1); heard the Trisagion ("holy, holy, holy"); saw the seraphim; and gained a sense of God's glory (6:1–4). When he became aware that he had come into Yahweh's presence, he confessed his defilement and that of his people, because he had seen "the King, the LORD of hosts" (6:1, 5), that is, the sovereign and glorious King of the whole world. The theophanic experiences of earthquake and smoke are manifestations of Yahweh's glory and a visible reminder that his glory encompasses the whole of creation (6:3).

Isaiah confesses that he and his people are defiled "of lips." His sensitivity to ritual purity is fully in line with God's expectation of a transformed community (4:3–4). The defilement in question appears to be more than ritual, though, as he addresses Israel's systemic injustice by which they become guilty of bloodshed and of uttering lies with their lips (59:3; cf. 1:11–17; 29:13). His experience of cleansing is a sign-act symbolically conveying the need for all people to discern their defilement and to submit to God's cleansing and forgiveness (4:4; 64:6).

The call narrative also introduces the reader to the purpose of Isaiah's mission (Isaiah 6). He is God's agent warning Israel of the coming desolation of the land and of the decimation of the population (6:11–13). The theme of desolation (6:11) opens and closes the book of Isaiah (1:7; 64:10). The prophetic mission was to provoke Israel[39] to show her the rebelliousness of her heart. The people had readily assumed that they were the children of the covenant (1:2–3) and that their obedience to Moses (1:10–15) was pleasing to God. Isaiah's message, with its imagery, argumentation, and complexity, was to inflame Israel, to reveal her hardness of heart, and to raise up a believing remnant, the "holy seed" (6:10; 29:10–13; 30:2; 32:3–4; 35:5; 44:18; 59:9–10; cf. Mark 4:11–12; John 12:39–40; Acts 28:26–27; cf. Romans 9–11).

God promises to protect Judah by the sign of Immanuel. The Immanuel prophecy (Isa. 7:14) is given in the context of events that rattled King Ahaz and shook Judah (see "Historical Factors" on p. 251). In fact, the promise of God's Immanuel presence with Judah (8:8, 10) is set within the context of other names. Isaiah explains that he and his children are "signs" to God's people (8:18). The significance of the name Isaiah ("salvation is from Yahweh [alone]") permeates the message of the book. The names of his own children—Shear-jashub ("a remnant shall remain," 7:14; cf. 10:20–22) and Maher-shalal-hash-baz ("the spoil of the two kings will quickly be taken," 8:1–4, my trans.)—signify the demise of the Aramean and Israelite alliance against Judah and the favor of the Lord upon a small remnant from Israel and Judah. The name of the child called Immanuel ("God is with us") signifies God's grace to Judah in that she survived the Syro-Ephraimite alliance and continued her political life for another 150 years after the fall of Samaria and Damascus (7:14; 8:8, 10). Isaiah hints at the identity of the child by the close association with his son, Maher-shalal-hash-baz, and by the mention of a Davidic child (9:6–7). The focus on Hezekiah in Isaiah 36–39 suggests that Isaiah saw him as a figuration of Immanuel. It was not given to Isaiah

---

[39] Torsten Uhlig argues that the book of Isaiah "enacts their restoration as 'the servants of the Lord,' the children of Zion (Isa. 54:17; Isa. 65:13–16)." "Too Hard to Understand? The Motif of Hardening in Isaiah," in Firth and Williamson, *Interpreting Isaiah*, 82.

to associate Immanuel with the Lord Jesus Christ, but he would have rejoiced at the presence of God in the flesh in Jesus Christ (Matt. 1:21–22; cf. 1 Pet. 1:10–12).

God commands Isaiah not to fear circumstances, as King Ahaz did (Isa. 7:2, 9), but to consecrate the Lord alone (8:11–13), because his word is reliable (8:10). Isaiah centers his hope on the Lord and also on the messianic expectations of a person with wisdom, power, faithfulness, righteousness, and peace (9:6–7; 11:1–9). This royal agent of the house of David will be endowed with God's Spirit (11:3), by whose power he will bring in the reality of God's plans for the Davidic dynasty, in which nations will participate and evil will have no place (11:9–16). Thus, Zion will be established as God's holy mountain (11:9).

A psalm of thanksgiving for God's deliverance celebrates the transformation of Yahweh's wrath into his comfort and salvation, cast in the imagery of the first exodus (Isaiah 12; cf. Exodus 15; Rev. 15:3–4). Isaiah holds out comfort and salvation to a people who have been struck by Yahweh's anger. Their outcries of pain will change to joy. Instead of being afraid of their oppressors, they will call upon the nations to witness Yahweh's salvation. Though they have spurned the Holy One of Israel and his instruction (Isa. 1:4; 5:24), the Lord commits himself to dwell again with his people in Zion (12:6).

Oracles concerning[40] the Nations (Isaiah 13–23)

The message of the desolation of Israel and Judah and the anticipation of her reversal of fortunes (Isaiah 1–12) anticipate God's sovereignty over the nations in judgment and in salvation. The oracles concerning the nations serve as a reminder that the God of the exodus is the Lord of the nations. God directed his judgment against the Egyptians when he delivered Israel at the Red Sea to evoke the response of awe for Yahweh. These oracles concerning the nations serve to remind God's people of his power and grace (14:1–2). God is sovereign over oppressive nations (Assyria/Babylon, Isaiah 13–14; 21; cf. 46–48), over troubling nations (Moab, Isaiah 15–16; cf. 25:10–12; Aram, Isaiah 17; Edom, Isaiah 34; 63:1–6; cf. Obad. 1), over powerful nations (Cush and Egypt, Isaiah 18–20), as well as over Jerusalem (Isaiah 22) and Tyre (Isaiah 23).[41] The oracles extend not only judgment but also hope to the nations, particularly Israel's two powerful nemeses: Assyria/Babylon and Egypt. They, too, will share in the heritage of God's people (19:24–25). God confirms his purposes for Zion (14:32; 18:7), the Davidic dynasty (16:5), and his blessing of the nations (19:25).

The nations constitute a major theme in Isaiah. Like Israel and Judah, they are subject to God's wrath but also to his mercy and comfort (14:1–2). On the one hand, his wrath extends to all humanity because all have sinned and are guilty of conceit (2:6–22; Isaiah 13–23; 24). On the day of the Lord, they experience God's leveling (2:12–21) because humanity as a whole is nothing but "breath" (2:22) and all have failed to keep his instruction (24:5). On the other hand, God's kingdom comes to earth when the nations

---

[40] The oracles are *concerning* the nations and surprisingly not against them.
[41] See Willem A. VanGemeren, *Interpreting the Prophetic Word: An Introduction to the Prophetic Literature of the Old Testament* (Grand Rapids, MI: Zondervan, 1990), 264–66.

receive Yahweh's instruction and submit to him (2:2–4). They, too, will receive God's blessing (19:25), enjoy the eschatological banquet (25:6), and the end of shame and death (25:7). Isaiah opens the doors to Yahweh's salvation for all (56:1–8; cf. 55:1) in order to impress upon all their need to learn God's way of salvation and life.[42]

The World Aflame and Zion's Fame (Isaiah 24–27)

It is difficult to find the common elements between these four chapters, and yet they share images that project a sense of harmony at the conceptual level: the destruction of the city of humans (Isaiah 24) and the glory and fame of God's city (Isaiah 25–26). These chapters have been called "The Isaiah Apocalypse," but they actually lack the typical apocalyptic features.

Judgments on particular nations (Isaiah 13–23) give way to a global judgment (Isaiah 24). Desolation comes to the whole earth (24:1–13) because all humans have broken God's law. The judgment eerily suggests the days of Noah (24:18–19; cf. Genesis 6–8; Isa. 54:9; Matt. 24:37–39). The image of a forlorn city represents the whole earth (Isa. 24:10–12). Human joys disappear and turn to cries, and the song of the ruthless comes to an end (24:8; 25:5). The cosmic desolation is a macrocosm of the desolation of Zion. All have sinned and exact glory for themselves, including Zion. Isaiah is all-inclusive as he prophesies the desolation of Zion (Isaiah 1–12), the desolation of the nations (Isaiah 13–23), and the desolation of the earth (Isaiah 24).

The prophet symbolically represents the remnant in his longing for redemption (24:16a). He catches a glimpse of God's kingdom: "the LORD of hosts reigns on Mount Zion and in Jerusalem, and his glory will be before his elders" (24:23b). The vision of God's kingdom assures the godly of his faithfulness (25:1–5). They rejoice in anticipation of the consummation of God's kingdom on earth. He is their refuge from the storm (25:4–5; cf. 4:6). His kingdom is symbolized by a banquet on Mount Zion where he invites all nations to a feast of fine food and wine (25:6–8) and by the removal of all shame, including death, and of forms of wickedness symbolized by Moab (25:10b–12). God's people burst out with joy (25:9–10a).

The image of the strong city stands in contrast to the ruined city (26:1–27:1; cf. 24:10–12). The citizens of the city (Zion) put their trust in Yahweh. During persecution, they may have to go into hiding, but they are confident that Yahweh will deliver them. They take up a song of Zion (cf. 12:2; Psalms 46; 47; 87). The prophet prays that God's people may persevere in wisdom (Isa. 26:7–11). His people will "live" (26:19) in a world free from evil, which is symbolically represented by leviathan, the dragon, and the coiling serpent (27:1; cf. 65:25).

In addition to the urban image of the city, Isaiah employs the image of the vineyard. It will be renowned for its productive vines (27:2–6; cf. 5:1–7;[43] 65:8; John 15:1–8) that spread out over the whole earth.

---

[42] Richard S. Schultz, "Nationalism and Universalism in Isaiah," in Firth and Williamson, *Interpreting Isaiah*, 122–44.

[43] Marvin Sweeney, "New Gleanings from an Old Vineyard: Isaiah 27 Reconsidered," in *Early Jewish and Christian Exegesis: Studies in Memory of William Hugh Brownlee*, ed. Craig A. Evans and William F. Stinespring, Scholars Press Homage Series (Atlanta: Scholars Press, 1987), 52–66.

Six Oracles of Woe: Desolation and the Restoration of Zion (Isaiah 28–33)

These oracles confirm that the political, social, and moral life of Judah under Hezekiah was little different from that of the northern kingdom before her exile. Both kingdoms faced the threat of Assyria and responded with self-confidence by not turning to Yahweh. Their hardness of heart found expression in numerous political ambitions.[44] The people rebelled, defiled the land, mocked the Holy One of Israel, rejected his instruction, were blind and deaf, were incapable of understanding divine revelation, and did not consult Yahweh in their political schemes (28:9–10, 13–22; 29:9–14, 15–17; 30:1–11, 16–17; 31:1–3; 32:9–13). They were religious but had no comprehension of the Holy One of Israel.

The oracles clarify both Yahweh's ability to deliver his people (29:6) and his intentional delay (30:18). These oracles afflict the comfortable and comfort the afflicted. God looks for people who learn to wait for and to trust in Yahweh (30:18; cf. 28:5–6). The story of the farmer confirms the necessity of desolation before a harvest can be expected (28:24–29).

The prophet details the theology of self-confidence, mockery, and autonomy in Israel (Isaiah 28) and in Jerusalem (Isaiah 29–31). Yahweh can save his people but purposes to delay[45] his salvation (30:18) because his people have abandoned the Holy One of Israel and must learn to rest in him alone: "In returning and rest you shall be saved; in quietness and in trust shall be your strength" (30:15; cf. Jer. 6:16; Matt. 11:28). But God, the teacher, does not give up on them. Through his instruction (Isa. 30:20–21; cf. 48:17–18), he will transform sorrow into rejoicing (30:18–26; cf. 31:6).[46] Oppression comes to an end (30:31–33; 31:8–9) when he establishes his kingdom (30:26). He inflicts wounds like a lion (31:4) but protects his people like a bird hovering over its nest (31:5).

The judgment of Zion could have brought her to a violent end (29:1–4; 30:12–14). But Yahweh renews his promise to protect his people, to deliver them, and to annihilate the Assyrian opposition (29:5–8; 30:25, 27–28; 31:4–5; 33:1–3). Isaiah portrays the restoration of Zion as a reversal in expectations. After all, she will be Yahweh's dwelling place, full of justice and righteousness (28:5–6, 16–17; 30:15–20; 32:1–5; 33:5–6; cf. 1:21; 4:2–6).

God is exalted in both judgment (33:10–14) and salvation (33:5–6). In judgment God is a "consuming fire" coming against his own people and against all who oppose him (30:27–33; 33:14; cf. Heb. 12:29). He inspires people with awe by his judgments on earth. The oracles of woe describe his coming in images of fire, thunderstorms, hail, and earthquake (Isa. 29:6; 30:27, 30; 33:14–15). Though he delays his salvation (30:18; cf. ESV "wait," NIV "long for"), at his appointed time "he will fill Zion with justice and righteousness" (33:5) and will extend his salvation and wisdom to all who fear him (33:5–6; cf. 29:23), acknowledge his holiness, and receive his instruction

---

[44] David J. Reimer, "Isaiah and Politics," in Firth and Williamson, *Interpreting Isaiah*, 84–103.

[45] So Hebrew; see Tanakh, "the Lord is waiting to show you grace. . . . Happy are all who wait for him." Cf. NIV "Yet the Lord longs to be gracious to you; . . . Blessed are all who wait for him."

[46] Karin Finsterbusch, *JHWH als Lehrer der Menschen: Ein Beitrag zur Gottesvorstellung der Hebräischen Bibel*, Biblisch-Theologische Studien 90 (Neukirchen-Vluyn: Neukirchener, 2007).

(29:22–23). They need not be afraid of the consuming fire because he is the source of their salvation: "For the LORD is our judge; the LORD is our lawgiver; the LORD is our king; he will save us" (33:22).

In offering his salvation God invites the righteous to look at Zion as the symbol of his presence (28:16) and at Yahweh as the standard of wisdom, justice, and righteousness (28:6, 17; 30:18; 32:10; 33:5). When God inaugurates a new age, his people will be consecrated to him and live in awe of his holiness (29:23). He will be their teacher (ESV, NIV "teachers") whom they will obey (30:19–22), whose grace they will see (30:23–26). He will exact vengeance on their enemies (30:27–33). The new age will transform society into a righteous and just world (32:1–8). God's people may experience tribulation, and their cities and fortresses may fail, but the Spirit of the Lord will inaugurate an era of righteousness and peace. He will bring order out of chaos (32:14–20). Yahweh's kingdom will be characterized by excellence, justice, salvation, wisdom, and the fear of the Lord (33:5–6).

Isaiah also details the qualities of the "holy" remnant. They are the humble who respond to Yahweh's revelation, stand in awe of him, and rejoice in the Holy One of Israel (29:18–24; 30:19–21). Their sins are forgiven, and they are healed (30:22–26; 33:24). Isaiah also portrays a people renewed by God's purification of society (28:16–17; 29:18–24), by leadership given to justice and righteousness (32:1–8), and by the transforming power of the Spirit of God (32:15–20). Theirs will be the promises of rest (28:11–12; 30:15), healing, and forgiveness (33:24; cf. 4:2–6; 30:22–26). Only those who respond in awe and in a transformed lifestyle of wisdom need not fear his coming as a "consuming fire." The Lord will protect and provide for all who live righteously and speak with integrity (33:15; cf. 10:1–2; Psalms 15; 24). They will behold the beauty of the Lord and experience his kingdom of healing and forgiveness (Isa. 33:17–24).

Visions of Vengeance and Vindication (Isaiah 34–35)

The prophecy in Isaiah 34–35 gives the contrastive perspectives of desolation and restoration. Edom represents the nations in judgment (see 63:1–6); it undergoes upheaval and desolation because of God's vengeance (34:8). In contrast, God transforms the wilderness of his people into a garden by manifesting his glory (35:1; cf. 29:17–24). In place of the desert, symbolic of the exilic existence, a garden with a road leads to Zion, the city of God. God's redeemed people enter Zion with thanksgiving (35:6–10). The vision of the transformation of the desert is part of the new exodus imagery with its distinctive vocabulary, themes, and images. It anticipates the imagery developed in Isaiah 40–55; it is a world of hope and comfort (see Isaiah 12).

The Hezekiah Narrative: Zion's Preservation and Doom (Isaiah 36–39)

By including the Hezekiah narrative, the prophet makes a distinctive contribution. The account connects well with the preceding and the following chapters.[47] On the one hand,

---

[47] See Christopher R. Seitz, *Zion's Final Destiny: The Development of the Book of Isaiah: A Reassessment of Isaiah 36–39* (Minneapolis: Fortress, 1991); Peter R. Ackroyd, "Isaiah 36–39: Structure and Function," in *Studies in the Religious Tradition of the Old Testament* (London: SCM, 1987), 105–20.

Isaiah presents God's fidelity to his plans and purposes for Jerusalem. He is "with" Jerusalem (Immanuel), he is sovereign over the nations (Assyria), and he reveals his grace to Judah through the godly Hezekiah (Isaiah 36–37). Yahweh is with Hezekiah during his illness (Isaiah 38). Unlike his father Ahaz, Hezekiah turns his political and personal problems over to the Lord and waits for his salvation. Unlike his great-grandfather, Uzziah, who died a sick man, Hezekiah is restored from his disease. Hezekiah symbolically functions as a model of godliness and of the ideals of the Davidic monarchy. Yet he, too, failed by relying on Babylon for a political-military solution (Isaiah 39), thus opening the door to the prophecy of Judah's exile (39:5–7). Jerusalem would survive another century but would eventually be destroyed at the hand of the Babylonians (586 BC).[48]

The Message of Isaiah 40–66

Though traditionally divided into two sections (Isaiah 40–55(54); 56(55)–66), Isaiah 40–66 evidently takes the form of an extended argument that may be analyzed in three sections: 40–48; 49–55(54); and 56(55)–66. Chapters 40–66 reveal an amazing thematic unity and development,[49] building on motifs and themes found in Isaiah 1–39. The shift in chapters 40–66 is not one of authorship but of movement. The prophecy addresses the exilic situation spoken of in Isaiah 39, yet the theme that distinguishes and unites chapters 40–66 is the revelation of God's character. He is the God of all comfort whose wrath turns to compassion, justification, and reconciliation (cf. 12:1–6). Out of the self-revelation of Yahweh, Isaiah develops interconnected themes that echo those in Isaiah 1–39. This thematic variation reveals the complexity of Isaiah and argues against simple comparisons or contrasts.

The good news in Isaiah is the self-disclosure of the Lord. He reveals himself as Creator, King, Redeemer, and Savior:

[I am] your Redeemer, the Holy One of Israel. (Isa. 41:14; 43:14; 48:17;
    cf. 44:6; 49:26; 54:5)

I am the LORD, your God,
    the Holy One of Israel, your Savior. (43:3)

I am the LORD, your Holy One,
    Israel's Creator, your King. (43:15)

Thus says the LORD, the King of Israel and his Redeemer, the LORD of hosts:
    "I am the first and I am the last; besides me there is no god." (44:6)

I, the LORD, am your Savior, your Redeemer,
    the Mighty One of Jacob. (49:26; 60:16)

I am . . . (42:8; 48:12)

---

[48] The book of Isaiah nowhere assumes the destruction of Jerusalem. John Walton has argued that the transposition of Isaiah 38–39, which occurs chronologically before Sennacherib's desolation of Judah, suggests that the book intentionally links the prophecy of exile with the subsequent chapters. The reordering of the historical sequence makes sense in Isaiah but not in Kings. He concludes that Kings was written after Second Isaiah. John H. Walton, "New Observations on the Date of Isaiah," *JETS* 28, no. 2 (1985): 129–32.

[49] Seitz, "Isaiah 1–66," 105–26.

He is the God of all comfort (40:1; 49:13; 51:3, 12; 52:9; 57:18; 61:2; 66:11–13; cf. 12:1–6; 2 Cor. 1:3). He is the Creator who has absolute sovereignty over his creation (40:26), rules wisely over the nations in accordance with his plan (40:8), judges the enemies of his people (40:23–24), hides himself from Israel (40:27), and strengthens those who wait for him in faith (40:31).

The prophet uses relational metaphors for Yahweh's historic bond with his people. He is Israel's father (63:16; 64:8; cf. 1:2), mother (42:14; 49:15; 66:13), husband (50:1; 54:1–5; cf. 50:1–3; 62:4), and teacher, who alone can bless his people (48:17–19; cf. 30:20). The new relationship with Israel involves the making of a "covenant of peace" (54:10) with a new community of Spirit-filled individuals (44:3–4) who in successive generations live by his word and are truly righteous (59:20, 21; 60:21–22).

This new relationship is also confirmed by the giving of new names to the people, to Zion, and to the land: "the city of righteousness, the faithful city" (1:26); "My Delight Is in Her" (62:4); "Married" (62:4); "The Holy People" (62:12); "The Redeemed of the Lord" (62:12); and "Sought Out, A City Not Forsaken" (62:12).

Isaiah 40–48

The well-known opening words "comfort, comfort" (40:1) shape the Isaianic proclamation (see 12:1; 40:1; 49:13; 51:3, 11; 52:8–9; 54:1; 55:12; 66:13). He presents us with the incomparable God who forgives his people (40:2), and who manifests his glory to humanity (40:3–5). His word is true (40:8). He is the divine Warrior rewarding his people who wait for him (40:9–11, 31). He is the Creator and sovereign of the world in whose presence human and religious structures collapse (40:12–26). The everlasting God is tireless in his concern for his people (40:27–31). Isaiah describes the calling of Cyrus to participate in the "new" era of redemption that will end the dominance of Babylon, so that her captives may go free (Isaiah 41; 44:28–47:15). The redemption of Israel is likened to a second exodus (41:17–20) as God confirms the election of Israel as his servant (41:8–10). God's purposes are unwavering, his word stands, and his love for Israel is gracious. Though Israel responds with questions and remains deaf and dumb, the Lord entices her with a plethora of promises to confirm her mission to be his "servant" and witness to the nations (Isaiah 41–44). He seals the promises with his Spirit (44:1–5; cf. 42:1), so that all will know him from generation to generation. In stating these promises and expressions of God's commitment, the prophet ridicules the powers of religious structures (Isaiah 40–44). God's word alone has a power that dwarfs the supposed powers of religious superstitions (44:25–28). God's salvation lasts (45:17), whereas Babylon's power will come to an end (Isaiah 45–47).

The transformation of God's people. The spiritual transformation of the people is one of the most remarkable reversal patterns in Isaiah.[50] Israel's hardness to the way

---

[50] Willem A. VanGemeren and Andrew Abernethy, "The Spirit and the Future: A Canonical Approach," in *Presence, Power, and Promise: The Role of the Spirit of God in the Old Testament*, ed. David G. Firth and Paul D. Wegner (Downers Grove, IL: IVP Academic, 2011), 321–45.

of the Lord is proverbial. They were religious but did not call upon his name. Yet Isaiah 40 opens with words of comfort. Alluding to the covenant formula, he calls them "my people" (40:1) and declares himself to be "your God" (40:1). He offers them forgiveness, the end of exile, and the manifestation of his glory (40:1–5). He promises them a new era marked by the experience of redemption (vindication), deliverance from the subjugation of Babylon, and his presence (43:14–21). He calls them to be his "servants" and his witnesses to the nations so that his praise will be heard throughout creation.

Yahweh's invitation to serve as his witnesses ("servants") to and instructors of the nations is met with complaints, questions, doubts, and objections (Isaiah 40–48).[51] Their objections are met by extensive polemics against idolatry, proofs of Yahweh's excellence in creation and history, and promises of renewal to all who wait for his salvation (40:31). But Israel cannot comprehend that Yahweh is the incomparable God. Isaiah confronts their unbelief or syncretistic mindset by belittling polemically and satirically the alleged powers of the gods. Paganism warps our relationship with the transcendent God and the ethical values that reflect the image of God in humans (44:20).

Though Israel remains deaf and blind (42:18–19), Yahweh confirms his commitment to them and his choice of Jacob to be his servant (41:8; 43:10, 20). He promises an inner transformation by the Spirit (44:1–5), so that they may bring his instruction, rule, and justice to the nations (42:1–4). He calls them to be his witnesses to the nations (43:10). Though they have lost the blessings flowing out of his promises (48:17–19; cf. Rom. 10:12), he opens the doors to himself and to a new future. Isaiah 48 climactically calls on Israel to listen, lest they lose out again (48:17–18). Yahweh's instruction has the potential for wisdom ("the way of the LORD"; see Gen. 18:19; Deut. 4:6–8), and its effects are righteousness, peace, and joy (Isa. 48:17–19; cf. Rom. 14:17). Israel could have received the blessings promised to Abraham (Isa. 48:19). Instead they hardened themselves against the Lord and suffered the consequences (42:24).

Yet Isaiah 49–66 amplifies the proclamation of the good news. God promises a new covenant ("covenant of peace") with the benefits of righteousness, peace, and population explosion (54:10–17). He further assures them that it will be accomplished according to his will (51:4–5). God's word is true (40:8; 55:10–13), and his instruction in justice and righteousness will go forth to the nations (51:4–5). Isaiah 55 renews the free offer of the good news with a second appeal to listen to the Lord (55:1–3), to seek him (55:6–9), and to wait for the unfolding of his salvation (55:4, 10–13). God's mission will be completed by his servant(s).

The faithful servant of the Lord. The servant theme in Isaiah is multifaceted because it extends from chapters 40 to 66. The portrayal of the servant is much more complex than the four servant songs (42:1–4; 49:1–6; 50:4–9; 52:13–53:12). It is also broader

---

[51] Rikk E. Watts, "Consolation or Confrontation? Isaiah 40–55 and the Delay of the New Exodus," *TynBul* 41 (1990): 31–59.

than the traditional identification of the servant with the Lord Jesus Christ because Isaiah speaks of Israel as the servant of the Lord who is not only called to instruct the nations (2:1–4) but is also described as deaf and blind and in need of divine forgiveness (42:18–22). Some have identified the servant with Cyrus, who is called "my shepherd" and "his anointed" (44:28; 45:1; cf. 41:2, 25). Though both Israel and Cyrus were called to serve the Lord's purposes, the task of God's servant is yet more enduring and transcendent than that of Cyrus or Israel (41:1–6; 44:28–47:15).

Isaiah moves from rebellious and unbelieving Israel to the idealization of the servant in the projection of a "suffering servant." He also projects a community of "servants" of the Lord (54:17) who follow in the footsteps of the suffering servant through their loyalty and suffering. All who seek Yahweh are called his "servants" (65:8–10; cf. 51:1), including a remnant from the nations (56:6).[52] Theirs is a great inheritance (54:17; 57:13b). God promises to remove their shame and give them a double inheritance for the harsh punishment they have endured (61:7; cf. 40:2). They will enter Zion (the new creation) as their sorrow turns to laughter (65:19; cf. 35:10; 51:10; Rev. 21:4) and their shame to blessing (Isa. 65:21–23). God will dwell with them. He will guide, comfort, and heal them (57:14–19).

Proclamation of comfort: Preaching, teaching, and witnessing. Isaiah directly connects the proclamation of suffering with the revelation of the good news of the glorious coming of God's kingdom. Yahweh had planned not only the appalling experiences of exile but also the glorious redemption that would follow (43:12). The proclamation of good news seeks to bring comfort and to remedy the experience of exile by promising God's people the presence of God's kingdom of peace, salvation, and joy: "How beautiful upon the mountains are the feet of him who brings good news, who publishes peace, who brings good news of happiness, who publishes salvation, who says to Zion, 'Your God reigns!'" (52:7; cf. 40:2, 9; 41:27; 62:11).

The messengers bring "comfort" to Zion (40:1). The identity of the comforters is less important than the task. Regardless, the usage of the first person ("I") in 48:16b, 49:1–13; 50:4–9; 61:1–3 has raised many questions on the identity. Isaiah is intentionally enigmatic. The "I" has been identified with Isaiah himself, with a symbolic reference to the prophetic movement, with a particular prophet such as Jeremiah, and with the Lord Jesus. For his part, the prophet associates the ministry of comfort vaguely with the servant/servants of the Lord.[53] While not denying the christological significance of the messenger(s), I have argued for a connection between the Head (Jesus) and the body (the church).[54] The servants are "agents" in completing God's mission. They anticipate and follow the Lord Jesus in their ministry. Their importance lies in their fidelity to Yahweh and in their witnessing to the execution

---

[52] The NIV obfuscates this designation by the translation "to worship him" instead of "to be his servants."

[53] W. A. M. Beuken argues that the "seed" motif (6:13b) finds its continuance in the servant theme in Isaiah 56–66 in "The Main Theme of Trito-Isaiah: The Servants of YHWH," *JSOT* 47 (1990): 67–87. See also his article "Servant and Herald of Good Tidings: Isaiah 61 as an Interpretation of Isaiah 40–55," in *The Book of Isaiah*, ed. J. Vermilion, BETL 81 (Leuven: Leuven University Press, 1989), 411–40.

[54] VanGemeren, "Our Missional God, 198–217. See my discussion on John Calvin's interpretation of Isa. 61:1 in the "Figuration of the Servant of the Lord" on p. 267.

of God's word (promises), their teaching, and their proclamation. They witness to the veracity of God's revelation (40:8; 55:10–11). The servants are faithful to God's instruction (cf. 30:20–21), serve him well, and model true discipleship through suffering (50:4–9). They experience humiliation and shame and await his vindication (49:6–7; 52:13–53:12; cf. 42:1–4; Rom. 8:32–39). This pattern marks the Lord Jesus Christ who spoke of these three markers of his ministry found throughout the Old Testament: suffering, glory (resurrection), and a witness to the nations (Luke 24:25–27, 44–48). Faithfulness to God's word lies at the heart of his ministry, just as it also marked the apostolic ministry (cf. Acts 6:4).

The task of the servant of the Lord is not only to witness to God's truthfulness but also to be a faithful instrument of the word through a ministry of teaching and proclamation. He is a Spirit-endowed *teacher* who instructs people in the just and righteous ways of God's kingdom (Isa. 42:1–4). Nations long for his instruction (42:4; cf. 2:5), and Yahweh will receive glory from his instruction (42:21). He is also a Spirit-empowered *preacher* of the good news of God's comfort to all who mourn (61:1; 62:1; cf. 48:16b). His mission is twofold: (1) to bring Israel back into a covenantal relationship, and (2) to bring God's light to the nations (42:6; 49:6). Moreover, he is a witness to the veracity of Yahweh's word in judgment and in salvation. He is called to be a *witness* to the nations (55:4–5). His witness is to the nations at large as he challenges their false claims and defends Yahweh's integrity (43:1–13; 44:8–20; 55:4–6), and as he offers them the good news of the gospel of forgiveness and participation in his kingdom.

Despite all of God's promises, confrontations, and exhortations, Israel is slow to react. She is marked by a history of unbelief and idolatry. The prophet confronts the deaf servant, Israel, with her idolatrous ways, calls her to listen to Yahweh, and holds out the vision of the spiritual transformation of the people by God's Spirit. Though Israel has missed God's blessings in the past because she did not heed Yahweh's instruction (48:17–19), the new exodus opens up a new era of redemption (48:20–21).

The new exodus. Isaiah distinguishes between two parts of Zion's story: the former things and the latter or new things (42:9; 43:18; 48:3; 65:17). The incomparable God plans and then executes his plan (40:8; 55:10–11; cf. 8:10), unlike the idols or false gods (41:21–24; 43:9; 48:3–5). He foretold the exile, and it happened. He also spoke of the restoration from exile (42:9–13), and it happened. The end of exile inaugurates an eschatological era, characterized by the victory of God, the glory of Zion, and his presence with his people (65:17–25). It is the vision of a new Zion, a new creation (66:20–22). The new era is likened to a second (or new) exodus (43:18–21), to Zion/ the New Jerusalem (65:18–19; 66:8–14), and to a new creation (65:17; 66:21). The new exodus portrays the process of redemption in the imagery of a return from the nations (exile, Diaspora) with Zion as their destiny.

The image of the new exodus is a helpful paradigm. In the first exodus, Yahweh brought Israel out of Egypt as they left "in haste," despoiling the Egyptians of their treasures. They had witnessed ten signs ("plagues") of God's sovereignty over Egypt, but they soon rebelled in the wilderness. They grumbled and were disobedient, but Moses, the servant of the Lord, interceded and suffered on behalf of Israel. In the end he could not bring Israel into her rest, and Joshua succeeded him in the conquest of the land. However, Israel rarely experienced the potential blessing, as they were the object of the curses of the covenant until they went into exile. The new exodus is a pattern based on the first exodus. It helps us to understand not only the theology of Isaiah but also that of the New Testament. Our Lord and the apostles explain and develop the understanding of "the gospel of the Lord Jesus Christ" in the light of Isaiah's teaching on the new exodus.

Isaiah 49–55(54)

The promised future is not restricted by Israel's past failure. God commits himself to alter Israel's rebellious course by the ministry of a true servant of the Lord. This suffering servant is a paradigm of loyalty. He is called both to minister to unfaithful Israel and to bring a light to the nations (49:6–7). His loyalty is tested through suffering, abuse, and death (52:13–53:12; cf. 50:4–9). The reader apprehends with greater clarity God's determination to bring about the new era. The ministry of the faithful servant (Isaiah 49; 50; 52:13–53:12) and the promise of the glory of Zion provide the structure to these chapters with their focused promises of everlasting salvation, Zion's future (restoration and population explosion), and the glorious manifestation of Yahweh's power in a Red Sea–like redemption.[55] The God of all comfort (49:13–16) will not forget his people. He will bring them to Zion, and they will witness the manifestation of his great power and glory. Isaiah likens the restoration of Zion to the glory of the garden of Eden (51:3). Great will be the joy of his people (49:13; 51:3, 11; 52:8–9; 54:1; 55:12). Her population will explode exponentially, and they will be the objects of God's mercy and love and the recipients of his covenant of peace (54:1–10). This section closes with a vision of restored Zion and the mention of "the heritage of the servants" of the Lord (54:10–17), followed by exhortations to turn to the Lord "for mercy and forgiveness" (55:1–7) with the promise that God's marvelous plans will open up a new world for his servants (55:8–13).[56] Chapter 55 is Janus-like, serving as a hinge connecting chapters 54 and 56.[57]

The ministry of God's servant. Who, then, is the true servant of the Lord? We have observed that Isaiah presents various aspects of the servant that are in tension with each other.[58] He speaks of the faithful servant (49:1–5) and the deaf and dumb servant (42:18, 19), God's appointment of Israel and Cyrus, the loyal servant (singular) and servants (plural) of the Lord. He presents the reader with the tension between Yahweh's empowerment of the servant in his mission (42:1–4) and Yahweh's direct

---

[55] Williamson, "Isaiah, Book of," 369.
[56] He Sung Lee, "The Inheritance of the Servants in Isaiah 40–66: A Text-Linguistic Analysis" (PhD diss., Trinity Evangelical Divinity School, 2007).
[57] Sweeney suggests that chap. 55 may introduce the last part of Isaiah. *Tanak*, 287–88.
[58] Tryggve N. D. Mettinger called attention to the compositional integrity of the alleged "servant songs" within the text of Isaiah 40–55. See "Die Ebed-Jahwe-Lieder: Ein fragwürdiges Axiom," *ASTI* 11 (1978): 68–76.

execution of the mission (51:4–5; cf. 42:21). Isaiah also speaks of the servant as an individual and as a community (Israel), descriptively (42:1–4; 52:13–53:12) and autobiographically (i.e., in the first person, 48:16b; 49:1–9; 50:4–9). Further, he portrays the servant with doubts, questions, and disputations (40:12–31; 41:9–17), while pointing to the servant's trust in Yahweh during his suffering (50:7–9). Finally, he contrasts the success of Cyrus's mission and the perceived failure of the suffering servant, who only succeeds in his mission after his death (44:24–45:7; 52:13–53:12).[59]

Both rebellious Israel and the cynical nations oppose the faithful servant. He faces such challenges by the power of the Spirit (42:1; 48:16b; see 61:1; cf. 11:1), in humility (42:2–4), and as one taught by the Lord (50:4–5), but his mission is of little success (48:16b; 49:1–13; 50:4–9). Like Moses, he questions the validity of the mission but accepts it. He is commissioned by the Lord and empowered by his Spirit (48:16b), and in the course of his ministry, he suffers (49:1–13; 50:4–9), but he entrusts himself to Yahweh. In the climactic poem of the suffering servant (52:13–53:12), the servant is reckoned with sinners and dies the death of infamy. Yet his mission is a success because the Lord accepts and rewards his sacrifice (53:11–12).[60]

Figuration of the servant of the Lord. In reading the magnificent texts about the agency of the servant, students of Isaiah have readily identified a connection between the enigmatic servant figure in Isaiah and Moses, the prophet himself, the prophetic movement, and Jesus. John Calvin cautioned interpreters not to identify the servant in Isaiah 61:1 too readily with the Lord Jesus Christ. He argued in favor of associating the ministry of Isaiah and of God's servants with the *mission* of the Lord Jesus Christ. He wrote:

> As Christ explains this passage with reference to himself, so commentators limit it to him without hesitation, and lay down this principle, that Christ is introduced as speaking, as if the whole passage related to him alone. The Jews laugh at this, as an ill-advised application to Christ of that which is equally applicable to other prophets. . . . But this is not inconsistent with the application of this statement to other prophets, whom the Lord has anointed; for they did not speak in their own name as individuals, or claim this authority for themselves, but were chiefly employed in pointing out the office of Christ, to whom belongs not only the publication of these things, but likewise the accomplishment of them. This chapter ought, therefore, to be understood in such a sense, that Christ, who is the Head of the prophets, holds the chief place, and alone makes all those revelations; but that Isaiah, and the other prophets, and the apostles, contribute their services to Christ, and each performs his part in making known Christ's benefits. And thus we see that those things which Isaiah said would be accomplished by Christ, have now been actually accomplished.[61]

---

[59] See Richard E. Averbeck, "Christian Interpretations of Isaiah 53," in *The Gospel according to Isaiah 53: Encountering the Suffering Servant in Jewish and Christian Theology*, ed. Darrell L. Bock and Mitch Glaser (Grand Rapids, MI: Kregel, 2012), 33–60.
[60] See the fine study on this topic in Bock and Glaser, *The Gospel according to Isaiah 53*.
[61] Calvin, *Commentary on Isaiah*, comment on Isa. 61:1.

Notice that Calvin does not take the prophecy in a predictive way. He describes the task as something the prophets and the apostles share. They serve the Lord Jesus in this manner. Like Calvin, I propose that what is true about all of God's servants is so much more true of the Lord Jesus. His disciples discerned that Jesus was more than a prophetic servant. He is God and the messiah of God.[62] Yet Jesus is the suffering servant who executes God's mission in the company of Moses, the prophets, the sages, and the apostles. They, too, were obedient and were tested. Still, Isaiah's suffering servant is very different from them, because he is God himself, is without sin, and has carried God's wrath on our behalf. His suffering is vicarious in a unique way as he brings in forgiveness, redemption, justification, and all the benefits of the new relationship with the Father for the "many," for "the transgressors" (53:12). In the execution of his mission, Jesus incarnates Isaiah's suffering-servant theme throughout his ministry and through his vicarious death and glorious resurrection. He is the Messiah (agent) of God and the head of a large body of faithful servants commissioned to bring the good news of the coming of God's kingdom, to summon people to call on the name of the Lord in faith, and to await their glorious salvation and vindication from the Lord of glory.

The New Testament contextualizes Isaiah's prophecies by helping its readers connect the dots. Through Jesus's ministry and teaching, they discover the providential patterns embedded in the prophetic word. In Matthew's account, Jesus inaugurates the Isaianic mission as "the Immanuel" who truly saves and brings forgiveness as God incarnate (Matt. 1:21–23). He is "the Christ, the Son of the living God" (Matt. 16:16). In Mark's account Jesus is closely identified with the gospel of the kingdom. Mark opens his gospel with these words, "the beginning of the gospel of Jesus Christ" (Mark 1:1; cf. Isa. 40:9), which, within the framework of Isaiah's message, Mark further defines as the nearness of the kingdom and the expected responses of faith and repentance (Mark 1:14–15).[63] Luke defines the ministry of Jesus and of the apostles as inclusive of preaching, restoration, and comfort (Luke 4:17–19) by citing Isaiah 61:1–3, which also incorporates other Isaianic texts.[64] The apostle Paul calls himself the "servant" of the Lord Jesus, as he too identifies himself with the Isaianic mission, "a servant of Christ Jesus, called to be an apostle, set apart for the gospel of God. . . . God is my witness, whom I serve with my spirit in the gospel of his Son" (Rom. 1:1, 9). He also identifies himself with the servant commissioned to bring light to the nations (Acts 13:47; cf. Isa. 42:6; 49:6).

Isaiah 56(55)–66

In this final section of the book, Isaiah ties together motifs, themes, and emphases found throughout Isaiah 1–55. The prophet restates his teaching from Isaiah 1–39.

---

[62] See the excellent study by Williamson, *Variations on a Theme*.

[63] Craig A. Evans, "From Gospel to Gospel: The Function of Isaiah in the New Testament," in *Writing and Reading the Scroll of Isaiah: Studies of an Interpretive Tradition*, ed. Craig C. Broyles and Craig A. Evans, VTSup 70 (Leiden: Brill, 1997), 2:651–92.

[64] See David W. Pao and Eckhard J. Schnabel, "Luke," in *Commentary on the New Testament Use of the Old Testament*, ed. G. K. Beale and D. A. Carson (Grand Rapids, MI: Baker Academic, 2007), 287–90.

God is constant in his commitment to justice and righteousness (56:1a). He expects social justice as an expression of true religion (1:11–20; cf. 58:6–12) and hates idolatry, greed, and self-fulfillment (2:6–9; 5:8–30; cf. 56:9–57:13a), for which reasons Israel has come under judgment (5:24–30; cf. 66:3–6). Isaiah also correlates God's promise of redemption (56:1b) with a lifestyle of godliness. The promised redemption is a restatement of the good news in Isaiah 40–55 that God's kingdom and vindication are coming (51:1b; cf. 45:8; 51:6, 8).[65] Moreover, the contrasts between God's condemnation of Israel (56:9–57:13a) and his acceptance of the nations (58:2–8) form an arch with God's favor on the nations and his abandonment of Zion (2:2–6).

Isaiah opens the way of wisdom to anyone who is thirsty and hungry to receive instruction (55:1–3). His language invites associations with the way of wisdom, such as that found in the Psalms. The blessing pronounced on all members of the human race who respond wisely to Yahweh's invitation is reminiscent of the Psalter's blessing pronounced on all who find refuge in God (56:2; 57:13b, cf. Ps. 1:1; 2:12b), and the affirmation of Yahweh's everlasting judgment on sinners reinforces this theme (Isa. 57:20–21; cf. Ps. 1:6; 2:12a). Isaiah charges Israel with duplicity because her worship is empty, lacking humility or justice (Isa. 58:1–5; cf. 1:10–24; Mic. 6:8). Israel stands guilty before God (Isa. 59:1–8; cf. 1:2–4).

Yet the world of Isaiah 56–66 is different, particularly in the way it treats the theme of the servants of the Lord. Like the suffering servant, the new community of godly servants experiences shame, ridicule, and persecution (66:3–6). In their laments they speak of persecution (57:1), guilt and failure (59:9–15), and alienation from God (63:7–64:11). As in the Psalms, their laments are not just for themselves but also for their fellow Israelites. Yahweh's response affirms that he will be with all who take refuge in him (57:13b–19), that he alone will bring them salvation (59:1, 16–21), and that the light of his salvation will shine brightly and transform the population of Zion (58:6–14; 60:1–22). Surprisingly, Gentiles are accepted as God's "servants" (56:6), celebrate the Sabbath (56:6; 66:23), and are invited to God's "holy mountain" (56:5, 7; cf. 57:13b; 66:20), where the Lord accepts their prayers and sacrifices (56:7). At the conclusion of this section, we find the promise that non-Jews may serve as God's priests (66:18–21). Hence, the "servants" of the Lord constitute a new community from Israel and the nations. They suffer for the sake of Zion and continue the mission of the suffering servant as God's chosen spokespersons, priests, and leaders (Isaiah 61).

God promises the vindication of his suffering servants (59:15b–21). The framing of the laments and the oracles of salvation define more explicitly the nature of God's servants and their rewards. God promises to be the Savior of all in Israel who repent from their transgression and of all people who fear him (59:19, 20). Three dimensions open up vistas to chapters 56(55)–66: God's salvation, the nature of the true servants of the Lord, and their entrance into the glory of Zion and of the new creation.

---

[65] See the earlier discussion on the double meaning of *righteousness* in Isaiah under "Figuration" (p. 253).

The Salvation of the Lord. God makes many promises in order to encourage his faithful servants, such as the inheritance of the holy mountain (Zion; cf. 56:7); entrance into his presence (57:14–15); his "dwelling" with them (57:15); healing, comfort, joy, and peace (57:18–19); and the exclusion of evildoers (48:22; 57:20; 66:24). But he also states the requirement of living by justice, righteousness, and holiness (Isaiah 58). The expectations are too great because his servants are unable to live up to his requirements (59:9–15). The vision of Zion's glory quickly disappears because many in Israel claimed to be servants of the living God without comprehending the cost of discipleship (58:1–12). The true servants observe the unlikelihood of perpetuating the vision because their fellow servants are corrupt and are suffering (57:1; 59:1–8). They cry out to the Lord for salvation because they are unable to live redemptively for the sake of Zion (59:9–15).

God responds to their lament by involving himself in the final resolution between appearance and reality. He commits himself to save his servants, to set them apart gloriously, to work in them monergistically, and to secure the vision of Zion's glory once and for all. Isaiah portrays God's coming as a Warrior with a breastplate, a helmet, and garments in order to bring in an everlasting and victorious righteousness (59:16–17). He will separate the righteous from the wicked and those who serve him from those who do not (59:18). He alone determines who belongs to Zion and who does not. Salvation is his alone!

The name Isaiah may be symbolic for the central message of the book. It means, "salvation is Yahweh's (alone)." When Yahweh condescends to meet the human condition, he renews all who wait for him (51:4; 64:4; cf. 8:17; 40:31). He reveals his glory (40:5). He is the divine Warrior who victoriously brings in righteousness, salvation, and all its benefits (59:15b–19). He renews the covenant with his servants (59:21; 60:21–22; 62:9–11; cf. 54:13), gives them the prophetic Spirit and the word (59:21; cf. Deut. 18:18; Isa. 44:3), restores the splendor of Zion (60:1–22), constitutes them as a righteous community, and empowers the proclamation of comfort by his Spirit (61:1–8; 62:1–12). The Lord graciously reverses the original judgment of the decimation of his people (6:13), with the promise of an increase in number and vitality (60:22). Instead of the image of their being cut down like an oak (6:13), Isaiah likens the new people of God to "the branch of my planting" (60:21) and to "oaks of righteousness, the planting of the LORD" (61:3; cf. 6:13; 54:13–14). They are the "holy seed" (6:13b; cf. 65:23).

The new community. Throughout the book we find marks of the new community. The last section (Isaiah 56–66) delineates more distinctly the qualities of God's "servants." All people, including eunuchs and Gentiles, are invited to "be his servants" (56:1–7).[66] The Lord promises to accept their sacrifices and prayers (56:7; cf. Mark 11:17), whereas he had rejected the pious busyness of Judah (Isa. 1:12–15). Isaiah keeps the door open for Israel (56:8).[67] In these chapters, Isaiah encourages God's servants to persevere to

---

[66] The NIV translation, "all who worship him," should be rendered "to be his servants."
[67] Childs wisely observes that the identity of the flock in Isa. 56:8 is not the issue. Jesus (John 10:6), like Isaiah, "denotes a similar openness to the further ingathering, but with a purposefully undefined referent." *Isaiah*, OTL (Louisville: Westminster John Knox, 2001), 459.

the end. God will triumphantly establish his kingdom, but he also expects his servants to advance his cause by living wisely: "Keep practicing justice and righteousness, because my [ultimate] salvation is coming and my [final] triumph is about to be revealed" (56:1, my trans.).[68] In keeping with the argument of the book, he ties together the salvation of the Lord (Isaiah 49–55) and the importance of living wisely (Isaiah 1–39).

The marks of the new community flow out of God's salvation. Because of God's love and power, the servants of the Lord constitute a new community of joy, glory, and praise (61:3–4, 7). Instead of living in shame and servitude, they share in the glory of Zion's restoration (Isaiah 60), in the wealth of the nations (60:5–7, 11; 66:12), and in a ministry of intercession on behalf of the nations (61:4–6). God confirms the covenant with them and with their children (61:8–9; cf. 59:21). They are his blessed people (61:9; 65:23; cf. 44:3). All these and more benefits (rewards) belong to the servants of the Lord. These are evidence of God's salvation, which is likened to the wedding array of the bride and groom (61:10), to a priestly adornment (61:10), and to a lush garden (61:11; cf. 1:30; 60:21).

The new names associated with Zion (cf. 1:26; 60:18) portray her as God's beloved people (62:5) and display the transformation of her shame into glory: "My Delight Is in Her," "Married, "The Holy People, The Redeemed of the LORD; . . . Sought Out, A City Not Forsaken" (62:4, 12; cf. 1:26; 60:18). The Lord confirms his promise to protect and to provide for his "bride" (62:5, 8–9; cf. 65:20–25) and to come to his people, to enter Zion, and to be with his people (62:12; cf. Ex. 19:6).

The future lies open to a remnant from Israel and from the nations[69] who trust in Yahweh, serve him faithfully, seek his kingdom, and are characterized by humility. All people, including eunuchs and Gentiles, are invited to "join" (suggesting a Levitical status) to Yahweh and to be his "servants"[70] by the practice of justice and righteousness (56:1; cf. Matthew 25), by the consecration of the Sabbath (Isa. 56:2, 4, 6; 58:13–14; 66:23), by loving him, and by participating in the covenant (56:1–7). The Lord promises to accept their sacrifices and prayers (56:7; cf. Mark 11:17), whereas he had rejected the pious religiosity of Judah (Isa. 1:12–15), including Sabbath observance (1:13). The Lord commits himself to his "servants" in covenant, in glory, and in salvation.

They receive the prophetic Spirit and the word (59:21) and are constituted a righteous community (60:21–22). A final lament (63:7–64:12) receives a climactic response. Yahweh confirms that he is just in his vengeance against the rebels and faithful in the vindication of his servants (Isaiah 65–66). The new creation is a divine reordering of this world in which righteousness, peace, and joy in the Holy Spirit are found on earth but without any remainder of rebellious, autonomous, and foolish people. God's acts of judgment and salvation assure his servants of his final victory over evil. His servants will inherit the new creation and receive citizenship in the New Jerusalem, Zion (Isaiah 65–66).

---

[68] See the earlier discussion under "Literary Factors" (p. 252).
[69] Childs, *Isaiah*, 459.
[70] The NIV translation, "all who worship him," should be rendered "to be his servants."

Zion and the New Creation. The new Zion is transcendent and immanent. Isaiah has likened Zion, the earthly city of David, to a whore because of her filth, unrighteousness, and infidelity (1:21). In the vision of God's coming to be with his people, Zion is a transcendent city. As Zion was the city of David, the new Zion is renowned for the presence of God. God is gloriously present when his people experience his transcendent qualities of righteousness, faithfulness, peace, and quietness (32:15–20; cf. 54:11–17; 60:17, 21; 61:8). God has promised to remove all causes of evil, anguish, and shame from his people (60:19–20).

The Zion imagery extends to the whole of creation because of the radical and transcendent nature of God's kingdom. As Zion is the mother of all the servants of God (cf. Psalm 87; Gal. 4:26), she knows no geopolitical boundaries. She is a microcosm of a world without evil, enemies, or ethnic rivalry. It is a world of love and righteousness. Hence, Isaiah readily moves from the city (Zion) to the new creation.

Yahweh renews his covenantal commitment to his people in the promise of his presence and blessing. Isaiah speaks of the transformation of the Davidic covenant (55:3–6), opening up leadership to all of God's servants. Like David, they are his ambassadors of the new Zion (55:3–5). He expects them to maintain justice and to guard the covenant (56:1–2), to serve him wholeheartedly (56:6), to find refuge in the Lord (57:13b), to keep the *mission* of Zion alive by proclaiming the good news of God's kingdom (Isaiah 61–62), and to suffer on for the sake of the *vision* of Zion's glory (62:1; 63:7–64:12; 66:5; cf. 57:4).

Isaiah speaks of the new era in images of a city (Zion; Isaiah 60; cf. 1:26–27; 26:1–2; 54:11–17), the garden of Eden (51:3), a new creation (65:18; 66:22), light and glory (60:1–3, 10, 13, 19–20; 66:18), the wealth of the nations (60:5–9, 11, 16–17, 18; 66:12), and joy (35:10; 60:15). It is the experience of reversal from deprivation to comfort, from anguish to restoration, from captivity to freedom, from shame to beauty, from mourning to joy, from despair to praise, from ruins to rebuilding, from being reviled by the nations to being honored, and from exile to the inheritance of a portion of God's world (61:1–7). It is an era of service. Great is the reward for those who serve him well as his royal ambassadors in a rebellious world. All God's people are called to serve their Savior as royal ambassadors. They are his priests, prophets, and royal leaders of the nations (61:1–11; cf. 55:3–5).

A lament (63:7–64:12) fittingly closes the grand central vision of Zion's glory (59:16b–63:6). God had promised to hasten his salvation and has commissioned his servants to proclaim, to prepare for, and to await his coming and Zion's imminent transformation (60:22; 61:1–62:12). But they live in the tension between the promise and its realization. The servants lament, confess, hope, and wait expectantly (63:7–64:12). They mourn while longing for redemption. The final two chapters assure the servants of God's care for his own. He will come to avenge them from the wicked (66:1–6, 15–17, 24) and to vindicate his servants (66:7–15). Theirs is the vision of the new creation, the New Jerusalem (65:17–18; cf. Revelation 21).

As the servants await God's salvation, they live in the tension between joy in the vision of the new world (Isa. 65:13–25) and mourning for the present world. God will vindicate his servants who persevere to the end (65:8–16) and hold onto his word (66:2; cf. Rev. 2:3; 3:5, 12, 21; 21:7). The righteous who find God to be their only refuge as they trust in his ultimate redemption (Isa. 57:13b) will see the glory of the Lord: his presence and shepherding care, his healing, and his restoration (58:9–11). Instead of life in exile—likened to darkness, dead vegetation, desert, and ruins—their new situation is likened to bright light, to a lush garden with fresh water, to a glorious city, and to a new creation (51:3; 58:11–12; 60:1–3; 61:11; cf. Revelation 21).

They already indwell the vision of being "at home" with their victorious Savior in Zion.[71] Their experience creates a deep longing for God's glorious and unhindered presence. God's servants will experience the beauty of Zion, symbolized by the bright light of God's presence (Isa. 60:1–3, 19–20) and the blessedness of a world without sinners and victimizers (63:1–6; 65:13–15; 66:15–17). The absence of evil, including the dwarfing of the "serpent" (65:25), is the guarantee that nothing will spoil God's lasting redemption.[72] The last verse (66:24) is a solemn reminder of the severe and eternal punishment that awaits the rebels. God's judgment is severe, but his mercy is even more relentless.

APPROACHING THE NEW TESTAMENT

Isaiah is full of surprises. In the first part (Isaiah 1–39), he shocks Israel by charging Zion with defilement, desecration, and prostitution, while at the same time opening the gates of Zion to nations instructed in the way of the Lord (1:21–2:4). He threatens Israel with judgment by the Holy One of Israel yet promises them the comfort and presence of God (Isaiah 1; 12). He envisions a new community of people who are cleansed and consecrated and who experience God's glorious presence (4:2–6; 12:6). He clarifies that the Lord will bring about a new and glorious Zion whose citizens walk in the light of the Lord (2:5), where righteousness and justice provide a shelter for humanity (32:1–5). Such an era can only come by the agency of the Spirit of God, who comes from on high to renew the Davidic dynasty to be an agent of justice and righteousness (11:1–9) and to renew the earth as a home of righteousness (32:15–20; cf. 2 Pet. 3:13).

In the second part (Isaiah 40–66), Isaiah presents a complex figuration of a faithful servant. He is endowed with the Spirit of the Lord to bring about everlasting righteousness (42:1–4), but he suffers injustice for the sake of many (52:13–53:12). He combines the power of the Spirit with suffering to create the vision of the suffering servant, whose wounds bring healing to people (52:13–52:12).

The vision of Isaiah makes clear that salvation comes from God alone. God will vindicate his faithful servants who will enjoy the liberation of Zion and the end of all evil (59:16b–60:22; 63:1–6; cf. 4:2–6). He also charges Zion's citizens to live up to their calling. After all, the "servants" of the Lord (54:17b) are the "seed" (or "offspring")

---

[71] See Richard J. Mouw, *When the Kings Come Marching In: Isaiah and the New Jerusalem*, 2nd ed. (Grand Rapids, MI: Eerdmans, 2002).
[72] Donald E. Gowan, *Eschatology in the Old Testament* (Edinburgh: T&T Clark, 2000).

of the suffering servant (53:10). They are empowered by the Spirit and constitute a remnant from Israel and the nations (44:1–4;[73] 56:6–7; 59:21), who are commissioned to proclaim, teach, and witness to the veracity of God's word of comfort (61:1–3). They are blessed by the Lord (60:21; 65:23), the subjects and objects of comfort (61:1–3), and heirs of God's holy mountain (the new Zion) and of the new creation (57:13b). They will endure together with the new heaven and earth (66:22). They await the fulfillment of God's promise to speed up the vindication of his servants (60:22).

But why are we still waiting for Immanuel to "redeem captive Israel"? First, God is training his servants in righteousness. As Abraham waited for the city of God (Heb. 11:10), his children also wait for the glorious redemption and revelation of Zion (Rev. 21:1). In Christ they are already members of Zion (Heb. 12:22–24), but they await the full revelation of the city of God (Gal. 4:26; Rev. 21:1–3). Like the new creation, Zion is here and not yet here.

Second, the final and climactic judgment of "Babylon the great" still lies in the future (Rev. 18:2). Though Christ judges the nations of the earth in history, there will be a final and triumphant shaking of the world (Heb. 12:26–28; Revelation 19–20). God gives grace by demonstrating his patience and by calling people to turn to him (2 Pet. 3:9).

Third, God is faithful and free in the execution and timing of the redemption of Zion. He has the power to hasten the redemption (Isa. 60:22; cf. 58:8–14) and the power to delay (30:18; 59:1; cf. Heb. 10:37; Rev. 10:6). Paradoxically, the Lord expects his people to be agents of his redemption (Isa. 59:2–15) and thus to hasten their own redemption (Isaiah 58). The consummation is hastened by every person who calls on the name of the Lord and becomes his redemptive agent (2 Pet. 3:11b–13). We wait until the full number of the children of God come home (2 Pet. 3:9).

Fourth, while waiting for the consummation of our salvation, Christians must grow in character, perseverance, and hope (Rom. 5:1–5). By dwelling in the Scripture, the servants of the Lord learn to dwell with Isaiah and to walk with the Lord Jesus and his apostles by incarnating the lifestyle of the suffering servant in their lives through preaching, teaching, and witnessing to the gospel of Christ. Though we cannot return to the early Christian community, we may well learn from their contextualization of Scripture. Richard Beaton describes the early church as a community that defined "the theological significance of Jesus, his life, death, and resurrection" in terms of Isaiah: "Isaiah was a favorite text that offered many answers."[74] It is indeed the fifth Gospel.

SELECT BIBLIOGRAPHY

Abernethy, Andrew T. *The Book of Isaiah and God's Kingdom: A Thematic-Theological Approach*. NSBT. Downers Grove, IL: InterVarsity Press, 2016.

---

[73] See Joseph Blenkinsopp, *Isaiah 40–55: A New Translation with Introduction and Commentary*, AB 19A (New York: Doubleday, 2002), 233–34.
[74] Richard Beaton, "Isaiah in Matthew's Gospel," in Moyise and Menken, *Isaiah in the New Testament*, 63–78.

Beale, G. K., and D. A. Carson, eds. *Commentary on the New Testament Use of the Old Testament*. Grand Rapids, MI: Baker Academic, 2007.

Beaton, Richard. *Isaiah's Christ in Matthew's Gospel*. SNTSMS 123. New York: Cambridge University Press, 2002.

Beyer, Bryan E. *Encountering the Book of Isaiah: A Historical and Theological Survey*. EBS. Grand Rapids, MI: Baker Academic, 2007.

Blenkinsopp, Joseph. *Isaiah 1–39: A New Translation with Introduction and Commentary*. AB 19. New York: Doubleday, 2000.

———. *Isaiah 40–55: A New Translation with Introduction and Commentary*. AB 19A. New York: Doubleday, 2002.

———. *Isaiah 56–66: A New Translation with Introduction and Commentary*. AB 19B. New York: Doubleday, 2003.

Bock, Darrell L., and Mitch Glaser, eds. *The Gospel according to Isaiah 53: Encountering the Suffering Servant in Jewish and Christian Theology*. Grand Rapids, MI: Kregel, 2012.

Chapman, Stephen B. *The Law and the Prophets: A Study in Old Testament Canon Formation*. FAT 27. Tübingen: Mohr Siebeck, 2000.

Childs, Brevard S. *Introduction to the Old Testament as Scripture*. Philadelphia: Fortress, 1979.

———. *Isaiah*. OTL. Louisville: Westminster John Knox, 2001.

———. *The Struggle to Understand Isaiah as Christian Scripture*. Grand Rapids, MI: Eerdmans, 2004.

Darr, Katheryn Pfisterer. *Isaiah's Vision and the Family of God*. Louisville: Westminster John Knox, 1994.

Firth, David G., and H. G. M. Williamson, eds. *Interpreting Isaiah: Issues and Approaches*. Downers Grove, IL: IVP Academic, 2009.

Goldingay, John E. *Isaiah*. NIBCOT 13. Carlisle, UK: Paternoster, 2001.

Lim, Bo H. *The "Way of the Lord" in the Book of Isaiah*. LHBOTS 522. London: T&T Clark, 2010.

Motyer, J. A. *Isaiah: An Introduction and Commentary*. TOTC 18. Downers Grove, IL: InterVarsity Press, 1999.

———. *The Prophecy of Isaiah: An Introduction and Commentary*. Downers Grove, IL: InterVarsity Press, 1993.

Moyise, Steve, and Maarten J. J. Menken, eds. *Isaiah in the New Testament*. NTSI. London: T&T Clark, 2005.

Oswalt, John M. *The Book of Isaiah: Chapters 1–39*. NICOT. Grand Rapids, MI: Eerdmans, 1986.

———. *The Book of Isaiah: Chapters 40–66*. NICOT. Grand Rapids, MI: Eerdmans, 1998.

Pao, David W. *Acts and the Isaianic New Exodus*. Biblical Studies Library. Grand Rapids, MI: Baker Academic, 2002.

Paul, Shalom M. *Isaiah 40–66: Translation and Commentary*. ECC. Grand Rapids, MI: Eerdmans, 2012.

Seitz, Christopher R. *Figured Out: Typology and Providence in Christian Scripture*. Louisville: Westminster John Knox, 2001.

———. *Isaiah 1–39*. IBC. Louisville: John Knox, 1993.

———. *Prophecy and Hermeneutics: Toward a New Introduction to the Prophets*. STI. Grand Rapids, MI: Baker, 2007.

————, ed. *Reading and Preaching the Book of Isaiah*. Philadelphia: Fortress, 1988.

————. *Zion's Final Destiny: The Development of the Book of Isaiah: A Reassessment of Isaiah 36–39*. Minneapolis: Fortress, 1991.

Smith, Gary V. *Isaiah 1–39*. NAC 15A. Nashville: Broadman, 2007.

————. *Isaiah 40–66*. NAC 15B. Nashville: B&H, 2009.

VanGemeren, Willem A. "Our Missional God: Redemptive-Historical Preaching and the Missio Dei." In *Living Waters from Ancient Springs: Essays in Honor of Cornelis Van Dam*, edited by Jason Van Vliet, 198–217. Eugene, OR: Pickwick, 2011.

Webb, Barry G. *The Message of Isaiah*. The Bible Speaks Today. Downers Grove, IL: InterVarsity Press, 1997.

————. "Zion in Transformation: A Literary Approach to Isaiah." In *The Bible in Three Dimensions: Essays in Celebration of Forty Years of Biblical Studies in the University of Sheffield*, edited by David J. A. Clines, Stephen E. Fowl, and Stanley E. Porter, 65–84. JSOTSup 87. Sheffield: JSOT Press, 1990.

11

Jeremiah

Peter Y. Lee

INTRODUCTION

The book of Jeremiah is the second of the three major prophetic books within the Hebrew canon. This prophetic book is an anthology of oracles that the Lord communicated through Jeremiah the son of Hilkiah (Jer. 1:1) using various literary genres during the most tumultuous times in the history of the southern kingdom of Judah. Jeremiah calls for the people of God to repent of their violation of the covenant or to face the consequences of their sins, namely their exile and the destruction of the city of Jerusalem. At the same time, he proclaims the magnificence of the covenant blessings of God. The recipients of these blessings are not limited to Judah alone. Remarkably, they extend not only to wayward Israel but also to the surrounding Gentile nations. The initial phase of these blessings occurs in the highly anticipated Judean restoration to the Israelite homeland of Canaan, but the true reality of the Lord's covenant promises see their fullest realization in the coming of Christ, the true messianic "Branch" of David (23:5; 33:15). Although the curse sections dominate the book quantitatively, the qualitative worth of the blessings is a bright beacon of hope in what would otherwise be dismal prophecies of doom.

Of all the prophetic figures within the Old Testament canon, Jeremiah demonstrates the struggles and heartaches that result from an impossible task that would only be fulfilled through supernatural means.

BACKGROUND ISSUES

Historical Setting

The book of Jeremiah takes place during a time of transition in the history of both the ancient Near Eastern world and, more narrowly, the kingdom of Judah. In the world at large, the major imperial power at the opening of the book was the neo-Assyrian Empire, which dominated the ancient world from 934–610 BC. During that time, the kings of Assyria reestablished their dominance by reconquering territorial lands that had belonged to their empires of the past (during the Old Babylonian period from 1894–1595 and the Middle Babylonian period of the Kassites from 1595–1155). It was specifically in the reign of Tiglath-pileser III (2 Kings 15:29; 16:7; 1 Chron. 5:26; 2 Chron. 28:20) that the Assyrian empire began to expand their geopolitical territories beyond their previously occupied lands into new areas.[1] The northern kingdom of Israel was directly affected by this new policy and ultimately fell to the powers of the newly growing superpower (see 2 Kings 17).

Yet as quickly as the neo-Assyrian empire grew to strength, so also it quickly collapsed, the reasons for which are not entirely understood. The death of Ashurbanipal in 626 BC, the last of the great Assyrian rulers, signaled the appearance of a newly rising Babylon presence. In alliance with the Medes, the great Babylonian king Nabopolassar (626–605 BC) began a series of lightning strikes against major Assyrian strongholds. By 614 BC, the city of Ashur fell, and then Nineveh in 612 BC. By 610 BC, nearly all Assyrian military resistance was crushed, and Babylon established herself as the new imperial sovereign of the ancient world.

The year of Ashurbanipal's death (626 BC) was also the inaugural year of Jeremiah's prophetic ministry, which lasted approximately forty years. A few years later, in 621 BC, the law book of Moses (presumably some form of the book of Deuteronomy; see 2 Kings 22) was discovered as the temple was being renovated. At this time, Jeremiah did not carry the prophetic weight and status that he would later possess. However, he was influenced by these reforms, which had a direct impact on the message that he gave to his fellow Judeans (Jer. 11:2, 3, 6). He prophesied words of warning and imminent destruction from "the peoples of the north" (6:22–26), whom he later identified as Babylon (20:4–5).

It was during this time that Egypt also began to resurge as a major political power under the rules of Pharaoh Psammetichus (664–610 BC) and Pharaoh Neco (610–594 BC). It was Neco who marched into the Canaanite coastal plains to assist the beleaguered Assyrians in their conflict against Babylon, now under the leadership of the prince-elect Nebuchadnezzar II, in the battle at Carchemish in 605 BC (Jer. 46:1–2). The Judean king Josiah, however, intervened in this Egyptian campaign and attempted to stop Neco at Megiddo.[2] He failed and was killed in battle (2 Kings 23:29). His son, Jehoahaz II, was made king (he is called Shallum in Jer. 22:10–12), but he was deposed by Neco after a very brief reign of three months and taken to prison in Egypt where he died. In his place Neco placed the brother of Jehoahaz, Jehoiakim (609–597 BC), on the throne of Judah (2 Kings 23:34).

---

[1] For a more detailed history of the expansion of the neo-Assyrian empire, see Amélie Kuhrt, *The Ancient Near East: c. 3000–330 BC*, Routledge History of the Ancient World (New York: Routledge, 1995), 1:478–92. For a more general and broader overview of the history, see Dominique Charpin, "History of Ancient Mesopotamia: An Overview," in *Civilizations of the Ancient Near East*, ed. Jack M. Sasson (Peabody, MA: Hendrickson, 2000), 2:807–29.

[2] It is possible that Josiah saw the rise of Babylon as a challenge to the persistent Assyrian threat to Judah, which had made its ways into the outskirts of Jerusalem a half century earlier in the time of Hezekiah (2 Kings 18). Conceivably, his attempt to halt the northern march of Neco at Megiddo was to prevent him from assisting Assyria in their struggle with Babylon.

At Carchemish the Egyptians were soundly defeated, securing Babylon's position as the new major power in the ancient world. This also made Judah and King Jehoiakim vassals under the rule of Nebuchadnezzar. Whereas Jehoiakim is given a very brief treatment in the book of Kings (2 Kings 24:1–6), the book of Jeremiah gives him a much more extensive (albeit not very flattering) description. He is portrayed as a political opportunist with a "heart only for your dishonest gain, for shedding innocent blood, and for practicing oppression and violence" (Jer. 22:17). It was during his reign that Jeremiah delivered the second of two temple sermons (Jeremiah 26). Jehoiakim ignored the prophetic writings of Jeremiah (Jeremiah 36) and even cut his scroll into pieces and had it burned, which resulted in a judgment oracle against him—the Lord would punish him, and no son of his would rule in his place (36:29–31). For three years, he was forced to be a tributary to Babylon (2 Kings 24:1), which he would have found particularly repulsive given that Egypt gave him the kingship of Judah. Throughout his reign, therefore, he rebelled against Babylon, despite the warnings of Jeremiah. Ultimately, this led to the Babylonian invasion in 597 BC and his removal from the throne. At the time of Jehoiakim's death, Jeremiah said, no one would mourn for him, and his body would be buried with animals outside the city of Jerusalem (Jer. 22:18–19).

As Babylon prepared to enter Jerusalem in 597 BC, Jehoiachin was enthroned in place of his father Jehoiakim (the book of Kings is silent on precisely how this transition took place; see 2 Kings 24:8–17). His reign lasted only three months. When the Babylonian forces finally entered Jerusalem to impose sanctions upon Jehoiakim for violating the treaty, they found his son Jehoiachin upon the throne instead. According to Jeremiah 22:24–30, his removal from the throne by Babylon represented the final stage of the divine curse upon his father. Nebuchadnezzar replaced him with his uncle Zedekiah (597–586 BC), but despite an oath of allegiance to Babylon, Zedekiah rebelled by seeking out support from Egypt. This led to another insurgence by Babylon in 586 BC, which proved to be decisive in its destructive scope upon Zedekiah, the kingdom of Judah, the city of Jerusalem, and the Solomonic temple. Jeremiah pleaded for Zedekiah to surrender to Babylon peacefully (Jeremiah 36, 37, 38), knowing that this would preserve Judah's survival and avoid unimaginable destruction. For this reason, Jeremiah was seen as a traitor who turned against his people and was thus thrown into prison (Jeremiah 37–38). Because of Jeremiah's apparently pro-Babylonian message, Nebuchadnezzar treated him with great respect. Once he was released from prison, he ended up serving alongside the new governor of Judah, Gedaliah. But when Gedaliah was murdered, Jeremiah and his cohort, Baruch, were taken forcibly by rebels into Egypt, where they spent their final days.

Text of Jeremiah

The growing interest in the book of Jeremiah in academia may be largely due to the recently discovered copies of the book within the Qumran library,[3] although its

---

[3] Six fragmentary copies of the book of Jeremiah have been discovered in Qumran. One was discovered in Cave 2 and the remaining five in Cave 4. See Maurice Baillet, "Textes des grottes 2Q," in *Les "Petites Grottes" de Qumrân: Exploration de la Falaise, les Grottes 2Q,3Q,5Q,6Q,7Q a 10Q, le Rouleau de Cuivre*, ed. Maurice Baillet, Jozef Tadeusz Milik, and

complex compositional history had been a well-documented fact even prior to the Dead Sea Scrolls discovery. Other than the book of Samuel, no other Old Testament book presents as complex a text-critical issue than Jeremiah. It comes down to us in two different versions that are witnessed in the Septuagint and the Masoretic text respectively. Although the majority of the divergences between the two are slight and minor, there are some glaring issues.[4] For example, the Septuagint version is approximately one-eighth shorter than the Masoretic text version. The most outstanding difference is the location of Jeremiah's "oracle to the nations." In the Septuagint it is located immediately following Jeremiah 25:13, where the list of nations appears in a different order than in the Masoretic text. In the Masoretic text, the oracle to the nations is found at the end of the book, in Jeremiah 46–51.

STRUCTURE AND OUTLINE

Unlike some of its prophetic colleagues, the book of Jeremiah exhibits an elusive literary organization. This may be due to its complex compositional history. Among commentators, very few share a similar proposed structure. Thus many resonate with the comments of John Bright when he states that any reader of this book may conclude that he is reading "a hopeless hodgepodge thrown together without any discernible principle of arrangement at all."[5]

On a broad, panoramic perspective, the book does apply some themes, and thus certain general divisions can be discerned. The book displays a broad chronological order in that Jeremiah 1, the call of the prophet, occurs at the beginning of the ministry of Jeremiah, while the latter portions of the book clearly occur toward the close of his prophetic work. From the vantage point of genre, the so-called "confessions of Jeremiah" tend to be concentrated within Jeremiah 11–20,[6] while the prophet's dealings with Judean kings is found largely in Jeremiah 36–39 and the accounts that immediately follow the fall of Jerusalem in Jeremiah 40–44. Furthermore, certain sections maintain literary solidarity. The oracle to the nations in Jeremiah 46–51 is an outstanding example of this, as is the Book of Consolation in Jeremiah 30–33. In fact, Jeremiah 26–44 seems to be a biographical account at various stages in the ministry of Jeremiah, although large portions are dedicated to the final days of Jerusalem and its ultimate destruction.

Given these observations, we will use the following organization in our analysis of the book:[7]

Roland de Vaux, DJD 3 (Oxford: Clarendon, 1962), 62–69; Emanuel Tov, "4QJer[a], 4QJer[b], 4QJer[c], 4QJer[d], 4QJer[e]," in *Qumrân Cave 4 X: The Prophets*, ed. Eugene Ulrich et al., DJD 15 (Oxford: Clarendon, 1997), 145–207. J. Gerald Janzen used the designation "4QJer[b]" for the three fragments later denoted in DJD as 4QJer[b] (4Q71), 4QJer[d] (4Q72a), and 4QJer[e] (4Q72b). *Studies in the Text of Jeremiah*, HSM 6 (Cambridge: Harvard University Press, 1973). In their work on these Jeremiah texts, Emanuel Tov and Esther Eshel realized that these three fragments belonged to several separate manuscripts, and thus Janzen's earlier terminology has been replaced in DJD in favor of this new, updated one.

[4] For a list of the differences between the Septuagint and Masoretic text versions and their relation to the Qumran copies of the book of Jeremiah, see Jack R. Lundbom, "The Book of Jeremiah," in *ABD* 3:707–9.

[5] John Bright, *Jeremiah: A New Translation with Introduction and Commentary* AB 21 (Garden City, NY: Doubleday, 1965), lvi–lvii.

[6] The term *confessions* is not entirely accurate. It would be better to call these *complaints*. Although the list of these "confessions" vary among commentators, the general consensus includes the following: Jer. 11:18–12:6; 15:10–12, 15–21; 17:9–10, 14–18; 18:18–23; 20:7–12, 14–18.

[7] This organization is similar to that of J. A. Thompson, *The Book of Jeremiah*, NICOT (Grand Rapids, MI: Eerdmans, 1980), ix; see also Tremper Longman III, *Jeremiah, Lamentations*, NIBCOT 14 (Peabody, MA: Hendrickson, 2008), 16. Note, though, that I group together several sections that both commentators keep distinct.

Jeremiah 1–25 is the opening section that begins with the prophetic call of Jeremiah (Jeremiah 1) and ends with a summation of this section (Jeremiah 25). According to 1:1, the inauguration of his prophetic ministry is dated to the thirteenth year of the reign of Josiah, approximately 626 BC. The date of the prophetic oracle that comes to Jeremiah in 25:1 is "the fourth year of Jehoiakim the son of Josiah, king of Judah," which is approximately 605 BC. This date is the year in which the Lord instructed Jeremiah to "take a scroll and write on it all the words that I have spoken to you against Israel and Judah and all the nations, from the day I spoke to you, from the days of Josiah until today" (36:2). It is conceivable that the opening twenty-five chapters of the book constituted the original writings of Jeremiah as mentioned in 36:2. Of course, the canonical shape of Jeremiah 1–25 would not reflect this (possibly) original form, as many additions were later included and other editions obviously made. However, I suggest that this opening portion contains a literary spine that was originally a collection of prophetic oracles against Judah.

Included in this section is the prophetic call of Jeremiah (Jeremiah 1), which I would parse out from the rest of the section (Jeremiah 2–25). This call of Jeremiah is significant and worthy of separate treatment since it sets his prophetic agenda and reveals the message that Jeremiah communicated to the people of God during his ministry.

Jeremiah 2–25 is a collection of oracles pronouncing warnings, words of condemnation, and pending destruction from an "army of the north" (1:11–16; 4:6–6:30). The content, not the chronological order, stands out as noteworthy in this section. Jeremiah uses various images (e.g., agriculture, marital infidelity, craftsmanship) and genres to express the sins of Judah against the Lord and to make a strong appeal for repentance, lest they face the destructive wrath of God in the invasion of a foreign power. However, time passes and Jeremiah fails to solicit that response, leaving the curse of exile as the only remaining option, which is exactly what happens. Thus, Jeremiah 2–25 parallels the vision of the "boiling pot" from 1:13–16, which in turn reflects the judgment language in 1:10 of "plucking up and breaking down" and "destroying and overthrowing." Interlaced within this section, however, are extraordinary oracles of hope that anticipate the Book of Consolation in Jeremiah 30–33 (see 3:12–18; 3:19–4:4; 4:27; 12:14–17; 16:14–21; 23:1–8; cf. 1:11–12, 17–19). The final passage in this section (25:15–38) turns the prophet's attention from the people of God to the nations. The oracle to the nations, found in Jeremiah 46–51 in the Masoretic text, was most likely located in the Jeremiah 25 literary vicinity in an earlier version of the book. By ending with this focus upon the "ends of the earth" (25:31), Jeremiah 2–25 concludes with the same cosmic focus as the entire book of Jeremiah in the canonical version.

Jeremiah 26–29 is a biographical description of several personal conflicts in the life of Jeremiah, in particular his dealings with false prophets and the struggles that he faced with them.

Jeremiah 30–33, or what is often referred to as the Book of Consolation, is enclosed by two large biographical narratives (Jeremiah 26–29; 34–45). It provides some of the most majestic pictures of the blessings of God and restored hope. The predominant theme in this section takes its cue from 30:3 where the Lord promises to "restore the fortunes of my people, Israel and Judah." The image found here is a fully restored northern and southern kingdom (33:23–26). The blessings extend even beyond the borders of both Israel and Judah as even the nations receive the Lord's favor (30:18; cf. chaps. 46–51). This section can be further subdivided: whereas Jeremiah 30–31 records a series of blessing oracles of restoration and hope, so Jeremiah 32–33 is composed of two oracles that come to Jeremiah while he is "shut up in the court of the guard" (32:2; 33:1).

Jeremiah 34–45 is a biographical narrative of the ministry of Jeremiah during the final days of the southern kingdom of Judah and the events in Judah after the destruction of the city of Jerusalem in 586 BC. Jeremiah 34–38 focuses on Jeremiah's engagement with the two significant Judean kings in these last days; it is arranged in a chiastic order where Jeremiah 34 describes Jeremiah's dealings with Zedekiah, Jeremiah 35–36 with Jehoiakim, then Jeremiah 37–38 again with Zedekiah. Jeremiah 39–44 recounts the actual collapse of Jerusalem and the events that occurred in the city in the days immediately afterward. During this time Gedaliah ruled as governor (Jeremiah 39), and anti-Babylonian factions rebelled, leading to Gedaliah's assassination (Jeremiah 40) and the escape of these Judean rebels to Egypt (Jeremiah 42–44). Jeremiah 45 ends this section abruptly with a prophecy concerning Baruch.

Jeremiah 46–51 is the aforementioned oracle to the surrounding nations. Jeremiah 52, which is dependent on 2 Kings 24:18–25:30 and Jeremiah 39:1–10, includes Judah in this litany of nations receiving divine blessings and curses.

In summary, the structure of the book of Jeremiah is as follows (see fig. 3): Jeremiah 1 is the prophetic call "to pluck up and to break down, to destroy and to overthrow, to build and to plant" (1:10); this imagery provides a thematic panorama of the entire book. Jeremiah 2–25 is the true prophetic word of Jeremiah that speaks of the "plucking up," "breaking down," "destroying," and "overthrowing" that the Lord will bring against his people. This is contra the false prophets who say that such condemnation and wrath either will not occur or else will be brief (Jeremiah 26–29). Jeremiah 30–33 is the blessed word of hope of the new covenant that will "build" and "plant" the people back in their homeland; the Lord will accomplish this through his messianic King, the "Branch" of David. This is contra the false kings of Judah, specifically Jehoiakim and Zedekiah, whose reigns resulted in Judah's destruction (Jeremiah 34–45). The cosmic scope of the work of God is envisioned in the final section in the oracle to the nations (Jeremiah 46–52).

MESSAGE AND THEOLOGY

It is helpful to begin with a summary description of the content of Jeremiah's true message so that we can see how the individual parts of the book come together to

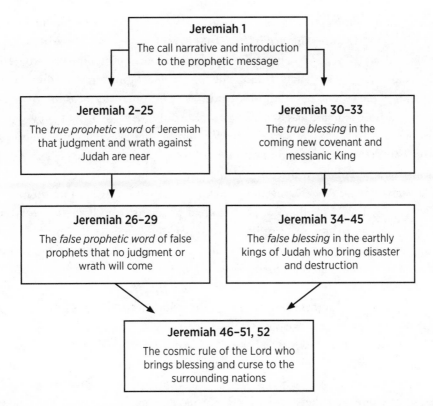

Figure 3

form a prophetic whole. After discussing this initial summary, we will explore other themes in the book in more detail.

Summary of Covenantal Themes

The overarching unity of the book is based largely upon the ways in which Jeremiah administers the various divine covenants that are in play during his days.

Prosecutor of the Mosaic Covenant

A careful reading of Jeremiah, particularly Jeremiah 2–25, shows that one of Jeremiah's prophetic functions was to prosecute the covenant lawsuit of the Lord against his people (see the use of the verb ריב, meaning "to bring a lawsuit," in 2:9; 25:31). There are two parts to this lawsuit. The first is a general call to repentance (3:12, 14, 22; 18:11–12; cf. 3:7; 4:3), which Jeremiah offers to the people of God prior to any invasion by a foreign nation or any forced relocation or exile. If they heed this call and genuinely repent of their sins, they will avoid the pending destruction by this invading army of the north (4:1–2).[8] However, if they do not repent, then their

---

[8] Geerhardus Vos suggests that this period of repentance as a response to the prophetic word describes not only the first stage of Jeremiah's ministry but also the entire prophetic movement from the time of Samuel until the writing prophets in the middle of the eighth century BC. In this sense, he refers to them as "reorganizers" and "reconstructionists." *Biblical Theology: Old and New Testaments* (Edinburgh: Banner of Truth, 1975), 188–89.

destruction is inevitable. In spite of sincere and passionate pleas from Jeremiah, Judah remains adamantly unrepentant (3:10; 5:1–3; 8:5).

This leads to the second stage of the prophet's prosecutorial ministry—to declare the covenant curse of destruction and exile. Nothing can prevent this from happening now; it is unavoidable. Judah may pray, fast, and offer sacrifices in attempts to appease the Lord's anger, but it will be to no avail (14:11–12). Not only will the Lord not listen to the prayers of the people, but he will also ignore the prayers of the prophet (7:16–20). It is within this second part of the prophetic lawsuit that the Lord instructs Jeremiah to discontinue his prayerful intercession on behalf of the people. The unavoidable coming of covenant curse is made even more poignant in 15:1 where the Lord says that even if the great prophets from Israel's history (specifically Moses and Samuel) were to intercede on Judah's behalf, even they would not convince Judah to repent, nor would it deter the Lord from bringing his divine wrath against them. The time for intervening prayer has passed. It failed to bring about the needed response. Only covenant curse remains.

This twofold development (warning and judgment) was not unique to Judah; it was a common legal practice in the ancient world. Whenever suzerains faced a rebellious vassal, they would send their royal messengers to prosecute a covenantal lawsuit. The prosecution of such a lawsuit parallels the two stages in Jeremiah's prophetic ministry as earlier outlined: a stage-A period of warning followed by a stage-B execution of covenant sanctions. At the stage-A level, covenant sanctions can still be avoided if the defiant vassal reacts properly by repenting, reconforming, and recommitting to the terms of the treaty. If not, this leads to stage B of the lawsuit, where the sanctions of the treaty can no longer be avoided—their execution is inevitable, and the vassal can do nothing to hinder or prevent them.

Herald of the New Covenant

Yet the promise of a "restoration of fortunes" (29:14; 30:3, 18) that results from a repentant heart remains. Even in exile, if Judah were to repent, then the Lord would restore them to their homeland and give them the covenantal blessings (4:1–2; 15:19). Such restoration is impossible, however, since the intrinsic fallen nature of the human heart is the underlying cause of Israel and Judah's sins. Idolatry and covenant breaking are only symptoms of this deeper spiritual condition (Gen. 6:5; Ps. 51:1–2; cf. Rom. 3:10–18, 23). What they need is direct, divine intervention to give them a new, transformed heart. Only then can they truly repent of their sins and turn to the Lord by faith. In other words, if their fortunes are going to be reversed, then the Lord must reverse them (Jer. 30:3, 13; 31:23; 32:44; 33:26; cf. 48:47; 49:6, 39), for Judah cannot do this on their own.

This reality leads to the second function of Jeremiah's prophetic role. Not only does he prosecute the two-stage covenantal lawsuit of the Lord, but Jeremiah also heralds the blessings of the Abrahamic covenant—which come to their fullest realization in the new covenant (31:31–34). In this covenantal administration of grace, the repentance that Israel and Judah were unable to manifest in the previous administration (i.e., the Mosaic covenant) is described as a sovereign work of God in their hearts. It is the Lord who provides this new heart of repentance by "heal[ing their] faithlessness" (3:22). What the people need is a "circumcised heart" (4:4; 9:26; cf. 4:14; 5:23; 11:8; 13:10), and that is what the Lord gives them (31:33; 32:39).

The twofold function of Jeremiah's prophetic ministry—prosecuting the Mosaic covenant and heralding the blessings of the new covenant—summarizes not only the work of Jeremiah but also the prophetic enterprise as a whole. These prophet-figures are emissaries who represent the divine Creator-King (2 Chron. 36:15–16; cf. Ex. 4:15; 7:1; Hag. 1:13; Mal. 3:1). As such, they serve two functions. On the one hand, they are plenipotentiary messengers who are called by the Lord to prosecute the Mosaic covenant, specifically the book of Deuteronomy. The history of Israel is a record of one covenantal violation after another. Not only their leaders were guilty of this but also the people. The patience of the Lord persisted throughout their generations, and he sent emissaries with his divine word calling them to repent of their ways lest they suffer the curse of the covenant. However, every covenantal means to bring about their repentance ended in failure, leaving Israel with "no remedy" (2 Chron. 36:16). Although the initial stage of this prosecution was a call to repentance, it ends with the execution of covenant sanctions—exile. As the northern kingdom of Israel was exiled in 722 BC, so also exile became the fate for rebellious Judah in the south. Jeremiah delivered this message with great passion and eagerly sought the repentance of his own people—but failed.

At the same time, Jeremiah and the prophets were not left with merely a word of woe and wrath. They were also given the prestigious duty to be heralds of the blessings of the Abrahamic covenant, which Jeremiah saw coming in the new covenant (Jer. 31:31–34; cf. Deut. 30:1–14; Jer. 32:37–41; Ezek. 11:16–20; 36:24–28).

A Message "From Repentance to Redemption"

The work of Jeremiah Unterman in his monograph *From Repentance to Redemption*[9] is helpful in developing a historical progression of the prophetic ministry of Jeremiah. From the beginning of his prophetic ministry (626–597 BC), Jeremiah administered stage A of the prophetic lawsuit, that is, the call to repentance. Sadly, Judah did not take his message to heart. From 597 to 586 BC, Jeremiah shifted his focus and engaged in stage B of the prophetic lawsuit, that is, informing Judah of the inevitability of the covenant curse sanctions. The final stage belongs in the period of the destruction of the city of Jerusalem and the temple. In the midst of such utter despair, the prophet boldly proclaimed the message of redemption and hope. This hope for restoration was still based upon Judah's repentant heart (Jer. 15:19). However, that repentance was now understood as a covenant blessing (3:19ff; 24:7; 31:22, 32;

---

[9] Jeremiah Unterman, *From Repentance to Redemption: Jeremiah's Thought in Transition*, JSOTSup 54 (Sheffield: JSOT Press, 1987). Unterman, however, does not take into account the covenantal background in Jeremiah's prophecy. The fact that he is able to discern a meaningful historic development without the covenant foundations is remarkable. For another helpful treatment on the themes of repentance and redemption, see Thomas M. Raitt, *A Theology of Exile: Judgment/Deliverance in Jeremiah and Ezekiel* (Philadelphia: Fortress, 1977).

32:37) resulting from the Lord's work of circumcising the heart (Deut. 30:6; Ezek. 11:19; 36:26; cf. Jer. 31:33; 32:39). Through this renewed heart, the people of God would be redeemed and would receive the blessings of the new covenant that would be revealed in the "last days."

The Prophetic Call of Jeremiah

The book of Jeremiah moves from the superscription that provides the historical setting of his ministry (1:1–3) to the actual call of the prophet (1:4–16). This call narrative can be subdivided into the commission of Jeremiah (1:4–10) and the content (message) he is to deliver (1:11–19). It is a highly stylized call as it brings together into a literary unity several significant and prophetically related texts (e.g., Isa. 6:7; Deut. 18:18). This section ends with vivid images showing how the Lord will protect the prophet in the midst of the intense hostility that he will eventually face (1:17–19). Because this prophetic call introduces several themes that permeate the book, its importance cannot be overstated.

The Commissioning of Jeremiah (Jer. 1:4–10)

The call of Jeremiah is similar to the prophetic call of Isaiah and Ezekiel. This is significant since the formation of a true prophet of the Lord requires a properly and divinely initiated call. According to Deuteronomy 18:15–22 (to which Jeremiah's call narrative repeatedly alludes), specifically Deuteronomy 18:15, 18, it is the Lord who will "raise up a prophet" from among the Israelites. In other words, one cannot presume to be a prophet or declare oneself a prophet; only the Lord can form a prophet. Therefore, this prophetic call is a necessary prerequisite to being a true prophet of the Lord. According to Meredith G. Kline, this divine call is the first of three components needed in the formation of a prophet.[10]

The second essential component is an entrance into the heavenly council (Isa. 6:1–7; Ezekiel 1; cf. Exodus 3–4; 24; Ps. 82:1; Revelation 4–5); although distinct from the first, this second component would hardly have been distinguishable in the experience of the prospective prophet. Jeremiah specifically states that this is a necessary requirement for a true prophet and says its absence is a mark of the false prophets of his day. Jeremiah 23:18 says concerning those false prophets, "For who among them has stood in the council of the LORD to see and to hear his word, or who has paid attention to his word and listened?" In other words, Jeremiah says that these prophets lack this experience of standing within the angelic "council of the LORD." The true prophet of the Lord brings the true word of the Lord, and it is in the divine assembly that he receives this divine word. Therefore, anyone who has not entered into this council cannot properly communicate the word of God; rather, he speaks his own words—he speaks presumptuously (Deut. 18:21–22). Although the Old Testament does not record every true prophet entering into the heavenly

---

[10] Meredith G. Kline, *Images of the Spirit* (Eugene, OR: Wipf and Stock, 1999), 57–59.

council, Jeremiah 23:18 provides a universal negative that clearly implies that every true prophet must have this experience.

The third and final component in the formation of a true prophet is a special endowment of the Spirit. Since prophets communicate the divine message of the Lord, their words are inspired by the Spirit (see Neh. 9:30; Zech. 7:12; 2 Pet. 1:21; cf. Num. 11:29–30; Judg. 6:34; 1 Chron. 12:18–19; 2 Chron. 24:20; Hos. 9:7).

The prophetic call for Jeremiah begins with his commission in Jeremiah 1:4–10. This is a beautiful poetic description of the care with which the Lord "formed" Jeremiah even in the womb for the purpose of being his appointed messenger to his people. Thus Jeremiah was "consecrated" to the Lord and "appointed . . . a prophet to the nations" (1:5). Yet he reacted to this call with timidity and uncertainty, brought on by two weaknesses he perceived within himself: his inability to speak and his youth (1:6). This is very reminiscent of the call narrative of Moses, the paradigm prophet, in Exodus 3–4, where he made similar excuses. In light of the rediscovery of the Mosaic law code in the early stage of Jeremiah's ministry, it seems that Jeremiah is being portrayed as the renewed Moses carrying forth the Deuteronomic law. This is why the call narrative alludes so heavily to Deuteronomy 18:15–22 and also why the book of Jeremiah has a strong affinity with the book of Deuteronomy—a Deuteronomic consciousness.

The Lord responds chiastically to Jeremiah. Regarding his youth (Jer. 1:6b), the Lord encourages him to fulfill his prophetic task and promises that his divine presence will be with him (1:7–8). Regarding his inability to speak (1:6a), the Lord responds by alluding to two powerful passages (1:9). The first is Isaiah 6. The Lord stretches out and touches the lips of Jeremiah—an act evocative of Isaiah 6:7, where the prophet Isaiah's lips were consecrated by an angelic figure touching them with burning coals. Although Jeremiah's experience differed in that the Lord (not an angel) touched his lips, the two encounters are clearly related to each other. The second passage alluded to is Deuteronomy 18:18, where the Lord says, "I will put my words in his [the prophet's] mouth." This allusion shows the reader that the prophetic ministry of Jeremiah is in the same tradition not only of Isaiah but also of Moses. In fact, the phrase in question in Jeremiah 1:9 is identical to Deuteronomy 18:18 (נָתַתִּי דְבָרַי בְּפִיךָ). Deuteronomy 18:18 demonstrates that the prophets of Israel do not speak their own opinions or words but rather the very words of God, and that is the very understanding of the prophetic word that is placed in the "mouth" of Jeremiah. The success of a prophet's ministry, therefore, depends not on his inherent abilities, strength, or eloquence but on his knowing the presence of the Lord and clearly articulating his divine word. Thus the Lord's response provides the proper supernatural perspective for Jeremiah as he begins what will be a very difficult prophetic task.

The goal of Jeremiah's ministry is summarized in Jeremiah 1:10 with the use of four verbs of judgment ("uproot," "tear down," "destroy," "overthrow") and two of blessing ("build," "plant"). The blessing image of "building" culminates the imagery of the destruction and rebuilding of the destroyed temple and city of God, while the "planting" imagery has strong messianic associations for Jeremiah. Thus in 23:5–6 and 33:15, Jeremiah prophesies a time after the exile (in the new covenant era) when the Lord will raise up a "righteous Branch." The word for "Branch" is צֶמַח. The verbal form of this noun occurs in 2 Samuel 23:5, which describes the activity of the messianic Son of David as "prospering" (יַצְמִיחַ, literally "branching out") the will of the Lord. The word צֶמַח is prevalent in other prophetic books with the same messianic significance (see especially Zech. 3:8; 6:12, which allude to Jer. 23:5; see also Isa. 4:2; 11:1; Ezek. 17:22–24). These two themes of the restored temple/city and the messianic royal line play a vital role in the kingdom theology of the holy Scriptures. Jeremiah's commission is given a cosmic dimension since the recipients of his word are not only the immediate people of Judah but also the nations (Jer. 1:5; cf. Jeremiah 46–51). Jeremiah 1:10 explicitly states that the Lord has set Jeremiah up to be "over nations and over kingdoms." It is clear, therefore, that the Lord's work of "tearing down" and "planting" extends beyond the people of Judah to include the nations. The reign of this messianic "Branch" will extend beyond his immediate ethnic people and will cover the nations.

The Content of Jeremiah's Message (1:11–19)

After the commissioning of Jeremiah, the Lord provides two visual signs that illustrate the prophetic message he is to deliver (1:11–16). The first is an almond branch (1:11–12). There is a similarity between the Hebrew words for "almond tree" (שָׁקֵד) and for the "watching" (שֹׁקֵד) of the Lord over his word. This wordplay is meant to remind Jeremiah and his audience that the oracular word of God is being "watched" by the Lord himself and that he will be the One who will ensure its fulfillment. As true as this is, one must ask, what is the "word" that he is watching over? The majority of commentators take this sign as referring only to the *general* notion that God has guaranteed that he will fulfill his word. This interpretation seems oddly tautologous. The superscription (1:1–3) had already stated that these "words of Jeremiah" are the "word of the Lord." Since the word of the Lord can never go unfulfilled—indeed, only the words of false prophets ever do—why would this need to be restated?[11] I suggest an alternative interpretation. The arboreal nature of this first sign parallels the "planting" description mentioned earlier in 1:10. This connection suggests that the word that God assures will come about is the anticipation of the coming "Branch" of David and his glorious kingdom, where the annual blooming of this almond tree would regularly remind the people of this fact. Instead of a general description of the reliability of prophecy, this first sign parallels the positive content of Jeremiah's message, which is guaranteed to be fulfilled because God is overseeing this promise.[12]

---

[11] See William L. Holladay, *Jeremiah*, Hermeneia: A Critical and Historical Commentary on the Bible (Philadelphia: Fortress, 1986), 1:38, who asks the same question.

[12] See Derek Kidner, *The Message of Jeremiah: Against Wind and Tide*, The Bible Speaks Today (Downers Grove, IL: InterVarsity Press, 1987), 27, where he refers to the second sign of the boiling pot as a word of "judgment," but adds, "here is hope." See also Roland K. Harrison, *Jeremiah and Lamentations: An Introduction and Commentary*, TOTC 21 (Downers Grove, IL: InterVarsity Press, 1973), 55, where he says, "this first vision has a positive ring to it, having as its subject an almond rod, the first tree to bud in spring."

Whereas the first sign is meant to show the reliability of the prophetic word (specifically the coming of the messianic Branch), so the second sign illustrates the second message that Jeremiah was called to deliver (1:13–16). This sign is a boiling pot that is facing away from the north, which is interpreted as the destruction of God's idolatrous people by northern invaders (1:16). Just as this pot is filled with boiling water that is overflowing, so also disaster from the north will flood over the land of Judah to devastate the city of Jerusalem and its surrounding areas (1:15). This image is intended to warn God's people that the judgment of God is indeed coming against them and that their identity as the covenant people will not exempt them from it. Later, Jeremiah identifies this invading army as the kingdom of Babylon under the reign of Nebuchadnezzar (Jer. 20:4–6).

The bipartite function of Jeremiah's prophetic ministry—articulated earlier as (1) prosecuting the lawsuit of the Lord, and (2) heralding the coming of the new covenant (see "Prosecutor of the Mosaic Covenant" on p. 283 and "Herald of the New Covenant" on p. 284)—parallels the two concrete images of the almond tree and the boiling pot. As the former represents the coming blessings of the new covenant, so the latter represents the judgment of God. This message of judgment and promise is summarized not only in the two signs of 1:11–16 but also in the twofold purpose statement of the prophetic task in 1:10, "to pluck up and to break down, to destroy and to overthrow" and "to build and to plant."

The Judgment from the North

The image of an invading foreign power from the north is prominent throughout the prophecy of Jeremiah (3:18; 6:22; 10:22; 16:15; 23:8; 31:8). The most outstanding example of this image is found in 4:5–6:30, which describes at length the coming "boiling pot" (1:15–16) from the north that will destroy Judah unless they repent of their sins. Jeremiah likens Judah's sin to a stallion neighing for his neighbor's wife (5:8). They have become rebellious and hard of heart. Even the kings, who are to lead and teach the people the ways of the Lord (5:26–27; cf. Deut. 17:18–20), are as corrupt and evil as the people; they have spurned their royal duties as caregivers to the needy in order to seek their own selfish gains and vainglory (Jer. 5:28). Not a single man does justice or seeks truth (5:1; cf. Genesis 18–19). They have forsaken the Lord and sworn allegiance to "no gods" (Jer. 5:7; cf. Deut. 32:21). Jeremiah calls for the nation to repent (Jer. 4:8; 6:26; cf. 4:14), but "their ears are uncircumcised, they cannot listen; behold, the word of the LORD is to them an object of scorn; they take no pleasure in it" (6:10b).[13] In fact, they are determined to not repent (5:3). Thus the Lord is filled with wrath and ready to call upon the armies of the north (6:22).

Jeremiah vividly describes this destructive hoard in this passage: they are devouring beasts (4:7; 5:6), a mighty military machine with an intimidating inventory of weapons of war (5:16), cruel without mercy. Indeed, "the sound of them is like the

---

[13] The imagery of "uncircumcised" ears alludes to Deut. 30:6, where the Lord says he will "circumcise" the heart. The lack of circumcision in this passage suggests that Judah's inability to heed Jeremiah's call to repentance is due to a lack of divine work within them.

roaring sea" (6:23). The Lord himself calls this foreign army of chaos against his own people. In 4:5 it is the Lord who cries out for the trumpet blast to signal the foreign invaders to begin their assault. Similarly, 4:13 states, "he comes up like clouds; his chariots like the whirlwind," and Tremper Longman correctly identifies the "he" as referring not to Babylon or any foreign king or military general but to the Lord arising as a chariot rider to bring judgment upon his people.[14] Again, though the epithet "rider of the clouds" is commonly applied to Baal in Ugaritic texts,[15] in this case it refers to the true Rider of the clouds, the Lord God.[16] Later in 20:11, the Lord is even called a גִּבּוֹר עָרִיץ, "dread warrior."[17] Jeremiah 25:9 is most compelling since the Lord engages in חֵרֶם warfare against his own people Judah (cf. Ex. 32:25–29; Deut. 13:15; Isa. 43:28; 63:7–14; Jer. 21:5). To portray the Lord as Judge executing the curse-sanctions of the covenant, the prophet uses this theme of the Lord as a divine Warrior leading this army from the north in combat against his own chosen people.

All these images are significant for Judah. Judah should not interpret their pending demise as the victory and supremacy of Marduk, the high god of Babylon, over against Yahweh, the God of Judah. Rather, their agony is a direct result of their covenantal infidelity, and the Lord is exercising his sovereign authority over all the world to utilize a pagan nation like Babylon (and thus their lesser deity) to fulfill his divine will and purpose. He is that powerful!

The Temple Sermon

Jeremiah delivers this sermon at the "gate of the LORD's house" (Jer. 7:2) by divine command to issue the following message to the people: *destruction is imminent and having the temple in your midst will not save you.* The people respond by threatening Jeremiah's life, forcibly taking him to court, and demanding his execution (26:7–11; cf. Deut. 22:19). The sermon appears in two locations, Jeremiah 7:1–8:3 and 26:1–24, and though the date of this sermon is unknown, the near duplicate found in 26:1–24 is dated "at the beginning of the reign of Jehoiakim" (26:1). Whether these two accounts record two proclamations of a similar message or one event told from two different perspectives cannot be determined with total confidence. What is clear, however, is that the presence of an immediate threat to the people causes them to turn to the temple for refuge from foreign assault.

One can nearly feel the banging of Babylon upon the doorsteps of Judah as the people turn to the temple and presume that this will protect them from any far-off invaders, simply because it is "the temple of the LORD, the temple of the LORD, the temple of the LORD" (7:4). Jeremiah warns them of this false comfort. They cannot

---

[14] See Longman, *Jeremiah, Lamentations*, 48–49. See also Tremper Longman III and Daniel G. Reid, *God Is a Warrior*, SOTBT (Grand Rapids, MI: Zondervan, 1995), 48–60, where they describe the Lord at war against "unfaithful Israel."
[15] See *CTA* 3.4.48, "What enemy rises against Baal / foe against the Rider of the Clouds"; cf. *CTA* 2.4.8; 2.4.29; 3.3.32–36; 6.3.6–7.
[16] Deuteronomy 33:26 says that Yahweh "rides through the heavens to your help, through the skies in his majesty." Psalm 104:3 states that God "makes the clouds his chariot" and "rides on the wings of the wind." See also Dan. 7:13–14, where the "one like a son of man" comes to the Ancient of Days "with the clouds of heaven." To this divine figure is "glory," "an everlasting dominion, which shall not pass away," and a kingdom that "shall not be destroyed."
[17] Cf. Isa. 9:6 (Masoretic text 9:5), where the expected messiah is given a litany of royal epithets, one being אֵל גִּבּוֹר, literally, "God a warrior."

engage in religious formalism while committing atrocities against the Lord and expect no consequences. They have neglected proper care for sojourners and orphans; they have even shed innocent blood (7:6). Worse yet, idolatry! In other words, Jeremiah condemns those who justify a life of debauchery and selfish hedonism while appearing with an outward form of godliness. In this case, they have drawn false comfort in thinking that the Lord will not destroy his own holy city of Jerusalem because it is the location of his own temple. Therefore, they turn to it not as a fortress of security but rather as a place of localized divine favor. To be near this temple is to be safe because the Lord will not permit any harm to come to his own home—or so they think.

Such presumptions, while false, are understandable. Jeremiah 7:10 states that the temple bears the name of the Lord. The memory of their own distant history could also lead to this false sense of complacency. Recall that Hezekiah faced invaders from Assyria nearly a century earlier in Sennacherib and his armies to the northern borders of Judah (2 Kings 18–19). Yet the Lord saved Judah that day by sending his angel, who struck down over 185,000 Assyrians, thus forcing Sennacherib to retreat back to Nineveh. The Lord did not spare Judah's northern sister of Israel (2 Kings 17; 18:9–10), but he did save Judah. Why? Perhaps it was because the true house of the Lord—the temple—was in Jerusalem and not in Samaria. The answer may not have been completely clear to the Judeans of Jeremiah's day. Regardless, they knew that the Lord saved them in the days of Hezekiah. Therefore, it would have been reasonable for them to think that the Lord would do the same in the days of Jehoiakim since it was the same temple. But God tells them that possession of this temple will not save them. As he was willing to destroy his sanctuary in Shiloh during the priestly ministry of Eli, so he will not hesitate to do the same here. After all, it is just a house, but his spiritual presence is much more profound and will be realized in the coming new covenant.

At that time, Judah had abused the worship in the temple and misunderstood its cultic significance. According to 7:21–29, the Lord tells them that their sacrifices have become meaningless since they use them to rationalize their sins. God wanted them to utilize the sacrificial system in the case of disobedience but not to justify lawlessness (7:22–23). They had forgotten that there is a virtue more important to the Lord than sacrifice—obedience. They believed that they could engage in the most heinous of immoral activities as long as they could offer sacrifices to atone for that sin. To partake in such cultic rituals, even something as theologically rich and profound like the sacrifices, with an antinomian heart was to empty that ritual of its true meaning.

Conflict with False Prophets

Jeremiah 23:9–24:10 and Jeremiah 26–29 describe the conflict between this true prophet and the false prophets of Israel. Apparently, these false messengers claim to have visions from the Lord, yet these are lies (23:25b)—they have acted presumptuously (Deut. 18:20). In reality, they lack the mark of a true prophet, namely entrance into the heavenly council of God (Jer. 23:18, 22). Therefore, they give a false message of peace when in reality the "storm of the Lord," his "wrath," and "a whirling tempest" (23:19) are what will come. The logic of these false teachers is that the Lord would dare not destroy his own house; Jeremiah counters this false hope in his temple sermon in Jeremiah 7 and 26 (see "The Temple Sermon" on p. 290). Thus this false message leads the people astray from true worship (23:32). For this reason, these false prophets will eat bitter food and drink poisoned water (cf. 9:15), and Judah is told not to listen to or obey them (23:16).

Two specific false prophets stand out as causing particular havoc to Jeremiah—Hananiah in Jeremiah 27–28 and Shemaiah in Jeremiah 29. Whereas the conflict between Jeremiah and Hananiah is presented as a narrative, his conflict with Shemaiah is described through an exchanging of personal letters between Jeremiah in Jerusalem and Shemaiah in Babylon. Deuteronomy warns of the rise of such false prophets, and Jeremiah 26–29 must be read in light of those warnings (Deut. 13:1–5; 18:20–22).

Several factors become clear within this section: (1) the message of these false prophets is diametrically opposed to that of Jeremiah; (2) the people are enamored with the positive optimism of the false prophetic word that depicts Jeremiah's words as increasingly negative by comparison; and (3) Jeremiah suffers greatly in body and spirit not only at the hands of the people but also at the hands of these false teachers.

The modern era of the church shares a disturbing similarity to the ministry of Jeremiah—both reject the call to repentance by divinely appointed preachers in favor of a false message of optimism that denies divine wrath. Yet what choice did Jeremiah have? To withhold this message would have provided comfort in his earthly life yet torment unto his soul (Jer. 20:9), since it would have resulted in the destruction of his beloved people. Although they eventually rejected his message with prejudice, the minimal comfort for Jeremiah was that they, at the very least, heard his message of repentance. Otherwise, their exile would have been based on their forgetfulness and ignorance and on his cowardice. The good news that these ancient Judeans needed was precisely a call to repentance. They did not want it, nor did they appreciate it. Still, they needed it desperately. If indeed it is true that the "feet of those who bring good news" is "beautiful" (Isa. 52:7; Rom. 10:15; cf. Nah. 1:15), it is only perceived as such after an initial period of intense loathing and apparent revulsion. This message of the book of Jeremiah, therefore, is a reminder of the great necessity of the ministerial call to proclaim the gospel message and the sober reality of the consequences that may result from it.

Conflict with False Kings

The kingship of Josiah was the last positive influence on the kingdom of Judah. His successors were dysfunctional failures, and their combined kingships not only undid the work of reforms inaugurated by Josiah but also aggravated the Lord's wrath, accelerated the looming exile, and brought on the final days of the southern monarchy. Jeremiah's conflict with these ungodly kings is recorded in two different sections:

Jeremiah 21:1–23:8 and Jeremiah 34–44. The first section is a series of prophetic oracles against these post-Josianic kings. It is organized chiastically as follows:

a Zedekiah—"The LORD is [our] righteousness" (21:1–14)
  b Unnamed king (22:1–9)
    c Shallum (Jehoahaz) (22:10–12)
      d Jehoiakim (22:13–23)
    c' Coniah (Jehoiachin) (22:24–30)
  b' Unnamed "shepherd" (23:1–2)
a' "Branch"—"The LORD is our righteousness" (23:3–8)

The a-sections counter the negative kingship of Zedekiah (whose name means "The LORD is [our] righteousness") with the picture of the eschatological king, the messianic "Branch of David," whose name is "The LORD is our righteousness" (23:6). The b-sections parallel two unnamed Judean kings (22:1–9; 23:1–2), whose failures to attend to the needs of their people resulted in their rejection. The c-sections describe two ungodly kings (22:10–12; 22:24–30), each of whom are referred to by a different name than what is found in the royal annals (Shallum for Jehoahaz and Coniah for Jehoiachin). The center section recounts the demoralizing kingship of Jehoiakim (22:13–23).

Jeremiah 34–44 is a biographical narrative that describes the failed monarchies of the kings of Judah and their disastrous impact upon both the nation and the prophet. Whereas Jeremiah 34 is concerned with the reign of Zedekiah, so Jeremiah 35–36 is concerned with the reign of his predecessor Jehoiakim. Jeremiah 37–38 jumps ahead again to the days of Zedekiah and Nebuchadnezzar's raid on the city of Jerusalem, during which Jeremiah was falsely imprisoned. Finally, Jeremiah 39–44 records the fall of the city and the subsequent events that immediately follow. All these accounts contrast with the preceding section, the Book of Consolation (Jeremiah 30–33; see the following section), which prominently describes the rise of the messianic "Branch" of David, who will rule justly, save the people of God, and provide a secure dwelling (33:15–16). By following this glorious portrayal of the ideal son of David, the failures of the Judean kings stand out even more prominently.

The Book of Consolation

The academic community has titled Jeremiah 30–33 the Book of Consolation. This is due to the subject matter of the "book" that Jeremiah was instructed to write in 30:2. With the exception of a few passages (see 1:11–12, 17–19; 3:12–18; 3:19–4:4; 4:27; 12:14–17; 16:14–21; 23:1–8), the bulk of the first half of the book of Jeremiah reiterates the threat of exile and citywide destruction caused by the people's rebellion. The prophetic images portrayed in the Book of Consolation, however, are strikingly different. In fact, they are some of the richest and most remarkable in all the Old Testament. Given the physical, emotional, political, and theological trauma that Judah had experienced during the Babylonian siege upon the blessed city and temple of God, they needed a powerful message of hope to outweigh their sense of loss and agony. As dire as those curses of the covenant were upon the people, they do not outshine the radiance and majesty of the new covenant blessings (31:31–34) found within these chapters. This "book" may even rival the magnificence of the more well-known prophecies in Isaiah 40–66. Where Isaiah speaks of a suffering servant, Jeremiah alludes to the rise of the triumphant messianic "Branch" (Jer. 33:15; cf. 23:5). Amazingly, the recipients of these oracles are "my people, Israel and Judah" (30:3, 4; 31:27, 31; 33:7, 14; cf. 32:30, 32). The highly anticipated restoration, therefore, includes not merely the southern kingdom but also her longtime rebellious sister (cf. 3:6–18). This newly united Israel receives the blessings of the new covenant, which will also be the time when a new messianic son of David will be seated upon the throne. Although the immediate fulfillment of these new covenant promises were typologically fulfilled in the restoration at 538 BC, the true realization of these blessings will not take place until the "last days" (30:24; Heb. 1:2; cf. Deut. 4:30; Acts 2:17; 1 John 2:18) with the coming of the true messianic Branch, the Lord Jesus Christ. Along with his eternal kingship will come the greater land promises of the new heavens and new earth (Isa. 65:17; 66:22; 2 Pet. 3:13; Rev. 21:1) with a greater city "whose designer and builder is God" (Heb. 11:10; cf. Jer. 30:18).

Perhaps the most intriguing aspect of the Book of Consolation is its brevity—it only covers four chapters, a mere eight percent of the entire book of Jeremiah. This brevity contrasts with Jeremiah 2–26, which hammers away at the flinty hearts of the stiff-necked, unrepentant people for nearly twenty-five chapters, and with Jeremiah 34–45, which contributes an additional twelve chapters describing the failings of the post-Josianic kings with the same stubborn heart. And these sections do not even account for the "tearing down" of the nations in Jeremiah 46–52, seven more chapters. The content within the Book of Consolation mirrors the repetitive nature of the previous twenty-nine and succeeding nineteen chapters. Only, what recurs is wave after wave of one oracle after another portraying the overwhelming grace of God as articulated in the promises of the new covenant and the coming Messiah. It is extraordinary to consider that the Lord needed only four chapters to accomplish what forty-eight chapters could not do, namely to bring about a repentant heart unto life. In spite of any quantitative, literary imbalance, the quality found within these four chapters outweighs, outshines, and outmagnifies the other forty-eight and thus tips the prophetic pendulum toward the side of glory.

New Covenant Promise

Arguably, the book of Jeremiah is most famous for its prophecy of the promise of a new covenant order in 31:31–34. It is cited in the New Testament on several occasions (Heb. 8:8–12; 9:15; 12:24; cf. Luke 22:20; 1 Cor. 11:25; 2 Cor. 3:6). Hebrews 8:8–12 is particularly helpful since it sees the new covenant as superior to the old with Jesus as the superior High Priest from a superior priestly order (i.e., Melchizedek; cf. Ps. 110:4; Heb. 7:1–28). Thus the new covenant era that is so highly anticipated is the era of the ministry of the Spirit-filled church. The references to the "house of

Israel" and the "house of Judah" in Jeremiah 31:27, 31, 33 (cf. 30:3–4) are examples of prophetic idiom, where old covenant terms are used to express a new covenant reality—in this case, the church.

Jeremiah contrasts the new covenant with the covenant made with the forefathers at Sinai. The "old covenant" is good but unstable since its effectiveness depends on Israel's conformity to it (31:32).[18] This new covenant will not differ in content since the laws are very much the same between the old and the new. Thus the new covenant is superior not in that it is absent of law and thus justifies a quasi-antinomian lifestyle. It has the same moral laws as the old. What differs is the transformation within the people so that they can now conform to the good law of the Lord. This is a significant point. If the fragility of the Mosaic covenant is caused by its dependence upon the obedience of a stonehearted people, then what good is this glorious restoration if they are returning to that same covenantal arrangement? If it failed once, it will fail again because the essential issue has not been addressed. A new covenant is needed; the *new covenant* is needed. The superiority of the new covenant is that it addresses the issues that the old covenant order did not, could not, nor was intended to.

The new covenant varies from the old on three grounds (31:33–34). First, it is written not on tablets of stone but on the hearts of the people; thus, they will hold to the law of God (31:33). This promise is an allusion to Deuteronomy 30:6 and the work of the Lord in "circumcising the heart." Jeremiah captures the same theological reality of heart transformation with the use of a different image. Instead of a heart "circumcised," he sees a heart *inscribed*. Since the law of God is now internalized within the individual believer and no longer external upon hardened stone, it is "near you" (Deut. 30:14a). More than that, "it is in your mouth and in your heart"; the purpose of this internalization is "so that you can do it" (Deut. 30:14b). Thus, in the new covenant, the commandment is "not too hard for you, neither is it far off" (Deut. 30:11). There is no need to go to heaven or across the depths to retrieve the power to conform to this command, for the messianic "Branch" has come down to us and has risen from the grave and has thus become the end of the law (Rom. 10:4, 6–7; cf. Deut. 30:11–13).

The previous covenantal order was a good gift because from it came a knowledge of sin (Rom. 3:20; Gal. 3:19). However, what Israel needed was a new heart that can "cause you to walk in my statutes and be careful to obey my rules" (Ezek. 36:27; cf. Deut. 4:30). The Mosaic code could not do this. Therefore, Israel and Judah rebelled and were exiled. The call to obedience remains in the new covenant, but that obedience is now a blessing of the covenant that the believer receives. Notice that the Lord is the only agent throughout this passage: "I will make a new covenant" (Jer. 31:31); "I will put my laws in their hearts"; "I will write it" (31:33). This divinely initiated transformation of the heart marks the substantial difference between the two covenantal administrations. The apostle Paul summarizes the superiority of

---

[18] Hebrews 8 provides an inspired commentary on the relation between the old and new covenant. Notice that in 8:8, the author of the book of Hebrews says that God finds fault in "them," referring to the members of the old covenant community; he does not say that God found fault in "it" (i.e., the old covenant).

this internalization of the law in Romans 8:3–4, "For God has done what the law, weakened by the flesh, could not do. By sending his own Son in the likeness of sinful flesh and for sin, he condemned sin in the flesh, in order that the righteous requirement of the law might be fulfilled in us, who walk not according to the flesh but according to the Spirit."

Second, they will no longer need a teacher since they will all, from the least to the greatest, know the Lord (Jer. 31:34a). This blessing logically flows from the first. If the people have the law of the Lord within them so that they can conform to it, they will have a greater understanding of the Lord since the law is a reflection of his moral character. The external locale of the old covenant code prevented the people from truly "knowing the Lord"—that is, coming to a deep, covenantal, intimate understanding of who he is as their Lord and Redeemer. Again, the law was not intended to do this. In the new covenant context, however, the Lord is the One who transforms the heart so that the people now desire to "know the Lord"—that is, to love him and thus desire to obey his holy commandments. According to Deuteronomy 6:4–10, the task before heads of households was to teach such obedience to the next generation. The failure to do this is a tragic testimony in the Former Prophets (see Judg. 2:9–11; 1 Sam. 3:13; 8:3). Such a task was daunting and, in retrospect, impossible within the context of that covenantal setting. The beauty of the new covenant is that the Lord has already renewed the hearts of his people, and thus they no longer need to be taught. God's people, from the least to the greatest, have that knowledge of him as their Savior.

The third and final blessing that makes the new covenant different from the old is the promise that the Lord "will forgive their iniquity" and "remember their sin no more" (31:34b). The Lord can only do so because of the once-for-all sacrifice of the messianic Priest-King. From the perspective of those in exile, these are extraordinary words of blessing and hope. They had been bombarded with the preaching of Jeremiah for years that showed them their sinful ways, their guilt in violating the covenant, their rejection of the one and only living God for idols, which are no gods at all. While in exile, suffering the consequences of their sins, they receive a word that these sins will be forgiven by faith in the Lord. It is hard to overemphasize the ecstasy of joy this prophecy would have had on its ancient audience. It has the same effect upon those in our day as well.

The "Messianic" Branch

The pinnacle of all new covenant blessings is found in Jeremiah 33:14–18. The reason for the citywide restoration and heart transformation of the people is because in the days of the new covenant, God will fulfill his promise to the house of Israel and the house of Judah by raising up the righteous "Branch" of David (Isa. 11:1; Zech. 3:8; 6:12).[19] This arboreal image was already mentioned in Jeremiah 23:5–6 and 30:9, 21. Unlike the previous kings of Israel and Judah, whose royal annals record their inability to fulfill their duties as lord protectorates and devotees of Yahweh (Deut. 17:14–20),

---

[19] See Isa. 4:2; 6:13, where the remnant is called "the branch."

this "Branch" will judge righteously and save Jerusalem. As we saw earlier in Jeremiah 23:5–6, his name is "The LORD is our righteousness," which is a pun on the name of the last king of Judah, Zedekiah, whose name also means "The LORD is [our] righteousness" (33:16). Interestingly, this oracle includes the promise of a perpetual priesthood as well (33:21b).[20] The mentioning of both an eternal kingship and priesthood highly suggests that this royal "Branch" will also serve as a priest—a Priest-King union in one figure.

It is helpful to compile the prophetic data from Jeremiah 30–33 and place them in their proper place in the panorama of the history of redemption (see fig. 4 [p. 298]). At the time this oracle was given to the people, the northern kingdom had been in exile for well over a century, and the southern kingdom was either in or near exile. Yet the prophetic material in this section assures the people that a time is coming when the Lord will restore both Israel in the north and Judah in the south to their homeland and rebuild their desolated capital. The covenantal administration that governs life in this new era will not be the same as the old, which was breakable. Rather, in this new covenant, the Lord will transform their hearts so that they will repent and obey the Lord's commands. This is not an era of anarchy; a king will be given, but not any normal king. The history of Israel's monarchies testifies to their weakness and failures, so much that they led the people farther away from the Lord and added to their troubles. But in this new covenant era, the Lord will bring forth an ideal king, the messianic "Branch" who will provide life and salvation. This "Branch" will be none other than the Lord himself who "is our righteousness" (33:15).

Although the immediate expectation for the readers of this prophecy is to see its fulfillment in a postexilic setting (i.e., the era of Ezra, Nehemiah, Zerubbabel, and the postexilic prophets Haggai, Zechariah, and Malachi), that is not the case. At least, that restoration is not the fullest reality of the promises portrayed in Jeremiah 30–33. It is only typological of a grander level of fulfillment that we see in the days of Jesus of Nazareth, who is the true Priest-King, the true Branch. The coming of Christ marks the "latter days" (30:24) that the Book of Consolation mentions as the historical-redemptive setting of these covenantal fulfillments.

The kingdom that this Messiah brings comes in two stages (see fig. 4 [p. 298]), the first marked by his incarnation, his expiatory and propitiatory death on the cross, and his resurrection-ascension-coronation unto glory. His redemptive work during his earthly ministry provides the foundation upon which the hearts of God's people can be "circumcised" (Deut. 30:6) and thus be given "one heart and one way" (Jer. 32:39). His redemptive work is also the basis upon which he is declared righteous (1 Tim. 3:16). This in turn is the grounds upon which believers are also declared "righteous" (cf. Rom. 3:21–22; 5:12–19; Phil. 3:9). Indeed, "the LORD *is* our righteousness" (Jer. 23:5–6; 33:15). Thus the kingdom that he brings at this preliminary stage is present but internalized within the hearts of God's people. However, at his return, the second stage, his kingdom will be revealed externally in consummated and visual glory, and the Promised Land of life and abundance—the new heavens and

---

[20] Numbers 25:13 speaks of such a covenant.

new earth (Isa. 65:17; 66:22; 2 Pet. 3:13; Revelation 21–22; cf. Rom. 4:13; 1 Pet. 1:4–5) along with the new city of Jerusalem (31:38–40)—will now be given as an "imperishable, undefiled, and unfading" inheritance (1 Pet. 1:4) to his blessed people.

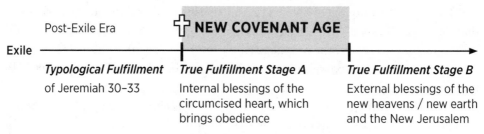

Figure 4

Oracle to the Nations

The finale to the book of Jeremiah brings the prophetic word to the foreign nations surrounding Judah, including oracles against Egypt (46:1–28), the Philistines (47:1–7), Moab (48:1–47), Ammon (49:1–6), Edom (49:7–22), Damascus (49:23–27), Kedar and Hazor (49:28–33), Elam (49:34–39), and Babylon (50:1–51:64). The final oracle to the nations is against Judah (52:1–34).

Like Judah, the nations have also angered the Lord in their prideful acts of injustice and immorality. Thus God will judge them also. However, the descriptions of judgment against the nations were already applied to Judah throughout the book. For example, these foreign nations are described as being "exiled" from their native lands (46:19, 26 [Egypt]; 48:9 [Moab]; 49:3 [Ammon]; 49:19–21 [Edom]; cf. 13:19 [Judah]). As with Judah, Nebuchadnezzar is the primary agent whom the Lord uses to desolate and deport the nations (46:2 [Egypt]; 49:28 [Kedar and Hazor]; 49:36 [Elam];[21] cf. 21:2 [Judah]). The pain connected with the destruction of their homes is equivalent to "a woman in her birth pains" (48:40–41 [Moab]; 49:22 [Edom]; 49:24 [Damascus]; 50:43 [Babylon]; cf. 4:31; 13:21–22; 30:6 [Judah]). As a result of Nebuchadnezzar's dominance, their lands will be made a "waste" (46:19 [Egypt]; 48:1, 20 [Moab]; 49:3 [Ammon]; 49:13 [Edom]; 49:33 [Kedar and Hazor]; cf. 2:15; 4:7, 20; 7:34; 25:11–12; 44:6 [Judah]).

These nations will not only experience the curse of the Lord's wrath but will also know the blessing of the new covenant. Again, as with the curses, so these blessings are similar to those given to Judah. There will be severe destruction, but a small remnant will survive (49:11 ["fatherless," "widows" in Edom]; cf. 39:10; 52:16 [Judah]). In a remarkable image, Jeremiah says the Lord mourns and weeps that such judgment must be meted out at all (48:31 [Moab]; cf. 9:10; 14:17–18 [Judah]). Yet in the future the nations will return to their homelands (46:26 [Egypt]). This restoration is described as a "reversal" or "restoration of fortunes" (48:47 [Moab]; 49:6

---

[21] The reference to "my throne" being in Elam refers to the throne of Nebuchadnezzar, who functions as the servant of the Lord (Jer. 25:9).

[Ammon]; 49:39 [Elam]; cf. 29:14; 30:3, 18; 31:23; 32:44; 33:7, 11, 26 [Judah]). In fact, the Lord will so renew these nations that their cities will be "the city of my joy" (49:25 [Damascus]; cf. 31:38–40 [Judah]). Finally, the reception of these blessings will occur in the same "days" as for Judah, the "latter days" (49:39 [Elam]; cf. 30:24 [Judah])—that is, the days of the new covenant. Blessings for the nations are not a dominant theme, but they are present, offering a glimmer of hope.

The overall effect of these descriptions is to identify the experiences of the foreign nations with those of Judah. As both Judah and the nations suffer through the pains of destruction and exile, so they also come to rejoice in the blessings of the Lord. Recall that the recipients of the new covenant promises are specified as "Israel" and "Judah" (30:3–4; 31:27–34), envisioning a renewed, unified Israel with a newly repentant and circumcised heart (31:33; 32:29). In light of the blessings given to the nations, this newly formed people of God must also account for the inclusion of the Gentiles into the "tents of Jacob" (30:18; cf. Gen. 9:27). Thus the new Israel is not one composed of ethnic stock or blood lineage. All those who come to trust in the messianic Branch of David, regardless of their ethnic or national identity, now make up this new Israel of God (Rom. 9:6–8; Gal. 3:29; cf. Rom. 4:11–12). The promise made to Abraham so many years earlier (Gen. 12:2–3), that the Lord would make him into a "great nation," will finally be realized in the new covenant era, and he will be made a "blessing to all the nations" (Gal. 3:8; cf. Gen. 12:3).

APPROACHING THE NEW TESTAMENT

As mentioned earlier, the life of Jeremiah has intrigued students of the Old Testament due to the prophet's clearly articulated passion. We know very little about the details of the life of Jeremiah, but we have ample materials that reveal his internal emotional state—more than any other Old Testament prophet. What we have in the book of Jeremiah, therefore, is not a sequential narrative of historical events but rather a wondrous insight into the psyche of a prophetic messenger and the strain that such a ministry places upon that individual.

There is a physical burden. Often, Jeremiah's life is used as a symbol to communicate the Lord's sovereign message. He is called to purchase a loincloth only to bury it, rendering it unusable; the "spoiling" of the loincloth parallels how the Lord will "spoil" the pride of his people (Jer. 13:1–9). He is commanded to wear an animal's yoke-bar (27:2), which corresponds to the way in which Nebuchadnezzar will place Judah and the surrounding nations under "the yoke." He is prohibited from marrying and thus having children (16:1–4) since nothing but destruction will come upon the inhabitants of the land. All these social eccentricities are intended to remind both Jeremiah and Israel of the curse they will endure.

There is also a heavy emotional burden on the prophet. Interestingly, in some moments his actions and thoughts cannot be clearly distinguished from those of the Lord. For example, 4:19–22 records the tormenting cries of an anguished speaker who laments the sins of the city of Jerusalem. Who is this speaker? Probably Jeremiah but possibly the Lord.[22] The text does not make this clear—an ambiguity that should be taken as divinely intended (see also 8:18–9:11). This demonstrates a radical and close identification between the great Suzerain and his suffering messenger.[23] The heart of Jeremiah, then, is also unveiling the heart of the Lord.

The ambiguity of speakers is only one example of several that illustrate how the prophet and the divine Sovereign share similar experiences. The Lord says that these people, in turning against Jeremiah, have turned against him (12:8). Both weep and mourn for the people (Jeremiah in 9:1; 13:17; the Lord in 9:10; 14:17; Luke 19:41). In his insightful article "The Tears of God in the Book of Jeremiah," David Bosworth states that in the book of Jeremiah the Lord weeps more than the prophet and that the few occasions of the prophet's weeping embody the tears of the Lord. Therefore, he suggests that the book of Jeremiah is not about the "weeping prophet" but about the "weeping God."[24]

Perhaps the most striking shared portrait is the suffering servant; that is, there is a righteous-sufferer motif associated with the Lord and with Jeremiah. In Jeremiah 11:19 the prophet is portrayed as being like a "gentle lamb led to the slaughter." This image reminds the reader of another figure described in nearly the same way, the suffering servant in Isaiah 53:7.[25] Terence Fretheim makes important nuances to this identification. He suggests that while Jeremiah sees himself as innocent of the hostility he receives from his kinsmen, he does not claim "vicarious import for his suffering."[26] In other words, although Jeremiah shares a similar experience as the suffering servant in Isaiah, there is no redemptive value in the sufferings of Jeremiah for the people—he does not atone for their sins. In the book of Isaiah, the servant is one who is "despised and rejected by men; a man of sorrows, and acquainted with grief" (Isa. 53:3). In the book of Jeremiah, the suffering servant is the prophet Jeremiah himself whose "joy is gone; grief is upon me; my heart is sick within me" (Jer. 8:18). In the case of Jeremiah, the prophet is called to experience and share in the same rejection and oppression that the eschatological suffering servant will experience centuries later as the sacrificial "Lamb of God" (John 1:29, 36). In fact, Jeremiah 24 depicts the prophet falsely accused of crimes, facing a bloodthirsty mob eager to condemn him to death, standing before royal officials who see his innocence yet succumb to the will of the masses and imprison him. This sequence of events is reenacted in the city of Jerusalem later in the history of redemption, only it is the Lord himself in his incarnate form who endures these trials during the final days of his earthly life as recorded in the New Testament Gospels.

---

[22] Commentators differ on the identity of this speaker. Kidner says it is the Lord. *The Message of Jeremiah*, 42. However, Harrison (not to mention the majority of commentators) says it is the prophet. *Jeremiah and Lamentations*, 75–76. See also C. F. Keil, *The Prophecies of Jeremiah*, trans. David Patrick, Biblical Commentary on the Old Testament (Grand Rapids, MI: Eerdmans, 1968), 1:114; Leslie C. Allen, *Jeremiah*, OTL (Louisville: Westminster John Knox, 2008), 69. Robert P. Carroll suggests the speaker could be either the land or the people. *Jeremiah*, OTL (Philadelphia: Westminster, 1986), 167.

[23] See the comment by Longman: "It is probably best, therefore, to understand these verses [4:19–21] as the prophet's lament followed by an answer from God [4:22], but the ambiguity does remind us of the close connection between God and his spokesperson." *Jeremiah, Lamentations*, 50.

[24] David A. Bosworth, "The Tears of God in the Book of Jeremiah," *Bib* 94, no. 1 (2013): 24–46.

[25] Whereas Isa. 53:7 uses כְּשֶׂה for "lamb" without a descriptive modifier, Jer. 11:19 uses כְּבֶשׂ with אַלּוּף, "trusting." The remaining vocabulary is identical though in a different word order; cf. Ps. 44:22.

[26] Terence E. Fretheim, *Jeremiah*, SHBC (Macon, GA: Smyth and Helwys, 2002), 189–90.

Jeremiah's identification with the sufferings of the Lord is established early in his prophetic career with his call. Remember that he descended from a priestly family in the city of Anathoth (Jer. 1:1). After the discovery of the law and the subsequent Josianic reforms, Jeremiah was called to preach a message of repentance throughout the cities of Judah, including his hometown. According to 11:21–23, the priests of Anathoth clearly abhorred this message of Jeremiah. Not only did they attempt to prevent him from carrying out his prophetic task of proclaiming the divine word, but they also warned that he would do so at the risk of his very life. It was to his own kin that the prophet was called to preach his message of wrath and condemnation that made him a "man of strife and contention to the whole land" (15:10). Thus some of the persecution and rejection that Jeremiah faced came not merely from his fellow countrymen but specifically from members of his very own family. Such hardship reflects another Prophet who "came to his own, and his own people did not receive him" (John 1:11).

The overall effect of the shared suffering between the Lord and his prophet portrays Jeremiah as one invited by the Lord to experience and know his suffering as a righteous sufferer. According to 1 Peter 4:12–13, to experience this "fiery trial" is not something that should be taken as unusual in the life of a believer but as expected; he says that "to this you have been called" (2:21). Indeed, according to the apostle Peter, to know such righteous suffering is to "share Christ's sufferings." This is the reason, the cause, the rationale for why believers can rejoice (4:13; cf. Phil. 4:4). To what extent are believers eager to "be conformed to the image of his Son" (Rom. 8:29)? We desire to know our union with Christ in his justification (1 Tim. 3:16), sanctification (Romans 6), and glorification (1 Corinthians 15). These are spiritual blessings in Christ that we receive willingly by the grace of God, but are we also willing to know Christ in his suffering and to see this also as a gracious gift? This is difficult and goes against our natural inclination to avoid pain and heartache. Yet to know one (his glory) without the other (his suffering) will not give us a holistic knowledge of our Savior because his life and ministry included both. Christ himself summarized his life as suffering to glory, and this two-part summation applies also to the entirety of the Old Testament Scriptures (Luke 24:26, 46; cf. Phil. 2:5–11; 1 Pet. 1:10–11).

Although 1 Peter 4:12–13 does not explicitly refer to Jeremiah, the principle he espouses there can be applied to the prophet nonetheless—he "fellowshiped" with Jesus in fullness, meaning in his suffering and also in glory. For this reason, he can be considered a man endowed with extraordinary grace.[27] Jeremiah could claim to have a deep union with his Suzerain since they knew similar agony. To not have such heartache would deny Jeremiah the richness of this fellowship. For that reason, this prophet can say that he has a "joy that is inexpressible and filled with glory" (1 Pet. 1:8).

---

[27] See Phil. 1:29, where the apostle Paul also calls both the faith and the suffering of believers a gift of grace from God; cf. Phil. 3:10; 1 Pet. 4:13.

SELECT BIBLIOGRAPHY

Allen, Leslie C. *Jeremiah*. OTL. Louisville: Westminster John Knox, 2008.

Bosworth, David A. "The Tears of God in the Book of Jeremiah." *Bib* 94, no. 1 (2013): 24–46.

Bright, John. *Jeremiah: A New Translation with Introduction and Commentary*. AB 21. Garden City, NY: Doubleday, 1965.

Brueggemann, Walter. *A Commentary on Jeremiah: Exile and Homecoming*. Grand Rapids, MI: Eerdmans, 1998.

———. *The Theology of the Book of Jeremiah*. New York: Cambridge University Press, 2007.

Calvin, John. *Commentaries on the Book of the Prophet Jeremiah and the Lamentations*. 5 vols. Grand Rapids, MI: Baker, 1993.

Carroll, Robert P. *Jeremiah*. OTL. Philadelphia: Westminster, 1986.

Dearman, J. Andrew. *Jeremiah/Lamentations*. NIVAC. Grand Rapids, MI: Zondervan, 2002.

Driver, Samuel R. "The Double Text of Jeremiah." *The Expositer* 9 (1889): 321–37.

Fretheim, Terence E. *Jeremiah*. SHBC. Macon, GA: Smyth and Helwys, 2002.

Harrison, Roland K. *Jeremiah and Lamentations: An Introduction and Commentary*. TOTC 21. Downers Grove, IL: InterVarsity Press, 1973.

Holladay, William L. "The Background of Jeremiah's Self-Understanding: Moses, Samuel, and Psalm 22." *JBL* 83, no. 2 (1964): 153–64.

———. *Jeremiah*. 2 vols. Hermeneia: A Critical and Historical Commentary on the Bible. Philadelphia: Fortress, 1986–1989.

Janzen, J. Gerald. "Double Readings in the Text of Jeremiah." *HTR* 60, no. 4 (1967): 433–47.

———. *Studies in the Text of Jeremiah*. HSM 6. Cambridge: Harvard University Press, 1973.

Keil, C. F. *The Prophecies of Jeremiah*. 2 vols. Vol. 1 translated by David Patrick. Vol. 2 translated by James Kennedy. Biblical Commentary on the Old Testament. Grand Rapids, MI: Eerdmans, 1968.

Kidner, Derek. *The Message of Jeremiah: Against Wind and Tide*. The Bible Speaks Today. Downers Grove, IL: InterVarsity Press, 1987.

Longman, Tremper, III. *Jeremiah, Lamentations*. NIBCOT 14. Peabody, MA: Hendrickson, 2008.

Lundbom, Jack R. "The Book of Jeremiah." In *The Anchor Bible Dictionary*, edited by David Noel Freedman, 3:707–9. New York: Doubleday, 1992.

———. *Jeremiah: A New Translation with Introduction and Commentary*. 3 vols. AB 21A–21C. Garden City, NY: Doubleday, 1999–2004.

———. *Jeremiah: A Study in Ancient Hebrew Rhetoric*. 2nd ed. Winona Lake, IN: Eisenbrauns, 1997.

McConville, J. Gordon. *Judgment and Promise: An Interpretation of the Book of Jeremiah*. Winona Lake, IN: Eisenbrauns, 1993.

Raitt, Thomas M. *A Theology of Exile: Judgment/Deliverance in Jeremiah and Ezekiel*. Philadelphia: Fortress, 1977.

Ryken, Philip G. *Courage to Stand: Jeremiah's Message for Post-Christian Times*. Phillipsburg, NJ: P&R, 2009.

Schreiber, Mordecai. *The Man Who Knew God: Decoding Jeremiah*. Lanham, MD: Rowman & Littlefield, 2010.

Thompson, J. A. *The Book of Jeremiah*. NICOT. Grand Rapids, MI: Eerdmans, 1980.

Unterman, Jeremiah. *From Repentance to Redemption: Jeremiah's Thought in Transition*. JSOTSup 54. Sheffield: JSOT Press, 1987.

12

Ezekiel

Michael G. McKelvey

INTRODUCTION

The book of Ezekiel has long been considered an enigma in the Christian church. The very mention of the prophet's name provokes intimidation. Its sensational imagery, obscure language, and challenging message (just to name a few characteristics) have created significant obstacles for those who have sought to understand this book. Who is this eccentric prophet? Why is his work so different from the other two major prophets (Isaiah and Jeremiah)? Why are his words so mysterious and perplexing?

Interpreting the book of Ezekiel is filled with challenges. There are textual difficulties,[1] linguistic challenges,[2] and genre considerations (e.g., poetry, narrative, prose), including the issue of apocalypticism.[3] However, the reader should not be afraid to study this prophetic text. Some of the details may challenge the careful reader, but if the overall message of Ezekiel is understood and kept in view, then Christians from all walks of life can profit from this great work.

BACKGROUND ISSUES

Authorship

The prophet Ezekiel of the sixth century BC has traditionally been considered the author of the book that bears his name, and for a long time, the apparent unity of the

---

[1] R. K. Harrison notes, "The text of Ezekiel has been poorly preserved, due partly to the fact that obscurities in the language, as well as technical expressions and *hapax legomena*, have led copyists into frequent error. The Septuagint is often very valuable in attempts to correct the Hebrew, but nevertheless it must be used with great care." *Introduction to the Old Testament* (Grand Rapids, MI: Eerdmans, 1977), 854. In addition, the Septuagint is approximately 4–5 percent shorter than the Masoretic text. This may simply reflect two different textual traditions in circulation at the time of the Greek translation of Ezekiel.
[2] See Carl Gordon Howie, *The Date and Composition of Ezekiel*, SBLMS 4 (Philadelphia: SBL, 1950), 47–68, for his study of the apparent Aramaic influence on the book of Ezekiel.
[3] Pieter De Vries, "Ezekiel: Prophet of the Name and Glory of YHWH—The Character of His Book and Several of Its Main Themes," *JBPR* 4 (2012): 107–8. See also D. Brent Sandy and Martin G. Abegg Jr., "Apocalyptic," in *Cracking Old Testament Codes: A Guide to Interpreting Literary Genres of the Old Testament*, ed. D. Brent Sandy and Ronald L. Giese Jr. (Nashville: Broadman, 1995), 177–96, and especially their discussion on Ezekiel 38–39 (190–93).

book went unquestioned. Even among early critical scholarship, the book's coherence was relatively accepted, but over the last century, some scholars have challenged the book's unity.[4] For example, in 1930 Charles Cutler Torrey suggested that the book was written under the pseudonym "Ezekiel" as late as the third century BC.[5] Working from the assumption that Daniel 1–6 was composed ca. 245 BC, Torrey argued that since "the atmosphere of Ezekiel is manifestly that of Daniel, Joel, and the last chapters of Zechariah," the best date would be shortly after 246 BC.[6] However, as De Vries observes,

> There are no compelling reasons to date the prophecies ascribed to Ezekiel to a period after the prophet's death. It is certain that no text in Ezekiel discusses any problems that occurred after exile. There is no text in Ezekiel that alludes to the return as an historical fact or to the capture of Babylon by the Persians. All the events that are described and all the prophecies that are given fit within the reign of Nebuchadnezzar.[7]

Others have argued that since Ezekiel was a prophet living in Babylon, chapters 8–11 cannot originate from him because they are set in the geographical context of Jerusalem. Such a setting, however, does not preclude the possibility that these chapters originated from the prophet. In fact, when one considers that these chapters are "visions of God" (8:3) received by the prophet, the argument fails to convince. Scholarship may minimize the possibility of "visions of God," but the content and perspective of these chapters do not necessitate that the author lived in Jerusalem *at the time of their writing.*

Additionally, some have questioned the mental health of the prophet because of his dramatic and otherworldly visions. His unusual actions have also caused some to wonder about his psychological stability.[8] While the book is filled with incredible, even distasteful, acts and perplexing symbolism, it remains mere speculation and conjecture to diagnose the prophet based upon what he has written, especially when examining him by our modern Western citeria. So it seems best to let the book speak for itself and examine the prophet based upon his calling and ministry.

Ultimately, the view that Ezekiel is, in fact, the author of this material is the most well-reasoned view because of the following arguments. First, Block notes, "All the prophecies are written in a first-person, autobiographical style, suggesting that they may be based on Ezekiel's personal *memorabile.*"[9] Second, "Confirmation of the appropriateness of Ezekiel's prophecies to the period and place to which they are described comes from Jeremiah. The description of the mood and expectations of the exiles given in Jeremiah 29—his letter to them—could not better illustrate the

---

[4] See De Vries, "Ezekiel: Prophet of the Name and Glory of YHWH," 94–96, for a brief summary of both the modern critical movement on Ezekiel and the responses that argue for the book's unity and a sixth-century dating.

[5] Charles Cutler Torrey, *Pseudo-Ezekiel and the Original Prophecy*, YOSR 18 (New Haven, CT: Yale University Press, 1930), 99.

[6] Torrey, *Pseudo-Ezekiel*, 97; see 71–101 for his complete discussion concerning the date of the book.

[7] De Vries, "Ezekiel: Prophet of the Name and Glory of YHWH," 96.

[8] For a discussion on Ezekiel's mental health, see Tremper Longman III and Raymond B. Dillard, *An Introduction to the Old Testament*, 2nd ed. (Grand Rapids, MI: Zondervan, 2006), 361–62.

[9] Daniel I. Block, *The Book of Ezekiel Chapters 1–24*, NICOT (Grand Rapids, MI: Eerdmans, 1997), 20.

setting assumed in Ezekiel's prophecies."[10] Third, the content and atmosphere of the book does not suppose a later date than the historical period it presents.[11] In the end, as Duguid notes, "When the text is allowed to speak for itself, it conveys a coherent and consistent worldview that addresses the situation of those exiled from Judah in the sixth century B.C."[12]

Historical Background and Audience

While the prophet Ezekiel (whose name means "God strengthens") is not mentioned in the Old Testament outside of this book, the work itself provides significant detail about the man and the time in which he served. According to 1:1–3, he was a priest living with his wife (see 24:15–27) in exile in the land of Babylon by the Chebar canal[13] near Nippur. He was from a priestly family, the son of Buzi, and apparently belonged to the upper echelons of Judahite society in Jerusalem, which was taken into Babylon in the second deportation in 597 BC. If "the thirtieth year" in verse 1 refers to Ezekiel's age, then it is likely that he was born around 623/22 BC.[14] Though he was a priest, he likely never served in the temple since priests did not serve until they were thirty years of age. However, he would have been intimately familiar with the priesthood, Holiness Code, and sacrificial system. Instead of entering into the temple priesthood at age thirty, he received a prophetic calling. So in Ezekiel the reader encounters the interesting combination of prophet and priest. The mixture of these two roles manifests itself as Ezekiel proclaims God's word and as the book frequently alludes to priestly imagery, especially the temple. The prophet ministered no less than twenty years (593–571 BC).[15]

The superscription of 1:1–3 also reveals the geographic location of the prophet ("among the exiles by the Chebar canal," 1:1), the time in which he ministered ("the fifth year of the exile of King Jehoiachin," 1:2), and that the hand of the Lord was upon him as he saw visions of God and received "the word of the LORD" (1:1, 3). Additionally, this passage forces the reader to consider how the prophet and the exiles came to be in the land of the Chaldeans in the first place.

For years both the northern kingdom of Israel and the southern kingdom of Judah were involved in the wider political upheaval of the ancient Near East. The Assyrians destroyed the northern kingdom of Israel when they demolished the capital city of Samaria in 722 BC. Assyria rose to its zenith with Ashurbanipal's reign, but after his death (ca. 627 BC), the empire deteriorated in less than twenty years.[16] The Assyr-

---

[10] Moshe Greenberg, *Ezekiel 1–20: A New Translation with Introduction and Commentary*, AB 22 (Garden City, NY: Doubleday, 1983), 14.

[11] Greenberg, *Ezekiel 1–20*, 15.

[12] Iain M. Duguid, *Ezekiel*, NIVAC (Grand Rapids, MI: Zondervan, 1999), 25.

[13] Ralph H. Alexander explains, "This 'River' has been identified by many with the *naru kabari* (mentioned in two cuneiform texts from Nippur), a canal making a southeasterly loop, connecting at both ends with the Euphrates River." *Ezekiel*, in *The Expositor's Bible Commentary*, ed. Frank E. Gaebelein (Grand Rapids, MI: Zondervan, 1986), 6:742.

[14] Harrison, *Introduction*, 838; Peter C. Craigie, *Ezekiel*, Daily Study Bible (Philadelphia: Westminster, 1983), 3.

[15] These dates are based on the "fifth year of the exile of King Jehoachin" and the last prophecy, which is dated to April 571 BC (Ezek. 29:17). For tables of dates in the book of Ezekiel, see Greenberg, *Ezekiel 1–20*, 8; Douglas Stuart, *Ezekiel*, The Communicator's Commentary: Old Testament (Dallas: Word, 1989), 16.

[16] For a discussion on the death of Ashurbanipal and the collapse of Assyria, see John Bright, *A History of Israel*, with an introduction and appendix by William P. Brown, 4th ed. (Louisville: Westminster John Knox, 2000), 314–15.

ian capital of Niniveh fell in 612 BC at the hand of Babylon (and its allies), a rising power in the ancient Near East. Babylon's leader, Nabopolassar (r. 625–605 BC), and his son Nebuchadnezzar continued the campaign for power, which eventually led to the Battle of Carchemish in 605 BC between the superpowers Babylon and Egypt. However, in order for Egypt to engage with Babylon, they needed to cross the Levant, which meant passing through territory belonging to Judah.

In the land of Judah, King Josiah began his reign in 639 BC, and in late 622 BC, his religious reforms commenced after the book of the law was found in the temple. Josiah is considered a good king in Israelite history, but his reign ended in 609 BC when the Egyptian army, led by Pharaoh Neco, sought to pass through ancient Israel to battle against Babylon. Disapproving of the Egyptian advance, Josiah rode out with his army to deny passage to the Egyptians but died in the battle at Megiddo in 609 BC (see 2 Kings 23:28–30). Following this defeat, Egypt gained control of Judah as a vassal nation, and Neco removed Jehoahaz (Josiah's second son) from the throne of Jerusalem. He then placed Eliakim (Josiah's oldest son) on the throne and gave him the name Jehoiakim. Eventually, under the leadership of Nebuchadnezzar (r. 605–562 BC), Babylon gained a decisive victory over Egypt at the Battle of Carchemish (605 BC). As a consequence, Judah came under the power of the Babylonians, who deported the Judahite upper class to Babylon that same year (605 BC).[17]

Judah's conflict with the Chaldeans, however, did not end at this point. King Jehoiakim eventually refused to pay tribute to Nebuchadnezzar, which led to the Babylonian siege of Jerusalem and the death of Jehoiakim in 598 BC.[18] This rebellion prompted a second deportation of much of the nobility in Jerusalem (including Ezekiel), as well as King Jehoiachin,[19] in 597 BC. Understandably, the prophet Ezekiel dates the events of his book in terms of the exile of Jehoiachin (e.g., 1:2; 8:1; 20:1; 29:17).[20] Nebuchadnezzar placed Mattaniah (the third son of Josiah) upon the throne in Jerusalem, likely to serve as a puppet king, and renamed him "Zedekiah." One might think Zedekiah would have learned from his predecessors, but that was not to be. Surrounded by a circle of pro-Egyptian nobility in Jerusalem, Zedekiah in time rebelled against Babylon, leading to the final siege against Jerusalem and the city's fall in 586 BC. Zedekiah fled through a breach in the city's walls but was captured, brought to Nebuchadnezzar, and forced to witness his own sons' executions before his eyes were gouged out and he was finally taken into exile (Jer. 39:1–10; 52:1–11). Thus, Judah's nationhood was terminated, and the Babylonian captivity fully dawned. It would not be until 539 BC that the Persian King Cyrus would decree that the Jewish people could return to the land of their forefathers.

Ezekiel's ministry spans the preexilic and exilic periods, from 593 BC to Jeru-

---

[17] Included in this first deportation (605 BC) were Daniel and his three friends.

[18] Jehoiakim may actually have been murdered by some of his own advisors and soldiers (cf. Jer. 22:18–19; 36:30–31). See Bright, *A History of Israel*, 327; Merrill C. Tenney, ed., *The Zondervan Pictorial Encyclopedia of the Bible*, vol. 3, *H–L* (Grand Rapids, MI: Zondervan, 1975), 420.

[19] Jehoiachin, son of Jehoiakim, reigned for three months after the death of his father.

[20] This dating likely shows that Ezekiel views Jehoiachin as the rightful king of Judah and not his uncle Mattaniah/ Zedekiah. Jehoiachin was the crucial link to the continuation of the Davidic line (cf. Jer. 52:31–34; Matt. 1:11–12); see Block, *Ezekiel 1–24*, 6.

salem's fall in 586 BC, with his final prophecy dating to 571 BC. The prophet saw his visions of Jerusalem's demise come to fruition. Even though many of his early prophecies concerned the fall of Judah's capital and his words may have made their way to Jerusalem, his primary audience was the upper classes of Judahite society living as captives in southern Mesopotamia. It was Ezekiel's job to communicate what God was going to do to Jerusalem, why he was doing it, what he would eventually do to the nations, and then how he would restore his chosen people. With that said, the structure of this book comes into focus.

STRUCTURE AND OUTLINE

The book of Ezekiel has been outlined in various ways by scholars, but most perceive a threefold division. In chapters 1–24, the coming doom against Jerusalem is announced.[21] Chapters 25–32 show the prophet's attention drawn to the coming judgment against the nations. Finally, chapters 33–48 reveal the restoration of the people of God. A detailed outline for the three divisions of this prophetic work appears below.

I. Judgment Coming to Jerusalem (1:1–24:27)
    A. The prophet's vision and call (1:1–3:27)
    B. Prophecies against Jerusalem (4:1–7:27)
    C. Vision of the temple in Jerusalem (8:1–11:25)
    D. Further prophecies against Jerusalem (12:1–18:32)
    E. A lament (19:1–14)
    F. Israel's rebellion (20:1–22:31)
    G. Two adulterous sisters (23:1–49)
    H. Siege of Jerusalem and the death of Ezekiel's wife (24:1–27)
II. Judgment Coming to the Nations (25:1–32:32)
    A. Ammon (25:1–7)
    B. Moab (25:8–11)
    C. Edom (25:12–14)
    D. Philistia (25:15–17)
    E. Tyre and Sidon (26:1–28:26)
    F. Egypt (29:1–32:32)
III. Restoration of God's People (33:1–48:35)
    A. Ezekiel the watchman and Jerusalem's fall (33:1–33)
    B. Total restoration (34:1–37:28)
    C. Gog and Magog (38:1–39:29)
    D. Renewed temple, renewed life, renewed land (40:1–48:35)

This structure clearly shows a pattern—from calamity to redemption, from cursing to blessing. Israel is a nation chosen by God to be in covenant with him. Their disobedience through the centuries has brought his judgment upon them. God will no longer tolerate their wickedness and will bring judgment upon them by means of

---

[21] Stuart notes that "the vast majority of the first twenty-four chapters is given over to the message that Jerusalem will fall to the Babylonians—a message told and retold dozens of times, from every conceivable angle, again and again and again." *Ezekiel*, 15.

the surrounding nations. Interestingly, this trajectory regarding Israel's waywardness and God's chastisement using foreign nations was set all the way back in Deuteronomy 29–31. The repetition of disobedience and punishment (see Joshua–Kings) has now culminated in the threatened judgment. However, those nations who conquer Israel and Judah are not guiltless before the Lord and will have to pay for their own iniquity. So God declares through Ezekiel that judgment is coming for them as well, and not only for the nations named in the book. Those various nations stand as representatives of the whole world, for God will call all mankind to account for their deeds (see Ezekiel 18; Jer. 18:7–10). However, for the sake of his name, God will keep his covenant with the forefathers of Israel and will establish his people in a land of peace and righteousness—a land where God himself will be in their midst, never to depart again (Ezekiel 40–48).

MESSAGE AND THEOLOGY

Creation, De-creation, and Re-creation

The message of the book of Ezekiel should be more closely examined in view of the structure. It has been noted that the key to understanding Ezekiel is the glory of God and the temple. Thus Freedman writes, "The theme of the Temple runs through the entire book, and is the key to its unity. In a sentence, it is the story of the departure of the glory of God from the Temple, and its return."[22] As one considers these themes, an overarching pattern clearly appears from the beginning of the book to its conclusion. For instance, consider Ezekiel's vision of the glory of God in chapter 1. This passage is remarkably descriptive as Ezekiel sees a visible theophany of Yahweh, a manifestation of the presence of God. It begins with "a stormy wind [that] came out of the north, and a great cloud, with brightness around it, and fire flashing forth continually, and in the midst of the fire, as if it were gleaming metal." This language brings to mind the theophanic appearances of God in the form of a storm so often recorded in Scripture.[23] With the mention of cloud and fire, it may very well recall the appearance of God on Mount Sinai when he displayed his visible glory to Israel and entered into covenant with the nation (see Ex. 19:9, 18).[24]

Then Ezekiel describes the four living creatures who have human "likeness," each one with four faces and four wings (1:5–6). These creatures also have beastly qualities (1:7–11). They go straight forward, wherever the spirit goes, without turning (1:12). The living beings glow with fire, and "lightning" comes forth from the fire (1:13). As the vision continues, Ezekiel describes a picture of wheels beside the creatures, a wheel within a wheel (1:15–16). They likewise go in any of the four directions without turning (1:17), and their rims are tall and full of eyes (1:18). This theophanic vision continues with wondrous portrayals of the characteristics and movements of these heavenly beings. They appear to characterize the nature and

---

[22] David Noel Freedman, "The Book of Ezekiel," *Int* 8, no. 4 (1954): 456.
[23] Leslie C. Allen, *Ezekiel 1–19*, WBC 28 (Waco, TX: Word, 1994), 24.
[24] The imagery from Sinai is very fitting since the Mosaic covenant provides the backdrop for how God is dealing with Israel. The Mosaic covenant will be further discussed later.

attributes of the Almighty, and the final verse of the chapter confirms this point of the vision: "Such was the appearance of *the likeness of the glory of the* LORD. And when I saw it, I fell on my face, and I heard the voice of one speaking" (cf. "the glory of the LORD" in 3:12, 23).

The next major description of the glory of God is found in Ezekiel 10, which features the same language to describe the theophanic presence of God. This description occurs in the context of chapters 8–11, when Ezekiel has a vision of Jerusalem and the temple.[25] Ezekiel 10 begins,

> Then I looked, and behold, on the expanse that was over the heads of the cherubim there appeared above them something like a sapphire, in appearance like a throne. And he said to the man clothed in linen, "Go in among the whirling wheels underneath the cherubim. Fill your hands with burning coals from between the cherubim, and scatter them over the city." And he went in before my eyes. Now the cherubim were standing on the south side of the house, when the man went in, and a cloud filled the inner court. And *the glory of the* LORD went up from the cherub to the threshold of the house, and the house was filled with the cloud, and the court was filled with the brightness of *the glory of the* LORD. And the sound of the wings of the cherubim was heard as far as the outer court, like the voice of God Almighty when he speaks. (10:1–5)

The scene continues with language and imagery that mirrors chapter 1—a wheel within a wheel and four living creatures. In fact, Ezekiel says in 10:20, "These were the living creatures that I saw underneath the God of Israel by the Chebar canal; and I knew that they were cherubim" (see also 10:15). However, the most notable purpose of this chapter is to explain that the glory of God is leaving the temple and Jerusalem:

> Then *the glory of the* LORD went out from the threshold of the house, and stood over the cherubim. And the cherubim lifted up their wings and mounted up from the earth before my eyes as they went out, with the wheels beside them. And they stood at the entrance of the east gate of the house of the LORD, and *the glory of the God of Israel* was over them. (10:18–19)

The presence of God, which comes to dwell in the Mosaic covenant with his people (first in the tabernacle [Ex. 40:34–38],[26] and then in the temple [1 Kings 8:10]), is now departing from the temple, the people, and the land. Yahweh's departure reveals the extent of punishment that Israel's iniquity has brought upon the nation (cf. Deut. 28:15–68). With this drastic picture proclaimed to the people, Ezekiel's words continue to indict Jerusalem until the city falls (Ezekiel 24). Without the presence of God, they are completely lost (cf. Exodus 32).

---

[25] Interestingly, "the glory of the God of Israel" is also mentioned in Ezek. 8:4 at the beginning of the vision of Jerusalem. The same phrase also occurs in 9:3 in the context of the temple.

[26] See Ex. 40:34–38: "Then the cloud covered the tent of meeting, and *the glory of the* LORD filled the tabernacle. And Moses was not able to enter the tent of meeting because the cloud settled on it, and *the glory of the* LORD filled the tabernacle. Throughout all their journeys, whenever the cloud was taken up from over the tabernacle, the people of Israel would set out. But if the cloud was not taken up, then they did not set out till the day that it was taken up. For the cloud of the LORD was on the tabernacle by day, and fire was in it by night, in the sight of all the house of Israel throughout all their journeys." See also 1 Kings 8:10–11: "And when the priests came out of the Holy Place, a cloud filled the house of the LORD, so that the priests could not stand to minister because of the cloud, for *the glory of the* LORD filled the house of the LORD."

After the fall of Jerusalem in Ezekiel 24, the prophet's focus turns to the surrounding nations. They will be punished for their wickedess as well. God's "vengeance" (24:8) will come upon them since they stood by, watched, or participated in Judah/Jerusalem's demise. Many nations are mentioned, but extended prophecies appear for Tyre and Egypt. Now the factor that distinguished between Israel and the nations was that God's presence was with his people and not the nations. So their judgment can also be said to arise from their sin and the lack of God's presence or glory among them. Interestingly, in 28:22, God says he will manifest his "glory" in Tyre through judgment. So as with Israel, without the presence of God, the nations are completely lost.

These oracles prepare the reader for the final section of the book (Ezekiel 33–48), in which God restores his people to the land, the temple is rebuilt, and the glory of God returns. In chapter 40, Ezekiel sees "visions of God" in which a new temple arrives. The prophet perceives "a man whose appearance [is] like bronze" (40:3), the same language describing the glory of God in 1:7, and the man tells him to proclaim what he sees to Israel. The new temple is then described in the remainder of chapter 40 through chapter 42. These accounts are followed by a grand picture of the glory of God filling the new temple in Ezekiel 43. The prophet says that "the vision I saw was just like the vision that I had seen when he came to destroy the city, and just like the vision that I had seen by the Chebar canal. And I fell on my face" (43:3). He continues, "As *the glory of the* Lord entered the temple by the gate facing east, the Spirit lifted me up and brought me into the inner court; and behold, *the glory of the* Lord *filled the temple*" (43:4–5; see also 44:4). Hence, the glory of God returns to the new temple, and the Lord says that "this is the place of my throne and the place of the soles of my feet, where I will dwell in the midst of the people of Israel forever" (43:7). No longer will anyone bring defilement, for God will cleanse the land and reestablish his people (Ezekiel 43–48). And as this third section of the book highlights through reoccuring statements, God will dwell in the midst of the temple, the city, and the people (see 37:26–28; 43:7, 9; 48:35). Overall, the book shows that after a time of judgment and purification, the Lord will return to his people and dwell with them forever. Yahweh will be their God, and they shall be his people (34:24, 30; 36:28; 37:23).

In light of the preceding outline and discussion, the thematic structure of the book of Ezekiel appears to follow a larger, reoccurring pattern in Scripture. This pattern can be desribed as *creation, de-creation,* and *re-creation,*[27] and is notably seen in the first three chapters of Genesis where God creates (Genesis 1–2),[28] where man through disobedience de-creates (Gen. 3:1–19), and where God promises to re-create (Gen. 3:15). The pattern continues with the flood narrative (Gen. 6:1–9:17), Moses's birth narrative

---

[27] Some may prefer the categories of creation, fall, and redemption, but the theological concepts are synonomous.
[28] The Hebrew word for "likeness" (דְּמוּת) occurs twenty-five times in the Old Testament, including three times in Genesis (1:26; 5:1, 3) and sixteen times in Ezekiel (1:5 [2x], 10, 13, 16, 22, 26 [3x], 28; 8:2; 10:1, 10, 21 [2x]; 23:15). In each case (except Ezek. 23:15), Ezekiel employs this term in the context of describing God. Genesis uses it in 1:26 and 5:1 in reference to the "likeness" of God. Thus the use of this term strengthens the link between the biblical account of creation and the book of Ezekiel.

(Ex. 1:8–2:10), the Exodus and Red Sea crossing (Ex. 3:1–15:18),[29] and Israel's crossing of the Jordan (Joshua 3–5). At the macrolevel, the entirety of Scripture follows this framework; from Genesis 1 to Revelation 22, a clear pattern of creation, de-creation (fall), and re-creation (redemption) reoccurs throughout the whole of God's Word.

Apparently, the book of Ezekiel also follows this arrangement. Ezekiel 1 displays God's glory among the people whom he has made for himself. Then God's glory leaves the temple, the city, and the people, signifying the removal of his presence (cf. the driving of Adam and Eve out of the garden away from the presence of the Lord in Gen. 3:22–24).[30] The prophet concludes the book with the promise of the glory of God returning to the temple (Ezekiel 43) and, in the final verse, of the Lord dwelling in the midst of the city: "And the name of the city from that time on shall be, 'The LORD Is There'" (48:35). Therefore, the book's outline is intimately tied to its message: The people whom God has created will be de-created because of their sin, but they will one day be re-created to dwell with God, and he with them, forever.

Before moving on, it must be noted that within this promised new creation there remains an essential role for the Davidic king. The Lord promises to seek out his people and says, "And I will set up over them one shepherd, my servant David, and he shall feed them: he shall feed them and be their shepherd. And I, the LORD, will be their God, and my servant David shall be prince among them. I am the LORD; I have spoken" (34:23–24). God also promises in 37:24, "My servant David shall be king over them, and they shall all have one shepherd."[31] Thus, the message of Ezekiel links the messianic Davidic king with the emergence of this new creation (cf. 2 Cor. 5:17; Gal. 6:15).

God's Holiness

One of the most important attributes of God expressed in the Old Testament, which the book of Ezekiel highlights, is his *holiness*.[32] From the prophet's vision in chapter 1 to the latter part of the book with its description of the new temple, the holy nature of Yahweh obtains prominence in this prophetic work. The root Hebrew word for "holy" or "to sanctify" occurs some fifty-one times, displaying significance. However, the occurence of this root by no means comes close to displaying the full concept of the *holy* God present in the book.

For instance, the transcendent[33] nature of God can be included within this

---

[29] Ezekiel 16:8 says, "When I passed by you again and saw you, behold, you were at the age for love, and I spread the corner of my garment over you and covered your nakedness; I made my vow to you and entered into a covenant with you, declares the Lord GOD, and you became mine." Note the context of Ezekiel 16.

[30] Interestingly, Eden is mentioned in Ezek. 28:13; 31:18.

[31] Note also Ezek. 37:22: "And I will make them one nation in the land, on the mountains of Israel. And one king shall be king over them all, and they shall be no longer two nations, and no longer divided into two kingdoms."

[32] See the book of Leviticus. Note especially Lev. 19:1–2: "And the LORD spoke to Moses, saying, 'Speak to all the congregation of the people of Israel and say to them, You shall be holy, for I the LORD your God am holy.'"

[33] The concept of trascendence needs to be further explained. Some use the idea of transcendence as expressing "that God is so far above us . . . that we can say nothing, at least positive, about him." However, John Frame argues that the biblical concept of transcendence refers to "God's majesty and holiness." As Frame states, "the transcendence of God is best understood, not primarily as a spatial concept, but as a reference to God's kingship. . . . If, therefore, we are to use the language of transcendence and immanence, it would be best to use *transcendence* for God's royal control and authority, and *immanence* for his covenant presence." In other words, the transcendent and immanent natures of God are not mutually exclusive. John M. Frame, *The Doctrine of God* (Phillipsburg, NJ: P&R, 2002), 110, 104, 106. See Frame's fuller discussion on 103–15.

discussion of God as set apart and distinct. The description of the heavenly beings and the other worldly phenomena in Ezekiel 1, 10, and 43 distinguish the Lord from all creation. Yahweh is above and distinct from creation, set apart from everything in such a way that it takes symbolic, supernatural "visions" to convey what mere words cannot. After reading such descriptions, one is left confounded with how to vizualize and construct this portrayal of the Most High. The point of God being holy comes through loud and clear, and it leaves the reader speechless. This seems to be the author's purpose: To fill his audience with wonder, fear, awe, and amazement at the God of Israel.

God loves his people and is intimately involved in both their lives and the affairs of the nations. So not only his transcendence but also his involvement reveals his holiness. In other words, his holiness serves as a backdrop and disjunction to the rebellion and sinfulness of man. How these two opposites exist in God's good creation is the tension we observe in Ezekiel. God is loving and holy, and he has chosen a people who are not loving and holy, but rather the very opposite. Therefore, their relationship is worked out through judgment, mercy, and redemption via the terms of the covenant. God is ultimately seeking to purge his people from their sin to make them righteous so that they might dwell with him, and he with them, forever. Therefore, the character of God is the driving force behind God's outworking of his covenant plans.

God's Sovereignty

Ezekiel paints a vibrant picture of God's control over all things, including Israel and the nations. In fact, he rules over the affairs of the nations in order to bring about his sovereign purposes. One of those purposes is to make himself and his sovereignty and dominion known on the earth. The phrase "they will know that I am the LORD" or similar expressions occur numerous times throughout the book as if they were a refrain (e.g., 2:5; 5:13; 6:7; 17:24; 24:24; 25:7; 37:28). Another saying (or sayings similar to it) that indicates God's sovereignty is "I the LORD have spoken" (e.g., 17:24; 21:17, 32; 22:14; 24:14; 36:36; 37:14). The very fact that Yahweh speaks guarantees fulfillment. Such a concept recalls the spoken word of God at creation, when everything came into existence by divine imperative (see Genesis 1).

These themes stress that what has happened and is happening to Israel and Judah reflects no lack of dominion on God's behalf. Quite the contrary, the past and present circumstances actually reveal the sovereignty of God (cf. Deuteronomy 29–31). The destruction of Jerusalem comes about because God has willed it. It follows from the penalties for disobedience—thus Ezekiel notes several times that the people have broken the covenant (Ezek. 16:59; 17:13–19; 44:7). In the Mosaic administration, the people of Israel became a nation that would receive blessings for obedience and cursings for rebellion (see Deuteronomy 27–28). God's judgment, which they are now experiencing, reveals the penalties for covenant unfaithfulness. The people are destroyed by the very hand that made them—Yahweh's hand. However, his sovereignty also continues in the promise of restoration and forgiveness through a new and everlasting covenant (20:37; 34:25; 37:26). Yahweh will cleanse his people and reestablish them for his name's sake.

God's Mercy and Grace

The judgment of God upon his people does not undermine his *mercy* and *grace*. The purging of the nation will bring about a holy people who will forever dwell with God and know his goodness. Ezekiel clearly reveals that not all of God's people will be cut off. As one example, in Ezekiel 5 the Lord commands the prophet to cut off his hair and beard. He is to weigh and divide the hair into thirds and then burn a third of it with fire, strike a third of it with the sword, and scatter a third of it to the wind. Then God says, "And you shall take from these a small number and bind them in the skirts of your robe. And of these again you shall take some and cast them into the midst of the fire and burn them in the fire. From there a fire will come out into all the house of Israel" (5:3–4). Ezekiel's act symbolizes God's sparing a remnant, who will inherit the promises of God. He will make his covenant with them (20:37) and they will receive the promise of a new heart and spirit (36:24–28), a new Davidic king (37:24–25; 45:7), and God's glorious presence (48:35). So the words of Habakkuk ring true in Ezekiel: in wrath, God remembers mercy (Hab. 3:2).

Additionally, God shows his grace "for the sake of his name." In Ezekiel 20:9, the Lord speaks of delivering the rebellious people of Israel from Egypt and says, "But I acted *for the sake of my name*, that it should not be profaned in the sight of the nations among whom they lived, in whose sight I made myself known to them in bringing them out of the land of Egypt" (see also 20:14, 22, 28, 44; 36:21–23). God is jealous for his name, and he will bring to pass all that he has said: "And my holy name I will make known in the midst of my people Israel, and I will not let my holy name be profaned anymore. And the nations shall know that I am the LORD, the Holy One in Israel. . . . Therefore thus says the Lord GOD: Now I will restore the fortunes of Jacob and have mercy on the whole house of Israel, and I will be jealous for my holy name" (39:7, 25). Therefore, God's grace and mercy to Israel (and the nations) depend not upon the worthiness of man but upon God's holy name alone.

Man's Sinfulness and Responsibility

When earlier considering the holiness of the Lord, we briefly mentioned the unholiness of man, but mankind's *sinfulness* in Ezekiel warrants further consideration. Israel's unfaithfulness to their covenant Lord provides the impetus for this prophetic work. Ezekiel is a covenant lawyer, a prosecuting attorney bringing indictment after indictment against them for their iniquity. From idolatry to Sabbath breaking (see Ezekiel 22), the people are called to account for their wickedness. The special relationship that Israel has with Yahweh exacerbates their infidelity. They were specially chosen to be the Lord's people and his bride, but they have turned away from him to go after other gods. Notably, Ezekiel exemplifies the nation's adulterous nature in chapter 23 with the picture of two sisters who played the harlot, Oholah and Oho-libah. Ezekiel 23:4 states that Oholah is Samaria (the former capital of the nothern kingdom of Israel) and Oholibah is Jerusalem (the capital of Judah). The rest of the chapter vividly describes their desire for someone or something other than the Lord and his rule, just before the fall of Jerusalem is announced in Ezekiel 24. Israel and Judah were so sinful that God calls Sodom their sister and even states that they were worse than Sodom: "within a very little time you were more corrupt than they in all your ways" (Ezek. 16:47).[34]

Ezekiel does not restrict human sinfulness to God's covenant people. The nations are included in God's reckoning of mankind's wickedness. The second major part of the book concentrates upon the foreign nations and Yahweh's judgment of them. So there remains in this work a universal perspective of man's fallenness and his impending doom, and lest someone blame another for his or her predicament, the Lord even directly addresses *individual responsibility*. In Ezekiel 18 the Lord deals with Israel's tendency to blame previous generations for their present plight (18:2). God says, "Behold, all souls are mine; the soul of the father as well as the soul of the son is mine: the soul who sins shall die" (18:4). From here, the Lord explains that the person who seeks him and lives righteously will live, but the one who does evil will die. God will even forgive if someone repents of his or her evil ways and seeks righteousness (18:21–23). If, however, someone lives righteously and then turns away from God to evil, he will die for his guilt (18:24). In this way, Yahweh declares the options to all individuals, and it remains each one's responsibility to choose life or death.

APPROACHING THE NEW TESTAMENT

The authors of the New Testament rely heavily upon the book of Ezekiel's imagery and theology. Nowhere is this reliance more prevalent than in Johannine literature. The apostle John's use of this prophetical work reverberates throughout his Gospel and the book of Revelation. As one studies John's use of Ezekiel, it becomes clear that the apostle saw the fulfillment of Ezekiel's prophecies in the coming of Christ, including both his first and second comings. However, contrary to some interpreters who take a very literalistic view of this Old Testament prophet, the apostle John saw spiritual and symbolic fulfillment in the person of Jesus as the new temple, the place where God's glory will dwell eternally.

To begin with, consider John's portrayal of Jesus as the Temple of God. In John 1:14, John writes, "And the Word became flesh and dwelt among us, and we have seen his glory, glory as of the only Son from the Father, full of grace and truth." The word translated "dwelt" literally means "to tabernacle," which echoes the image of the tabernacle where God's presence dwelt in Israel. Also, John says that "we have seen his *glory*," an allusion to Ezekiel's reoccurring theme that the glory of God rep-

---

[34] Interestingly, Lam. 4:6 also describes the sin of Israel as worse than the sin of Sodom: "For the iniquity of the daughter of my people Is greater than the sin of Sodom, Which was overthrown as in a moment, And no hands were turned toward her" (NASB).

resents the presence of God. Later, after Jesus's first cleansing of the temple, Christ says, "Destroy this temple, and in three days I will raise it up" (2:19). John then informs us that the temple to which he was referring is "his body" (2:21). Once again, the glory of God / God's presence dwells in Jesus's bodily form, the true Temple.[35]

The apostle does not stop there. Having shown Jesus as the New Temple, John then reveals through the account of the Samaritan woman at the well that Jesus provides "living water" (4:7–25, see esp. 4:10, 13–15). Also, in John 7:37–38, Jesus stands up on the last day of the Feast of Booths and says, "If anyone thirsts, let him come to me and drink. Whoever believes in me, as the Scripture has said, 'Out of his heart will flow rivers of living water.'" These statements that Jesus provides "living water" apparently refer to the new eschatalogical temple in Ezekiel 47, which yields water that makes everything live. That same water even turns the salt water of the Dead Sea to fresh water, causing it to teem with life. Clearly, John sees Jesus as Ezekiel's eschatological temple who gives living water to all who will come to him.

The book of Revelation provides even more connections with the book of Ezekiel.[36] From the beginning to the end of Revelation, John seemingly has his eye on Ezekiel's work. The description of Jesus's divine appearance in Revelation 1:15 relies clearly on imagery from the Old Testament prophet. His feet as burnished bronze and voice sounding like the roar of many waters reflect Ezekiel 1:7 and 43:2 respectively. Revelation 4–6 also alludes to the book of Ezekiel (see Ezekiel 1; 10; 43:1–5) in John's description of the presence of God with "the four living creatures" (Rev. 4:6–11) and their actions in Revelation 5 and 6. This allusion pictures the grandeur of God's holy presence in the heavenly realms. Later, in Revelation 10:8–11, the apostle John is commanded to take the scroll and eat it. It was "sweet as honey" in his mouth, which clearly echoes the command for Ezekiel to eat the scroll, which was "as sweet as honey" (Ezek. 3:1–3). Also, the mention of Gog and Magog in Revelation 20:8 recalls the prophecy in Ezekiel 38–39 against "Gog, of the land of Magog" (38:2). John pronounces in Revelation 20 that Satan will be released from prison after a thousand years and will gather the deceived "nations that are at the four corners of the earth, Gog and Magog, to gather them for battle" (20:8). The proclamation of God's judgment upon these places in Ezekiel finds eschatological fulfillment in the final judgment of God upon mankind.

In addition, the book of Revelation ends in a dramatic fashion by revealing that Ezekiel's eschatalogical temple is not a literal building but the Lord Jesus Christ himself. In the final description of the New Jerusalem, John writes, "And I saw no temple in the city, for its temple is the Lord God the Almighty and the Lamb" (Rev. 21:22). Revelation 22:1–2 continues the passage with a depiction of the river of life: "Then the angel showed me the river of the water of life, bright as crystal, flowing from the throne of God and of the Lamb through the middle of the street of the city;

---

[35] See also Col. 3:19; 2 Cor. 4:6; Heb. 1:3.

[36] Since every possible connection between Ezekiel and Revelation cannot be considered in a chapter of this length, only the main allusions will be noted. For an extended discussion on the temple in Ezekiel 40–48 and its connection with the New Testament (especially Revelation), see G. K. Beale, *The Temple and the Church's Mission: A Biblical Theology of the Dwelling Place of God*, NSBT 17 (Downers Grove, IL: InterVarsity Press, 2004), 335–64.

also, on either side of the river, the tree of life with its twelve kinds of fruit, yielding its fruit each month. The leaves of the tree were for the healing of the nations." In this text, John borrows from Ezekiel's vision of water flowing from the temple: "And on the banks, on both sides of the river, there will grow all kinds of trees for food. Their leaves will not wither, nor their fruit fail, but they will bear fresh fruit every month, because the water for them flows from the sanctuary. Their fruit will be for food, and their leaves for healing" (47:12). John concludes his account with the eschatalogical depiction of the new heavens and earth and the New Jerusalem, and at its center the presence of God and of the Lamb providing living water for the city.

In this way, the canon of Scripture concludes in a manner similar to the way in which it began. God creates all things, and he places humanity in a position to rule over creation. God's presence dwells with his people in the garden in Eden, which has the Tree of Life and the tree of the knowlegde of good and evil. Humanity falls into sin and loses God's special presence. God, however, promises his redemption (Gen. 3:15), and the rest of the Bible recounts God's faithfulness in keeping his promise to "dwell with" his people forever. As the Bible ends, we are shown that through Jesus, God dwells with his people, and he will do so forever. God spiritually regenerates his people. Then he will re-create all things and dwell at the center of his new creation—and the Tree of Life will be there. God and his Son—the true Temple and the Lamb—will never depart from their people. Thus, redemption will be complete, and salvation will be brought to final consummation.

While the book of Ezekiel presents challenges for every reader, its overall presentation delivers a glorious statement of God's work in redemptive history. Though the people of Israel have failed to keep Yahweh's covenant, he will not fail to bring about his promises. So while the people have and will experience judgment for sin, they will also experience his mercy and grace. Ezekiel's work does not mince words in terms of the consequence of rebellion—the time for exile has come. That reality, however, is not the last word. The reader finds himself awaiting an eschatological change that will make everything right—re-creation! With this glorious expectation of the coming glory of God, the Major Prophets are concluded, only to have some of these main themes repeated in the Minor Prophets and then find their ultimate fulfillment in Jesus Christ and his new covenant. In the end, God reveals his sovereign love to mankind, and those who receive it will glory in the presence of God forever.

Select Bibliography

Alexander, Ralph H. *Ezekiel*. In *The Expositor's Bible Commentary*, edited by Frank E. Gaebelein, 6:737–996. Grand Rapids, MI: Zondervan, 1986.

Allen, Leslie C. *Ezekiel 1–19*. WBC 28. Waco, TX: Word, 1994.

———. *Ezekiel 20–48*. WBC 29. Dallas: Word, 1990.

Beale, G. K. *The Temple and the Church's Mission: A Biblical Theology of the Dwelling Place of God.* NSBT 17. Downers Grove, IL: InterVarsity Press, 2004.

Block, Daniel I. *The Book of Ezekiel Chapters 1–24.* NICOT. Grand Rapids, MI: Eerdmans, 1997.

———. *The Book of Ezekiel Chapters 25–48.* NICOT. Grand Rapids, MI: Eerdmans, 1998.

Boadt, Lawrence. "Textual Problems in Ezekiel and Poetic Analysis of Paired Words." *JBL* 97, no. 4 (1978): 489–99.

Bright, John. *A History of Israel.* With an introduction and appendix by William P. Brown. 4th ed. Louisville: Westminister John Knox, 2000.

Craigie, Peter C. *Ezekiel.* Daily Study Bible. Philadelphia: Westminster, 1983.

De Vries, Pieter. "Ezekiel: Prophet of the Name and Glory of YHWH—The Character of His Book and Several of Its Main Themes." *JBPR* 4 (2012): 94–108.

De Vries, Simon J. "Remembrance in Ezekiel: A Study of an Old Testament Theme." *Int* 16, no. 1 (1962): 58–64.

Duguid, Iain M. *Ezekiel.* NIVAC. Grand Rapids, MI: Zondervan, 1999.

Freedman, David Noel. "The Book of Ezekiel." *Int* 18, no. 4 (1954): 446–71.

Greenberg, Moshe. *Ezekiel 1–20: A New Translation with Introduction and Commentary.* AB 22. Garden City, NY: Doubleday, 1983.

Harrison, R. K. *Introduction to the Old Testament.* Grand Rapids, MI: Eerdmans, 1969.

Hill, Andrew E. and John H. Walton. *A Survey of the Old Testament.* 2nd ed. Grand Rapids, MI: Zondervan, 2000.

Howie, Carl Gordon. *The Date and Composition of Ezekiel.* SBLMS 4. Philadelphia: SBL, 1950.

Joyce, Paul M. *Divine Initiative and Human Response in Ezekiel.* JSOTSup 51. Sheffield: JSOT Press, 1989.

Longman, Tremper, III, and Raymond B. Dillard. *An Introduction to the Old Testament.* 2nd ed. Grand Rapids, MI: Zondervan, 2006.

MacRae, Allen A. "The Key to Ezekiel's First Thirty Chapters." *BSac* 122, no. 487 (1965): 227–33.

Stuart, Douglas. *Ezekiel.* The Communicator's Commentary: Old Testament 18. Dallas: Word, 1989.

Torrey, Charles Cutler. *Pseudo-Ezekiel and the Original Prophecy.* YOSR 18. New Haven, CT: Yale University Press, 1930.

Zimmerli, Walther. "The Message of the Prophet Ezekiel." *Int* 23, no. 2 (1969): 131–57.

13

The Twelve

Daniel C. Timmer

INTRODUCTION

What is the Book of the Twelve? This question is not as simple as it may seem. How one answers this question depends primarily on the following considerations: (1) The authorship of these books—is God involved in authoring them, or are they purely human productions? (2) The way that God communicates to us through them—besides their verbal nature, do the books as a collection have a hermeneutically significant "shape"? In what follows, we will first address these introductory questions in reverse order and then move on to consider the content of the Twelve in light of our responses to them.

BACKGROUND ISSUES

Evidence for the "Shape" of the Twelve?

We begin with the order of the Twelve. Peterson summarizes possible rationales for the orders of the Twelve as *chronology* (though Joel is problematic), *catchwords* (though while these could be original, most think that they were added after the books were composed and thus are redactional links), *length* (though Joel's brevity and Zechariah's length make this problematic), and even *geography*.[1] Peterson himself suggests that the Twelve are a "thematized anthology" focused on the day of the Lord (though Jonah raises problems in this regard), so that their most evident shared characteristic is material, not formal.[2]

Each of these explanations has some merit, while some are more convincing than others. All the same, it is not necessary to choose one to the exclusion of others.

---

[1] David L. Peterson, "A Book of the Twelve?" in *Reading and Hearing the Book of the Twelve*, ed. James D. Nogalski and Marvin A. Sweeney, SymS 15 (Atlanta: Scholars Press, 2000), 6. See also my earlier exploration of this question in Daniel C. Timmer, *The Non-Israelite Nations in the Book of the Twelve: Thematic Coherence and the Diachronic-Synchronic Relationship in the Minor Prophets*, BibInt 135 (Leiden: Brill, 2015), 16–19.
[2] Peterson, "A Book of the Twelve?," 10.

Further, unless the most convincing rationale has significant hermeneutical import (which is not the case with geography, for example), we don't need to be unduly troubled by uncertainty. In any case, the prophets and those who collected them, as well as their New Testament interpreters, left us no clear indication of their rationale, so the importance of their shape should not be overstated.

Extant Orders of the Twelve

To guard against conjecture, especially since the "shape" of the Twelve *is* often credited with hermeneutical significance, we must also keep in mind the various orders of the collection attested to in history. Around the middle of the second century BC, Sirach referred to a collection without specifying its order: "May the bones of the twelve prophets send forth new life from where they lie" (49:10; cf. *Baba Bathra* 14b/15a). So first, it is clear that the collection existed well before the New Testament era. But in what order? The available historical evidence demonstrates a considerable diversity of arrangements. Table 18 summarizes the various attested orders.[3]

Jones conveniently summarizes the data as follows: "One arrangement, reflected in manuscripts of the Septuagint, has survived only in translation [the 12 are followed by Isaiah, Jeremiah . . . Ezekiel in the Septuagint]. Yet another, seen in 4QXIIa, survived only as an archaeological artifact. Finally, only one arrangement, that of the Masoretic text, has survived as a continuing textual tradition in Hebrew."[4] Various explanations have been offered for the arrangement of the Septuagint and of 4QXII,[5] and it is also not certain that Jonah follows Malachi in the 4QXII fragments.[6] While these and other details await resolution, the most recent evaluations of the data suggest that multiple literary editions of the Twelve existed near the turn of the era.[7]

Significance of the Varying Orders

These varied orders, particularly that of the Septuagint, are important for several reasons. First, the oldest extant evidence, from Qumran, attests to an order that differs slightly from the Masoretic text (assuming that Jonah indeed follows Malachi in 4QXII per Jones's arguments).[8] Second, while the Septuagint translators inevitably

---

[3] Following Marvin A. Sweeney, "Sequence and Interpretation in the Book of the Twelve," in Nogalski and Sweeney, *Reading and Hearing the Book of the Twelve*, 52n7. More evidence from Qumran exists; see Russell Earl Fuller, "The Form and Formation of the Book of the Twelve," in *Forming Prophetic Literature: Essays on Isaiah and the Twelve in Honor of John D. W. Watts*, ed. John W. Watts and Paul R. House, JSOTSup 235 (Sheffield: Sheffield Academic Press, 1996), 86–101.

[4] Barry A. Jones, "The Book of the Twelve as a Witness to Ancient Biblical Interpretation," in *Reading and Hearing the Book of the Twelve*, 69. For more on 4QXIIa, see the references in Aaron Schart, "Reconstructing the Redaction History of the Twelve Prophets: Problems and Models," in Nogalski and Sweeney, *Reading and Hearing the Book of the Twelve*, 37n16.

[5] See Thomas Römer, "Introduction," in *Two Sides of a Coin: Juxtaposing Views on Interpreting the Book of the Twelve / the Twelve Prophetic Books*, ed. Ehud Ben Zvi and James D. Nogalski, Analecta Gorgiana 201 (Piscataway, NJ: Gorgias Press, 2009), 5n10. On 4QXIIa, see further Odil Hannes Steck, "Zur Abfolge Maleachi—Jona in 4Q76 (4QXIIa)," *ZAW* 108, no. 2 (1996): 249–53.

[6] See Jones, "The Book of the Twelve as Witness," 69; Philippe Guillaume, "The Unlikely Malachi-Jonah Sequence (4QXIIa)," *JHebS* 7 (2007): article 15.

[7] See for this conclusion George J. Brooke, "The Twelve Minor Prophets and the Dead Sea Scrolls," in *Congress Volume: Leiden 2004*, ed. André Lemaire, VTSup 109 (Leiden: Brill, 2006), 19–43; Martin Beck, "Das Dodekapropheton als Anthologie," *ZAW* 118, no. 4 (2006): 558–81. The orders are helpfully tabulated in Philippe Guillaume, "A Reconsideration of Manuscripts Classified as Scrolls of the Twelve Minor Prophets (XII)," *JHebS* 7 (2007): article 16, p. 9.

[8] Redditt counters this point by arguing that "the people at Qumran are known to have changed the order of other biblical books to suit their own needs: specifically in the Psalms Scroll, the Habakkuk Pesher, the Temple Scroll, and the Great Isaiah

Septuagint (Vaticanus) (fourth century AD)	Masoretic Text (L) (ca. AD 1008)	*Martyrdom and Ascension of Isaiah* 4:22 (ca. AD 75–175)	*Lives of the Prophets* (first century AD)	4QXII (fragments a, b, g) (ca. 150 BC)	Mur 88 (ca. AD 75)
Hosea	Hosea	Amos	Hosea	Joel	
Amos	Joel	Hosea	Micah	Amos?	
Micah	Amos	Micah	Amos	Obadiah	
Joel	Obadiah	Joel	Joel		Jonah
Obadiah	Jonah	Nahum	Obadiah	Nahum	Micah
Jonah	Micah	Jonah	Jonah	Habakkuk	Nahum
Nahum	Nahum	Obadiah	Nahum		
Habakkuk	Habakkuk	Habakkuk	Habakkuk	Zephaniah	Habakkuk
Zephaniah	Zephaniah	Haggai	Zephaniah	Haggai	Zephaniah
Haggai	Haggai	Zephaniah	Haggai		Haggai
Zechariah	Zechariah	Zechariah	Zechariah	Malachi	Zechariah
Malachi	Malachi	Malachi	Malachi	Jonah?	

Table 18

worked from Hebrew manuscripts consistently tied to the proto-Masoretic text tradition and attempted to translate them faithfully, they did not feel obliged to follow the order eventually reflected in the Masoretic tradition (assuming it was available to them). Jones is therefore wise to offer a cautious conclusion: "It is better to speak not so much of any 'original' arrangement of the Twelve, but rather of an original *diversity* of arrangements in circulation among Jewish communities of the final centuries before the common era."[9]

Jones draws a further inference from this data that leads us to consider the hermeneutical significance of the order of books in a collection: "The diversity of ancient arrangements of the Twelve appears to support Ben Zvi's argument that the Twelve is a collection of individual books of varied arrangement rather than a single unified work of definitive shape."[10] This brings us to the question of how to approach the Twelve *as a collection*: should our hermeneutic take account of the Twelve's order and its rationale(s)—that is, its "shape"?

This question gets at the nature of a "text," which is no simple question.[11] In the case of the Twelve, it is best to formulate an answer inductively, beginning with the collection itself. Ben Zvi notes that in the *pesharim* from Qumran the readers/writers "were aware of the fact that the twelve prophetic books were written in one scroll

---

Scroll." Paul L. Redditt, "The Formation of the Book of the Twelve: A Review of Research," in *Thematic Threads in the Book of the Twelve*, ed. Paul L. Redditt and Aaron Schart, BZAW 325 (Berlin: de Gruyter, 2003), 9.

[9] Jones, "Book of the Twelve as a Witness," 69.

[10] Jones, "Book of the Twelve as a Witness," 69.

[11] See Ludwig Morenz and Stefan Schorch, eds., *Was ist ein Text? Alttestamentliche, ägytologishe und altorientalistische Perspektiven*, BZAW 362 (Berlin: de Gruyter, 2012).

but yet considered them separate works,"[12] and thus he stresses the fact that each book in the Twelve has its own title.[13] All textual traditions, of course, recognized this reality—none of the Twelve lacks an introduction separating it from the preceding book. However much other factors unify the collection on a literary level, then, they were never sufficient to incline scribes or translators to eliminate the titles that divide the books, which shows that each book of the Twelve has the same literary integrity as Isaiah or Jeremiah.

Ben Zvi also criticizes a single-book approach to the Twelve for creating literary unity from factors that carry limited significance, such as link words.[14] Thus even if for the moment we bracket the literary and hermeneutical importance of titles, Ben Zvi argues that the features that some have proposed as sufficient to make the Twelve a unified work are inadequate. For example, Nogalski proposes that Hosea and Joel be read together in part because the words "this," "inhabitants," "wine," "vine," and "grain" appear in Hosea 14 and Joel 1. Ben Zvi responds as follows:

> It is most unlikely . . . that the intended and primary readers of these two texts not only (a) noticed the repetition of four very common words among hundreds in the relevant texts—a feat for which they would have had to look at these texts in a very a-contextualized manner—and even (b) added to these four a combination of "this" and "these" but also (c) thought that such a repetition created a sense of textual bond between these two texts that outweighed the most salient and overt differences between the two texts.[15]

This is not to deny that the books share significant similarities, particularly on the literary and linguistic levels. Ben Zvi himself suggests the likelihood of there being, among twelve individual books all authored in the same "social group" (but not necessarily simultaneously), "a (largely) shared discourse, a common linguistic heritage, implied 'intertextuality,' and shared literary/ideological tendencies."[16] Still, the integrity of a literary text, identified in large part by its title and distinct historical setting, is not something that can easily be discounted (by minimizing the importance of titles) or replaced (by means of catchwords).

Still other arguments have been put forward in favor of reading the Twelve as a literary unity. Schart, for example, understands Sirach 49:10 to refer to a book (in the sense that we use the word today). He also suggests that since the Qumran copies of the Twelve leave only three lines rather than a partial column blank before the beginning of a new book, they present the twelve "writings" as part of a single "book."[17] Schart draws an analogy with the formation of the Psalter: since both have been extensively redacted, both have been significantly unified. However, he admits, since only the Psalter has a single title for the whole collection, the lack of a single

---

[12] Ehud Ben Zvi, "Twelve Prophetic Books or 'The Twelve'?: A Few Preliminary Considerations," in Watts and House, *Forming Prophetic Literature*, 131.
[13] Ben Zvi, "Twelve Prophetic Books?," 137.
[14] Ben Zvi, "Twelve Prophetic Books?," 140.
[15] Ben Zvi, "Is The Twelve Hypothesis Likely," in Ben Zvi and Nogalski, *Two Sides of a Coin*, 88.
[16] Ben Zvi, "Twelve Prophetic Books?," 155.
[17] Aaron Schart, "Das Zwölfprophetenbuch als redaktionelle Großeinheit," *TLZ* 133, no. 3 (2008): 227–28.

superscription over the Twelve means we can expect less unity in the Twelve than in the Psalter or a prophetic "book" like Isaiah, Jeremiah, or Ezekiel.[18]

At least two critiques should be brought at this point. First, in his argument from Sirach, Schart seems to have assumed what he seeks to prove, namely, that when Ben Sira refers to a "book," he means a unified, essentially single composition.[19] Second, with respect to the Qumran evidence, one could argue that the presence of the super-scriptions in the Qumran copies of the Twelve obviated the need to begin a new column, since the end of one book and the beginning of the next were already sufficiently clear.

The Interpretative Significance of the Shape of the Twelve

Where does all this leave us? To summarize our findings thus far, (1) there were various orders for the Twelve prior to the New Testament era; (2) the rationale for any of these orders has proven very elusive; (3) arguments in favor of reading the Twelve as one, unified work must overcome the literary significance of the titular introduction that begins each book; and (4) arguments in favor of reading the Twelve as one, unified work must provide semantically significant grounds for such unity (i.e., more than isolated catchwords, remembering that meaning arises from combinations of words).

These points bring us back to our earlier question: is there an intentional "shape" to the Twelve that should guide its interpretation? These four considerations should give us pause, but one or two more challenges remain. Approaches to the Twelve that accord hermeneutical significance to the literary order of the collection and its resultant "shape" must give historical or theological grounds for taking one order as exclusively significant and must develop a hermeneutic of "shape" that relates responsibly to linguistic communication. Sailhamer has undertaken this latter task by drawing an analogy with a film—a whole created by assembling various sections, a *montage*—but the analogy with film fails to convince because the multiple authors he proposes for the Twelve differs from the single authorship of the film.[20] Similarly, the claim that the Masoretic *order* is inspired lacks a sufficient hermeneutical explanation, and the New Testament offers no evidence that canonical order has hermeneutical significance. Finally, the fact that the influential canon approach of Childs defines textual meaning as "a function of a cultural system rather than an expression of intention" encourages us to adopt an approach that recognizes the primacy of the text's verbal-semantic content, and especially its linguistically and historically grounded meaning, over its nonverbal "shape."[21]

---

[18] Schart, "Großeinheit," 228. Paradoxically, he takes the similar titles of the "D-corpus" (Hosea, Amos, Micah, Zephaniah) as evidence of their shared redactional origin. Schart, "Großeinheit," 233. This is a very slim basis on which to propose the comprehensive redaction that this subcorpus, and eventually the Twelve, underwent.

[19] Heath Thomas makes a similar argument: he suggests that "bones" "presumably implies that this coherent book (the bones serve as a framework for a body) and the message of that book were to instill hope" but assumes that only one prophet's bones are in view. "Hearing the Minor Prophets: The Book of the Twelve and God's Address," in *Hearing the Old Testament: Listening for God's Address*, ed. Craig G. Bartholomew and David J. H. Beldman (Grand Rapids, MI: Eerdmans, 2012), 360.

[20] John H. Sailhamer, *Introduction to Old Testament Theology: A Canonical Approach* (Grand Rapids, MI: Zondervan, 1995), 214, followed by Stephen G. Dempster, *Dominion and Dynasty: A Biblical Theology of the Hebrew Bible*, NSBT 15 (Downers Grove, IL: InterVarsity Press, 2003), 33–35.

[21] Brevard Childs, "Response to Reviewers of *Introduction to the Old Testament as Scripture*," *JSOT* 16 (1980): 52. For critical responses to Childs's work over the way it configures the text's relation to history and meaning, see Dale A. Brueggemann,

In light of these points, while we can appreciate various links and similarities between the collection's constituent books, for our investigation of the Twelve, we will first limit our hermeneutical horizon to each individual book and then explore the coherence of the books (among themselves but more importantly with the rest of the Christian Canon) on the basis of their common divine authorship and their shared focus on a single, unified history of redemption.

The Unity and Diversity of the Twelve

The decision to approach the Twelve as a collection that is not redactionally unified will appear to some to be an open door to hermeneutical incoherence. For various reasons, many have argued that the collection as we have it resulted from a complex process of redaction spanning centuries. Wolfe sees the Twelve as the accretion of thirteen layers, including a "day of Yahweh" layer, even though his reconstruction generally follows the chronology suggested by the books' opening lines.[22] Schart's approach reaches similar conclusions.[23] Wöhrle takes as a cornerstone of his theory the existence of an exilic "Book of the Four" or D-corpus (Hosea, Amos, Micah, and Zephaniah), which is indebted to 2 Kings 17 (Hosea and Amos), 2 Kings 18 (Micah), and 2 Kings 22–25 (Zephaniah).[24] Nogalski reached similar conclusions a few years earlier.[25]

It may be admitted that redaction would, in theory, contribute coherence to the text. On the other hand, redactional additions are often identified by virtue of their perceived theological incoherence with respect to their contexts. More important, when the redaction of individual sections takes precedence over the final form of the text, the verbal authorial discourse of each individual book *as a book*—with its literary, historical, and theological facets and coherence—comes in danger of being overwritten. Furthermore, without presenting in detail the arguments against redactional approaches, we can briefly note that the vast complexity of most such theories reduces their probability to worrisome levels.[26] Moreover, many of the criteria for identifying redactional additions are circular[27] or unconvincing.[28]

"Brevard Childs' Canon Criticism: An Example of Post-Critical Naiveté," *JETS* 32, no. 3 (1989): 311–26; Iain W. Provan, "Canons to the Left of Him: Brevard Childs, His Critics and the Future of Old Testament Theology," *SJT* 50, no. 1 (1997): 1–38; John N. Oswalt, "Canonical Criticism: A Review from a Conservative Viewpoint," *JETS* 30, no. 3 (1987): 317–25.

[22] As summarized by Schart, "Reconstructing," 42.

[23] As summarized by Schart, "Reconstructing," 42.

[24] Jakob Wöhrle, "Joel and the Formation of the Book of the Twelve," *BTB* 40 (2010): 128; see also his *Die frühen Sammlungen des Zwölfprophetenbuches: Entstehung und Komposition*, BZAW 360 (Berlin: de Gruyter, 2006), and *Der Abschluss des Zwölfprophetenbuches: Buchübergreifende Redaktionsprozesse in den späten Sammlungen*, BZAW 389 (Berlin: de Gruyter, 2008).

[25] James D. Nogalski, *Literary Precursors to the Book of the Twelve*, BZAW 217 (Berlin: de Gruyter, 1993), and Nogalski, *Redactional Processes in the Book of the Twelve*, BZAW 218 (Berlin: de Gruyter, 1993).

[26] In Landy's words, "a proposal with two-thirds (2/3) probability will decrease to four-ninths (4/9) at the second stage and to only 16 in 81 chances of being correct in the third stage." Francis Landy, "Three Sides of a Coin: In Conversation with Ben Zvi and Nogalski, *Two Sides of a Coin*," *JHebS* 10 (2010): article 11, p. 17n52. See in more detail Joshua Berman, "A Response: Three Points of Methodology," *JHebS* 10 (2010): article 9, pp. 42–49, esp. 43–44. Berman argues that if a conclusion rests on multiple factors, "we must compute the likelihood of each factor, and multiply them, for a final determination of probability." "A Response," 43.

[27] It seems that the dual role of redaction has not been sufficiently explored, especially since at the level of the book it indicates discontinuity while at the level of the collection it indicates unification. Can a redaction that is by definition poorly anchored in its host-text simultaneously lend coherence to the larger collection in which its host-text was taken up? Jeremias's observation that redactional interplay can go in both directions further complicates the question. Jörg Jeremias, "The Interrelationship between Amos and Hosea," in Watts and House, *Forming Prophetic Literature*, 172–86.

[28] See Benjamin D. Sommer's trenchant critique of the frequent practice of dating a text to a period in which social or other factors are thought to favor its production in "Dating Pentateuchal Texts and the Perils of Pseudo-Historicism," in

Our reasons for preferring an approach to each book as it stands (i.e., in its final form, which is the only extant form) rather than as a collection of discordant redactional bits are thus the same reasons for preferring an approach to each book as a literary unity rather than part of a twelve-chapter book. In other words, our hermeneutical point of departure must take account of the fundamental fact that each book of the Twelve *is a book*. The reader is thus obliged to attempt to understand each book as a unity before, failing that, being forced to turn to its constituent parts (redactional approaches) or to the literary whole of which it is a part ("shape" approaches) as the primary locus of meaning and coherence. Belief in the text's inspiration and in its joint divine-human authorship confirms the value of a book-focused approach because such a doctrine of Scripture places importance on the historical rootedness and coherence of the divine-human communication these books record and present.

Ultimately, of course, we want to do justice to the unity *and* diversity of these books, and a book-focused approach seems to still be the best way to do so. Shaped-canon approaches run the risk of obscuring historical diversity and referentiality, while redactional approaches run the risk of overstating literary or theological variety. Therefore the following exploration of the Twelve will approach each book both as an individual composition *and* as part of a larger collection while rooting meaning in each book as an integral whole. This approach is anchored in the little empirical data we have—namely, explicit attributions of authorship or date (e.g., the regnal notices in various incipits)—or in a book's more general historical setting (e.g., Babylon's rise as observed by Habakkuk). In the absence of contrary evidence, this approach proposes that the constituent books of the Twelve came into being *independently* and does not insist that they were transformed into a single work before (or after) Ben Sira mentions "the bones of the twelve prophets." Nor does it interpret link words, shared citations (e.g., of Ex. 34:6–7), and other coherence-favoring phenomena as evidence of a later, imposed coherence. Instead, in this approach we are content to view such data *first of all* in light of each book's inherent literary unity and conceptual coherence before considering how that book relates to the other books in the collection. Ultimately, the coherence of the individual book, of the collection of which it is part, and of the Canon as a whole can be guaranteed only by its ultimate divine authorship.

MESSAGE AND THEOLOGY
Theme

A theme is the statement that a work is making about its subject.[29] Thus the majority of the secondary elements in the text must have meaningful relationships with the theme in order for the work to be semantically coherent and to communicate effectively. While a focus on theme might seem to dispense too quickly with compositional

---

The Pentateuch: International Perspectives on Current Research, ed. Thomas B. Dozeman, Konrad Schmid, and Baruch J. Schwartz; FAT 78 (Tübingen: Mohr Siebeck, 2011), 85–108.

[29] Jason T. LeCureux, *The Thematic Unity of the Book of the Twelve*, Hebrew Bible Monographs 41 (Sheffield: Sheffield Phoenix, 2012), 27. See the longer discussion of theme and thematic coherence in Timmer, *The Non-Israelite Nations*, 4–11.

elements that have been the focus of much careful redactional and source-critical work, it is simply the expression in methodological terms of the axiom that meaning arises from combinations of words and that the primary semantic unit is the sentence rather than the word.[30]

Unfortunately, choosing which themes to explore in the Twelve involves sacrificing both detail (since following numerous themes would be terribly lengthy) and simplicity (since no single theme does justice to the majority of the Twelve's content). The day of Yahweh is probably the best single optic with which to survey the Twelve, but as we shall see, it is a very polyvalent concept and so is more a metatheme than a simple theme. The simpler themes we will explore bear important relationships to the day of Yahweh but also allow us to capture more detail, especially in the case of books which make limited or no use of the day of Yahweh (e.g., Jonah, Nahum, Haggai).[31]

Chronology

The varied dates of each of the books that constitute the collection of the Twelve encourage us to explore the Twelve by means of something other than its literary order.[32] Accordingly, our thematic survey will generally follow chronological lines, largely because chronology seems to be the predominant (but not sole) organizing scheme of the Twelve.[33] This affirmation is simply an inductive argument based on the incipits of Hosea, Amos, (arguably) Jonah, Micah, Nahum (dated per 3:8 and Nineveh's fall in 612), Zephaniah, Haggai, and Zechariah. Among these eight books, six offer clear dates while two others are fairly precise. Moreover, the superscriptions of Hosea, Amos, Micah, and Zephaniah are very similar, as are the superscriptions of Haggai and Zechariah, and together they establish a rough historical sequence from the middle of the eighth century to the end of the sixth century. In general this chronology provides a plausible order for the composition or setting (if not collection and redaction) of the books that make up the Twelve.[34]

Two limits to this diachronic approach should be noted. First, while we expect later prophets to develop or elaborate on themes touched upon by earlier prophets, we must allow a given author's perspective to determine how the theme in question is treated. The fact that a later book's perspective on a given point seems less developed

---

[30] As James Barr explains, "The linguistic bearer of the theological statement is usually the sentence and the still larger literary complex and not the word or the morphological and syntactical mechanisms." *The Semantics of Biblical Language* (Oxford: Oxford University Press, 1961), 269. More traditional linguistic scholars also identify the sentence (rather than the word) as the prime semantic unit: "molecularity is not a requirement but a finding: not a hypothetical universal canon, but a formal characterization which mirrors an empirical discovery. Hence it can operate as a constraint on the attempts to produce a theory of meaning in respect of biblical languages." Arthur Gibson, *Biblical Semantic Logic: A Preliminary Analysis*, 2nd ed., BibSem 75 (Sheffield: Sheffield Academic Press, 2001), 212. Gibson goes on (214) to cite Michael Dummett, "What Is a Theory of Meaning? (II)," in *Truth and Meaning: Essays in Semantics*, ed. Gareth Evans and John McDowell (Oxford: Oxford University Press, 1976), 79: "The difference between a molecular and a holistic view of language is not that, on a molecular view each sentence could, in principle, be understood in isolation, but that, on a holistic view, it is impossible fully to understand any sentence without knowing the entire language, whereas, on a molecular view there is, for each sentence, a determinate fragment of the language a knowledge of which will suffice for a complete understanding of that sentence."

[31] Dempster suggests "the impending eschaton" as the metatheme for the Twelve and proposes as distinct themes sin and judgment, an impending day of eschatological disaster, the restoration of all things, and David. *Dominion and Dynasty*, 182–88.

[32] See for this Brooke, "The Twelve Minor Prophets"; Beck, "Das Dodekapropheton als Anthologie." The orders are helpfully tabulated in Guillaume, "A Reconsideration of Manuscripts," 9.

[33] Rolf Rendtorff calls it "an explicit chronological framework." "How to Read the Book of the Twelve as a Theological Unity," in Nogalski and Sweeney, *Reading and Hearing the Book of the Twelve*, 76.

[34] Schart, "Großeinheit," 230. Joel remains difficult to integrate on this basis; see Wöhrle, "Joel."

or more developed than an earlier book's is not sufficient to disprove or prove its later date. Second, we must also allow for some books to be dated only tentatively and thus must view their integration into a diachronic scheme with greater restraint than others.[35]

The overall coherence of the Twelve, ultimately rooted in its inspiration, provides a sufficient basis for a thematic survey of the corpus (unity). It also allows us to assert the uniqueness of each constituent book on the basis of its historical context and semantic content (diversity). Under this overarching unity, then, we can give unrestricted attention to diachronic development across the corpus and the unique facets or characteristics of each book.

Sin in Israel and Judah

Without wanting to give an overly dour cast to the prophetic writings, we must still note that their raison d'être (at least in terms of the immediate cause) was almost inseparable from the sin that increasingly characterized much of Israel and Judah in the eighth century and later.[36] As early as the ministries of Amos and Hosea (mid-eighth century), the northern kingdom had established a record of deviancy (first royal, then popular) that reached back to the time of Jeroboam I (1 Kings 12:25–33) and showed no signs of changing. In fact, Amos underlines that despite increasingly severe punishment (the fivefold cycle of unsuccessful discipline in Amos 4:6–11 echoes the fivefold cycle of worsening covenant sanctions in Lev. 26:14–39), Israel has persisted in her sin so that superlative punishment is now unavoidable (Amos 4:12).[37] Hosea gives Israel's sin a very vertical, Godward aspect when he summarizes it under the metaphor of marital infidelity, and Hosea too recognizes that severe punishment is unavoidable (Hos. 1:4, 6, 8; 10:13–15; 13:4–8).

While the southern kingdom of Judah remained more faithful for a time (Hos. 11:12), it did not take to heart the punishment of the north that it witnessed. Micah, writing around the end of the eighth century, ties a theophany of global significance directly to the sins of the northern and southern kingdoms alike (1:2–5). Micah's critique is far-ranging and includes social injustice (2:1–2, 8–9), a rejection of the prophets' message (2:6), and the abuse of social and religious power (3:1–11; 7:3), among other things (note also 5:10–14; 7:9).

Notably, the prophets' ministries, and even covenantal sanctions, produced little amelioration in terms of Israel's or Judah's sinful behavior. Well over a century after the writing prophets took up their public ministries, Habakkuk is gravely troubled by the violence of late seventh-century Judah and its deadening effect on Yahwistic

---

[35] For example, Joel lacks any clear means by which to date the book. The significance of the lexical links between Joel and Amos notwithstanding, it is very difficult to establish that such links imply chronological proximity.

[36] Patrick D. Miller notes, "At least by the eighth century, prophetic oracles came to be directed against *various segments of society* or against the *society as a whole*." "The World and Message of the Prophets: Biblical Prophecy in Its Context," in *Israelite Religion and Biblical Theology: Collected Essays*, JSOTSup 267 (Sheffield: Sheffield Academic Press, 2000), 519.

[37] While some theologians still assert Wellhausen's dictum that the prophets can be understood without the law, this is nearly impossible to establish. The prophets routinely make reference to Pentateuchal law and to the covenantal relationship of which it is part. See Gene M. Tucker, "Prophecy and Prophetic Literature," in *The Hebrew Bible and Its Modern Interpreters*, ed. Douglas A. Knight and Gene M. Tucker, BMI 1 (Chico, CA: Scholars Press, 1985), 325–68, esp. 331.

revelation, teaching, and practice (Hab. 1:2–4). About the same time, Zephaniah pronounces judgment on those guilty of religious syncretism or outright worship of other gods (Zeph. 1:4–6) while contradicting the false impression that Yahweh is complacent or lax (Zeph. 1:12).

Perhaps most surprisingly, even the exile of the southern kingdom by Babylon in 586, which entailed the catastrophic destruction of the Jerusalem temple and the interruption of the Davidic line, did little to change the hearts of those who survived (though one can perhaps infer from the absence of archaeological evidence that idolatry became much less common after the exile).[38] The postexilic prophets thus continue to focus on the spiritual and moral condition of the returnees just as did their preexilic predecessors. Indeed, the book of Zechariah begins with a call to repentance that puts the returned community on par with their forebears, who refused to repent and so suffered judgment (Zech. 1:2–6). Haggai, speaking in the year 520, asserts that within two decades of the people's return, covenantal curses are already reappearing (Hag. 1:6). Finally, Malachi (probably ministering in the fifth century), focuses his longest condemnation on a corrupt priesthood (Mal. 1:6–2:9), while Joel, which likely dates to the fifth or fourth century, limits itself to the problem of insincere repentance (Joel 2:12–13).

The Sins of the Non-Israelite Nations

The sins of the non-Israelite nations are typically identified as pride (Hab. 2:5; Zeph. 2:8, 10), violence (whether against Israel or Judah, as in Joel 3:2–3, 5–6; Amos 1:11–12; or against each other, as in Amos 2:1–3; Hab. 2:12–13), and rebellion against Yahweh (Nah. 1:9–15, esp. 1:9, 11). Several of the nations around Israel and Judah subjugated these two relatively small nations from time to time and so were occasionally their suzerains (Hos. 10:6; 12:1). While the prophets do not condemn this status quo itself, they imply that something is inherently sinful in the way that the nations subjugate Israel and Judah; hence even the "pax Persia" is condemned by Zechariah (1:11–12).[39] There is no significant development in terms of the sins that characterize the nations in the pre- and postexilic periods, but in terms of prophetic eschatology, some of the nations will see radical transformations (see "Repentance of Non-Israelite Nations" on p. 333).

Punishment of the Sins of Israel and Judah

The idea of sin's punishment follows logically upon the resounding condemnations of the prophets. The paradigm of the Sinai covenant made clear the link between sin and punishment (Leviticus 26; Deuteronomy 27–28), and the prophets regularly

---

[38] Edwin M. Yamauchi notes, "Since the beginning of the Persian era not a single piece of evidence has been found for any pagan cults in Judah and Samaria." "Ezra and Nehemiah, Books of," in *New Dictionary of Biblical Theology*, ed. T. Desmond Alexander and Brian S. Rosner (Downers Grove, IL: InterVarsity Press, 2000), 293. Contrast this with the view of H. Niehr, who argues that a variety of biblically proscribed religions were practiced in postexilic Yehud. "Religio-Historical Aspects of the 'Early Post-exilic' Period," in *The Crisis of Israelite Religion*, OtSt 42 (Leiden: Brill, 1999), 239–41.
[39] See further J. Gordon McConville, *God and Earthly Power: An Old Testament Political Theology, Genesis–Kings*, LHBOTS 454 (London: T&T Clark, 2006).

availed themselves of this link. In his commentary on Hosea–Jonah, Stuart notes verbal and other links between dozens of passages in the first six books of the Twelve and a list of twenty-seven categories of curses derived from the Pentateuch. Our brief survey of some prophetic condemnations will show that this covenantal logic permeates the Twelve.[40]

As early as Hosea (4:3; 8:13; 9:3, 17), exile is unavoidable because of Israel's covenantal infidelity (Hosea 1). Micah insists that Israel and Judah will be exiled because of their violations of the covenant (Mic. 1:6, 16). About a century later, Zephaniah (1:13) announces a wide range of covenantal sanctions against Judah that together express the holistic destruction of exile.

While the postexilic prophets continue to condemn their audiences for their sins, threats of (a second) exile as punishment for sin are notably absent from their writings. This is not because the Sinai covenant is no longer in force but because these prophets see the exile as a mere precursor of an ultimate judgment on sin. While the preexilic prophets do speak of exile, they too see it not as ultimate but rather as a harbinger of things to come in the day of Yahweh. Note, for example, how Zephaniah's announcement of exile is followed immediately by a statement that the day of Yahweh is near (Zeph. 1:16) and how the whole context of Zephaniah 1 puts the exile in that larger context (Zeph. 1:2–3).

This shift from a historical or partial perspective to one that is eschatological or complete will appear in our study of the theme of deliverance as well, and it highlights a crucial dynamic in the eschatology of these books. The shift is *from* a paradigm determined by the national, ethnic identity of God's people (Israel and Judah) and their relationship with him on the basis of the Sinai covenant (before and after exile) *to* a paradigm in which ultimate judgment and deliverance come upon people irrespective of their national or ethnic identity. As a result, it destabilizes the Sinai paradigm (belonging to a nation) in favor of the Abrahamic paradigm (benefitting from the promises made to Abraham regardless of nationality).

This transition is perfectly captured by the concept of the *remnant*, which appears regularly throughout the Twelve. Note, first of all, that the remnant is very clearly an inner-Israel distinction[41]—the concept all by itself destabilizes the Sinai paradigm's national aspect.[42] Second, prophets use this inner-Israel distinction most effectively in contexts where they discuss ultimate punishment and ultimate deliverance. There is a historical remnant, according to some of the Twelve (e.g., Amos), but it does not escape exile. Not only were the vast majority of Israel and Judah exiled, but those who were left remained in the land at the discretion of their captors, not because of any moral or spiritual qualification.

The remnant that appears in contexts of ultimate judgment—and survives—is of

---

[40] Douglas K. Stuart, *Hosea–Jonah*, WBC 31 (Waco, TX: Word, 1987), xxxiii–xl.
[41] The concept is also used in connection with non-Israelite nations, but in such cases, of course, it serves simply to distinguish between the ultimate outcomes of judgment and deliverance without directly destabilizing the Sinai paradigm.
[42] This is not to suggest that the concept is foreign to the Sinai paradigm (cf. Ex. 32:25–29; 1 Kings 19:18) but rather that in a postexilic context without king, territory, or sovereignty, the shift from an empirical Israel to a spiritual Israel is more developed than in nonprophetic literature.

a different nature. Amos makes very clear that Israel will be sifted in a global process led by Yahweh in which "all the sinners of my people shall die by the sword" but not the smallest grain (of the remnant) will fall to the ground (Amos 9:8–10). Much later, Malachi makes the same inner-Israel distinction. Those Israelites who think it is worthless to serve Yahweh and who think that his justice can be thwarted will be completely destroyed. On the other hand, and in the same process, those Israelites who "fear Yahweh's name" (an expression that consistently describes those in a genuine relationship with Yahweh[43]) will be made his possession in terms reminiscent of Exodus 19, the classic text describing Israel's formation as a theocratic nation.[44]

Punishment of the Sins of the Non-Israelite Nations

The Twelve also affirm that God will punish the sins of the non-Israelite nations. The first thing to note is that this judgment is based on moral grounds: the nations will be punished because they have *sinned*, not because they are not Israelite. The historical judgments announced against the nations can be extensive, as when Amos announces the destruction of the royal infrastructure of Aram, the Philistine pentapolis, and other entities (Amos 1–2). Other punishments are not easily identified as either historical or eschatological (e.g., Obadiah; Zephaniah 2), in part because at least some of the nations concerned have a typological role (e.g., Edom in Obadiah; Assyria in Nahum). Finally, in a number of passages non-Israelite nations, usually characterized by stubborn opposition to Yahweh, meet with ultimate destruction (Joel 3; Mic. 5:8; Habakkuk 3; Hag. 2:20–22; Zech. 14:12–15).

Repentance of Israel and Judah

There is no doubt that repentance is a prominent theme in the Twelve. It is quite pronounced in Hosea (2:2b, 7; 14:1), Amos (5:14–16, 24), Haggai, and Malachi (especially due to the six-dispute structure), and it is also important in Joel (1:5, 8, 11, 14; 2:12–17), Micah (6:8), Zephaniah (1:7, 11; 2:1–3), and Zechariah.[45] The fact that preexilic and postexilic prophets alike press repentance upon their audiences means that repentance plays an important role in connection with both historical and ultimate punishment or deliverance.

Repentance does not guarantee deliverance from historical judgment (Joel 2:14; Amos 5:15; Jonah 3:9; Zeph. 2:3).[46] Still, the close association between repentance and "life" in Amos (5:4, 6, 14), for example, suggests (especially in light of Deuteronomy 30) that true repentance transcends particular, limited historical judgments and

---

[43] See, for example, Roland E. Murphy, *The Tree of Life: An Exploration of Biblical Wisdom Literature*, 3rd ed. (Grand Rapids, MI: Eerdmans, 2002), 16; Deryck Sheriffs, *The Friendship of the Lord* (Carlisle, UK: Paternoster, 1996), 162–64; and Joachim Becker, *Gottesfurcht im Alten Testament*, AnBib 25 (Rome: Päpstliches Bibelinstitut, 1965). Sheriffs concludes, "The spirituality of the 'fear of the Lord' is both the deep inward orientation and its practical outcome in behavior." *Friendship*, 164; similarly 92–93.

[44] Every other time that the term *possession* is used with God as its owner, it refers to Israel; cf., e.g., Ex. 19:5; Deut. 7:6.

[45] LeCureux makes this concept the primary theme of the Twelve in *The Thematic Unity of the Book of the Twelve*.

[46] While Zeph. 2:1–3 seems to contradict the claim that repentance delivers from the day of Yahweh, it may be that the aspect of the day of Yahweh in view is not its fully eschatological consummation but something less. It would be strange, not to say theologically problematic, if those exhorted to repent who have upheld justice and are meek would be fully destroyed by Yahweh.

deliverance from them. Hosea 14 also notably links repentance and abandoning other gods in whom Israel had trusted with the finding of full life in Yahweh. Repentance in the Twelve is thus often associated with both historical and eschatological outcomes. In Micah a chastened Israel draws nearer to God through *historical* punishment and awaits the *ultimate* manifestation of his righteousness (Mic. 7:8–10) that involves the complete pardon of her sins (7:20). Habakkuk experiences the same existential tension, feeling (at least by way of anticipation) the weight of Babylon's punitive attacks in the late seventh and early sixth centuries (Habakkuk 1) while awaiting the eschatological vindication that comes to the one who trusts in God's promise and that will fully establish perfect justice (Habakkuk 2–3).

This robust theology of repentance probably derives from the fact that the Twelve call for a holistic repentance that leads to complete submission to and trust in Yahweh. This is not to say that these prophets think just anything merits the term *repentance*. On the contrary, Joel mentions only one sin that (by default) must account in large part for the judgments that the book announces, and that sin is half-hearted repentance (2:12–13). Similarly, the repentance contemplated by the community in Hosea 6:1–3 seems inauthentic in light of what follows in 6:4, and that repentance contrasts sharply with the closing of the book where they request pardon, reject foreign help and deities, and exhibit complete contentment with Yahweh alone.[47]

A good way to integrate the theme of repentance into our understanding of the Twelve is to connect it to the inner-Israel distinction explored earlier, the remnant. Calls to repentance require the reader to respond—the call must be rejected or heeded, and the Twelve make clear the sharply contrasting outcomes of these two possible responses. The call to repent is also striking for its presence in postexilic writings, because it demonstrates that the return to the land is of no value if the people have not returned to Yahweh (Zech. 1:3).[48] The theme of repentance thus parallels the concept of the remnant, destabilizing Israel's external identity as Yahweh's covenant partner in favor of an internal disposition.

Repentance of Non-Israelite Nations

The book of Jonah constitutes the only instance of a non-Israelite nation repenting outside an eschatological context in the Twelve. While Nineveh's repentance was doubtfully a full-fledged conversion to Yahweh,[49] the historical setting provided by the link to Jonah son of Amittai makes it hard to resist the conclusion that even Nineveh could repent in ways that Israel in the eighth century consistently did *not*.

While the repentance of the Ninevites is hard to evaluate precisely, no such ambiguity appears in the case of the non-Israelite sailors in Jonah. Through a network of allusions to passages that distinguish between faithful and unfaithful *Israelites* (especially Pss. 115:3; 135:6), the author leaves no doubt that these formerly polytheistic sailors

---

[47] Geerhardus Vos offers an unparalleled exposition of this passage in *Grace and Glory: Sermons Preached in the Chapel of Princeton Theological Seminary* (Edinburgh: Banner of Truth, 1994), 1–24.
[48] LeCureux, *The Thematic Unity of the Book of the Twelve*, 238.
[49] See especially John H. Walton, "The Object Lesson of Jonah 4:5–7 and the Purpose of the Book of Jonah," *BBR* 2 (1992): 47–57.

become faithful worshipers of Yahweh.[50] Apart from the interesting questions that this raises about Israel's missionary role (cf. Deut. 4:6), the reader cannot escape the conclusion that non-Israelites with absolutely no Yahwistic background can change completely and be counted among those who "revere Yahweh" (although the text is otherwise silent about the process of repentance).

The repentance of some non-Israelite nations in the eschatological future appears rarely in the Twelve. (There is, of course, no need to limit ourselves to the Hebrew word group for "repent" since a variety of words and expressions can articulate the same concept.) However, since Yahweh's transformation of the nations is relatively common in the collection, and since this transformation inevitably involves a subjective, internal component, repentance is very frequently taken for granted. In Amos 9, for example, "all the nations who are called by my name" are inducted into the Davidic kingdom that Yahweh will restore (Amos 9:11–12), but not a word is said of their repentance. The same is true of the non-Israelite "peoples" in Zephaniah 3:9, who by some unspecified means no longer assault God's people as they did in Zephaniah 2 but now "call on Yahweh's name" and serve him "shoulder to shoulder." Zechariah too includes several passages that surely presuppose repentance but do not explicitly mention it. These passages include some nations being joined to Yahweh and becoming his people (Zech. 2:11) and also feature Zion's would-be eschatological attackers becoming worshipers of Yahweh (Zech. 14:16).

The only clear examples of eschatological repentance on the part of the nations are the seeking of Yahweh of hosts in Jerusalem by "many peoples and strong nations" (Zech. 8:20–22) and the similar turn toward Zion (in terms of direction) on the part of the nations in Micah 4:1–4 (cf. the parallel in Isa. 2:1–4). Both passages notably include worship of Yahweh and submission to him in their description of the nations, and so they require the reader to see this change as part of a holistic repentance that makes them faithful worshipers of Yahweh.

Deliverance of Israel, Judah, and the Remnant

As we take up a last Israel-focused theme, we continue to work with the historical/eschatological distinction and the inner-Israel distinction dictated by the remnant concept.[51] These two distinctions allow us to assert, for example, that there was historical deliverance from exile without having to say that the return to Yehud (i.e., Judah) was either the full accomplishment of prophetic eschatology or proof that all those who returned had repented and become faithful worshipers of Yahweh. Indeed, the reality "on the ground" in the postexilic period, at least as Haggai, Zechariah, Malachi, and Joel present it, would quickly force us to abandon such a simplistic approach to fulfillment. The two distinctions just mentioned thus allow us to say that those who returned were indeed a remnant but one not identical to *the* eschatological remnant that would be finally and fully manifested on the day of Yahweh.

---

[50] See Daniel C. Timmer, *A Gracious and Compassionate God: Mission, Salvation and Spirituality in the Book of Jonah*, NSBT 26 (Downers Grove, IL: InterVarsity Press, 2011), 72–74.

[51] Note, however, that redefining collective terms like "Israel" can accomplish the same thing, as seen in Hosea.

As we have already seen, the postexilic prophets continue to look forward to that day *and continue to anticipate the remnant's appearance* in that final denouement.

Mainly because of the typological, anticipatory nature of earlier deliverances from sin and its consequences, including the return from Babylonian exile, this section focuses on the eschatological deliverance that the Twelve associate with the end of the age. The link between the circumcision of the heart and "life" in Deuteronomy 30:6, as well as the clear connection of this internal change to the return from exile, suggests that whatever historical, external realizations of deliverance appeared in Israel's experience, these were not the end of the matter.[52]

Here we will again proceed chronologically through the Twelve and note how they describe this ultimate deliverance in various ways. Hosea, as we've noted, foresees a repentant Israel finding her full satisfaction and life in Yahweh (Hosea 14). Amos speaks of the renewed Davidic line and of the peaceful integration of foreign nations alongside the renewal of the land in terms drawn from the Sinai covenant (Amos 9:11–15). The same elements of reign and victory over enemies appear in Micah, which includes a strong note of forgiveness at the end of the book and subsumes the whole under the promise to Abraham (Mic. 7:18–20). Nahum's focus on Assyria near the middle of the seventh century is generally historical, but the opening hymn connects deliverance from Yahweh's holy vengeance with trust in him in a much more general and universal framework (Nah. 1:7–8). Where Habakkuk raises concerns about the injustice of Babylon, a response appears first through a series of woes that focus faith on Yahweh's reign (Hab. 2:20) but comes into full view in the theophanic hymn of Habakkuk 3, where Yahweh arrives in splendor to save his people and his anointed while destroying "the wicked." Zephaniah's description of the deliverance Yahweh will bring focuses on the dispositions, behavior, and status of those who survive his judgment: he restores worship (Zeph. 3:10), removes pride (3:11), and creates humility and trust (3:12), and those who are delivered "do no injustice and speak no lies" (3:13) while receiving universal "praise and renown" from Yahweh. All this takes place in a pastoral setting in which renewed Israel is free from all danger and fear and in which Yahweh exults over his delivered people in the most profound way (Zeph. 3:13b–17).

In the postexilic period, Haggai describes facets of Israel's ultimate deliverance in two primary ways: (1) the glory of the latter temple will exceed that of Solomon's temple (Hag. 2:6–9), and (2) Yahweh will overthrow "the throne of kingdoms" and "the strength of the kingdoms of the nations" while elevating Zerubbabel (Hag. 2:22). Zechariah's presentation of Israel's future is notoriously complex, in part because it is multifaceted. Deliverance includes the rebuilding of Jerusalem (1:16–17), the scattering of the nations who oppressed "Judah, Israel, and Jerusalem" (1:18–21), Yahweh taking up his residence among his people (2:5, 11–12; 8:3), the sending of Yahweh's "servant the Branch" to rule and serve as priest (Zechariah 3; 5), the destruction of sinners and the removal of sin from the land (Zechariah 5), and the deliverance of

---

[52] This is not to say, however, that the imagery of return never appears in contexts describing eschatological deliverance; note Zeph. 3:20.

Jerusalem from all attacks once and for all (Zechariah 14). Malachi's confrontational tone means that his description of deliverance is carefully couched in terms making clear that it will come only to those who truly revere Yahweh and that God will establish an intimate relationship with that remnant (3:17), bringing them healing and well-being (4:1–3). Finally, Joel also invites his audience to repent before announcing the coming salvation for those who call on the Lord's name (Joel 2:32), the destruction of the nations who oppose Yahweh and his people (Joel 3:1–16), and the renewal of the land crowned by Yahweh's taking his place as King among them (Joel 3:17–21).

Despite the wide variety of contexts and images used to describe Israel's eschatological deliverance in the Twelve, a common constellation revolves around internal purification of the remnant and the consummation of their relationship with Yahweh on the one hand, and the reestablishment of Jerusalem as Yahweh's royal city/temple on the other. The larger context is the purified or renewed land/earth, free of sin and sinners through the destruction of both Israelites and non-Israelites who refuse to submit to Yahweh.

Deliverance of Some among the Non-Israelite Nations

Despite the fact that many of their descriptions of the remnant's deliverance include the destruction of "the nations" or the like, the Twelve also affirm at a number of points that some non-Israelites will participate in the same deliverance as Israel. This means, obviously, that not *all* non-Israelites are doomed to destruction in prophetic eschatology. But how do we explain this apparently contradictory perspective? How can the nations be destroyed for their sins in some contexts while being delivered in others?

In a word, the "nations" are defined differently in each context. When a prophet foresees that some of them will turn to Yahweh, deliverance naturally follows. Recall especially their repentance in Micah 4 and Zechariah 8, already mentioned, but also the more numerous descriptions of their transformation into worshipers of Yahweh. Conversely, when a prophet foresees ongoing resistance to God and his people, this group of "nations" is to be punished for their rebellion. For example, in Joel 3 *nations* language refers to a group that refuses to submit to Yahweh and in fact persists in rebellion, even accepting Yahweh's invitation to war with the intention of retaliating against him (Joel 3:4, 9–11). In such contexts, a categorical moral evaluation like "their evil is great" (Joel 3:14) often makes clear that this group's moral and spiritual failings are key, while its ethnicity is incidental.

With this dual definition of the "nations" in mind, we turn to a diachronic survey of the theme of the nations' deliverance. Amos 9 foresees the integration of some non-Israelites "who are called by my name" into the renewed Davidic kingdom (9:12). Most frequently, the collocation "call [God's] name over" has as its object either Jerusalem[53]/the temple[54] (about ten times) or Israel[55] (about five times). When used

---

[53] On Jerusalem, see Jer. 25:29; Dan. 9:18, 19.

[54] On the temple, see 1 Kings 8:43 (= 2 Chron. 6:33); Jer. 7:10, 11, 14, 30; 32:34; 34:15.

[55] Of Israel, the description is voiced by Moses (Deut. 28:9–10); by God (2 Chron. 7:14); and by Daniel (Dan. 9:19). Isaiah 63:19 uses it to say that because of her judgment, Israel has become like "those over whom you never ruled, over whom your name was never called." Israel uses it of herself in Jer. 14:9. Exceptionally, Jeremiah uses it of himself in Jer. 15:16.

of a people group with God as the verbal subject, the phrase consistently denotes Yahweh's ownership of his covenant people.[56] This relationship was established not through military conflict but through a unilateral offer of a covenant relationship that Israel accepted, so Amos is essentially speaking of the integration of non-Israelites into the people of God. The deliverance they enjoy is thus identical to that of the remnant in the same context (described earlier). Micah's treatment of the nations, originating a few decades later, foresees some of them repenting and entering a peaceful relationship with Yahweh, Israel, and all other nations (Mic. 4:1–4) in language drawn from 1 Kings 4:25 or Leviticus 26:6 (notably, both texts speak of *Israel's* historical or eschatological benediction).

Zephaniah's description of the non-Israelite nations' deliverance is probably limited to Zephaniah 3:9, where only one divine action is mentioned: "I will give the peoples a pure lip." The expression "pure lip" is very rare (Job 33:3 only; cf. Pss. 15:3; 24:4; Prov. 10:8, 11, 32; Isa. 33:15). The closest conceptual parallels are Hosea 2:17, which speaks of removing Baal's name from unfaithful Israel (cf. Zeph. 1:4–6), and Isaiah 6:5, which speaks of a cleansing from sin by means of touching a coal from the altar on the lips (plural). A good case can be made that "purify" is not primarily cultic but moral or ethical when paired with heart or hands, and Irsigler is probably correct that it "means a comprehensive moral-religious purification."[57] The phrase "call on Yahweh's name" (with a variety of prepositions) can describe various types of communication with Yahweh, but in light of Zephaniah 2:11, the most reasonable meaning is a new relationship with Yahweh.[58] This is confirmed by the expression "serve Yahweh" in 3:9, which is also frequently contrasted with serving other gods.[59]

The deliverance of the nations in Zechariah is essentially identical to that of the remnant. Finally, Malachi makes several predictions that the nations will worship Yahweh acceptably and that Yahweh's name "will be great among the nations" (1:11, 17). The book's focus on the flaws of the returned community probably accounts for why Malachi develops those pregnant statements no further.

APPROACHING THE NEW TESTAMENT

A ready bridge between the Twelve and the New Testament appears if we consider the day of Yahweh as the point at which the kingdom of God begins to irrupt in a new way into this world.[60] The preaching of Jesus preserves the priority of Israel as the original covenant partner of Yahweh, yet Jesus makes clear that one enters the kingdom not by Jewish birthright but rather by way of radical repentance. Identifying himself as the consummation of the Old Testament's varied promises, Jesus becomes

---

[56] A. S. van der Woude, "שם," *TLOT*, 1363; C. J. Labuschagne, "קרא," *TLOT*, 1162; Sandra L. Richter, *The Deuteronomic History and the Name Theology: lešakkēn šemō šām in the Bible and the Ancient Near East*, BZAW 318 (Berlin: de Gruyter, 2002), 84–85.

[57] Hubert Irsigler, *Zefanja*, HThKAT (Freiburg: Herder, 2002), 374.

[58] F. L. Hossfeld and E.-M. Kindl, "קרא," *TDOT*, 13.113. In light of Zephaniah's penchant for moving backward through Genesis, Gen. 4:26 is an interesting cotext.

[59] H. Ringgren, "עבד," *TDOT*, 10.384–87.

[60] See further the very helpful treatment in Thomas, "Hearing the Minor Prophets," 372–78.

the nucleus of a new Israel, and his position as such constitutes the grounds for God's judgment of his people Israel, while the delay of immediate judgment for the whole world makes possible the proclamation of the gospel to the ends of the earth. Jesus's followers constitute the firstfruits of the eschatological remnant and are identified by and with his perfect obedience and substitutionary death, thus becoming part of a new "Israel" that is simultaneously in continuity and discontinuity with the old. This discontinuity on the one hand and the preaching of the gospel to the Gentiles on the other gradually but emphatically do away with the Sinai covenant as the basis for a restored relationship with the God of Israel. The New Testament thus brings to a conclusion the destabilization of the Sinai-based identity of the people of God, witnesses to the arrival of a new covenant that consummates the Abrahamic covenant in particular (Romans 4; Galatians 3–4), and unveils the mystery at the heart of the historical unfolding of God's saving purposes (Eph. 3:4–10).

Select Bibliography

Albertz, Rainer, James Nogalski, and Jakob Wöhrle. *Perspectives on the Formation of the Twelve: Methodological Foundations – Redactional Processes – Historical Insights.* BZAW 433. Berlin: de Gruyter, 2012.

Barton, John. "The Day of Yahweh in the Minor Prophets." In *Biblical and Near Eastern Essays: Essays in Honour of Kevin J. Cathcart,* edited by Carmel McCarthy and John F. Healey, 68–79. JSOTSup 375. Sheffield: T&T Clark, 2004.

Ben Zvi, Ehud. "Twelve Prophetic Books or 'The Twelve': A Few Preliminary Considerations." In *Forming Prophetic Literature: Essays on Isaiah and the Twelve in Honor of John D. W. Watts,* edited by John W. Watts and Paul R. House, 125–56. JSOTSup 235. Sheffield: Sheffield Academic Press, 1996.

Conrad, Edgar W. *Reading the Latter Prophets: Toward a New Canonical Criticism.* JSOTSup 376. London: T&T Clark, 2003.

House, Paul R. "The Character of God in the Book of the Twelve." In Nogalski and Sweeney, *Reading and Hearing the Book of the Twelve,* 125–45.

———. *The Unity of the Twelve.* JSOTSup 97; BLS 27. Sheffield: Almond, 1990.

McComiskey, Thomas E., ed. *The Minor Prophets: An Exegetical and Expository Commentary.* 3 vols. Grand Rapids, MI: Baker, 1992–1998.

Nogalski, James D. "The Day(s) of YHWH in the Book of the Twelve." In Redditt and Schart, *Thematic Threads,* 192–213.

———. *Literary Precursors to the Book of the Twelve.* BZAW 217. Berlin: de Gruyter, 1993.

———. "Reading the Book of the Twelve Theologically: The Twelve as Corpus: Interpreting Unity and Discord." *Int* 61, no. 2 (2007): 115–22.

———. *Redactional Processes in the Book of the Twelve.* BZAW 218. Berlin: de Gruyter, 1993.

Nogalski, James D., and Ehud Ben Zvi, eds. *Two Sides of a Coin: Juxtaposing Views on Interpreting the Book of the Twelve / the Twelve Prophetic Books.* With an introduction by Thomas Römer. Analecta Gorgiana 201. Piscataway, NJ: Gorgias, 2009.

Nogalski, James D., and Marvin A. Sweeney, eds. *Reading and Hearing the Book of the Twelve*. SymS 15. Atlanta: Scholars Press, 2000.

Redditt, Paul L. "Recent Research on the Book of the Twelve as One Book." *CurBS* 9 (2001): 47–80.

Redditt, Paul L., and Aaron Schart, eds. *Thematic Threads in the Book of the Twelve*. BZAW 325. Berlin: de Gruyter, 2003.

Rendtorff, Rolf. "How to Read the Book of the Twelve as a Theological Unity." In Nogalski and Sweeney, *Reading and Hearing the Book of the Twelve*, 75–87.

Roth, Martin. *Israel und die Völker im Zwölfprophetenbuch: Eine Untersuchung zu den Büchern Joel, Jona, Micha und Nahum*. FRLANT 210. Göttingen: Vandenhoeck & Ruprecht, 2005.

Schart, Aaron. "Das Zwölfprophetenbuch als redaktionelle Großeinheit." *TLZ* 133, no. 3 (2008): 227–46.

Seitz, Christopher R. *The Goodly Fellowship of the Prophets: The Achievement of Association in Canon Formation*. Acadia Studies in Bible and Theology. Grand Rapids, MI: Baker Academic, 2009.

Timmer, Daniel C. *The Non-Israelite Nations in the Book of the Twelve: Thematic Coherence and the Diachronic-Synchronic Relationship in the Minor Prophets*. BibInt 135. Leiden: Brill, 2015.

14

Psalms

Mark D. Futato

INTRODUCTION

The book of Psalms opens the third division of the Hebrew canon, a division the New Testament labels as "the Psalms" along with "the Law of Moses" and "the Prophets" (Luke 24:44). The purpose of this third division of the Hebrew canon is *to instruct God's people* in how to live out the covenant.[1] The book of Psalms is a perfect introduction to this third division, because as we shall see, the purpose of the book of Psalms is *to instruct God's people* in how to experience the abundant life for which God has created and redeemed them.

This instruction comes in many particular forms in the book of Psalms, such as hymns, laments, songs of thanksgiving, songs of confidence, wisdom psalms, and divine-kingship psalms. The individual psalms were written by many different people in many different places over a long stretch of time, and most of them were originally composed as human words to God. But under the superintendence of the Holy Spirit, these human words to God were transformed into God's word to humans in order to instruct them in how to experience the abundant life in all of life's varied circumstances, whether the depths of despair or the heights of joy. Certainly one of the reasons why the book of Psalms has been so cherished by God's people throughout the centuries is the fact that it brings to expression all of life's experiences. John Calvin certainly understood this when he said, "I have been accustomed to call this book, I think not inappropriately, 'An Anatomy of all the Parts of the Soul'; for there is not an emotion of which anyone can be conscious that is not here represented as in a mirror. Or rather, the Holy Spirit has drawn to the life all the griefs, sorrows,

---

[1] Miles V. Van Pelt, "Biblical Theology: Old Testament: Structure of the Christian Bible," BiblicalTraining.org, accessed September 22, 2015, https://www.biblicaltraining.org/library/structure-christian-bible/biblical-theology/van-pelt-blomberg-schreiner.

fears, doubts, hopes, cares, perplexities, in short all distracting emotions with which the minds of men are want to be agitated."[2]

The instruction provided by the book of Psalms is found not only in the individual psalms but also in the book as a whole, for if it is true anywhere that the whole is greater than the sum of its parts, it is true in the book of Psalms. The book of Psalms is not a random anthology of discrete poems but an intentionally shaped collection with instruction embedded in the whole.

I think it fair to summarize the instruction provided by the book of Psalms in three words: *our God reigns*. As we grow in believing this truth and in keeping the divine principles taught in the book of Psalms, we grow in experiencing the abundant life so graciously provided by our King.

BACKGROUND ISSUES

History of Composition

From the composition of the first psalm to the completion of the book of Psalms as a whole, there was a period spanning about one thousand years. Psalm 90 is "A prayer of Moses, the man of God," and may be the oldest psalm, dating back to about 1400 BC. Psalm 137 begins, "By the waters of Babylon, there we sat and wept, when we remembered Zion." This psalm goes back at least to the Babylonian captivity, but the ending of the psalm leads to the conclusion that Psalm 137 likely dates to the postexilic era and may have been written as late as 400 BC.

While we cannot trace the process with precision, there were no doubt collections of various psalms that were later put together with other collections, and these collections were then put together with yet other collections, until the book of Psalms reached its final form.[3] For example, in the well-known collection consisting of Psalms 120–134, all the psalms share the same title, "A song of ascents." There were also numerous collections of Davidic psalms, like Psalms 3–41 and 51–70. Positioned between these two collections is a collection of psalms "of the Sons of Korah" (Psalms 42–49). A collection of psalms "of Asaph" (Psalms 73–83) is followed by another collection of psalms "of the Sons of Korah" (Psalms 84–88). The point here is not to trace the process in any detail but simply to indicate that the composition of the book of Psalms was complex and spanned a long period.

Authorship

Obviously, in light of the history of composition, no one author wrote the book of Psalms. The individual psalms were composed by numerous people at numerous times in numerous places.

A fair number of psalms seem to indicate authorship by placing a name after a Hebrew preposition that can be translated "of." So, for example, we have psalms "of

---

[2] John Calvin, *Commentary on the Book of Psalms*, trans. James Anderson (Grand Rapids, MI: Baker, 1979), 1:xxxvi–xxxvii.
[3] For more on the collecting of the Psalms, see Ernest C. Lucas, *Exploring the Old Testament*, vol. 3, *A Guide to the Psalms and Wisdom Literature* (Downers Grove, IL: InterVarsity Press, 2003), 25–28, and William P. Brown, *The Psalms*, IBT (Nashville: Abingdon, 2010), 85–107.

David," "of Asaph," "of Solomon," and so on. But a couple of considerations lead us away from a hard and fast conclusion that this "of" necessarily and always indicates authorship in the modern sense of that term. One consideration is the phrase "of the Sons of Korah." While possible, it is unlikely that a group of people composed an individual psalm. The word "of" in this phrase seems to mean "associated with" in some sense, and may refer to those who either collected or were responsible for preserving the groups of psalms with this title.

A second consideration is the use of "of" in Proverbs 1:1, "The proverbs of Solomon," which again may lead a modern reader to conclude that Solomon was the author of the book as a whole, but this would be an erroneous conclusion. Proverbs 25:1 refers to "more Proverbs of Solomon which the men of Hezekiah king of Judah copied," so Proverbs 25:1–29:27 was not put together until around 700 BC, some two hundred or more years after Solomon. The book of Proverbs also contains wisdom material from a group of people known as "the wise" (see Prov. 22:17 and 24:23), as well as the "words of Agur son of Jakeh" (Prov. 30:1) and the "words of King Lemuel" (Prov. 31:1a), so not all the "proverbs of Solomon" were authored by Solomon. The "words of King Lemuel" are of special interest, because while the "of" might lead a modern reader to think that King Lemuel was the author of these words, this too would be an erroneous conclusion, since they are "An oracle that his mother taught him" (Prov. 31:1b). The ancients obviously used "of" plus a name in a way that cannot be restricted to authorship in the modern sense.

This is not to say that "of" never refers to authorship. For example, the title of Psalm 18 states that it is "of" David, "who addressed the words of this song to the LORD on the day when the LORD rescued him from the hand of all his enemies." When read in the context of 2 Samuel 22:1 ("David spoke to the LORD the words of this song") and 2 Samuel 23:1 ("these are the last words of David: The oracle of David"), this title leads to the conclusion that David was the author of Psalm 18. So while "of" plus a name in the titles of various psalms may refer to authorship, this is not necessarily or always the case.[4]

Genre

As modern songs can be placed into various categories—such as classical or country or blues—and as modern literary works can be placed into various categories—such as short story or biography or fantasy—so individual psalms can be placed into various categories. We call these categories genres. In terms of literature, a genre is simply a group of texts that share common characteristics.[5]

In the broadest terms, we can say that the Hebrew Bible is composed of two genres: prose and poetry. There are various subgenres of poetry[6] in the Hebrew Bible,

---

[4] For more on the Davidic authorship of the Psalms, see Willem A. VanGemeren, *Psalms*, vol. 5 of *The Expositor's Bible Commentary, Revised Edition*, ed. Tremper Longman III and David E. Garland (Grand Rapids, MI: Zondervan, 2008), 33–34.
[5] Richard N. Soulen and R. Kendall Soulen, *Handbook of Biblical Criticism*, 3rd ed. (Louisville: Westminster John Knox, 2001), 66.
[6] For more on the poetry of the Hebrew Bible, see Mark D. Futato, *Interpreting the Psalms: An Exegetical Handbook*, HOTE (Grand Rapids, MI: Kregel, 2007), 23–55.

psalms being just one of them. But not all psalms are the same. The psalm genre can also be further divided into subgenres.

The three main psalms genres are the hymn, the lament, and the song of thanksgiving. These three genres articulate three major movements in life: the hymn for when all is well, the lament for when something is wrong, and the song of thanksgiving for when what was wrong has been set right.[7] Each of these genres has its own structure and content.[8]

The hymn[9] typically opens with an invitation to praise God for the fact that all is well.[10] This invitation is then followed by the praise of God, that is, the confession of the praiseworthy character and actions of God in creation and redemptive history. The hymn typically concludes with an affirmation of faith or renewed invitation to praise God.

The lament typically moves from the negative to the positive, from plea to praise.[11] The lament asks why: "Why am I in this trouble?" In this way an amazing and at times brutal *honesty* characterizes the lament. The lament also asks what: "What do I want God to do for me in this situation?" Here the lament is characterized by *concreteness*. The request for help corresponds to the nature of the trouble articulated in the lament. The petitioner may ask for forgiveness, healing, vindication, deliverance, sustenance, and so forth. While the dominant tone is dark, the lament ends with light.[12] The lament may close with a note of confidence or trust, with an assurance that God will grant the request made, or with a promise to praise God once the trouble is over.

The song of thanksgiving typically has three sections: an intention to give thanks; a recitation of the past trouble, call for help, and deliverance; and a concluding expression of thanks.[13] Because the central section of a song of thanksgiving mirrors a lament, one might confuse a song of thanksgiving for a lament. Some positive note at the beginning will usually suffice for distinguishing the two. Because both songs of thanksgiving and hymns praise God, one might confuse a song of thanksgiving for a hymn. However, the redemption celebrated in the song of thanksgiving refers to a redemption in one's personal history rather than in redemptive history, as is the case in the hymn.[14]

There are a number of reasons for paying attention to the genre of a psalm.[15] Here I want to mention just one of the more important reasons: genre gives us a window into a christological reading of the Psalms.[16] When the hymns praise God as our Creator or Redeemer, they are speaking of Christ, who is Creator of all (John 1:3) and

---

[7] For a detailed discussion of this concept, see Walter Brueggemann, *The Message of the Psalms: A Theological Commentary* (Minneapolis: Augsburg, 1984).

[8] For more details, see Futato, *Interpreting the Psalms*, 146–60.

[9] For more details, see Mark D. Futato, "Hymns," in *Dictionary of the Old Testament: Wisdom, Poetry & Writings*, ed. Tremper Longman III and Peter Enns, IVP Bible Dictionary Series 3 (Downers Grove, IL: IVP Academic, 2008), 300–305.

[10] Examples of the hymn are found in Psalms 8, 19, 29, 33, 65, 67, 68, 93, 96, 98, 100, 103, 104, 105, 111, 113, 114, 117, 135, 145, 146, 147, 148, 149, 150.

[11] Examples of the laments are found in Psalms 3, 5, 6, 7, 13, 17, 22, 25, 26, 27, 28, 38, 39, 42, 43, 44, 51, 54, 55, 56, 57, 59, 61, 63, 64, 69, 70, 71, 74, 79, 80, 83, 86, 88, 89, 102, 109, 120, 130.

[12] There are two exceptions: Psalms 44 and 88.

[13] Examples of songs of thanksgiving are found in Psalms 18, 30, 34, 40, 41, 66, 92, 116, 118, 124, 138.

[14] For a discussion of other genres, see Futato, *Interpreting the Psalms*, 160–73.

[15] Futato, *Interpreting the Psalms*, 141–45.

[16] Futato, *Interpreting the Psalms*, 173–81.

Redeemer of all (Gal. 3:13). When the laments ask, "why have you forsaken me?" we hear the words of our Great High Priest (Matt. 27:46). And when they offer up prayers and pleas with loud cries and tears, they point us to Jesus (Heb. 5:7). Because the Father answered the agonizing prayers of the Son (Heb. 5:7), we know that he will answer our prayers in due time. And in the praise of thanksgiving, we hear the leader of the band (Heb. 2:12).[17]

STRUCTURE AND OUTLINE

Lamentation to Praise

Genre not only gives us a window into a christological reading of the Psalms, it also gives perspective on the shape of the book of Psalms. The Hebrew title for the book of Psalms is ספר תהלים ("book of praises"). This title might seem strange, given that the book of Psalms contains more laments than any other genre. So why did the ancients call this book the "book of praises"?

While it is true that the book of Psalms contains more laments than any other genre, it is also true that it is weighted in the front with laments and at the end with hymns.[18] Thus the book of Psalms follows a macromovement from lamentation to praise, from suffering to glory. This movement mimics the movement in the laments themselves, which move from plea to praise. The ancients understood this, which is why they did not call the book "the book of lamentations" but "the book of praises."

Seeing this macromovement also gives us a window into a christological reading of the book of Psalms as a whole. Luke 24:26 records that after his resurrection Jesus taught the two men on the road to Emmaus the macromovement of his own life: "Was it not necessary that the Christ should suffer these things and enter into his glory?" The macromovement of the book of Psalms anticipates the macromovement in the life of Jesus, so not just individual psalms show us Christ, but the book of Psalms as a whole is a portrait of his life.

Once we see that the book of Psalms is a portrait of the life of Christ, we can then see a portrait of our own lives in this book. While we may experience different kinds and degrees of suffering in this life, suffering is not our destiny. We have not been created for suffering, nor have we been redeemed for suffering. We have been created for glory, and we have been redeemed for glory. The book of Psalms teaches us that our destiny is glory. As Psalm 30:5 says, "weeping may tarry for the night, but joy comes with the morning."

Five Books

A second perspective on the shape of the book of Psalms is found in the ancient division of the Psalms into five "books": book 1 (Psalms 1–41), book 2 (Psalms 42–72),

---

[17] We could discuss three other psalm genres, psalms of trust, kingship psalms, and wisdom psalms. For more information on these, see Futato, *Interpreting the Psalms*, 160–73.

[18] I believe this insight goes back to Claus Westermann, *Praise and Lament in the Psalms*, trans. Keith R. Crim and Richard N. Soulen (Atlanta, GA: John Knox, 1981), 257. It is now a commonly held view; see Tremper Longman III and Raymond B. Dillard, *An Introduction to the Old Testament*, 2nd ed. (Grand Rapids, MI: Zondervan, 2006), 255; J. Clinton McCann, *A Theological Introduction to the Book of Psalms: The Psalms as Torah* (Nashville: Abingdon Press, 1993), 53.

book 3 (Psalms 73–89), book 4 (Psalms 90–106), and book 5 (Psalms 107–150). The ends of books 1–4 have been clearly marked by the placing of doxologies at the ends of the final psalm in each book.[19] Psalms 146–150 serve not only as the doxology that ends book 5 but also as the grand doxology that brings the entire book of Psalms to a conclusion.

Since 1985, scholars have been studying the shape of the book of Psalms or the intentional arrangement of the Psalms as a book.[20] The psalms that lie at the seams of the five books give us important clues for the shape of the book as a whole.

There is a general consensus that Psalms 1 and 2 have been placed at the beginning of the book of Psalms to serve as a twofold introduction to the book, with Psalm 1 giving us the purpose of the book and Psalm 2 giving us the overall message. One reason for separating out these two psalms as introductory is the fact that, unlike the psalms that follow in book 1, these first two psalms have no titles. In addition, the two are bound together by a number of literary features, such as an *inclusio* that uses the word אַשְׁרֵי ("blessed") in the first verse of Psalm 1 and in the last verse of Psalm 2, tail linkage that uses the words דֶּרֶךְ ("way") and אבד ("perish") in the final verse of each psalm, and a play on the word הגה ("meditate/plot") in 1:2 and 2:1. The significance of the twofold introduction and the five-book structure will be drawn out in the next section.

MESSAGE AND THEOLOGY

Purpose

In Psalm 1 we find the first half of the twofold introduction to the book of Psalms. This psalm communicates the purpose of the book as a whole.

Torah as Instruction

In the introduction to his commentary on the book of Psalms, John Calvin emphasizes the instructional nature of the book of Psalms. The Psalms "*teach* us the true method of praying aright," and by them we are "*taught* the right manner of praising God"; they are

> replete with all the precepts which serve to frame our life to every part of holiness, piety, and righteousness, yet they will principally *teach* and train us to bear the cross. . . . [W]e find here general commendations of the goodness of God, which may *teach* men to repose themselves in him alone, and to seek all their happiness solely in him; and which are intended to *teach* true believers with their whole hearts constantly to look to him for help in all their necessities.[21]

---

[19] Scholars debate whether these doxologies were originally part of the poems or were added later as independent pieces. While certainty is not possible, I think it is better to see them as independent poems added at these particular junctures to punctuate the closing of each book.

[20] This approach goes back to Gerald H. Wilson, *The Editing of the Hebrew Psalter*, SBLDS 76 (Chico, CA: Scholars Press, 1985). For a survey of the history of this approach, see David M. Howard Jr., *The Structure of Psalms 93–100*, BJSUCSD 5 (Winona Lake, IN: Eisenbrauns, 1997), 1–19. See also Nancy L. DeClaissé-Walford, *Reading from the Beginning: The Shaping of the Hebrew Psalter* (Macon, GA: Mercer University Press, 1997); J. Clinton McCann, ed., *Shape and Shaping of the Psalter*, JSOTSup 159 (Sheffield: Sheffield Academic Press, 1993).

[21] Calvin, *Psalms*, 1:xxxviii–xxxix. Emphasis mine.

Calvin's emphasis on the Psalms as instruction is consonant with the teaching of Psalm 1, which sets the stage for our reading of the rest of the Psalter.[22]

While the Hebrew word תּוֹרָה (*torah*, Ps.1:2) is most frequently translated with the English word "law," this is not always the best translation. The ESV, for example, translates תּוֹרָה twelve times with the English word "teaching"[23] and eight times with the English word "instruction."[24] "Teaching" and "instruction" are particularly appropriate translations in wisdom contexts, and Psalm 1 has numerous points of contact with the wisdom tradition, including the אַשְׁרֵי ("blessed") formula and the use of the "two paths" image. In keeping with this approach, the TNK rightly translates תּוֹרָה in Psalm 1:2 with "teaching": "the teaching of the LORD is his delight, and he studies that teaching day and night."

Torah in Two Places

If we want to delight in and meditate on the Lord's instruction, we need to know where to find this instruction. It is found in two places.

On the one hand, this instruction is found in the five books of Moses. Since the book of Psalms reached its final form sometime in the postexilic era and around the time Chronicles and Ezra–Nehemiah were completed, the way in which the phrase "the תּוֹרָה of the LORD" is used in those books should give us insight into its use in Psalm 1. For example, 2 Chronicles 34:14 refers to "the Book of the Law [תּוֹרָה] of the LORD given through Moses," while Nehemiah 8:1 refers to "the Book of the Law [תּוֹרָה] of Moses, which the LORD had commanded for Israel." Putting these together, we come to the conclusion that in the postexilic era "the תּוֹרָה of the LORD" referred to the "the תּוֹרָה of Moses," that is, the five books of Moses. So the one wanting to delight in and meditate on the "instruction [תּוֹרָה] of the LORD" would meditate on the five books of Moses.

On the other hand, this instruction is also found in the five books of the Psalms. Here we need to ask why the ancients divided the book of Psalms into five books rather than four or six. The answer seems to be that just as the five books of Moses are "the תּוֹרָה of the LORD," so are the five books of the Psalms. While Calvin's understanding of this phrase in the context of Psalm 1 is not identical with mine, he well articulates the main point: "He [the psalmist] must, therefore, be understood as meaning to exhort the faithful to the reading of the Psalms also."[25] Edward J. Young is, therefore, correct in my opinion when he says,

> Moreover, we are mistaken when we regard the entire Psalter as designed for the usage of the Temple. That some Psalms were so used cannot be denied, but it is interesting to note that liturgical directions are lacking for many of the Psalms. The Psalter, rather, is primarily a manual and guide and model for the devotional needs of the individual believer.[26]

---

[22] McCann, *Theological Introduction*, 13–21.
[23] Psalm 78:1; Prov. 1:8; 3:1; 4:2; 6:20, 23; 7:2; 13:14; 31:26; Isa. 1:10; 8:16, 20.
[24] Deuteronomy 17:11; 2 Sam. 7:19; Job 22:22; Isa. 30:9; Mal. 2:6, 7, 8, 9.
[25] Calvin, *Psalms*, 1:4.
[26] Edward J. Young, *An Introduction to the Old Testament* (Grand Rapids, MI: Eerdmans, 1949), 309.

In other words, the primary purpose of the book of Psalms is to serve as an instruction manual for the godly. But to what end?

Torah for Well-Being

The first word in the book of Psalms, אַשְׁרֵי ("blessed"), is a keyword in the Psalter, appearing in all five books of the Psalms. What does this word mean in this context?

To begin, אַשְׁרֵי ("blessed") is the opposite of אבד ("perish"). The poet teaches us this by placing these two words at the opposite ends of Psalm 1, with אַשְׁרֵי ("blessed") being the first word in the poem, while אבד ("perish") is the last word in the poem. This contrast is underscored by the fact that אַשְׁרֵי ("blessed") and אבד ("perish") begin with letters at the opposite ends of the alphabet: אַשְׁרֵי ("blessed") begins with the first letter of the Hebrew alphabet (*aleph*), while תּוֹבֵד ("perish")—an inflected form of the term אבד found at this location—begins with the last letter of the Hebrew alphabet (*taw*). The author of Psalm 1 is not the only poet to have used this technique to contrast אַשְׁרֵי ("blessed") and אבד ("perish"); the author of Psalm 112 has done so as well.[27] But the fact that אַשְׁרֵי ("blessed") is the opposite of אבד ("perish") only helps us if we have a proper understanding of the word אבד ("perish") in context.

In context, the Hebrew word אבד ("perish") means "to come to nothing." Note first of all that it is not the wicked who אבד ("perish"), but rather, it is "the *way* of the wicked" that perishes. This is similar to the other occurrence of this word pair at opposite ends of a poem (Psalm 112), where it is "the longings of the wicked" that אבד ("perish"). The NIV in my estimation rightly translates the verb אבד in this context with "will come to nothing" (112:10). As the "longings" of the wicked come to nothing (112:10), so does their "way" or lifestyle (1:6). Note in the second place that in Psalm 1 the wicked are "like chaff," and in a word, chaff is good for nothing. So in context אבד in Psalm 1:6 means "to come to nothing."

Since אבד means "to come to nothing" and is the opposite of אַשְׁרֵי, it must mean something like "amount to something." What this "something" is finds amplification in the simile of a tree (1:3). The righteous are "like a tree" (i.e., they are full of life); "planted" (i.e., they have endurance); "by streams of water" (i.e., they are tapped into abundant resources); "that yields its fruit in season" (i.e., their lives are productive); "and its leaf does not whither" (i.e., these characteristics go on into old age). In summary, "In all that he does, he prospers" (1:3; cf. 92:12–15).

To be "blessed" is thus to have well-being in every area of life. This well-being is what humanity had before the fall and is what Jesus came to restore, as he said, "The thief comes only to steal and kill and destroy. I came that they may have life and have it abundantly" (John 10:10). So we can say in summary that the purpose of the book of Psalms is to serve as an instruction manual for experiencing the abundant life that God intends both in creation and in redemption.

---

[27] After the initial "Praise the LORD," the first word in the poem is אַשְׁרֵי ("blessed") and the last word is תּוֹבֵד ("perish").

Message

The dominant theme in the book of Psalms is the kingship of God. We see this both in the teaching of Psalm 2—the second half of the twofold introduction to the book of Psalms—and in the teaching of the five-book structure of the Psalter as a whole.

Our God Is King

Psalm 2:4 refers to God as "he who sits in the heavens." This is a picture of God as King, reigning over his creation from his heavenly throne. We encounter this same picture elsewhere in the book of Psalms, as in, for example, Psalm 29:10:

> The LORD sits enthroned over the flood;
> the LORD sits enthroned as king forever.

Then there is Psalm 47:8:

> God reigns over the nations;
> God sits on his holy throne.

Or consider Psalm 93:1–2:

> The LORD reigns, he is robed in majesty;
> the LORD is robed; he has put on strength as his belt;
> Yes, the world is established, it shall never be moved.
> Your throne is established from of old;
> you are from everlasting.

This is the overarching message of the book of Psalms: *the Lord reigns*, or *our God is King*.

Psalm 2 goes on to teach that this kingship of our God is exercised through his anointed one. The anointed one in the book of Psalms is predominantly the king, and the king is predominantly David. For example, Psalm 18:50 says,

> Great salvation he brings to his king,
> and shows steadfast love to his anointed,
> to David and his offspring forever.

This anointed one God calls "my King" (2:6). And God promises that one day his anointed King will inherit the nations. As I explain elsewhere,

> Since there was never a time when God ruled all nations of the earth through the Davidic monarchy, we are not to interpret this text as a description of some particular *historical* situation. Rather, this text paints an *ideological* picture of God's intention for the nations of the world against the backdrop of historical reality. God's intention for the nations is that they *all* experience the truly happy life articulated in the final line of Psalm 2: "But what joy [אַשְׁרֵי] for all who take refuge in him!" (NLT).[28]

---

[28] Futato, *Interpreting the Psalms*, 75.

Since this ideal was never experienced during the Davidic monarchy, Psalm 2 is not only ideological but also eschatological in the sense that "the proclamation of God's universal reign amid circumstances did seem to deny it and belie it."[29] Psalm 2 is also eschatological in the sense that it is pointing to that future day when there truly will be "joy for all who take refuge in him" (2:12b NLT). Psalm 2 thus points us forward to the coming of Jesus, the ultimate Anointed One, who, in the words of Scripture, comes "that they may have life and have it abundantly" (John 10:10), or who, in the words of the hymn "Joy to the World," "comes to make his blessings flow far as the curse is found."

Our King Is Coming

The eschatology inherent in Psalm 2 is drawn out in the fivefold division of the book of Psalms. The message that *our God is King* was desperately needed by those who first used the book of Psalms in its completed form. The movement from lamentation to praise, from suffering to glory, that we have already examined dovetails nicely with the message contained in the fivefold division of the book of Psalms.

Ancient Israelite faith stood on two pillars, the temple and the Davidic monarchy. It is almost impossible for us to imagine the crisis of faith that ancient Israelites experienced at the demise of both the temple and the monarchy in the midst of the Babylonian captivity. Likewise, it is hard to imagine the elation of the postexilic community when the temple was rebuilt (Ezra 6:16). "No comparable joy, however, was experienced at a reenthronement of a Davidic king, for this pillar continued to lie in ruins throughout the postexilic era."[30] The book of Psalms was edited in its final form to teach the postexilic community how to experience an abundant life in the absence of the Davidic king and his reign promised in Psalm 2.

With Psalm 2, book 1 opens the book of Psalms with a coronation hymn that inaugurates the Davidic covenant.[31] While there were numerous troubles along the way (e.g., see Psalm 3), Psalm 41 closes book 1 with a strong affirmation that the promises made in Psalm 2 are being fulfilled (see 1 Kings 8:24, 56). Psalm 41 opens with אַשְׁרֵי ("blessed"), forming an *inclusio* with Psalm 1 and identifying David as the blessed man of that psalm. Psalm 41:11 confirms God's "delight" in David, which corresponds to David's "delight" in God's instruction in 1:2:[32]

> By this I know that you delight in me;
>> my enemy will not shout in triumph over me. (41:11)

This verse in the context of the whole psalm also affirms that the promises made to David in Psalm 2 are being fulfilled.

But what would happen to the promises at David's death? Could they be effectively transferred to David's successor? Psalm 72 brings book 2 to a close with an affirma-

---

[29] J. Clinton McCann, *Psalms*, in *The New Interpreter's Bible* (Nashville: Abingdon, 1996), 4:668.
[30] Futato, *Interpreting the Psalms*, 80.
[31] Gerald H. Wilson, *Psalms*, vol. 1, NIVAC (Grand Rapids, MI: Zondervan, 2002), 111; VanGemeren, *Psalms*, 64.
[32] The Hebrew verb (חפץ) is the same in both verses.

tion that the covenant made with David has indeed been effectively transferred to Solomon. It is not coincidental that Psalm 72 is "of Solomon," whether this means by Solomon or about Solomon. In any case, now Solomon is caring for the weak (72:4) as the successor of David, who is likewise portrayed as caring for the poor in 41:1 at the close of book 1. In addition, Psalm 72 describes Solomon with imagery that recalls the imagery of Psalm 1:

> Let the mountains bear prosperity for the people,
>   and the hills, in righteousness. . . .
>
> May he be like rain that falls on the mown grass,
>   like showers that water the earth!
> In his days may the righteous flourish,
>   and peace abound, till the moon be no more! . . .
>
> May there be abundance of grain in the land;
>   on the tops of the mountains may it wave;
>   may its fruit be like Lebanon;
> and may people blossom in the cities
>   like the grass of the field! (72:3, 6–7, 16)

And Psalm 72:8–11, 15 tells us that Solomon is now the great king who rules over the nations, promised in Psalm 2. Solomon is thus now the blessed man of Psalm 1 and the anointed king of Psalm 2. By the end of book 2, the Davidic covenant has been successfully transferred to David's successor, King Solomon.

Psalm 89:49 brings book 3 to a close on a quite different note. It is easy to hear in this dark word the anguish of the postexilic community experiencing the absence of a Davidic king:

> Lord, where is your steadfast love of old,
>   which by your faithfulness you swore to David?

This anguish is intensified against the backdrop of the opening of Psalm 89, which celebrates the promises made to David (89:1–29). The covenant promises given to David in Psalm 2 and transferred to Solomon in Psalm 72 seem to have come to naught.

Books 1–3 raise the question, how do we live in the absence of the messianic king? Books 4–5 answer that question in two ways: faith and obedience.

At the heart of book 4 is a series of psalms that celebrate God's kingship:

> The Lord is king! (93:1 NLT)

> For the Lord is the great God,
>   and a great King above all gods. (95:3)

> Declare among the nations, "The Lord is king!" (96:10 TNK)

> The Lord is king! (97:1 NLT)

Make a joyful symphony before the LORD, the King! (98:6 NLT)

The LORD is king! (99:1 NLT)

On the heels of the agonizing cry of Psalm 89 comes the repeated affirmation that God is King. Thus book 4 teaches that we are to live by faith in the reign of God even when the evidence is to the contrary, as was the case in the postexilic community, when there was no Davidic king and when Israel was a small and poor province in the dominant and pagan Persian Empire.

At the heart of book 5 is Psalm 119, with its overwhelming emphasis on living in keeping with God's Torah, or instruction. The faith called for in book 4 is a faith that obeys in book 5. And this obedience finds particular expression in the proper worship of God, as the grand doxology of Psalms 146–150 make clear. While the postexilic community may not have a Davidic monarch on the throne, they have in the rebuilt temple the essence of King David, who lived to praise and worship the divine King (Psalm 145). So how does one live in the absence of the messianic king (books 1–3)? He or she lives by trusting and obeying with an obedience that culminates in the worship of the divine King (books 4–5).

But there is more. Books 4–5 also teach us to live with hope, hope that the King is coming. The kingship psalms in book 4 celebrate the coming of the divine King "to judge" the earth (96:11–13; 98:7–9). The word used for "judge" in these psalms (שׁפט) means "to pass judgment" in some contexts, but in others it means "to rule/govern."[33] This verb "designates an action that restores the disturbed order of a . . . community."[34] The kingship psalms in book 4 instill hope that the divine King will come to put all things in right order.

Whereas book 4 instills hope that the divine King will come, book 5 instills hope that the messianic king will come. Psalm 132 asks God to remember David and all his hardships (132:1) and not to reject the "anointed one" (132:10). This plea is followed by an affirmation of the promise made to David (132:11) and a promise from the Lord himself:

> There I will make a horn to sprout for David;
>   I have prepared a lamp for my anointed.
> His enemies I will clothe with shame,
>   but on him his crown will shine. (132:17–18)

For the postexilic community this is a word of hope that God will keep his promise to the household of David (cf. 1 Sam. 2:10; 2 Sam. 22:3)

This word of hope also comes to expression in Psalm 118:26, which says, "Blessed is he who comes in the name of the LORD." First-century Jews believed that the one coming in the name of the Lord was the messianic king of Israel, as is clear from John 12:13, "Blessed is he who comes in the name of the Lord, even the King of

---

[33] *HALOT*, 4:1624, 1625.
[34] G. Liedke, "שָׁפַט," in *TLOT*, 3:1393.

Israel!" And they believed that the one to come was also the "horn" promised in Psalm 132:17, as Zechariah said in Luke 1:68–69,

> Blessed be the Lord God of Israel,
> for he has visited and redeemed his people
> and has raised up a horn of salvation for us
> in the house of his servant David.

There is a wonderful coherence in the book of Psalms from start to finish. The message of the book of Psalms is that our God is King and our King is coming to transform our suffering into glory and to bless all who take refuge in him (2:12) with a truly abundant life (1:1).

APPROACHING THE NEW TESTAMENT

The question is often raised as to which of the psalms are messianic. The answer can be either *none* or *all*.

If by messianic one is thinking of psalms that directly predict some dimension of the life and work of Jesus the Messiah without any reference to someone in the Old Testament (such as David), then the answer is *none*.[35] Consider Psalm 2:7–9.

> I will tell of the decree:
> The Lord said to me, "You are my Son;
> today I have begotten you.
> Ask of me, and I will make the nations your heritage,
> and the ends of the earth your possession.
> You shall break them with a rod of iron
> and dash them in pieces like a potter's vessel."

This language originally applied to the royal covenant made with David and his descendants.[36] Or consider the opening line of Psalm 22, "My God, my God, why have you forsaken me?" Based on the title, "A Psalm of David," these words originally articulated King David's feelings at a point in his life when he felt utterly abandoned by God. Before moving to the New Testament, the reader must understand a given psalm in its original context with its original reference.[37]

On the other hand, it is fair to say that all the psalms are messianic. From the perspective of genre, the Creator and Redeemer we praise in the hymns finds sharp focus in the person and work of Christ, who is Creator of all (John 1:3) and Redeemer of all (Gal. 3:13). And while David certainly felt abandoned by God, it is Jesus who was truly abandoned by his Father for our sake, which he made clear when he called out, "My God, my God, why have you forsaken me?" (Matt. 27:46). And in the praise of

---

[35] See Psalms 2, 16, 22, and 110 for examples of psalms that some would understand as predicting the person and work of Christ to the exclusion of any reference to an ancient historical figure.

[36] Mark D. Futato, *The Book of Psalms*, in vol. 7 of the Cornerstone Biblical Commentary series, ed. Philip W. Comfort (Carol Stream, IL: Tyndale, 2009), 35.

[37] Bruce K. Waltke, "A Canonical Process Approach to the Psalms," in *Tradition and Testament: Essays in Honor of Charles Lee Feinberg* (Chicago, IL: Moody, 1981), 3–18.

thanksgiving, we hear the voice of the leader of the band (Heb. 2:12).[38] While the kingship psalms that focus on the human king certainly referred to David and his descendants in their original contexts, psalms like Psalm 2 clearly point forward to the coming of Jesus, the ultimate messianic King, who is the "begotten" Son (John 3:16 KJV) against whom the nations raged (Acts 4:25–26) but who will inherit the nations (Heb. 1:2).

Whether a psalm refers to the depths of a psalmist's suffering or the heights of his glory, it is in the suffering and glory of Jesus that the fullness of such psalms is displayed. As Luke 24:26 records, after his resurrection Jesus taught the two men on the road to Emmaus, asking them, "Was it not necessary that the Christ should suffer these things and enter into his glory?" Not only can each individual psalm be read as messianic but also the book as a whole is a portrait of Christ; the flow of the book from lamentation to praise, from suffering to glory, reveals to us a pattern of Christ's life and of our destiny as we are united to him by grace through faith.

SELECT BIBLIOGRAPHY

Allen, Leslie C. *Psalms 101–150*. 2nd ed. WBC 21. Nashville: Thomas Nelson, 2002.

Bellinger, W. H. *Psalms: A Guide to Studying the Psalter*. 2nd ed. Grand Rapids, MI: Baker Academic, 2012.

Brown, William P. *The Psalms*. IBT. Nashville: Abingdon, 2010.

Brueggemann, Walter. *The Message of the Psalms: A Theological Commentary*. AOTS. Minneapolis: Augsburg, 1984.

Bullock, C. Hassell. *Encountering the Book of Psalms: A Literary and Theological Introduction*. EBS. Grand Rapids, MI: Baker Academic, 2001.

Calvin, John. *Commentary on the Book of Psalms*. Translated by James Anderson. 5 vols. Grand Rapids, MI: Baker, 1981.

DeClaissé-Walford, Nancy L. *Introduction to the Psalms: A Song from Ancient Israel*. St. Louis, MO: Chalice, 2004.

———. *Reading from the Beginning: The Shaping of the Hebrew Psalter*. Macon, GA: Mercer University Press, 1997.

Futato, Mark D. *The Book of Psalms*. In vol. 7 of the Cornerstone Biblical Commentary series. Edited by Philip W. Comfort. Carol Stream, IL: Tyndale, 2009.

———. "Hymns." In *Dictionary of the Old Testament: Wisdom, Poetry & Writings*, edited by Tremper Longman III and Peter Enns, 300–305. IVP Bible Dictionary Series 3. Downers Grove, IL: IVP Academic, 2008.

———. *Interpreting the Psalms: An Exegetical Handbook*. HOTE. Grand Rapids, MI: Kregel, 2007.

———. *Joy Comes in the Morning: Psalms for All Seasons*. Phillipsburg, NJ: P&R, 2004.

———. "Psalms 16, 23: Confidence in a Cup." In *The Psalms: Language for All Seasons of the Soul*, edited by Andrew J. Schmutzer and David M. Howard, 231–36. Chicago, IL: Moody Publishers, 2013.

---

[38] Reggie M. Kidd, *With One Voice: Discovering Christ's Song in Our Worship* (Grand Rapids, MI: Baker, 2005).

———. *Transformed by Praise: The Purpose and Message of the Psalms*. Phillipsburg, NJ: P&R, 2002.

Goldingay, John. *Psalms*. 3 vols. BCOTWP. Grand Rapids, MI: Baker, 2006–2008.

Kidner, Derek. *Psalms*. 2 vols. TOTC 14a–b. Downers Grove, IL: InterVarsity Press, 1973–1975.

Longman, Tremper, III. *How to Read the Psalms*. Downers Grove, IL: InterVarsity Press, 1988.

Mays, James Luther. *Psalms*. IBC. Louisville: John Knox, 1994.

McCann, J. Clinton, ed. *The Shape and Shaping of the Psalter*. JSOTSup 159. Sheffield: Sheffield Academic Press, 1993.

———. *A Theological Introduction to the Book of Psalms: The Psalms as Torah*. Nashville: Abingdon, 1993.

Miller, Patrick D., Jr. "The Beginning of the Psalter." In McCann, *The Shape and Shaping of the Psalter*, 83–92.

———. *Interpreting the Psalms*. Philadelphia: Fortress, 1986.

VanGemeren, Willem A. *Psalms*. Vol. 5 of *The Expositor's Bible Commentary, Revised Edition*, edited by Tremper Longman III and David E. Garland. Grand Rapids, MI: Zondervan, 2008.

Waltke, Bruce K., and James M. Houston. *The Psalms as Christian Worship: An Historical Commentary*. Grand Rapids, MI: Eerdmans, 2010.

Waltke, Bruce K., James M. Houston, and Erika Moore. *The Psalms as Christian Lament: A Historical Commentary*. Grand Rapids, MI: Eerdmans, 2014.

Westermann, Claus. *The Psalms: Structure, Content & Message*. Minneapolis: Augsburg, 1980.

Wilson, Gerald H. *The Editing of the Hebrew Psalter*. SBLDS 76. Chico, CA: Scholars Press, 1985.

———. *Psalms*. Vol. 1. NIVAC. Grand Rapids, MI: Zondervan, 2002.

Young, Edward J. *An Introduction to the Old Testament*. Grand Rapids, MI: Eerdmans, 1949.

15

Job

Richard P. Belcher Jr.

INTRODUCTION

The book of Job is complex. Its author works hard to consider the difficult issues related to human tragedy and suffering. All people in all times have experienced at least some measure of tragedy and suffering, which makes the questions with which this book wrestles universal in nature. In spite of various interpretive challenges in the book of Job, its message remains relevant for God's people who live in a fallen world and continue to hope and wait for the renewal of all things.

BACKGROUND ISSUES

Historical Context

The book reflects a period that coincides with the patriarchal era (roughly 2000–1700 BC). The evidence for this dating includes the following: (1) Job's wealth was measured in livestock (Job 1:3); (2) Job functioned as a priest for his family by offering sacrifices on their behalf (1:5); and (3) the death of Job was described like the death of Abraham in two ways. First, it was recorded that Job lived 140 years, which is in line with the length of the lives of the patriarchs—Abraham lived 175 years, Isaac 180 years, and Joseph 110 years. Second, Abraham is described at his death as "an old man and full of years" (Gen. 25:8), and Job is described as "an old man, and full of days" (Job 42:17).

It is also clear that Job was not an Israelite. He is from the land of Uz (1:1), which probably refers to the area of Edom. Lamentations 4:21 clearly associates Edom with Uz. And Job is also called "the greatest of all the people of the east" (Job 1:3), which is probably a reference to his wealth in 1:2,[1] but the phrase "people of the east" refers to the areas of Edom, Moab, and Ammon.

---

[1] Francis I. Anderson, *Job*, TOTC 13 (Downers Grove, IL: InterVarsity Press, 1976), 80.

Job was probably not an Israelite, but he certainly believed in the God of Israel. The names or titles that Job employed for God confirms for us his belief in the God of Israel. The book uses the name Yahweh, the covenant name of God, only sparingly,[2] but the name Shaddai, which was associated with the patriarchs (Gen. 17:1; 28:3; 35:11; 43:14; 48:3; 49:25; Ex. 6:3), occurs more often in the book of Job than in the rest of the Old Testament.[3]

Some also debate whether Job was an actual historical figure. Many scholars consider the prose tale of Job 1–2 to be a folktale that presents a fictional story.[4] The comment in Ezekiel 14:14 connects Job with a hero of prehistory called *Dan'el* from the Ugaritic texts. Also, the beginning of the book of Job parallels the beginning of Nathan's parable to David in 2 Samuel 12:1.[5] The events of the book seem to be unrealistic with a series of tragedies hitting Job all at once. And finally, Job and his friends communicate in poetry, which is not the normal way people speak to each other.

There are good reasons, however, to understand Job to be a historical figure. The beginning of the book of Job, "There was a man," also parallels the way that Judges 17 and 1 Samuel 1 begin, two passages relating historical events about historical individuals. The name Dan'el in Ezekiel 14:14 is more likely a variant form of the name Daniel, which better fits the point Ezekiel is making.[6] Also, the events of Job 1 are not unrealistic if God, angels, and Satan really exist. And the poetic speeches in the dialogues may function to give the book more emotional appeal because poetry stimulates the imagination and the emotions more than prose.[7]

The book of Job does not make any claim concerning its authorship, and the date of composition is unknown. The fact that events of the book appear to fit into the patriarchal period has led some to conclude that Moses may have been the author.[8] Others prefer the era of Solomon because wisdom literature flourished at that time,[9] or the time of Isaiah due to possible connections with this prophet.[10] Because Job is mentioned by name in the book of Ezekiel (Ezek. 14:14), we may consider the era of this prophet as the latest possible date for composition.

Scholars have proposed a variety of arguments to determine the date of the book's composition. For example, the Hebrew text of Job at Qumran was written in a paleo-Hebrew script, like the Pentateuch, which some argue supports Mosaic authorship. Certain parallels between Job and other books of the Bible are used to support a date during the period of the monarchy. For example, Job 28 is similar to Proverbs 8, and Job 7:17 may allude negatively to Psalm 8. However, wisdom tradi-

---

[2] The name Yahweh occurs twenty-three times in the book of Job (Job 1:6–9, 12, 21; 2:1–4, 6–7; 12:9; 38:1; 40:1, 3, 6; 42:1, 7, 9–12).

[3] The title Shaddai occurs forty-eight times in the Old Testament. Thirty-one of these occurrences (65 percent) appear in the book of Job.

[4] Norman Whybray, *Job*, Readings—A New Biblical Commentary (Sheffield: Sheffield Academic Press, 1998), 9–11.

[5] Tremper Longman III raises these issues in *Job*, BCOTWP (Grand Rapids, MI: Baker, 2012), 32–34.

[6] Daniel I. Block shows that the biblical figure Daniel makes more sense than the Ugaritic figure Dan'el. *The Book of Ezekiel Chapters 1–24* (Grand Rapids, MI: Eerdmans, 1997), 448.

[7] Tremper Longman III and Raymond B. Dillard, *An Introduction to the Old Testament*, 2nd ed. (Grand Rapids, MI: Zondervan, 2006), 233.

[8] Gleason Archer, *A Survey of Old Testament Introduction*, 2nd ed. (Chicago: Moody Press, 1974), 456.

[9] Edward J. Young, *An Introduction to the Old Testament* (Grand Rapids, MI: Eerdmans, 1952), 309.

[10] John E. Hartley, *The Book of Job*, NICOT (Grand Rapids, MI: Eerdmans, 1988), 13–15, 19.

tions are both ancient and international, so the use of this criterion is not entirely decisive.[11] Others have argued that the message of the book would fit well into the exilic or postexilic period, encouraging God's people in the midst of their own tragic losses and suffering.[12] However, the emphasis on the innocence of Job's suffering does not fit well with the fact that Israel is in exile because of her sin. Also, any connections to Edom and its wisdom would be difficult to substantiate after the fall of Jerusalem because of Edom's actions against "her brother Jacob" (cf. Obadiah 11) when Jerusalem fell.[13] This connection would make an earlier date of the book more likely than a later date. Given the inconclusive nature of the evidence, many scholars prefer not to ascribe a date to the book's composition.[14] Perhaps the book of Job was composed or became prominent during the reign of Solomon, though the actual events recorded therein may date to earlier centuries.

The Genre of Job

Some questions concerning both the genre and the structure of this book impact interpretation and meaning. Genre discussions involve comparisons of the book of Job with literature from other nations that deal with the suffering of the righteous and the issue of theodicy—the defense of God's justice in the face of evil. Such comparisons work to identify similarities and differences between the literature. For example, several Egyptian works have been compared to Job, including "The Protests of the Eloquent Peasant," "The Admonitions of Ipu-wer," and "A Dispute over Suicide."[15] These pessimistic texts protest the breakdown of society where people long for death and the gods cannot be found.[16] As R. K. Harrison notes, a major difference between the Egyptian literature and Job is that the Egyptian literature relates questions of injustice to *human* perversions of the divinely established order, meaning that disillusionment with the gods is not prominent.[17] Job, on the other hand, wrestles with the perceived injustice of the actions of God in this world.

Several works from Mesopotamia have also been compared to Job. The work *A Man and His God*, which comes from about 2000 BC, is a first-person complaint to God concerning undeserved suffering. The protagonist claims that his god is neglecting him, and he seeks a hearing from the deity so that his suffering might be relieved. A confession of sin leads to restoration. This work differs from the book of Job because it does not raise the question of divine justice; instead, it takes the perspective that people, being sinners, deserve whatever misfortune befalls them.[18]

---

[11] For the best argument that Job uses Psalm 8 in an ironic way, see Will Kynes, *My Psalm Has Turned into Weeping: Job's Dialogue with the Psalms*, BZAW 437 (Berlin: de Gruyter, 2012). He also discusses the use of Psalms 1; 39; 73; 107; and 139 in the book of Job.

[12] Gerald H. Wilson, *Job*, NIBCOT 10 (Peabody, MA: Hendrikson, 2007), 2.

[13] Hartley, *Job*, 19.

[14] Longman and Dillard, *Introduction*, 225.

[15] For the Egyptian texts see Pritchard, *ANET*, and William K. Simpson, ed., *The Literature of Ancient Egypt: An Anthology of Stories, Instructions, Stelae, Autobiographies, and Poetry*, trans. Robert K. Ritner et al., 3rd ed. (New Haven, CT: Yale University Press, 2003).

[16] Katharine J. Dell, *Job: Where Shall Wisdom Be Found?* (Sheffield: Sheffield Phoenix, 2013), 51.

[17] R. K. Harrison, *Introduction to the Old Testament* (Grand Rapids, MI: Eerdmans, 1969), 1025. For individual comparisons of the Egyptian works with the book of Job, see Hartley, *Job*, 7–8. Dell also recognizes that Job defies genre classification. *Job*, 33.

[18] Hartley, *Job*, 8.

The Babylonian Theodicy, from about 1000 BC, is an acrostic dialogue between a sufferer and his friend. The sufferer relates his troubles to a friend, cites examples of injustice, and deduces that those who neglect god prosper while the pious become destitute. The friend tries to restrain the sufferer's bitterness and recommends prayer and just conduct. Like Job, this work recognizes the inadequacy of simplistic solutions concerning reward and punishment in the face of suffering, but it gives no solution to the dilemma.[19]

The work that may be most like the book of Job is *I Will Praise the Lord of Wisdom*, also called *The Babylonian Job*, which dates to about 1300 BC. In this work, a wealthy man is suddenly reduced to horrible suffering and so laments his condition in gruesome detail. Although he had lived piously, he suffered like the ungodly, and the gods were not answering him. He is eventually restored, and in gratefulness he offers praise to Marduk. But this work also differs from Job: it is a monologue instead of a dialogue, and the sufferer does not rebuke or condemn his god.[20]

Although the book of Job does consider the problem of unjust suffering, a careful comparison of these works with Job ultimately displays Job's unique status. This uniqueness is expressed well by Anderson:

> Job stands far above its nearest competitors, in the coherence of its sustained treatment of the theme of human misery, in the scope of its many-sided examination of the problem, in the strength and clarity of its defiant moral monotheism, in the characterization of the protagonists, in the heights of its lyrical poetry, in its dramatic impact, and in the intellectual integrity with which it faces the "unintelligible burden" of human existence. In all this Job stands alone. Nothing we know before it provided a model, and nothing since, including its numerous imitations, has risen to the same heights. Comparison only serves to enhance the solitary greatness of the book of Job.[21]

In order to understand the book of Job better, scholars sometimes highlight different aspects of the book. For example, Job's response to suffering, including his response to his friends, takes the form of a lament. Westermann terms the book of Job the dramatization of a lament, which is not pure lament but a story with a lament element.[22] Recognizing the lament element of Job's response is helpful, but it is doubtful that lament can explain the whole book. A lament is only one of the responses to suffering that occurs in the book of Job. In addition to lament, we find the well-known wisdom poem in chapter 28 and Job's assertions of innocence in chapters 29–31. By way of contrast, Habel highlights the legal aspect of Job's call for a trial before God and calls the book a disputation.[23] Job does call for a hearing before God, and there is a legal element related to the guilt or innocence of Job, but once again, this legal element does not explain the totality of the book. God does vindicate Job, but it does

---

[19] Ernest C. Lucas, *Exploring the Old Testament*, vol. 3, *A Guide to the Psalms and Wisdom Literature* (Downers Grove, IL: InterVarsity Press, 2003), 133.
[20] Hartley, *Job*, 8; Lucas, *Guide to the Psalms and Wisdom Literature*, 132.
[21] Anderson, *Job*, 32.
[22] Claus Westermann, *The Structure of the Book of Job: A Form-Critical Analysis* (Philadelphia: Fortress, 1981), 1–13.
[23] Norman C. Habel, *The Book of Job*, OTL (Philadelphia: Westminster, 1981), 54.

not happen in the setting of a courtroom. It is important to view the book as a whole, which makes the overall structure of the book an important clue to its message.

STRUCTURE AND OUTLINE

The book of Job is not difficult to outline, but how the different parts relate is a debated topic. An analysis of the structure of Job helps to identify the book's genre and clarify its message.[24] The following outline delimits the major sections of the book:

  I. Prologue (1:1–2:13)
  II. Job's Lament (3:1–26)
  III. The Cycle of Speeches (4:1–27:23)
  IV. The Wisdom Poem (28:1–28)
  V. Job's Last Speech (29:1–31:40)
  VI. Elihu's Speeches (32:1–37:24)
  VII. God's Speeches and Job's Response (38:1–42:6)
  VIII. Epilogue (42:7–17)

The prologue and epilogue were written in Hebrew narrative (prose), but the rest of the book, made up of speeches, was composed using Hebrew poetry. Some argue that the original story contained only the prologue and the epilogue, which told the tale of a man who was tested by God through suffering but remained faithful and was subsequently rewarded for his faithfulness with material blessings.[25] But it is questionable whether the prologue and the epilogue by themselves make a complete story. The dialogues are necessary for the argument of the book.[26] Other questions relate to the response of Job, who is compliant in the first two chapters but laments his situation in chapter 3 and then begins to question God in his discussion with his friends. How do we best explain these important changes?

The cycles of speeches also raise questions. For example, the third cycle is incomplete, and the identity of the speaker toward the end of this cycle is unclear. Scholars also debate the function of the wisdom poem in chapter 28 and the purpose of the Elihu speeches in chapters 32–37. Does Elihu really say anything different from the friends of Job? Does he move the argument forward? What is the purpose of his speeches? Job's response to God's speeches is also debated. Does Job repent? And if so, of what does he need to repent? Answers to these questions certainly impact the message of the book of Job.

There is no doubt that the book of Job is about suffering, but the book does not answer the question of why there is suffering. When God answers Job, he does not explain to him what went on in the heavenly council in chapters 1 and 2. The book is more about how to respond to suffering, which is at the heart of the debate between Job and his friends. They raise several issues, but a major issue concerns the question of where wisdom can be found. Are the friends correct that Job is suffering

---

[24] Longman and Dillard, *Introduction*, 227.
[25] Habel mentions this view. *Job*, 25.
[26] Anderson, *Job*, 43.

because of his sin? Is Job right in the assertions of his innocence? Does Job go too far in some of the things he says about God? Job's crisis of suffering generates a dispute concerning how to explain his suffering, which also touches upon Job's relationship with God. The issue of wisdom is at the heart of the book, for wisdom is the ability to apply truth to particular situations. Where is wisdom found in this debate between Job and his friends? This question is ultimately answered in the wisdom poem in chapter 28 and in God's response to Job's suffering in chapters 38–42. In light of this brief overview, the designation "wisdom dialogue" appropriately characterizes the various content of the book, highlighting Job's response to suffering as he leads the reader to consider the source of true wisdom.[27]

MESSAGE AND THEOLOGY
The Prologue (Job 1–2)

The prologue is foundational for the rest of the book. It provides readers with important background information, some of which is unknown to Job and his friends. The book opens with a description of Job. He is presented as a man who is blessed by God with wealth and children. Job is characterized as a man of integrity, blameless and upright, concerned about the welfare of his children. It is significant that the book begins by affirming the character of Job because his friends will call into question his character when he experiences hardship and suffering.

The next section of the prologue (1:6–22) gives the reader insight into the heavenly council as the sons of God present themselves to Yahweh. These "sons of God" refer to angels. At this particular heavenly council Satan is present. The Hebrew noun שָׂטָן with the definite article has been translated "the adversary" or "the accuser."[28] Some debate whether it is appropriate to see in this adversary the one later identified in Scripture as the Devil. No doubt later revelation gives a fuller picture of the role and purposes of Satan, and the description in Job 1–2 fits with subsequent descriptions (1 Chron. 21:1; Zech. 3:1–2; Matt. 4:1–11; John 8:44; Rev. 12:9). He is presented as an outsider to this council by the addition of the word "also" (Job 1:6) and by the description of his activity as roaming about the earth (1:7). But more important, he attacks Job's character and, indirectly, the character of God.

God takes the initiative with Satan by bringing up the character of Job. God affirms the character of Job as blameless and upright and calls him "my servant" (Job 1:8), a term used for other faithful followers of God, such as Abraham, Moses, and David. Satan responds by saying that Job fears God because God has blessed him with good things. If those blessings would be taken away, then Job would curse God (1:11).[29]

---

[27] Longman and Dillard use the term "wisdom debate." *Introduction*, 232.

[28] The term שָׂטָן has the definite article, which suggests that it is functioning as a title. Hartley, *Job*, 71. But the article can also be used with a proper name. Bruce K. Waltke and Michael P. O'Connor, *An Introduction to Biblical Hebrew Syntax* (Winona Lake, IN: Eisenbrauns, 1990), 249. Elmer B. Smick argues that the article stresses the root meaning of the term, which he understands as "the adversary" or the "accuser." *Job*, in *The Expositor's Bible Commentary*, ed. Frank E. Gaebelein (Grand Rapids, MI: Zondervan, 1988), 4:881.

[29] The word translated "curse" in the first two chapters of Job is actually the Hebrew word for "bless" (ברך). This is called a euphemism, a literary device to heighten the radical nature of this unmentionable sin by employing an antonym to describe it. Habel, *Job*, 88.

Satan challenges the character of God by implying that people only love God for what he does for them, which implies that God is unworthy of being loved by virtue of who he is. Satan also challenges the faith of Job by identifying it with self-interest. Job's piety is only a result of his prosperity. God gives Satan the authority to take away Job's blessings. He loses everything he has except his wife and his life. Even his children are taken away (1:12–19). Job's response to this calamity is a humble submission to God's sovereignty: "The LORD gave, and the LORD has taken away; blessed be the name of the LORD" (1:21). This confirms the statement, "In all this Job did not sin or charge God with wrong" (1:22).

The second heavenly council (2:1–6) is very similar to the first. God again raises Job's situation to Satan, confirms Job's character, and then states, "He still holds fast his integrity, although you incited me against him to destroy him without reason" (2:3). This statement does not mean that Job's ordeal has no purpose but rather that there is no cause in Job that has brought on this suffering. Satan responds by saying that God has not really hurt Job because he still has his health, but if God takes that away, Job will curse him to his face (2:4–5). Once again God authorizes Satan to take away Job's health, but he must spare his life. Job's illness is described in 2:7–8. He is full of sores all over his body and finds himself sitting in the ashes, probably a reference to where the garbage is burned. He is separated from the community because of his illness. Even though his wife encourages him to curse God and die, Job again responds in humble submission to God's will and does not sin with his lips (2:10).

The first response of Job's three friends is excellent (2:11–13). They come to sympathize and to comfort Job, and at first they accomplish those goals. They go to be with Job where he is sitting in the ashes, and they sit with him for seven days, mourning and weeping with him. Perhaps most important, they do not speak a word. They are silent, but their presence with Job demonstrates their concern for him. Job feels secure enough in their presence to unload the burden of his heart.

Job's Lament (Job 3)

Major changes occur in chapter 3. The prose ends, and the poetry begins. The divine perspective of chapters 1–2 is gone, leaving the reader with a limited, human perspective. Also, Job's response to his suffering changes. Chapter 3 opens with a jolting statement in light of what has transpired in chapters 1–2. The first two chapters focused on whether Job would curse God (1:11, 2:5, 2:9). Job did not curse God, and the narrator makes clear statements that Job did not sin with his lips. So when chapter 3 opens with the words "Job opened his mouth and cursed," the reader is somewhat surprised. Does Job curse God?

Job 3 contains a curse (3:1–10) and a lament (3:11–26). Job curses the day of his birth (3:1), and by calling for darkness to overtake his birthday, he expresses the desire that it be obliterated from existence. Job's lament continues the theme of cursing and, unlike most lament psalms in the book of Psalms, lacks a movement toward praise. The "why" questions continue Job's desire for nonexistence by questioning why he did not die at birth so that he would now be at rest. Job's way is hidden, which means he has lost the meaning and purpose to life, and he feels "hedged" in by God (3:23). Satan had used this term to refer to God's protection of Job (1:10), but Job feels trapped in his situation of suffering with no way out. Instead of waiting for God, Job longs for death (3:21). Job 3 ends with Job's self-centered perspective on his life situation, for it is full of "my" and "I" as he moves from a God-centered outlook in chapters 1–2 to a self-centered outlook in chapter 3.

Job's response to his suffering changes in chapter 3. The humble, submissive Job becomes the questioning, protesting Job. This change in Job's view of his suffering shows that suffering can impact the way people view life. In the crisis of suffering, many have wrestled with how God can be both good and all-powerful, for they reason that if God is good and all-powerful, then such tragedies of suffering would not happen. Some even go so far as to change their view of God.[30] Job himself recognizes that his words are sometimes rash because of the great grief and anguish he is experiencing (6:2). He will also at times question God's justice in light of his own innocent suffering, but he does not curse God[31] or turn away from him.

In light of Job's change of response, an important distinction needs to be made that will help the reader understand different parts of the book of Job. It is clear from Job 1–2 that Job is not suffering because he has done something wrong. God declares that Job is blameless and that Satan has incited God against Job without cause. This can be called point A. However, Job does not always respond correctly or appropriately from within the situation of suffering. Job sins with his mouth in some of the things he says in response to his suffering. This can be called point B. Some things in the book of Job are said in response to point A. Job is correct concerning the main point of contention with his friends that he is not suffering because of specific sin in his life, which helps explain God's statement in Job 42:7. But God does accuse Job of speaking of things he does not understand (38:2) and of calling into question God's justice (40:8), which refers to how Job has responded once he was faced with his suffering (point B).

The Speeches of the Friends (Job 4–25)

The book of Job includes three cycle of speeches with Eliphaz and Bildad each making three speeches, Zophar making two speeches, and Job responding to each of the speeches. The third cycle is incomplete because it lacks a third speech by Zophar and attributes some words to Job that seem foreign to his earlier thoughts. Although some try to make a complete third cycle, an incomplete third cycle serves a literary purpose within the book of Job.

The friends try to help Job understand his suffering, but it becomes apparent that they believe Job must be suffering because of something he has done. In response to

---

[30] In his best seller *When Bad Things Happen to Good People* (New York: Anchor, 1981), Harold Kushner comes to the view that God is good but not all-powerful; otherwise, tragedies, such as his son dying from progeria (rapid aging), would not happen.

[31] To curse one's birthday is to curse something of the past that cannot be changed; it is a parody of a curse and is Job's way of saying that he wished he had never been born.

some of Job's statements, they seek to uphold the justice of God, which must mean that Job has sinned to bring on his suffering. They cannot reconcile God's justice with Job's assertions of integrity. The friends make many true statements about God, but they stumble when they try to apply those statements to Job's situation. In other words, the main problem is the application of theology, which is a matter of wisdom.

Eliphaz is the first to respond to Job's outburst of chapter 3. He seeks to comfort Job by reminding him of his fear of God and the integrity of his ways as his source of confidence (4:6). However, he also raises the issue that a person who sows trouble will reap it (4:8), perhaps a response to Job's statement of wanting trouble to be hidden from his eyes (3:10). In this first speech Eliphaz does not confront Job directly but makes allusions to Job's situation that raise the issue of Job's integrity. For example, he states that the children of the fool are far from safety, the harvest of the fool is eaten by others, and the thirsty pant after the wealth of the fool (5:2–7). Thus Eliphaz says some things that are true on a general level (4:8; 5:17) but applies them wrongly to Job's situation. Job is not reaping what he has sown because of sin in his life.

In his second speech Eliphaz becomes more confrontational by pointing out that Job's own mouth condemns him (15:6) and by offering a poem on the fate of the wicked (15:20–35), who give birth to trouble. His third speech tries to pinpoint Job's wickedness by listing examples of things that Job may need to confess as a way to get Job to acknowledge his sin (22:5–9).

Bildad takes up the cause of God's justice in order to defend it. God punishes the wicked and blesses the righteous, which makes it clear that Job's children must have sinned (8:4) and that Job is suffering because of his sin. Job cannot be blameless because God would not reject a blameless man (8:20). Bildad also gives a graphic description of the fate of the wicked in arguing that the lamp of the wicked is snuffed out (18:5–21). In his third speech, which is very short (25:1–6), he attacks Job's claims of innocence.

Zophar seeks to get Job to understand the way God works in the world. If Job would only repent, he could enjoy the peaceful security of repentant sinners (11:13–20). But without repentance only the fate of the wicked awaits Job, which he describes graphically (20:6–29). Zophar does not offer a third speech.

The Speeches of Job (Job 6–26)

Job responds to each of his friends' speeches. It is helpful to remember that he is suffering, and thus his words may not always be logical (6:1–3). At times Job despairs because of what he is experiencing, and at other times he makes bold statements. Sometimes he speaks directly to the friends, and sometimes he speaks directly to God.

Several themes can be highlighted in Job's speeches. First, Job desperately wants a chance to present the case of his integrity before God, but he also despairs that such an event will ever happen, or if it does take place, that no one can hope to win an argument with God (9:3, 14–20). Second, Job continues to assert that he is innocent (9:15; 16:17; 23:11–12), even as he perceives that God is part of his problem. God is a hunter who pursues his prey so that death is Job's only hope (6:4–10). God has no regard for the blameless or wicked but destroys them both. In fact, God mocks the calamity of the innocent (9:22–23). Such statements call into question God's justice. Third, Job explores the complexity of God's ways in the world so that his view of God is not limited to the mechanical view of deed and consequence that the friends present, which opens the door to hope in God's sovereignty (Job 24). Fourth, Job speaks some surprising statements of hope. He asserts, "when he has tried me I shall come out as gold" (23:10); "though he slay me, I will hope in him" (13:15);[32] and "I know that my Redeemer lives. . . . In my flesh I shall see God" (19:25–26).[33]

The End of the Cycle of Speeches (Job 27–31)

After Bildad speaks for the third time (Job 25) and Job answers him (Job 26), Zophar offers no third speech. According to the text, two speeches of Job remain. Job 27:1 states, "Job again took up his discourse," a phrase that also covers chapter 28, which has no heading. Job 29–31 is Job's final speech, which is introduced with "Job again took up his discourse" (29:1).

Scholars see several problems with this layout. Some want to complete the third cycle of speeches by taking something Job says in chapter 27 and making it Zophar's third speech. Job 27:13–23 gives a description of the demise of the wicked that sounds very much like what the friends have argued earlier, even specifying that if the children of the wicked are multiplied, it is for the sword (27:14). However, there is no evidence that these words were ever the words of Zophar, and the text clearly identifies them as the words of Job.

The sequence of speeches can be explained. An incomplete third cycle is evidence that the debate between Job and his friends has collapsed. They have made no progress in the argument and found no resolution to the question. Instead, each side has become entrenched in their position, and they have ended up hurling insults back and forth at each other. Job has even called his friends miserable comforters who offer long-winded speeches (16:1–3). Bildad feels insulted because Job has treated them as stupid (18:4), and his short speech ends by calling "man"

---

[32] The ESV, NKJV, NIV, and NASB translate this verse as an affirmation of faith. The textual issues involved in the translation of this verse leave room for other options. The RSV translates 13:15 as an affirmation of resignation: "Behold, he will slay me; I have no hope." Hartley translates it as an affirmation of uncertainty: "If he were to slay me, I would have no hope." *Job*, 221. Habel translates the verse as an affirmation of perseverance: "Yes, though he slay me, I will not wait." *Job*, 725. Either the affirmation of faith or the affirmation of perseverance fits the context of Job's confidence to continue to argue his ways before God (13:15b) and his confidence of salvation (13:16).

[33] There is much debate concerning when Job believes he will be vindicated by his kinsman-redeemer (גֹּאֵל). The interpretation of these verses hinges on the meaning of "upon the earth" (literally, "dust") in 19:25 and on whether "in my flesh" should be translated "without my flesh" (19:26). One view is that Job's vindication comes after his death. Some understand 19:25–26 as a direct reference to the resurrection as Job's ultimate hope, but others understand the passage as falling short of a full statement of bodily resurrection while still affirming that Job has the hope of a favorable meeting with God after death. Anderson, *Job*, 194. Another view is that Job is confident that after his death a kinsman-redeemer will perform the proper rituals to preserve his name and patrimony for posterity. In this way he will avoid the death of the wicked, who are not given proper funerary rites. Matthew J. Suriano, "Death, Disinheritance, and Job's Kinsman-Redeemer," *JBL* 129, no. 1 (2010): 49–66. It is also possible to argue that Job is confident of vindication before his death, even as he sits on the heap of ashes. Vindication before death is what takes place at the end of the book. However, Job's hope of vindication is phrased in such a way that it speaks of our ultimate hope in light of the resurrection of Jesus Christ. Hartley, *Job*, 297. Our Redeemer lives, and even though our flesh is destroyed in the grave, we have the hope that in our resurrected bodies we shall see God.

a maggot (25:6). The debate has collapsed and the argument has come to an end. However, Job offers further words in which he seems to agree with the friends' argument that the wicked will get what comes to them (27:13–23). It seems strange that Job would here echo the argument of the friends. It could be that he is quoting the friends' "meaningless talk" (a translation of 27:13).[34] It could be that Job is instructing the friends by turning the argument back upon them, warning them that what they have argued could happen to them.[35] This works if the friends are seen as the enemy (27:7) who will receive the portion of the wicked (27:13). But perhaps it is no more complicated than the fact that on a general level Job agrees with the argument of the friends concerning the ultimate demise of the wicked, which he asserts in chapter 27. The problem has been the application of the argument to Job's situation.

The poem on wisdom (Job 28) highlights that although human ingenuity can do a lot of good things, it does not know how to find wisdom. Human beings also do not fully comprehend the worth of wisdom. The only one who understands the way to wisdom is God, who has given to man the foundation for wisdom: the fear of the Lord (28:28). Job 28 stresses that wisdom is unattainable on the human level, which is a judgment on the speeches that have already been given by Job and his friends. They have not spoken with wisdom. If wisdom is only found in God, then it is imperative that God would speak wisdom to this situation.

Job's final words before God speaks come in chapters 29–31. He gives an account of his glorious past when he was a respected man of the community, God was his friend, and life was full of blessing (Job 29). He contrasts that with his humiliating present condition where he suffers contempt from worthless fools, suffers affliction from the hand of God, and suffers from a life full of turmoil and sorrow (Job 30). Job's final assertions of his integrity come in the way of self-imprecation (Job 31). Job lists certain wicked behaviors and calls down upon himself negative, horrible consequences if he has done any of those wicked deeds. In doing so, Job vigorously asserts his innocence and tries to force the hand of his accuser. God must either activate the curse of the oath or clear the one who takes the oath. Should God remain silent, Job would be cleared by not being cursed.[36]

Elihu's Speeches (Job 32–37)

God does not immediately respond to Job; instead, Elihu steps into the debate. Elihu has not entered the discussion because he is younger than Job's three friends, but he becomes angry when the argument between Job and the three friends collapses. He is angry at the friends because they were not able to answer Job even though they declared him to be in the wrong (32:3–4). He is angry with Job because he justified himself rather than God (32:2). Elihu promises a different approach. Job need not

[34] Robert L. Alden, *Job*, NAC 11 (Nashville: Broadman, 1993), 265.
[35] Layton Talbert combines the quotation view with the idea that this section is an imprecation against the enemies, who would be Eliphaz, Bildad, and Zophar. *Beyond Suffering: Discovering the Message of Job* (Greenville, SC: Bob Jones University Press, 2007), 149–50.
[36] Hartley, *Job*, 406.

fear him because he too is a "piece of clay" (33:6). He also quotes the words of Job as a basis for his argument (33:9; 34:5; 35:2), which has the potential for clearing up misunderstandings between them. Thus Elihu offers the possibility of finding wisdom on the human level.

Elihu's argument is difficult to evaluate. The key question is whether he truly advances the argument, or whether he basically operates with the same perspective of the friends even though he may emphasize things the friends did not. Scholars evaluate Elihu in various ways. Some are very negative toward him and understand him to be pompous, bombastic, and arrogant.[37] Others are more positive and argue that he provides a partial answer to the words of Job. His fundamental argument differs from the friends because he emphasizes that affliction is a matter of God's grace for the sufferer's benefit rather than a product of God's displeasure. Also, the fact that five chapters are devoted to Elihu—more than to any one of the other three friends—must mean that he has something beneficial to say, and the fact that God does not answer him would seem to suggest that God is pleased with his argument.[38] An interesting nuance on the positive view is that Elihu deals with the response of Job once he is in the situation of suffering (point B) and does not deal with the main argument of whether Job is suffering because he has sinned (point A).[39]

Others take a mixed view of Elihu. They recognize that Elihu uses a different approach than the friends and that he does have a broader view of the purpose of suffering, but in the final analysis Elihu's argument lines up with the friends' basic argument. Several of his statements seem to agree with the argument of the friends (33:9–13, 26–28; 34:11, 37; 36:7–11). For example, in seeking to uphold the justice of God, he affirms that God repays a man according to his work (34:11–20) and that Job has added rebellion to his sin by speaking words without insight (34:35–37). It is difficult to limit the latter statement of adding rebellion to sin to what Job has said in response to his suffering (point B). Job has added words of rebellion (point B) to his sin (point A).

The Elihu speeches function to demonstrate that human wisdom falls short, which shows the need for God to answer. If twenty-five chapters can be given over to a debate that collapses (Job 3–27), five chapters can be devoted to showing once again the limits of human wisdom. It is true that Elihu's emphasis on the majesty of God prepares Job for God's response, but Elihu also downplays the possibility that God will respond to Job. He states that God has answered Job without Job perceiving it (33:14) and that God has no compelling need to enter into litigation or to answer the formal complaints of people like Job (34:23; 35:13–14). What a surprise, then, when God does respond to Job. Thus God may not answer Elihu directly, but he does answer him indirectly simply by actually speaking to Job.

---

[37] Cyril S. Rodd, *The Book of Job*, Narrative Commentaries (Philadelphia: Trinity Press International, 1997), 63.
[38] William Henry Green, *Conflict and Triumph: The Argument of the Book of Job Unfolded* (Carlisle, PA: Banner of Truth, 1999), 118–36; Talbert, *Beyond Suffering*, 163–74.
[39] Talbert, *Beyond Suffering*, 170.

God's Speeches, Job's Response, and the Epilogue (Job 38–42)

When God does speak, he addresses Job directly. In God's first speech (38:1–40:2) he accuses Job of darkening counsel by words without knowledge (38:2). Job has spoken of things he has not understood. He has questioned God, but now God will question Job. The first speech is a barrage of questions that focus on God's rule over creation. The purpose is to remind Job of the power and glory of God over against Job's limited knowledge and understanding of the world. The panorama of creation stands over against the self-centered focus of Job at the end of chapter 3.

In responding to God's first speech (40:3–5), Job admits that his knowledge is limited and that he has no answer to God's questions. He puts his hand over his mouth, which shows that he will no longer speak or take up a new line of argument. Thus he feels the impact of God's speech, but he does not yet renounce anything he has said, which makes a second speech of God necessary.[40]

God's second speech (40:2–41:34) raises the question of God's justice in ruling the world and whether Job has the ability and power to govern the world. God asks Job, "Will you condemn me that you may be in the right?" (40:8). This question is followed by God's exhortations for Job to exercise power in the world by dealing with the proud and the wicked (40:10–14). God uses two examples to further support his point: Behemoth and Leviathan. Some regard these two creatures as physical animals. God describes Behemoth to Job as "which I made as I made you" (40:15). The habitat of Behemoth is described as a river and his food as grass. The physical description of both animals gives the impression that they are physical animals (40:16–18; 41:14–17). Scholars debate what animals are being described.[41] However, other things are said about these two creatures that go beyond what we would say about a literal animal. There are hints of this in Behemoth when he is called the first of the works of God (40:19).[42] These hints are expanded in the description of Leviathan, who has flaming torches coming out of his mouth and smoke coming out of his nostrils (41:18–21). Such descriptions cause some to understand Behemoth and Leviathan as mythological creatures.[43] Perhaps we need not choose between these two options. The purpose of God's second speech is to convince Job that God is Lord of the moral order, which lends weight to the contention that Behemoth and Leviathan, in part, symbolically represent evil powers.[44] The point is that Job does not have the power to govern a world full of wickedness and injustice.

---

[40] Hartley, *Job*, 518.

[41] Behemoth has been described as the hippo or the elephant, but the description of the tail as "stiff like a cedar" (40:17) has caused some to question these identifications. One suggestion is that the reference is to the sexual organ because the loins (40:16) were considered the seat of procreative power. August H. Konkel, *Job*, in vol. 6 of the Cornerstone Biblical Commentary series (Carol Stream, IL: Tyndale, 2006), 231. Others have argued for some kind of dinosaur. Allan Steel, "Could Behemoth Have Been a Dinosaur?" *Journal of Creation* 15, no. 2 (2001): 42–45. Leviathan is understood to be a crocodile.

[42] Smick takes this as a reference to a unique cosmic creature such as the Accuser (Satan) mentioned in the prologue. *Job*, 4:911.

[43] Marvin H. Pope, *Job: A New Translation with Introduction and Commentary: Introduction, Translation, and Notes*, 3rd ed. AB 15 (Garden City, NY: Doubleday, 1973), 320–22. For a refutation of the mythological view, see Robert Gordis, *The Book of God and Man: A Study of Job* (Chicago: University of Chicago Press, 1965), 569–72. For a response to Gordis, see Robert S. Fyall, *Now My Eyes Have Seen You: Images of Creation and Evil in the Book of Job*, NSBT 12 (Downers Grove, IL: InterVarsity Press, 2002), 127–28.

[44] Smick, *Job*, 4:888, 906, 911. See also Fyall, *Creation and Evil in Job*, 129–37, 157–68. Fyall argues that throughout Job are references to the netherworld and that they culminate in Behemoth (identified with Mot the god of death) and Leviathan (identified with Satan).

There is debate about the nature of Job's second response to God (42:1–6), which revolves around the meaning of the terms מאס and נחם in 42:6. The former term can mean "refuse, reject," and the latter term can mean "regret, be sorry, comfort." Some understand Job's statement not as repentance but as a change in his stance so that he is willing to drop his suit against God.[45] But in light of what God says to Job in 38:2 and 40:8, it is better to see Job's response here as repentance. God calls Job to account for words that called into question God's justice. However, concerning the main point of contention between Job and the friends, Job was right that he was not suffering because of some sin in his life. This explains God's statement to the friends in 42:7: "you have not spoken of me what is right, as my servant Job has." God is angry with the friends, who must offer burnt offerings and seek Job's intercession for them. A final confirmation that Job was right in the basic point of contention with the friends is that Job intercedes for them while he is still in suffering. Job is restored after he prays for his friends (42:10).

Some are troubled by the lavish restoration Job receives from God, as if this confirms the view of the friends that righteousness is always rewarded by God, which would contradict the purpose of the book. Plus, the restoration of Job could leave the impression that Job's suffering was not that significant because now everything is well and good. Several points put Job's restoration into perspective. The restoration is evidence that God had not forsaken his servant. Also, it is clear that Satan is wrong about Job; thus both Job's honor and God's honor are vindicated.[46] Job's restoration by God allows for restoration with his family (42:11). Finally, Job's restoration should remind all of God's people who are suffering that even though the reason for their suffering may not be known, there is hope for restoration.

We learn from Job that God is not obligated to explain to us the whys of our suffering; rather, the important thing is how we respond to suffering. A common human response to suffering is to question God's purposes. The lament psalms are full of questions, and Habakkuk registers his deep concerns about the lack of justice with God. Many times questions arise because people do not see the covenant promises of God demonstrated in their lives. However, it is also important that questions come to an end as a person willingly submits to the sovereignty of God. Surely this may take place over a period of time, but eventually Habakkuk comes to the place where he asserts that "the LORD is in his holy temple; let all the earth keep silence before him" (2:20).

APPROACHING THE NEW TESTAMENT

Job is presented in James 5:11 as a person who was steadfast under great trial. He is a picture of one who suffers unjustly. Just as his friends could not comprehend how someone who was blameless could endure such suffering, so those at the foot of the cross could not comprehend how one who was being crucified could be the Son of

---

[45] William J. Dumbrell, "The Purpose of the Book of Job," in *The Way of Wisdom: Essays in Honor of Bruce K. Waltke*, ed. J. I. Packer and Sven Soderlund (Grand Rapids, MI: Zondervan, 2000), 96–97.
[46] Smick, *Job*, 4:1056.

God: "He trusts in God; let God deliver him now, if he desires him. For he said, 'I am the Son of God'" (Matt. 27:43). Jesus's suffering is much greater than Job's suffering, for Jesus suffers for the sake of others, with the great hope that he "shall see his offspring" and "shall prolong his days" for "the will of the LORD shall prosper in his hand" (Isa. 53:10).

The followers of Jesus are promised that they too will suffer for his sake, and they see, more clearly than Job saw, the confident hope of vindication because of the resurrection of Christ. Not only does Jesus take upon himself our sin, sickness, and suffering, but he calls us to take up our cross daily to follow him. The coming restoration for the followers of Jesus will be so much greater than Job's restoration, for we will experience the fullness of the kingdom when Christ comes again in glory. Even so, come quickly Lord. Amen.

SELECT BIBLIOGRAPHY

Alden, Robert L. *Job*. NAC 11. Nashville: Broadman, 1993.

Anderson, Francis I. *Job*. TOTC 13. Downers Grove, IL: InterVarsity Press, 1976.

Belcher, Richard P., Jr. "Suffering." In *Dictionary of the Old Testament: Wisdom, Poetry, & Writings*, edited by Tremper Longman III and Peter Enns, 775–81. IVP Bible Dictionary Series 3. Downers Grove, IL: InterVarsity Press, 2008.

Dell, Katharine J. *Job: Where Shall Wisdom Be Found?* Sheffield: Sheffield Phoenix, 2013.

Dumbrell, William J. "The Purpose of the Book of Job." In *The Way of Wisdom: Essays in Honor of Bruce K. Waltke*, edited by J. I. Packer and Sven Soderlund, 91–105. Grand Rapids, MI: Zondervan, 2000.

Fyall, Robert S. *Now My Eyes Have Seen You: Images of Creation and Evil in the Book of Job*. NSBT 12. Downers Grove, IL: InterVarsity Press, 2002.

Gordis, Robert. *The Book of God and Man: A Study of Job*. Chicago: University of Chicago Press, 1965.

Green, William Henry. *Conflict and Triumph: The Argument of the Book of Job Unfolded*. Carlisle, PA: Banner of Truth, 1999.

Habel, Norman C. *The Book of Job*. OTL. Philadelphia: Westminster, 1985.

Hartley, John E. *The Book of Job*. NICOT. Grand Rapids, MI: Eerdmans, 1988.

Kynes, Will. *My Psalm Has Turned into Weeping: Job's Dialogue with the Psalms*. BZAW 437. Berlin: de Gruyter, 2012.

Konkel, August H. *Job*. In vol. 6 of the Cornerstone Biblical Commentary series. Edited by Philip W. Comfort. Carol Stream, IL: Tyndale, 2006.

Longman, Tremper, III. *Job*. BCOTWP. Grand Rapids, MI: Baker, 2012.

Rodd, Cyril S. *The Book of Job*. Narrative Commentaries. Philadelphia: Trinity Press International, 1997.

Smick, Elmer B. *Job*. In *The Expositor's Bible Commentary*, edited by Frank E. Gaebelein, 4:843–1060. Grand Rapids, MI: Zondervan, 1988.

Steel, Allan. "Could Behemoth Have Been a Dinosaur?" *Journal of Creation* 15, no. 2 (2001): 42–45.

Suriano, Matthew J. "Death, Disinheritance, and Job's Kinsman-Redeemer." *JBL* 129, no. 1 (2010): 49–66.

Talbert, Layton. *Beyond Suffering: Discovering the Message of Job*. Greenville, SC: Bob Jones University Press, 2007.

Westermann, Claus. *The Structure of the Book of Job: A Form-Critical Analysis*. Philadelphia: Fortress, 1981.

Wilson, Gerald H. *Job*. NIBCOT 10. Peabody, MA: Hendrikson, 2007.

16

Proverbs[1]

Willem A. VanGemeren

INTRODUCTION

The title of the book is a translation of the Hebrew word מִשְׁלֵי, "the proverbs [of Solomon]," a shortened form of the superscription (Prov. 1:1). These proverbs or short sayings define the genre of the bulk of the book (10:1–31:10). The English title, Proverbs, is derived from the Latin Vulgate title, *Proverbia*.

Proverbs is an invitation to pursue the path of godly wisdom, though it does not intend to deal with all the complexities raised by life. Job, Ecclesiastes, many of the psalms, and to some extent the whole of the Old Testament encourage the godly to pursue wisdom (or holiness). As God revealed more and more of himself, the body of wisdom grew exponentially. The revelation of God in Christ ties all the pieces together, and James, our Lord's brother, instructs the followers of Jesus not to forget the ancient path of wisdom (cf. James 1:5; 3:13, 15, 17).

Wisdom instruction in Israel was intended to lead people to be in awe of the Lord (Prov. 1:7), to seek fellowship with him by trusting in him (3:5–6), and to incarnate the way of justice, righteousness, and commitment on earth. Proverbs develops the Mosaic themes of wisdom and folly, life and death, and blessing and curse. The knowledge of God taught by Moses and the Prophets receives its complement in the sapiential (from the Latin *sapientia*, meaning "wisdom") Writings. All parts of the Old Testament canon prod its readers to see God in relation to all aspects of life. As part of the Writings, Proverbs contains sapiential instructions by which God's people may discern wisdom and apply it to a great variety of situations.

---

[1] This essay is in gratitude to Reformed Theological Seminary-Jackson, where I was privileged to teach from 1978–1992, and is dedicated to the "valiant" young men from Christ Church (PCA, Normal/Bloomington, IL), who spent many mornings in our gardens learning the way of wisdom in Proverbs and in creation, and to the students at Colombo Theological Seminary (Sri Lanka), who joined me on the path of wisdom in the fall of 2014.

Background Issues

Authorship and Date

The superscription of the book mentions Solomon: "The proverbs of Solomon, son of David, king of Israel" (1:1). The title gives the impression that Solomon authored the whole book of Proverbs. The threefold mention of Solomon's name (1:1; 10:1; 25:1) furthers this impression. However, the mention of the wise men (22:17; 24:23) and of two non-Israelite kings (Agur, 30:1; Lemuel, 31:1) argues against such a conclusion.

Solomon is the paragon of Israelite wisdom (cf. Matt. 12:42). The Solomonic contribution hails from the tenth century BC, while the process of collecting and organizing the book took centuries. But how much comes from Solomon? Kitchen attributes Proverbs 1–24 to Solomon. He understands the linkage of 1:1 and 10:1 as original and favors to read the assignation to Solomon (ca. 950 BC) as part of the original text. The next heading (25:1) links the second part of the book with a collection of Solomonic sayings that were gathered during the time of Hezekiah (chaps. 25–29; ca. 700 BC). Kitchen supports his conclusion by arguing from comparative data in the ancient Near Eastern proverbial collections that chapters 1–24 (Solomon I) and chapters 25–29 (Solomon II) are Solomonic, though collected at different times. Kitchen favors an early date for the composition of the whole book (ca. 700 BC).[2]

Longman and others see a Solomonic nucleus, while recognizing that a collection attracts other collections and generally undergoes redactional processes. Longman concludes, "if one regards the indications within the book, the origins of the book of Proverbs might be associated with Solomon, but its redaction continued for centuries afterward."[3] It could be dated to the postexilic era, a suggestion favored by Van Leeuwen.[4] Supporting this postulate are two other pieces of evidence. First, some proverbs repeat material with minor variations; for example, "The words of a whisperer are like delicious morsels; they go down into the inner parts of the body" (18:8; cf. 26:22). Others reveal a significant change in expression; compare 10:2, "Treasures gained by wickedness do not profit, but righteousness delivers from death," with 11:4, "Riches do not profit in the day of wrath, but righteousness delivers from death."[5] These changes may indicate fluidity in the tradition.[6] Second, the Masoretic text and the Septuagint reveal different structures and significant variations. In brief, the Masoretic text and the Septuagint are identical in order for Proverbs 1:1–24:23. From this point on, they differ. The Septuagint inserts the sayings of Agur (30:1–14) before the "sayings of the wise" (24:23–34), continues with 30:15–31:9 (numerical sayings and the sayings of Lemuel), and inserts the sayings collected by Hezekiah's

---

[2] K. A. Kitchen, "Proverbs 2: Ancient Near Eastern Background," in *Dictionary of the Old Testament: Wisdom, Poetry & Writings*, ed. Tremper Longman III and Peter Enns, IVP Bible Dictionary Series 3 (Downers Grove, IL: IVP Academic, 2008), 552.

[3] Tremper Longman III, "Proverbs," in Longman and Enns, *Dictionary of the Old Testament: Wisdom, Poetry & Writings*, 540.

[4] Van Leeuwen understands the process of collecting and editing to be drawn out from the days of the early monarchy into the Hellenistic period. The wordplay on the Greek word *sofia* in 31:27 suggests the Hellenistic period. Raymond C. Van Leeuwen, *Proverbs*, in *The New Interpreter's Bible*, ed. Leander E. Keck (Nashville: Abingdon, 1997), 5:21.

[5] See Daniel C. Snell, *Twice-Told Proverbs and the Composition of the Book of Proverbs* (Winona Lake, IN: Eisenbrauns, 1993).

[6] Also compare 14:12 with 16:25 and 20:6 with 27:13.

men (25:1–29:27) before the concluding poem of the virtuous woman (31:10–31). The Septuagint varies at other points from the Masoretic text as each include additional verses missing in their counterpart. Thus, the evidence of the Septuagint suggests that the Masoretic text form was not as fixed by 700 BC as Kitchen suggests. At the very least, it is safe to say that the book as a whole became a part of the Canon well before the dawn of the New Testament era and that the wisdom tradition remained alive in Judaism and in the teachings of our Lord and of his apostles.[7]

Social Context

The social context of wisdom varies widely from Babylon to Egypt. In the Babylonian tradition, scribes belonged to a "tablet house," received support from the royal court, and gradually rendered their services to the wealthy. In Egypt the locus of the wisdom tradition was the "house of life" connected with a temple. Both Babylonian and Egyptian scribes were professionals who transmitted and helped shape their cultures over millennia.

In the ancient Near East, wisdom was located in "schools" constructed for the purpose of training government officials, religious functionaries, and business executives. They functioned in the court or temple setting and learned the protocol of court life in preparation for serving the bureaucracy.

No evidence for such schools has been found in ancient Israel. The social context of Israel's wisdom tradition is likely the home. It is suggested that the proverbs and wisdom tradition of Israel come from a number of different contexts: the family, work (agriculture), and government (court). Wisdom, though international by nature, was transmitted at the tribal/family level. The paradigm of parents exemplifying wisdom and teaching their children in the context of the family forms the basis of Israel's democratized religious structure (Gen. 18:19; Deut. 6:7). From within the family context, children would also learn to observe their parents in many different contexts: at home, in the field, in business, in court, and in government.[8] A lifestyle characterized by awe for Yahweh would serve as a model for future generations and would open for them the way of wisdom. Proverbs 4 supports the family context by the repetition of the wisdom instruction of the grandfather through the father to the grandson (4:3–9).

Wisdom in the Ancient Near East[9]

Israel was not the only nation with a wisdom tradition. Israel's neighbors also had long-standing wisdom traditions. The Sumerians collected proverbs (ca. 2500 BC),

---

[7] Witness the apocryphal writings (Wisdom, Sirach, and sections of Baruch) and the Mishnah (Pirqe Avot; i.e., "Sayings of the [Jewish] Fathers"). See Richard J. Clifford, SJ, *Introduction to Wisdom Literature*, in *The New Interpreter's Bible*, 5:14–16.
[8] G. I. Davies raises the possibility of schools in ancient Israel. "Were There Schools in Ancient Israel?," in *Wisdom in Ancient Israel: Essays in Honour of J. A. Emerton*, ed. John Day, Robert P. Gordon, and H. G. M. Williamson (Cambridge: Cambridge University Press, 1995), 199–211.
[9] See further Tremper Longman III, "Proverbs 1, Book of," in Longman and Enns, *Dictionary of the Old Testament: Wisdom, Poetry & Writings*, 545–47; *How to Read Proverbs* (Downers Grove, IL: InterVarsity Press, 2002), chap. 6; Kitchen, "Proverbs 2," 552–66; Michael V. Fox, *Proverbs 1–9*, AB 18A (New York: Doubleday, 2000), 19–27; Roland E. Murphy, *Proverbs*, WBC 22 (Nashville: Thomas Nelson, 1998), 287–94.

and the Babylonians copied these lists together with their translation. Concurrently, the cultured Egyptians relished wisdom instructions, such as "The Instruction which a Man made for his Son" and the thirty instructions of Amenemope. The genre of Egyptian instruction was popular for several millennia among the elite to ensure that their "sons" would advance in their careers. The discovery of the instruction of Amenemope created a stir because it revealed remarkable parallels with Proverbs.[10] The purpose of the instruction was to inculcate "the teaching of life, the testimony for prosperity, all precepts for intercourse [interaction] with elders, the rules for courtiers, to know how to return an answer to him who said it . . . to rescue him from the mouth of the rabble, revered in the mouth of the people."[11] This instruction also revealed close parallels with "the sayings of the wise" in Proverbs 22:17–24:34.[12] Kitchen, however, argues strenuously that there is no clear dependency on the Egyptian sayings in the first Solomonic collection (Proverbs 1–24).[13] He concludes, "there is nothing to exclude his drawing upon and even reformulating topics from Amenemope any more or less than any other source."[14] It is true that Egyptian instruction sought to maintain a world order of righteousness and right. While Israel's wisdom also aims at righteousness, it uniquely associates righteousness with the fear of the Lord and with the wisdom lifestyle and worldview that result from this relationship.[15]

Genre[16]

Proverbs shares genre characteristics with other wisdom literature in the ancient Near East. It is largely made up of instructions, sayings (proverbs), and admonitions. This literature works to reveal ways of looking at the world through the aperture of a short, pithy saying or proverb.

Instructions and Admonitions

The genre of wisdom instruction is specifically found in Mesopotamian and Egyptian literature. It occurs in two forms: title and text (type A) and title, prologue, and text (type B). These forms appear in Proverbs as well. Type A is found in chapters 10–31 and type B in chapters 1–9, though scholars show no agreement on the number of instructions. In the book of Proverbs, the instructions genre shapes chapters 1–9, in which the father (and mother) address the son to prepare him for life (1:8). The instruction consists of an invitation to listen, a warning or exhortation, and words

---

[10] Fox, *Proverbs 1–9*, 72–73.

[11] Pritchard, *ANET*, 421–25.

[12] See "Words of the Wise" on p. 393.

[13] Kitchen, "Proverbs 2," 552–64.

[14] Kitchen, "Proverbs 2," 565. Longman agrees with Kitchen's evidence and his conclusion. Longman, "Proverbs 1, Book of," in Longman and Enns, *Dictionary of the Old Testament: Wisdom, Poetry & Writings*, 547. Murphy concludes that while the biblical writer may have known Egyptian sources, he may have relied on wisdom sayings that were "common property, as it were, throughout the ancient Near East." Murphy, *Proverbs*, 294. But Fox concludes that the influence of Amenemope was extensive. *Proverbs 1–9*, 73.

[15] Some sayings of Amenemope also suggest a more internal application of wisdom. Longman, *How to Read*, 67. Longman concludes that the Old Testament sages "never simply or uncritically borrowed ideas from the broader cultural setting. Rather they adapted them to their own religious values." *How to Read*, 77.

[16] See T. Hildebrandt, "Proverbs, Genre of," in Longman and Enns, *Dictionary of the Old Testament: Wisdom, Poetry & Writings*, 528–39.

of encouragement that should motivate the child to guard his heart for wisdom. The instructions contain parental admonitions and prohibitions with promise or threat (1:10–19; 3:7–8). Lady Wisdom's instructions reinforce the parental instructions, highlighting the folly of not listening to her (1:20–33), her presence at creation (8:1–36), and the invitation to the banquet in the house of Lady Wisdom in contrast to the cheap entertainment of Lady Folly (9:1–18).

In Egypt a king (father) would leave instructions for his successor (son) for the purpose of succeeding in life by finding harmony between one's life and the established order of the gods. Cooperation with this order entitled the sage to the blessing of the gods. The social order was to reflect the larger order of nature. Proverbs, too, includes sayings pertaining to court protocol (14:35; 16:12–15; 20:1–2, 8, 26; 25:1–7) but insists that the fear of kings is derivative (24:21). Young men excelling in godly wisdom could take their place before kings, even foreign kings. Such was the case with Joseph and Daniel.[17]

Sayings

The genre of individual proverbs, aphorisms, or wisdom sayings is that of a two-line saying called מָשָׁל (*mashal*) in Hebrew.[18] A proverb draws comparisons from the world of humans and from nature. The observation is a snapshot of reality, one that represents reality at a particular time and place. The proverb is like a winged insect.[19] Once spoken or applied, the speaker may catch the spirit of the proverb or miss it, just like trying to catch a fly. Over time it becomes more apparent to what extent the proverb was "caught" in a particular time or situation.

Hildebrandt summarizes several features of the proverbial sayings in Proverbs. A saying may be defined as a short, pithy statement that transmits an intergenerational observation cast in various figures of speech, communicating through a relatively fixed literary form that is yet free in poetic variation.[20] For example, the image of the balance and weights comes from the world of business: "A false balance is an abomination to the LORD, but a just weight is his delight" (11:1). This short, pithy saying fixes an observation made by folks at one time and transmits it through usage to other generations.

Sayings become readily detached from the original situation and are reattached in collections of proverbs to be applied to many new situations, so that "the virtual potential of this collected proverb may be realized in a multitude of ways when it is recontextualized in each new interactional situation."[21] Observe the connection between the proverb on weights within the context of sayings pertaining to humility, integrity, and righteousness:

---

[17] Longman, *How to Read*, 74–75, 92–100.
[18] This lexeme is related to the verb מָשַׁל, meaning "be like, resemble" or "rule." The Hebrew word for "proverb," מָשָׁל, signifies a great range of sayings, from a satirical statement (Isa. 14:1) to a very short story (24:32–34). The proverbial saying is a pithy saying that encapsulates a truth. All proverbs are sayings, but not all sayings are proverbs in the broad sense.
[19] James L. Crenshaw, *Old Testament Wisdom: An Introduction*, 2nd ed. (Louisville: Westminster John Knox, 1998), 56.
[20] Van Leeuwen, *Proverbs*, 529. See also Crenshaw, *Old Testament Wisdom*, 1–4.
[21] Hildebrandt, "Proverbs, Genre of," 530.

> A false balance is an abomination to the LORD,
>   but a just weight is his delight.
> When pride comes, then comes disgrace,
>   but with the humble is wisdom.
> The integrity of the upright guides them,
>   but the crookedness of the treacherous destroys them.
> Riches do not profit in the day of wrath,
>   but righteousness delivers from death.
> The righteousness of the blameless keeps his way straight,
>   but the wicked falls by his own wickedness.
> The righteousness of the upright delivers them,
>   but the treacherous are taken captive by their lust. (11:1–6)

Sayings have a metaphorical significance, because they can be used in many situations. Through imagery and repetition of themes, they bring up many associations calling for discernment and poetic imagination. Hildebrandt describes categories of conceptual space (wisdom) that mark the vocabulary and themes in Proverbs.[22] The interconnectedness of sounds, parallelism, and figures of speech (metonymy, metaphor, hyperbole, synecdoche, and personification) creates a metaphorical world open to all who enter the riches of Israel's wisdom tradition by the fear of the Lord. Thus the sayings with their parallelism, terseness, and imagery require the reader to "slow down" and discern its interpretation and meaning.[23] Van Leeuwen insightfully speaks of liminality (i.e., a point of transition) and worldview.[24] The way of wisdom opens people up to the pathway of wisdom by which they experience a transition from a cultural worldview to a more transcendent (metaphorical) worldview.

Proverbs are often cast in contrastive ways so as to create different perspectives. The wise son is contrasted to the foolish son in association with the gladness of the father and the sorrow of the mother: "A wise son makes a glad father, but a foolish son is a sorrow to his mother" (10:1). The following verse enhances the contrast by the antithesis of the perceived benefits associated with wickedness and righteousness, "Treasures gained by wickedness do not profit, but righteousness delivers from death" (10:2). The following verse grounds the ways of wisdom and folly in relationship with the Lord and thus brings together ethics and theology: "The LORD does not let the righteous go hungry, but he thwarts the craving of the wicked" (10:3). Since the parents' reaction of gladness or sorrow to the son's respective wisdom or folly is important to the son (10:1), how much more important is God's response to human wisdom and folly. It is an issue of life and death.

"Better Than" Sayings

The "better than" sayings compare the two ways of wisdom (righteousness) and folly (wickedness). Wisdom is "better than" silver and gold (3:13–14; 8:10–11, 19; 16:16;

---

[22] Hildebrandt, "Proverbs, Genre of," 533.
[23] Longman, *How to Read*, 37–46.
[24] Raymond C. Van Leeuwen, "Liminality and Worldview in Proverbs 1–9," *Semeia* 50 (1990): 111–44.

22:1), even when one has to live humbly (15:16–17; 16:8, 19; 17:1; 19:1, 22; 28:6). The first such saying in the Solomonic collection (Proverbs 10–24) is 12:9: "Better to be lowly and have a servant than to play the great man and lack bread." The next set of sayings also encourages contentment (15:16–17). The number of sayings increases in chapter 16 (16:8, 16, 19, 32). These Solomonic "better than" sayings build a strong case for the excellence of humility, the fear of the Lord, love, righteousness, wisdom, and patience together with a lifestyle of simplicity, if not poverty, over against a life of feasting, treasure, revenue, riches, and might, enjoyed together with trouble, hatred, injustice, and lack of self-control.[25] These sayings realistically create a paradoxical tension between expectations and the reality grounded in the trust of the Lord (3:5–7; 11:28; 16:20; 22:19; 28:25–26; 29:25).[26]

Numerical Sayings

The numerical saying takes several forms. It may simply list three or four examples, or the device may take the form of *x plus one*. Both are a striking way to call the reader's attention to the examples. They are not intended to be comprehensive but rather encourage the reader to observe similar examples in real life. The list of abominations to the Lord takes the form of six plus one (6:16–19). The sayings of Agur use the numerical sayings extensively: two (30:7, 15), three (30:15–16), three plus one (30:18–20), and four (30:24–28).

Alphabetic Acrostic

An alphabetic acrostic concludes the book of Proverbs (31:10–31) with a hymn celebrating a heroine: womanhood dressed in the idealized garb of Lady Wisdom. Proverbs 2 is a poem reminiscent of the alphabetizing acrostic in that it has twenty-two verses and consists of one long sentence. It has the total number of letters of the Hebrew alphabet (twenty-two), but it is not an acrostic. Rather, the number twenty-two suggests a comprehensive view of wisdom. Wisdom is familiar (cultural), but divine wisdom is beyond human grasp. It is a gift.

Beatitudes

Beatitudes differ from blessings. A blessing (ברך) is an expression of potentiality and vitality, whereas a beatitude (אַשְׁרֵי) is an expression of felicity or a wish for true happiness. Though translated as "blessed" in the ESV, אַשְׁרֵי could well be rendered as "happy."[27] The beatitude occurs in a context of admonition and encouragement to pursue the way of wisdom though the road may be difficult. The book of Psalms begins with such an expression (Ps. 1:1). Proverbs encourages the pursuit of wisdom

---

[25] Longman concludes, "While many proverbs associate lasting wealth with the wise, other proverbs implicitly acknowledge that when a choice must be made between wealth and wisdom, one is much better off with wisdom (Prov 16:16)." *How to Read*, 89.

[26] Bruce Waltke uses the expression "counter-proverbs." "Do Proverbs Promise Too Much?," *Andrews University Seminary Studies* 34, no. 2 (1996): 319–36.

[27] The word ברך ("bless") suggests potentiality and vitality, as in Prov. 5:18: "Let your fountain be blessed (בְּרוּךְ), and rejoice in the wife of your youth."

as the way to true happiness: "Blessed is the one who finds wisdom, and the one who gets understanding. . . . She is a tree of life to those who lay hold of her; those who hold her fast are called blessed" (Prov. 3:13, 18; cf. 8:32; 14:21; 16:20; 20:7; 28:14).

The Situational Nature of the Sayings

Promises and threats appear to be categorical, but in reality they are situational at the human level and subject to divine sovereignty. The sages were confident about the value of life with God and held on to God's promise of life, even when faced with great distress.[28] On the one hand, the sayings suggest a confident boldness as expressed in Brueggemann's *In Man We Trust*.[29] That is one reason why we enjoy the book of Proverbs. They take some of our questions and doubts away. But Proverbs also wants to deconstruct our familiar world by inviting humans to observe, evaluate, and draw conclusions. Reality takes off the cultural blinders as it asks tough questions. Instead of absolutizing the sayings into principles, we must recognize the complexity of life and the situations in which a saying applies or does not apply. The individual proverbs require wisdom in their application and a humble spirit that confesses that what was thought, said, or done in one situation may not be right in another set of circumstances.[30] Wisdom reminds its practitioner of how limited is one's cognition and field of vision and how extensive is one's bias, prejudice, and foregone conclusion. In other words, wisdom is *proximate*. It is a step in the direction toward divine righteousness that God grants by grace and revelation in the face of human injustice, concern with self, and peer pressure. The best-known example is found in two contradictory admonitions: "Answer not a fool according to his folly, lest you be like him yourself. Answer a fool according to his folly, lest he be wise in his own eyes" (26:4–5; cf. 26:7, 9).[31]

Issues in the Translation and Interpretation of the Sayings

The translation of proverbial sayings is made difficult by their compact style, use of ellipsis, and terse expression. Murphy translates the proverbs as literally as possible, while still making sense of the sayings. He leaves out words that are generally added to bind the sayings together. For example, he renders Proverbs 11:24 as "There is one scattering, and still the richer, and one sparing only the poorer," while the ESV smooths out the translation with added words: "One gives freely, yet grows all the richer; another withholds what he should give, and only suffers want." Murphy leaves the ambiguity of the Hebrew intact. The verb "scattering" may suggest sowing seed in the field or may be interpreted as giving gifts (so ESV).[32] Similarly, compare his

---

[28] See Jon D. Levenson's Jewish view on the God of life in *Resurrection and the Restoration of Israel: The Ultimate Victory of the God of Life* (New Haven, CT: Yale University Press, 2006).

[29] Walter Brueggemann, *In Man We Trust: The Neglected Side of Biblical Faith* (Richmond, VA: John Knox, 1972).

[30] See Longman, *How to Read*, 18.

[31] Longman rightly cautions against the potential of inappropriate applications: "Experience, observation, instruction, learning from mistakes and, most importantly, revelation—all these lay the groundwork for reading the text, reading people, and reading the situation." *How to Read*, 57.

[32] Bruce K. Waltke rejects the sowing translation on the ground that the verb פזר is used of giving gifts and of the scattering of people, bones, or favors. *Proverbs 1–15*, NICOT (Grand Rapids, MI: Eerdmans, 2004), 506. Van Leeuwen reads Prov. 11:24 in connection with verses 25 and 26 under the topic of rich and poor. He advances the paradoxical relationship

reading of 22:16 ("One oppressing the poor for his enrichment; one giving to the rich—only for impoverishment") with the ESV ("Whoever oppresses the poor to increase his own wealth, or gives to the rich, will only come to poverty").[33] Murphy is quite helpful in resisting a periphrastic rendering, arguing that other literature demands the same caution: "one would keep the literal wording and refuse to bowdlerize for the sake of clarity."[34] After all, proverbial sayings are poetic and "are best appreciated if 'prosaic' features are not inserted into them."[35]

STRUCTURE AND OUTLINE

Proverbs is an anthology of anthologies. It contains wisdom instructions (1:1–9:18), an anthology of Solomonic wisdom sayings (10:1–22:16), words of the wise (22:17–24:34), a second anthology of Solomonic wisdom sayings collected at the time of Hezekiah (25:1–29:27), and several wisdom poems (30:1–31:31). The book of Proverbs is composed of many different parts edited into its final form. Introductory formulas allow us to clearly identify seven parts:

   I. Prologue, Instructions, and Admonitions (1:1–9:18)
  II. The Proverbs of Solomon (10:1–22:16)
    A. Part 1 (10:1–15:33)
    B. Part 2 (16:1–22:16)
 III. Words of the Wise (22:17–24:22)
  IV. More Words of the Wise (24:23–34)
   V. Solomonic Proverbs Collected by the Men of Hezekiah (25:1–29:27)
  VI. Oracle of Agur (30:1–33)
 VII. Oracle of Lemuel (31:1–31)

MESSAGE AND THEOLOGY

In the following discussion, we will first describe three broad dimensions of the sapiential tradition and then explore the message of Proverbs following the structure outlined above.

Three Sapiential Dimensions

Israel's sapiential tradition involves three dimensions: (1) a transcendent illumination from God (the fear of the Lord); (2) discernment and application of God's wisdom

---

between generosity and enrichment by reading 11:25 as an expansion of 11:24a and 11:26 as an expansion of 11:24b. Van Leeuwen, *Proverbs*, 119–20. Waltke reads 11:24 as a janus connecting 11:23–27. The larger cotext aids in the interpretation. He comments that 11:23–27 defines "what is right in terms of serving community, not self," and that 11:24–26 brings together "paradoxes, in which two entities are brought into a surprisingly and seemingly contradictory relation in order to clarify subject matter that is not obvious." *Proverbs 1–15*, 507, 506.

[33] Whose wealth is increased, the rich or the poor? Murphy leaves it ambiguous: "his own wealth." *Proverbs*, 116–17. The ESV explains that the oppressor is made wealthier. Another issue lies in the connection between the two lines. The ESV suggests that the oppressor of the poor or the giver (of bribes) to the rich will be impoverished in the end. The TNK clarifies it further: "To profit by withholding what is due to the poor / is like making gifts to the rich—pure loss." It explains oppression as the act of "withholding what is due to the poor." This denying the rights of the poor is interpreted by the second line. It is like making gifts (bribes) to the rich. The paradox lies in the withholding of rights of the poor and the privileging of the rich as a way to advance oneself. It is foolish and will end up in a loss anyway.

[34] Murphy, *Proverbs*, 253.

[35] Murphy, *Proverbs*, 254.

to transcultural (ecumenical, interhuman) issues; and (3) transformation within the self and in relationship with God and others.

A Transcendent Illumination from God: The Fear of the Lord

The greatest virtue set forth in the book of Proverbs is the fear of the Lord. All are invited to enter the path of wisdom through the fear of the Lord. It is fear rather than dread. Fear is the response of awe that attracts the God-fearers to know God. He is the Maker of humans and the Creator of the world (3:19–20). He gave order to this world, maintains his creation, and reveals his wisdom in everything that exists and has come into being (8:22–31). The basic requirement of Israelite wisdom is "the fear of the Lord" (1:7), which is better understood as "awe" for Yahweh,[36] the indefinable and incomprehensible One. Awe is an awareness of God's "otherness," his holiness.

God is both revealed and hidden. Creation reveals a greater order than is humanly comprehensible. It brings harmony (stability) and chaos (earthquakes, tsunamis) together into a greater order that God sees as beautiful, but it often leaves humans with a sense of futility or hopelessness. Proverbs addresses the first level of understanding God: the God of revelation and harmony. Other wisdom books (Job and Ecclesiastes) address the more complex world: the world of God's hiddenness.

The fear of the Lord also comes to expression in dependency on and trust in the Lord (Prov. 3:5–6). A life of trust is more than passive waiting. It requires the diligent search for his wisdom (Proverbs 2). This search requires an openness to understand, discern, and transcend the lot of humanity by walking with the Creator and Giver of life. In communion with God, his human creatures find life (9:32–35; cf. 3:13–17) within limitations.

The fear of the Lord provides the door to apprehend that all life is centered on the Creator, through whom individuals may gain understanding and wisdom (1:7; 9:10). Humans can only realize their purpose when they live within God's order (3:13–20; 8:22–31). The fear of the Lord is an expression of awe for God, and through this awe, personal and communal concerns become secondary to the joy of entering into God's glorious presence revealed in creation, worship, and a lifestyle of ethical obedience. The fear of the Lord brings together cult (religion) and culture, the sacred and the secular, the divine and the human. It is not a fear of God but a cognizance of God's incomprehensibility and a joy of walking in his presence. Through the fear of the Lord, the "righteous" person relates to his Maker continuously in openness, integrity, and authenticity (23:17). In God's presence one becomes more aware of life and of the issues of life (1:29; 10:27; 19:23; 22:4), because the Lord delights in his children who walk with him in humility and wisdom (15:33; 16:6–7; 22:4). The mention of the fear of the Lord at the beginning (1:7) and end of Proverbs (31:30) ties the whole book together as both men and women are encouraged to embody the fear of the Lord.[37] He takes the upright into his inner circle.[38] As they embrace

---

[36] Marvin A. Sweeney, *Tanak: A Theological and Critical Introduction to the Jewish Bible* (Minneapolis: Fortress, 2012), 402.
[37] See Murphy, *Proverbs*, 254–58.
[38] The ESV renders 3:32, "the upright are in his confidence."

wisdom, they love their God and find their utmost joy in him (4:6–8). It is a lifestyle of commitment and love that the parents (4:6; 5:1–2) and Lady Wisdom (8:17) encourage young people to enter, so that they might value all relationship in the light of their love of and commitment to wisdom.

The wisdom tradition flows out of the worship of the one God, Maker of heaven and earth. Israel's worship (cult) was centered on Yahweh, the Creator and Redeemer, the God of Israel and of the nations, and on his exclusive claims (right) to receive worship from his human creatures. His authority extends to all of life and to the whole world. Nature reveals God's wisdom on a universal and royal scale (3:19–20). He has left the clear imprint of his nature to bear witness to his wisdom and to call on people to desire him and his wisdom (24:3–4; cf. Ps. 33:8–9). The repeated calls of Lady Wisdom invite human creatures to observe, listen to, and trust in the way of the Creator (Prov. 8:1–36) so that they may feast in the "house" of wisdom as a microcosm of the macrocosm of the world (9:1). The wise find in creation the wisdom of God as nature invites them to discover the grand scheme of things. If humans do not heed the invitation, they gradually find themselves on the self-destructive way of folly (14:1) and hardened to wisdom (1:7).

Human culture is directly related to the nature of worship, because submission to God or the lack thereof produces a corollary development in culture—ethics (21:3, 7; cf. Ps. 115:8; 135:18; Rom. 1:28–32). Worship (cult) and culture (ethics) are closely interconnected in Israel's wisdom tradition (see especially the epistle of James). Wisdom is "the art of living honestly together with others before God."[39] The two ways of wisdom and of folly are radically opposed to each other. Wisdom, what James calls "pure and faultless," is unlike "worthless" religion (James 1:26–27 NIV), and it reveals itself by its ethics or way of life, whether it be "earthly, unspiritual, of the devil" or "from heaven" (James 3:15–18). The way of wisdom in humans affirms God's purpose for creation in cult and in culture. Van Leeuwen observes, "The life of the Christian community, therefore, will not be fully 'Christian' until our entire lifestyle is shaped in harmony with God's order for creation and consciously dedicated to honor and serve the Lord."[40]

Discernment and Application of God's Wisdom

The heading of the book significantly connects wisdom with royalty: "The proverbs of Solomon, son of David, king of Israel" (Prov. 1:1). Solomon is a prime example of ecumenical sovereignty. He developed his reputation as a wise king when he listened carefully to the conflicting story of the two prostitutes (1 Kings 3:16–27). The news of the verdict spread through all Israel: "they held the king in awe, because they saw that he had wisdom from God to administer justice" (1 Kings 3:28). The pursuit of justice, righteousness, and equity is an expression of royal wisdom (Prov. 1:3; 8:15–16; cf. Ps. 72:1–2). It is also "ecumenical" in the sense that a king cannot

---

[39] Murphy, *Proverbs*, 276; see 269–77.
[40] Ray C. Van Leeuwen, *Book of Proverbs*, in *The New Interpreter's Bible*, ed. Leander E. Keck (Nashville: Abingdon, 1997), 5:208.

be obligated to one part of the country or to one class of people over against another. The story of the two prostitutes demonstrates that Solomon was truly concerned with wise judgment for all people.

The international character of wisdom also opens the search for wisdom into other worlds: biology (e.g., flora, fauna, ecosystems), economics, agriculture, politics, culture, and so forth. Solomon, for example, was known for his wisdom internationally. People from many nations came to visit him because his wisdom was unrivaled (1 Kings 4:30–32). Moreover, Solomon was known for his collection and knowledge of plants, trees, and animals (4:33). Though unstated, it may be assumed that Solomon enjoyed a royal garden and zoo. For example, 1 Kings mentions the import of apes and baboons (10:22) to Solomon's international reputation of wisdom (10:23–24).[41]

Solomon's ecumenical sovereignty included understanding and discernment. As justice penetrates the minds and scheming of people, so wisdom extends these skills to all areas of life. Jurisprudence requires an apprehension of global justice, competence in the application of the law, and the gift of contextualizing the laws through wise judgment. "Wisdom is always prudential, conducive to the individual's well-being," Fox notes, "but it weighs the effect of an action on others as well. It is an ethical quality, never merely instrumental. It is also a quality of character, for it entails not only the knowledge of the right ends but also the will to pursue them."[42] Israel's wisdom tradition helped shape a culture of investigation, exploration, and discovery.

All human beings reflect the image of God. The unity of the human race is a basic tenet in Israel's wisdom tradition. God is the Maker of all human beings, whether poor or rich (Prov. 14:31; 17:5; 22:2). Oppression and injustice are blasphemy of his holy name, because he has made both the oppressor and the oppressed: "Whoever oppresses a poor man insults his maker, but he who is generous to the needy honors him" (14:31). The same goes for any thoughts, acts, or words that create divisiveness between people, because they introduce chaos into the fabric of humanity (13:10; 17:14; 26:17, 21). The fear of the Lord is restorative (8:13). Wisdom is associated with life, blessing, obedience, integrity, and a God-given security, happiness, and meaning for life.[43] Folly is associated with the polar opposites: death, curse, crookedness, corruption and violence, ruin and death, and sorrow. Through the divinely ordered path of wisdom, God's children are restored to the garden of Eden, as they take hold of the Tree of Life, because "[wisdom] is a tree of life to those who lay hold of her" (3:18).

Because of their creational and transcultural perspective, Israel's wisdom sayings show that wisdom can be applied widely to all human situations. These sayings

---

[41] Jon D. Levenson marshals evidence from the ancient Near East that would suggest that "gardens, especially royal gardens, are not simply decorative. They are symbolic, and their religious message is very much involved with that of the Temple in or near which they are not infrequently found. Gardens present and preserve natural things in a form that is so unnatural that it is free from chaos, decay, and death." *Resurrection and the Restoration of Israel*, 86. Stager speaks of "the ecumenical sovereignty of the ruler." He argues that the king demonstrated his transcultural and international perspective and that the world of nature was an extension of his sovereignty. Lawrence E. Stager, "Jerusalem and the Garden of Eden," *Eretz-Israel* 26 (1999): 186–88.

[42] Fox, *Proverbs 1–9*, 9, 29.

[43] Crenshaw interprets wisdom as propriety: a "conduct that secured existence." *Old Testament Wisdom*, 11, 68–72.

remain applicable over time and in different cultural and geographical settings. The purpose of Proverbs and of Israel's wisdom tradition is not to provide a way of wisdom for pious Israelite boys only; it is an invitation for all people to pursue the way of wisdom in all situations, at any time, and in any place (1:2–7).

Transformation within the Self and in Relationship with God and Others

While Israel shared the cultural world of the ancient Near East, her wisdom tradition is rooted in a unique theological framework. Only the knowledge of the Holy One opens the door to wisdom (9:10), and thereby humans learn to know themselves as God's creatures who may walk with him and come to know him better through his revelation in creation and through their engagement with his creation.[44]

Humans are accountable to God, and yet he determines the course of human lives and history. He utilizes the righteous and the wicked to accomplish his purposes. Humans may come to know God's ways over time, but a great gulf will always remain. Humans propose their plans and counsels, but Yahweh determines the execution and correlation of all human activity. Thus, "the plans of the heart belong to man, but the answer of the tongue is from the LORD," and "many are the plans in the mind of a man, but it is the purpose of the LORD that will stand" (16:1–2; 19:21).

Proverbs, as with all Scripture, teaches that there are consequences for one's actions. The nature of divine retribution remains a mystery. Wisdom does not answer questions such as, When and how does God reward and punish? Why does he delay judgment and vindication? What is the connection between individual and communal rewards and punishment? Are blessings and curses a direct or indirect intervention of God? And why does God permit wickedness to thrive at the expense of the godly? Murphy writes that the deed-consequence approach is a "distraction" because it takes away from the radical contrasts of folly versus wisdom and of wickedness versus righteousness.[45] A better approach is character-consequence, which focuses on the contrast between the righteous and the wicked. In God's time both receive their just deserts, because God is patient and gracious in his justice.

The character of a person is tested and shaped by every thought of the heart, action, speech, and response to situations. In some ways, particular acts and words are secondary, because it is the person's being ("heart," or character) that is truly at stake (4:23–27). A wise person may speak and act wrongly, learn from the wrong, and grow in character over time through wise observation and discernment. Proverbs encourages growth in character (virtue) by the constant and vigilant pursuit of wisdom with the promise of life, freedom within limits, and true happiness (contentment).[46]

However, Proverbs does not offer these promises simplistically. It is fully cognizant of the complexity of life, the deceptive power of wealth and riches, and the inequities of this world. In the words of Murphy, "Divine justice, and hence, human

---

[44] Gerhard von Rad treats Israel's search for reality in terms of the search for analogies, act-consequence relationships. *Wisdom in Israel* (Nashville: Abingdon, 1972), 144–76.

[45] Murphy, *Proverbs*, 267.

[46] Crenshaw sees the limits of human reason as a legacy of wisdom, which forced people to face life realistically. *Old Testament Wisdom*, 184.

suffering, remains a mystery, and the struggling of the sages must be appreciated in that light."[47] Agur confesses his failure in apprehending wisdom (30:2–3) in the light of Yahweh's wisdom. Yahweh's wisdom in a sense is incomprehensible (30:4–5). Nevertheless, Proverbs invites all people to fear the Lord, to trust in him, to receive his grace, and to live as royal creatures in their heavenly Father's grand world.[48]

The theology of the book of Proverbs is not easy to define because wisdom casts a comprehensive and overarching reach into all aspects of life. We have seen that wisdom connects God, humans, and his creation. The theological framework of wisdom is largely developed in chapters 1–9.[49] Proverbs touches on many topics: God, wisdom, cosmic order and chaos, humanity and the individual (thoughts, acts, speech), the fear of the Lord, the nature of seduction, the two ways, character, ethics, freedom and limitations, divine sovereignty, and the problem of evil.[50] These topics flow out of the "central assumption . . . that God has made the world, an order within which the human race must learn to live."[51] In addition, Proverbs has many thematic developments that further define the framework and the topical comments.[52]

The Prologue, Instructions, and Admonitions (Prov. 1:1–9:18)[53]

Prologue (Prov. 1:1–7)

The prologue introduces Solomon as the main persona of the book. Not only is he the author of many proverbs (1:1; 10:1; 25:1), but the weight of his royal wisdom hangs over the whole book. The introduction (1:2–7) sets forth the purposes, nature, comprehensiveness, objects, and forms of wisdom. A series of infinitives calls attention to the purpose of the book of Proverbs: that the reader might *know, receive, give,* and *understand* wisdom instruction in its many different forms. The goal of the instructions and sayings is relational, cognitive, and educational. But note that wisdom is a particular form of cognition.[54] It is more than rational deductive or inductive thinking[55] because it begins with God and takes the creational order into account. Wisdom includes cognition, reasoning, and emotional intelligence.[56] Above all, it is

---

[47] Murphy, *Proverbs*, 269.

[48] Proverbs bears witness to the joy of living in relationship with God in Christ. Jesus is the Logos, who is God, who was with God, who created all things, who witnessed to the new life in communion with God (*perichoresis*) through self-humiliation and suffering (*kenosis*), and who invites people to enter into the divine realm of grace, forgiveness, compassion, and justice. He is the way to God, to the knowledge of self, and to a vital relationship with others. See the final section of this chapter for the connection between wisdom and Jesus.

[49] See Hee-Suk Kim, "Proverbs 1–9: A Hermeneutical Introduction to the Book of Proverbs" (PhD diss., Trinity Evangelical Divinity School, 2010).

[50] Richard J. Clifford lists eight themes as major emphases in the Hebrew wisdom literature: God, cosmic order, creation, wisdom, the effects of human choice, the two ways, the problem of evil, and the personification of wisdom. *Introduction to Wisdom Literature*, 5:8–14. Longman suggests the following themes in Proverbs: money, sexuality, and speech. *How to Read*, 117–55.

[51] Clifford, *Introduction to Wisdom Literature*, 5:8.

[52] Crenshaw speaks of a "certain indescribable quality" of biblical wisdom and attempts to further define this quality. *Old Testament Wisdom*, 15.

[53] Kitchen argues that the prologue with its many exhortations to listen was characteristic of the second millennium, which suggests the unity of chapters 1–24. He favors the Solomonic connection with these chapters and concludes that they are best understood as representative of the earliest Mesopotamian wisdom tradition rather than the Egyptian. "Proverbs 2," 554–59. For a contrary point of view, see Fox, *Proverbs 1–9*, 72–3.

[54] Fox, *Proverbs 1–9*, 3.

[55] R. E. Clements rightly brings out the larger agenda of wisdom: "it sought to draw religious activity under the umbrella of a wider social and conceptual framework." "Wisdom and Old Testament Theology," in Day, Gordon, Williamson, *Wisdom in Ancient Israel*, 286.

[56] Longman connects wisdom with emotional intelligence that helps people navigate through life. *How to Read*, 15–16.

the search for a transcendent wisdom that comes from above and gives illumination for how to enhance life; to shape a royal, ecumenical, and virtuous character; to create an imaginative awareness of the world; to open a person up to God and to others; and to deal effectively and wisely with seductive and enticing schemes that take the life out of a person, destroy relationships, fragment communities, and close in one's personal and social world.[57]

Instructions (Prov. 1:8–2:22)

Wisdom offers herself from many directions. The narrator (1:2–7), the parents (1:8), and Lady Wisdom (1:20)—a personification of divine wisdom—call on all to heed wisdom as the supreme good. Why? Wisdom directs them to cultivate a relationship with God and people, to keep them away from distractions and seductions, and to grow in character (justice, righteousness, and equity; mercy and patience; faithfulness and commitment; see 1:3; 2:9; 3:3). Their instructions and appeals constitute an extensive argument for the pursuit of wisdom.

The prologue invites the "simple" and the "young" to set out for wisdom, and those advanced in wisdom to increase in it (1:4, 5). In the instructions, the parents address their son ("my son," 1:8; "sons," 4:1), whom they had already instructed in wisdom in his earlier days (1:8), and encourage him to continue his walk on the way of wisdom. Lady Wisdom[58] addresses her audience both as "sons" (8:32) and as "simple ones" (1:20), a designation for lads who had received some instruction in wisdom. These young people had not yet committed themselves to pursue and love wisdom (1:20; 9:4–6). The voices of the narrator, the parents, and Lady Wisdom join together in inviting the reader to turn toward wisdom with its attending qualities of truth, purpose, and life, and to turn away from folly with its negative associations of deception, seduction, alienation, and death. In their vivid portrayal of the benefits of wisdom, they direct the young men to a perspective on God, the world, opportunity, vitality, communion, and community (1:33; 2:20–21; 3:5–8, 13–18). They also warn the young men of the consequences of not listening: anguish, sudden destruction, alienation, and loneliness (1:17–19, 29–32; 2:22).

They admonish them to seek, find, and stay on the path of wisdom, and to stay away from life's seductions (3:7). On the one hand, they warn against the entrapments resulting from peer pressure (1:8–19) and commonly received wisdom (1:20–33). Both forms keep people content with life on earth but do not prepare them for the demands of life. In a lengthy sentence consisting of twenty-two Hebrew verses, the father calls on his son to pursue wisdom first, because in the process of the search, God reveals the fear of the Lord, the path of wisdom, and the character of righteousness

---

[57] Crenshaw interprets Israel's wisdom from a humanistic perspective. He writes, "Wisdom is the reasoned search for specific ways to assure well-being and the implementation of those discoveries in daily existence. Wisdom addresses natural, human, and theological dimensions of reality, and constitutes an attitude toward life, a living tradition, and a literary corpus." Elsewhere he speaks of a tension between self-reliance and trust in God's mercy." *Old Testament Wisdom*, 15, 51. See also von Rad, *Wisdom in Israel*, 113–37.

[58] Crenshaw rightly understands the "sex appeal" of the image of Lady Wisdom for young men: "The highly erotic language associated with wisdom certainly justifies this understanding of the image. . . . Through her, God communicates life-giving knowledge in the living present." *Old Testament Wisdom*, 82.

(2:1–11). Commitment to and communion with God not only keeps one from associating with immoral men and women whose paths lead to death (2:12–19, 22) but also opens the door to life with God and the godly (2:20–21).

Instructions (Proverbs 3–4)

The nature of wisdom is further developed in chapters 3–4. The constant search for wisdom brings about a life of divine vitality as one submits in trust to the Lord and to his fatherly correction (3:1–12). Wisdom manifests itself in commitment to the Lord's instruction (3:1–2), in a life of devotion (3:3–4), in a constant trust in God (3:5–8), in honoring God's name (3:9–10), and in submission to his fatherly discipline (3:11–12). God's gifts are many, because he restores his children to enjoy communion with him and to experience the joy of life and true happiness. After all, God is the Creator of an orderly world (3:19–21) and invites his wise children to take hold of the Tree of Life (3:13–18). They are truly happy, for they find all they need for life in God's gift of wisdom. The admonitions (3:21–35) describe what a life of wisdom might look like.

The endowment of wisdom is God's gift from one generation to another (4:1–9). The father instructs his son in the same manner that he received instructions from his father. The admonition focuses on the search and benefits of wisdom. Wisdom is the aim of life, because in this search one grows in commitment to the Lord. Through the personification of wisdom as a lover, the young person is enticed to make Lady Wisdom the greatest love by courting her with a lifestyle of commitment, respect, and affection (4:6–9). The instruction details the two ways: the way of wisdom and the way of folly (4:10–27). The way of wisdom is the path of light, "which shines brighter and brighter until full day" (4:18). But darkness gradually overtakes the fools (4:19).

Instructions (Proverbs 5–7)

The instructions in chapters 5–7 warn against the folly of seductions. These include sexual immorality (5:1–23; 6:20–37; 7:1–27), financial and legal entanglements (6:1–5), a self-indulgent lifestyle (6:6–11), and other forms of depravity (6:16–19). These are examples of seduction that take away life and keep one from seeking wisdom.[59] The problems associated with any form of inappropriate dependency are so immense that one begins to understand the significance of freedom within limitations. The way of wisdom opens the traveler to vistas of freedom, life, and happiness. Such is a life that is dependent on the Lord. It is paradoxical that a life of trust in the Lord creates the greatest freedom. It is a freedom not to be captive to greed; that is, it is a contentment with one's life.

Therefore, the wise person accepts limitations readily, whether they come in the form of admonitions, instructions, divine sanctions, personal choices, or restrictions

---

[59] Moses, the prophets, the Lord Jesus, and the apostles warn and threaten people who find themselves on such a road. For example, Jesus and Paul connect folly with the sinful nature that keeps people out of God's kingdom (Matt. 15:19; Gal. 5:19–21).

imposed by people or circumstances. Such limitations keep them safe from the seduction of bad choices. The wise pass through a threshold in time and space that opens them to a metaphorical world that shapes their worldview.[60] This experience serves as a point of transition in the journey from folly to wisdom. It offers a perspective on divine reality that protects the inner life ("the heart," 4:23–27). Wisdom offers a set of limitations and expectations that shapes one's character and being. It is the offer of an "ordinary" life but with a vitality and meaning from on high.[61]

The caution against the adulterous and promiscuous woman is a realistic warning to keep from entanglements that may kill the "heart" and derail one's life from the path of wisdom. As such, "the woman" is a metaphor for the entrapments of folly (Proverbs 5–7). Similar cautions are found in the ancient Near East, but young people in the service of Yahweh are particularly warned, lest they stray from the fear of the Lord.[62]

Instructions and an Invitation (Proverbs 8–9)

We meet Lady Wisdom again in chapters 8 and 9. The voice of the parents has guided the son to walk on the path of wisdom (Proverbs 1–7). Lady Wisdom transcends the voice of the parents. She addresses all human beings at any time and place, because she, unlike the parents, is transcendent and preexistent. She enjoyed a special relationship with the Creator and was herself present at creation. Lady Wisdom was God's counselor (8:30),[63] she and rejoiced in the creation of human beings (8:31). As God brought everything into being in wisdom and unto wisdom (8:22–29), Lady Wisdom invites all human beings to listen, because she, who was with the Creator at creation, still awaits humans to walk the path of life (8:32–36).[64] She is God's agent in bringing justice and righteousness on earth.

In her final exhortations, Lady Wisdom urges people to enter her "house," a metaphor for the security and communion given to all who partake of wisdom. The imagery of a royal banquet prepared for her guests suggests a relationship of intimacy and protection (9:1–2; cf. Isa. 25:6; Matt. 22:1–14). The image of the house further suggests associations with the cosmos. Yahweh created the world ("house"), and Wisdom participated in its creation. In so doing, Wisdom built her house (the cosmos) for people to enjoy and occupy. Her house was complete, being structured on seven pillars. The number seven is reminiscent of the creation story, where seven indicates the completion of God's work (Gen. 2:1–3).[65] Unlike Lady Wisdom, Lady

---

[60] Van Leeuwen, "Liminality and Worldview," 111–44.
[61] Michael Horton, *or.di.na.ry: Sustainable Faith in a Radical, Restless World* (Grand Rapids, MI: Zondervan, 2014).
[62] Longman, *How to Read*, 72–74.
[63] Contra ESV, "a master workman." Van Leeuwen writes that the counselor is "Wisdom personified as the king's architect-adviser, through whom the king puts all things in their proper order and whose decrees of cosmic justice are the standard for human kings and rulers (v. 15)." *Proverbs*, 94–95.
[64] The unique place of Wisdom in relation to God is rightly interpreted as the second person of the Trinity. He is the Logos of John's Gospel who presents himself as full of glory, light, and wisdom. The Hebrew verb may be rendered as "begat," which has been interpreted as the creation of wisdom as a special creation and, hence, was used by Arius to support his argument that Jesus is God's special creature, not the Creator. Athanasius argued against Arius and helped define the nature of Jesus's incarnation. A preferable interpretation is "possessed me" (ESV) or, as Waltke renders it, "brought me forth." Waltke, *Proverbs 1–15*, 127–39.
[65] See further Van Leeuwen, *Proverbs*, 102–3.

Folly invites people without having prepared her house or banquet. Her life is easy, but all who follow her come to nothing (Prov. 9:13–18). The reminder of the fear of the Lord—"The fear of the Lord is the beginning of wisdom, and the knowledge of the Holy One is insight" (9:10)—forms an *inclusio* with 1:7: "The fear of the Lord is the beginning of knowledge; fools despise wisdom and instruction."

The Proverbs of Solomon (Prov. 10:1–22:16)
Part 1: Contrastive Sayings (Prov. 10:1–15:33)

The proverbs in this collection are largely antithetical: "A wise son makes a glad father, but a foolish son is a sorrow to his mother. Treasures gained by wickedness do not profit, but righteousness delivers from death" (10:1–2). These proverbs affirm hope rather than promising riches, honor, or long life. By affirming the benefits of wisdom, the author encourages readers to wait for God's ultimate justice in the face of pervasive evil in the world. The fear of the Lord and wise living are oases during the pilgrimage of life. For example, "Better is a little with the fear of the Lord than great treasure and trouble with it. Better is a dinner of herbs where love is than a fattened ox and hatred with it" (15:16–17). These proverbs contrast the righteous with the wicked, good with evil, and wisdom with folly. Human beings are held accountable for everything they do and say, because actions have consequences. Since they are a part of God's created order, they may enhance, maintain, or destroy his order by the pursuit of folly, indolence, injustice, greed, or pride. A wise person is set apart by his humility, openness to counsel, justice, and integrity. The fool falls because of hubris, egocentricity, injustice, and waywardness (11:1–3). The wise bring about peace in human relations and thus restore order. Fools rejoice in duplicity and divisiveness and thus destroy God's order. They "damage the bond of common humanity."[66] All will witness or experience the consequences of their actions, though it may take many years and several generations to observe God's justice. Time will show God's approval and disapproval of human beings.

Wise people accept limitations. Though crowned with divine glory and dignity, "humanity's freedom is limited by the constraints of righteousness, service of God, and the good of creation," van Leeuwen observes.[67] The transgenerational witness and pursuit of wisdom make limitations more acceptable because the child has learned to embrace the virtues and values of wisdom (13:1; 14:26). To the contrary, folly is met with punishment, discipline, and divine rejection (10:27, 29; 11:20; 12:2, 22; 14:2; 15:9, 11). God rewards and punishes justly (15:3). As a father delights in a wise son (10:1), so the Lord delights in all who fear him (11:20; 15:22).

Wisdom and godliness belong together. Wisdom leads to life, whereas injustice and lack of compassion characterize the way of death. The fear of the Lord and the way of wisdom are both associated with God's life-giving and sustaining power (10:11, 16, 17, 19; 11:19; 12:28; 13:3, 14; 14:27; 15:4). Oppression of the marginalized is

---

66 Van Leeuwen, *Proverbs*, 121.
67 Van Leeuwen, *Proverbs*, 128.

not only wrong but is also a rejection of the Creator (14:31). This truth implies that the wise should not keep company with fools but should rather enjoy rich relations with like-minded people (13:20).

Proverbs 12 is a good example of the contrastive perspectives recorded in chapters 10–15. The proverbs encourage growth in character through self-discipline and living in God's presence. The wise person receives instruction, discipline, and wisdom (12:1, 15, 23) because he is a lover of God. He receives God's favor and his protection (12:2, 13, 14). He is established, like a tree (12:3, 7, 12; cf. Ps. 1:2). God provides his needs (Prov. 12:11). In his family life he is blessed with "an excellent wife" (12:4; cf. 31:11). Joy marks such a person (12:20). His thoughts, speech, and actions are characterized by justice and truth (12:5, 17, 19, 22). He is redemptive in his relationships with others (12:6, 18, 25, 26). He shows mercy even to animals (12:10). He is not vindictive (12:16) but rather committed to peace (12:20). People will take note of a person of integrity (12:8), and God delights in his servant (12:22). Though he may experience troubles, he is delivered from them (12:13, 21). The Lord's intervention on behalf of the wise is apparent. Van Leeuwen comments, "God is the one who rewards human works. . . . God's mysterious hand is present in the process of the world God has made."[68] The wise have qualities of leadership (12:24) with a life-giving presence (12:28).

The fools are brutish, inhumane, and animal-like. They reject discipline and recoil at any hindrance on their path of freedom (12:1). They gradually lose their grounding in life (12:3, 7; cf. Ps. 1:4). They are far away from God because they are under his condemnation (Prov. 12:2). Their freedom leads to dissipation, corruption, opportunism, and deception (12:5–6, 8, 22; cf. 1:16–19). They make bad choices about marriage (12:4). They have little regard for people, let alone animals (12:10).

The fool hates instruction (12:1). He is deceptive and duplicitous, so that his words, thoughts, and counsel cannot be trusted (12:5, 8). He is opportunistic and narcissistic (12:6, 12, 20, 23). He is unjust and inhumane. Even his mercy is mean (12:10). Whatever he pursues is worthless (12:11). His speech is not only deceptive (12:17) and hurtful (12:18), it is a web of lies (12:13). He may not perceive his own crookedness (12:15, 26), and when caught, he is filled with anxiety and makes every attempt to untangle the mess (12:16, 25). He may even try to get by with indolence but not without dire consequences (12:24, 27). Tragedy will befall the fool. His way will not succeed forever because he walks contrary to God's order (12:3, 19). He may fail in his family relationships and be put to shame (12:4). He sows unrighteousness and harvests its fruit (12:21). Though the fool is active and creates perceptions of wealth and well-being, death confronts him everywhere (12:25, 28). Pretention is his game, but in the end it will fail him (12:9). On the other hand, directly and indirectly, he is the object of God's condemnation (12:2, 22). He is perceived to be strong, but his days are numbered (12:7). His ways are abhorrent to the king of the universe (12:22).

---

[68] Van Leeuwen, *Proverbs*, 126.

Chapter 13 opens with a contrast between people who love wisdom and discipline (13:22; cf. 10:1) and those who are greedy (13:1–4). Wise young people accept limits set by parents and demonstrate wisdom in their speech. They enjoy the benefits of life without sacrificing their integrity to satisfy cravings. In their search for right relationships, they hate duplicity (13:5), but fools experience shame and self-destructive living (13:6). Wealth and poverty are perceptions of reality rather than reality itself (13:7–8). Wealth may be taken away or create trouble. It may be useful, but the poor experience less trouble. The "light" of life continues to burn in the wise, whereas the wicked experience darkness (13:9). Strife and occupation with prosperity are twins of folly, but wisdom gives birth to diligence and is open to advice (13:10–11).

Proverbs 13:12–19 must be read together. Though hope deferred creates difficulties in life, true fulfillment may be experienced through wisdom rather than folly (13:12, 19). The wise receive instruction and counsel because they bring about life (13:13–14). Rejection of instruction brings about shame and ruin (13:15, 18). The two ways go in opposite directions: wisdom, joy, and life belong together, and so do folly, trouble, and death (13:12–19). The company one keeps confirms the direction of the way (13:20). The enduring nature of wisdom is set over against the short-lived enticement of folly (13:21–22). There are no guarantees in life, because injustice may rob the poor of the pleasures of life (13:23). However, profit is secondary to contentment in life (13:25). Discipline and instruction belong together, but harsh discipline is to be used only in extreme situations (13:1, 13–14, 24).

Part 2: God and King Sayings (Prov. 16:1–22:16)

The largest proverbial collection on God and king is at the center of the book. The midpoint of the book is 16:17: "The highway of the upright turns aside from evil; whoever guards his way preserves his life." How true! The image of the highway suggests the way of wisdom that leads to life and away from evil. In this section, Yahweh ("the LORD") and king sayings occur more frequently than in the previous section (Proverbs 10–15). The first seven verses open with a focus on the Lord. The king sayings follow and intersect with the Yahweh sayings in 16:10–15.

These sayings reveal the close connection between a godly and wise king and the Lord. Both the Lord and the king have the gift of speech and judgment (16:1–2, 10). God weighs the spirit and holds people accountable for just scales and balances (16:2, 11). The Lord judges arrogance to be an abomination and punishes the guilty (16:5). The righteous king keeps the throne by righteousness, knowing that evil in his kingdom is abominable to the Lord (16:12). This close connection establishes the hierarchy in relationships. The good ruler represents the Lord in a righteous rule and thus encourages the pursuit of wisdom in his kingdom (16:13–14). His kingship receives God's blessing, likened to life and rain (16:14, 15; cf. Ps. 72:6–7).

At the same time, the sayings invite the wise to enter into the domain of kings. Their plans, ways, works, righteousness, and steps are in the Lord's hands. He weighs, guides, and blesses whatever his wise children pursue. They are active and deliberative but subject to him. Proverbs teaches that "guidance" is not passive. It is the active pursuit of wisdom in life with the assurance that the Lord will direct the steps of his children. Wisdom consists of both planning and trusting the Lord, awaiting the outcome of God's blessing while taking personal responsibility for one's decisions. The Lord is King. His royal decrees establish his kingdom, but humans, including kings, may advance or hinder his kingdom. Even when they hinder his kingdom, God's purposes are still advanced. The guilty, though, will receive their punishment, because they are held responsible for their actions (Prov. 16:5).

Wisdom eschews arrogance. God is in control of all human actions and disposes whatever humans execute to accomplish his own purposes. Humans may accomplish much, but they have no reason for pride. After all, God is working out his purposes in and through humans. Pride sets up a person for a fall (16:18). Wisdom is at home with humility (16:19). The wise express themselves in discernment and "good sense" (16:21, 22), conveying the state of the heart punctuated with "sweetness of speech," "gracious words" (16:21, 24), and self-control (16:32). Royalty is God's gift to the wise, whose "gray hair" is like "a crown of glory" (16:31). The arrogant person "plots evil" and executes his plans with a speech that is "like a scorching fire" (16:27). He is dishonest and does not rest until he separates friends and creates divisiveness (16:27–30).

Words of the Wise (Prov. 22:17–24:22)

These sayings have been associated with the Egyptian instruction of Amenemope (see "Wisdom in the Ancient Near East" on p. 375), but I agree with the assessment of many scholars who do not see Egyptian influence in these sayings. The sayings appear in the form of admonitions with encouraging or discouraging motivations, such as, "Incline your ear, and hear the words of the wise, and apply your heart to my knowledge, for it will be pleasant if you keep them within you, if all of them are ready on your lips" (22:17–18). This theology connects with the wisdom framework that includes the fear of the Lord: "That your trust may be in the LORD, I have made them known to you today, even to you" (22:19). The mention of "thirty sayings of counsel and knowledge" has been connected with the "thirty" sections of Amenemope's instructions, but the thirty sayings cannot readily be identified.[69] Waltke makes a valiant attempt by dividing the text into four sections composed of thirty sayings:[70]

1. Sayings 1–11: Wealth (22:22–23:11)
2. Sayings 12–20: An obedient son (23:12–24:2)
3. Sayings 21–25: Strength in distress (24:3–12)
4. Sayings 26–30: Relations with the wicked (24:13–22)

---

[69] The mention of "thirty sayings" is an attempt to fit these sayings from Proverbs with the thirty sayings in the Egyptian sayings of Amenemope. The NIV note gives the alternate rendering "excellent sayings." Kitchen takes the phrase idiomatically as "already." Kitchen, "Proverbs 2," 561.

[70] Waltke, *Proverbs 15–31*, 225–88.

The purpose of the instructions is stated specifically: "to make you know what is right and true, that you may give a true answer to those who sent you" (22:21). The sayings aim to cultivate the quality of reliability and honesty in service to others.

More Words of the Wise (Prov. 24:23–34)

This brief collection covers a person's public and private life: fairness in justice without discrimination or vindictiveness (24:23–26, 28–29) and diligence in providing food for one's family (24:27, 30–34).

Solomonic Proverbs Collected by the Men of Hezekiah (Prov. 25:1–29:27)

This collection is best approached in two parts: chapters 25–27 and chapters 28–29.[71] The king sayings in the first part consider the sovereignty of kings and then one's public and private demeanor. The sayings encourage deliberative thinking and raise the bar for one's public demeanor: compliance (25:2–5), humility (25:6–7), justice (25:8–10, 18), critical acumen (25:11–12), faithfulness (25:13–14), patience (25:15), contentment (25:16, 27), detachment (25:17), discernment (25:19–20), generosity (25:21–22), resistance to vindictiveness (25:23–25), perseverance (25:26), and self-control (25:28). As the antithesis of wisdom, folly is utterly inappropriate. The fool receives his just deserts (Proverbs 26). Chapter 27 further delineates several distinctive features of wisdom in opposition to folly. Folly shows up in boasting and self-praise (27:1–2), provocation (27:3), wrath and jealousy (27:3–4), flattery (27:5–6), lack of discernment (27:7), a boisterous spirit (27:14), and divisiveness (27:15–16). Wisdom is committed to the home (27:8), cultivates friendship[72] (27:9–10), is open to counsel (27:5, 17), and grows in wisdom and prudence (27:11–13), industry (27:18, 23–27), transparency (27:19), and submission to testing (27:21–22).

Chapters 28–29 are largely antithetical proverbs like the first Solomonic collection of sayings in chapters 10–15. They also draw distinctions between the righteous and the wicked, as in 28:1, "The wicked flee when no one pursues, but the righteous are bold as a lion." Moreover, the contrast between folly and wisdom is rooted in a submission to God's instruction. The repetition of "law" (*torah*) in these two chapters is remarkable for Proverbs (28:4, 7, 9; 29:18). Torah and wisdom are thus correlative and divide humanity into two communities: those who forsake the law and those who uphold the law (28:4, 7, 18). Torah also correlates with the prophets (29:18). In the absence of a prophetic voice, wisdom provides a sufficient framework for maintaining God's order. The wise maintain and advance the divine order (28:14; cf. Ps. 1:1–2). The way of wisdom is marked by discipline (Prov. 29:15–21) that accords with divine revelation (29:18). In contrast, oppression and corruption lead to destruction and dysfunctionality (28:2–28; 29:1–27), because people make rules that benefit the group that lives in the fear of humans (29:25). Their words (promises) are ineffective (29:19–20, 25). Human society cannot extricate itself from the

---

[71] See Van Leeuwen, *Proverbs*, 215.
[72] See Sung-Jin Kim, "Teaching on Friendship in the Proverbs of Solomon (Prov 10:1–22:6 and Prov 25–29): A Text-Linguistic Study" (PhD diss., Trinity Evangelical Divinity School, 2012).

experiences of injustice because justice is ultimately eschatological: "Many seek the face of a ruler, but it is from the LORD that a man gets justice" (29:26). Those who trust in Yahweh will find safety, rest (29:25), and happiness (cf. 29:18).

Oracle of Agur (Prov. 30:1–33)[73]

This chapter divides into two parts: the oracle of Agur, son of Jakeh (30:1–14), and the numerical sayings (30:15–33). Agur is a critical thinker who stimulates the reader with his questions and enigmatic words. The opening words, "I am weary, O God; I am weary, O God" (30:1), are problematic. In Hebrew it literally reads, "to Ithiel, to Ithiel" (JPS 1917, TNK), or with Murphy, "I am not God, I am not God." Is Agur a skeptic or a reflective believer? Does he deny the existence of God, or is he overtaken with awe of God? Agur confesses his humanity and the loftiness of wisdom. Humans are on earth, whereas the "Holy One" is in heaven. God is the Creator who holds all creation together, but Agur seeks to know him through a series of questions that end with a riddle, "What is his name, and what is his son's name?" (30:4). Agur has already answered his own question. He is a "son of Jakeh." The name Jakeh (or Yak[q]eh) is an acronym that stands for "Yahweh is holy." The God of all wisdom is Yahweh, the Holy One, who graciously invites people to learn wisdom from him. They, like Agur, are treated as sons of God.[74] Agur has spoken "words" (30:1), but his words are unlike God's word (30:5). Agur's view of God as holy and lofty is also to be connected with the God who reveals himself (30:7). God's word is true. Hence, Agur prays that he may learn to be content with his daily bread, lest he profane God's name (30:7–9). He reflects on human relations (servant-master, child-parent, victim-oppressor). In each case, people exalt themselves against humanity and disturb God's order. Great is their provocation of the name of God.

The numerical sayings (30:15–33) provide a series of reflections on God's creation that bring the reader back to the greatness and mysteriousness of God. He is incomprehensible. He permits order and chaos to coexist. The final exhortation warns against folly and pride, which put "pressure" on people and upset order in creation (30:33).

Oracle of Lemuel (Prov. 31:1–31)[75]

This chapter is also divided into two parts: the oracle of King Lemuel (31:1–9) and the song of the virtuous woman (31:10–31). The royal (mother's) instruction is unique in the ancient Near East. It is reminiscent of the opening instructions (Proverbs 1–9) and forms a magnificent closure together with the hymn celebrating womanhood (31:10–31). The mother instructs her son to keep from sexual seduction

---

[73] The extent of Agur's words is uncertain. Some take it to cover the whole chapter.

[74] See Murphy, *Proverbs*, 229.

[75] The variant order in the Septuagint suggests that the final hymn may not have been authored by Lemuel but was associated with 31:1–9 because of the speech of the king's mother and because of the verbal association with 31:3: "Do not give your strength to women, your ways to those who destroy kings." The Hebrew word for "strength" here is the same as that found in 31:10, 29, there translated "excellent" or "valor." This wordplay contrasts immoral women (31:3) with the virtuous woman.

(31:3; cf. 2:16–19; 5:7–14; 6:24–35; 7:6–27; 23:20–28), to avoid obnoxious partying (31:4–7; cf. 2:12–15; 4:17; 20:1; 21:17; 23:30–35), and to commit himself to justice and righteousness (31:8–9), because injustice is associated with sexual immorality (23:20–35). She, however, does not prohibit the use of wine. She channels it from the powerful to the victims who have so little joy in life. Wine is God's blessing (3:9–10; cf. 9:2, 5).

The song of the virtuous woman is an alphabetic acrostic hymn in praise of wisdom as portrayed by the excellence of qualities. The portrait has been anticipated in several proverbs (12:4; 18:22; 19:14; cf. 5:15–19; Ruth 3:11). Moreover, the hymn summarizes the qualities of wisdom as portrayed by virtues, activities, and speech that exemplify the best of wisdom. The repetition of the word "strength" (ESV excellent[ly], Prov. 31:10, 29; cf. 31:17, 25) unifies the poem. Wisdom of this type is best viewed as a fulfillment of Genesis 2. This woman is trustworthy, good, and beneficent (Prov. 31:11–27). She is industrious, filled with vitality, kind, considerate, and generous (31:13–22, 24, 26–27). She is majestic, strong, reputable, dignified, humble (31:17, 20–23, 25), intelligent, shrewd, and wise (31:10–31). She fears the Lord (31:30) and receives the praise of her husband, family, and the community (31:28–31).

APPROACHING THE NEW TESTAMENT

The New Testament presents Jesus as the incarnate Wisdom of God. He is the Teacher, the One greater than Moses (Matt. 11:28–29). He is the preexistent Logos who existed before creation (John 1:1; cf. Prov. 8:22–23; John 17:5). Like Lady Wisdom, Jesus invites people to follow him and to eat and drink with him (John 1:36–38; 6:35; cf. Prov. 9:2–5). Jesus is the incarnation of the transcendent God, who enters culture and ministers in a transcultural manner. He revealed his own transformative growth in wisdom and obedience to the Father (Luke 2:40; Heb. 4:15; 5:9).

Paul argues that true wisdom is revealed in the cross, "Christ the power of God and the wisdom of God" (1 Cor. 1:24), because the folly of the cross reveals that "the foolishness of God is wiser than men, and the weakness of God is stronger than men" (1:25). He is the fullness of God's glory, by whom and in whom all things exist (Col. 1:15–17). Jesus Christ is the wisdom of God incarnate. He was before creation and is the Creator (1:16–17). Jesus Christ, the revelation of the wisdom of God, is the Creator, the Revealer of wisdom, the Head of the church, and the Alpha and Omega, the beginning and the end. The past, present, and future are secure in him. Christians, being united with Jesus, receive transcendent, transcultural (royal, ecumenical), and transformational wisdom. They are the body, and he is the Head who holds everything together (1:18–23). The Old Testament path of wisdom leads to Jesus Christ, but it also demands that we pay attention to the Old Testament voices that, together with the revelation in the New Testament, help us to comprehend the excellence of wisdom.

The path is narrow but highly exalted. Who can understand the wisdom that is from above? James writes,

But the wisdom from heaven is first pure, then peaceable, gentle, open to reason, full of mercy and good fruit, impartial and sincere. And a harvest of righteousness is sown in peace by those who make peace. (3:17–18)

God's wisdom is made visible in humans when they reflect the light and life of Jesus Christ on earth.

SELECT BIBLIOGRAPHY

Aitken, Kenneth T. *Proverbs*. Daily Study Bible. Philadelphia: Westminster, 1986.

Atkinson, David. *The Message of Proverbs: Wisdom for Life*. The Bible Speaks Today. Downers Grove, IL: InterVarsity Press, 1996.

Blenkinsopp, Joseph. *Wisdom and Law in the Old Testament: The Ordering of Life in Israel and Early Judaism*. 2nd ed. Oxford Bible Series. Oxford: Oxford University Press, 1995.

Blocher, Henri. "The Fear of the Lord as the 'Principle' of Wisdom." *TynBul* 28 (1977): 3–28.

Brown, William P. *Character in Crisis: A Fresh Approach to the Wisdom Literature of the Old Testament*. Grand Rapids, MI: Eerdmans, 1996.

———. *Wisdom's Wonder: Character, Creation, and Crisis in the Bible's Wisdom Literature*. Grand Rapids, MI: Eerdmans, 2014.

Clements, R. E. *Wisdom for a Changing World: Wisdom in Old Testament Theology*. Berkeley Lecture Series 2. Berkeley, CA: BIBAL, 1990.

———. *Wisdom in Theology*. Didsbury Lectures. Grand Rapids, MI: Eerdmans, 1992.

Clifford, Richard J. *The Book of Proverbs and Our Search for Wisdom*. Père Marquette Lecture in Theology. Milwaukee, WI: Marquette University Press, 1995.

———. *Proverbs*. OTL. Louisville: Westminster John Knox, 1999.

Crenshaw, James L. *Old Testament Wisdom: An Introduction*. 2nd ed. Louisville: Westminster John Knox, 1998.

———, ed. *Studies in Ancient Israelite Wisdom*. Library of Biblical Studies. New York: Ktav, 1976.

Estes, Daniel J. *Hear, My Son: Teaching and Learning in Proverbs 1–9*. NSBTE. Grand Rapids, MI: Eerdmans, 1997.

Fox, Michael V. *Proverbs 1–9*. AB 18A. New York: Doubleday, 2000.

———. *Proverbs 10–31*. AB 18B. New York: Doubleday, 2009.

Garrett, Duane A. *Proverbs, Ecclesiastes, Song of Songs*. NAC 14. Nashville: Broadman, 1993.

Hubbard, David Allan. *Proverbs*. The Communicator's Commentary: Old Testament 15A. Dallas: Word, 1989.

Kidner, Derek. *The Wisdom of Proverbs, Job, and Ecclesiastes: An Introduction to Wisdom Literature*. Downers Grove, IL: InterVarsity Press, 1985.

Longman, Tremper, III. *How to Read Proverbs*. Downers Grove, IL: InterVarsity Press, 2002.

———. *Proverbs*. BCOTWP. Grand Rapids, MI: Baker Academic, 2006.

McKane, William. *Proverbs: A New Approach*. OTL. Philadelphia: Westminster, 1970.

Murphy, Roland E. *Proverbs*. WBC 22. Nashville: Thomas Nelson, 1998.

———. *The Tree of Life: An Exploration of Biblical Wisdom Literature*. ABRL. New York: Doubleday, 1990.

———. *Wisdom Literature: Job, Proverbs, Ruth, Canticles, Esther*. FOTL 13. Grand Rapids, MI: Eerdmans, 1981.

Perdue, Leo G. *Proverbs*. IBC. Louisville: John Knox, 2000.

Schultz, Richard L. "Unity and Diversity in Wisdom Theology? A Canonical and Covenantal Perspective." *TynBul* 48, no. 2 (1997): 271–306.

Van Leeuwen, Raymond C. *Proverbs*. In vol. 5 of *The New Interpreter's Bible*, edited by Leander E. Keck. Nashville: Abingdon, 1997.

von Rad, Gerhard. *Wisdom in Israel*. Nashville: Abingdon, 1972.

Waltke, Bruce K. *Proverbs 1–15*. NICOT. Grand Rapids, MI: Eerdmans, 2004.

———. *Proverbs 15–31*. NICOT. Grand Rapids, MI: Eerdmans, 2005.

Westermann, Claus. *Roots of Wisdom: The Oldest Proverbs of Israel and Other Peoples*. Louisville: Westminster John Knox, 1995.

17

Ruth

John J. Yeo

INTRODUCTION

The book of Ruth has all the earmarks of a great story. The reader is taken on a journey complete with drama and suspense. Its characters are fascinating. They develop and change as the plot meanders through unexpected twists and turns. The reader is drawn into the narrative and gets caught up in all its complexity. We care about the protagonists and are affected by the events that happen to them. The book, however, not only touches the heart but also impresses the mind. Its inspiring redemptive message makes us think deeply about its theological implications. The cumulative effects of its literary artistry together with its theological profundity make the book of Ruth one of the most enjoyable yet instructive stories ever written. It also has much to teach us with regard to our redemption in Christ, for Ruth not only directs us to King David but ultimately points us to David's greater Son—Jesus, the Messiah.

BACKGROUND ISSUES
Date, Authorship, and Genre

The historical context of the book suggests a preexilic date. In fact, most interpreters favor a preexilic date for the book: Daniel Block believes Ruth was written by an author living in the former northern kingdom of Israel who hoped that his fellow northerners might identify themselves with the revived Davidic house during the reign of King Josiah.[1] Jack Sasson similarly suggests a Josianic date for the book.[2] Edward Campbell favors a ninth-century BC date around the time of King Jehoshaphat's

---

[1] Daniel I. Block, *Judges, Ruth*, NAC 6 (Nashville: Broadman, 1999), 598.
[2] Jack M. Sasson, *Ruth: A New Translation with a Philological Commentary and a Formalist-Folklorist Interpretation*, 2nd ed., BibSem 10 (Sheffield: Sheffield Academic Press, 1995), 251.

reform.[3] Robert Hubbard slightly prefers a preexilic date, while Murray Gow believes that the author was the prophet Nathan during the reign of King David.[4] And Kirsten Nielsen claims that the author was part of the royal court within the period of the Davidic dynasty, correctly asserting that "the majority prefer a preexilic date, but agreement ends there."[5] Interpreters who favor a postexilic date for the book include Robert Holmstedt and Frederic Bush, who opt for the early Persian period (ca. 530s BC).[6] K. Lawson Younger Jr. and Katharine Sakenfeld take an intermediate position between a late preexilic to an early postexilic date.[7]

According to Jewish tradition, the Babylonian Talmud states, "Samuel wrote the book which bears his name and the book of Judges and Ruth" (*Baba Bathra 14b*). The same document later declares, "Samuel wrote the book which bears his name. But is it written in it, 'Now Samuel was dead' [cf. 1 Sam. 25:1]? It was completed by Gad the seer and Nathan the prophet" (*Baba Bathra 15a*). In general, evangelicals have been skeptical about the Jewish talmudic tradition regarding the authorship of Ruth. Edward J. Young asserted that "this view [of Samuel as the author of Ruth] . . . , while possible, is unlikely, since the genealogy in Ruth 4:22 seems to imply that David was a well-known person."[8] Young, however, believed that it was written during David's lifetime.[9] Mark Rooker similarly notes,

> This [talmudic] tradition has been rightly contested since Samuel died before David became king (1 Sam. 28:3), and Ruth 4:22 presupposes that David was a well-known figure at the time of writing. It does suggest that the book of Ruth had a long-standing tradition of being viewed as a preexilic composition. The fact that Solomon is not mentioned in the genealogy (4:18–22) would lend support to the view that the work was composed during David's lifetime before he ascended to the throne (2 Sam. 2:1–4:12).[10]

Tremper Longman III and Raymond B. Dillard also dismiss the possibility that Samuel authored the book of Ruth because he lived too early.[11] Robert L. Hubbard Jr. writes, "The Talmud credits the book to Samuel, but such an attribution cannot be correct. The book must originate after David's rule (4:17b), and he reigned some years after Samuel's death. . . . In our view, the evidence favors a date in the period of the Monarchy (tenth-sixth centuries BC)."[12] In sum, it is apparent that these

---

[3] Edward F. Campbell Jr., *Ruth: A New Translation with Introduction, Notes, and Commentary*, AB 7 (New York: Doubleday, 1975), 28.

[4] Robert L. Hubbard Jr., *The Book of Ruth*, NICOT (Grand Rapids, MI: Eerdmans, 1988), 35; Murray D. Gow, *The Book of Ruth: Its Structure, Theme, and Purpose* (Leicester, UK: Apollos, 1992), 208–10.

[5] Kirsten Nielsen, *Ruth: A Commentary*, OTL (Louisville: Westminster John Knox, 1997), 29.

[6] Robert D. Holmstedt, *Ruth: A Handbook on the Hebrew Text*, Baylor Handbook on the Hebrew Bible (Waco, TX: Baylor University Press, 2010), 39; Frederic Bush, *Ruth/Esther*, WBC 9 (Dallas: Word, 1996), 30.

[7] K. Lawson Younger Jr., *Judges and Ruth*, NIVAC (Grand Rapids, MI: Zondervan, 2002), 390; Katharine D. Sakenfeld, *Ruth*, IBC (Louisville: Westminster John Knox, 1999), 5.

[8] Edward J. Young, *Introduction to the Old Testament* (1949; repr., Grand Rapids, MI: Eerdmans, 1989), 338.

[9] Young, *Introduction*, 338.

[10] Eugene H. Merrill, Mark F. Rooker, Michael A. Grisanti, *The World and the Word: An Introduction to the Old Testament* (Nashville: B&H Academic, 2011), 301.

[11] Tremper Longman III and Raymond B. Dillard, *An Introduction to the Old Testament*, 2nd ed. (Grand Rapids, MI: Zondervan, 2006), 147.

[12] William S. LaSor, David A. Hubbard, Frederic W. Bush, *Old Testament Survey: The Message, Form, and Background of the Old Testament*, 2nd ed. (Grand Rapids, MI: Eerdmans, 1996), 52.

evangelicals make the assumption that Samuel could not have authored the book of Ruth because (1) Samuel had died before David ascended the throne; (2) the inclusion of the genealogy at the end of the book appears to suggest that David was already a well-known figure; and (3) the genealogy was likely composed after his reign. In other words, as Longman had succinctly surmised, Samuel lived too early.

The talmudic tradition regarding the authorship of Ruth is, however, not as untenable as proposed. In agreement with Rooker, the point that the genealogy at the end of Ruth never mentions Solomon argues in favor of the book being written before Solomon's ascension to the throne and not after.[13] More significantly, God had specifically ordered Samuel to anoint David as king (1 Sam. 16:1) because he rejected Saul (1 Sam. 15:11, 23, 26, 28). And just as Saul was anointed privately (1 Sam. 10:1) and then made king publicly (1 Sam. 10:9–27), so it was with David (private anointing: 1 Sam. 16:1, 13; public anointing: 2 Sam. 5:3). The only substantive differences between Saul and David were that (1) David was anointed twice (privately and publicly) while Saul was anointed once (privately), and (2) Samuel died before David's ascension to the throne. But the latter detail that Samuel had died before David's actual reign in 2 Samuel 5 is irrelevant to the question of Samuel's authorship of Ruth since Samuel already knew that God had chosen David as the anointed king over Israel (cf. 1 Sam. 15:28; 16:1, 13; 28:17). In point of fact, one of the central and collective theological themes in the books of Judges, Ruth, and 1 Samuel is to legitimize David as the true king of Israel in the face of Saulide oppression (see "Genre" on p. 403).

Furthermore, the record of Samuel's death in 1 Samuel 25:1 is no indication that he could not have authored the majority of 1 Samuel. In fact, *Baba Bathra 15a* takes into consideration Samuel's death and then specifies the subsequent prophets who completed the history of David's life: Gad the seer and Nathan the prophet. It is interesting to note that 1 Chronicles 29:29–30 validates this tradition regarding the written account of David's life: "Now the acts of King David, from first to last, are written in the Chronicles of Samuel the seer, and in the Chronicles of Nathan the prophet, and in the Chronicles of Gad the seer, with accounts of all his rule and his might and of the circumstances that came upon him and upon Israel and upon all the kingdoms of the countries."[14] This is also confirmed by the fact that the books of Samuel–Kings served as the primary source materials for the Chronicler's account of Israel's history for the postexilic community.[15]

Samuel as Author

The theme of kingship serves as a thematic *inclusio* that bookends the entire book of Ruth,[16] and this theme plays a prominent role in Samuel's ministry. The story opens with

---

[13] Merrill, Rooker, and Grisanti, *World and the Word*, 301.

[14] Gleason Archer states, "While other written records are not referred to by name, it is quite likely that the official archives were consulted, including the 'Acts of David' composed by Samuel, Nathan, and Gad (according to the statement in 1 Chron. 29:29)." *A Survey of Old Testament Introduction*, rev. ed. (Chicago: Moody Press, 1994), 314.

[15] Merrill, Rooker, and Grisanti, *World and the Word*, 81.

[16] For a brief description of *inclusio*, see David A. Dorsey, *The Literary Structure of the Old Testament: A Commentary on Genesis–Malachi* (Grand Rapids, MI: Baker, 1999), 32–33.

Elimelech (1:1–2), whose name means, "My God is King," and it ends with a genealogy that climaxes with King David (4:18–22). The introduction focuses on Elimelech and his ill-fated decision to leave Bethlehem in order to sojourn in the land of Moab. The reader is prompted to view Elimelech's decision negatively since the story happened during the era of the judges.[17] Elimelech "did that which was right in his own eyes" by forsaking the Promised Land and moving his family to the fields of Moab, where Yahweh proceeded to judge him and his two sons. Bereaved of her husband and sons, Naomi returned with her daughter-in-law, Ruth, to Bethlehem, where they experienced God's abundant provision and redemptive faithfulness. The depravity and lawlessness of the time is held in stark contrast to the hero in the story, Boaz, who is characterized as being a faithful, Torah-keeping Judahite who becomes the kinsman-redeemer for Naomi (and Ruth) by fulfilling the duty of a levirate. The redemption of Naomi and Ruth, therefore, serves as a foil to the dark downward spiral of the book of Judges. Michael Moore observes, "Interpreted in its canonical-historical context . . . the book of Ruth appears to be a masterfully crafted response to the politics of despair in Judges. Ruth's short-story structure is the perfect vehicle for subverting this despair."[18] The story's ultimate hope is directly focused on King David (4:17, 22). David is the answer to the pivotal issue raised in Judges—"Israel had no king."[19]

In the book of 1 Samuel, the theme of kingship is also conspicuously foregrounded. In 1 Samuel 8–10, the Israelites asked God for a human king like the other nations (8:5, 20), but God was deeply offended by their request because he was Israel's King (8:7–8; 10:19). From its inception, the nation had been a theocracy, not a monarchy or democracy. Thus the people, by their presumptuous request, had rejected God's reign over them. God, therefore, reluctantly gave Israel their first king (8:22; 9:16; 10:9–26). The man who was chosen looked the part, but he lacked faith and obedience toward God. In the course of his reign, Saul, a Benjaminite from Gibeah (9:1, 21; 10:26), dismembered a pair of oxen and sent them to all the tribes of Israel in order to assemble the nation for holy war against the Ammonites (11:4–8). This act paralleled the occasion in which the Levite dismembered his concubine in order to call all Israel for holy war against the Benjaminites (cf. Judges 19). The purpose of the comparison is clear: it was intended to diminish Saul's credibility as king by associating him with the lawless and wicked Benjaminites who came from his hometown of Gibeah. Furthermore, it also foreshadowed Saul's future acts of wickedness and disobedience as Israel's first king.[20]

The overall theological message that begins to emerge from Judges, Ruth, and 1 Samuel is one that legitimizes King David as Israel's true and divinely chosen king (see table 19).[21]

---

[17] Cf., for example, Iain M. Duguid, *Esther and Ruth*, Reformed Expository Commentary (Phillipsburg, NJ: P&R, 2005), 131–32.

[18] J. Gordon Harris, Cheryl A. Brown, Michael S. Moore, *Joshua, Judges, Ruth*, NIBCOT 5 (Peabody, MA: Hendrickson, 2000), 300.

[19] Hubbard, *Ruth*, 84.

[20] Edward J. Young, *My Servants, the Prophets* (Grand Rapids, MI: Eerdmans, 1952), 81.

[21] For a fuller treatment of the comparisons between Judges 17–21 and the book of Ruth, see Harris, Brown, and Moore, *Joshua, Judges, Ruth*, 294–96, 300–305; and Eugene H. Merrill, "The Book of Ruth: Narration and Shared Themes," *BSac* 142, no. 566 (1985): 131–33.

	Judges	Ruth	1 Samuel
Tribe of Judah	Judahites: exalted	Faithful Judahites: Boaz and David	Judahite: King David, "a man after [God's] own heart"
Tribe of Benjamin	Benjaminites: vilified/judged		Benjaminite: King Saul, about whom God said, "I have rejected him from being king"
Cities of Significance	Benjaminites: Gibeah (rape and murder)	Judahites: Bethlehem (redemption)	Saul: Gibeah David: Bethlehem
Call to Holy War	Levite dismembered concubine; holy war against Benjaminites		Saul dismembered pair of oxen; holy war against Ammonites

Table 19

This chart demonstrates that the talmudic claim that Samuel authored the books of Judges, Ruth, and the first portion of 1 Samuel is at least possible, if not highly probable.[22] It also helps the interpreter grasp the significance of the central theological theme of kingship found in these books: the legitimation of David's reign.

Genre

The genre of Ruth should be regarded as a short story with an apologetic focus. Some interpreters have inappropriately classified the book as a novella. The term *novella*, however, misrepresents the genre of Ruth since it assumes that the story is categorically fictional. Lee Humphreys clarifies: "The major characters of a novella may be historical figures, and events from history may be incorporated into the plot. But it must be stressed that the intent is not to report historical activity. The historical figures and events are caught up into an imaginative fabric produced by the creative activity of an author."[23] By contrast, the short story has four basic characteristics: (1) it possesses a distinctive literary style that employs elevated prose and semipoetic rhythmic elements; (2) its content deals with the lives of "typical people" and contains valuable historical information; (3) the purpose of the short story is to entertain and instruct; and (4) the audience appreciates the author's creativity in wedding the story's message and literary artistry.[24] Hubbard correctly asserts, "unlike novella the short story allows for the historical accuracy of the narrative. . . . While the skill of the storyteller is quite evident, the heart of the story is historical."[25]

That Ruth is a factual short story also supports the assertion that it functioned historically as an apology for David's reign. Block nicely summarizes this point:

---

[22] Merrill states, "While this tradition cannot be validated there is nothing inherently improbable about it." Merrill, "The Book of Ruth," 139n9.

[23] W. Lee Humphreys, "Novella," in *Saga, Legend, Tale, Novella, Fable: Narrative Forms in Old Testament Literature*, ed. George W. Coats, JSOTSup 35 (Sheffield: JSOT Press, 1985), 87.

[24] Hubbard, *Ruth*, 47.

[25] Hubbard, *Ruth*, 48.

Like the Book of Judges, the Book of Ruth should be interpreted as a historio-graphical document. It describes real experiences of real people in real times at real places. The storyteller does indeed exhibit great literary skill and promote a particular ideology, but to relegate the book to the shelf of fiction is to miss the primary point of the book—honoring David by remembering the noble charac-ters in his family history. Accordingly, the Book of Ruth is best classified as an independent historiographical short story.[26]

Placement in the Canon

The canonical status of the book of Ruth was recognized from the beginning. The Babylonian Talmud in *Tractate Melilla 7a* notes that Ruth, Esther, and the Song of Songs "make the hands unclean," which means that they deemed these books as holy and authoritative canonical works.[27] Four fragments among the Dead Sea Scrolls also signify its importance to the Qumran community.[28]

The relevant sources reflect two basic traditions for the location of Ruth in the Canon. The first tradition places Ruth in the Prophets, immediately after Judges. The Septuagint witnesses to this tradition, which also appears to be accepted by Josephus. He wrote in *Against Apion* 1.8 that there were twenty-two canonical books, which would have required Ruth to have been counted with Judges, and Lamentations with Jeremiah.[29] The second tradition places Ruth among the Writings (the Former Prophets in the Jewish canon) and has a number of variants with it. The fourth book of Esdras, from about the same time as Josephus, reckons the number of canonical books at twenty-four, thus giving Ruth and Lamentations independent status.[30] In the vast majority of Hebrew manuscripts and published editions, Ruth is placed as the first of the five *Megilloth* (or "five scrolls," also including the Song of Songs, Lamentations, Ecclesiastes, and Esther), and they are read liturgically at annual Jew-ish festivals.[31] In the Ben Asher family of manuscripts, this group as a whole appears after Proverbs. According to Block, "This arrangement is propitious, for it places the story of Ruth immediately after the alphabetic celebration of wifely nobility in Prov 31:10–31. . . . The arrangement in the majority of Hebrew manuscripts, however, contradicts the order of books in several Talmudic lists, most notably *Baba Bathra* 14b, which places Ruth ahead of Psalms at the beginning of the Writings."[32] Younger surmises that the debate over the two traditions centers on which one is older and original. He notes that both traditions arose within different elements of the Jewish community and existed side by side until the fourth century AD. Although there ap-pears to be no definitive way to tell which of the two has priority, it seems evident that the earliest Jewish tradition treated the book as an entity.[33]

---

[26] Block, *Judges, Ruth*, 603.
[27] Block, *Judges, Ruth*, 588.
[28] Block, *Judges, Ruth*, 588.
[29] Barry G. Webb, *Five Festal Garments: Christian Reflections on the Song of Songs, Ruth, Lamentations, Ecclesiastes, and Esther*, NSBT 10 (Downers Grove, IL: InterVarsity Press, 2000), 52.
[30] Webb, *Five Festal Garments*, 52.
[31] Block, *Judges, Ruth*, 589.
[32] Block, *Judges, Ruth*, 589.
[33] Younger, *Judges and Ruth*, 392.

STRUCTURE AND OUTLINE

I. Prologue: Disobedience in the Royal Line (1:1–5)
II. Act 1: The Punishment and Predicament for the Royal Line (1:6–22)
III. Act 2: The Hope of a Kinsman-Redeemer for the Royal Line (2:1–23)
IV. Act 3: The Unexpected Complication for the Royal Line (3:1–18)
V. Act 4: The Redemption of the Royal Line (4:1–17)
VI. Epilogue: The Ancestry of the Royal Line (4:18–22)[34]

MESSAGE AND THEOLOGY

Ruth 1

Prologue: Disobedience in the Royal Line (Ruth 1:1–5)

The book of Ruth is set in the era of the "Judges Period."[35] This negative detail alerts the readers that the same moral depravity and spiritual apostasy that prevailed during that dark period of Israel's history was also present in Bethlehem at the outset of this story. The narrator also informs the readers that because of a famine in Bethlehem, a man named Elimelech took his wife, Naomi, and his two sons, Mahlon and Chilion, to sojourn in the fields of Moab.

Famines are often intrinsically tied to the curses of the Mosaic covenant (e.g., Deut. 32:24; 2 Sam. 21:1; 1 Kings 8:37; 2 Kings 6:25–33; Jer. 15:2; 18:21). The mention of the famine in Bethlehem, therefore, is both ironic and instructive. The name of the ancient town of Bethlehem (Hebrew for "house of bread") was well deserved due to its plentiful crops.[36] But Israel's failure to keep God's covenant brought about God's righteous judgment, which meant the "house of bread" had been diminished to a "house of crumbs."

Elimelech stood at a crossroads. He could stay in Bethlehem and trust God to provide or seek greener pastures elsewhere. The narrator makes clear, however, that Elimelech and his family not only chose to sojourn in Moab but also remained there and did not return to Bethlehem (Ruth 1:2). Elimelech's choice should not be viewed as a neutral or an indifferent decision, especially in the eyes of God. In effect, it was paramount to denying the divine covenant promise made to Abraham that God would give the land of Canaan to his descendants (cf. Gen. 12:1–7; 15:12–19). Moreover, the Israelites left the "fields/plains of Moab," where they ratified the covenant renewal recorded in the book of Deuteronomy, before they crossed the Jordan in order to conquer Canaan under Joshua's leadership. While it is true that some tribes remained in the Transjordan region, Deuteronomy plainly states that Moab was not a part of the Promised Land. Additionally, Moab had a tainted history as far as Israel was concerned. Duguid notes,

> The Moabites had originated out of an incestuous relationship between Lot and his older daughter (Gen. 19:30–38); their king Balak had hired Balaam to curse Israel when they came out of Egypt (Num. 22–24); their women had been

---

[34] This outline of the book of Ruth is a modification of Block's in *Judges, Ruth*, 587.
[35] As Hubbard notes, "Israel remembered the 'Judges Period' (ca. 1200–1020 BC)—the time between Joshua's death (Judges 1:1) and the coronation of Saul (1 Sam. 10)—as an era of frightful social and religious chaos." *Ruth*, 84.
[36] Hubbard, *Ruth*, 85.

a stumbling block to Israel in the wilderness, seducing them to the worship of false gods (Num. 25); and they had recently oppressed the Israelites in the days of Eglon (Judg. 3).[37]

Thus, Elimelech's choice to flee the famine in Bethlehem was a clearly sinful decision, because he, like the others in the period of the Judges, did what was right in his own eyes since there was no king in Israel (cf. Judg. 17:6; 21:25).

To compound the severity of Elimelech's sin, his two sons, Mahlon and Chilion,[38] married Moabite women. Block correctly points out that

> these marriages must be interpreted in light of Mosaic prohibitions against marriage with pagans, particularly Deut. 7:3–4. The Moabites are not listed with these Canaanite nations, but since they were the people of Chemosh, a foreign God, the spirit of the law would have them included. . . . Naomi's sons lived in their married state for ten years but without fathering any children. The barrenness of Ruth and Orpah too must be interpreted as evidence of the punitive though hidden hand of God (Deut. 28:18).[39]

Accordingly, in a matter of five short verses (1:1–5), Elimelech and his two sons died. Their deaths must be interpreted as God's judgment on their disobedience to his law. Early Jewish exegesis plainly took the series of tragic events as the results of divine retribution. The Targum for Ruth attributed the deaths of Naomi's sons to the marriages, while the Midrash (*Ruth Rabbah* 2.10) and the Babylonian Talmud (*Baba Bathra* 91a) attributed them to the earlier sin of fleeing Judah.[40] In support of this interpretation, Naomi herself unambiguously declared three times that God had punished her and, by implication, had judged her husband and her two sons as well (cf. Ruth 1:13, 20, 21).

The Punishment and Predicament for the Royal Line (Ruth 1:6–22)

Naomi, bereft of her husband and two sons, decided to return to Bethlehem because she heard that Yahweh had visited the people with "bread" (1:6, my trans.). There is an interesting "empty/full" contrast in this section. In 1:1, God had punished Israel by sending a famine upon the land. In 1:6, however, God "visited" Israel with an abundance of crops, namely barley (1:22; 2:17; 3:2, 15, 17) and wheat (2:23). Bethlehem—the "house of bread"—had been fully replenished.[41] Hubbard explains that when the verb "to visit" (פקד) is combined with Yahweh as its subject, "it conveys the idea that God evaluates the loyalty of his vassal people and, as a result, either punishes them for rebellion (e.g., Ex. 20:3; Jer. 6:15; Hos. 1:4; Amos 3:2) or rewards their loyalty by improving their circumstances."[42] In other words, Ruth 1:6

---

[37] Duguid, *Esther and Ruth*, 132.
[38] Although the meaning of the names of Elimelech's sons, Mahlon and Chilion, is uncertain, Block suggests that Mahlon's name may be related to חָלָה ("to be sick"), thus the name "Sickly," while Chilion's name is constructed from the root כָּלָה ("to be finished, come to an end"), which would render his name "Frailty, Mortality." Block, *Judges, Ruth*, 625.
[39] Block, *Judges, Ruth*, 629.
[40] Cf. Hubbard, *Ruth*, 95n18; Campbell, *Ruth*, 58.
[41] Block, *Judges, Ruth*, 631.
[42] Hubbard, *Ruth*, 100.

is a reversal of 1:1; it marks a progression from famine/emptiness (i.e., God's judgment) to harvest/fullness (i.e., God's grace/favor).

As Naomi and her daughters-in-law, Orpah and Ruth, began their journey to the land of Judah, Naomi strongly implored them to return to the homes of their mothers (1:8–13, 15) and to their gods (1:15). The background for Naomi's plea is the story of Judah and Tamar (Genesis 38) and the "levirate marriage" law of Deuteronomy 25:5–10—both of which highlight women's economic reliance on men. The dire situation of these bereft women should not be overlooked. Naomi correctly perceived that her plight was, indeed, hopeless. In fact, Naomi tacitly grouped herself among the dead when she exclaimed to her daughters-in-law, "May the LORD deal kindly with you, as you have dealt with the dead and with me" (Ruth 1:8). In a subtle, yet perceptible manner, Naomi declared that she was as good as dead due to her lack of a husband or sons. Block writes, "Naomi acknowledges that in the world in which they all live security and well-being were directly dependent upon a link with some male. The death of a husband meant the loss of one's economic support base and the severing of connections to the kinship structures. Widowhood often meant inevitable alienation and destitution."[43] In light of her patriarchal and agrarian setting, it is no wonder that Naomi attempted to persuade her daughters-in-law to return to their mothers' houses.

The most difficult aspect of Naomi's plight, however, was her recognition that Yahweh had punished her family. Naomi complained that her plight was more bitter for her than for her daughters-in-law because "the hand of the LORD has gone out against me" (1:13). Although Naomi correctly acknowledged that God had punished her family for their unrepentant sins, she failed to see that the God who "visits" his people with curses (e.g., famine, barrenness, death) also "visits" them with blessings (e.g., harvest, redemption, birth, life) when they repent.

Heeding Naomi's airtight logic, Orpah decided to return to her mother's house and to her Moabite gods (1:14–15). Orpah's name is conjecturally "associated with *'ōrep*, 'neck' from which is derived the Jewish midrashic explanation that she turned her neck/nape on her mother-in-law."[44] Ruth, however, did not turn her back on Naomi. Instead, she implored Naomi not to urge her to abandon her. In a poignant statement of Ruth's commitment to Naomi and to Naomi's God, Ruth maintained the following confession of faith:

a   Do not press/urge me to leave you,
    or to turn back from following you.
  b   For wherever you go, I will go;
      And wherever you stay, I will stay.
    c   Your people will be my people,
      And your God, my God.
  b'   Where you die, I will die;

---

[43] Block, *Judges, Ruth*, 634.
[44] Block, *Judges, Ruth*, 628. Cf. also *HALOT*, s.v. "עָרְפָּה." The meaning of Ruth's name is difficult to ascertain. Block states, "A derivation from a root *rwh*, 'to soak, irrigate, refresh,' hence 'refreshment, satiation,' is more likely." *Judges, Ruth*, 628.

> And there shall I be buried.
> a' Thus may Yahweh do to me and more so—
> Nothing but death will separate me from you![45]

Ruth's emotive statement is known in the ancient Near East as a "self-maledictory oath."[46] By swearing in the name of Yahweh, Ruth pronounced a curse upon herself if she did not fulfill the terms of her covenant vow.

As both Naomi and Ruth entered Bethlehem (1:19), the entire city was abuzz as the women asked one another, "Is this Naomi?" Having overheard them, the question upset Naomi because her name is rendered "the Pleasant One." Her resentful response in 1:20 is revealing: "Do not call me Naomi; call me Mara, for the Almighty has dealt very bitterly with me. I went away full, and the LORD has brought me back empty. Why call me Naomi, when the LORD has testified against me and the Almighty has brought calamity upon me?" The Hebrew word מָרָא (*Mara*) is derived from a verb meaning "to be bitter."[47] In essence, Naomi, "the Pleasant One," had returned from Moab as "the Bitter One." Her speech clearly highlights contrastive elements: Naomi left Bethlehem "full" (with her family intact) when the city was "empty" (due to famine), but she returned "empty" (with no husband or sons) when Bethlehem had become "full" (in the midst of the harvest season).

Ruth 2

The Hope of a Kinsman-Redeemer for the Royal Line (Ruth 2:1–23)

As chapter 2 begins, the narrator reveals that God had preserved for Naomi a relative within Elimelech's family. Boaz, whose name is likely related to "strength,"[48] is described to be "a worthy man." Although the Hebrew phrase may refer to a "mighty man" or "military hero" (as in Judg. 6:12 where it refers to Gideon), the book never depicts Boaz as a warrior. Instead, Boaz is seen as a "man of substance" or "wealth,"[49] as well as a godly man who is worthy of respect and dignity (cf. Ruth 2:4).

In the opening dialogue, Ruth asked Naomi permission to glean in a field where she might find favor in the owner's sight (2:2). Ruth's request was appropriate because God, in his grace, provided for aliens, orphans, and widows during the harvest season. Block explains, "harvesters [were] deliberately [to] leave the grain in the corners of their fields for these economically vulnerable classes and not go back to gather (*liqqēt*) ears of grain they might have dropped (Lev. 19:9, 10; 23:22; Deut. 24:19)."[50] Upon Naomi's affirmative response, Ruth "happened to come to the part of the field belonging to Boaz, who was of the clan of Elimelech" (2:3). It is interesting to note that the phrase may be translated "her chance chanced upon."[51]

---

[45] Younger, *Judges and Ruth*, 424.
[46] For a concise explanation of the "self-maledictory oath" from ancient Near Eastern and biblical perspectives, see Meredith G. Kline, "The Two Tables of the Covenant," *WTJ* 22, no. 2 (1960): 143–44.
[47] Block, *Judges, Ruth*, 645.
[48] For possible meanings regarding Boaz's name, cf. Campbell, *Ruth*, 90–91.
[49] Block, *Judges, Ruth*, 651.
[50] Block, *Judges, Ruth*, 652.
[51] Block, *Judges, Ruth*, 653.

However, the context makes clear that this was not a simple case of luck or fate. The narrator intentionally repeats that Boaz was in Elimelech's extended family (cf. 2:1, 3), by which the original audience would have understood that he could serve as a "kinsman-redeemer" to Naomi and, by extension, to Ruth. Moreover, the fact that Ruth was hopeful to find a man "in whose sight she might find favor" (2:2) also foreshadows Boaz's kindness toward her as a kinsman-redeemer. The combination of both of these elements—a gracious man and a close relative—is necessary for the story to have a "happy ending."[52]

The rest of act 2 deals with Boaz's desire to protect and provide for Ruth and her mother-in-law. It is apparent from Boaz's own words (cf. 2:11) that he had heard of Naomi and Ruth's plight by the talk spreading throughout the city (cf. 1:19–21). Boaz had also learned from his foreman that Ruth had worked much of the day, seldom taking opportunities to rest (2:7). Boaz then addressed Ruth gently, urging her not to leave his field but rather to stay close to his young maidens as they reaped behind the harvesters (2:8). Ruth, overwhelmed by Boaz's favor (חסד, *hesed*), asked, "Why have I found favor in your eyes, that you should take notice of me, since I am a foreigner?" (2:10). Boaz answered,

> All that you have done for your mother-in-law since the death of your husband has been fully told to me, and how you left your father and mother and your native land and came to a people that you did not know before. The LORD repay you for what you have done, and a full reward be given you by the LORD, the God of Israel, under whose wings you have come to take refuge! (2:11–12)

Boaz responded to Ruth with favor (חסד, *hesed*) because of what he had been told regarding her undying commitment toward Naomi, her people, and her God. Duguid notes, "Covenant faithfulness (*hesed*) is a key term in the Book of Ruth and in the Bible generally. It is a hard word to translate because it includes so many things: love, grace, mercy, kindness—all of the positive acts of devotion that flow out of a covenantal relationship."[53]

Boaz went above and beyond the call of duty required by the law in order to allow the widow, the poor, and the alien to glean in his field (cf. Lev. 19:9, 10; 23:22; Deut. 24:19). He even instructed his men to deliberately pull out some of the barley stalks from the sheaves so that she could glean them also (Ruth 2:16).[54] At the end of the day, Ruth gleaned and threshed so much grain that it equaled an "ephah of barley" (about 5.8 gallons or 22 liters, 2:17) or roughly 30 to 50 pounds![55]

Upon returning home to Naomi, Ruth presented her with the leftover roasted grain and the day's gleaning (2:18). Surprised by the amount of grain Ruth brought home, Naomi inquired, "Where did you glean today? And where have you worked? Blessed be the man who took notice of you" (2:19). Upon Ruth's revelation that she

---

52 Block, *Judges, Ruth*, 654.
53 Duguid, *Esther and Ruth*, 163.
54 Note that Ruth fits all three categories.
55 Bush, *Ruth/Esther*, 133.

had gleaned in Boaz's field, Naomi immediately recognized that Boaz was a near kinsman-redeemer (גֹּאֵל). For the first time since the deaths of her husband and two sons, Naomi acknowledged God's covenant faithfulness, manifested in his gracious provision of a near kinsman: "May he [i.e., Boaz] be blessed by the LORD, whose kindness has not forsaken the living or the dead!" (2:20). This declarative statement of blessing highlights Naomi's "fullness" in contrast to the "emptiness" she experienced in the first half of the story. It represents the turning point where despair turns into hope and fulfillment.

Ruth 3

The Unexpected Complication for the Royal Line (Ruth 3:1–18)

In chapter 3 Naomi conceived of a plot to help speed things along between Boaz and Ruth. Naomi knew that Boaz looked upon Ruth with favor, but she did not know if he was interested in fulfilling the role of the kinsman-redeemer. According to Leviticus 25:25–55, a kinsman-redeemer was obligated to redeem (or "buy back") his relatives who had fallen into debt and had sold themselves into slavery.[56] The circumstances surrounding Naomi and Ruth, however, were not akin to the kinsman-redeemer laws found in Leviticus 25.[57] In addition, Deuteronomy 25:5–10 described a situation where the kinsman-redeemer was obligated to marry the widow in order to raise up a child for a brother who had died childless. Duguid remarks, "In this way, the inheritance would continue to be associated with the name of the man who had died."[58] Although Boaz was not technically Elimelech's immediate brother, the levirate law still applied to Boaz precisely because the law codes found in the Old Testament were not comprehensive.[59]

Was Boaz then obligated to marry Ruth? While it is true that Boaz was a close relative, it was also true that no legal demands bound him to act. Furthermore, "the law didn't address the issue of foreigners who had illegally married into the family and what obligations, if any, a kinsman redeemer had toward them."[60] Why then had Ruth found so much favor in Boaz's eyes? Why did he go above and beyond what was required of him in the law of God? Naomi's plan would get to the heart of the matter. She would intentionally force his hand in order to find out if he intended to fulfill the role of a kinsman-redeemer.

Naomi's plan was for Ruth to approach Boaz at the threshing floor and request that he take her as his wife. But in order to make the best possible impression, Naomi instructed Ruth to wash, anoint herself, and put on her best clothing (Ruth 3:3).[61] Naomi then directed Ruth to enter the threshing floor by stealth after Boaz had finished his work for the day and had satisfied himself with food and drink (3:3).

---

[56] Cf. Paul Copan, *Is God a Moral Monster? Making Sense of the Old Testament God* (Grand Rapids, MI: Baker, 2011), 124–34.

[57] Bush, *Ruth/Esther*, 137.

[58] Duguid, *Esther and Ruth*, 163.

[59] Bush, *Ruth/Esther*, 168.

[60] Duguid, *Esther and Ruth*, 163.

[61] Some commentators have taken Naomi's sense of "bathe, anoint, dress up" as possibly dressing her as a bride. Cf. Hubbard, *Ruth*, 202.

When he retired for the night, Ruth was to take note of where he lay down. She would then uncover his feet and lie down until he woke to tell her what to do (3:4). Naomi's directive to wait until Boaz had finished working, eating, and drinking was as shrewd as it was wise.

Ruth did exactly as Naomi had instructed her to do (cf. 3:6–7). She uncovered Boaz's feet and lay near the soles of his feet waiting for him to awake. Some commentators take this gesture to be seductive and risqué.[62] Moreover, they inappropriately blame Naomi for devising a plan whereby Ruth would instigate a sexual encounter with Boaz under the guise of a marriage proposal.[63] These interpreters also tend to perceive Ruth's act of uncovering Boaz's "feet" as a euphemistic and veiled reference to her uncovering his genitals. But this is clearly an example of eisegesis, where the interpreter has read something into the text rather than extracting the meaning out of it. Block correctly states, "It seems that Naomi is advising Ruth to uncover Boaz's lower limbs [including feet, legs, and thighs], probably exclusive of his genitals, and then go and lie down herself. . . . The choice of [feet] actually draws the reader's attention away from the genitals and diffuses it over the limbs as a whole."[64] In addition, the contextual use of the word "feet" in 3:8 demands that its referent be simply Boaz's feet!

The symbolic act of uncovering Boaz's feet, however, has much less to do with his feet and more to do with the edge or hem of his robe. Block helpfully elucidates, "The word כָּנָף is gloriously ambiguous, referring not only to the wings of a bird but also to a skirt, the corners of one's flowing garments."[65] In fact, the idea of a man covering a maiden with the edge of his garment is best understood in light of Ezekiel 16:8: "When I passed by you again and saw you, behold, you were at the age for love, and *I spread the corner of my garment over you* and covered your nakedness; I made my vow to you and entered into a covenant with you, declares the Lord God, and you became mine." The Ezekiel passage refers to the marriage covenant between Yahweh and his bride, Jerusalem/Israel. The metaphorical "spreading of the garment" over the woman is to cover her nakedness, not to expose or exploit her sexually. God is clearly portrayed as the gracious covenant Husband in whom Israel may find refuge and solace under "the shadow of [his] wings [plural form of כָּנָף]" (Pss. 17:8; 36:7; 57:1; 63:7).

Sometime in the middle of the night, something startled Boaz, and he awoke to find a woman lying at his feet (Ruth 3:8). Because it was too dark to tell, he asked, "Who are you?" Ruth responded, "I am Ruth your servant. Spread your wings over your servant, for you are a redeemer." The term translated "redeemer" in the ESV (גֹּאֵל) may also be rendered "near kinsman-redeemer." Ruth recognized Boaz as a kinsman-redeemer because she was hoping that he would fulfill his levirate duty as

---

[62] Admittedly, chapter 3 does contain language capable of double entendre. Bush, *Ruth/Esther*, 155. Words that have sexual overtones in the Hebrew Bible are used repeatedly throughout the chapter.

[63] Cf. D. R. G. Beattie, "Ruth III," *JSOT* 5 (1978): 39–51; and Charles Halton, "An Indecent Proposal: The Theological Core of the Book of Ruth," *SJOT* 26, no. 1 (2012): 30–43. A perusal of the scholarship on Ruth 3 will show that this is the minority view.

[64] Block, *Judges, Ruth*, 686.

[65] Block, *Judges, Ruth*, 691. Cf. *HALOT*, s.v. "כָּנָף."

a near relative. The most amazing aspect of Ruth's request is not that a woman had proposed to a man (which was really unheard of)[66] but that Ruth had boldly challenged Boaz to make good on the blessing he himself had spoken earlier in Ruth 2:12! Boaz had declared that Yahweh would bless Ruth for all the good she had done for her mother-in-law, and he even employed the metaphor of her coming under his wings for refuge. Webb similarly concludes, "In the previous episode Boaz had expressed the wish that Yahweh, under whose 'wings' Ruth had come to take refuge (2:12), would richly reward her. . . . Now Ruth challenges him to translate pious words into action by being the means by which the blessing will be fulfilled."[67]

Boaz was not only interested, he was elated and relieved to know that Ruth was proposing marriage to him, especially since he was an older man (3:10). Boaz responded to her, "And now, my daughter, do not fear. I will do for you all that you ask, for all my fellow townsmen know that you are a worthy woman" (3:11). The epithet "worthy woman" corresponds with an earlier parallel statement describing Boaz as a "worthy man" (2:1). These characterizations reveal that Boaz and Ruth were morally impeccable people who lived above the immorality that was so endemic to the period of the Judges. This made them a perfect match.[68]

Boaz, however, knew that another younger kinsman stood in the way (3:12–13). The unexpected complication of a nearer kinsman-redeemer is a shock and a twist to the plot. It adds tension and suspense to an otherwise happy ending. The conclusion and resolution must wait until the morning. In the meantime, no one must know of Ruth's secret rendezvous with Boaz at the threshing floor. Webb explains, "The possibility of scandal certainly exists, and is implicitly acknowledged by Boaz's directive that no-one should know of the visit (3:14). But the only misconduct of which they could justly be accused is of pursuing their relationship so far without first consulting the nearer kinsman."[69]

Before Ruth returned home, Boaz filled her shawl with six measures of barley (3:15–17). This gesture of kindness was not only consistent with how well Boaz had treated Ruth during harvest time but also revealed his intent to fulfill his role as the kinsman-redeemer for both Naomi and Ruth. The emptiness that typified their lives in Moab was coming to an end. Boaz would serve as the instrument by which God would bring fullness and covenantal blessings. As Ruth recounted the evening's events to her mother-in-law, Naomi knew that Boaz was a willing participant just as she had anticipated. Interestingly, Naomi's statement that "the man will not *rest* but will settle the matter today" (3:18) coincides with her earlier statement, "My daughter, should I not seek *rest* for you, that it may be well with you?" (3:1). Boaz would "not rest" until Ruth was "resting" in his household as his wife. The only unknown variable was what the nearer kinsman would decide.

---

[66] Duguid, *Esther and Ruth*, 172.
[67] Webb, *Five Festal Garments*, 46.
[68] Duguid, *Esther and Ruth*, 178. This fact further underscores our view that nothing sexual occurred at the threshing floor.
[69] Webb, *Five Festal Garments*, 47–48.

Ruth 4

The Redemption of the Royal Line (Ruth 4:1–17)

Chapter 4 begins with Boaz seated at the gate of the city of Bethlehem. The narrator does not say when Boaz arrived at the city gate, but it must have been the same day as the threshing floor encounter with Ruth. The narrator does, however, reveal by Boaz's actions that he is not only a man of his word (cf. 3:13) but also a man on a mission.

With Boaz waiting for the nearer kinsman-redeemer to appear, the Hebrew expression הִנֵּה ("Behold") suggests that the man came walking by the gate as soon as Boaz sat down. Block's comments are apt and insightful: "In 3:13, when Boaz had suggested to Ruth that he would take action in the morning, he had invoked the name of Yahweh in an oath as a sign of his determination to resolve the issue quickly. Now Yahweh ensures the quick resolution of the matter by sending him [i.e., the kinsman-redeemer] by the gate just as Boaz was sitting down."[70] In other words, God's hidden hand of providence was revealed in the timing of the nearer kinsman's appearance.

Interestingly, Boaz addressed the nearer kinsman-redeemer informally. The ESV translates the Hebrew phrase פְּלֹנִי אַלְמֹנִי as "friend," but the TNK rendering of "So-and-so" is preferred. The phrase is actually a wordplay known as *farrago* in which a combination of meaningless rhyming words produces a new idiom.[71] The purpose of the wordplay was to conceal the man's identity.

Boaz then took ten elders of the city and called them to sit in order to be witnesses to his transaction with the nearest kinsman-redeemer. Ruth 4:2–4 recounts what happened:

> And he took ten men of the elders of the city and said, "Sit down here." So they sat down. Then he said to the redeemer, "Naomi, who has come back from the country of Moab, is selling the parcel of land that belonged to our relative Elimelech. So I thought I would tell you of it and say, 'Buy it in the presence of those sitting here and in the presence of the elders of my people.' If you will redeem it, redeem it. But if you will not, tell me, that I may know, for there is no one besides you to redeem it, and I come after you." And he said, "I will redeem it."

The overwhelming majority of interpreters agree that the idea of Naomi "selling" the piece of land that belonged to Elimelech needs to be qualified. While it would be imprudent to discuss these questions exhaustively at this point, we need to at least explain what Boaz intended in his statement here. Along with the passages Leviticus 25:25–55 and Deuteronomy 25:5–10, discussed under "Ruth 3," Numbers 27:9–11 is also pertinent to our discussion.

The broader context of the Numbers passage relates the case of Zelophehad, who had died leaving behind five daughters but no sons. His daughters approached Moses to adjudicate their case, pleading with him to allow them as women to take possession of the land because there was no male heir to continue their father's name

---

[70] Block, *Judges, Ruth*, 705.
[71] Block, *Judges, Ruth*, 705–6.

within their clan. The significance of this law in Numbers 27:9–11 as it relates to Naomi is that the deaths of Elimelech, Mahlon, and Chilion left no immediate male heir in her family. The law intended that the land stay within the clan of the deceased man. Even if a daughter was to inherit the property, Numbers 36:6–9 stipulated that she must marry within "the clan of the tribe of their father" because the land could not be transferred outside the father's tribe to that of another. Therefore, the law allowed the land to be given to the "nearest kinsman of his clan," which is what Boaz was making known to Mr. "So-and-so." Duguid explains,

> Boaz is really saying something like this: "Naomi has a field. She needs to sell it to raise money to live on. If there were a kinsman redeemer, however, he could buy that field and keep it in the family. Of course, the buyer would ultimately get to add property to his own inheritance, provided that there are no children involved. You are the first in line . . . are you interested?"[72]

The plot of the story at this point takes an unexpected twist because the nearest kinsman was willing to redeem (Ruth 4:4). It appears that Boaz and Ruth would not marry after all. But this was not the end of the story. Boaz added an important proviso to the purchase of the land: "The day you buy the field from the hand of Naomi, you also acquire Ruth the Moabite, the widow of the dead, in order to perpetuate the name of the dead in his inheritance" (4:5). The law regarding the levirate was also linked to the inherited estate. Younger notes, "Where the land has already been alienated (as in the case of Elimelech), redemption of it 'triggers' the levirate duty."[73] In other words, the purchase of the land activated the necessity for the kinsman-redeemer to marry Ruth the Moabite, the widow of the dead man, so that they could raise up a child who would eventually inherent the field when he grew up.

Upon hearing Boaz's surprising addendum to the offer, the nearest kinsman changed his mind (4:6). According to Duguid, Mr. "So-and-so" backed away from the deal because if "there were to be a child from the relationship with Ruth, the redeemer would lose the field and there would be no benefit to his own children and estate to compensate for the costs involved in taking care of Naomi and Ruth."[74] The nearest redeemer was, therefore, unwilling to take the risk necessary in order to properly care for them as the law required. Duguid insightfully asserts, "The irony is that by seeking to protect his future legacy in this way, Mr. So-and-So ended up leaving himself nameless, missing out on having a share in the biggest legacy of all: a place in God's plan of salvation."[75] By contrast, Boaz wasted no time in completing the transaction:

> Now this was the custom in former times in Israel concerning redeeming and exchanging: to confirm a transaction, the one drew off his sandal and gave it to the other, and this was the manner of attesting in Israel. So when the redeemer

---

[72] Duguid, *Esther and Ruth*, 181–82.
[73] Younger, *Judges and Ruth*, 476.
[74] Duguid, *Esther and Ruth*, 182.
[75] Duguid, *Esther and Ruth*, 182.

said to Boaz, "Buy it for yourself," he drew off his sandal. Then Boaz said to the elders and all the people, "You are witnesses this day that I have bought from the hand of Naomi all that belonged to Elimelech and all that belonged to Chilion and to Mahlon. Also Ruth the Moabite, the widow of Mahlon, I have bought to be my wife, to perpetuate the name of the dead in his inheritance, that the name of the dead may not be cut off from among his brothers and from the gate of his native place. You are witnesses this day." (Ruth 4:7–10)

According to Younger, "The nearer redeemer (גֹּאֵל) removes his sandal and hands it to Boaz as a symbolic act declaring his abdication of his own right of redemption."[76] With the green light now available to him, Boaz forthrightly made the purchase of Elimelech's land and acquired Ruth the Moabite, the widow of Mahlon. The irony associated with the nearer redeemer's abdication is foregrounded by the fact that he is the only nameless person in the entire chapter—a chapter that is primarily about the preservation of names and legacies.[77]

The scene at the gate closes with the blessing of the townspeople and their overwhelming approbation of their marriage (4:11–12). Their blessing consisted of three main elements. In the first blessing, the elders hoped that Ruth's womb would be fruitful and would build Boaz's house as Rachel and Leah did for Jacob (4:11). In the second blessing, the elders wished that Boaz's name would become famous and be remembered in Bethlehem. This would come true because in Ruth 4:13, it states, "So Boaz took Ruth, and she became his wife. And he went in to her, and the LORD gave her conception, and she bore a son." Duguid correctly points out, "Although for ten years Ruth had been unable to bear a son for Mahlon, through the Lord's intervention she conceived and bore a son for Boaz."[78] The opening of the womb is consistent with God's covenant blessings as recorded in Leviticus 26:9 and Deuteronomy 28:4. The son, according to Ruth 4:14, was blessed by the women in Bethlehem to become renowned not only in Bethlehem but also in all of Israel. In the third blessing, the elders invoked the story of Perez, who was born to Tamar and Judah (Genesis 38).

The son coming into Boaz's house was not only to preserve his name but also to bring comfort and provision for Naomi. Thus the townswomen said to Naomi, "He shall be to you a restorer of life and a nourisher of your old age, for your daughter-in-law who loves you, who is more to you than seven sons, has given birth to him" (Ruth 4:15). Their statement foreshadowed the climax of the story. Naomi's grandson would be the answer to the tragic loss of her husband and two sons. In Moab, she had considered herself among the dead (cf. 1:8). With the hopeful birth of her grandson, he would be "a restorer of life" and "a nourisher" of her old age. But this could not have happened without her daughter-in-law who displayed her undying love to Naomi even in the most desperate of circumstances. By God's sovereign grace, Ruth

---

[76] Younger, *Judges and Ruth*, 478.
[77] Duguid, *Esther and Ruth*, 183.
[78] Duguid, *Esther and Ruth*, 183.

helped to redeem Naomi from destitution and certain death. In this way, Ruth was indeed worth more than seven sons!

The story concludes with the realization of the hopes of the elders and the towns-women: "Then Naomi took the child and laid him on her lap and became his nurse. And the women of the neighborhood gave him a name, saying, 'A son has been born to Naomi.' They named him Obed. He was the father of Jesse, the father of David" (4:16–17). The townswomen name the baby Obed, which is fitting for the end of the story, for his name has the sense of "provider, guardian" (cf. Mal. 3:17). In the final scene, Naomi is seen holding Obed on her lap and is said to take care of him in his young age. As Obed grows and Naomi ages, he will be the one to provide and guard his grandmother. Naomi's "emptiness" has been reversed. The "fullness" of God's grace and blessing has come to Naomi in Obed's birth—for she who was childless now has a son.[79] The story proper ends with a short genealogy that runs from Obed to Jesse and then to David.

Epilogue: The Ancestry of the Royal Line (Ruth 4:18–22)

The book of Ruth concludes with a fuller genealogy (4:18–22) than the one given in 4:17. The author intentionally gives the genealogy of David twice. The shorter genealogy in 4:17 logically connects Obed to David and reveals how God sovereignly redeemed Naomi and brought about the birth of Obed, who became the grandfather of King David. The coda of 4:18–22 goes further and "links the events of the story with the line that would build the house of Israel more than any family since the time of Jacob, the line of David."[80] The book of Ruth, therefore, is not merely a love story between Boaz and Ruth or a tale of a destitute widow's redemption but a historical account that relates the background of the king of Israel with the intention of legitimizing his reign.

Approaching the New Testament

According to Archer, the kinsman-redeemer serves as a messianic type for the following reasons: (1) he must be a blood relative (even as the incarnate Christ became a blood relative to humankind via the virgin birth); (2) he must have the means to redeem the forfeited inheritance (even as Christ alone had the merit to redeem sinners); (3) he must be a willing redeemer (even as Christ willingly laid down his life for sinners); and (4) he must be willing to marry the wife of a deceased kinsman (which typifies the marriage relationship between Christ and his church).[81] Similarly, Duguid states that Boaz is a type of Yahweh as the Redeemer:

> He [God] is the Redeemer behind the human redeemer [Boaz] in Ruth and Naomi's story. This is also what the Lord has done for each of us. He is the Redeemer behind each of our own personal salvation stories. He sought each of us while we

---

[79] Cf. Younger, *Judges and Ruth*, 484.
[80] Duguid, *Esther and Ruth*, 186.
[81] Archer, *Survey of Old Testament Introduction*, 309.

were utterly lost. Not only did he make us *feel* valuable; in Christ, God actually made us valuable. It is not just Ruth's story that turned out to be part of a much bigger narrative than she ever imagined. Your story and my story are also woven into the bigger tapestry of what God is doing in Jesus Christ.[82]

Waltke goes even further and notes that a canonical interpretation invites the interpreter to read the Old Testament typologically: "The intertexuality of Ruth with the New Testament suggests that Boaz foreshadows Christ, while Naomi and Ruth foreshadow the union of ethnic Israel and of Gentiles in the church. Naomi of Judah and Ruth of Moab typify the union of ethnic Israel and Gentiles respectively in the church, and Boaz typifies Christ."[83] Boaz is a type of Christ because "he sacrificed himself financially to give Naomi and Ruth land and an inheritance in perpetuity. Jesus Christ, the greater antitype, sacrifices his blood to give his church a regenerated earth and eternal life."[84] Waltke concludes, "'Boaz' gave the dead immortality: by his sacrifice he bought back those who verged into death and debt and secured a 'Ruth,' his Gentile bride. 'Boaz' brought his 'bride' into final rest. As Boaz brought Naomi and her family rest (see Ruth 1:9; 3:1), so David brought Israel rest, and Christ gives the church rest."[85]

SELECT BIBLIOGRAPHY

Archer, Gleason. *A Survey of Old Testament Introduction*. Rev. ed. Chicago: Moody Press, 1994.

Beattie, D. R. G. "Ruth III." *JSOT* 5 (1978): 39–51.

Block, Daniel I. *Judges, Ruth*. NAC 6. Nashville: Broadman, 1999.

Bush, Frederic. *Ruth/Esther*. WBC 9. Dallas: Word, 1996.

Campbell, Edward F., Jr. *Ruth: A New Translation with Introduction, Notes, and Commentary*. AB 7. New York: Doubleday, 1975.

Copan, Paul. *Is God a Moral Monster? Making Sense of the Old Testament God*. Grand Rapids, MI: Baker, 2011.

Dorsey, David A. *The Literary Structure of the Old Testament: A Commentary on Genesis–Malachi*. Grand Rapids, MI: Baker, 1999.

Duguid, Iain M. *Esther and Ruth*. Reformed Expository Commentary. Phillipsburg, NJ: P&R, 2005.

Gow, Murray D. *The Book of Ruth: Its Structure, Theme, and Purpose*. Leicester, UK: Apollos, 1992.

Halton, Charles. "An Indecent Proposal: The Theological Core of the Book of Ruth." *SJOT* 26, no. 1 (2012): 30–43.

---

[82] Duguid, *Esther and Ruth*, 191–92.
[83] Bruce K. Waltke, *An Old Testament Theology: An Exegetical, Canonical, and Thematic Approach*, with Charles Yu (Grand Rapids, MI: Zondervan, 2007), 867–68.
[84] Waltke, *An Old Testament Theology*, 868.
[85] Waltke, *An Old Testament Theology*, 868.

Harris, J. Gordon, Cheryl A. Brown, and Michael S. Moore. *Joshua, Judges, Ruth*. NIBCOT 5. Peabody, MA: Hendrickson, 2000.

Holmstedt, Robert D. *Ruth: A Handbook on the Hebrew Text*. Baylor Handbook on the Hebrew Bible. Waco, TX: Baylor University Press, 2010.

Hubbard, Robert L., Jr. *The Book of Ruth*. NICOT. Grand Rapids, MI: Eerdmans, 1988.

Humphreys, W. Lee. "Novella." In *Saga, Legend, Tale, Novella, Fable: Narrative Forms in Old Testament Literature*, edited by George W. Coats, 82–96. JSOTSup 35. Sheffield: JSOT Press, 1985.

Kline, Meredith G. "The Two Tables of the Covenant." *WTJ* 22, no. 2 (1960): 133–46.

LaSor, William S., David A. Hubbard, and Frederic W. Bush. *Old Testament Survey: The Message, Form, and Background of the Old Testament*. 2nd ed. Grand Rapids, MI: Eerdmans, 1996.

Longman, Tremper, III, and Raymond B. Dillard. *An Introduction to the Old Testament*. 2nd ed. Grand Rapids, MI: Zondervan, 2006.

Merrill, Eugene H. "The Book of Ruth: Narration and Shared Themes." *BSac* 142, no. 566 (1985): 130–41.

Merrill, Eugene H., Mark F. Rooker, and Michael A. Grisanti. *The World and the Word: An Introduction to the Old Testament*. Nashville: B&H Academic, 2011.

Nielsen, Kirsten. *Ruth: A Commentary*. OTL. Louisville: Westminster John Knox, 1997.

Sakenfeld, Katharine D. *Ruth*. IBC. Louisville: Westminster John Knox, 1999.

Sasson, Jack M. *Ruth: A New Translation with a Philological Commentary and a Formalist-Folklorist Interpretation*. 2nd ed. BibSem 10. Sheffield: Sheffield Academic Press, 1995.

Waltke, Bruce K. *An Old Testament Theology: An Exegetical, Canonical, and Thematic Approach*. With Charles Yu. Grand Rapids, MI: Zondervan, 2007.

Webb, Barry G. *Five Festal Garments: Christian Reflections on the Song of Songs, Ruth, Lamentations, Ecclesiastes, and Esther*. NSBT 10. Downers Grove, IL: InterVarsity Press, 2000.

Young, Edward J. *Introduction to the Old Testament*. 1949. Reprint, Grand Rapids, MI: Eerdmans, 1989.

———. *My Servants, the Prophets*. Grand Rapids, MI: Eerdmans, 1952.

Younger, K. Lawson, Jr. *Judges and Ruth*. NIVAC. Grand Rapids, MI: Zondervan, 2002.

18

Song of Songs

Miles V. Van Pelt

INTRODUCTION

The Song of Songs is located in the third section of the Hebrew Bible: the Writings.[1] This section deals with topics related to life in the covenant—that is, how to think and live as God's people, in God's world, and according to his Word. Many of the books in this section are poetic wisdom compositions (Job, Proverbs, Ecclesiastes, and a number of the psalms), and the Song of Songs is one of them.

Its position in the Hebrew Scriptures is strategic. The Song of Songs appears after Proverbs and the book of Ruth. Proverbs ends, in chapter 31, with King Lemuel setting forth the character of a "virtuous woman" (lit. "woman/wife of strength"). The wisdom narrative that follows identifies Ruth as just such a woman (Ruth 3:11).[2] The Song of Songs appears in a way that the woman of the Song, the hero of the composition, is likely to be conceived of in the same manner, as a virtuous woman of strength. In other words, Proverbs 31 works to describe the importance of a good marriage partner, and the Song of Songs works to describe a good marriage relationship.

Given that wisdom literature is grounded in creation and the created order, it should come as no surprise that this genre gives considerable attention to the topic of marriage (examples include Prov. 2:16; 5:15–20; 6:26, 32; 7:5; 30:18–19; Eccles. 2:8; 7:26; 9:9). A corresponding significance appears in the creation of the woman

---

[1] Unless otherwise indicated, Scripture quotations in this chapter are my own translation.
[2] The designation "woman of strength" (אֵשֶׁת הַיִל) appears only three times in the Hebrew Bible, twice in Proverbs (12:24; 31:3) and once in Ruth (3:11). Ruth is the only woman in Scripture to receive this explicit designation. Based upon its placement in the Hebrew canon, it appears that Ruth is intended to function as the illustration of the ideal woman presented in Proverbs 31. In our English Bibles, this connection is obscured by Ruth's narrative-chronological [mis]placement after the book of Judges and by the inconsistency of Bible translations. For example, the ESV translates this designation as "excellent wife" in Proverbs but as "worthy woman" in Ruth. The NASB (1995) and the NIV (1984) are better with, respectively, "excellent wife" and "wife of noble character" in Proverbs and "woman of excellence" and "woman of noble character" in Ruth. The KJV is helpfully consistent with "virtuous woman" in all three instances. However, readers rarely notice this connection because of the [mis]placement of the book of Ruth after the book of Judges in our English Bibles.

recorded in Genesis 2. In Genesis 2:18, the Lord God made a shocking statement. He declared that something was "not good" on day six of creation. We know from Genesis 1:31 that day six was set apart from the previous five days; it was not just "good" (cf. Gen. 1:4, 10, 12, 18, 21, 25) but "very good." There was man in the garden of God's presence with all his resource needs met, but the status of his situation remained "not good." According to the presentation in Scripture, the creation of the woman and the marriage covenant (Gen. 2:21–25) was what finally transformed day six from "not good" to "very good." It could be said that the "building" of the woman and the marriage covenant serves as the climax of creation on day six and the beginning of human history. Thus, it is important to observe that marriage and the family are prefall, creational institutions woven into the very fabric of culture and the means by which the cultural mandate (Gen. 1:28) was to be fulfilled. By way of contrast, the institution of marriage was *not* a result of the fall or a means by which humanity better coped with a world that had fallen into sin. Marriage as the one-flesh relationship established by God on day six of creation became the covenantal, human paradigm by which he would relate to his people, both in this world and in the world to come.[3]

The fact that God created man and woman as (very good!) sexual beings, that this reality was to be expressed in the covenant of marriage, and that by analogy this covenantal relationship became the dominant way by which God would relate to his people, has caused difficulty for those who have labored to interpret the Song of Songs. In fact, no other book in the Old Testament has suffered at the hands of interpreters throughout history like the Song of Songs. Interpretations range from carnal, erotic love poetry to sublime, otherworldly descriptions of the divine-human relationship, and almost everything in between.

On the one hand, marriage and sexuality are legitimate aspects of creation and certainly deserve attention in biblical (and nonbiblical) wisdom literature. As such, many interpreters have argued that the Song of Songs deals with this very topic and that all the body parts and descriptions of sexual activity are just that, wise considerations of marriage and sex. On the other hand, some have considered such a "natural" approach indelicate, inappropriate, or just plain carnal. These interpreters have preferred a more "supernatural," allegorical interpretation of the Song. With this interpretation, the Song constitutes an allegorical description of the covenantal relationship between God and his people, whether Yahweh and Israel or Jesus and the church. Proponents argue that this interpretation is more theologically suitable for Scripture as it describes and provokes love for our covenant Lord.

The swing of the pendulum from allegorical to natural interpretations in our modern context has resulted in the "functional decanonization" of the Song of Songs.[4] The

---

[3] See Rev. 19:7, "Let us rejoice and exult and give him the glory, *for the marriage of the Lamb has come, and his Bride has made herself ready,*" and Rev. 21:2, "And I saw the holy city, new Jerusalem, coming down out of heaven from God, *prepared as a bride adorned for her husband*" (ESV).

[4] D. M. Carr states, "This increasingly exclusive focus on the literal sense of the Song has corresponded with the functional decanonization of the Song in those sections of the church and synagogue which have been most deeply influenced by historical-critical method." "The Song of Songs as a Microcosm of the Canonization and Decanonization Process," in *Canonization and Decanonization: Papers Presented to the International Conference of the Leiden Institute for the Study*

current popularity among scholars for the more natural interpretation of the book has resulted in a corresponding demise in the use of this book in public worship and Christian education. In other words, because of the book's sexually oriented language and our overly religious conceptions about the nature of the church, we simply ignore the Song, even though we recognize its presence in the Canon and render lip service to its inspiration and authority. This is a serious charge and a regrettable situation for the church. For this reason, modern attempts to revive the allegorical approach persist as a means to rescue this text from homiletical neglect.[5]

In this introduction, however, we will argue that the Songs of Songs is a canonical work of poetic wisdom literature that considers the important topic of human marriage. In our modern context, the consideration of marriage—including its definition, status, and legitimate participants—demands careful consideration from Scripture. Since wisdom literature reflects on the application of God's Word to God's world, who is better qualified to instruct about the reality of marriage than the One who created this "very good" institution? However, it is important to note that this approach does not preclude application to the divine-human covenant relationship that is biblically and intentionally analogous to it (cf. Ezekiel 16; 23; Hosea 1–3; 1 Corinthians 7; 2 Corinthians 11; Ephesians 5; Colossians 3; Rev. 19:7, 21:2). Covenant life finds its ultimate meaning in our covenant Lord, Jesus Christ. To interpret Scripture in any other way would contradict the clear and forceful teaching of Jesus and the apostolic witness (cf. John 5:39–40; Luke 24:25–27, 44–45; Acts 28:23–34; Rom. 1:1–3; 1 Pet. 1:10–11).

BACKGROUND ISSUES

Authorship and Date of Composition

The questions of authorship and date are closely related. There are basically two options. Either Solomon wrote the book in the tenth century BC, or an anonymous author wrote sometime between the tenth and fifth centuries BC.

Traditionally, authorship of the Song was attributed to Solomon, the son of David, the third and final monarch of Israel's united kingdom. Solomon reigned over Israel from approximately 970–930 BC. The biblical account of his reign is recorded in 1 Kings 1–11 and 1 Chronicles 29–2 Chronicles 9. The following evidence supports the *possibility* that Solomon is the author of the Song of Songs:

(1) The superscription in Song of Songs 1:1 may indicate that Solomon was the author—"The Song of Songs, *which is by Solomon* [אֲשֶׁר לִשְׁלֹמֹה]." The Hebrew preposition that appears with the proper name Solomon may be used to indicate authorship. The use of this same preposition with a proper name is employed with some frequency in the book of Psalms. For example, it appears in the superscription at the beginning of Psalm 3: "A song *by David* [לְדָוִד] when he fled from Absalom"

---

of Religions (LISOR), Held at Leiden 9–10 January 1997, ed. A. van der Kooij and K. van der Toorn, with an annotated bibliography compiled by J. A. M. Snoek, SHR 82 (Leiden: Brill, 1998), 184–85.
[5] A recent attempt is represented by James M. Hamilton Jr., *Song of Songs: A Biblical-Theological, Allegorical, Christological Interpretation* (Fearn, Ross-Shire, Scotland: Christian Focus, 2015).

(3:1). Additionally, Psalms 72 and 127 both feature the same authorial superscription "by Solomon." However, the indication of authorship is not required by this preposition. It may also indicate that the Song was written *about* Solomon, or that it was *dedicated to* Solomon.

(2) Solomon is the only person named in the Song. In addition to the superscription (1:1), Solomon's name appears six more times (1:5; 3:7, 9, 11; 8:11–12). The Hebrew text also includes several wordplays that are connected to the name Solomon. For example, in 1:7 the ESV translation "for why" (שַׁלָּמָה) is a unique Hebrew construction with the exact same consonants as the proper name Solomon (שְׁלֹמֹה). Additionally, the designation "Shulammite" (שׁוּלַמִּית) in 7:1 (twice) appears to be a feminine form of Solomon's name and may mean something like "Solomonite" or "one who belongs to Solomon." The appearance of Solomon's name in the Song certainly does not require Solomon to be the author. At the very least, however, we can affirm that the Song is *about* Solomon at some level.

(3) In addition to Solomon's name, several other features in the Song are connected with his person and kingdom. On five occasions, a male figure in the Song is identified as the "king" (1:4, 12; 3:9, 11; 7:6). In 3:9 and 3:11 the king is specifically identified as Solomon. The Song also mentions the king's bed (1:12), chambers (1:4), royal guard (3:7–8), carriage (3:9), crown (3:11), harem (6:8–9), and vineyard (8:11). Other connections with Solomon include the chariots of Pharaoh (1:9), the tower of David (3:4), and the location of Jerusalem (1:5; 2:7; 3:5, 10; 5:8, 16; 6:4; 8:4). Additionally, the frequent mention of spices, perfumes, wealth, and flora in the Song corresponds with Solomon's kingdom and wisdom endeavors. By itself, the information presented in this paragraph does not require Solomon to be the author of the Song. However, whoever did write the Song would have had intimate knowledge of Solomon, the trappings of his court, and similar educational background and intellect.

(4) Solomon was a gifted and prolific author of poetic and wisdom literature. It is recorded that God granted Solomon wisdom to such a degree that he surpassed all who came before him and all who would come after him (1 Kings 3:28; cf. 1 Kings 4:29–34; 5:7, 12; 10:4–8, 23; 11:41). Solomon applied his wisdom to many different areas of life, but one of those areas was the production of literature:

> [Solomon] was wiser than any other man, including Ethan the Ezrahite—wiser than Heman, Calcol and Darda, the sons of Mahol. And his fame spread to all the surrounding nations. He spoke three thousand proverbs *and his songs numbered a thousand and five.* He described plant life, from the cedar of Lebanon to the hyssop that grows out of walls. He also taught about animals and birds, reptiles and fish. Men of all nations came to listen to Solomon's wisdom, sent by all the kings of the world, who had heard of his wisdom. (1 Kings 4:29–34 [Heb. 5:9–14] NIV)

First Kings 4:32 [Heb. 5:12] records that Solomon wrote over one thousand songs during his lifetime, not to mention three thousand proverbs (cf. Prov. 1:1; 10:1; 25:1). The Hebrew word used for "song" (שִׁיר) in this text is the same word that appears in

Song of Songs 1:1, "The Song of Songs," or the "Best Song."[6] Once again, this connection proves not that Solomon was the author of the Song of Songs but rather that he had the required background and ability. In fact, according to the biblical record, it can be reasonably argued that no other person in human history had better gifts or experience than Solomon to serve as the author of this superlative composition.

(5) The love poetry contained in the Song of Songs is related to love poetry found in Egypt dating from approximately 1305–1150 BC, just *before* the era of Solomon.[7] As a wisdom collector, Solomon may have become familiar with this literature (cf. 1 Kings 4:30). Additionally, Solomon traded with Egypt (1 Kings 10:28–29; cf. Song 1:9), and he allied himself to Egypt by way of royal marriage: "And Solomon became the son-in-law of Pharaoh, king of Egypt, and he married the daughter of Pharaoh and he brought her to the city of David" (1 Kings 3:1). Solomon's connection to Egypt by royal alliance, trade, and marriage may have put him in contact with a genre of love poetry that provides the background for some of the material that appears in the Song of Songs. A connection of this type does not require dependence or anything like our modern category of plagiarism. It does, however, establish the possibility of influence and adaptability in the hands of a skilled wisdom poet.

By way of conclusion, no single piece of evidence proves with absolute certainty that King Solomon is the author of the Song of Songs. However, the cumulative force of the body of evidence presented here identifies Solomon as the best possible candidate for authorship.

Genre

According to the superscription (1:1), the Song of Songs is just that, a song (שִׁיר). This same designation appears in the superscription for many of the psalms in the book of Psalms (e.g., Psalms 30, 45, 46, 48, 65, 66, 67, 75, 76, 83, 88, 92, 108, 120–134; see also 28:7; 33:3; 40:3[4]; 96:1; 98:1; 137:3; 144:9; 149:1). The frequency with which this designation appears in the book of Psalms suggests that this particular genre would have been well-known in ancient Israel. Its association with Solomon in the same superscription (לִשְׁלֹמֹה) also suggests a connection with wisdom literature.

Wisdom literature exhibits a variety of distinct and adaptive genres. Proverbs features proverbial sayings. Job is a poetic wisdom dialogue with a dramatic narrative frame, and the book of Psalms includes wisdom psalms (e.g., Psalms 36, 37, 49, 73, 78). Given its placement in the Hebrew canon, even the book of Ruth may be understood as a wisdom narrative. In light of the variety and adaptability of genre in biblical wisdom literature, classifying the Song of Songs as *a poetic wisdom song* seems entirely appropriate.[8]

---

[6] The construction "The Song of Songs" in Hebrew is used to indicate the superlative (i.e., the best of something). Similar constructions in the Hebrew Bible include "slave of slaves" or "lowest slave" (Gen. 9:25), "holy of holies" or "most holy" (Ex. 29:37), "the God of gods" or "the supreme God" (Deut. 10:17), "the Lord of lords" or "the greatest Lord (Deut. 10:17), and "vanity of vanities" or "ultimate vanity" (Eccles. 1:2).

[7] COS, 1:125–30.

[8] The Song has also been described as a "canonical work of lyric poetry." Duane A. Garrett, *Song of Songs*, in *Song of Songs / Lamentations*, by Duane A. Garrett and Paul R. House, WBC 23B (Nashville: Thomas Nelson, 2004), 14; cf. 90–97. Others have similarly called it "an anthology of lyric love poetry." Tremper Longman III, *Song of Songs*, NICOT (Grand

The language is clearly poetic. Its imagery and style accord with the best examples of Hebrew poetry. Its designation as a song would indicate that the Song was originally composed for singing, but this does not mean that it must be sung in order to be understood (related examples would include Exodus 15 and Judges 5).

As noted earlier, the evidence for connecting this song with wisdom literature and with Solomon is significant. Its subject matter appears in both Proverbs (5:15–21; 30:18–19) and Ecclesiastes (2:1–11; 9:9). Additionally, the didactic section in Song of Songs 8:6–12 suggests an overall purpose or message for the book, much like Proverbs 1:2–6 and Ecclesiastes 12:9–13. In fact, the basic didactic strategy of the Song may mirror the collection and presentation of poetic texts in Proverbs 1–9. These features play a prominent role in the following identification of the purpose and message of the Song.

Proposed Setting

Many factors work together to determine the correct interpretation of the Song of Songs. Once these factors have been considered, both the translation and the exposition of the text are shaped by the adopted interpretation. Given the Song's complexity and poetic ambiguity, examining the Song's setting is vital for making sense of its language and imagery and for making a wise decision with regard to the interpretation of the Song. Careful consideration of the Song itself (internal evidence) suggests that the most likely setting is the royal harem of Solomon. Because we possess limited knowledge of ancient harem life, it is helpful to consider a text like Esther 2, which describes this institution in some detail.

According to Esther 2, young virgins were gathered into king Ahasuerus's harem (lit. "the house of women") and then supervised by male eunuchs (lit. "keepers of the women") and female attendants. These young women would undergo a series of preparatory treatments that included "six months with the oil of myrrh and six months with spices and cosmetics for women" (Est. 2:12). After a year of preparation, a young virgin would be selected from this part of the harem to spend a night with the king. Then in the morning, that woman, no longer a virgin, would return to another part of the harem, the place of the concubines. There she would live out her days in the royal harem, never returning to the king unless he summoned her by name (Est. 2:14).

Though the description of King Ahasuerus's harem in Esther 2 may not correspond exactly to the policies and procedures that governed King Solomon's harem, we can only imagine that the court of Solomon and his harem operated on a scale that surpassed that of Ahasuerus. The descriptions of cosmetics, spices, and oils in the Song correspond to the experience described in Esther. Additionally, the presence of guards and attendants appear both in the Song and in Esther 2.

The identification of Solomon's harem as the location of the woman in the Song

Rapids, MI: Eerdmans, 2001), 48–49; Michael A. Fishbane, *Song of Songs: The Traditional Hebrew Text with the New JPS Translation*, JPS Torah Commentary (Philadelphia: Jewish Publication Society, 2015), xxi; cf. Garrett, *Song of Songs*, 25–26. There is also the wedding song (*epithalamium*) interpretation. Additionally, Origen (and John Milton) considered the Song to be a drama. Cf. Marvin H. Pope, *Song of Songs: A New Translation with Introduction and Commentary*, AB 7C (Garden City, NY: Doubleday, 1977), 34–35.

is substantiated in several instances. For example, Song of Songs 6:8 describes the female occupancy of the harem: "There are sixty queens and eighty concubines and virgins without number." A similar description appears in the very next verse, "The daughters see her, and they bless her, the queens and the concubines [see her], and they praise her" (6:9b). The categorization of the harem women into three groups—queens, concubines, and virgins—corresponds to the description of Ahasuerus's harem in Esther 2. It also complies with the well-known and shocking description of Solomon's harem later in 1 Kings 11:3: "He [Solomon] had seven hundred royal wives and three hundred concubines."

The descriptions of the harem in Song of Songs 6:8 and 6:9 help to identify the enigmatic daughters of Jerusalem. They are not a background chorus, nor are they simply the young female inhabitants of the royal city. Note that the "virgins" (עֲלָמוֹת) in 6:8 appear as the "daughters" (בְּנוֹת) in 6:9, identifying the so-called "daughters of Jerusalem" as those virgins taken into Solomon's harem in order to be prepared as potential concubines.[9] In other words, the daughters of Jerusalem represent the virgins taken with the female protagonist of the Song into the harem of Solomon for training and preparation. This interpretation suits the harem context of the Song, and it avoids the creation of participant categories (e.g., a background chorus) that are foreign to the ancient context or the genre of the song.

In the final verses of the Song, Solomon's harem is described as a vineyard in Baal-hamon (בַּעַל הָמוֹן): "Solomon had a vineyard in Baal-hamon. He entrusted the vineyard to those who would guard it [i.e., eunuchs]. Each would bring in his fruit [i.e., a virgin] for a thousand pieces of silver" (8:11). However, the woman of the Song rejects both Solomon and harem life in the very next verse: "My vineyard, which belongs to me, is still before me. Keep your thousand [pieces of silver] and the two hundred for those who guard its fruit" (8:12). It is also worth noting that the location Baal-hamon appears only here in the Old Testament. However, it may not be a location at all but rather a satirical designation for Solomon's harem, literally translated "husband of a multitude." This is certainly a fitting description for the harem of Solomon (cf. 1 Kings 11:3; Song 6:8). It also implicitly condemns this reality as a violation not only of the covenantal regulations that governed kingship in Israel (cf. Deut. 17:17) but also of the original created order, in which one man and one woman were united in the one-flesh covenant of marriage (cf. Gen. 2:18–25).

Identifying the harem as the background for the Song also helps make sense of many enigmatic texts in the Song. For example, the opening verses of the Song describe a man whose lovemaking prowess was so famous that it provoked the admiration and love of the virgins (עֲלָמוֹת). In 1:2 we read the statement that "making love to you

---

[9] The connection between the "virgins" in 6:8 and the "daughters" in 6:9 is obscured by modern translations. For example, the feminine plural form בָּנוֹת (lit. "daughters") in 6:9 is translated as "young women" by the ESV and NIV and as "maidens" by the RSV, NASB, and NET. The KJV is helpfully accurate, "The *daughters* saw her." Thus, the categories for women residing in the harem in 6:8 include queens, concubines, and *virgins*. In 6:9 these same women are referred to as *daughters*, queens, and concubines. With the juxtaposition of virgins and daughters in 6:8 and 6:9, the author has provided readers with a helpful clue for identifying the so-called daughters [of Jerusalem] that appear throughout the Song (1:5; 2:7; 3:5, 10; 5:8, 16; 8:4).

[masculine singular] is better than wine" (cf. 1:4). This is followed by the statements, "Therefore *the virgins* love you" (1:3) and "rightly *they* love you" (1:4). Given the proposed harem context, the man famous for his lovemaking is Solomon. He is the desire of the virgins. His name appears in 1:1 and 1:5, and his royal chambers are mentioned in 1:4 (הֱבִיאַנִי הַמֶּלֶךְ חֲדָרָיו).

In Song of Songs 2 another man arrives, the woman's beloved, "leaping over the mountains, jumping over the hills" (2:8). However, this man does not have access to the woman. He is cut off by a wall and can only peer through the windows and lattice (2:9). He must call to her at a distance (2:10ff). Now for a man who can leap over mountains and hills, the obstacle of a wall should present no difficulty. However, this was no ordinary wall. Rather, it was the fortress of the harem, a well-guarded enclosure that would have been fortified to prevent access by other men.

The appearance of the man in Song of Songs 2 stands in contrast to the appearance of Solomon in Song of Songs 3. In the third chapter, Solomon arrives "from the wilderness" (3:6) with his portable bedroom surrounded by sixty warrior-eunuchs (lit. "men who have been seized by the sword") to be present for the "terror of the nights" (3:8). Upon Solomon's arrival in the harem, the women are summoned, "Come out and look upon King Solomon, O daughters of Jerusalem" (3:11). Here the virgin women, the daughters of Jerusalem, are summoned to appear before the king upon his arrival so he can select his next concubine. It is important to observe that the man in chapter 2 does not have access to the harem but that the man in chapter 3, identified as King Solomon, has full access to the virgins who have been prepared to become concubines and permanent members of the harem.

The identification of Solomon's harem, real or imagined, as the background for the Song will shape our interpretation of the Song. It places the Song in a context that explains the imagery, identifies the participants, and sheds light on the plight of the woman who is the hero of the Song.

STRUCTURE AND OUTLINE

There is a spectrum of opinion regarding the structure of the Song. At one end of the spectrum are those who argue that the Song consists of an indeterminate number of individual poems "of uncertain and often even of doubtful connection with one another."[10] At the other end of the spectrum are those who argue that the Song is a single "unified work with chiastic structure and is composed . . . for presentation by a male and a female soloist with a chorus."[11] The truth probably lies somewhere in between these two extremes. The Song's language, style, and content suggest a single, unified composition. However, there is no discernible plot and no original headings to

---

[10] Longman, *Song of Songs*, 43. Longman's assessment considers the Song to be "an anthology of love poems, a kind of erotic psalter" without "a strict narrative unity" (43). Scholars debate the total number of individual poems. Longman argues for twenty-three poems, Keel for forty-two, Goulder for fourteen, and Murphy for nine. Garrett, *Song of Songs*, 25–26. The paragraph markers in the Masoretic version of the Hebrew Bible divide the Song into twenty sections.

[11] Garrett, *Song of Songs*, 31–32. Other scholars who share a similar view regarding a chiastic structure for the Song include Alden, Dorsey, Exum, Shea, and Webster. Cf. Garrett, *Song of Songs*, 30–35.

identify shifts in vocal performance.[12] Furthermore, the proposed chiastic structures fail to correspond in any meaningful way and seem forced or imposed rather than clearly emerging from the language of the Song.

The Song's title in the superscription directs us to read this poetic composition as a single, unified song, "*The Song* [singular!] of Songs." If this is true, then we should expect to observe at least some structural markers to guide those who sing, hear, or read the text of the Song. One such device that appears to serve in this capacity is the so-called adjuration (NASB, ESV) or charge (KJV, NIV) of the woman: "I adjure you, O daughters of Jerusalem, by the gazelles or the does of the field, that you not stir up or awaken love until it pleases" (ESV). In addition to Song of Songs 2:7, this charge also appears at 3:5 and 8:4.[13] Technically speaking, the woman is placing the daughters of Jerusalem under an oath, and so literally, "*I put you under oath*, daughters of Jerusalem, by the gazelles or the does of the field, *if you stir up or arouse love before it is willing, [may you be cursed]*."[14] The statement in Hebrew is stronger than it comes across in most of our English translations, which makes it well suited to mark divisions in the text. Additionally, in all three occurrences, the oath is followed by the announcement of an individual's arrival (e.g, "behold, he is coming" in 2:8). It is proposed that the occurrence of this oath formula marks the ending of each major section and that the announcement of an individual's arrival marks the beginning of the next section. This scheme, therefore, divides the Song into four major sections:

    I. The Temptation of Solomon's Harem (1:2–2:7)
    II. The Arrival of True Love (2:8–3:5)
    III. The Arrival of Solomon (3:6–8:4)
    IV. The Arrival of the Woman (8:5–14)

This outline is expanded and explained in the following section, "Message and Theology." At this point, however, it is worth mentioning that three of the four major sections are relatively short, ranging only from ten to twenty-four verses. The third section is the longest section with sixty-eight verses divided into two subsections: 3:6–5:8 (thirty verses) and 5:9–8:4 (thirty-eight verses). The division of this subsection is marked and identified by the fourth oath, which is similar to but distinct from

---

[12] It is important to note that the headings and subheadings imposed by many modern translations do not appear in the Hebrew text. These headings are based on the editors' interpretation(s) of the Song. The oldest known headings of this type appear in Codex Sinaiticus (a fourth-century AD Greek manuscript).

[13] A similar oath formula also appears in Song 5:8 but is not counted with the three texts listed here for several reasons. First, it is not followed by the formulaic warning against stirring up or awakening love before it is ready; rather, the oath in 5:8 concerns finding and speaking to the woman's beloved. Second, the oath in 5:8 is not followed by the interrogative description of someone's arrival (cf. 2:8; 3:6; 8:5). Third, the oaths in 2:7 and 8:4 are preceded by the statement, "his left [hand] is under my head and his right [hand] embraces me" (2:6; 8:3), and the oaths in 2:7 and 3:5 include references to "the gazelles and the does of the field," perhaps functioning symbolically as witnesses to the oath. Finally, the oaths in 2:7; 3:5; and 8:4 constitute prohibitions (Do *not* stir up love!), while the oath in 5:8 functions positively as an admonition (Tell him that I am lovesick!). Thus, strong linguistic and contextual connections tie together the oaths in 2:7; 3:5; and 8:4 that do not occur for the oath in 5:8.

[14] For oath formulas of this type, see Blane Conklin, *Oath Formulas in Biblical Hebrew*, LSAWS 5 (Winona Lake, IN: Eisenbrauns, 2011), esp. 21–22, 29, 61. The appearance of the bracketed text above, *[may you be cursed]*, indicates that the biblical text normally omits the actual curse statement (the apodosis) in an oath formula of this type for the sake of propriety or discretion (i.e., language taboo).

the one that terminates the first three sections: "I put you under oath, daughters of Jerusalem, *if you find my beloved, what will you tell him?*" (5:8).[15]

MESSAGE AND THEOLOGY

Interpretation

As stated earlier, the Song of Songs is a poetic wisdom song. Biblical wisdom literature is rooted in creation and works to describe how to live in God's world according to God's Word. It is first about understanding how this world works and then about how to make good decisions in light of that knowledge. As such, the Song is neither an allegorical description of the divine-human relationship nor an "erotic psalter" without any didactic purpose except to praise the goodness of human sexuality.[16] The Song is not a drama, a play, or an opera. It is not a veiled account or interpretation of the history of Israel. There is no good evidence that it originally served in wedding ceremonies, funerals, or the cult. It does not read as myth.[17]

The Song of Songs is a poetic wisdom song that treats the topic of marriage and love from the perspective of a young woman. This woman has been taken into Solomon's harem in order to be trained as a potential concubine (cf. Esther 2). She is a woman presented with the possibility of wealth, luxury, ease, and prestige if she will only give up the biblical, creational standard of marriage and love (Gen. 2:18–25; Ex. 20:14; Prov. 5:15–21). The Song, therefore, presents two men: Solomon, set in the context of his court and harem, and another male figure known by the woman, her true love, sometimes identified as the shepherd (e.g., Song 2:16; 6:3). For this reason, this particular explanation is often labelled "the shepherd interpretation."[18]

In the opening verses, King Solomon is presented as a famous lover whose "lovemaking is better than wine"(1:2) and whom the young virgins love (1:3–4). But according to the woman, her beloved is unique, "like an apple tree among the trees of the forest" (2:3), and she is lovesick because of his absence (2:5). In Song 2:8–17, a male figure arrives who does not have access to the harem. A wall separates him from the woman, and he can only search for her by looking through the windows and lattice. When this man calls out to the woman, she is unable to come to him, and so he must go away and wait until the woman is able to leave the harem. By way of contrast, Solomon arrives in 3:6 with full access to the harem. He appears with

---

[15] See note 13 on p. 427.

[16] The designation "erotic psalter" comes from Longman, *Song of Songs*, 43. The traditional error with the interpretation of the Song excluded the natural reading of the text as it relates to human marriage and sexuality. The modern error operates at the other end of the spectrum, treating the Song as some sort of manual for sexual activity or as an aid to sexual arousal.

[17] In this introduction, I do not describe the history of the Song's interpretation, though I have alluded to it in the paragraph above. For those interested in this topic, some of the better treatments include Longman, *Song of Songs*, 20–49; Garrett, *Song of Songs*, 59–91; Provan, *Song of Songs*, 237–48; Hess, *Song of Songs*, 22–29; and the extensive treatment by Pope, *Song of Songs*, 89–229.

[18] For this interpretation, see Chaim Rabin, "The Song of Songs and Tamil Poetry," *SR* 3, no. 3 (1973): 205–19; Walter C. Kaiser Jr., "True Marital Love in Proverbs 5:15–23 and the Interpretation of Song of Songs," in *The Way of Wisdom: Essays in Honor of Bruce K. Waltke*, ed. J. I. Packer and Sven Soderlund (Grand Rapids, MI: Zondervan, 2000), 106–16; Provan, *Song of Songs*, 245–48.

royal retinue and accoutrement where the virgins (i.e., daughters of Jerusalem) are assembled for viewing and selection (3:11). Of the two male figures that the Song presents, Solomon has access to the harem in 3:6 and following, but the man appearing in 2:7 does not have access to the harem. This reality also explains the woman's rejection of Solomon and harem life in 8:11–12 but the presence of the woman together with her beloved earlier in that same chapter (8:5).

Simply put, while Solomon appears repeatedly and explicitly in the Song, he does not exemplify fidelity in the context of the covenant of marriage or the love that a permanent, exclusive relationship promotes. In other words, the figure of Solomon in the Song represents not the way of wisdom but rather the way of folly, or that which is evil in the eyes of the Lord (cf. 1 Kings 11:1–6). A similar style of wisdom instruction occurs in Proverbs 1–9. There a young man is instructed by his parents to choose between two ways, the way of wisdom or the way of folly, each of which is exemplified by two women: Lady Wisdom and Lady Folly. It is helpful to compare the descriptions of the two women in Proverbs and to observe that these passages share much in common, even vocabulary, with the Song. For example, the instruction in Proverbs 5:15–20 shares language and imagery with the Song (see also Prov. 3:13–18; 4:6–9):

> Drink water from your own cistern,
>   flowing water from your own well.
> Should your springs be scattered abroad,
>   streams of water in the streets?
> Let them be for yourself alone,
>   and not for strangers with you.
> Let your fountain be blessed,
>   and rejoice in the wife of your youth,
>   a lovely deer, a graceful doe.
> Let her breasts fill you at all times with delight;
>   be intoxicated always in her love.
> Why should you be intoxicated, my son, with a forbidden woman
>   and embrace the bosom of an adulteress?

The call to fidelity in Proverbs 5:15–20 is contrasted with the description of Lady Folly in Proverbs 7:4–27 (cf. Prov. 2:16–19; 5:3–8; 6:23–29; 9:13–18). The following selection is lengthy, but clearly exhibits connections in language and instruction with the Song:

> Say to wisdom, "You are my sister,"
>   and call insight your intimate friend,
> to keep you from the forbidden woman,
>   from the adulteress with her smooth words.
>
> For at the window of my house
>   I have looked out through my lattice,
> and I have seen among the simple,

I have perceived among the youths,
    a young man lacking sense,
passing along the street near her corner,
    taking the road to her house
in the twilight, in the evening,
    at the time of night and darkness.

And behold, the woman meets him,
    dressed as a prostitute, wily of heart.
She is loud and wayward;
    her feet do not stay at home;
now in the street, now in the market,
    and at every corner she lies in wait.
She seizes him and kisses him,
    and with bold face she says to him,
"I had to offer sacrifices,
    and today I have paid my vows;
so now I have come out to meet you,
    to seek you eagerly, and I have found you.
I have spread my couch with coverings,
    colored linens from Egyptian linen;
I have perfumed my bed with myrrh,
    aloes, and cinnamon.
Come, let us take our fill of love till morning;
    let us delight ourselves with love.
For my husband is not at home;
    he has gone on a long journey;
he took a bag of money with him;
    at full moon he will come home."

With much seductive speech she persuades him;
    with her smooth talk she compels him.
All at once he follows her,
    as an ox goes to the slaughter,
or as a stag is caught fast
    till an arrow pierces its liver;
as a bird rushes into a snare;
    he does not know that it will cost him his life.

And now, O sons, listen to me,
    and be attentive to the words of my mouth.
Let not your heart turn aside to her ways;
    do not stray into her paths,
for many a victim has she laid low,
    and all her slain are a mighty throng.
Her house is the way to Sheol,
    going down to the chambers of death.

The instruction in the Song of Songs is of the same type as that presented in Proverbs 7 but from the perspective of a woman who must choose between two men, both enticing in their own way but one leading to life and the other to death. As such, the instruction of the Song is intended to teach women how to make a wise choice in the selection of a husband and to resist the dangerous and deadly temptation of folly exemplified by Solomon with his offers of luxury, ease, and prestige characterized by harem life.

Message

The message of the Song is recorded in Song of Songs 8:6–10, in the context of the woman's arrival with her beloved (8:5) and her corresponding rejection of Solomon and harem life (8:11–12). By way of summary, the Song teaches that the biblical covenant of marriage is intended to promote love that is both rock solid (8:6a) and white hot (8:6b), and that this type of love endures hardship (8:7a), resists temptation (8:7b), and brings wholeness (8:10).

The wisdom of biblical marriage produces rock-solid commitment that is capable of enduring hardship and resisting temptation. The text of 8:6a reads, "place me like the seal on your heart, like the seal on your arm." The imagery of the seal is one of ownership and access. Seals were placed on documents, doors, vessels, or containers to mark ownership, responsibility, content, and access. "Sealing was a means of closing something from interference," the visible and public application of authority.[19] The unsanctioned breaking of a seal was met with punishment, curse, and even death. Biblical examples include the sealing of the lion's den in Daniel 6 so that only the king could open it, and the sealing of the scrolls with seven seals in Revelation 5 so that only Jesus could open them. Here in Song of Songs 8:6, the application of the seal to the heart and the arm perhaps represents the possession of one another in marriage, both emotionally (heart) and physically (arm). The apostle Paul affirms the same reality in 1 Corinthians 7:4: "The wife's body does not belong to her alone but also to her husband. In the same way, the husband's body does not belong to him alone but also to his wife."

The woman also explains that rock-solid covenant love is "strong like death, obstinate like the grave with zeal" (Song 8:6a). Though it may seem odd at first, the language of death and the grave aptly characterizes the rock-solid commitment of covenant life described by this woman. These symbols are intended to communicate that the marriage covenant is designed to be a permanent relationship. Covenant life of this type is a miraculous, supernatural work. Recall, for example, what Jesus said about marriage. The rock-solid union of marriage is something that "God has joined together" (Matt. 19:6; Mark 10:9); that is, there is a force behind this type of covenant life that God himself implements. It is powerful, even life producing. The wisdom of the Song teaches us that covenant life in marriage must be rock solid.

---

[19] *NIDOTTE*, 2:324.

The wisdom of the Song teaches us not only that covenant life in marriage must be rock solid but also that it must be white hot! Consider, for example, the text of Song of Songs 8:6b, "Its flames are flames of fire, the very flame of Yahweh."[20] The type of heat described here is the heat of physical intimacy created for the marriage relationship—that is, sexual intimacy. This is clear from the vast amount of physical or sexual descriptions in the Song. In fact, every chapter in the book is loaded with sexual imagery or descriptions of sexual activity or both. The heat of marital intimacy was designed not only to provide satisfaction and wholeness but also to protect from the enemy. That is, both rock-solid commitment and white-hot intimacy work together. Again, Paul reinforces this teaching for us in the New Testament: "For the wife does not have authority over her own body, but the husband does. Likewise the husband does not have authority over his own body, but the wife does. Do not deprive one another, except perhaps by agreement for a limited time, that you may devote yourselves to prayer; but then come together again, so that Satan may not tempt you because of your lack of self-control" (1 Cor. 7:4–5 ESV).

Rock-solid commitment makes white-hot intimacy possible. And white-hot intimacy fuels, protects, and supports rock-solid commitment. Traditionally, the church has done much to support the rock-solid commitment of biblical marriage and its permanent design. However, it has done little, if anything, to encourage, promote, or celebrate the heat of marital intimacy. On the other hand, the world loves, and unashamedly celebrates, the white-hot nature of sexual intimacy, but it despises the rock-solid commitment of marriage created as the context for this heat. Both positions, by themselves, are weak and endanger the covenant partners.

The wisdom of the Song teaches that both commitment and intimacy work together to secure, strengthen, and protect the marriage relationship. The Song makes this point in Song of Songs 8:7, where it states that "many waters [i.e., trials] cannot extinguish love, and rivers cannot flood it." When marriage is *both* white hot *and* rock solid, it is protected from shipwreck during the storm. Moreover, not only will trials threaten covenant life in this world, but so will temptations such as money, power, security, or freedom—here characterized by the wealth of a man's household: "if a man gave all the wealth of his house for love [i.e., Solomon], it would utterly scorn him" (8:7b). In other words, this type of love is not for sale. It cannot be bought, and only a fool would try to make such a purchase. The type of love promoted in the Song must be protected (8:8–9) because it promotes peace and wholeness (8:10). The message of the Song is summarized in table 20.

---

[20] The translation and interpretation of the expression "the very flame of Yahweh" in 8:6b is debated. Some take this to describe the origin or source of sexual intimacy, that this type of heat can only come from the Lord. Others take it to mean the degree of heat: it is super hot, the hottest possible heat (i.e., the superlative use of the divine name). Perhaps there is no need to distinguish. In both origin and degree, this type of love is a divine gift. But there may be more to it. When it comes to the fire of Yahweh in the Bible, both Old and New Testaments, we learn that God himself is a consuming fire (Deut. 4:24; Heb. 12:29). Yet note that this fire does not consume his people but rather protects them. It is the fire of God's presence and so also of his fellowship. But this same fire consumes God's enemies. And so in marriage, the heat of sexual intimacy was designed to protect the marriage by consuming the threat of an enemy through the production of satisfaction (1 Cor. 7:4–5) and the creation of wholeness (Song 8:10).

The Message of the Song: Song of Songs 8:6–10

Verse	Translation	Instruction
8:6a	Place me like the seal on your heart, like the seal on your arm; for love is strong like death, obstinate like the grave with zeal.	The commitment of marriage should be rock solid.
8:6b	Its flames are flames of fire, the very flame of Yahweh [or "the hottest possible flame"].	The intimacy of marriage should be white hot.
8:7a	Many waters cannot extinguish love, and rivers cannot flood it.	This type of love endures hardship.
8:7b–9	If a man gave all the wealth of his house for love, it would utterly scorn him. We have a younger sister . . .	This type of love resists temptation.
8:10	I am a wall, and my breasts are like the towers, and so in this way I have become in his eyes like one who brings forth [finds] wholeness [peace, shalom].	This type of love promotes satisfaction and wholeness.

Table 20

The Song's Content: A Summary

As indicated earlier (see "Structure and Outline" on p. 426), the message of the Song unfolds in four main sections, each of which is summarized in what follows. It is important to remember that each major section concludes with the woman placing the daughters of Jerusalem under oath (2:7; 3:5; 8:4) and that the next major section begins with the arrival of a different individual—the shepherd in 2:8, Solomon in 3:6, and the woman in 8:5.

By way of context, recall that the woman in the Song has been taken into Solomon's harem, where she must decide between a life as one of Solomon's many concubines (6:8–9) or a life of true love in the context of an exclusive marriage relationship (8:1–12). There are, therefore, two men represented in the Song, Solomon and the so-called shepherd (the woman's true love). Additionally, the woman of the Song finds herself among the daughters of Jerusalem, the other virgins in the harem complex training and preparing for the possibility of harem life. These are the voices of the Song.

The Temptation of Solomon's Harem (Song 1:2–2:7)[21]

The harem in 1:2–4, either collectively or by way of a harem attendant, instructs the woman regarding the fame of Solomon and the intoxication of his lovemaking skills. It is here that the woman is first tempted by the so-called benefits of harem life. The woman immediately objects in 1:5–7 based upon her appearance that has

---

[21] The text of Song 1:1 constitutes the superscription. It is not a part of the Song.

resulted from prolonged exposure to the sun and manual labor. She concludes with a statement of longing for her true love, the shepherd. The harem responds in 1:8–17 with an affirmation of the woman's beauty and the allurement of royal jewelry and perfume for beautification and decoration. Once again, the woman responds in 2:1–7 by affirming her preference for an exclusive relationship with the shepherd (e.g., a lily among thorns, an apple tree among the forest trees), and she concludes with another statement of longing. She is sick with love (i.e., lovesick) and so places the daughters of Jerusalem under oath not to force or provoke false love, or the love that she does not desire (2:7).

The Arrival of True Love (Song 2:8–3:5)

In this second main section of the Song, the woman's true love, the so-called shepherd, arrives in search of the woman in order to return with her. He is described as coming with strength and vitality, "leaping over the mountains, bounding over the hills" (2:8–9a). Upon arrival, the beloved shepherd searches for the woman, but he is prohibited from entering the harem. Such an act would have resulted in quick and certain death. He can only stand behind the wall looking through the windows and lattice (2:9b). In 2:10–17 the shepherd calls out to the woman. It is now spring, the time for love, and he invites her to return to their vineyard, the place for love. The woman responds in 2:16–17, first with a vow expressing her rock-solid commitment to the shepherd, "my beloved belongs to me, and I belong to him, the shepherd among the flowers" (2:16),[22] and then with a command to go and wait until she is able to come out to him (2:17). This section concludes in 3:1–4 with the first of two dream accounts in the Song (cf. 5:2–7). These accounts contain some of the most explicit sexual imagery in the Song and represent the woman's strong desire to be reunited and joined in marriage to the shepherd. Both dreams highlight the degree to which the woman longs for her shepherd and express the lovesick condition of the woman kept from the shepherd in the harem of Solomon. The shepherd has departed to the mountains where he waits for the arrival of the woman. The termination of this section is clearly marked by the repetition of the oath in 3:5.

The Arrival of Solomon (Song 3:6–8:4)

The third section of the Song is the longest. It is divided into two parts (3:6–5:8 and 5:9–8:4) by a secondary oath at 5:8, "I put you under oath, daughters of Jerusalem, if you find my beloved, what will you say to him? [Tell him] that I am lovesick."[23] It is a question and answer, not a prohibition as with the other three oaths.

Subsection one: The temptation of Solomon (Song 3:6–5:8). In this first subsection, Solomon arrives in royal splendor. He appears in a billow of perfume and incense,

---

[22] This vow may represent the covenantal expression of the marriage commitment, similar to the covenantal expression in Gen. 17:7–8; Jer. 31:33; 32:38, et al. See Rolf Rendtorff, *The Covenant Formula: An Exegetical and Theological Investigation*, trans. Margaret Kohl, OTS (Edinburgh: T&T Clark, 1998).

[23] See note 13 on p. 427.

accompanied by his royal bed and surrounded by palace warriors, likely the harem eunuchs—that is, those who have been "seized by the sword" (3:6–10). The virgins are assembled for selection in 3:11, and then Solomon works to woo the woman by way of flattery (4:1–8) and then with promises of love and lovemaking (4:9–5:1). The temptation of Solomon is followed by the second dream account in the Song (5:2–7), once again expressing the woman's profound longing for her shepherd. Like the previous dream account, this one is also filled with explicit sexual imagery designed to characterize the woman's longing for covenantal union with the beloved shepherd in opposition to Solomon. This first subsection concludes with the oath that marks the division at 5:8.

Subsection two: The temptation of the harem (Song 5:9–8:4). This second subsection begins with the daughters of Jerusalem inquiring of the woman. They want to know why her beloved shepherd is better than any other man, especially Solomon (5:9). The woman responds by describing the shepherd to the daughters of Jerusalem (5:10–16). The woman's answer provokes a second question, "Where has your beloved gone, O beautiful one among the women, where has your beloved turned, that we may search for him with you?" (6:1). The woman answers and also affirms her commitment to the shepherd by repeating her statement of covenant loyalty, "I belong to my beloved, and my beloved belongs to me" (6:2–3). Following this vow of loyalty, Solomon sets out to woo the young woman a second time (6:4–10). The woman refuses and desires to leave the harem (6:11–12). The daughters of Jerusalem join with Solomon to call the woman back, "return, return!" She has now created conflict in the harem among the virgins, a conflict described as the "dance of two armies" (7:1). Next, Solomon delivers his third and final attempt at wooing the young woman to become a part of his harem as a concubine (7:2–10a), but it does not work. She responds to the king, "I belong to my beloved, and his desire is for me" (7:10b). The rejection of Solomon is followed by the woman's invitation or call to the shepherd to return in order that they might depart together and be united in marriage (7:11–8:3). This section is concluded by the third appearance of the oath-curse directed at the daughters of Jerusalem (8:4).

The Arrival of the Woman (Song 8:5–14)

This final section constitutes the climax of the Song. In this section, the woman of valor (cf. Prov. 12:24; 31:3; Ruth 3:11) arrives with the beloved shepherd and sets before us the wisdom instruction presented by her experience. Her message is summarized in the chart "The Message of the Song" (p. 433). The woman arrives with her beloved shepherd, coming up from the wilderness, the place of testing (Song 8:5; cf. 3:6). The woman teaches that true love, the love of marriage described in Genesis 2:18–25, must exhibit rock-solid commitment and white-hot sexual intimacy in order to endure hardship and resist temptation (Song 8:6–9). Only this exclusive marriage commitment is capable of producing satisfaction, wholeness, and peace (8:10). As such, the woman rejects Solomon and harem life along with the temptations of wealth, luxury, ease, and prestige (8:11–12). The Song concludes with an invitation to the beloved, and those friends who would embrace her wisdom, to come away from the folly and temptation of harem life, or any other perversion of biblical marriage, in order to experience the type of love described by biblical wisdom (8:13–14).

Full Outline for the Song of Songs

Having explored the Song in detail, we are now ready to expand the outline:

I. The Temptation of Solomon's Harem (1:2–2:7)
   A. Temptation of the harem: A famous lover (1:2–4)
   B. Response of the woman: Unqualified (1:5–7)
   C. Temptation of the harem: Royal endowment (1:8–17)
   D. Response of the woman: Exclusive love (2:1–6)
   E. The oath-curse (2:7)
II. The Arrival of True Love (2:8–3:5)
   A. Arrival of the shepherd (2:8–9a)
   B. The shepherd locked out of the harem (2:9b)
   C. The shepherd calls the woman to return (2:10–15)
   D. The woman vows commitment: Go and wait for me (2:16–17)
   E. The woman's dream of longing and desire (3:1–4)
   F. The oath-curse (3:5)
III. The Arrival of Solomon (3:6–8:4)
   A. Subsection one: The temptation of Solomon (3:6–5:8)
      1. Solomon's arrival (3:6)
      2. Solomon's royal retinue (3:7–10)
      3. Virgins assemble (3:11)
      4. Solomon's first temptation (4:1–5:1)
      5. The woman's dream of longing and desire (5:2–7)
      6. The oath-request (5:8)
   B. Subsection two: The temptation of the harem (5:9–8:4)
      1. The harem's question: Why? (5:9)
      2. The woman's response: Desire (5:10–16)
      3. The harem's question: Where? (6:1)
      4. The woman's response: Commitment (6:2–3)
      5. Solomon's second temptation (6:4–10)
      6. The woman's response: Leave the harem (6:11–12)
      7. Solomon's third temptation (6:13[7:1 Heb.]–7:10a)
      8. The woman's response: Commitment and desire (7:10b)
      9. The woman calls the shepherd to return (7:11–8:3)
      10. The oath-curse (8:4)
IV. The Arrival of the Woman (8:5–14)
   A. Arrival of the woman with the shepherd (8:5)
   B. Wisdom instruction (8:6–10)
   C. Rejection of Solomon and harem life (8:11–12)
   D. Invitation to the wisdom of biblical marriage (8:13–14)

APPROACHING THE NEW TESTAMENT

The wisdom of love and marriage presented in the Song of Songs connects with the New Testament in several significant ways. First, both the Song and the New Testament affirm and promote marriage as an exclusive, covenantal relationship between one man and one woman (Matt. 5:27–32; Mark 10:8; 1 Cor. 6:16; 7:1–15; Eph. 5:31). Additionally, the New Testament also affirms that the marriage relationship should be both rock solid and white hot (1 Cor. 7:1–15; Heb. 13:14) and that together these realities protect and sustain the marriage relationship.

It is important to understand that the New Testament does not deny or diminish the importance of our physical bodies. In fact, the bodily resurrection of Jesus affirms their importance. Our bodies are temples of the Holy Spirit, and so we are taught, "Flee from sexual immorality. Every other sin a person commits is outside the body, but the sexually immoral person sins against his own body. Or do you not know that your body is a temple of the Holy Spirit within you, whom you have from God? You are not your own, for you were bought with a price. So glorify God in your body" (1 Cor. 6:18–20 ESV). For this reason, the wisdom of the New Testament demands that a Christian must not marry a non-Christian: "Do not be unequally yoked with unbelievers. For what partnership has righteousness with lawlessness? Or what fellowship has light with darkness?" (2 Cor. 6:14 ESV).

The importance of the marriage covenant is also highlighted by its use as a picture of the relationship between Yahweh and Israel in the Old Testament (Isa. 50:1; 54:4–8; 62:5; Jer. 2:2, 32–33; Ezekiel 16; Hosea 1–3) and between Christ and the church in the New (Eph. 5:22–32). This covenantal symbolism is intentional, typological, and rooted in the earliest parts of Scripture. It is no accident that the creation account in Genesis 2 climaxes on day six with the creation of the woman and the marriage covenant. This first marriage in the first creation points beyond itself to the ultimate marriage in the new creation, where both the New Jerusalem and the people of God are described as the bride of Christ: "Hallelujah! For our Lord God Almighty reigns. Let us rejoice and be glad and give him glory! For the wedding of the Lamb has come, and his bride has made herself ready" (Rev. 19:6b–7 NIV); "I saw the Holy City, the New Jerusalem, coming down out of heaven from God, prepared as a bride beautifully dressed for her husband" (Rev. 21:2 NIV; cf. 21:19; 22:17). The goodness and joy of marriage and sexuality anticipate the satisfaction, fulfillment, and wholeness of life in the coming kingdom (Song 8:10b; Rev. 21:1–4). In this way, the wisdom of the Song is not limited to the realities of this fallen world, nor does its instruction apply only to those who are engaged or married. As wisdom literature, even the Song of Songs can make us "wise for salvation through faith in Christ Jesus" (2 Tim. 3:15b ESV).

SELECT BIBLIOGRAPHY

Brady, Gary. *Heavenly Love: The Song of Songs Simply Explained*. Welwyn Commentary. Darlington, UK: Evangelical Press, 2006.

Carr, D. M. "The Song of Songs as a Microcosm of the Canonization and Decanonization Process." In *Canonization and Decanonization: Papers Presented to the International Conference of the Leiden Institute for the Study of Religions (LISOR), Held at Leiden 9–10 January 1997*, edited by A. van der Kooij and K. van der Toorn, with an annotated bibliography compiled by J. A. M. Snoek, 173–89. SHR 82. Leiden: Brill, 1998.

Curtis, Edward M. *Ecclesiastes and Song of Songs*. Teach the Text Commentary. Grand Rapids, MI: Baker, 2013.

Duguid, Iain M. *The Song of Songs: An Introduction and Commentary*. TOTC 19. Downers Grove, IL: InterVarsity Press, 2015.

Fishbane, Michael A. *Song of Songs: The Traditional Hebrew Text with the New JPS Translation*. JPS Bible Commentary. Philadelphia: Jewish Publication Society, 2015.

Garrett, Duane A. *Proverbs, Ecclesiastes, Song of Songs*. NAC 14. Nashville: Broadman, 1993.

———. *Song of Songs*. In *Song of Songs / Lamentations*, by Duane A. Garrett and Paul R. House. WBC 23B. Nashville: Thomas Nelson, 2004.

Griffiths, Paul J. *Song of Songs*. BTCB. Grand Rapids, MI: Brazos, 2011.

Hamilton, James M., Jr. *Song of Songs: A Biblical-Theological, Allegorical, Christological Interpretation*. Fearn, Ross-shire, Scotland: Christian Focus, 2015.

Hess, Richard S. *Song of Songs*. BCOTWP. Grand Rapids, MI: Baker Academic, 2005.

Jenson, Robert W. *Song of Songs*. IBC. Louisville: John Knox, 2005.

Longman, Tremper, III. *Song of Songs*. NICOT. Grand Rapids, MI: Eerdmans, 2001.

Noegel, Scott B., and Gary A. Rendsburg. *Solomon's Vineyard: Literary and Linguistic Studies in the Song of Songs*. AIL 1. Atlanta: Society of Biblical Literature, 2009.

O'Donnell, Douglas Sean. *The Song of Solomon: An Invitation to Intimacy*. Preaching the Word. Wheaton: Crossway, 2012.

Pope, Marvin H. *Song of Songs: A New Translation with Introduction and Commentary*. AB 7C. Garden City, NY: Doubleday, 1977.

Provan, Iain W. *Ecclesiastes, Song of Songs*. NIVAC. Grand Rapids, MI: Zondervan, 2001.

Stoop-van Paridon, P. W. T. *The Song of Songs: A Philological Analysis of the Hebrew Book* שִׁיר הַשִּׁירִים. ANESSup 17. Louvain: Peeters, 2005.

Webb, Barry G. *Five Festal Garments: Christian Reflections on the Song of Songs, Ruth, Lamentations, Ecclesiastes, and Esther*. NSBT 10. Downers Grove, IL: InterVarsity Press, 2000.

19

Ecclesiastes

Richard P. Belcher Jr.

INTRODUCTION

The book of Ecclesiastes challenges the modern reader. The fact that commentaries set forth several different ways to interpret this book is not surprising when its contents are examined. The book includes both positive and negative statements, and how those statements relate to one another is important but complicated. Some statements in the book also appear to be unorthodox, such as when the author denies that the wise one is any different from the fool (Eccles. 2:13–17), that human beings have any advantage over animals (3:19–21), or that there is any difference between the righteous and the wicked (9:1–2). The author refers to God only periodically throughout the book, but it is not certain that he brings God into the discussion in order to solve the problems with which he is wrestling (see 3:17–21; 9:1–2). Such are the challenges that await the student of Ecclesiastes.

BACKGROUND ISSUES

The Authorship of Ecclesiastes

Although there is little consensus on the major introductory issues related to Ecclesiastes, there appears to be substantial agreement that Solomon is *not* the author of the book. The major arguments *for* Solomonic authorship include the description of the author as "the son of David, king in Jerusalem" (1:1) and the statement "I . . . have been king over Israel in Jerusalem" (1:12). Solomon was the only immediate son of David who was king over (all) Israel reigning in Jerusalem. In fact, the phrase "son of David" refers to a biological son of David whenever it is used in the Old Testament.[1]

---

[1] Eric S. Christianson, *A Time to Tell: Narrative Strategies in Ecclesiastes*, JSOTSup 280 (Sheffield: Sheffield Academic Press, 1998), 129.

Additionally, the way the author describes his search in chapter 2 sets forth opportunities and activities available only to a king like Solomon: unrivaled wisdom (1:16), wealth in abundance (2:8), a tremendous retinue of servants (2:7), opportunities for carnal pleasure (2:3), and extensive building activities (2:4–6).

Although the text seems to affirm Solomonic authorship, most recent commentators have challenged this view for a variety of reasons. The statement in 1:16 presents some difficulty: "I have acquired great wisdom, surpassing all who were over Jerusalem before me." The problem with this statement is that there were few who reigned in Jerusalem before Solomon to whom he could compare his surpassing wisdom. Thus some scholars understand this statement to be a literary device, which is meant to provide a loose association with Solomon but not any strict identification.[2] On the other hand, the statement in 1:16 may be a way to express Solomon's unsurpassed wisdom. The phrase "all who were . . . before" can refer to someone who excels in something (cf. 1 Kings 14:9; 16:25, 30). In fact, it is used of Jeroboam negatively in this way in 1 Kings 14:9. There were not many kings before Jeroboam with whom to compare him, so the emphasis is likely on his exceptional wickedness in setting up the system of false worship in the northern kingdom subsequent to the division of Israel.[3] The emphasis in Ecclesiastes 1:16; 2:7; and 2:9 is on the unsurpassed wisdom and wealth of the narrator. This fits the picture of Solomon in 1 Kings 3:12, where something similar to Ecclesiastes 1:16 is stated: "none like you has been before you and none like you shall arise after you."

Another argument against Solomon is that the author does not speak as a king throughout the whole book. For example, in Ecclesiastes 4:1–3 the author laments all the oppression in the world and that there is no one to comfort the oppressed. Certainly a powerful king like Solomon could have done something to help the destitute. Additionally, 5:8–9 protests against the king and certain royal policies, and 10:20 assumes that the king is a suspicious bully. These statements seem to come from someone other than a king.[4] Thus, the author presents himself as Solomon at the beginning of the book, but other statements seem to call Solomonic authorship into question. In response, some have suggested that a king could be aware of mismanagement and oppression even within his own kingdom. The fact that no statement appears in 4:1–3 to rectify the oppression may suggest that in this case he is focused on observing what is taking place in the kingdom in order to draw conclusions concerning the futility of life. If the king himself is struggling with the futility of life, he might not have the energy or desire to deal with such oppression. Plus, we do know that Solomon mistreated his subjects in the latter part of his reign (1 Kings 12:14).

Some have suggested that the book of Ecclesiastes reflects a historical period when things were not going well for Israel, which may explain the somber mood of the book. Friedrich Delitzsch situates the book in the Persian period of the fifth

---

[2] Tremper Longman III, *The Book of Ecclesiastes*, NICOT (Grand Rapids, MI: Eerdmans, 1998), 57–58.
[3] Gleason L. Archer Jr., *A Survey of Old Testament Introduction* (Chicago: Moody Press, 1974), 485.
[4] Longman, *Ecclesiastes*, 5–6.

century BC,[5] as does C. L. Seow, based on certain economic realities reflected in the book.[6] Others argue that Qohelet (the Hebrew designation for the author of the book) was a Palestinian Jew of the third century heavily influenced by Greek thought. This would explain the more personal tone of the book and the abstract thinking, both of which are uncharacteristic of other wisdom literature in Scripture.[7] However, it is important to understand that none of the arguments situating Ecclesiastes in a certain historical time period are entirely conclusive. The somber tone of the book may have more to do with the outlook of the author than the particular period in which he lived. Thus, there is currently no consensus on the setting of Ecclesiastes due to the inconclusive nature of the arguments that attempt to prove literary or cultural dependence.[8]

The Hebrew of Ecclesiastes

The most compelling argument for a post-Solomonic date for Ecclesiastes is the nature of the Hebrew language used in the book. Delitzsch's statement has become famous: "If the book of Koheleth were of old Solomonic origin, then there is no history of the Hebrew language." He bases his argument on the use of rare words and words that are associated with later biblical Hebrew, including Aramaisms.[9] A. Schoors has argued that twenty-four different linguistic features demonstrate that the language of Ecclesiastes fits best into the postexilic period and that it shows traits of later Mishnaic Hebrew.[10] As such, most scholars argue that the Hebrew of Ecclesiastes does not fit the Hebrew of the preexilic period (usually designated Standard Biblical Hebrew) but is more characteristic of the Hebrew after the exile (commonly designated Late Biblical Hebrew). The language and style of the book is thought to represent the latest stage in the development of Hebrew found in the Bible. If this is truly the case, then Solomon could not have written the book.

The dominant view concerning the development of the Hebrew language from Standard Biblical Hebrew to Late Biblical Hebrew characterizes preexilic Hebrew as unduly monolithic, which then developed into postexilic Hebrew. Thus any Hebrew that is not in accord with Standard Biblical Hebrew (preexilic) either is postexilic or, if early, belongs to northern Israel as a distinctive dialect, much like the dialectical differences between northern and southern English in the United States.[11] Because Ecclesiastes does not match the characteristics of preexilic Hebrew as presented in this scenario, most scholars understand it to be postexilic and representative of Late Biblical Hebrew.

[5] Friedrich Delitzsch, *Ecclesiastes*, in *Commentary on the Old Testament*, vol. 6, *Proverbs, Ecclesiastes, Song of Solomon* (1872; repr., Grand Rapids, MI: Eerdmans, 1978), 212–15.

[6] C. L. Seow, *Ecclesiastes: A New Translation with Introduction and Commentary*, AB 18C (New York: Doubleday, 1997), 21–29.

[7] Michael V. Fox, *A Time to Tear Down and a Time to Build Up: A Rereading of Ecclesiastes* (Grand Rapids, MI: Eerdmans, 1999), 6–8.

[8] Roland E. Murphy, *Ecclesiastes*, WBC 23A (Dallas: Word, 1992), xlii.

[9] Delitzsch, *Ecclesiastes*, 6:190–99.

[10] A. Schoors, *The Preacher Sought to Find Pleasing Words: A Study of the Language of Qoheleth*, Part 2, *Vocabulary*, OLA 143 (Leuven: Peeters, 1992). See also C. L. Seow, "Linguistic Evidence and the Dating of Qohelet," *JBL* 115, no. 4 (1996): 650–54.

[11] Ian Young, "Evidence of Diversity in Pre-Exilic Judahite Hebrew," *HS* 38 (1997): 7–20.

The question is not whether there is a standard preexilic Hebrew that can be compared with a later postexilic Hebrew. Clearly one can demonstrate linguistic and grammatical developments between the two.[12] Rather, the question is whether Standard Biblical Hebrew represents the only possible linguistic option before the exile. Does the evidence allow for more diversity within the Hebrew language before the exile? Might other factors explain the language of Ecclesiastes? What if Standard (preexilic) Hebrew was not a widespread monolithic phenomenon but originated in the South during the united kingdom when a central administration was needed?

Substantial evidence supports a diverse linguistic situation in the development of Hebrew in the land of Canaan.[13] A diverse group of people lived in the area, and there is evidence that the people spoke different languages and dialects (Judg. 12:1–6).[14] Standard (preexilic) Hebrew appears to have originated in the early monarchy when the need for a central administration arose; thus, it is not to be identified with any particular dialect of the area. The standard prose that developed into this form of preexilic Hebrew likely sought to avoid Aramaic influences. However, since Israel and Aram certainly came in contact as early as 1100 BC, one should expect to find Aramaic influence before the exile. Thus Aramaic influence cannot be used to argue that a text is late. Additionally, in light of the fact that the Philistines were from the Aegean area and that the Assyrians had settled in Judah in the middle of the eighth century, Greek and Persian loanwords cannot be used to date a text as late on that basis alone. The language of Ecclesiastes may represent a local, literary dialect, exhibiting a simplified syntax distinct from the official Standard Biblical Hebrew. Thus, the language of Ecclesiastes may fit into a more diverse language situation characteristic of the preexilic period.[15] If this analysis of diversity in preexilic Hebrew is correct, then the Hebrew of Ecclesiastes cannot be used conclusively to date the book as a postexilic composition. One might even expect a book of a particular individual's personal reflections to be written in a less official form of the language.

STRUCTURE AND OUTLINE

Literary Analysis

Other important questions that relate to the authorship and interpretation of the book concern literary genre and the designation Qohelet. These questions also affect our understanding of the book's structure. In a discussion of the genre of Ecclesiastes, it is important to recognize that the book contains two types of writing. The first-person account of the author (1:12–12:7) is framed by a third-person prologue (1:1–11) and a third-person epilogue (12:8–14). The author introduces himself as Qohelet in

---

[12] Mark F. Rooker, *Biblical Hebrew in Transition: The Language of the Book of Ezekiel*, JSOTSup 90 (Sheffield: Sheffield Academic Press, 1990).
[13] Ian Young, *Diversity in Pre-exilic Hebrew*, FAT 5 (Tubingen: J. C. B. Mohr, 1993).
[14] Gary A. Rendsburg, *Diglossia in Ancient Hebrew*, AOS 72 (New Haven, CT: American Oriental Society, 1990), and "Morphological Evidence for Regional Dialects in Ancient Hebrew," in *Linguistics and Biblical Hebrew*, ed. Walter Ray Bodine (Winona Lake, IN: Eisenbrauns, 1992), 65–88.
[15] Ian Young, *Diversity in Pre-exilic Hebrew*; Ian Young and Robert Rezetko, *Linguistic Dating of Biblical Texts*, with the assistance of Martin Ehrensvärd, 2 vols. (London: Equinox, 2008).

1:12, which begins the first-person discourse. One might expect the book to begin with the self-introduction of 1:12, but someone else presents Qohelet's words (1:1) and then comments on them (12:9–14). Thus the terminology used to refer to the book becomes very important in order to avoid misunderstanding. The term Ecclesiastes refers to the whole book. The term Qohelet refers to the first-person discourse (1:12–12:7) framed by the third-person discourses.

There is currently no consensus on the genre of the book.[16] Ecclesiastes has been compared to many texts from the ancient Near East, including the Egyptian royal testaments,[17] the West Semitic royal inscriptions,[18] and Akkadian fictional autobiographies.[19] However, Ecclesiastes fits no single genre category from the ancient Near East neatly.[20] One prominent characterization of Ecclesiastes is "autobiography," which has been defined as "an account of the life (or part thereof) of an individual written by the individual himself." It is normally written in the first person and includes reminiscences of the individual's past.[21] Accordingly, Ecclesiastes can be identified as an autobiography cast in a narrative frame.[22]

The fact that the first-person account of Qohelet is framed by third-person narration raises significant questions that impact the interpretation of the book. For example, what is the relationship between the first-person autobiography (1:12–12:7) and the third-person framework (1:1–11; 12:8–14)? Some have suggested that the author of the epilogue (12:8–14) is also responsible for the first-person discourse, meaning that one person wrote the whole work.[23] However, it seems better to understand the third-person frame to be from a different hand. This view is supported by the shift from the first person to the third person in the epilogue and by the fact that the epilogue comments on the words of Qohelet. Although it is possible that someone could comment on his own work and speak about himself in the third person, it is not likely one would do so in the middle of a first-person sentence, as in 7:27, where there is a third-person intrusion ("Qohelet says" [my trans.]).[24]

Given this literary analysis, we suggest the following outline for Ecclesiastes:

    I. Prologue: Exploration of the Nature of the World (1:1–11)
   II. Qohelet's Autobiography (1:12–12:7)
      A. The search for meaning under the sun (1:12–6:12)
      B. Human limitation concerning knowledge (7:1–12:7)
  III. Epilogue: Evaluation of the Work (12:8–14)

---

[16] For a fuller discussion of genre and other introductory issues related to Ecclesiastes, see Richard P. Belcher Jr., *A Study Commentary on Ecclesiastes*, EP Study Commentary (Darlington, UK: Evangelical Press, 2014).

[17] Roland E. Murphy, *The Tree of Life: An Exploration of Biblical Wisdom*, 3rd ed. (Grand Rapids, MI: Eerdmans, 2002), 164–65.

[18] Y. V. Koh, *Royal Autobiography in the Book of Qoheleth*, BZAW 369 (Berlin: de Gruyter, 2006), 73–77.

[19] Tremper Longman III, *Fictional Akkadian Autobiography: A Generic and Comparative Study* (Winona Lake, IN: Eisenbrauns, 1991), 103–16.

[20] This is the conclusion of Koh, who offers an excellent discussion of the different possibilities for the genre of Ecclesiastes, especially literature that has a royal figure. *Royal Autobiography*, 72.

[21] Longman, *Fictional Akkadian Autobiography*, 40–41.

[22] Craig G. Bartholomew, *Reading Ecclesiastes: Old Testament Exegesis and Hermeneutical Theory*, AnBib 139 (Rome: Editrice Pontificio Istituto Biblico, 1998), 157; Longman, *Ecclesiastes*, 17.

[23] Delitzsch, *Ecclesiastes*, 6:429–30.

[24] Michael V. Fox, "Frame-Narrative and Composition in the Book of Qohelet," *HUCA* 48 (1977): 84.

The Term Qohelet

The term Qohelet (קֹהֶלֶת) is used to designate the author of the first-person discourse. It occurs in 1:1, 2, 12; 7:27; 12:8, 9, and 10. Most identify this expression as a feminine singular participle from the verb קהל, which means "to assemble." The most common translation is "preacher," which designates someone who gathers people into an assembly to speak to them. Another possibility is "teacher," which is more in line with the statement in 12:9 that Qohelet taught the people. Perhaps an even better option is to leave the term untranslated, simply Qohelet.

But why is the name Qohelet used if Solomon is the author? One suggestion is that Qohelet represents a new name given to Solomon later in his life after he repented from earlier sins.[25] However, there is no evidence that Solomon repented later in life, and Ecclesiastes is no confession of sin. Some argue that the author adopted this royal persona in order to demonstrate that not even Solomon would have fared any better in his search for meaning. However, the use of the term Qohelet suggests that the author is really not Solomon.[26] If the author wanted us to believe that he was Solomon, would he not simply have used the name Solomon throughout? However, if Solomon had written the first-person discourse during the period of his life when his wives had turned his heart away from the Lord (1 Kings 11:1–8), then this might explain the struggle in the book and what appears to be a drifting away from true wisdom. If Solomon, who had more wisdom than anyone, fell prey to the despair presented in the book, then it could happen to anyone.

Different Approaches to Ecclesiastes

A passage that encapsulates the difficulty of interpreting Ecclesiastes is 8:11–15. This text seems to outright contradict itself regarding whether the righteous and the wicked get their just rewards.[27] In 8:11 Qohelet observes that punishments for evil are often delayed, and in 8:12a he recognizes that sinners do evil and live long lives. But then he states just the opposite in 8:12b–13: it will not be well with the wicked, and his days will not be prolonged. Then in 8:14 Qohelet notes that the righteous are not rewarded for their righteousness and the wicked are not rewarded for their wickedness; rather, the righteous get what the wicked deserve and the wicked get what the righteous deserve. This is followed by a call to enjoyment in 8:15. The way that commentators handle the tension in these verses offers a small window into how they understand the message of the book as a whole.

---

[25] Charles Bridges, *A Commentary on Ecclesiastes*, Geneva Series (1860; repr., Edinburgh: Banner of Truth, 1985), ix–x, 1.

[26] Longman, *Ecclesiastes*, 6–7.

[27] The relationship between a person's deeds and the consequences of those deeds is called divine retribution. Qohelet struggles with the breakdown of the relationship between deeds and consequences, which makes it appear that the wicked do not get what they deserve. This raises questions concerning God's justice. For further discussion see Richard P. Belcher Jr., "Divine Retribution in Ecclesiastes: An Analysis of the Deed-Consequence Relationship with Implications for the Interpretation of the Book" (PhD diss., Westminster Theological Seminary, 2000).

The Heterodox Qohelet

Some have argued that Qohelet deviated from orthodox wisdom teaching and rejected the claim that wisdom could secure one's existence.[28] In this view, the positive statements in the book are to be understood as dogmatic corrections made by another hand in order to bring the message of Qohelet more in line with traditional wisdom thinking. Thus, several editors and viewpoints may appear in the first-person discourse. The first editor, or redactor, admired the thinking of Qohelet and so did not change anything. A second redactor was disturbed by Qohelet because it did not support traditional wisdom thinking, and thus he set out to make orthodox corrections to the work. In the example of 8:12–14, whereas 8:12a and 8:14 appear to deny the deed-consequence relationship, 8:12b–13 represent an orthodox correction validating that relationship.[29] However, one problem with this approach is that the corrective glosses do not really fulfill their intended purpose because the pessimistic statements still dominate the passage. For example, in 8:11–14, the denial of retribution (8:12a, 14) gets the last word, not the corrective gloss (8:12b–13). This also raises the question of why the redactors copied the book to begin with instead of suppressing it altogether.[30]

Others argue for some kind of dialogue in the book between Qohelet and traditional wisdom. Thus 8:12b–13 represents a quotation of traditional wisdom from which Qohelet dissents in 8:12a and 8:14–15.[31] One problem with the quotation view, however, is that clear criteria for identifying quotations do not exist. It is hard to identify a quotation unless there is some introductory statement, such as, "the sages say."[32]

The Orthodox Qohelet

This approach argues that the views of Qohelet agree fully with the views expressed in the book of Proverbs and that the statement in the epilogue "fear God and keep his commandments" (Eccles. 12:13) is the message of Qohelet himself. With this approach, the positive statements take precedence over the negative statements. Many early commentators on Ecclesiastes, both patristic and Jewish, took this view.[33]

Modern commentators who take this view include R. N. Whybray, Michael Eaton, Bruce Waltke, and Graham Ogden. For example, Eaton calls Ecclesiastes an essay in apologetics, which "defends the life of faith in a generous God by pointing to the grimness of the alternatives." God was left out of the picture for much of the

---

[28] James L. Crenshaw, *Ecclesiastes*, OTL (Philadelphia: Westminster, 1987); George A. Barton, *A Critical and Exegetical Commentary on the Book of Ecclesiastes*, ICC (1908; repr., Edinburgh: T&T Clark, 1971).

[29] Barton, *Ecclesiastes*, 45–46.

[30] Fox, *Rereading Ecclesiastes*, 18–19.

[31] Robert Gordis, *Koheleth, the Man and His World: A Study of Ecclesiastes* (New York: Bloch, 1955), 28, 95–96, 101–8, 287; Gordis, "Quotations in Wisdom Literature," *JQR* 30, no. 2 (1939): 123–47; see also Murphy, *Ecclesiastes*.

[32] Fox, *Rereading Ecclesiastes*, 20. See also Fox, "The Identification of Quotations in Biblical Literature," *ZAW* 92, no. 3 (1980): 416–31.

[33] Peter S. Knobel, *The Targum of Qoheleth*, in vol. 15 of *The Aramaic Bible*, ed. Martin McNamara (Collegeville, MN: Liturgical Press, 1991). Targums were Aramaic translations of the Hebrew text read in the synagogue alongside the reading of the Hebrew for people who no longer understood Hebrew. Some of these translations were not very literal. See also John Jarick, *Gregory Thaumaturgos' Paraphrase of Ecclesiastes*, SCS 29 (Atlanta: Scholars Press, 1990).

argument, which led to a very pessimistic view of life. However, God was suddenly introduced, and the pessimism gave way to joy and purpose. Instead of beginning with the premise of the fear of "the LORD" (hereafter Yahweh), Qohelet argued as a secularist in order to show that such a starting point would lead to meaningless-ness. The contradictions in the book draw our attention to Qohelet's viewpoint of faith expressed in 8:12b–13. Having shown the bankruptcy of the secularist approach, Qohelet allows the heavenly perspective to shine through in 8:12b–13. The epilogue summarizes the message of Qohelet and describes the implications of the life of faith.[34]

The main problem with the more positive view of the message of Qohelet is that the positive statements in the book are given precedence over the negative state-ments, even when the text seems to indicate the opposite. Although the positive calls to enjoyment increase in urgency as one reads the book, it is doubtful that they should be seen as theological affirmations of faith (see "The Calls to Enjoyment" on p. 451). The target of Qohelet is not secularism but the failure of wisdom by itself to produce what was promised. Qohelet is not beginning with secularism in order to demonstrate where it will lead. Rather, he engages in a sober struggle with wis-dom in order to understand what he observes in life. Thus, it is difficult to interpret 8:12b–13 as "winning the day" when that positive statement is surrounded by 8:12a and 8:14. Qohelet could have written the text differently, but he gave the negative statements the final word. It is thus difficult to see how 8:12b–13 would constitute Qohelet's response of faith.[35]

The Struggling Qohelet

The views considered under this heading allow the tensions expressed by Qohelet to stand without resolution. These tensions evidence the honest struggles experienced by Qohelet. The major question is which side of the tension ultimately wins out in 1:12–12:7.

Craig Bartholomew examines Ecclesiastes from a narrative standpoint. He argues that the juxtaposition of vanity (or meaninglessness) and the calls to enjoyment, contradictory answers given by Qohelet, create a gap that requires filling.[36] Eccle-siastes 8:11–14 juxtaposes the positive statements of 8:12b–13 with the negative statements of 8:11–12a and 8:14, and that juxtaposition creates a gap filled only at the end of the book by 12:13–14. Bartholomew argues that the narrator reads Qohelet positively and so arrives at a point of agreement with Qohelet in the state-ment "fear God and keep his commandments."[37]

Tremper Longman understands Qohelet to be a wisdom teacher struggling with

---

[34] Michael A. Eaton, *Ecclesiastes: An Introduction and Commentary*, TOTC 16 (Downers Grove, IL: InterVarsity Press, 1983), 44–45, 122–23, 156.

[35] Although Bruce Waltke recognizes the honest struggle that Qohelet is experiencing, he quotes Eccles. 8:11–13, omitting 8:14, and declares that Qohelet confesses faith against contrary evidence. Bruce K. Waltke, *An Old Testament Theology: An Exegetical, Canonical, and Thematic Approach*, with Charles Yu (Grand Rapids, MI: Zondervan, 2007), 961.

[36] Bartholomew, *Reading Ecclesiastes*, 238; Bartholomew, *Ecclesiastes*, BCOTWP (Grand Rapids, MI: Baker Academic, 2009), 79–82.

[37] Bartholomew, *Reading Ecclesiastes*, 170, 248–54.

the normative traditions of his people represented in the book of Proverbs. Pessimism permeates the book because Qohelet takes an "under the sun" approach, a limited perspective that fails to consider heavenly realities. In 8:12–15 Qohelet contradicts in 8:13 what he stated in 8:12a. In 8:12b–13 he states the traditional view of divine retribution, which Qohelet does not affirm, for he clearly questions that view in 8:14. Thus, Qohelet is a confused wise man whose thoughts are filled with tensions and contradictions as he struggles with traditional wisdom thinking. The epilogue sets forth a view contradicting Qohelet, identifying the dangers of speculative wisdom, and reinforcing the normative teaching of the Old Testament.[38]

Michael Fox argues that one must recognize the contradictions in the thought of Qohelet in order to bring the book's central concern into focus: the problem of the meaning of life. The contradictions Qohelet observes must be allowed to stand because they identify the obvious problems encountered in life. In 8:12–14 Qohelet describes both sides of an apparent tension without resolving them. He understands the principle of retribution (8:12b–13) and does not deny it, but he also recognizes that some situations violate the principle (8:11, 14).[39] The advice to "fear God and keep his commandments" (12:13–14) echoes fundamental elements of Qohelet's teaching with dogmatic certainty that is contrasted with the uncertainty of all knowledge in Qohelet. Such a conclusion becomes a call to tolerate the expression of unorthodox opinion, which allows everything to be heard as long as one finally reaches the orthodox conclusion.[40]

Bartholomew's approach provides a rationale for the epilogue that bridges the gap created by the tensions presented in the book. Although this approach may work on a broad scale for Ecclesiastes, it is not clear how it might work itself out in individual passages.[41] For example, in 8:11–15, a juxtaposition appears between sinners who will be punished with short life over against sinners who will not be punished with short life. One could argue that this disparity is ameliorated by 8:15, the call to enjoyment. Or when Qohelet juxtaposes wickedness in 3:16 with God's judgment in 3:17, the apparent disparity is amended by the negative assertions that humans are not different from beasts in 3:18–21. In other words, why does one have to wait until 12:13–14 for the gap to be filled? In most passages the negative assertions get the last word (as in 8:11–14). Both Longman and Fox recognize that a key element to Qohelet's thinking is the unresolved tension in his thought. In the final analysis, the best approach is to understand that Qohelet does not subordinate the anomalies of life and the breakdown of the principle of retribution to a higher principle for the sake of resolution. The troubles of life so dominate his thinking that he calls into question traditional thinking. The author of the epilogue, however, subverts Qohelet when he brings in the commandments and secret judgment of God (12:13–14).

---

[38] Longman, *Ecclesiastes*, 32–39.
[39] Fox, *Rereading Ecclesiastes*, 3, 51, 55–56, 134.
[40] Fox, "Frame-Narrative," 103–4.
[41] It is difficult to find clear statements in Bartholomew on how the gaps are to be filled in relationship to specific passages. *Ecclesiastes*, 81–82. After reading his book *Reading Ecclesiastes*, one would expect that his commentary on Ecclesiastes would include an application of this method to the book, but he discusses the role of gaps in only a few places.

MESSAGE AND THEOLOGY

The interpreter of Ecclesiastes needs to make several important exegetical decisions when approaching the book, decisions that will determine how the book is understood and used in the church. However, a number of hermeneutical keys help unlock the message of the book for Christians.

The Prologue

Several such keys are found in the prologue of the book (1:1–11). This section consists of the superscription (1:1), which announces the one who will be speaking in 1:12–12:7; the motto (1:2); the key question (1:3); and an introductory poem that elaborates on the motto (1:4–11). The purpose of the prologue is to introduce Qohelet and to prepare readers for Qohelet's message.

The Meaning of the Hebrew Word הֶבֶל *(hebel)*

The motto of the book contains the important Hebrew word הֶבֶל (*hebel*), which is used more than any other word in the book and represents Qohelet's primary affirmation regarding life. It occurs in a superlative construction in the motto that frames the book (1:2; 12:8). This superlative construction indicates something that is complete, absolute, and unqualified.[42] It is also the word that Qohelet keeps coming back to as he examines various aspects of life. But what does Qohelet mean by *hebel*?

The basic meaning of *hebel* is "breath," as seen in its use in Isaiah 57:13, where it parallels "wind" (רוּחַ). Most of the time it is used metaphorically. Temporally, it stresses the idea that something is fleeting or transient, like breath.[43] In Ecclesiastes, however, it may be best to understand *hebel* in the sense of significance. Qohelet wrestles with more than the fleeting nature of life. He also wrestles with the fact that life does not work the way it should, which constitutes the real heart of his struggle. As such, some understand *hebel* to mean "incomprehensible," which stresses that life is hard to understand. In this sense *hebel* may be translated as "mystery" or "enigma."[44] Another nuance of *hebel* as "incomprehensible" is the sense that life is not just hard to understand but altogether impossible to understand (8:17). Here the idea of *hebel* is expressed by the English translation "vanity," in the sense of futile, purposeless, or meaningless. Qohelet uses *hebel* to refer to scenarios where there is a disparity between rational expectations and actual consequences.[45] The view that *hebel* connotes "futility" is an old view, which has the support of certain ancient versions (the Greek Septuagint and its daughter translation, the Latin Vulgate), as well as many English translations (ESV, KJV, NASB, NIV, NKJV, NRSV). Both Christianson and Longman closely examine

[42] R. N. Whybray, *Ecclesiastes: Based on the Revised Standard Version*, NCB (Grand Rapids, MI: Eerdmans, 1989), 34–35.

[43] Daniel C. Fredericks, *Coping with Transience: Ecclesiastes on Brevity in Life*, BibSem 18 (Sheffield: JSOT Press, 1993), 30; Fredericks, *Ecclesiastes*, in *Ecclesiastes and the Song of Songs*, by Daniel C. Fredericks and Daniel J. Estes, ApOTC 16 (Downers Grove, IL: InterVarsity Press, 2010), 27–28.

[44] Staples translates הֶבֶל as "mystery," and Ogden uses "enigmatic" in the sense that life is not fully comprehensible. W. E. Staples, "Vanity of Vanities," *CJT* 1, no. 3 (1955): 143; Graham S. Ogden, *Qoheleth*, Readings—A New Biblical Commentary (Sheffield, JSOT Press, 1987), 17.

[45] Fox, *Rereading Ecclesiastes*, 36–42.

the use of *hebel* outside Ecclesiastes and conclude that it refers to something obviously false, futile, or empty.[46] This is perhaps the best way to understand *hebel* in Ecclesiastes.

The Main Question of the Book

The main question of the book appears in Ecclesiastes 1:3, "What profit is there for a person in all his labor for which he labors under the sun?" (my trans.). This basic question is repeated in 2:22; 3:9; and 5:16, and it contains two key ideas that are important for understanding the book.

"Under the sun." The importance of this phrase is demonstrated by the fact that it appears twenty-nine times throughout the book. It focuses the reader's attention on this world over against the heavenly realm, which is God's domain.[47] This phrase is commonly used with the Hebrew verbs translated "to do, make" (which stresses human deeds) and "to see" (which stresses human observation or understanding). The noun "work" (or "toil") also appears with some frequency. These words underscore the experience of humanity while alive, the observable world of work and other human activity. Thus the phrase "under the sun" limits Qohelet's thinking to this earthly life and the horizons of an earthly perspective without recourse to divine revelation or orientation. God is never brought in as a solution to the problems that plague Qohelet, even when there is a clear opportunity to do so, as in 9:1–2. Qohelet thus offers a realistic portrayal of a world that suffers under curse without the adjoining reality of God's providence.[48]

"Profit." The Hebrew word for "profit" (יִתְרוֹן) is a commercial term referring to surplus or gain, but it also has a wider meaning in Ecclesiastes when used with reference to wisdom (2:13). When two things are compared, the term refers to an advantage one thing might have over another thing (2:13; 3:19; 5:8; 6:8, 11; 7:11, 12; 10:10, 11). When יִתְרוֹן ("profit") is used by itself, it refers to any net gain that allows one to get ahead in life[49] or to a desired result produced by effort or labor. It is imperative to see that the basic answer to the question of 1:3 comes in 2:10–11, where a very important distinction appears. Qohelet considers all his activities and concludes that there is no "profit" under the sun. This observation is not a "temperamental over-reaction" or a "temporary disillusionment"[50] because Qohelet never wavers from this answer. However, Qohelet does recognize that even though there is no "profit" (יִתְרוֹן) from labor, there is a "portion" (חֵלֶק) that should be enjoyed. This "portion" (also translated "reward" or "lot") refers to all that one can expect in a world where human activity and effort do not achieve the desired results. Even though there is no profit to labor, one should enjoy the portion that does come from labor, because it is all that one can expect from this life.

---

[46] Christianson, *Narrative Strategies*, 79–80; Longman, *Ecclesiastes*, 62–64.
[47] Fox, *Rereading Ecclesiastes*, 165.
[48] Longman, *Ecclesiastes*, 39, 66.
[49] Fox, *Rereading Ecclesiastes*, 112.
[50] Fredericks, *Transience*, 52–53.

The Introductory Poem (Eccles. 1:4–11)

Scholars debate the meaning of this poem. Does it set forth the wonders of creation or the futility of nature? The tenor of the poem emphasizes the *frustration* of the activities described. In the natural world, the endless actions of the sun, rivers, and wind stress constant movement with no discernible purpose. The sun is weary in its course, the wind goes round and round, and the waters empty into the sea but never fill it. The emphasis is not simply that these natural elements repeat their cycles over and over but also that they have no purpose. So 1:8 describes certain human functions that, in the same way, are not achieving their purpose. The mouth, eyes, and ears fail in their actions. And then there is the important phrase "there is nothing new under the sun." It is difficult to give this phrase a positive meaning. Ecclesiastes 1:9–11 stresses the paralyzing repetition of the past. Thus history is going nowhere, and individuals are destined to live lives that can never achieve true fulfillment. This poem prepares the reader for the ensuing struggle of Qohelet where nothing in life works and everything falls short of expectation.

The Epistemology of Qohelet

It is important to examine the basis for Qohelet's conclusions about life and the role that experience plays in drawing those conclusions. In both Proverbs and Ecclesiastes, observation and reflection play a significant role in forming conclusions about life. For example, in Proverbs 24:30–34, the writer makes observations about a vineyard that was not kept, which is followed by reflection and then instruction (24:32; see also 7:6–23). In Proverbs, however, observation does not yield new knowledge but is used as an occasion for reflection and for the reinforcement of known principles.[51] In other words, the sages do not observe creation from a neutral standpoint but begin with the vantage point of divine revelation.[52] In the book of Proverbs, the question "How do you know?" is answered, "Because I learned it."[53]

Qohelet approaches wisdom differently in Ecclesiastes. He stresses the role of experience and the use of independent rational intelligence for drawing conclusions about life. The first-person (singular) form of the Hebrew verb ראה ("to see") is used twenty-one times in Ecclesiastes.[54] Six times it occurs with the Hebrew word for "all" (1:14; 4:1, 4; 7:15; 8:9, 17), which appears to emphasize the comprehensive nature of his observations. Qohelet investigates by observing, and thus experience is his primary source of knowledge as he observes, reflects, and draws conclusions.[55] Although the book includes statements concerning God and justice that are not based on experience (3:17; 8:12b–13), Qohelet does not use these statements to alter his conclusions based on experience. In Ecclesiastes, the question "How do you know?" is answered, "Because I observed it."[56] On this basis Qohelet's epistemology is best described as

---

[51] Fox, "The Epistemology of the Book of Proverbs," *JBL* 126, no. 4 (2007): 670–73, 683; Fox, *Rereading Ecclesiastes*, 80–81.
[52] Bruce K. Waltke, *Proverbs 1–15*, NICOT (Grand Rapids, MI: Eerdmans, 2004), 55.
[53] Fox, *Rereading Ecclesiastes*, 85.
[54] Eccles. 1:14; 2:3, 13, 24; 3:10, 16, 22; 4:1, 4, 7, 15; 5:12, 17; 6:1; 7:15; 8:9–10, 17; 9:13; 10:5, 7.
[55] Waltke with Yu, *Old Testament Theology*, 959; Fox, *Rereading Ecclesiastes*, 76–77.
[56] Fox, *Rereading Ecclesiastes*, 85.

autonomous, and his use of wisdom to investigate the world means that he will use the powers of reason in light of experience and observation to understand the world. Thus, one cannot assume that wisdom, as used by Qohelet, means the same thing as it does in the book of Proverbs. Rather, Qohelet's use of wisdom appears subversive because it is not rooted in the fear of Yahweh but is based on experience and observation.[57]

In Qohelet's search for meaning, wisdom is both an instrument ("by wisdom," 1:13) and the object of investigation. Qohelet does not privilege wisdom over foolishness but rather uses both in his search for meaning. For example, he states in 1:17, "I applied my heart to know wisdom and to know madness and folly." This approach is different from the method of investigation employed in Proverbs, or even Psalm 1, where God's way is the privileged starting point. Qohelet's starting point helps to explain the analysis of wisdom and folly in Ecclesiastes 2:12–17. He argues that wisdom is better than folly because it helps a person practically in life. But ultimately, wisdom is not better than folly because the fate of the fool will be his own. In considering death, Qohelet concludes that the wise one dies just like the fool (2:16). As such, there can be no guarantee that wisdom will lead to an honorable death after a long life (Gen. 25:8; Prov. 3:16). He laments, "Why then have I been so very wise?" and then asserts his hatred for life (Eccles. 2:15–17).

Everything that Qohelet examines in life fails to satisfy. The wise rarely experience the benefits of wisdom, and the fool rarely experiences the negative consequences of foolishness. This is a problem that Qohelet considers throughout the book (2:15–16, 26; 3:16–21; 5:5; 6:1–2; 7:15–18, 26; 8:10–14; 9:1–6; 11:9). He sees no difference between the wise person and the foolish person because they both ultimately suffer the same fate (2:15–16). Even more startling, humans appear to have no advantage over the animals because they too suffer the same fate (3:16–22). Additionally, there appears to be virtually no distinction between the righteous and the wicked in what people experience in life, for they all suffer the same fate (9:1–6). That same fate is death—particularly its manner, timing, and outcome.

In sum, the fact that the righteous do not always receive the promised blessings in this life and that the wicked do not receive the expected negative consequences constitutes a major reason for Qohelet's conclusion that there is no profit from human activity under the sun. Everything in this life is *hebel* because Qohelet does not take a perspective that reaches above the sun.

The Calls to Enjoyment

The first call to enjoyment comes in 2:24–26 after Qohelet has concluded that there is no profit in labor (2:10–11), that wisdom is ultimately no better than folly (2:13–17), and that he hated both life (2:17) and labor (2:18). He then concludes that there really is nothing better in life than to eat and drink and find enjoyment in life. The calls to enjoyment in Ecclesiastes are part of the "portion" in life that one should enjoy (3:22; 5:19; 9:7), but they are not the answer to life's struggles. They constitute the

---

[57] Bartholomew, *Ecclesiastes*, 269–77. He has an excellent discussion of Qohelet's epistemology.

author's resignation that life does not appear to work out according to expectation. Although the calls to enjoyment seem positive, they also have a negative side. In 2:26 Qohelet makes a statement very similar to Proverbs 13:22: The sinner works hard to gather things for the one who pleases God. However, he follows this observation with the statement, "this also is vanity and a striving after the wind" (Eccles. 2:26). The call to enjoyment in 3:22 comes after Qohelet's assertion that humans and animals share the same final destiny. The call to enjoyment in 5:18–20 ends with the assertion that God gives these good things to people in order to keep them occupied with enjoyment so that they will not contemplate the meaning(lessness) of life. The call to enjoyment in 9:7–10 is longer and more urgent than the other calls to enjoyment, but it ends with the statement that a person must enjoy these things now, with all his or her might, because there is no human activity after death.

Qohelet's View of God

Three passages are important for understanding Qohelet's view of God. The first two passages demonstrate that Qohelet recognizes God's existence but does not allow this reality to solve the so-called problems of life. In 3:16–22 Qohelet reflects on the injustice of life by asserting that wickedness is found in the place of justice (perhaps a reference to a court of law). He offers a theological reflection that God will judge the righteous and the wicked (3:17) but then observes that the destiny of human beings is no different from the destiny of animals (3:18–21). He follows this with a call to enjoyment that ends with a question concerning who can really know what is coming in the future. However, these observations are not brought to bear on the problem of injustice.

In 9:1–2 Qohelet states that the righteous, the wise, and their deeds are in the hand of God. Such a statement should be comforting because the hand of God brings protection and confidence to the righteous and to the wise (Ps. 138:7). However, Qohelet goes on to state that a person cannot really know whether love or hate awaits him in life because there is no difference between the righteous and the wicked. It does not really matter if a person is righteous or wicked, or good or evil, because these things do not appear to make any difference for what a person might experience in life. And so, being in the hand of God has no bearing on what happens to a person in life. In these two passages, Qohelet had the opportunity to show how God could make a difference, but in Qohelet's view, God is not the solution for life's troubles.

Ecclesiastes 5:1–7 is a passage that deals with the worship of God in terms of prayer and making vows. It concludes with a statement on the fear of God. A first inclination might be to understand this passage as teaching the traditional view of the fear of God—that people should approach God with reverence and awe. However, in light of the fact that Qohelet does not consider God a solution to life's difficulties, perhaps his view of God in 5:1–7 is not so positive. Instead of reverence for God, Qohelet may be urging caution before a God who cannot be counted on to solve life's problems. This section of the book (4:1–6:9) deals with the problem of unfulfilled expectations in life relating to political power (4:1–3, 13–16; 5:8–9), labor relationships (4:4–12), and money (5:10–6:9). And this theme of unfulfilled expectations sets the tone for how to understand 5:1–7. The fear of Yahweh in Proverbs represents reverence for God, which leads to a life submitted to God. However, the realities associated with the fear of God in Proverbs are questioned by Qohelet, such as finding the knowledge of God (Prov. 2:5), long life (Prov. 10:27), and strong confidence (Prov. 14:26). It is significant, therefore, that Qohelet never uses the divine name Yahweh ("the LORD") to refer to God, but rather uses the title Elohim, which reinforces the concept of a distant God. Thus, it is possible that Qohelet is expressing caution before a God who is no longer relevant to the problems of life. This view of God would certainly correspond to the period of Solomon's life when his wives had turned his heart away from Yahweh.

The Third-Person Epilogue

Finally, some answers to the problems of life appear in the third-person epilogue of the book (Eccles. 12:8–12). This final section constitutes an evaluation of the words of Qohelet. Although some translation issues affect the interpretation of these verses, the essence of the answer to the problems of life appears in 12:13–14. Here the fear of God is used in conjunction with the keeping of God's commandments, which was never the concern of Qohelet. Thus, the fear of God in this section is in line with the reverence for God expressed in the book of Proverbs. Additionally, the text indicates that the judgment of God will include the secret things that people do, a side of judgment that Qohelet does not explore. The epilogue does what Qohelet failed to do—to explain the apparent problems of life in light of the character of God. In other words, God is the One who reconciles the problems of life, even when individuals fail to discern the purposes of God in life.

The Danger of Speculative Wisdom

The first-person discourse (1:12–12:7) is written from an "under the sun" perspective and questions the meaning of life. The third-person epilogue (12:8–14) provides the answer to Qohelet's questions (12:13–14). How, therefore, does this book help people struggling with the meaning of life?[58] Eaton has observed that there are no other known examples of wisdom instruction like this one, juxtaposing two opposing worldviews.[59]

The struggle of Qohelet is not unknown to the rest of the Old Testament. The prophets Jeremiah and Habakkuk wrestle with it, the dialogues of Job with his friends center around it, and certain psalms explore it (e.g., Psalms 37; 49; 73). It is possible that someone can forfeit the very foundation of wisdom by trying to explain the problems of life, which elucidates the struggle in Psalm 73, a microcosm of Qohelet's struggle. Psalm 73 begins in verse 1 with the theological affirmation that God is good to Israel and to the pure in heart, but then the psalmist acknowledges that he almost stumbled because of the prosperity of the wicked (73:2–3). After describing the security and

---

[58] Waltke with Yu, *Old Testament Theology*, 950.
[59] Eaton, *Ecclesiastes*, 41.

prosperity of the wicked (73:3–12), he lays out some of the implications related to his struggle. The psalmist wonders whether it has been useless to live a life of purity before God (73:13). He talks about the anguish and the wearisome task of trying to understand this problem (73:16). He states that if he had continued down this path and had taught such things, he would have betrayed God's people (73:15). This is the danger of speculative, doubting wisdom, when the experiences and problems of life so dominate a person's thinking that he or she moves away from the very foundation of wisdom itself. In Psalm 73 a change occurs when the psalmist enters the temple and, from that renewed perspective, sees the true fate of the wicked.

In Ecclesiastes we are pointed back to the true foundation of wisdom in 12:13–14. The book of Ecclesiastes sets forth Qohelet's struggle "under the sun" to demonstrate the danger of speculative wisdom and to remind God's people about wisdom's true foundation: a reverent trust in God and his revelation. Solomon possessed more wisdom than anyone, and he was blessed by God (1 Kings 3:10–14), yet his heart was turned away from God to worship foreign gods (1 Kings 11:4–8). How does one explain what happened to Solomon? If the words of Qohelet represent Solomon's struggle, then we can understand why this struggle was preserved for God's people. If Solomon, who possessed more wisdom than anyone, fell prey to this problem, then it could happen to anyone.[60] In this way, the book of Ecclesiastes remains relevant for the church in every age as God's people struggle with the meaning of life in a fallen, broken world.

APPROACHING THE NEW TESTAMENT

It can be difficult to work through the book Ecclesiastes when one takes the "under the sun" approach to the first-person discourse (1:12–12:7). Only relative benefits are presented because there is no real answer to the problems of life until one comes to the epilogue (12:8–12). Thus it is imperative that the reader make connections to the epilogue, to other Old Testament scriptures, and to the New Testament in order to see the necessary "above the sun" perspective. There are many possible and important connections.

Qohelet accurately describes a world struggling under the effects of the curse of the fall. One of the key words of Ecclesiastes, *hebel*, is translated in the Greek Septuagint as ματαιότης, the same term used in Romans 8:20 to describe the subjection of creation to futility. The creation groans as it waits to be set free from the bondage of decay. However, futility will not have the last word because Jesus has taken upon himself the curse of the futility of life. The power of the new creation is demonstrated in the resurrection of Jesus from the dead. There is, therefore, something *new* under the sun. The work of creation has a purpose (Psalm 104). We are able to see beyond the earthly horizon of this world to the light of the glory of the new heavens and the new earth. When that day comes, the former things, which refer to the troubles of life, will no longer be remembered (Isa. 65:16–17).

---

[60] Waltke offers very perceptive comments on what happened to Solomon as he moved away from God's wisdom. Waltke with Yu, *Old Testament Theology*, 706.

When Qohelet speaks about the frustration that can accompany wisdom (Eccles. 1:18), remember the commandments that God has given for our benefit (12:13) and the perfect wisdom that comes from above and is manifested in Jesus Christ, the very Wisdom of God (1 Cor. 1:24). When Qohelet struggles with the frustrations that arise in labor (Eccles. 2:18–23), remember the exhortation of the apostle Paul that our labor is not in vain in the Lord (1 Cor. 15:58). When eating and drinking appear to be the only pleasure in this life (Eccles. 2:24–26), remember that whatever we do, including eating and drinking, we do for the glory of God (1 Cor. 10:31). When Qohelet struggles with the apparent injustice of life (Eccles. 3:16; 7:15; 8:11–14), remember the King of righteousness (Psalm 72) who has established righteousness (Isaiah 11; 1 Pet. 1:3–7; Rev. 21:4). When Qohelet denies that there is any difference between the destiny of humans and animals (Eccles. 3:19–21), remember that mankind only in his pride is like the beasts (Ps. 49:20). When Qohelet struggles with the fact that the righteous die like the wicked (Eccles. 2:16) and that there is no human activity after death (9:10), remember that God will ransom the righteous from the power of the grave (Ps. 49:15) and that Christ has conquered sin and death (1 Cor. 15:55–56). When a young person is cut down in the prime of life, remember that there is a God who is sovereignly working out his purposes even if we do not understand those purposes. To be certain, the problems of life can be overwhelming, but the Bible teaches that God brings comfort and relief.

When Sarah Longstreet died prematurely in a car accident, her parents wrote the following as part of her obituary:

> While most would call the car accident that took Sarah's life a "tragedy," her family knows that it was the case of God calling one of His children home. Certainly unexpected, but an indication that Sarah's work on earth was complete. For those who read of Sarah's accident and feel that a young life has been cut short, the Longstreets believe that Sarah would want them to know what the Bible says, "for me to live is Christ, and to die is gain." And she would challenge you to consider where you will spend eternity.[61]

The Longstreets were able to place the loss of their child within a worldview that included the sovereignty of a loving God, who is working out his purposes for their lives even in the midst of life's "tragedies."

SELECT BIBLIOGRAPHY

Bartholomew, Craig G. *Ecclesiastes*. BCOTWP. Grand Rapids, MI: Baker Academic, 2009.

———. *Reading Ecclesiastes: Old Testament Exegesis and Hermeneutical Theory*. AnBib 139. Rome: Editrice Pontificio Istituto Biblico, 1998.

---

[61] *The Charlotte Observer*, April 2001.

Belcher, Richard P., Jr. *A Study Commentary on Ecclesiastes*. EP Study Commentary. Darlington, UK: Evangelical Press, 2014.

Crenshaw, James L. *Ecclesiastes*. OTL. Philadelphia: Westminster, 1987.

Delitzsch, Friedrich. *Ecclesiastes*. In *Commentary on the Old Testament*. Vol. 6, *Proverbs, Ecclesiastes, Song of Solomon*, 179–441. 1872. Reprint, Grand Rapids, MI: Eerdmans, 1978.

Eaton, Michael A. *Ecclesiastes: An Introduction and Commentary*. TOTC 16. Downers Grove, IL: InterVarsity Press, 1983.

———. "Frame-Narrative and Composition in the Book of Qohelet." *HUCA* 48 (1977): 83–106.

———. "Qohelet's Epistemology." *HUCA* 58 (1987): 137–55.

———. *A Time to Tear Down and a Time to Build Up: A Rereading of Ecclesiastes*. Grand Rapids, MI: Eerdmans, 1999.

Fredericks, Daniel C. *Ecclesiastes*. In *Ecclesiastes and the Song of Songs*, by Daniel C. Fredericks and Daniel J. Estes. AOTC 16. Downers Grove, IL: InterVarsity Press, 2010.

———. *Qoheleth's Language: Re-evaluating Its Nature and Date*. ANETS 3. Lewiston, NY: Edwin Mellon, 1988.

Isaksson, Bo. *Studies in the Language of Qoheleth: With Special Emphasis on the Verbal System*. SSU 10. Stockholm, Sweden: Almqvist & Wiksell International, 1987.

Koh, Y. V. *Royal Autobiography in the Book of Qoheleth*. BZAW 369. Berlin: de Gruyter, 2006.

Longman, Tremper, III. *The Book of Ecclesiastes*. NICOT. Grand Rapids, MI: Eerdmans, 1998.

Murphy, Roland E. *Ecclesiastes*. WBC 23A. Dallas: Word, 1992.

Ogden, Graham S., and Lynell Zogbo. *A Handbook on Ecclesiastes*. UBS Handbook Series: Help for Translators. New York: United Bible Societies, 1997.

Schoors, A. *The Preacher Sought to Find Pleasing Words: A Study of the Language of Qoheleth*. Part 2, *Vocabulary*. OLA 143. Leuven: Peeters, 2004.

Seow, C. L. *Ecclesiastes: A New Translation with Introduction and Commentary*. AB 18C. New York: Doubleday, 1997.

———. "Linguistic Evidence and the Dating of Qohelet." *JBL* 115, no. 4 (1996): 643–66.

Whybray, R. N. *Ecclesiastes: Based on the Revised Standard Version*. NCB. Grand Rapids, MI: Eerdmans, 1989.

———. "Qoheleth, Preacher of Joy?" *JSOT* 23 (1982): 87–98.

Young, Ian. *Diversity in Pre-exilic Hebrew*. FAT 5. Tübingen: J. C. B. Mohr, 1993.

Young, Ian, and Robert Rezetko. *Linguistic Dating of Biblical Texts*. With the assistance of Martin Ehrensvärd. 2 vols. London: Equinox, 2008.

20

Lamentations

Peter Y. Lee

INTRODUCTION

The book of Lamentations is a collection of five poems that mourns the most tragic day in the history of Judah, the destruction of Jerusalem and the temple in 586 BC. This event would have a lasting and formidable effect upon the Judean consciousness, their literature and culture, even their theology. While the historical narrative that recounts the fall of the city is found in 2 Kings 25:1–21; Jeremiah 39:1–10; and 52:1–34, the description of the physical and spiritual trauma caused by this destruction is captured in Lamentations. It is impossible to overstate the significance of this event for Judah and the newly formed Judean state that arose from the ashes of this once-majestic city.

According to the prophets, the cause of this catastrophic event was the transgressions of the people. Although the poet of Lamentations—or the implied speaker(s) in the poems—does at times acknowledge that covenant violation brought on their demise (Lam. 1:5, 14, 22; 3:39, 42; 5:7, 16), this is not a dominant theme. There is no explicit call for repentance, as is frequently found within the Prophetic Books. What stands out is a graphic and at times disturbing depiction of a personified city brutalized and humiliated to an unimaginable degree. The experience of raw physical and emotional pain is memorialized, inscripturated, and canonized within this book for future generations to read. Thus the agony of those who suffered such torment cannot be forgotten; it cannot be ignored, nor can it be minimized. Moments of hope of restoration are few and far between. The first poem begins in lament and the final poem ends in lament. If there is a book in the holy Scriptures that allows believers to "weep with those who weep" and to ponder their pain within a God-centered context, it is the book of Lamentations.

Background Issues
Title, Authorship, and Historical Setting

In the ancient world titles to literary works were often derived from their opening word or words. This is the case here, where the exclamatory word אֵיכָה ("how," the first word of the Masoretic text version of Lamentations) serves as its title; it is also the first word found in three of its five poems (Lam. 1:1; 2:1; 4:1). The ancient versions, however, derived their title from the prominent theme in the book, namely lament. English Bibles follow the tradition of these ancient versions, thus the book title Lamentations.

Although the Masoretic text does not name the author of this work, several ancient versions do. The Greek Septuagint, the Latin Vulgate, and Jewish tradition specify Jeremiah as the author. This explains the canonical relocation of the book from the Writings to the position immediately after the book of Jeremiah in the Septuagint and the Vulgate, where it is also located in English translations (see "Canonical Position" on p. 459). The Old Testament canon itself also gives evidence for Jeremianic authorship. Consider 2 Chronicles 35:25, which states, "Jeremiah also uttered a lament for Josiah; and all the singing men and singing women have spoken of Josiah in their laments to this day. They made these a rule in Israel; behold, they are written in the Laments." Most likely this passage is the reason that rabbinic tradition connects the authorship of Lamentations with Jeremiah. Other considerations within Lamentations also support Jeremianic authorship. The destruction of the city seems to be described from the point of view of an eyewitness, which would place the book within the historical setting of Jeremiah. The "man who has seen affliction" in Lamentations 3 experiences many of the same types of persecutions as the prophet. There are also close literary parallels between Jeremiah and Lamentations (see Lam. 2:14/Jer. 5:31; Lam. 2:22/Jer. 6:25; Lam. 3:14/Jer. 20:7; Lam. 3:53/Jer. 38:6; Lam. 4:17/Jer. 2:36). Since the notion of Jeremiah as the author is old and enjoys support from early witnesses within and outside the book, it is not without merit.

However, the majority of scholars have either rejected or remain uncertain about this claim. Nothing in the Masoretic text tradition explicitly credits Jeremiah as the author (2 Chron. 35:25 is only an inference), unlike several psalms that appear to credit David as their author. The most persuasive argument against Jeremianic authorship is the lack of emphasis upon the sins of the people as the reason for the city's demise. The book of Jeremiah unequivocally attributes the cause of the city's destruction to the transgressions of the covenant community. While this connection can also be found in Lamentations, it is not the predominant theme. It is plausible, as some argue in response, that Jeremiah changed his focus once the city met its tragic end. Prior to the destruction of the city, Jeremiah's main prophetic task was to call for repentance in hopes of avoiding this tragedy (Jer. 18:6–8). After the city was destroyed, the sheer overwhelming sight of this once-great metropolis razed to the ground could have been more than he could bear. The writing of laments may have been a cathartic way to deal with the pain of a crushing event personally and theologically.

Another argument against Jeremianic authorship is related to the book's genre as an Israelite city lament. Laments for destroyed cities were commonly written not at the time of its destruction but rather in the near future at the time of its rebuilding. If this is true in the case of Lamentations, then this would date the book within the postexilic era, which would make any claims to Jeremiah as its author highly questionable.

For the reasons mentioned here, we can conclude that Jeremianic authorship of Lamentations is a reasonable but not necessary position to hold. I suggest, however, that the identity of the author of Lamentations is secondary to its content. Regardless of who wrote these poems, what we know with certainty is that the poet-author is consciously pondering the destruction of the city of Jerusalem. Either he witnessed the destruction firsthand and is living through the aftermath, or he is contemplating the destruction several generations after the fact as the city approaches a time of rebuilding. The poet-author expresses his lament through various "personas" within each of the five poems that compose the book. Whether these various personas represent the actual author cannot be determined, but they do reflect the heart of the people as they mourn the destruction of the city: Lamentations 1 and 2 describe the agony of the city of Jerusalem as an abused woman; Lamentations 3 presents two different personas, a "man who has seen affliction" and a suffering community; Lamentations 4 gives the perspective of a third-person eyewitness; and Lamentations 5 is a lament poem. Throughout each of the five lyrical works, there is a linguistic, thematic, and poetic consistency that suggests a single author whose thoughts are expressed through these personas.

This is contra the critical schools that want to see multiple compositions written by multiple authors. Even if a persuasive case could be made that the five poems came from five different authors, it still could not account for the fact that a single poet-editor must have compiled the poems into its current canonical shape. The diversity of personas, more likely, reflects the diversity of peoples who survived the Babylonian siege and remained in the city—all of whose laments are expressed in this book.

Canonical Position

There is no attested controversy over the inclusion of Lamentations within the biblical Canon. Its location within the Canon, however, differs among the ancient versions. Lamentations follows the book of Jeremiah in most ancient versions, such as the Septuagint and the Vulgate. As mentioned earlier, this placement is most likely related to its authorship. However, in the Hebrew canon, it is not found with the prophet Jeremiah. Rather, it is in the third section of the Hebrew canon, the Writings.

Notably, Lamentations is considered part of a smaller subset of five books called the *Megilloth* (Hebrew for "scrolls"). The other four are the Song of Songs, Ecclesiastes, Esther, and Ruth. Different criteria are used for the canonical location of these five books. Ruth is the first of the *Megilloth*. It is followed by the two books connected to Solomon—Song of Songs and Ecclesiastes. Lamentations and Esther follow, whereas Lamentations fits the poetic genre of the previous two and Esther fits the historical setting of the following two (Daniel, Ezra–Nehemiah). All five have become associated with various festivals and memorials in Jewish history and thus are used as lectionary readings at their respective feasts. Song of Songs is read at Passover, Ruth at Pentecost, Lamentations on the ninth of Ab, Ecclesiastes at the Feast of Booths/Tabernacles, and Esther at Purim. Once the liturgical connection was made with these books, the literary order was changed to match the calendrical order of the feasts—Song of Songs, Ruth, Lamentations, Ecclesiastes, Esther. Christian uses of these books remain both an academic and pastoral desideratum.[1]

As mentioned previously, Lamentations is read on the ninth of Ab (approximately in July or August), a day of fasting and mourning in the Jewish calendar. It was originally intended to commemorate the destruction of the city of Jerusalem in 586 BC. Later, it was also used to remember the destruction of the city in AD 70. Now it has expanded in its use to include all other disasters that have befallen the Jewish people, including the Holocaust in World War II.[2]

Poetic Features

It is ironic that a collection of poems expressing some of the most intense sorrows experienced at the lowest point in the history of Israel could also be a wondrous example of ancient verse. Yet that is what we have in Lamentations. There is no doubt that the events of 586 BC marked the nadir in the life of God's people. If there is any good that can be salvaged from this destructive event, it can be found only in the poems that remember it. The more destructive the event, the more elegant the poetry. One can almost sense that the beauty of the poetry brought a small level of relief for a poet who was suffering searing pain at the destruction of the great city (see "Mourning and Suffering" on p. 465).

The poetry in Lamentations uses typical features found in other examples of Hebrew poetry, such as parallelism, a rich use of images, and acrostic structures. The two pillars of Hebrew poetry—parallelism and meter—make up the standard approach to poetic analysis. Regarding parallelism, the academic community is currently conducting a lengthy discussion about its nature, which does not need to be repeated here.[3] Regarding meter, its understanding is much less stable. Although there is some variance in how Hebrew parallelism works, that diversity pales in comparison to the variance that exists within the area of Hebrew metrics. The majority of scholars are divided between the Budde/Ley/Sievers system of counting word-accents and the

---

[1] See Barry G. Webb, *Five Festal Garments: Christian Reflections on the Song of Songs, Ruth, Lamentations, Ecclesiastes, and Esther*, NSBT 10 (Downers Grove, IL: InterVarsity Press, 2000), whose thoughts provide a meaningful contribution to a Christian understanding and use of these books.

[2] Erhard S. Gerstenberger convincingly shows how Lamentations has been "cast into the liturgical shape of ceremonial mourning." *Psalms, Part 2, and Lamentations*, FOTL 15 (Grand Rapids, MI: Eerdmans, 2001), 473.

[3] For a helpful understanding of parallelism, see Adele Berlin, *The Dynamics of Biblical Parallelism*, rev. ed. (Grand Rapids, MI: Eerdmans, 2009). Adele Berlin's commentary on Lamentations is also highly recommended as an outstanding treatment of this biblical book. *Lamentations*, OTL (Louisville: Westminster John Knox, 2002).

Freedman/Cross system of counting syllables as the means by which to measure the meter of Hebrew poetry. A growing number of scholars, myself included, remain skeptical that Hebrew poetry had any meter at all.[4] Due to the elusiveness of this matter, no significant comment will be made except to note that several commentators have observed a possible Qinah, or "limping" meter, in Lamentations. The discovery of the Qinah meter is credited to Karl Budde; this meter is an imbalanced three-two rhythm that is common in Hebrew dirges.[5] A closer examination of the poetry reveals that such an imbalanced "meter" is present but inconsistent in Lamentations 1, steady in Lamentations 2–4, and nonexistent in Lamentations 5. Given the theme of lament within the book, to find such a varied metrical structure is not surprising.

Imagery—Personification

Luis Alonso Schökel says that "images are the glory, perhaps the essence of poetry, the enchanted planet of the imagination, a limitless galaxy, ever alive and ever changing."[6] In my estimation, Schökel overstates the significance of images in Hebrew poetry; however, they are truly more at home in poetry than in prose. For that reason, a greater density of images is expected in poetry, and that is the case with Lamentations. The abundance of vivid images contained within this book has been underappreciated and neglected in favor of its impressive acrostic structures (see "Structure and Outline" on p. 463). Yet the message of the book is expressed poignantly through these images, which evoke an emotional dismay from the reader. One could say that this is a book of images and that the images preach the message of the book.

One dominant image is the personification of the city of Jerusalem. In Lamentations 1–2 the city is depicted as a woman, a common motif used by ancient writers (see Queen Babylon in Isaiah 47). As in our world today, women functioned in various roles within Israelite society. The multifaceted duties of women allowed the ancient poet to use multifaceted metaphors to express the agony of a decimated city. Women, particularly widows, were to be cared for and tended to, but in Lamentations the treatment of the widowed city is traumatically opposite. Thus Jerusalem is alone in the night, weeping bitterly due to the devastation brought on by her transgressions. She who was once a loving bride had acted as a harlot. Thus the one-time queen of cities has now been reduced to a slave—abused, beaten, and publicly humiliated. These pictures evoke strong feelings of horror, suffering, and shame. It is precisely the use of the feminine persona that makes an already tragic event that much more tragic.

Lamentations 3 transitions from the feminine persona to two different images. The first is of a man who has been physically tormented and trampled by his enemies; the second is of an afflicted community that has not yet received the forgiveness of

---

[4] Michael O'Connor's system of syntactic constraints constitutes a fresh and persuasive assessment of the subject of meter that offers a helpful alternative to the earlier approaches mentioned above. *Hebrew Verse Structure* (Winona Lake, IN: Eisenbrauns, 1980).

[5] Karl Budde, "Das hebräische Klagelied," *ZAW* 2 (1882), 1–52. See also Paul R. House, *Lamentations*, in *Song of Songs / Lamentations*, by Duane A. Garrett and Paul R. House, WBC 23B (Nashville: Thomas Nelson, 2004), 308–10.

[6] Luis Alonso Schökel, *A Manual of Hebrew Poetics*, SubBi 11 (Rome: Editrice Pontificio Istituto Biblico, 2000), 95.

sins requested of the Lord. Many scholars have attempted to identify the "man who has seen affliction" (Lam. 3:1). However, such an approach of analysis is misleading. The man and the community, like the woman in Lamentations 1–2, represent the stricken city of Jerusalem.[7] The suffering of the city, therefore, is depicted from multiple perspectives—male/female, individual/community, righteous sufferer/repentant sinner. In so doing, the cries of the entire population of Jerusalem are given a voice in Lamentations. This makes the book applicable for any member of Judean society. In fact, anyone who has experienced a traumatic event has an understanding and sympathetic representative among the various voices/personas in this book.

Literary Genre

The longstanding title of Lamentations, as found in numerous ancient witnesses and in rabbinic tradition, is fitting given the theme and content of the book. However, scholars (particularly form critics) disagree on the specific genre of the poems within the book, generally proposing two views: a dirge and a communal lament. Qinah, the metrical limp mentioned earlier, is characteristic of the genre of a dirge, and although the existence of meter remains dubious, no one disputes that there was a tradition of Qinah poems (see 2 Chron. 35:25, which speaks of Qinoth, the Hebrew plural of Qinah). The Qinah genre also shares similarities with the communal lament; both express the pain and anguish of the poet or the community of God's people after a tragic event. They differ in that a Qinah sees little hope for restoration while a communal lament retains some hope for deliverance. The word *Qinah* does not occur in Lamentations, but this has not solved the genre issue for form critics since the book includes elements of both the Qinah and the communal lament—heartfelt mourning for the epic loss of the city yet a cautious anticipation for restoration.

Adele Berlin has furthered this discussion by suggesting that Lamentations transcends both genres and constitutes a new post-586 BC lament, which she calls a "Jerusalem lament."[8] She also suggests that several psalms exhibit the characteristics of a Jerusalem lament (Psalms 44; 69; 74; 79; 102; 137). According to Berlin, these newly formed laments were used to mourn the loss of the city of Jerusalem and particularly the destruction of the temple. These are in the same tradition as the ancient Mesopotamian city laments, the majority of which predate both Lamentations and the city-lament psalms mentioned earlier. She suggests that these laments are juxtaposed to the Zion psalms, which celebrate the city's architectural magnificence and its central theological significance in the life of Judah (see Psalms 46; 48; 50; 76; 84; 87; 122). With Judah in exile and the city in ashes, it would obviously pose problems to use such psalms. Prior to 586 BC, all Judeans were joyous; after 586 BC, all Judeans became mourners. They needed a song that captured the current state of their mourning hearts, one that gave them a religious context in which to express

---

[7] The book does contain allusions and intertextual references to the book of Job that portray this man in Job-like terms. For more details, see "Voice of the Righteous Remnant" on p. 467.
[8] Berlin, *Lamentations*, 24–25.

the sorrow associated with the loss of their capitol (Qinah) while at the same time providing a tinge of hope for restoration (lament). This was the occasion for the rise of these Jerusalem laments, best exemplified in the book of Lamentations.

STRUCTURE AND OUTLINE

Acrostic

Perhaps the most outstanding literary feature of Lamentations is its remarkable acrostic structure. In an acrostic the first consonants of each poetic unit (line, strophe) join together to form a specific pattern.[9] Lamentations implements an alphabetic acrostic. Of the five poems that compose the book, the first four (Lamentations 1–4) use this acrostic structure, though they vary slightly. Lamentations 1 is a perfect acrostic composed of twenty-two poetic units, with the first consonant in each section following in the successive order of the Hebrew alphabet. Lamentations 2–4, however, differs in that the ע and פ elements are in reverse order. Lamentations 3 adds another layer of poetic sophistication. Whereas in Lamentations 1–2 only the first consonant in each strophic unit follows the alphabetic acrostic, in Lamentations 3 each of the three poetic lines in each strophe follows the alphabetic pattern—a trifold acrostic. Thus the first three lines begin with א, the next three with ב, and so forth. The standard acrostic form returns in Lamentations 4 but with a quantitative difference. The strophes in Lamentations 4 have only two poetic lines, unlike the three-lined strophes in Lamentations 1–3. Lamentations 5 brings a sense of finale to the book by breaking from the acrostic structure, but it retains a connection with the previous four poems in that it is composed of twenty-two poetic lines paralleling the twenty-two strophes in Lamentations 1–4. Thus Lamentations 5 is the shortest of the five poems.

The acrostic structure clearly demonstrates an intentional design and purpose. It provides a literary stability to the book as a whole. This is unexpected since the message is one of instability, disorder, chaos, destruction, and suffering. The acrostic structure is the opposite—it is stable, fluid, and elegant. Barry Webb also observes this contrast between the theological message and the literary form when he says that it is "startling to discover that a book that portrays such radical disorientation should be one of the most ordered works in the Old Testament."[10] Within all the chaos, shame, and obliteration described within the book, a sense of order, control, and precision is sustained at a literary level. As there is a modicum of hope found in the Lord whose mercy is renewed daily (Lam. 3:22–23), so that same hope is expressed in the literary steadiness that reflects the true divine Poet of the book.

The use of the acrostic also has another profound effect upon the reader. As previously mentioned, Lamentations 3 differs from the acrostic in Lamentations 1–2 in that each line in each strophe begins with the consonant in which it is grouped. This well-stylized and cyclical use of the acrostic in Lamentations 3 causes the reader to slow down and encourages deeper meditation upon each poetic line. Such

---

[9] See David N. Freedman, "Acrostic Poems in the Hebrew Bible: Alphabetic and Otherwise," *CBQ* 48, no. 3 (1986): 408–31; Freedman, "Acrostics and Metrics in Hebrew Poetry," *HTR* 65, no. 3 (1972): 367–92.

[10] Webb, *Five Festal Garments*, 60.

an effect is interesting since the primary message of hope in the book is found in this chapter, specifically in 3:19–39. The literary design of the book leads readers through the first two poems at a steady pace until they reach the third: they mourn in the first; they are shocked by the divine origins of their suffering in the second; they are restored in the third. A burden is lifted as the reader finally comes to a sense of restoration in the midst of a litany of images of destruction and suffering. The acrostic structure allows the reader to slowly enter into this literary respite of momentary joy. Lamentations 4–5, however, returns to the mournful overtones characteristic of Lamentations 1–2, but with two significant and meaningful differences. First, each of these final two poems grows progressively and systematically shorter. The movement in the book transitions from three sixty-six-lined poems in Lamentations 1–3, with the acrostic slowing the reading pace in Lamentations 3, to a forty-four-lined poem in Lamentations 4 and then a twenty-two-lined poem in Lamentations 5. The pace of the poetry that slowed in Lamentations 3 picks up speed in the final two poems until it reaches a dramatic end that anticipates the end of the exile for Judah (Lam. 4:22) whose future is in the hands of their sovereign Lord, who reigns for eternity (Lam. 5:19–22).

Summary Outline

I. The Shame and Mourning of the City (Lamentations 1):
The themes that dominate this chapter are shame and remorse brought on by the rebellion of the city of Jerusalem. The city is personified as a woman, and the poet utilizes a plethora of female images to portray the curse of the covenant against Lady Jerusalem—a lonely widow, a dethroned queen reduced to the status of a maiden, a treacherous wife betrayed by her adulterous lovers, one sexually abused and stripped naked, and a ritually unclean menstruating woman.

II. The Lord as the Primary Agent of Wrath (Lamentations 2):
Whereas Lamentations 1 is more interested in the subjective misery of Judah, Lamentations 2 focuses on the agent of that misery—the Lord as the enemy of the personified city.

III. The Lament of the Afflicted Man and His Community (Lamentations 3):
This third poem changes the persona of the poem from the female voice of Lamentations 1–2 to a "man who has seen affliction under the rod of his wrath" (3:1). The man's perspective is in 2:1–39 and 2:48–66, while the community's is in 2:40–47. The suffering of the man is strikingly brutal. The description of the man also makes many allusions to the biblical Job, which gives the sense that he specifically represents the righteous remnant who are exiled due to their membership within the covenant community of Judah.

IV. The City Besieged (Lamentations 4):
Lamentations 4 shares similar characteristics with the poem in Lamentations 3 in that both graphically depict the physical effects of the exile upon the inhabitants of the city. The siege motif is prevalent in this poem, and its immediate impact upon the city is displayed using disturbing images.

V. Communal Lament Finale (Lamentations 5):
The book of Lamentations comes to a somewhat abrupt end with this final communal lament. The inhabitants of the city—men, women, and children—are mentioned as experiencing physical suffering from their enemies. They are discouraged and ill. Yet the poem ends with a glimmer of hope as it appeals to the Lord as their King to remember and restore them (5:19–22).

MESSAGE AND THEOLOGY
Mourning and Suffering

The book of Lamentations is about mournful loss, agonizing pain, and ongoing misery. This is the single most important theme in the book. While poetic analysis is helpful in appreciating its literary sophistication, it should not deter us from its more poignant content. No other book within the biblical Canon is as dark and depressing as this one. It says much about the Christian church (and the academic community) that they pay little to no attention to this book. Sunday school classes rarely tackle it. Pastors generally stray from it. The one exception is Lamentations 3:22, which mentions the renewing faithfulness of the Lord. That passage is well known; the remainder of the book is not. We can only ponder the reasons for this neglect, although it is not difficult to perceive why. It is due to the morbid depiction of suffering and pain. These are human experiences that many would rather not remember or reflect upon, yet they are sadly unavoidable. As such, Lamentations is a reminder of the excruciating anguish that characterizes life in a fallen world.

To study Lamentations is to remind us of that which we fight to avoid; the harsh reality, however, is that many in the church suffer a life ravaged and decimated by transgressions—all of which produces only agony and pain. Some are *unwilling* to acknowledge these distresses, but they can surface psychosomatically (cf. Psalm 32). Still others are *not able* to acknowledge them—these are the individuals represented in Lamentations. Extreme misery has a profound and powerful effect upon the frail human psyche. The sheer excruciating intensity of pain is often so overwhelming that it leaves us for an extended time in a state of emotional and spiritual deafness and dumbness. The apostle Paul says that there are moments when we suffer with such agony that all we can do is "groan" (Rom. 8:23). We want to share our pain, we need to share our pain, but we are unable to speak of our pain—it hurts that badly. We are encouraged to pray to the Lord in such times of trouble, but our senses are immobilized during those agonizing times. Those who have experienced the loss of loved ones or the severing of sincere and meaningful relationships, those who have endured a losing battle against physical illnesses and ailments, those who have attempted to live in godly obedience only to face rejection and scorn—in short, anyone who lives on planet earth knows of what I speak: a pain so painful that it cannot be expressed in human words.

Rarely do preachers preach from Lamentations when that is exactly what must be done for the very reasons described here. For the silent sufferer, this book (as well as the psalms of lament) provides what they desperately need—a voice to express their pain. If they suffer due to their transgressions, Lamentations provides the voice of confessors who acknowledge their wayward heart and seek covenantal restoration from the Lord, whose mercy is new every morning (3:22). For the broken and destitute, Lamentations gives them a lyrical setting to finally verbalize their pain. As Dobbs-Allsopp states so eloquently, "To come across language in which one finds one's own hurts and grief so precisely and accurately named and expressed can be a wonderfully consoling and forever transformative experience."[11] This voice occurs within a canonical and liturgical context to memorialize the traumatic events in 586 BC, as well as those tragedies that occurred before or occur afterwards.

So often we are told that our suffering needs an emotional and verbal outlet in order to release internal pressure. Frequently, that pain is too intense to be verbalized. During those times when we can voice our feelings, they generally come out explosively—in angry words that lash out without careful thought and sensitivity toward others. We feel that our pain gives us a legitimate right to selfish and sinful desires, which conversely results in more damage and more pain. Because of its liturgical use, Lamentations is not merely a cathartic expression of misery; it is not venting emotional angst for the sake of relieving pent-up, negative emotional energy. It is also more than stylish and well-ordered poetry. It is a collection of elegant *prayers* that have been scripted for the sufferer; it reflects the real state of their misery and allows them to finally verbalize these struggles directly to the Lord, to commune with him on the tragic matters of their lives—their frustrations and anguish—and to appeal to him for relief.

Sufferers are finally given a voice. These are not wasted words, because they are given a graceful, poetic form that is directed to the one and only Person who can help them. They continue to mourn. Although moments of levity and restoration may occur, Lamentations ends as it began, in suffering without relief. But as they focus on the Lord, it becomes clear to them that he is their "portion" (3:24). With that profound reminder, they realize that their hope is not found in the restoration of their city, nor is it even found in the termination of their pain. Hope is not found in the blessings of earthly comforts, which the exile has shown to be frail, weak, and unreliable. Only with a vertical perspective can they truly find hope. Simply put, they can mourn with hope because they mourn in the context of God-centered worship.

We cannot expect those in pain to immediately begin meditating on Lamentations and find spiritual healing within it. Again, Dobbs-Allsopp is helpful when he describes how the poet-author gradually brings the reader into the mourning experience of the book with care and sensitivity; ultimately, the reader is united with the personified mourners to form a new stricken and grieving community.[12] Recall that the book begins in Lamentations 1–2 with the personification of the destroyed city of Jerusalem in dialogue with the poet-narrator. We as readers witness this dialogue

---

[11] F. W. Dobbs-Allsopp, *Lamentations*, IBC (Louisville: John Knox, 2002), 35.
[12] Dobbs-Allsopp, *Lamentations*, 34–35.

as a third-party observer; the narrator describes the devastation upon the city, and Lady Jerusalem can only respond with a meager appeal: "O LORD, behold my affliction, for the enemy has triumphed" (1:9b). Lamentations 3 continues this urban personification but changes the gender perspective to that of a "man who has seen affliction" (3:1). Thus far, the reader does not take part in the hurting experiences of these personas—the pain is distant though disturbingly nearby. That changes in 3:40–47, where the voice of the poem shifts to the first-person plural pronoun *we*. The reader is no longer a third-party observer who can empathize with the female and male personifications; he is part of the suffering community and realizes that this book is not only *for* him but *about* him.

This initial shock of identifying with the agony of the man quickly subsides with the recurrence of the first-person singular in 3:48, returning the reader to an outsider perspective. However, Lamentations 3 has given a glimpse of the reader's internal anguish by identifying her with the afflicted man. The reader realizes that she is not alone; others share in her pain. That communal suffering continues in Lamentations 4, which expresses the agony of many who suffer defeat and pain at the hands of their enemies. The pronoun *we* returns once again in 4:17, and it remains throughout the fourth poem and is the dominant voice in Lamentations 5. The union of the reader with the suffering community is now complete. By the end of Lamentations, no longer is the pain depicted as that of others; this is the reader's pain; this is my pain. We are no longer alone, and there is comfort within a community, even one that shares similar struggles. Together they desperately appeal to their Lord as their source of comfort.

Voice of the Righteous Remnant

Lamentations 3 portrays the city of Jerusalem as a man "who has seen affliction" (Lam. 3:1), and commentators have unnecessarily proposed different suggestions for the identity of this man. In spite of a change in persona (from the feminine in Lamentations 1–2 to the masculine in Lamentations 3) and the shift from an individual to a community (within Lamentations 3), what is represented is the same throughout—the city of Jerusalem. Yet the third poem brings a significant distinction regarding the precise indentity of the corporate community. Whereas the sinful inhabitants of the city are embodied in the woman of Lamentations 1–2, it is possible that the man in Lamentations 3 represents the few righteous followers of the Lord who suffer the covenant curse of exile. Jeremiah 31:29–30 contrasts the life within the old covenant with that of the new covenant. In the old covenant order, although it was the fathers who "have eaten sour grapes" and suffer exile, their children share in this same fate, and so their "teeth are set on edge" (31:29). In contrast, in the new covenant, children are no longer to suffer the consequences of the previous generations, "but everyone shall die for his own iniquity," and "each man who eats sour grapes, his teeth shall be set on edge" (31:30). Thus a generation of Judeans are suffering the covenant curse of exile not because of their own sins. I suggest that the man of affliction in Lamentations 3 is to be understood as representing the same subgroup of Judeans as the children whose teeth are set on edge—they are a righteous remnant, the few who remained faithful to the Lord in the midst of moral and cultic decay but who were nonetheless exiled due to their corporate membership within the covenant community of Judah.

Three factors within the text support this suggestion. First is the apparent discrepancy between Lamentations 3:1–39 and 3:49–66 over the cause of the man's affliction. Both sections describe the physical suffering of an afflicted man, forming an *inclusio*, while 3:40–48 separates them and describes the suffering of a community. The first section (3:1–39) graphically depicts the man as physically brutalized by the Lord, yet 3:39 shows that he has no grounds to complain since he is suffering the "punishment of his sins." The second section (3:49–66) continues the pain of the afflicted man, yet the Lord afflicts him through the means of his enemies. Lamentations 3:53 is particularly startling since the man cries out that he has been hunted down like prey by his enemies even though this act is "without cause." He confesses that from his perspective, there is no reasonable explanation for this suffering; he is blameless. Whereas the first section (3:1–39) attributes his affliction to sin, the second (3:49–66) suggests that he suffers "without cause."

A proposed solution to this discrepancy leads to the second factor in the identity of this man. It is significant to observe that only 3:39 reveals the man's culpability in the opening section; his transgressions go curiously unmentioned in the previous thirty-eight verses. Lamentations 3:39 also introduces the following section, a corporate confession of sin. This third poem is a macroexample of poetic enjambment, where the thematic structure of the poem does not align with the acrostic structure. The thematic structure is most helpful here. Two rhetorical questions are issued in 3:37a and 3:39, with answers following in 3:37b–38 and 3:40–41 respectively; 3:42–47 develops the answer in 3:40–41 further. Notice also that the second question asks about "his sin" as an individual. The answer, however, is not from the individual man but from a collective of which he is a part (3:40–41, 42–47). Thus the perception of the poetry shifts from the individual man to the corporate community. The man is now envisioned as a member of a confessing body guilty of sin. The sin in view therefore is not his per se but his as part of the larger community of transgressors. As an individual he is afflicted "without cause" for he remained faithful to the Lord, unlike his idolatrous contemporaries and forefathers; as a member of the community he suffers the curse of the covenant, the "punishment of his sins."

The third and final factor to support the identity of the afflicted man as representing a righteous remnant is the affinity that he shares with the biblical figure of Job. Tremper Longman and Adele Berlin have made this observation, independent of each other.[13] The parallels between the two literary figures are striking. Table 21 shows their similarities.

---

[13] Berlin, *Lamentations*, 85–86; Tremper Longman III, *Jeremiah, Lamentations*, NIBCOT 14 (Peabody, MA: Hendrickson, 2008), 363–78.

Shared Description	Man of Affliction (Lamentations 3)	Job
Called הַגֶּבֶר	Lam. 3:1; the opening of the poem	Job 3:3; the first speech of Job
Crooked paths	Lam. 3:9	Job 19:8
Devoured by animals	Lam. 3:10; hunted by a bear and a lion	Job 10:16; hunted by a lion
Targeted by God's arrows	Lam. 3:12	Job 7:20; 16:12–13
Mocked by the nations	Lam. 3:14	Job 30:1, 9
Full of bitterness	Lam. 3:15	Job 9:18
Good to bear chastisement from God	Lam. 3:24–27	Job 5:16–18
Sitting in silence	Lam. 3:28	Job 2:13
Face in the dust	Lam. 3:29	Job 42:6
Healing in the future	Lam. 3:32	Job 5:18
God will not pervert justice	Lam. 3:33–36	Job 8:3
Both good and bad come from God	Lam. 3:38	Job 2:10
Blocked access to God	Lam. 3:44	Job 3:23

Table 21

As Job is an innocent man who struggles intense suffering, so the afflicted man in Lamentations 3 suffers similarly. It is tempting to think that the inspiration for the use of a male image was the person of Job. Although possible, the literary origins of this masculine image should not deter us from the pressing point that the poet-author is making: the city and its inhabitants are in extreme agony and pain. The nation as a whole violated the covenant mandates and thus has to suffer the curse sanctions of the covenant—citywide destruction and exile of Deuteronomic proportions. Within this sinful body are a few who remained faithful but are exiled due to their covenantal membership and not because of their personal transgressions. They suffer *in spite of* their fidelity. They are the righteous remnant who must endure suffering "without cause." The image of Job is a well-known figure who also knew such pain; thus he is a perfect model for the poet to use in representing an innocent sufferer.

While righteous sufferers are few and far between, this theme is prominent in the history of salvation. Joseph was sold into slavery for no fault of his own. Abraham was called to sacrifice his one and only son, Isaac. David was exiled from Jerusalem although he was a faithful servant of King Saul. The prophets as a whole represent servants of the Lord who suffer because of their obedient fulfillment of their divine duty to call the people to repentance. Several psalms of lament (e.g., Psalm 44) record such cries. The book of 1 Peter is addressed specifically to such a community. Even our Lord Jesus Christ addressed such believers in his Sermon on the Mount (Matt. 5:11–12). In the same way, within the exiled community were those few—Jeremiah, Baruch, Ezekiel, Daniel and his three companions—who never turned away from the Lord. The covenant violators suffer, and their cries are recorded within the majority of this book, including Lamentations 3:40–48. Within that mass are those righteous few who clung to the Lord and did not compromise. They also have a voice represented in Lamentations, namely, in this figure of the afflicted man.

Lamentations, in particular chapter 3, offers two qualitatively different cries that appear superficially the same. The one is the cry of a repentant sinner who appeals to the Lord for his forgiving mercies; the Lord will grant such a pardon, and the people will ultimately find comfort within it—although it may not come immediately. This is the corporate community in 3:40–48. The second is the cry of the righteous believer; his comfort is also found in the Lord but in a very different capacity. This is the man in 3:1–38/39, 49–66.

The apostle Paul reminds believers that their union is with a significant individual who suffered pain and agony "without cause." He was One who "knew no sin" (2 Cor. 5:21). Astonishingly, in Philippians 3:10–11 Paul expresses his desire to grow in the knowledge of Christ not only in his death but also in his suffering. While Lamentations is a literary union of the reader with the personas in the book, the apostle outlines a redemptive-historical union between Christ and his bride, the church. Therefore, not only do we have a High Priest who is able to sympathize with our suffering (Heb. 4:15), we are also called to identify with his suffering. The apostle Peter writes that insofar as we share in his sufferings, we can rejoice (1 Pet. 4:12–13). In fact, Peter says that this joy is "inexpressible and filled with glory" (1:8). Those who have known unspeakable pain can also know an unspeakable joy in Christ! To know the Lord as a righteous sufferer gives to the believer a holistic knowledge of Christ, who knew both suffering for righteousness and blessed glory. Lamentations reminds us that in our transgressions we must repent. Suffering, however, still results in faithful obedience to the Lord. During such times, it calls us to identify with the afflicted Man who knew agony in greater intensity than the "man who has seen affliction" in Lamentations 3. To know this man is to know comfort, for he is the Giver of comfort.

A Violent God?

The portrait of God in Lamentations is difficult for many since it flies in the face of broad evangelical concepts of God as a gentle and gracious Father. Scripture clearly teaches that he is indeed that and more. He is the faithful Shepherd who protects and leads his people into a land of everlasting prosperity (Ps. 23:1; Ezek. 34:12; Zech. 11:16; cf. 2 Sam. 7:7; Ps. 78:71; Isa. 40:11), a just and gracious king (Psalms 93–99; 110:1; 111), the almighty Creator (Gen. 1:1; Psalm 148; Prov. 8:22–30). The list of glorious epithets that tell us who he is and what he does for his covenant people is endless.

Such positive descriptions of God, however, are nearly absent in Lamentations. The afflicted man appeals to his endless mercy in 3:19–39; he is also depicted as a divine Arbiter who takes up the legal cause of the man in 3:58–59. But these glorious descriptions cannot mask the more destructive and disturbing portrayals of a violent deity. What stands out is a picture of the divine Sovereign in violent images. He is the God who inflicts incomparable pain (1:12); he "set fire to my bones" (1:13); he is a Warrior who ruthlessly assaults the "daughter of Zion" with a "bent . . . bow" (2:4). Throughout the entire book the Lord is the primary agent causing havoc in the city. We know that the siege of Babylon against Jerusalem is the historic event that lies behind the book. However, neither Babylon nor any of her officials are mentioned. The one possible exception is an implicit reference to them in 1:9–10; 3:49–66 where the afflicted man calls for the Lord to punish his enemies (implicitly Babylon). With the exception of this one very subtle implication, God himself is viewed as the cause of Judah's demise, so much so that he is even described as being like their "enemy" (2:4–5).

Although the main theme of Lamentations is one of suffering, the book implicitly connects that suffering with the people's transgressions. The sin of the people, while not pervasive, is present within the book (1:5, 8, 18, 22; 2:14; 3:39, 42; 4:6, 13; 5:7, 16). And while the author never makes a direct corollary between the painful experience of Judah and their covenant violation, that does not make it any less a reality. The afflicted man himself acknowledges that in light of his/their sins, "Why should a living man complain, a man, about the punishment of his sins?" (3:39).

In fact, by recognizing the Lord as the primary agent of covenantal justice, Lamentations partakes in the larger exilic and postexilic interest in clearing God of any impotence or wrongful action. Judah (and Israel before her) were destroyed and their people exiled not because of the superiority of foreign deities and not due to any arbitrary desires of the Lord but rather because of the sins of the people. Deuteronomy warned what would result from such covenant breaking; Lamentations mourns the fact that, indeed, that has come about (cf. 4:10; Deut. 28:53–57). God is not weak in comparison to Marduk; in fact, it is the total opposite. He is the One who executes the curse of the covenant against his rebellious people, while the people of Marduk are mere instruments of his divine will. His act of judgment against Jerusalem is therefore not capricious. In order for the Lord to honor his holy character, covenant transgressors must be penalized; this is a just act. He gave them countless opportunities to repent and change their ways, to conform to the covenantal standards by which they agreed to live by. They had violated that agreement over and over again. The only act left for the Lord was one of covenant sanction—and it was justly executed.

However, though it contains a mild "theodic" sense, Lamentations is not a theodicy in the truest sense of the word . While the broader Old Testament context gives reasonable covenantal explanations to justify the suffering of the city, the portraits of God as the divine Executor of justice in Lamentations is graphic—this is unavoidable.

Dobbs-Allsopp says that to read Lamentations as a theodicy is to overlook these "antitheodic sensibilities."[14] In other words, the violence associated with God's acts against Judah cannot be defended very easily. His point is an important one, and evangelicals cannot merely ignore that these graphic depictions of their God are present within this book. The God of Scripture is indeed a God vengeful for his glory. He is loving, gracious, and merciful, but he is also just and holy. These latter characteristics tend to be underappreciated in studies of the doctrine of God. As fellow human beings, our sympathies are for the sake of the brutalized and beaten in Lamentations. Our hearts go out to them and ponder what possible crime they could have committed to warrant this penalty. It seems too extreme and more than what any person deserves.

This sympathy, however, comes at a cost, a very expensive one at that. To see unjust treatment in Lamentations requires sacrificing the high value of the glory of a holy God. If the people are experiencing unjust pain, then the Lord is unjust since he is the primary cause of their agony. This approach downplays his holiness as an afterthought, or even an insignificant peripheral factor. But there is a higher virtue in the world than human empathy, a divine one. The poet of Lamentations recognizes this when he states that the "Lord is our portion" (Lam. 3:24) and that the Lord who is our portion is "holy, holy, holy" (Isa. 6:3).

A proper theology is the starting point for developing a proper mindset to understand these difficulties. The man in Lamentations 3 begins to find comfort not in the thought that his torment will end but in a theological meditation upon the nature of God (Lam. 3:19–39). It is blasphemous to think that we can offend his holy character without severe consequence. One will never begin to comprehend the violence in Lamentations (or throughout Scripture) until one first has a proper understanding of the holiness of God.

Approaching the New Testament

It should be noted that frequently those who struggle with this notion of a "violent" God also struggle with the wider concept of a vengeful God who punishes sin. In recent theological diatribes many evangelical theologians have fought to maintain that there is a propitiation required for sin where the wrath of a holy God must be satisfied. The Christian gospel is built upon the fact that such atoning work was accomplished by the sacrifice of Jesus Christ, the God-man, upon the cross (Rom. 3:25; 1 John 2:2; cf. Isa. 53:4–5). Those who dare to stand before his holy presence audaciously upon the measure of their own flawed good works will only come to realize too late that such "righteousness" is no righteousness at all before the One who is all-holy. A small picture of that wrathful God is manifested in Lamentations. If readers struggle with a God who honors his own holiness as depicted in Lamentations, then what are their thoughts of eternal condemnation and wrath? We must remember that the Christian gospel depicts an eternity for those who are without

---

[14] Dobbs-Allsopp, *Lamentations*, 29–30.

the righteousness of Christ in much more damning pictures than those painted in Lamentations. Thus is the sober reality of life away from the Lord.

However, the Christian gospel also offers an eternal city that is "imperishable, undefiled, and unfading" (1 Pet. 1:4), whose inhabitants are those who turned from their transgressions and embraced the Lord as their portion (Lam. 3:24). The unspoken lesson of Lamentations is to remind the reader that there is coming a glorified city of God "that has foundations, whose designer and builder is God" (Heb. 11:10). The earthly Jerusalem, although magnificent in its architecture and extravagant in its wealth, was frail and limited due to its fallen nature. As the writer of the book of Hebrews states, "here we have no lasting city, but we seek the city that is to come" (Heb. 13:14). The book of Lamentations has a limited application; it can only be used in a fallen world that mourns the devastation brought on by sin. There will be no such need in the New Jerusalem of the new covenant, for in that eschatological city "he will wipe away every tear from their eyes, and death shall be no more, neither shall there be mourning, nor crying, nor pain anymore" (Rev. 21:4).

SELECT BIBLIOGRAPHY

Berlin, Adele. *The Dynamics of Biblical Parallelism*. Rev. ed. Grand Rapids, MI: Eerdmans, 2009.

———. *Lamentations*. OTL. Louisville: Westminster John Knox, 2002.

Budde, Karl. "Das hebräische Klagelied." *ZAW* 2 (1882): 1–52.

Carmignac, Jean. "Étude sur les Procédés Poétiques des Hymnes." *RevQ* 2, no. 4 (1960): 515–32.

Dobbs-Allsopp, F. W. *Lamentations*. IBC. Louisville: John Knox, 2002.

Freedman, David N. "Acrostic Poems in the Hebrew Bible: Alphabetic and Otherwise." *CBQ* 48, no. 3 (1986): 408–31.

———. "Acrostics and Metrics in Hebrew Poetry." *HTR* 65, no. 3 (1972): 367–92.

Gerstenberger, Erhard S. *Psalms, Part 2, and Lamentations*. FOTL 15. Grand Rapids, MI: Eerdmans, 2001.

Green, M. W. "The Eridu Lament." *JCS* 30, no. 3 (1978): 127–67.

———. "The Uruk Lament." *JAOS* 104, no. 2 (1984): 253–79.

Gwaltney, W. C., Jr. "The Biblical Book of Lamentations in the Context of Near Eastern Literature." In *Scripture in Context 2: More Essays on the Comparative Method*, edited by William W. Hallo, James C. Moyer, and Leo G. Perdue, 191–211. Winona Lake, IN: Eisenbrauns, 1983.

House, Paul R. *Lamentations*. In *Song of Songs / Lamentations*, by Duane A. Garrett and Paul R. House. WBC 23B. Nashville: Thomas Nelson, 2004.

Longman, Tremper, III. *Jeremiah, Lamentations*. NIBCOT 14. Peabody, MA: Hendrickson, 2008.

McDaniel, Thomas F. "The Alleged Sumerian Influence upon Lamentations." *VT* 18, no. 2 (1968): 198–209.

Michalowski, Piotr. *The Lamentation over the Destruction of Sumer and Ur*. MC 1. Winona Lake, IN: Eisenbrauns, 1989.

O'Connor, Michael P. *Hebrew Verse Structure*. Winona Lake, IN: Eisenbrauns, 1980.

Provan, Iain W. *Lamentations: Based on the Revised Standard Version*. NCB. Grand Rapids, MI: Eerdmans, 1991.

Schökel, Luis Alonso. *A Manual of Hebrew Poetics*. SubBi 11. Rome: Editrice Pontificio Istituto Biblico, 2000.

Soll, Will. "Acrostic." In *The Anchor Bible Dictionary*, edited by David Noel Freedman, 1:58–60. New York: Doubleday, 1992.

Webb, Barry G. *Five Festal Garments: Christian Reflections on the Song of Songs, Ruth, Lamentations, Ecclesiastes, and Esther*. NSBT 10. Downers Grove, IL: InterVarsity Press, 2000.

21

Esther

Peter Y. Lee

INTRODUCTION

Because there are so many meaningful facets to the book of Esther, it is impossible to do justice to the book by focusing on only one. In part it is about a young Jewish girl, whose plight in life not only left her an orphan but also landed her in the foreign lands of Persia, where she ended up in a position of influence over the most powerful political figure of the day, Ahasuerus the king. To focus on the narrative of this young Jewess alone can distract from another significant plot point, the tension between Mordecai and Haman. This Haman is also called "the enemy of the Jews" (Est. 3:10; 9:24), whose personal clash with Mordecai led him to manipulate the Persian king into proclaiming an edict to annihilate not only his mortal enemy but also the Jewish people. We also are given insight into the internal operations of the Persian court, even the squabbles of the royal couple. Of course, one of the more significant aspects of this book is that it provides the origin, regulations, and prominence of the Jewish holiday of Purim. This is one of numerous festivals that occur, so many that the narrative exudes a *carnivalesque* aura.[1] This seems fitting given the excessive way in which Purim is celebrated. The preservation of the Jews also preserved covenantal promises made by the Lord to his people that can find their origins as far back as Genesis 3:15, the promise that the seed of the woman would come to crush the head of the Serpent. That seed would come through the line of the Jews.

Indeed, the book of Esther cannot be oversimplified. The interweaving of various thematic strands forms a literary beauty that distinguishes it from other Old Testament books, especially in the way it communicates its message. Not only is God never mentioned explicitly, but this book is also considered by many the most

---

[1] According to Jon D. Levenson, there are ten banquets. *Esther*, OTL (Louisville: Westminster John Knox, 1997), 3–5.

comical within the Canon—God draws laughter from the reader at the expense of a pagan king.

BACKGROUND ISSUES
Canonical Matters[2]

Studying the canonicity of Esther is difficult, largely because it unexpectedly omits any mention of God. The Jewishness of Esther is self-evident in that it expressly describes the providential preservation of their race and the establishment of their well-known holiday of Purim. Yet it is still odd for a Jewish text to be devoid of a *theos*. For these reasons, many commentators have considered Esther not only the most Jewish but also the most "secular" book within the biblical Canon.[3] Martin Luther famously denounced it, saying, "I am so great an enemy to the second book of Maccabees, and to Esther, that I wish they had not come to us at all, for they have too many heathen unnaturalities."[4] Early records of the Old Testament canon are inconclusive regarding its canonicity. Esther is not listed in the oldest catalog of canonical books by the Bishop of Melito of Sardis (ca. AD 180). Several prominent Eastern church fathers in the fourth century AD also omit Esther in their canonical lists (e.g., Athanasius and Gregory of Nazianzus); however, it is affirmed by the Councils of Hippo (ca. AD 393) and Carthage (ca. AD 397).

In addition, it is the only Old Testament book not found among the biblical texts discovered at Qumran.[5] Although the absence of copies may be due to the accidents of archaeological work and the result of the frail nature of manuscripts, and not due to any rejection by the ancient Qumran community, the majority of scholars believe that Esther was indeed not accepted as canonical because this would have conflicted with the Qumran calendar. Roger Beckwith insightfully points out that the Qumran community followed a 364-day calendar, which distributed the year into fifty-two weeks. In this system any day of the month will always fall on the same day of the week. Since Adar 14, the day of the Feast of Purim in Esther 9:17, 19, falls on the Sabbath, to accept Esther would cause a theological crux since it would describe the protagonists of Esther performing work on a day when it was prohibited.[6]

Regarding the Qumran evidence, one must remember that the Jews in Qumran were possibly a sectarian group (the Essenes) who separated themselves in protest against the teachings of the Pharisees in Jerusalem. If there is any merit to the argu-

---

[2] A distinction between the Septuagint and Masoretic text versions of Esther must be noted at the outset prior to any investigation of canonical matters with Esther. What follows applies only to the Masoretic text version. For issues related to the Septuagint version of Esther, see "Ancient Versions" on p. 478.

[3] See Roger T. Beckwith, *The Old Testament Canon of the New Testament Church and Its Background in Early Judaism* (Grand Rapids, MI: Eerdmans, 1985), 283–87.

[4] Martin Luther, *Table Talk of Martin Luther*, trans. William Hazlitt (London: David Bogue, 1848), 27.

[5] Lee Martin McDonald, however, comments that the copies of noncanonical writings discovered at Qumran do outnumber those of the biblical texts and that only a single copy of other canonical books have thus far been discovered (i.e., Proverbs, Ezra, and Chronicles). *The Biblical Canon: Its Origin, Transmission, and Authority*, 3rd ed. (Peabody, MA: Hendrickson, 2007), 109.

[6] Beckwith, *Canon*, 291–94. Adele Berlin points out that rabbinic Judaism had no problem of Purim (or any other holiday) falling on the Sabbath and that according to the Jewish calendar now in use, Adar 14 can never fall on the Sabbath. *Esther: The Traditional Hebrew Text with the New JPS Translation*, JPS Bible Commentary (Philadelphia: Jewish Publication Society: 2001), xlv.

ment that this Essene community opposed the canonicity of Esther due to calendar conflicts, then it is reasonable to presume that Esther was accepted as canonical among non-Essene Jews. Interestingly, Lee Martin McDonald mentions the discovery of proto-Esther texts (4Q550, 4Q550a, 4Q550b, 4Q550c, 4Q550d), which should give us pause before leaping to any definitive canonical conclusions regarding Esther in Qumran. This suggests that Esther was indeed accepted as canonical by the Jewish community at large during the Second Temple era prior to the Essene occupation of the community center by the Dead Sea.

Looking at the question from another angle, the significant comment by Josephus (ca. AD 100) in his *Contra Apion* 1.37–43 does not specify what books the Jews accepted as canonical, but it marks a canonical *terminus a quo* and a *terminus ad quem*: "From Moses' passing until Artaxerxes who was king of the Persians after Xerxes" (1.40). The reference to "Artaxerxes" is the historical period of Ezra and Nehemiah. It is possible that this includes Esther, which also relates events from the reign of Artaxerxes according to the Septuagint.

Within rabbinic Judaism a *baraita* on the order of the books in *Baba Bathra* 14b and the oldest of the Septuagint codices all include Esther in their canonical lists. The rabbinic scholars who met at Jamnia in ca. AD 90 discussed the canonicity of Esther, but this discussion was intended to justify the status quo of its canonicity, not to reject it.[7] The deduction, therefore, is that Esther was accepted as canonical (and thus authoritative) well before this gathering at Jamnia. The majority of scholars believe the canonization of Esther occurred around the second century BC.

Place in the Canon

In the Masoretic text Esther is considered part of the *Megilloth*, which is composed of the Song of Songs, Ruth, Lamentations, Ecclesiastes, and Esther. These five books were to be read at five major festal holidays in the Jewish liturgical year. Curiously, the order in the rabbinic tradition in *Baba Bathra* 14b scatters the five books throughout the third section of the Canon, the "Writings," where Esther seems to be grouped with the books of Daniel, Ezra–Nehemiah, and Chronicles.

Regarding the place of Esther in the *Megilloth*, Barry Webb points out that the liturgical reading of Esther at Purim occurs approximately one month before Passover, making the two festivals of Passover and Purim calendrical partners.[8] Although the cultic tone of the two are diametrically antithetical, the overall cause of celebration is interestingly identical—both celebrate deliverance of the sons of Abraham from imminent threat and extinction. Thus it is possible that the literary placement of

---

[7] Earlier scholarship viewed the "council" at Jamnia as equivalent to an authoritative ecumenical council meeting. Recent studies have disproven this theory. It is now properly understood as an academic gathering of scholars who were interacting on the state of Judaism absent the temple and thus is analogous to an academic conference. Also debunked is the theory that the Torah was canonized in ca. 400 BC, the Prophets in ca. 200 BC, and the Writings at Jamnia. Cf. Jack P. Lewis, "What Do We Mean by Jabneh?," *JBR* 32, no. 2 (1964): 125–32; Robert C. Newman, "The Council of Jamnia and the Old Testament Canon," *WTJ* 38, no. 3 (1976): 319–49; D. E. Aune, "On the Origins of the 'Council of Javneh' Myth," *JBL* 110, no. 3 (1991): 491–93.

[8] Barry G. Webb, *Five Festal Garments: Christian Reflections on the Song of Songs, Ruth, Lamentations, Ecclesiastes, and Esther*, NSBT 10 (Downers Grove, IL: InterVarsity Press, 2000), 111.

Esther not only follows a calendar order but also helps to communicate a major theme within the book by relating it to Passover: the deliverance by God from overwhelming enemies (see "Exodus Redux" on p. 492).

Ancient Versions

The comments made thus far have been based upon the Masoretic text of Esther. This version is distinct from the Septuagint, a Greek translation of a different Hebrew text from that of the Masoretic text. There is also another Greek text of Esther, referred to as the Greek Alpha text. Recent studies in Esther have embarked on detailed comparisons of these ancient versions, which have elucidated what early form this narrative might have taken before the Masoretic text and how these other versions took the forms as we currently have them. Since our interest is exclusively on the Masoretic text, the history of the development of the text of Esther need not concern us; however, some comment seems warranted on the differences between the Septuagint and the Masoretic text.[9]

Within the Septuagint are six passages not paralleled by the Masoretic text. The work of Jerome in his Latin Vulgate was significant in dealing with these passages and shaping Esther. Seeing that these six passages had no Hebrew parallel, he doubted their authenticity and thus canonicity. Consequently, he partitioned those six passages from the main body of Esther and placed them at the end of the book. By the time of the Protestant Reformation, these six passages were deemed noncanonical and excluded from Esther entirely. In the Roman Catholic Church, however, the Council of Trent affirmed these six "additions" as canonical in 1546 and grouped them together into a collection, giving them the title "The Additions of Esther."[10] It remains to this day as part of the Apocrypha of the Roman Church while noncanonical among Protestants.[11]

Historicity of Esther

The historical character of Esther has been a point of contention within the academic community. The majority of scholars see the narrative of Esther not as actual historical events of a Jewish community in the heart of a Persian urban capitol but rather as historical fiction. Adele Berlin uses the term "imaginative storytelling," where Esther shares certain similarities with Greek literary works in its portrayal of life in the Persian court.[12] Some of the reasons why the historical character is called into question are as follows:[13]

---

[9] The Alpha text is a Greek translation of an original Hebrew text that seems very different from the Masoretic text tradition. For a more detailed discussion of the interrelationships between the Alpha text, the Septuagint, and the Masoretic text versions of Esther, see David J. A. Clines, *The Esther Scroll: The Story of the Story*, JSOTSup 30 (Sheffield: JSOT Press, 1984). Clines's work was further developed by Michael Fox in *The Redaction of the Books of Esther: On Reading Composite Texts*, SBLMS 40 (Atlanta: Scholars Press, 1991). Also see Levenson, *Esther*, 27–34; Carey A. Moore, *Daniel, Esther, and Jeremiah: The Additions*, AB44 (Garden City, NY: Doubleday, 1977); Frederic Bush, *Ruth/Esther*, WBC 9 (Nashville: Thomas Nelson, 1996), 279–94.

[10] For a commentary on each of these six additions, see Moore, *Daniel, Esther, and Jeremiah*, 153–252; Levenson, *Esther*, 37–42, 74–77, 83–86, 86–88, 111–14, 134–36.

[11] For more on the differences between the Masoretic text and Septuagint versions of Esther, see Clines, *The Esther Scroll*, 169–74.

[12] Berlin, *Esther*, xv, xxviii–xxxii.

[13] In addition to these, Berlin adds that Esther would not have been able to keep her ethnic identity a secret, a plot point upon which the narrative is heavily dependent. *Esther*, xvii. However, I fail to see the impossibility of such a task. According to

1. There is no record of a Persian queen named Esther or of any Jewish queen of Persia, especially since queens came from noble Persian families, not ethnic minorities. In fact, the ancient Jewish historian Herodotus refers to the wife of Xerxes (Ahasuerus) as Amestris, not Vashti.
2. If Mordecai was taken into captivity with Jehoiachin (Jeconiah) as Esther 2:6 states, then he would be over one hundred years old during the events in the book of Esther.
3. The number of satrapies in Esther does not match those found among other records. While Esther 1:1 says that Ahasuerus had 127 satrapies (Dan. 6:1 also records 120), Herodotus and the inscriptions of Darius (the father of Xerxes) record 20 and 23–30 respectively.
4. No Persian king would act in the manner of Ahasuerus, who is depicted as an incompetent bumbler and easily manipulated by others around him.
5. To govern by instituting laws that are irrevocable makes governing impossible.
6. A royal edict to annihilate the Jews is contrary to Persian policies that tended to be benevolent to other ethnic groups, as illustrated in Cyrus's decree permitting the Jews to return to their homeland to rebuild their ancient city of Jerusalem and their temple (2 Chron. 36:21–22; Ezra 1:1–4).

Karen Jobes says that each of these particular critiques have a reasonable explanation, and thus the historical reliability of the narrative can be preserved. In her commentary she, in fact, addresses each point listed here. For example, regarding point 1, Jobes says that Vashti and Amestris (from Herodotus) are possibly one and the same person with two different names, where Amestris is Greek and Vashti Persian. Jobes also suggests that the name Vashti sounds similar to an Old Persian word meaning "beautiful woman," possibly making Vashti in Esther a literary reference to Amestris. Regarding the lack of reference to Esther in the Persian royal archives, Jobes notes that since the interest of these records was to trace the succession of a royal dynasty, it was customary to only mention wives who bore successors/sons to the throne and thus that all other concubines or wives were omitted.[14]

However, the greater argument used by the literary-critical school against the historicity of Esther is the fact that it reads like a highly stylized narrative, more akin to "imaginative storytelling" (Berlin's term) than historical writing. As we will see, one of the ways in which the structure of the book can be analyzed is as a story—with a plot that is developed, the characterization of the protagonists/antagonists, conflict resolution, and so forth (see "Structure 2: 'Problem-Based Plot'" on p. 485). For these reasons, it is alleged that Esther was not (nor should be) read as records of actual historical events, the presumption being that narrative and historicity are mutually exclusive. In other words, if a text is deemed to be a literary artifice, then

---

the Masoretic text of Esther, she shared her bed with a pagan king, partook of pagan foods and drink. In other words, she lived like a Persian queen and did not give her identity away by her outward conformity to biblical law. Her ethics may be called into question and even criticized, but she was surely able to preserve the secrecy of her true ethnicity. For an ethical evaluation of Esther, see Karen H. Jobes, *Esther*, NIVAC (Grand Rapids, MI: Zondervan, 1999), 114–15.

[14] Jobes, *Esther*, 66–67. Regarding point 2, see Jobes, *Esther*, 95; point 3, Jobes, *Esther*, 58–59; point 4, Jobes, *Esther*, 79; and point 5, Jobes, *Esther*, 78–79. Point 6 is raised by Berlin and not addressed by Jobes. Berlin, *Esther*, xvii. However, it would not be difficult to see that with a new king comes new policies. Also, part of the satiric portrayal of the king is to show how easily he can be manipulated. See "Comedy and the Sovereignty of God" on p. 490.

it cannot be a source of accurate and reliable historical record keeping of ancient peoples and events.[15]

Although the high literary quality of Esther is undeniable, it is unclear why a literary work cannot be both artistic narrative and reliable history. Such an assumption seems to impose more modern conceptions of historiography and literary critical theory upon ancient biblical writers who did not share the same dichotomy. At the very least, it would seem that one must prove that the ancients accepted such a dichotomy before it can be applied to the book of Esther.

In one sense, an "imaginative storytelling" approach to Esther would be counter to its designed intent. Clearly, one purpose that Esther served was to describe and justify the origins of Purim. The heroic acts of the Jewish remnant in Persia demonstrate that there are historical reasons to justify the practice of Purim. Such an explanation was necessary for the budding Jewish community of the Diaspora especially since the holiday lacked precedence within the old covenant legislation. If, however, the origins of this new holiday was based upon untrue historical events, then does this not call into question the validity of the holiday? Why should the Jews continue to observe it? Where did it come from? Logically, a case can be made, therefore, that the historicity of Esther is necessary, or at the very least, true unless proven otherwise.

Such an argument, however, must not neglect the clear literary quality of the narrative. There is little doubt that the author/editor of this text sways the emotions of the reader by using literary devices and techniques to raise hopes of resolution of conflicts, only to be disappointed with the results. So we cannot help but feel a letdown when we read about Mordecai's thwarting of the schemes of assassins against the Persian king only to see that his nemesis is rewarded instead. We scream at the text when we read of Esther inviting Ahasuerus and Haman to a private banquet yet withholding meaningful information that can save the Jews. We hold our breath only to be relieved later when she organizes a second banquet where she reveals the true enemy of both the Jews and Persia. Our earlier frustration in reading of Haman's apparent victory over Mordecai is satisfied when we read that Haman himself is hung by the very instrument he built for Mordecai's execution. Is all this elevated narrative writing? Indeed it is. Is it also historical recounting? Again, yes. In the same way that we can worship God as our Creator and Redeemer because he indeed did the work of creation and redemption, so Purim is a legitimate holiday for Jews because of the historical reliability of Esther.

---

[15] From this line of reasoning, not only is the historicity of Esther called into question but easily the entirety of Old Testament historical literature. Such thought is best reflected in the "minimalist" approach. According to this view, the majority of Old Testament historical narratives are fictitious accounts invented by Jewish writers during the Persian and Hellenistic periods. Thus the Old Testament contains very few, if any, reliable historical events or people. For a more thorough response to the minimalist approach to Old Testament historiography, see Iain W. Provan, V. Philips Long, and Tremper Longman III, *A Biblical History of Israel* (Louisville: Westminster John Knox, 2003), 1–107; Tremper Longman, "Storytellers and Poets in the Bible: Can Literary Artifice Be True?," in *Inerrancy and Hermeneutic: A Tradition, a Challenge, a Debate*, ed. Harvie M. Conn (Grand Rapids, MI: Baker, 1988), 137–50. A defense of the historicity of Esther in light of its literary nature can be found in Jobes, *Esther*, 30–37.

STRUCTURE AND OUTLINE

The author/editor is unknown, and the date of the book cannot be determined with great precision. It was most likely put into the form as we have it in the Hebrew canon no later than 400 BC, after the reign of Xerxes and before the Hellenization agenda of Alexander the Great in the fourth century BC.

It is possible that the author/editor used written materials as sources of the narrative—so Esther 10:2 mentions the "Chronicles of the kings of Media and Persia." Some scholars have alleged that there are three sources in the book—a Vashti, a Mordecai, and an Esther source.[16] Still, others see two sources that parallel the numerous doublets in the narrative, where the two have been interwoven into the final form of Esther as we have it today. Regardless of the various source theories of literary critics, this does not distract from the narrative cohesion of the book that many commentators recognize.

The structural cohesion of any literary work should be perceived in relation to the themes found within it. In other words, literary organization enhances the message, which means the two should not be mutually exclusive. The question at hand regarding the book of Esther is, what themes do we find within it and how does the literary organization highlight those themes? As there are several different motifs in this book, so there are various ways to analyze its organization. We should not feel pressure to commit to only one approach. Michael Fox prefers to speak of the book as "organizable" as opposed to being limited to merely one literary "organization."[17] Because of the overall unity in Esther, it is difficult to parse out sections and discern a literary substructure with absolute precision. Indeed, no such precision exists in any literary work, biblical or not. Again, Fox is helpful when he states that "the structures need not present neat, symmetrical, or hierarchical designs, for design is not their point. . . . There must simply be enough of a design to do the job assigned it."[18] All this should remind us that when dealing with literature, we are dealing with "organic" thought processes that cannot always be categorized with precise narrative units. Ancient (like modern) authors wrote freely and openly with the goal of communicating a certain message, not rigidly conforming to a literary standard. The duty for modern readers is to see the connection between the form of the literature and the message found within it.

Structure 1: Banquet Theme

In that regard I suggest that there are three meaningful literary structures in Esther.[19] The first is based upon the prevalent partying scenes so common in the book. Pivotal points arise that are significant to the development of the narrative, and it is noteworthy that these plot points frequently occur in the context of a banquet.

---

[16] See Clines, *The Esther Scroll*, 115–17; Fox, *Redaction of the Books of Esther*, 96–98.
[17] Michael V. Fox, *Character and Ideology in the Book of Esther*, Studies on Personalities of the Old Testament (Columbia: University of South Carolina Press, 1991), 153.
[18] Fox, *Character and Ideology*, 153.
[19] Fox, *Character and Ideology*, 153–63. Curiously, Fox says that he sees "four" structures, yet he only describes three.

Esther 1 begins with the Persian king Ahasuerus hosting two extravagant banquets, the first for the official elite of his empire (1:3) and the second for "the people present in Susa" (1:5). The excessiveness of these parties is encapsulated when they are described as continuing for 180 days and seven days, respectively, and as including drinking done in accord with the royal edict, "There is no compulsion" (1:8). Also, "the king had given orders to all the staff of his palace to do as each man desired" (1:8). Meantime, Queen Vashti organizes her own party (banquet 3) for the women of the palace (1:9). It is in the midst of all these banquets that an inebriated Ahasuerus summons his queen to flaunt her beauty before his guests. However, she refuses. This act of defiance portrays the most powerful political figure of the day, the monarch of the most powerful empire of the ancient world, as one who is unable to manage his own household. The king overreacts and foolishly (and humorously) attempts to resolve his own domestic squabble by issuing a national edict ordering "all women [to] give honor to their husbands" (1:20). All this takes place in the midst of a multiplicity of banquets.

Esther 2 opens with Ahasuerus calling for every beautiful young virgin in his realm to enter a competition to be the new queen in place of the dethroned Vashti (2:1–4). At this point, the main Jewish protagonists of the book, Esther and Mordecai, are introduced. Esther wins the favor of the king and becomes the new queen, which is the occasion for yet another banquet (banquet 4). Mordecai, serving at the gate of the king, discovers and reports an assassination plot against Ahasuerus, thus saving his life. However, Mordecai does not receive any recognition or rewards; rather, Haman, the "enemy of the Jews," is promoted to second in command of the empire.

Esther 3, for unspecified reasons, finds Mordecai at odds with Haman, refusing to pay him respect. Haman responds by plotting the destruction of not only Mordecai but the entire Jewish race (3:1–6). He casts פּוּרִים (*purim*), or lots, to determine the day of this mass execution. After manipulating the king by offering a bribe, Haman is able to win the favor of Ahasuerus, who issues a royal decree that permits the destruction of all Jews on Adar 13. While the city of Susa is thrown into chaos due to this edict, Haman and Ahasuerus celebrate with yet another feast—banquet 5.

Esther 4 describes Mordecai and the Jews as in mourning after hearing about the dreadful edict. Esther also is greatly disturbed. She is, however, mindful of Persian court practices that prohibit anyone from approaching the king unsummoned, and she fears using her position to influence the king (4:1–11). Mordecai, in what is clearly manipulative argumentation, persuades Esther to intercede nonetheless by reminding her that, though she may have risen to her position for this very reason, redemption will come to the Jews even without her involvement; they will survive while she will perish (4:12–14). Esther agrees to go to the king and encourages Mordecai to hold a three-day fast on her behalf (4:15–16).

Esther 5 depicts Esther as winning the favor of the king, who offers her whatever she wishes; however, she only requests that the king along with Haman attend a banquet that she is holding—banquet 6. At this party, the king repeats his offer to give whatever she desires, to which she again requests the presence of the same duo at a second banquet (5:1–8). Haman, thinking that the queen has such a high regard for him, boasts to his friends and his wife about his VIP invitation by Esther. Yet his ego is again bruised when Mordecai refuses to honor him. Haman's wife suggests that he order that Mordecai be impaled upon a giant stake, and he proceeds with preparations to his heart's malicious delight (5:9–14).

Esther 6 is a significant transition point. Whereas the first half of Esther saw difficulties for Mordecai, Esther, and their fellow Jews, so the second half describes dramatic reversals for them. It begins comically with Ahasuerus treating his insomnia by reading his royal annals. In so doing he learns of the assassination attempt on his life that was thwarted by Mordecai. As he is contemplating how to reward Mordecai for his act of loyalty, Haman "coincidentally" enters to seek permission from the king to execute the very man whom the king desires to bless. The king asks, "What should be done to the man whom the king delights to honor?" (6:6). Thinking that Ahasuerus is referring to him, Haman says that such a man should be honored as if he was a monarch. The king agrees. To Haman's shock, however, it is Mordecai who is honored. Dejected and humiliated, Haman returns home to seek counsel from his wife. Where previously she had a word of victory for Haman, his wife now has a more frightening message—he is doomed to fall before his foe.

Esther 7 begins with the banquet given by Esther for Ahasuerus and Haman (banquet 7). It is at this party that a series of quick-paced events follow with lightning speed. Esther reveals her true ethnic origins and appeals for the salvation of her people (7:1–4). The king discovers that Haman had manipulated him into issuing the aforementioned genocidal decree (7:5–6). He stomps out in a huff. Meanwhile, Haman falls on the couch where Esther was sitting, begging for his life (7:7). At that very moment, the king returns and thinks that Haman is assaulting his queen (7:8)! In an ironic twist the king has Haman hoisted upon the very stake that he had built for Mordecai (7:9–10).

Esther 8 finds Esther awarded Haman's estate and Mordecai promoted. The plight of the Jews, however, remains, and Ahasuerus is unable to reverse the previous edict (8:1–6). Instead, he permits Mordecai to issue a second edict that permits the Jews to defend themselves against their attackers on the very day that Haman had determined by lot (*purim*) to destroy them (8:7–14). Mordecai stands publically in the royal robes given to him by the king, to the pleasure of his fellow Jews. Thus they hold another banquet—banquet 8. Indeed, many Gentiles also identify themselves as Jews for fear of their reprisal.

Esther 9 marks that fateful day, Adar 13, the day of the Jewish genocide. However, the Jews win an overwhelming victory and defeat their foes (9:1–10). Even the ten sons of Haman are executed at the request of Esther (9:11–14). The Jews in the capitol of Susa celebrate their victory with a banquet on Adar 14 (9:15, 18), while the rest of the Jews throughout the empire follow with a feast on Adar 15 (9:16–17,

19). This marks banquets 9 and 10 in the book and the beginning of the new annual holiday of Purim (9:20–32).

Esther 10 closes the narrative with a lofty description of the success of Mordecai.

From this survey, it is clear that the motif of "banquet" (מִשְׁתֶּה) is a dominant theme within the book. To put it in perspective, Karen Jobes notes that מִשְׁתֶּה occurs twenty times in the book of Esther compared to twenty-four times in the rest of the Old Testament.[20] Michael Fox suggests the literary structure in figure 5 using the banquet theme as the central rubric in its organization.[21]

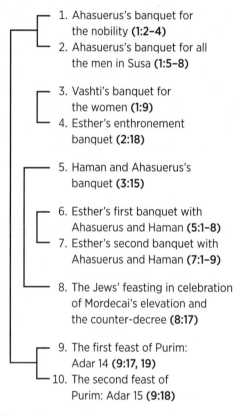

Figure 5

Certain banquets seem intentionally paired together. Fox correctly sees that banquets 1 and 2 have an obvious connection, as do banquets 9 and 10. There is also a correspondence between those two pairs that creates a literary *inclusio* for the book. Vashti's party (banquet 3) contrasts Esther's (banquet 4); whereas the first represents the final celebration for one queen (Vashti), the second marks the inauguration of another (Esther). Fox also correctly sees a pairing of banquets 5 and 8: the former celebrates Haman's diabolical plan to annihilate the Jews, which causes Mordecai

---

[20] Jobes, *Esther*, 40.
[21] Fox, *Character and Ideology*, 157. To Fox's proposed structure, Levenson suggests another layer of pairings that is complex and intriguing but unpersuasive. *Esther*, 5–6.

to mourn, and the latter celebrates Mordecai's promotion, which causes Haman to mourn. The parallelism between banquets 6 and 7 is self-evident. Thus, the structure of Esther follows the occurrences of these ten banquets that have been organized into five pairs. Since one purpose of the book is clearly to explain (and possibly justify) the newly established holiday of Purim, this is not surprising. Similar to the pairing of feasts in the narrative, so the celebration of Purim is to be observed over a pair of days that begin with a festive celebration.

Structure 2: "Problem-Based Plot"

A second structure is based upon the story-like character of Esther. In his analysis Michael Fox suggests that it can be viewed as a "sequence and segmentation of events." He proposes the following outline of a "chronological order": (1) the beginning (1:1–2:23), which sets the stage for the entire book; (2) the middle (3:1–9:19), which describes the narrative proper; and (3) the end (9:20–10:3), which establishes the holiday of Purim.[22]

Although Fox says that this approach is so obvious that it can be easily missed, it is not missed by Frederic Bush, who applies the theories of modern literary criticism to Esther (as well as to Ruth) and suggests that it is an example of a "problem-based plot" structure.[23] For Bush, Esther can be seen as subdivided into the following categories:

1. The setting (1:1–2:23), where the major characters of the narrative are introduced
2. The problem (3:1–15), which is the royal edict of genocide
3. Complicating/resolving incidents (4:1–7:10), where a series of complex issues arise that require immediate resolution without solving the major crisis
4. The resolution (8:1–9:5), where the schemed destruction of the Jews backfires against Haman
5. The denouement (9:6–32), which establishes the holiday of Purim as an annual practice for the Jewish people
6. The conclusion/coda (10:1–3), which is a word of praise for Mordecai

The book of Esther, therefore, can be read as a novella, which has unnecessarily given fuel to many scholars challenging its historicity (see "Historicity of Esther" on p. 478).

Structure 3: Reversal Theme

In addition to the banquet and narrative structures, the theme of reversal serves as another organizing principle. In general Esther is about the plight of the Jews who nearly suffer extermination. Yet the story twists, turns, and ultimately reverses the fortunes of the Jews, with their enemies suffering the fate initially planned for them while they institute a new holiday. Fox calls this theme *peripety*, which occurs when "the result of an action is actually the reverse of what was expected."[24] Reading the

---

[22] Fox, *Character and Ideology*, 154–56. He also subdivides his tripartite sections further into "acts" or "scenes."
[23] Bush, *Ruth/Esther*, 300–304. Bush applies the theories of John Beekman, John Callow, and Michael F. Kopesec, *The Semantic Structure of Written Communication* (Dallas: Summer Institute of Linguistics, 1981), §4.2.4.
[24] Fox, *Character and Ideology*, 158. Cf. Jobes, *Esther*, 40–41.

book from this perspective brings out an alternative literary structure, which high-lights the theme of reversal even further.

The work of Jon Levenson is helpful here.[25] He shows that chapter 6 is a pivotal point in the narrative, specifically Ahasuerus's struggle with his insomnia and his real-ization of the loyalty of Mordecai who had reported the earlier assassination attempt on his life (6:1–11). Prior to this event, the Jews faced one obstacle after another. After the king is awakened to the service of Mordecai, everything changes. Instead of facing total destruction, Mordecai and the Jews are delivered, even empowered to destroy those who threatened them. The immediate narrative surrounding the opening event of chapter 6 illustrates this reversal theme. Prior to chapter 6, Ahasuerus and Haman were invited to a banquet given by Esther (banquet 6 in figure 5). Haman boasted of his private invitation while Mordecai faced execution (5:1–14). Within chapter 6, it is Mordecai who is exalted and recognized by the king while Haman faces his own execution (6:10–13). Even the words of Haman's wife change drastically. Prior to chapter 6, she devises the method for executing Mordecai, which pleases Haman. Within chapter 6, she says somber words to Haman that suggest divine powers may be at work for Mordecai and thus against her doomed husband. This illustrates a larger correspondence of reversals that occur within Esther and are structured ac-cording to a chiastic schematic. Levenson proposes the following chiastic structure:[26]

a   Greatness of Ahasuerus (1:1–8)
   b   Two Banquets of the Persians (1:1–8)
      c   Esther Identifies as a Gentile (2:10–20)
         d   Elevation of Haman (3:1)
            e   Anti-Jewish Edict (3:12–15)
               f   Fateful Exchange of Mordecai and Esther (4:1–17)
                  g   First Banquet of the Threesome (5:6–8)
                     h   Royal Procession (6:1–14)
                  g'   Second Banquet of the Threesome (7:1–6)
               f'   Fateful Exchange of Ahasuerus and Esther (7:1–6)
            e'   Pro-Jewish Edict (8:9–14)
         d'   Elevation of Mordecai (8:15)
      c'   Gentiles Identify as Jews (8:17)
   b'   Two Banquets of the Jews (9:20–32)
a'   Greatness of Ahasuerus and Mordecai (10:1–3)

The first half of the book (sections a–g) depicts the challenges and negative cir-cumstances that face Esther, Mordecai, and the Jewish community, and the second half (sections g'–a') shows resolution to the numerous conflicts of the protagonists in the ultimate reversal of the edict of genocide that occasions the birth of a new festival. Thus the very structure of the book reinforces its message: the enemies of the Jews attempted to manipulate political powers for their destruction, but "the

---

reverse occurred: the Jews gained mastery over those who hated them" (9:1). These were days, therefore, that went "from sorrow into gladness and from mourning into a holiday" (9:22).

MESSAGE AND THEOLOGY

Since the message of a book cannot be divorced from its organization, I have already alluded to descriptions of the message in the preceding sections. Yet more can be said. Karen Jobes believes that preaching through the book of Esther is challenging if a verse-by-verse approach is taken. She suggests that preaching thematically is more helpful. Thus the sections delineated in what follows could be a proposed preaching outline.[27]

The Presence of God in the Absence of God

When we consider the message of the book of Esther, it is a bit awkward to call it a "theology" since the book is missing the most important element in a theological work—a *theos*. As stated earlier, Esther is most popularly known as the only book in the Old Testament (indeed, the entire Bible) that is devoid of any explicit mention of God. The divine name Yahweh does not occur, nor does the Hebrew word *elohim*, "God," or any other names of God. He is not addressed formally in prayers, praise, or dedications. In fact, there are no prayers at all in the book of Esther (though there is a fast in Est. 4:16). The absence of God is even more conspicuous when we compare the Masoretic text version with the other ancient versions of this book, such as the Septuagint, where God is not only mentioned by name but is directly involved as an active participant within the narrative. Why is God incognito?

The answer to that question is elusive. It would be safe, however, to presume that any Jewish text in the postexilic era, even one that does not mention God overtly, would have some theological significance. For a people who were so conscious about the Lord and the continuity of his covenantal promises to them during this period of restoration (Chronicles) and so concerned with a return to Mosaic orthodoxy and orthopraxy (Ezra–Nehemiah), it would be highly implausible for them to adopt a literary work that did not have some theological message. Consider also the events in the book. The Jews are threatened with genocide due to the manipulative deceit of Haman, "the enemy of the Jews" (Est. 3:10; 9:24). Had Haman's malicious plan succeeded, the theological impact would have been catastrophic. Recall that in the days of the garden of Eden, the Lord promised that a seed of the woman would come to crush the head of the Serpent (Gen. 3:15). The history of salvation traces the development of that line through Seth (5:3), Noah (5:28–29), Abraham (15:3–5), and the Judean king David (2 Sam. 7:12). Simply put, the blessed seed of the woman would come through the line of the Jews. In fact, in light of these various Old Testament passages, he *had* to come through the line of the Jews. If there were no Jews, then

---

[27] Jobes, *Esther*, 38. As an example of an attempt to "preach" through Esther in a more traditional way, see Iain M. Duguid, *Esther and Ruth*, Reformed Expository Commentary (Phillipsburg, NJ: P&R, 2005).

the line of descendants would be cut off. If that line were cut off, then there would be no seed of the woman, no coming son of Abraham, no future son of David, no Messiah, no Jesus! The impact of Jewish annihilation had not only immediate consequences upon the Jewish people but also a far-reaching effect upon the Christian gospel. If there was ever a time for the Lord to be directly involved in the affairs of his people, it was in the book of Esther. Yet, he is never mentioned!

The expectation is the complete opposite—for God to be mentioned constantly and persistently. Given the significant place of the narrative in the history of salvation, the need for God to actively engage in the affairs of his people is overwhelming. Too much is at stake. The author of the book of Esther could easily have written a literary work in which direct references to God could be found in every sentence on every page. That would definitely create a sense of God's presence. Or the author could take the radical opposite approach to communicate the same exact message—that is what we have here. One could say that the expectation for the explicit mention of God is so needed that the omission of his name is a silence so loud, it is deafening. The expected theological bomb blast is heard in its overwhelming, unexpected silence.

In other words, I suggest that the author of Esther created an awe-inspiring sense of the presence of God by creating a literary-theological vacuum. The effect of this vacuum is to remind the reader of the subtle activities of God, who would not abandon his people when they were in need of his sovereign grace the most. Indeed, the salvation of the Jews in Esther was due neither to the creative maneuverings of Mordecai nor to the courage of Esther. These heroes of faith were truly steadfast in their resolve, but behind the scenes of the earthly stage was the divine hand of the Lord, who orchestrated the totality of what is found in the book for his own glory and for the well-being of his people.

Divine Providence

The presence of God is established in the absence of God. He was there, and he faithfully continued to unfold his divine plan by more implicit means. For this reason the majority of commentators have properly seen that one of the prominent theological themes in this book is the divine providence of God. The narrative alludes to this message on several occasions. For example, after learning of Haman's despicable plan to annihilate the Jews, Mordecai appeals to Esther and alludes to providence as the means by which God will save his people: "And who knows whether you have not come to the kingdom for such a time as this?" (Est. 4:14). The wife of Haman also seems to be aware that the God of the Jews may be supporting Mordecai: "If Mordecai, before whom you have begun to fall, is of the Jewish people, you will not overcome him but will surely fall before him" (6:13). Even the use of "lots" suggests that God is in divine control and coordinating events according to his good and pleasing will.

It is significant to notice the ordinary means by which the Lord is working. Although he escapes human perception, he is very active in using the normal means of everyday life. He does not intercede by the use of the miraculous. What we would see as "coincidence" is actually the work of God's divine providence. It seems like "coincidence" that Mordecai happened to overhear the plot against Ahasuerus, or that Ahasuerus was reading about his own reign and stumbled upon that good deed of Mordecai, or that Haman was falling over Esther at the moment when the king stepped into the room. What seems as "chance" or even "luck" is in fact God overseeing all situations of life.

In this regard, the book of Esther has more in common with the life of believers today than any other book of the Bible. After all, we do not live in a time where we see a devastating deluge as an act of divine wrath (Genesis 6), nor do we see a smoking fire pot and flaming torch as theophanic manifestations of God (Genesis 15). We don't see God bringing fresh manna from the heavens (Exodus 16) or supernaturally providing life-giving water from a rock (Exodus 17). Although we live in a day without these extraordinary visuals of God's power, we should not be fooled. The absence of any direct references to God does not equate to a true theological absence of God. The Lord works in the life of his people in subtle yet powerful ways. It is more like the days of Esther. He is there; he is always there, even if we don't see him. During those times in life when it is difficult to discern his presence and we thus wonder about his providence in our lives, we are to remember the book of Esther and bear in mind what it teaches us—he is there, he is always there, and he is always working for our good, even if we cannot see him, even if no one mentions him.

The Theme of Reversal

The theme of reversal is one way in which we see God working for his people. In Esther, Haman manipulates, coerces, even bribes royal officials in order to achieve his wicked desire—the destruction of Mordecai and the Jews. He nearly succeeds. At the moment when victory seems at hand, the story turns on its head. Mordecai is exalted and praised by the monarch while Haman ends up executed (see "Structure 3: Reversal Theme" on p. 485).

This theme of reversal is found not only in the book of Esther but throughout the entirety of Scripture. One easily thinks of the reversal in the garden of Eden; the Lord comes after the violation of the original covenant of works to judge his creation, but he takes this as an opportunity to herald a coming "seed" who will crush the head of the Serpent. At the dawn of destruction comes life. Think also of Israel on the coast of the Red Sea. The pharaoh of Egypt is storming against them with weapons of war. Israel has no escape route. All looks lost. Yet the Lord turns this into an event that would remain the grandest demonstration of his work of redemption prior to Christ. Even the Christian gospel witnesses to the Lord as a God of reversal. The death of Christ on the cross is the lowest point of human history, yet God reverses the fortunes of Christ in his triumphant resurrection. All those in union with Christ also die to sin but live in Christ. The book of Esther testifies again that there is nothing that can halt the Lord from accomplishing his divine plan.

Without the explicit mention of God in Esther, we can only presume that these events occurred under divine oversight. Such a presumption is fully warranted. In fact, God was not merely a passive observer who occasionally stepped in when necessary; he was the One who planned these events to occur as they did. After reading Esther once, we are encouraged to reread it again, realizing that "the reverse occurred" (9:1) and the Jews' "sorrow [turned] into gladness and [their] mourning into a holiday" (9:22) because God is the Governor of all creatures, actions, and circumstances in the everyday events of life.

Esther encourages us to do the same at the end of each day of our lives. The Lord is there and is actively involved in every moment of every event of every hour of every day. There is never a moment when he is far off or distant. Our human senses are frail and weak; they are poor instruments for measuring the divine presence or his sovereign providential preservation of our lives. We are called to look at our day and are reminded that the difficulties we face that are so frequently turned into blessings are due to the mercy and grace of an invisible God.

Comedy and the Sovereignty of God

If there is a book of the Bible that shows that God has a sense of humor, it is the book of Esther. Unfortunately, the humor of the book is often missed. Modern Christian thought on the book of Esther is best captured by the literary critic H. L. Mencken when he described God as "a comedian performing before an audience who is afraid to laugh."[28] The book of Esther is comedy. It is intended to bring out laughter from its readers. Where else can you find a powerful political figure who attempts to instill obedience in his wife by constitutionally declaring as the law of the land that all wives must honor their husbands (1:10–20)? This is ludicrous since obedience cannot be litigated. Instead of achieving its intended goal, this royal decree broadcasts to the entire Persian realm how this powerful monarch is unable to tame the passions of his own wife. Any married couple would easily see the irony and humor in this scene. Esther also records that this monarch finds the solution to his insomnia in reading about his own reign (6:1). This is equivalent to the pastor who finds listening to his own sermons a quick-and-easy way to fall asleep!

Readers miss the comedy in Esther largely because of misconceived notions about the inspired Word. We expect books in the holy Scriptures to be serious (i.e., somber) with a life-altering message. The message in Esther is indeed life-transforming, but it is not presented with the same tenor as found in other books. Humor is viewed as banal and profane and thus inappropriate for the Word of God. To miss this humor, however, is more than unfortunate because the comedic aspects are not incidental but rather central to the message. As Berlin states, "We cannot appreciate the story fully unless we realize that it is meant to be funny."[29]

---

[28] H. L. Mencken, *A Book of Burlesques* (New York: Knopf, 1920), 203; Mencken, *A Mencken Chrestomathy* (New York: Knopf, 1949), chap. 30. This quotation has been incorrectly attributed to the eighteenth-century French philosopher Voltaire.
[29] Berlin, *Esther*, xviii. Berlin lists various kinds of comedies as theorized by literary critics. She says that the most accurate kind of comedy to describe Esther is a *farce*, which she defines as "a type of comedy designed to provoke the audience to

The comedy of the book comes at the expense of the Persian king and his court, as seen in some of these humorous descriptions. One purpose of this humorous spirit is to deflate the power of the Persian empire, specifically the king, who is portrayed as an incompetent bumbler. Here is the most powerful figure of the known world of the day. There is no higher authority on earth than the seated King Ahasuerus. Yet even at the height of his power and wealth, he is unable to manage his own court officials, his own concubines, even his own wife. He is more easily misled, fooled, and mocked than he is respected, feared, and adored. He is more a court jester than a king. Esther is not primarily intended to critique Ahasuerus but rather to show that even the most powerful figure of the earth, whose wealth is unmatched in a kingdom that reaches to the farthest points of the world, cannot be compared to the God of the Jews, whose authority is established even without mentioning his name.

Within the royal court, it is Haman, the king's second in command, whose exploits are laughable. Some of the funniest scenes of the book are at Haman's peril. Ahasuerus, having learned of Mordecai's prevention of the assassination plot, calls in Haman and asks what honor should be bestowed upon a loyal servant of the king. Thinking that the king had him in mind, Haman answers by saying that one so dedicated should be given all the privileges, honor, and wealth of the royal office. To his dismay, the king turns and blesses Mordecai, sending Haman mourning like a beaten young school boy (6:1–12). His malicious plans backfire, and he is ultimately executed. This reversal recalls Psalm 2, where the nations "rage" against the Lord and his anointed servant. However, such threats and challenges are so weak against the Lord of glory that he can't help but "laugh" at their devices and schemes (2:4). The one laughing is not only the reader but also the Lord. Indeed, the thought that any creature is capable of undermining the sovereign will of God is so ridiculous, it is comic. We cannot help but laugh—and to laugh with the Lord.

The Seed of the Serpent vs. the Seed of the Woman

The nature of the tensions in Esther comes more clearly into view when we see it in the context of redemptive history. For example, the conflict between Mordecai and Haman is a postexilic clash reminiscent of Saul and Agag in 1 Samuel 15. This is obvious since Haman is specified as an "Agagite" (Est. 3:1, 10; 8:3, 5; 9:24) and Mordecai a descendent of "Kish," whose most famous son was Saul (1 Sam. 9:1, 3; 14:51; cf. 10:11, 21). Where Saul failed to fulfill the will of the Lord in executing Agag, Mordecai does not. Thus tucked within the resolution of the conflict between Mordecai and Haman is the resolution of the previous rivalry.[30]

---

simple, hearty laughter. . . . To do so it employs highly exaggerated or caricatured character types, puts them into impossible and ludicrous situations, and makes free use of broad verbal humor and physical horseplay." *Esther*, xviii–xxii.

[30] We must be cautious, however, when we contemplate the aggression of the Jews in Esther. Saul's failure to execute Agag in 1 Samuel 15 is part of the Deuteronomic commentary on Israel's failure to follow the mandates of חֵרֶם (*herem*), or the "ban." In Deut. 20:1–20, the regulations for חֵרֶם (*herem*), Moses states that it applies only within the land of Canaan, which is a type of the kingdom of God (20:16–20). Outside the land, Israel is called to initially extend an offering of peace. If the foreign nation rejects and attacks, Israel is permitted to defend themselves (20:10–15). It is the latter that applies in Esther. The engagement of Jews against their oppressors is not a continual cleansing of the land where they fulfill their duties as a kingdom of priests (Ex. 19:6). Rather, they were acting for the peace of the city (e.g., Mordecai's thwarting the attempted assassination of Ahasuerus) until that city became hostile to them. According to Deuteronomy 20, they are permitted to engage in self-defense, which is what they do.

The conflict between Saul and Agag finds its source even further back in redemptive history since Agag is a descendent of Amalek (1 Sam. 15:20). Recall that Exodus 17:8–16 describes how the Amalekites opposed the Israelite journey from Egypt to Sinai. As a curse against them, the Lord tells Moses to record this battle as a reminder to Israel that "I will utterly blot out the memory of Amalek from under heaven" (Ex. 17:14; cf. Deut. 25:17–19). The "blotting out" of Amalek occurs in the book of Esther. Yet this conflict between Israel and Amalek can be traced even further back since Amalek is a descendent of Esau (Gen. 36:12). Esau's clash with Jacob is one of the numerous examples of the greater conflict between the seed of the woman and the seed of the Serpent of Genesis 3:15. Thus Haman's aim to annihilate the Jews witnesses once again the attempts made by the wicked seed to nullify the redemptive seed of life. God, however, preserves that seed, which climaxes in the true seed of the woman in the person of Jesus Christ.

Exodus Redux

It was briefly mentioned earlier that the events in Esther are linked canonically with Passover in the book of Exodus (see "Place in the Canon" on p. 477). A careful analysis confirms that they are linked thematically as well. For example, both describe the redemption of God's people. In both the Lord uses a particular individual as the primary instrument of his redemptive activities (Moses/Esther). Both "mediators" are reluctant to act (Exodus 3–4 / Est. 4:11–14). Both "mediators" have support in their task (Aaron/Mordecai). In each case a pagan king needs to be persuaded (pharaoh/Ahasuerus). They both result in the establishment of a new festival (Passover/Purim). Finally, Esther highlights the palpable reality of the exile in the Jews of Persia by explicitly connecting the Jews (specifically Mordecai) with the exile of Jeconiah (a.k.a. Jehoiachin) in Esther 2:6. Recall that the writing prophets described the restoration from exile as a second exodus (Isaiah 40–55; Jer. 31:1–26). Thus, by portraying the events of Esther as another exodus, the history of Old Testament Israel ends in the same way it began.

This analysis should not neglect the obvious discontinuities and difficulties—the Jews are still in exile in spite of the heroic acts of Mordecai and Esther. This is a reminder to the reader that although there was an "exodus redux" in Esther, there is still to come a *true* exodus where the Lord will establish a *true* restoration of the *true* people of God. We are given a small glimpse of this hope in the narrative of this book.

Approaching the New Testament

There is at least one event recorded in the Gospels that has an affinity with the book of Esther. In Matthew 14:1–11 (cf. Mark 6:17; Luke 3:19), Herod the tetrarch was placed in a similar position as Ahasuerus: both rulers were forced to act due to the alluring effects of a woman. In the case of Herod it was the daughter of Herodias; for Ahasuerus, Esther. Where Herod "promised with an oath to give her whatever she might ask" (Matt. 14:7), Ahasuerus offered Esther "even to the half of my kingdom" (Est. 5:3, 6; 7:2). It is difficult not to see a literary allusion to Esther in this Gospel account. In Esther the authority and powers of the royal monarch are comically undermined by the ease in which a woman can lure him. The same effect is found in the Gospels.

In a broader sense, the book of Esther reminds New Testament readers of their true identity as disciples of Christ—they are all "sojourners and exiles" (1 Pet. 2:11; cf. Heb. 11:13) in a hostile world, just like Esther. Our true citizenship is not of this world; rather it is "in heaven, and from it we await a Savior, the Lord Jesus Christ" (Phil. 3:20).

The most obvious observation cannot and should not be ignored. Without the book of Esther, there would not only be no Messiah, there would also be no Jewish writers to preserve the New Testament texts for us. So much of the New Testament was written by Jewish writers to defend the true identity of Jesus of Nazareth as the messianic Son of David, the true Prophet, the eschatological High Priest, God incarnate, and so forth. Thus, when "approaching the New Testament" from the perspective of the book of Esther, we do well to remember that without the events of the book of Esther and the preservation of the Jews, there would be no "approach to the New Testament" because we would not have a New Testament.

Select Bibliography

Beckwith, Roger T. *The Old Testament Canon of the New Testament Church and Its Background in Early Judaism.* Grand Rapids, MI: Eerdmans, 1985.

Berg, Sandra Beth. *The Book of Esther: Motifs, Themes, and Structure.* SBLDS 44. Missoula, MT: Scholars Press, 1979.

Berlin, Adele. *Esther: The Traditional Hebrew Text with the New JPS Translation.* JPS Bible Commentary. Philadelphia: Jewish Publication Society, 2001.

Bush, Frederic. *Ruth/Esther.* WBC 9. Nashville: Thomas Nelson, 1996.

Clines, David J. A. *The Esther Scroll: The Story of the Story.* JSOTSup 30. Sheffield: JSOT Press, 1984.

Duguid, Iain M. *Esther and Ruth.* Reformed Expository Commentary. Phillipsburg, NJ: P&R, 2005.

Fox, Michael V. *Character and Ideology in the Book of Esther.* Studies on Personalities of the Old Testament. Columbia: University of South Carolina Press, 1991.

———. *The Redaction of the Books of Esther: On Reading Composite Texts.* SBLMS 40. Atlanta: Scholars Press, 1991.

Jobes, Karen H. *Esther.* NIVAC. Grand Rapids, MI: Zondervan, 1999.

Levenson, Jon D. *Esther.* OTL. Louisville: Westminster John Knox, 1997.

McDonald, Lee Martin. *The Biblical Canon: Its Origin, Transmission, and Authority.* 3rd ed. Peabody, MA: Hendrickson, 2007.

Moore, Carey A. *Daniel, Esther, and Jeremiah: The Additions.* AB 44. Garden City, NY: Doubleday, 1977.

Provan, Iain W., V. Philips Long, and Tremper Longman III. *A Biblical History of Israel.* Louisville: Westminster John Knox, 2003.

Radday, Yehuda T. "Chiasm in Joshua, Judges, and Others." *LB* 27/28 (1973): 6–13.

Webb, Barry G. *Five Festal Garments: Christian Reflections on the Song of Songs, Ruth, Lamentations, Ecclesiastes, and Esther.* NSBT 10. Downers Grove, IL: InterVarsity Press, 2000.

22

Daniel

Richard P. Belcher Jr.

INTRODUCTION

The book of Daniel is complex and challenging. It is a combination of historical narrative and apocalyptic vision. The narrative covers those events in the life of Daniel while he was living in Babylon, and the apocalyptic visions look forward to the future of God's people. Adding to the complexity, this book was written in both Hebrew and Aramaic, indicating both the particular (Hebrew) and universal (Aramaic) significance of Daniel's message. The God of Israel has a plan for his people that will include the nations of the world. No matter what God's people face in this world, they have the assurance that God's purposes will prevail. God will defeat every foe, and his people will participate with him in that victory.

BACKGROUND ISSUES

Daniel's life covers a period that includes the end of the kingdom of Judah, the exile of God's people to Babylon, the fall of Babylon to Persia, and the decree of Cyrus to allow God's people to return to Israel (approximately 605 to 538 BC). Daniel spent most of his life in Babylon. He was taken to Babylon in the deportation of 605 BC, after Babylon had defeated Egypt in the Battle of Carchemish. Young men from Judah were retrained in the Babylonian way of life to serve in the kingdom of Babylon. Daniel rose to a place of prominence within Babylon and was brought in to speak to Belshazzar on the very night that Babylon fell (539 BC). Daniel also held a high position in the Persian government. He received his vision of the seventy weeks just before the end of the exile. The events recorded in Daniel 1–6 come from this historical period.

While Daniel 1–6 contains history, Daniel 7–12 contains apocalyptic literature. These final chapters speak about events that were future to the time in which Daniel lived.[1] Some of these final chapters describe the Greek period of the Maccabean revolt (168–164 BC), and some describe the establishment of God's kingdom in the ministry of Jesus. Because the events depicted in these chapters speak to the future, many argue that this section of Daniel could not have been written until after the events of the Greek period.[2] Skepticism about the historicity of Daniel was first expressed by Porphyry in the late third century AD, who argued that Daniel was composed by someone in Judea during the rule of Antiochus IV Epiphanes (170–164 BC). This viewpoint anticipated the modern critical view that became prevalent during the Enlightenment and that represents the current critical consensus that the book of Daniel came from the Maccabean period.[3]

Responses to the questions of date and authorship will depend upon presuppositions concerning God's ability and willingness to reveal the future to his prophets. The Old Testament, however, is clear about this issue. For example, Isaiah, in comparing and contrasting God with the idols, asserts that Yahweh declares the end from the beginning (Isa. 46:8–11) and tells his people beforehand what will occur so that they will not attribute it to their idols (42:8–9; 44:7–8). Part of the message of the book of Daniel is that the God of Israel is Lord over the nations and their kings. He is working out his sovereign plans and purposes in history despite Israel's experience in exile. The power of the Babylonian kings seems invincible, but God is the One who gave Jehoiakim into the hand of Nebuchadnezzar, king of Babylon (Dan. 1:2). Nebuchadnezzar himself confesses that the kingdom of Israel's God is everlasting and that none can hinder his purposes (4:34–35). Daniel 2 demonstrates the failure of the Babylonian wise men and presents the God of Israel as the source of all wisdom. He is the One who reveals deep and hidden things and who has made known to Daniel the dream of Nebuchadnezzar and its interpretation. Since the God of Israel is the Lord of history and the One who reveals deep and hidden things, then there is no problem understanding that the book of Daniel actually came from the hand of Daniel decades—even centuries—before the apocalyptic events in the book took place.[4] To deny this aspect of God's ability is to make him no different from the idols that he opposes. It also neglects the clear testimony of Scripture and impugns the wisdom and character of God.[5]

---

[1] Apocalyptic literature is a type of prophecy that is eschatological (looks to the end of time), is revelation given through an angelic mediator, is characterized by unusual imagery, is many times given in the context of oppression, and is sometimes pseudonymous. See Tremper Longman III and Raymond B. Dillard, *Introduction to the Old Testament*, 2nd ed. (Grand Rapids, MI: Zondervan, 2006), 386–88; D. Brent Sandy and Martin G. Abegg Jr., "Apocalyptic," in *Cracking Old Testament Codes: A Guide to Interpreting Literary Genres of the Old Testament*, ed. D. Brent Sandy and Ronald L. Giese Jr. (Nashville: Broadman, 1995), 177–97.

[2] Carol A. Newsom, *Daniel*, OTL (Louisville: Westminster John Knox, 2014).

[3] Otto Eissfeldt calls the late date of Daniel "an assured position of scholarship." *The Old Testament: An Introduction* (New York: Harper and Row, 1965), 517. For the view that the events described in Daniel do not match up with the historical events described, see John J. Collins, *A Commentary on the Book of Daniel*, Hermeneia: A Critical and Historical Commentary on the Bible (Minneapolis: Fortress, 1993), 24–25. For a defense of the historicity of Daniel, see R. K. Harrison, *Introduction to the Old Testament* (Grand Rapids, MI: Eerdmans, 1969), 1112–27. It is unlikely that the book of Daniel was completed in the second century because Daniel is referred to as authoritative by the literature of the second century. Harrison, *Introduction*, 1107.

[4] Tremper Longman III shows that the prophecies of Daniel in chapters 7–12 are delivered by Daniel in the first person, which makes an implicit claim to have originated in the sixth century. He also argues that pseudonymity fails when applied to the book of Daniel because the only way that Daniel's intention as demonstrated in the text can be achieved would be to dupe the audience into believing he was a true prophet. *Daniel*, NIVAC (Grand Rapids, MI: Zondervan, 1999), 22–23.

[5] James M. Hamilton Jr., *With the Clouds of Heaven: The Book of Daniel in Biblical Theology*, NSBT 32 (Downers Grove, IL: InterVarsity Press, 2014), 30–40. Hamilton gives a robust defense of the authorship of Daniel against those who argue

STRUCTURE AND OUTLINE

There are several different ways to approach the structure of the book of Daniel. The most basic division occurs between the narrative of chapters 1–6 and the apocalyptic visions of chapters 7–12. The narratives of Daniel 1–6 deal primarily, though not exclusively, with the events of exile as experienced by Daniel and his comrades in Babylon. The visions of chapters 7–12 cover events that are future to the time of Daniel, with an emphasis on the persecution of God's people in the Maccabean era or at the end of time.

Another possible division of the book relates to the languages in which the book was written. The division according to language (Hebrew and Aramaic) overlaps the division between the narratives and the apocalyptic visions. Part of the book was written in Aramaic (2:4b–7:28), and the rest of the book was written in Hebrew (1:1–2:4a; 8:1–12:13). Most of the material in the Aramaic section deals with kings who usurp their authority and must be humbled by God. Chapters 2 and 7 are distinct in that they each present a dream characterizing history from the Babylonian empire (612–539 BC) to the Roman empire (31 BC–AD 476 [in the West]; 31 BC–AD 1453 [in the East]). The Hebrew chapters cover events that are more relevant to the experience of God's people in exile. Daniel 1 describes life in exile and Daniel 8 and 10–12 deal with the persecution that occurs in exile, perhaps in connection with the Maccabean period. Chapter 9, like chapters 2 and 7, also covers that same period of history from the Babylonian kingdom to the Roman kingdom but from the standpoint of the extended exile. Chapters 8 and 10–12, which appear to focus on the persecution of the Maccabean era, establish a paradigm for the persecution that will occur at the end of the period described in chapters 2, 7, and 9. Based on the emphases of these chapters, the book of Daniel deals with the difficulties of living faithfully in exile; the persecution of God's people in exile; and the hope that God is the sovereign Ruler, who is more powerful than the kings of the nations and who will one day deliver his people by a great and mighty victory.

MESSAGE AND THEOLOGY

Daniel 1: Living Faithfully in Exile

The first chapter of Daniel sets the scene for the rest of the book by describing a momentous event in the history of Judah. With the demise of Assyria, Babylon became the next superpower under the leadership of Nabopolassar (658–605 BC), with Nebuchadnezzar (605–562 BC) bringing Babylon to the height of its power. The year 605 BC was an important year as Babylon and Egypt were each seeking to control the area of Syria. Babylon defeated Egypt at the Battle of Carchemish, which gave Babylon control over Syria and opened up Palestine to Babylonian dominance. Nebuchadnezzar besieged Jerusalem, changing Israel's allegiance from Egypt to Babylon. Jehoiakim, the king of Judah, now paid tribute to Nebuchadnezzar, who

---

that it does not matter whether the book is written in the sixth or second century, such as John E. Goldingay, *Daniel*, WBC 30 (Dallas: Word, 1989), and Ernest C. Lucas, *Daniel*, ApOTC (Downers Grove, IL: InterVarsity Press, 2002).

had come into the city and carried off vessels from the temple along with some of the royal family and nobility. This was Israel's first deportation to Babylon, and it is the event described at the beginning of Daniel 1, specifically as it relates to Daniel, one of the young men taken captive into exile. Although Daniel's experience of reeducation in the Babylonian way of life would not be the universal experience of Jewish exiles, his experience of living faithfully in exile served as an example for other Jews living in Babylon.

Daniel 1:1–7 describes the events of the first deportation. From a human point of view, it looks like the Babylonian gods are more powerful than Yahweh, the God of Judah. Nebuchadnezzar takes the city where the name of Yahweh is said to dwell, and he marches right into the temple of Yahweh and carries off vessels from the house of Judah's God. These vessels are placed in the house of his own god as a trophy of his victory (1:1–2). Babylon also takes some of the royal family and the nobility, including "youths without blemish, of good appearance and skillful in all wisdom, endowed with knowledge, understanding learning" (1:4).[6] They are immersed in the Babylonian way of life, which means learning about Babylonian religion, eating Babylonian food, and being given new Babylonian names. Their new names were meant to give them new identities. This reeducation process would take three years, and at the end of that time they would stand before the king. In this way, Babylon took the best from the youth of Jerusalem to retrain them in the Babylonian way of life for service in the Babylonian empire. These events raise the question of whether a Jewish person living in exile can keep his or her Jewish identity and remain faithful to God.

Although Daniel and his companions are immersed in the Babylonian way of life, he decides to take a stand with regard to partaking of the king's food and drink (1:8–16). The reason stated is to avoid defilement: "Daniel resolved that he would not defile himself with the king's food, or with the wine that he drank" (1:8). No doubt some of the king's food would have violated the food laws of Leviticus 11, for all food in Babylon or Assyria was ritually unclean (Ezek. 4:13; Hos. 9:3–4).[7] However, the regulations in Leviticus would not have covered the wine. Another source of defilement could be that the food and wine were offered to the pagan gods of Babylon. However, this would also be true of the vegetables they were eating.[8] Certainly the judgment of exile entails the difficulty of avoiding defilement, especially related to food (see Amos 9:3). The reason that Daniel may have chosen to take a stand on the issue of the king's food could be that food was the easiest way to resist giving total allegiance to the king. This move would also show that the Babylonian food or way of life does not bring success but that God gives success to those who are loyal to him. At the end of ten days, the period of testing, Daniel and his friends are found in better appearance than those who ate the king's food.

---

[6] Goldingay points out that taking the young men and nobility to Babylon may have had several purposes, including to confirm Judah's vassal status to Babylon, to discourage Judah from rebelling, to bring the future leadership of Judah under the influence of Babylon, and to employ the young men in the Babylonian court. *Daniel*, 15.

[7] Joyce G. Baldwin, *Daniel*, TOTC 21 (Downers Grove, IL: InterVarsity Press, 1978), 81–82.

[8] Goldingay, *Daniel*, 18.

The last part of Daniel 1 (1:17–21) demonstrates that God is sovereignly working out his purposes for his people. God is the One who gave Jehoiakim along with the vessels from the temple into the hand of Nebuchadnezzar (1:2). God is the One who gave Daniel favor in the eyes of the eunuch so that he was willing to listen to Daniel's proposal concerning the king's food (1:9). God is the One who blessed Daniel and his friends so that at the end of the period of testing they looked healthier than those who were eating the king's food. God is the One who gave Daniel and his companions skill in literature and in wisdom and understanding in dreams and visions so that the king found them ten times better than all the magicians in the kingdom of Babylon (1:17, 20). The following chapters of the book show the wisdom of God to be more powerful than the wisdom of Babylon.[9] Daniel 1:21 states that "Daniel was there until the first year of King Cyrus." This narrative conclusion teaches that God is sovereign over the kings and nations of the earth, even over the powerful king of Babylon. Powerful kings and nations come and go, but Daniel, because of his God, outlasts Babylon. This statement gives hope to the exiles that God will bring his people back from exile, as Cyrus will issue the decree to allow them to return to their land. This also gives hope to God's people today who know that God is always more powerful than any nation in any era. Our God is able to depose kings, preserve his people, and fulfill his promises. The message of Daniel 1 is that we can be faithful in exile, living in the world but not of the world, because God is sovereign over the nations to carry out his purposes to bless his people.

Daniel 3 and 6: Living Faithfully in Exile Even unto Death

In Daniel 3 and 6 Jewish exiles are threatened with death unless they abandon the worship of God. In Daniel 3 Nebuchadnezzar sets up a gold image for all to worship. The chapter features a great deal of repetition. For example, the titles for all the officials gathered for the dedication of the image are mentioned twice, as are the musical instruments employed for the event. This repetition demonstrates how significant the event is for Nebuchadnezzar, creating enormous pressure on Shadrach, Meshach, and Abednego to bow down to this image. To refuse to bow down would demonstrate disloyalty to the king, bringing hefty repercussions: anyone who refuses to bow down to the image is to be cast into a fiery furnace.

The events of Daniel 6 occur near the beginning of Darius's reign (539 BC) and describe how Darius will govern the kingdom. There will be 120 satraps scattered throughout the kingdom with three high officials over them. Daniel is appointed as one of the three officials. Not only is Daniel a high official, but the king also plans to put him over the whole kingdom (6:1–3). The other high officials and satraps seek to find something against Daniel so they can accuse him before the king. However, they can find nothing because of his faithful character. They decide to attack his religious observance of prayer but not directly. Instead, they maneuver the king to sign a decree that no one can make a petition to any god or man besides the king

---

[9] Goldingay, *Daniel*, 24.

for a period of thirty days, or they will be cast into a den of lions. King Darius signs the document without realizing that the officials are trying to harm Daniel (6:4–9).

In both chapters, the Jewish exiles choose death rather than abandon their allegiance to God. In Daniel 3 they refuse to bow down to the image. Nebuchadnezzar tells them what will happen to them if they do not bow down by asking the question, "Who is the god who will deliver you out of my hands?" (3:15). They affirm that they will not bow down to the image and that they are willing to be cast into the fiery furnace. The three men are bound in their cloaks, tunics, and hats and are thrown into the furnace. In chapter 6 Daniel goes to his room to pray with his window open toward Jerusalem, as he did every day, even though he knows that the decree has been signed by the king. The difference in chapter 6 is the king's response. In Daniel 6 the king is distressed over the situation and seeks to rescue Daniel. However, the law of the Medes and the Persians cannot be changed, even by the king. The king's only choice is to have Daniel thrown into the den of lions, and to commit Daniel to his God to deliver him.

In both chapters the exiles are delivered from the certainty of death. In Daniel 3 Nebuchadnezzar is shocked to observe four men walking in the furnace.[10] They are not bound, and they are not harmed by the fire. In fact, when Shadrach, Meshach, and Abednego come out from the furnace, their hair is not singed, their cloaks are not burned, and they do not smell like fire. Similarly, in chapter 6, after a night of sleepless fasting, the king discovers that the God of Daniel has delivered him from the mouth of the lions.

Finally, in both Daniel 3 and 6 the king issues decrees in favor of the worship of Yahweh because he is a God who delivers his people. The words of Nebuchadnezzar emphasize that no other god is able to deliver in the way that the God of Israel can deliver, and that the servants of this God are willing to set aside the king's command and yield up their bodies to death. The decree of Darius states that all in his kingdom are to fear the God of Daniel because he is the living God whose kingdom shall never be destroyed. He also emphasizes God's power to deliver. These great kings are made to recognize the power of the one true God. The kingdom of this God is the everlasting kingdom.

Daniel 4 and 5: Living Faithfully in Exile— God Rules over the Kings of This World

Daniel 4 and 5 record the account of two kings who exalt in their own power and are then brought low by the power of God. The king of Daniel 4, Nebuchadnezzar, is restored to his position, but the king of Daniel 5, Belshazzar, loses his kingdom that very night.

In Daniel 4 Nebuchadnezzar is at the height of his success as the king of Babylon (4:4). He has a dream that the wise men of Babylon cannot interpret, so he brings in Daniel to interpret. In the dream, Nebuchadnezzar sees a tree that becomes strong

---

[10] For a discussion of the identification of the fourth figure in the furnace, see "Appendix B: The Role of Heavenly Beings in Daniel."

and visible to the whole earth. It provides food for all (4:10–12). Then an angel comes down from heaven and proclaims that the tree should be cut down, which results in its fruit being scattered and the beasts and birds fleeing from its protection. However, the stump of the tree is left and is bound with a band of iron and bronze amid the grass of the field (4:13–15). The description that follows fits the description of a person (4:15b–16). This individual is to be wet with the dew of heaven, his portion is to be with the beasts in the grass of the earth, his mind is to be changed into the mind of a beast, and seven periods of time are to pass over him. In the interpretation of the dream, Daniel identifies the tree with Nebuchadnezzar, who will be cut down. Daniel ends the interpretation of the dream with an exhortation for the king to repent from his sins by practicing righteousness and showing mercy to the oppressed in order to extend his prosperity.

In Daniel 5 King Belshazzar gives a great feast on the night that the kingdom of Babylon falls to the Persians. In that feast they bring out the golden vessels that Nebuchadnezzar had taken from the temple in Jerusalem (Daniel 1), and they drink wine from them in praise of the gods of gold, silver, bronze, iron, wood, and stone. Immediately, the fingers of a human hand appear and write on the wall opposite a lampstand in the sight of the king. When the king sees the handwriting, his countenance changes, and he falls apart physically (5:6). The wise men of Babylon cannot read the writing, so Daniel is brought in. He chastises Belshazzar for not learning from the example of Nebuchadnezzar (Daniel 4). He should have humbled himself before God, but instead he has lifted himself up against the Lord of heaven by not giving honor to his name.

The writing on the wall appears (in Aramaic) as *mene, mene, tekel,* and *parsin.* These words are related to weights, *mene* to the mina and *tekel* to the shekel. *Parsin* either refers to the noun for "half" or is a play on the word Persia. Daniel interprets the writing on the wall with the meaning that the kingdom of Babylon has been weighed, found wanting, and will be destroyed.

Daniel recalls God's judgment on Nebuchadnezzar in order to warn Belshazzar (5:18–23). A year after Nebuchadnezzar had a dream, while he was boasting of his great accomplishments, the events described in the dream overtook him. The description of what happened to the king appears in 4:33: "He was driven from among men and ate grass like an ox, and his body was wet with the dew of heaven till his hair grew as long as eagles' feathers, and his nails were like birds' claws." At the end of the designated period of time, the king looked up to heaven, and his reason returned to him. Nebuchadnezzar had been humbled by these events and was subsequently restored to his kingdom.

After Nebuchadnezzar was restored, he offered praise to the God of Israel. In fact, in Daniel some of the most powerful kings on earth provide remarkable theological statements about God. Nebuchadnezzar's statements come in 2:46–47; 3:29–30; and 4:34–37, and Darius's statements come in 6:25–27. There is some debate concerning what these statements signify about the men who uttered them. Did these powerful kings come to a saving knowledge of the God of Israel? Most scholars recognize that this is a difficult question to determine with certainty. It is hard to know if Darius's statement that God "is the living God, enduring forever; his kingdom shall never be destroyed, and his dominion shall be to the end" (6:26) is just a recognition that the God of Israel is above other gods or is a denial that other gods exist.[11] The same is true for Nebuchadnezzar's statements in Daniel 2 and 3. When Nebuchadnezzar states to Daniel, "your God is God of gods and Lord of kings, and a revealer of mysteries," he is acknowledging that Israel's God is more powerful than the other gods and that he is sovereign over the kings of the earth.[12] It appears, however, that the king is still a polytheist—that is, he believes in many gods. After all, in chapter 3 he builds an image to be worshiped.

Most scholars take the same view of Nebuchadnezzar in Daniel 4. When he is restored, he proclaims praise and honor to the One "who lives forever, for his dominion is an everlasting dominion, and his kingdom endures from generation to generation" (4:34). Perhaps these words "fall short of penitence and true faith,"[13] but there are some interesting aspects to Nebuchadnezzar's confession in Daniel 4. His praise of God echoes other biblical texts such as Psalms 115:3; 145:13; Isaiah 14:27; 40:17; 43:12; 45:9.[14] It is also significant to observe that the king offers praise after he has been humbled by God. This is not a decree like those issued as in Daniel 2 and 3. These words are spoken in the first person. The king does not witness something in others, but he himself experiences humbling and restoration by the God of Israel. His words of worship come from his experience with God. And finally, the king's knowledge of God progresses through these chapters: in 2:47 he says to Daniel "your God is God of gods"; in 3:28 he states, "Blessed be the God of Shadrach, Meshach, and Abednego"; and in 4:34 he proclaims, "I blessed the Most High, and praised and honored him who lives forever." The king moves from speaking about the God of Israel to offering his own words of worship and praise to the God of Israel. Thus some understand more going on here than Nebuchadnezzar just adding the God of Israel to the pantheon of gods that he worships.[15] However, the purpose of such statements in the mouth of powerful kings may also be to offer encouragement to God's people in exile. The king represents hostile foreign powers humbled before the God of Israel.[16] The most powerful king on earth has acknowledged that there is a kingship greater than his own and that the God of Israel does whatever he pleases. In this way, God extends hope to his people. God uses human kings for his purposes: to bring judgment and to display his glory.[17]

---

[11] Hardly any commentators understand Darius's statement to be a confession of faith in the true God. Most comment that he perceives the God of Israel to be the highest God among other gods. E.g., Edward J. Young, *The Prophecy of Daniel: A Commentary* (Grand Rapids, MI: Eerdmans, 1949), 139; Andrew E. Steinmann, *Daniel*, ConcC (St. Louis, MO: Concordia, 2008), 323; among others.

[12] Newsom, *Daniel*, 84.

[13] Baldwin, *Daniel*, 116.

[14] Baldwin, *Daniel*, 116; Newsom, *Daniel*, 149.

[15] Young argues for progress in the knowledge of God in Nebuchadnezzar's understanding. *Daniel*, 113–14. Newsom adds that Nebuchadnezzar is presented in a positive role as a redeemed sinner. *Daniel*, 149.

[16] Baldwin, *Daniel*, 94. As I write this, the Islamic State of Iraq and Syria (ISIS) is destroying the Christian church in Iraq. It would be such an encouragement to the Christians if a leader of ISIS would make the same proclamations that Nebuchadnezzar made about the God of Israel in Daniel.

[17] Goldingay, *Daniel*, 97.

Daniel 2 and 7: Living Faithfully in Exile with the Assurance of the Victory of God's Kingdom

Daniel 2 and 7 cover the same sweep of history in four kingdoms, with Daniel 7 providing more details concerning the fourth kingdom and the victory of God's people. In Daniel 2 Nebuchadnezzar has a dream that he is unwilling to reveal to the wise men of Babylon (2:9).[18] He wants the wise men to discover the dream as evidence of their ability to provide an accurate interpretation. Of course, the wise men are unable to reveal the dream (2:10–11), so the king commands that all the wise men of Babylon be destroyed. Daniel asks for time in order that he might make known the dream and its interpretation to the king. What seems impossible from the standpoint of the wise men of Babylon will not be impossible for God, who reveals the dream and its interpretation to Daniel. God is the source of wisdom. He reveals mysteries that will come to pass when the kingdom of God is established. God also has the power to move history from one epoch to another, to depose and establish kings. God's wisdom is greater and more powerful than Babylonian wisdom. The exiles do not need to be impressed with the wisdom of Babylon because their God reveals mysteries and is in control of the kings of the nations.

The dream in Daniel 2 consists of an image made from various metals. This image has a head of gold, chest and arms of silver, a middle and thighs of bronze, legs of iron, and feet of iron and clay. This image is broken into pieces by a stone not made by human hands, which strikes the image at its feet. This stone becomes a great mountain that fills the whole earth.

The dream in chapter 7 comes to Daniel and consists of four beasts coming out of the great sea. These beasts are hybrid animals that represent four future kingdoms. The fourth beast goes unnamed but is described as terrifying and dreadful. It has ten horns with a little horn that arises and speaks great things. Judgment takes away the rule of this beast, and God's universal kingdom is established.

Scholars debate the identification and timing of the events portrayed in these two chapters. The two main options are the Greek period and the Roman period. Most agree that the head of gold (2:32) and the first beast, described as a lion with eagles' wings (7:4), is Babylon (626–539 BC). Following Babylon comes an inferior kingdom represented by the chest and arms of silver (2:32) and a beast like a bear raised on one side (7:5). These two depictions likely represent the Median empire (612–549 BC). The description of this kingdom is limited because the Medes did not play a major role in Jewish tradition. The third kingdom, represented by bronze (2:39) and the leopard with four heads and four wings (7:6), is Persia (549–330 BC). The fourth kingdom (7:7–8) is Greece (323–146 BC).[19] This kingdom differs

---

[18] The king's statement about the dream is understood in various ways, based on the meaning of the word אַזְדָּא in 2:5, 8. The Septuagint takes it as a verb with the meaning "depart," which would mean the king has forgotten the dream. Keil and Delitzsch argue for the meaning "let the word from me be known," in the sense of "be it known to you," based on the old Persian word *azanda*. Carl Friedrich Keil and Franz Delitzsch, *Daniel*, in *Commentary on the Old Testament*, vol. 9, *Ezekiel, Daniel* (Grand Rapids, MI: Eerdmans, 1978), 90. However, the best understanding of this word is "certain," with the idea that this matter is certain to the king: they will be destroyed if they do not tell him the dream and the interpretation. Young, *Daniel*, 60.

[19] Newsom, *Daniel*, 81. Most of the connections of the image to the Greek period are taken from Newsom.

from the previous kingdoms in terms of its destructiveness. In 7:19–22 it is described as terrifying, dreadful, and exceedingly strong with great iron teeth, while in 2:40 the kingdom is described as strong like iron, shattering all things. These depictions highlight the violent and destructive impact of the Hellenistic conquest of the Persian empire by Alexander the Great (356–323 BC). Each chapter emphasizes different things about this kingdom. In 2:41–42 the legs made from iron and clay represent a divided kingdom. As such, after the death of Alexander the Great, the kingdom was divided into four sections: Cassander ruled Macedonia and Greece; Lysimachus ruled Thrace and Asia Minor; Ptolemy ruled Egypt, Palestine, and Cyprus (launching the Ptolemaic Dynasty); and Seleucus ruled Syria, Babylon, Persia, and India (founding the Seleucid empire). The mixing of iron and clay refers to dynastic intermarriages between the Ptolemies and the Seleucids as a way to unite these kingdoms. The vision of Daniel 7 emphasizes the Seleucid kingdom. The ten horns represent totality, and the little horn is Antiochus IV Epiphanes. The uprooting of three horns probably refers to specific historical events from that period.[20]

In Daniel 2 the stone cut from a mountain without human hands represents a divine kingdom that lasts forever. Some, however, prefer to understand this period of time as God's rule manifested through the earthly sovereignty of a revived kingdom of Israel, perhaps the nucleus of this kingdom coming from the Diaspora community.[21] In Daniel 7 the fourth beast is destroyed in the context of judgment and the establishment of an everlasting kingdom. The Ancient of Days describes God as Judge, with dominion given to a human-like figure, "one like a son of man."[22]

This particular interpretation of the image identifies the four kingdoms as Babylon, Media, Persia, and Greece. There are, however, problems with this interpretation. For example, the book of Daniel understands the Medes and the Persians to be one kingdom, as seen in the phrase "the law of the Medes and the Persians" (6:8).[23] Additionally, the establishment of an everlasting kingdom that will never be destroyed is difficult to identify during the kingdom of Greece. However, this depiction does fit the Roman kingdom because Christ sets up his kingdom at that time, which is an eternal kingdom that will eventually destroy all human kingdoms.[24]

A better interpretation of these dreams understands the Medes and the Persians as a single kingdom, so that the four kingdoms represent Babylon, Medo-Persia, Greece, and Rome. In Daniel 2 Babylon as the head of the image is the pinnacle of the human kingdoms. As one moves down the image, the materials that make up the image become inferior. Medo-Persia is represented by the chest and arms of silver and is called inferior (2:39). The third part of the image, middle and thighs of bronze, can

---

[20] Newsom, *Daniel*, 226.

[21] Newsom, *Daniel*, 83.

[22] Many who take this view of chapters 2 and 7 see the "son of man" as either a symbolic representation of the people of Israel or an angelic being such as Michael the archangel. Newsom, *Daniel*, 235–36.

[23] Young has an extensive discussion of the major issues related to the identification of the fourth kingdom. "Appendix V," in *Daniel*, 275–94.

[24] The fact that Rome and other human kingdoms are not destroyed by Christ's kingdom is because the kingdom Christ establishes has two phases. It is a spiritual kingdom entered into by faith that will eventually be established in its fullness when Christ comes again. The New Testament will specifically draw a connection from these figures and concepts in Daniel 7 to Christ and his kingdom.

be identified with Greece and is said to cover the whole earth. The fourth kingdom of Rome, represented by the legs of iron and the feet of part iron and part clay, is a divided kingdom. Iron mixed with soft clay does not hold together. As such, they will mix with one another in marriage, but the kingdom will not hold. This refers to the intermarriage among ethnic groups within the kingdom that will threaten the stability of the kingdom.[25]

In Daniel 7 the first beast represents Babylon but specifically Nebuchadnezzar, who is compared to a lion and an eagle (Jer. 4:7; Lam. 4:19; Ezek. 17:1–3). The plucking off of the wings and the standing on two feet is probably a reference to his humiliation described in Daniel 4. The second beast is like a bear, raised on one side with three ribs in its mouth, a reference to the Medo-Persian kingdom. The raised side refers to the ascendancy of Persia over Media with the ribs referring to the conquests of this kingdom. The third beast is the leopard with four wings and four heads so that it can move swiftly in either direction, a reference to Greece and perhaps to its four divisions stretched over much of Europe and Asia. The fourth beast is not identified with an animal. It is different from all the beasts that went before it. The interpretation of this dream focuses on the fourth beast, Rome. The ten horns are kings that shall arise, with the little horn being a king who puts down three other kings. This horn blasphemes God and makes war on the saints by seeking to change the laws and worship of God (7:24–25).

The key issue with the fourth beast is the relationship between the beast, the ten horns, and the one horn that supplants three horns. Although there are a variety of ways to interpret the ten horns, most interpretations understand the vision as pointing to the arrival of an Antichrist, represented by the little horn.[26] In the New Testament, the spirit of antichrist is described as present in anyone who does not confess that Jesus is from God (1 John 2:18, 22; 4:5; 2 John 7). However, there is also an Antichrist that is still coming (1 John 2:18).[27]

The dreams of Daniel 2 and 7 highlight the establishment of a kingdom that shall never be destroyed. The stone in Daniel 2 that strikes the image represents a divinely established kingdom that will bring an end to the other kingdoms by breaking them in pieces. In Daniel 7 the power of the fourth beast and the little horn that arises from it will be demolished by the judgment of the Ancient of Days, who will give an everlasting kingdom to "one like a son of man" (7:13) and to the saints of the Most High (7:27). The character of this kingdom is divine. The kingdom in Daniel 2 is not

---

[25] Steinmann, *Daniel*, 155.

[26] For different views on how the fourth beast and the little horn culminate in the Antichrist, see Keil and Delitzsch, *Daniel*, 9:286; John F. Walvoord, *Daniel: The Key to Prophetic Revelation* (Chicago: Moody Press, 1971), 161–63; Young, *Daniel*, 148–50. An exception to this view would be Jay E. Adams and Milton C. Fisher, who argue that the little horn of the fourth beast is not the Antichrist but Nero Caesar of the first century. In this approach passages such as the Olivet Discourse (Matthew 24; Mark 13; Luke 21), 2 Thess. 2:1–12, and the book of Revelation primarily have to do with the destruction of the temple in Jerusalem in AD 70 and not the second coming of Christ. *The Time of the End: Daniel's Prophecy Reclaimed* (Woodruff, SC: Timeless Texts, 2000), 17–26.

[27] Scholars who understand the epistles of John to speak of an individual Antichrist who will come in the future include I. Howard Marshall, *The Epistles of John*, NICNT (Grand Rapids, MI: Eerdmans, 1978), 150, and Stephen S. Smalley, *1, 2, 3 John*, WBC 51 (Waco, TX: Word, 1984), 100. For the view that the New Testament teaches a coming Antichrist, see Anthony A. Hoekema, *The Bible and the Future* (Grand Rapids, MI: Eerdmans, 1979), 149–62. For an analysis that understands 1 John as undermining the view of a future Antichrist, see Kenneth L. Gentry Jr., *He Shall Have Dominion: A Postmillennial Eschatology* (Tyler, TX: Institute for Christian Economics, 1997), 383–87.

like human kingdoms.[28] The kingdom in Daniel 7 is given to the One who exhibits the traits of deity as he comes on the clouds of heaven and receives a universal kingdom with complete dominion. Jesus came proclaiming this kingdom (Mark 1:15). It is a spiritual kingdom (John 18:36) that will one day fill the whole world (Matt. 13:31–32). This kingdom was established by the Son of Man, who came to offer his life a ransom for sinners (Matt. 20:28) and promised to come back one day on the clouds of heaven (Matt. 26:64). Only then will the saints receive the fullness of the kingdom, when every knee bows to the Son (Phil. 2:9–11).

Daniel 9: Living Faithfully in Exile While Looking for the Completion of Salvation

Daniel 9 contains the well-known and highly disputed vision of seventy weeks. In the first year of the reign of Darius (539 BC), Daniel is reading the prophet Jeremiah concerning the seventy-year exile. Daniel understands that the seventy years of exile are near their end. He responds with a prayer of confession for the sins of the people (9:3–19). The result of Israel's disobedience enacted the curses of the Mosaic covenant (Leviticus 26; Deuteronomy 27–28), and Daniel is concerned that the purpose of the judgment of exile has not yet had its effect on God's people to provoke them to repentance. The prayer ends with a plea to God to hear his prayer and to show mercy.

In the context of this prayer, Daniel is given the vision of the seventy weeks. In Leviticus 26, God declares that if the people do not listen to God when he sends covenant curses upon them, then he will continue striking them sevenfold for their sins. The phrase "sevenfold for your sins" occurs several times in that chapter (Lev. 26:18, 21, 24, 28). As the seventy-year exile is coming to an end, God gives a vision to Daniel that expands the period of exile sevenfold. This indicates that the exile is not coming to an end, but that an additional seventy weeks of exile are needed.

Daniel is told what the seventy weeks will accomplish in Daniel 9:24, a full and lasting salvation. In the vision, the seventy weeks are broken up into three unequal sections: seven weeks, sixty-two weeks, and one week. The significance of these weeks and their divisions has provoked significant debate. When do the weeks start? Should the years be understood as a literal 490 years? Does the anointed prince come after the first period of seven weeks or after the periods of seven weeks and sixty-two weeks?

The Beginning of Daniel's Seventy Weeks

The debate begins with determining the starting point for the seventy weeks. According to the text, it corresponds to the going forth of a word to restore and rebuild Jerusalem (9:25). Many have considered the decree of Cyrus in 538 BC (2 Chron. 36:23; Ezra 1:2–4) to represent this starting point. Others reject this view because

---

[28] Young shows that the character of the stone is different from the character of the other kingdoms in its origin (divine versus human), its duration (eternal versus temporary), and its power (unconquerable versus being overcome by each succeeding kingdom). *Daniel*, 79.

this decree did not specify the rebuilding of the city.[29] So scholars have examined other decrees by subsequent kings to see if they mention the rebuilding of the city. Possible candidates include the decree of Darius (519 BC), which confirms the decree of Cyrus (Ezra 6:6–12); the decree of Artaxerxes to Ezra (458 BC) authorizing him to go to the land of Palestine (Ezra 7:11–26); and the decree of Artaxerxes given to Nehemiah (445 BC) authorizing the rebuilding of the city (Neh. 2:1–8). Because the decree of Artaxerxes specifically mentions the rebuilding of the city, many scholars pinpoint 445 BC as the beginning point of the seventy weeks.[30] And yet, the decree of Artaxerxes in 445 BC is far removed from Daniel's situation. Since the seventy weeks are given in response to Daniel's prayer, one would expect the prophecy to be relevant to Daniel's prayer for restoration.[31] The later dates (after 538 BC) are thus too far removed from Daniel's prayer.

The official decree of Cyrus may only mention the rebuilding of the temple, but the evidence suggests that he also had the rebuilding of the city of Jerusalem in view. For example, in Isaiah 44:28, Yahweh calls Cyrus "my shepherd" who will fulfill "all my purpose," and Cyrus is quoted as saying of Jerusalem, "She shall be inhabited." Isaiah 45:13 likewise records that the one who sets the exiles free "shall build my city." According to Isaiah, therefore, the work of Cyrus included the rebuilding of the city of Jerusalem.

Beginning the seventy weeks with the decree of Cyrus in 538 BC requires that the weeks be understood symbolically, not literally. For this reason, some find this view problematic, arguing that the seventy weeks of Daniel should be understood as a literal period of 490 years culminating in the ministry of Christ.[32] A literal period of time requires a starting point of 458 or 445 BC for the seventy weeks (see "Appendix A"). However, there are good reasons not to take these seventy weeks as a literal period of time. First, the word *weeks*, in the plural, generally signifies an ordinary week of seven days (Gen. 29:27; Dan. 10:2–3).[33] However, this designation is used in a metaphorical way in Daniel 9, for the restoration will surely not take place in a literal seventy periods of seven, or seventy literal weeks, which is less than a year and a half.[34] Second, the numerical designation *seventy* corresponds to the jubilee pattern, which many understand as a symbolic pattern.[35] Seventy sabbatical years would constitute ten jubilees, signifying fulfillment and completeness.[36]

---

[29] Walvoord, *Daniel*, 224–28.

[30] For other interpretive options, see "Appendix A: The Seventy Weeks of Daniel 9."

[31] Vern S. Poythress, "Hermeneutical Factors in Determining the Beginning of the Seventy Weeks (Daniel 9:25)," *TJ*, n.s. 6, no. 2 (1985): 134.

[32] This view takes the Hebrew word for "weeks" to be a unit of seven. In light of the prophecy coming at the end of the seventy-*year* exile, the unit of seven is taken as a period of 490 years. Gleason L. Archer Jr., *Daniel*, in *The Expositor's Bible Commentary*, ed. Frank E. Gaebelein (Grand Rapids, MI: Zondervan, 1985), 7:112.

[33] Young, *Daniel*, 195.

[34] Steinmann, *Daniel*, 452.

[35] Hamilton gives several reasons why the seventy weeks should not be taken in a literal manner, including the way "seventy years" is used in Ps. 90:10 and Isa. 23:15 and the use of numbers in Ezekiel 4. *Daniel in Biblical Theology*, 122–25.

[36] Both Poythress and Kline show that the immediate context of Daniel 9 would lead one to expect that the decree would be issued not long after Daniel's prayer. Poythress, "Seventy Weeks," 133–34; Meredith G. Kline, "The Covenant of the Seventieth Week," in *The Law and the Prophets: Old Testament Studies Prepared in Honor of Oswald Thompson Allis*, ed. John H. Skilton (Nutley, NJ: Presbyterian and Reformed, 1974), 452–62. Seventy weeks can also be used in a nonliteral sense as a technical term for a sabbatical cycle. Thomas McComiskey, "The Seventy 'Weeks' of Daniel against the Background of Ancient Near Eastern Literature," *WTJ* 47, no. 1 (1985): 42.

The Translation of Daniel 9:25

By comparing the translations provided in table 22, it becomes apparent that we can translate Daniel 9:25 a couple of different ways, which in turn impacts the interpretation of the "seventy weeks." The translation of the ESV complies with the Masoretic accent system appearing in our Hebrew Bibles. In the ESV, the anointed prince appears after the first seven weeks. The NASB and NIV translations do not follow the Masoretic accent system, and the anointed priest appears after the sixty-two weeks that follow the first seven weeks. Generally speaking, those who follow the ESV understand the seventy weeks to culminate in the Antichrist, while those who follow the NASB and NIV see the work of Christ as the culmination of the seventy weeks.

ESV	NASB (1995)	NIV (1984)
Daniel 9:25: Know therefore and understand that from the going out of the word to restore and build Jerusalem to the coming of an anointed one, a prince, there shall be seven weeks. Then for sixty-two weeks it shall be built again with squares and moat, but in a troubled time.	*Daniel 9:25:* So you are to know and discern *that* from the issuing of a decree to restore and rebuild Jerusalem until Messiah the Prince *there will be* seven weeks and sixty-two weeks; it will be built again, with plaza and moat, even in times of distress.	*Daniel 9:25:* Know and understand this: From the issuing of the decree to restore and rebuild Jerusalem until the Anointed One, the ruler, comes, there will be seven "sevens," and sixty-two "sevens." It will be rebuilt with streets and a trench, but in times of trouble.

Table 22

A system of accents and vowels were added to the consonantal text of the Hebrew Bible by a group of scribes known as the Masoretes in the second half of the first millennium AD. This system of notation was designed to preserve the reading tradition of the biblical text. Though they are not inspired, they do provide a very important witness to the original text and its interpretation. However, there are instances, supported by good evidence, where it is preferable not to follow this ancient system, and this appears to be one such case.[37] As such, the following interpretation of Daniel's seventy weeks corresponds to the translation of the NASB and NIV.

The period of sixty-nine weeks includes the rebuilding of the temple and the city, and the troubled times that occur from Cyrus's decree to the coming of Christ. Scholars do not completely agree about how to decipher the period, but the first period of seven weeks ends either with Nehemiah or Malachi.[38] The Anointed One, who is identified as a prince after the sixty-two weeks, is Christ, the Messiah.

Those who take a symbolic view of the seventy weeks understand the last period of the final week in different ways, although they agree that the cutting off of the

---

[37] Roger T. Beckwith argues that the accents of the Masoretic text were a Jewish reaction to the messianic view among Christians. "Daniel 9 and the Date of Messiah's Coming in Essene, Hellenistic, Pharisaic, Zealot, and Early Christian Computation," *RevQ* 10, no. 4 (1981): 522. This view is denied by McComiskey. "The Seventy 'Weeks' of Daniel," 20–22.
[38] Young takes the end of this period as Ezra and Nehemiah. *Daniel*, 205. Hamilton has the period end with Malachi but includes Ezra and Nehemiah in it. *Daniel in Biblical Theology*, 131.

Anointed One refers to the death of Christ. One view is that the last week describes the ministry of Christ and the results of that ministry, which leads to the destruction of the temple in AD 70.[39] This approach understands 9:26–27 in a parallel way. Christ is referred to in 9:26a and 9:27a, and the destruction of the temple is referred to in 9:26b and 9:27b.[40] Another view is that the last period of seven can be divided into two periods. The first half refers to the death of Christ and the destruction of Jerusalem in AD 70. The last half encompasses the whole period of the church to the second coming of Christ.[41] In this view the events described in 9:27b refer to a coming Antichrist who appears near the end of history.[42] In this way, the seventy weeks bring an end to the exile and usher in the consummation of all things, including complete salvation (9:24).

Daniel 8 and 10–12: Living Faithfully in Exile during Intense Periods of Persecution

Daniel 8 and 10:1–12:4 describe events corresponding to the persecution of Antiochus IV Epiphanes during the Greek period (170–164 BC). However, these visions also point beyond these particular events. Daniel 8 describes an intense period of persecution that foreshadows a future time of persecution. Daniel 10:1–12:4 appears to move beyond the Greek period to the resurrection. In both visions, Daniel is alarmed by what he sees, but in Daniel 10 the alarm is much greater. In the vision of 10:1–12:4, more detail is provided, the events are described in more familiar terms (not with beasts but with kings), and the end reached is the final resurrection.

These two visions overlap and discuss many of the same events. The Persian kingdom in Daniel 8 is presented as a ram that does as he pleases and becomes great. It has two horns, which are identified as the kings of Media and Persia. One horn is higher than the other, and the higher one, a reference to Persia, comes up last (Dan. 8:3–4, 20). Daniel 11:1–2 goes further in describing Persia by discussing four of its kings,[43] with the fourth king becoming very strong through his wealth. Going back to Daniel 8, the rise of the Grecian kingdom is described as a male goat with a conspicuous horn between his eyes, a reference to the first king of Greece, Alexander the Great. The goat strikes the ram, breaks its two horns, and becomes great. However, the large horn is also broken and is replaced by four horns, an allusion to the division of the kingdom into four parts after the death of Alexander (8:5–8, 21–22; cf. 11:3–4). After this division, two parts of the kingdom battle for supremacy over the

---

[39] Young, *Daniel*, 217–20.
[40] For a detailed analysis that sets forth the view that 9:26 and 9:27 should be understand as parallel to each other, see Peter J. Gentry and Stephen J. Wellum, *Kingdom through Covenant: A Biblical-Theological Understanding of the Covenants* (Wheaton, IL: Crossway, 2012), 550–62. Dispensationalists understand 9:26–27 to unfold in a chronological way, with a gap between the sixty-ninth week and the seventieth week, ending with the Antichrist. Walvoord, *Daniel*, 230–31.
[41] Hamilton, *Daniel in Biblical Theology*, 131–32. Kline states that the second half of the seventieth week is the age of the new covenant, the church in the wilderness for a time, times, and half a time (Rev. 12:13–14). "The Seventieth Week," 468. Hamilton understands Dan. 9:26–27 in a chronological way that ends with the Antichrist, but he sees no need for a gap between the sixty-ninth and seventieth weeks because in his view the seventieth week covers the final period between the first and second coming of Christ.
[42] Hamilton, *Daniel in Biblical Theology*, 131–32.
[43] There is debate concerning the identification of the four kings of Persia. The Persian kings mentioned in the Bible are Cyrus, Darius, Xerxes, and Artaxerxes. Newsom, *Daniel*, 339.

land of Palestine. Daniel 11 fills in some of the details before describing the rise of a king of the north, the little horn of Daniel 8. Daniel 11:5–20 depicts the struggles between the kings of the north (the Seleucid kingdom of Syria) and the kings of the south (the Ptolemaic kingdom of Egypt). These struggles affect the glorious land of Palestine when Antiochus III, king of the north, causes turmoil among the Jewish people (11:14) by setting himself up in the land with the intent to destroy it (11:16). But neither he nor his son succeed (11:18–20).[44]

The description of Antiochus IV Epiphanes is given in Daniel 8:9–12, 23–25, and 11:22–35. He is the little horn[45] that grew exceedingly great. What is said about the little horn of Daniel 8 is expanded in Daniel 11. He is arrogant and boastful. He is a "king of bold face" who exalts himself as usurper of the throne (8:23; cf. 11:21), and he exalts himself against the God of heaven (8:11). He advances himself through intrigue and deceit, and he makes war on the saints of God and the worship of God (8:24–25; 11:23, 30–32). These passages describe Antiochus's attempt to unify the empire through the imposition of Greek culture on the land of Palestine. These measures bring about a desecration of the temple and its sacrificial system through stopping the legitimate sacrifices and demanding that unclean animals be sacrificed. He also sets up an idol in the temple called the abomination that makes desolate.[46] These events lead to the intense persecution of God's people (8:12). Even some of the "faithful" will stumble through the persecution of sword, flame, captivity, and plunder (11:33). A major purpose of the description of these events is to show God's people that they will face intense periods of persecution in the future.[47]

The visions of Daniel 8 and 11 cover the desecration of the Jewish temple by Antiochus. The vision of Daniel 8 states that the transgression that makes desolate in the sanctuary will last for 2,300 evenings and mornings, and then the sanctuary will be restored (8:13–14). The angel interpreting the vision does not comment on this period but simply asserts that it is true (8:26).[48] The vision in Daniel 11 follows the events of history up to 11:35, which ends with the attempt of Antiochus to force the Jews to abandon their ways. This will be a time to refine and purify God's people.

There is some debate concerning the events described in 11:36–45. Clearly the events pertaining to Antiochus IV are no longer in view. This ambiguity opens up other possibilities, such as Herod the Great, events surrounding the fall of Jerusalem, and the Antichrist.[49] Although important, the specific identity of this period does not greatly affect the ultimate meaning and outcome. The focus for these verses is

---

[44] Longman, *Daniel*, 276–77.

[45] Young shows why the horn of Daniel 8 is not the same horn described in Daniel 7. *Daniel*, 276–77.

[46] Antiochus IV himself entered the temple in 169 BC. Baldwin, *Daniel*, 159.

[47] Reading 1 Maccabees can give one a sense of the opposition to the Jewish people and the pressure on them to conform to practices that go against the law of God during this period of history.

[48] The 2,300 evenings and mornings are understood by some as six years (Young, *Daniel*, 174–75), by others as 1,150 days or about three and a quarter years (Newsom, *Daniel*, 267), and by others as a symbolic period (Goldingay, *Daniel*, 213). There is general agreement that this period refers to the restoration of the temple after its defilement by Antiochus IV.

[49] Of the different views concerning Daniel 11:36–45, Mauro holds that it is a description of Herod's reign, Parry that it is a description of the Jewish revolt against Rome that led to the destruction of Jerusalem in AD 70, and Young and Walvoord that it is a description of the Antichrist. Philip Mauro, *The Seventy Weeks and the Great Tribulation: A Study of the Last Two Visions of Daniel and of the Olivet Discourse of the Lord Jesus Christ* (Choteau, MT: Old Paths Gospel Press, n.d.), 140–50; Jason T. Parry, "Desolation of the Temple and Messianic Enthronement in Daniel 11:36–12:3," *JETS* 54, no. 3 (2011): 485–526; Young, *Daniel*, 246–53; Walvoord, *Daniel*, 270–80.

the king who will magnify himself against every god and speak astonishing things against the God of gods (11:36). He will come into the glorious land where tens of thousands will fall. He will make his final stand against Jerusalem during a great period of trouble that has never before been experienced. However, this king will come to an end, and God's people will be delivered. The glorious victory and vindication of God's people in the resurrection is finally described (12:1–3). Thus, 11:36–45 appears to be a description of the end, either directly or typologically.

The book of Daniel does not end with the resurrection. The vision continues with the question, "How long shall it be till the end of these wonders?" (12:6). The answer comes, "for a time, times, and half a time" (12:7). This response causes Daniel to state that he does not understand the outcome of these things (12:8). Daniel is told to inquire no further because the words do not have immediate application to him. They are sealed up until a time when they will be read and understood.[50] The book ends with a set of cryptic numbers. There will be 1,290 days from the time the regular burnt offering is taken away and the abomination that makes desolate is set up (12:11). The one who waits and arrives "at the 1,335 days" will be blessed (12:12). Some take these numbers to be describing the time of Antiochus IV (168–165 BC).[51] Another view is that they refer to the destruction of Jerusalem in AD 70.[52] Still others take these numbers to refer to the second half of the seventieth week of Daniel 9, which is described in the book of Revelation as 1,260 days (Rev. 11:3; 12:6; 13:5). The extra thirty days may refer to the period needed for the judgment of the nations, and the 1,335 days brings one to the millennial reign of Christ on the earth.[53] Another approach is to take the 1,335 days as referring to the whole period of the opposition to God's kingdom until the consummation, with the 1,290 days referring to the most severe period of persecution.[54] These views read the numbers as referring to a period of intense persecution, which can be understood typologically as a description of the end of history. The point is that God's people will persevere until the end. When persecution in exile comes, and come it will, God's people take comfort in his sovereign control over history and its certain end with the great victory of resurrection.

APPROACHING THE NEW TESTAMENT

Like Daniel, we are still living in exile today. Peter can address the recipients of his letter who are scattered across Pontus, Galatia, Cappadocia, Asia, and Bithynia as the "elect exiles" (1 Pet. 1:1). He identifies them as "born again to a living hope through the resurrection of Jesus Christ from the dead, to an inheritance that is imperishable, undefiled, and unfading, kept in heaven for you" (1 Pet. 1:3–4). This inheritance has not yet been fully received by God's people, but it will be revealed

---

[50] Young, *Daniel*, 360–61.
[51] Newsom, *Daniel*, 367.
[52] Mauro, *The Seventy Weeks*, 177–79.
[53] Walvoord, *Daniel*, 295.
[54] Young understands this period of persecution to refer to Antiochus IV, which is a type of the persecution under the Antichrist. *Daniel*, 263.

in the last time. In the present time the church will be tested by various trials as it waits for the full revelation of its inheritance. Living in exile means living during the period in which the fullness of the kingdom has not yet come. As Israel looked forward to a coming One who would be given the throne of David and his kingdom (Luke 1:33), so we look forward to the coming of this One to bring the full salvation that he has accomplished. Thus we live in a period of redemptive history much like Israel in exile, except that in our case, the fullness of revelation has come (Heb. 1:1). However, we are still in need of exhortation and warning lest we fail to receive the promise through unbelief (1 Cor. 10:1–2; Heb. 4:1–13). We are still pilgrims in this world because we have not yet reached our final destination. Thus the message of Daniel is still relevant for us today—not that we would imitate the actions of Daniel in his cultural context but that we would imitate the faithfulness of Daniel in light of our own current exile.

SELECT BIBLIOGRAPHY

Adams, Jay E., and Milton C. Fisher. *The Time of the End: Daniel's Prophecy Reclaimed*. Woodruff, SC: Timeless Texts, 2000.

Anderson, Robert. *The Coming Prince: The Marvellous Prophecy of Daniel's Seventy Weeks Concerning the Antichrist*. 14th ed. Grand Rapids, MI: Kregel, 1954.

Archer, Gleason L., Jr. *Daniel*. In *The Expositor's Bible Commentary*, edited by Frank E. Gaebelein, 7:1–157. Grand Rapids, MI: Zondervan, 1985.

Baldwin, Joyce G. *Daniel*. TOTC 21. Downers Grove, IL: InterVarsity Press, 1978.

Beckwith, Roger T. "Daniel 9 and the Date of Messiah's Coming in Essene, Hellenistic, Pharisaic, Zealot, and Early Christian Computation." *RevQ* 10, no. 4 (1981): 521–42.

Collins, John J. *A Commentary on the Book of Daniel*. Hermeneia: A Critical and Historical Commentary on the Bible. Minneapolis: Fortress, 1993.

Gentry, Peter J., and Stephen J. Wellum. *Kingdom through Covenant: A Biblical-Theological Understanding of the Covenants*. Wheaton, IL: Crossway, 2012.

Goldingay, John E. *Daniel*. WBC 30. Dallas: Word, 1989.

Hamilton, James M., Jr. *With the Clouds of Heaven: The Book of Daniel in Biblical Theology*. NSBT 32. Downers Grove, IL: InterVarsity Press, 2014.

Harmon, Allan M. *Daniel*. EP Study Commentary. Darlington, UK: Evangelical Press, 2007.

Hoekema, Anthony A. *The Bible and the Future*. Grand Rapids, MI: Eerdmans, 1979.

Keil, Carl Friedrich, and Franz Delitzsch. *Daniel*. In *Commentary on the Old Testament*. Vol. 9, *Ezekiel, Daniel*, 1–506. 1872. Reprint, Grand Rapids, MI: Eerdmans, 1978.

Kline, Meredith G. "The Covenant of the Seventieth Week." In *The Law and the Prophets: Old Testament Studies Prepared in Honor of Oswald Thompson Allis*, edited by John H. Skilton, 452–69. Nutley, NJ: Presbyterian and Reformed, 1974.

Longman, Tremper, III. *Daniel*. NIVAC. Grand Rapids, MI: Zondervan, 1999.

Lucas, Ernest C. *Daniel*. ApOTC. Downers Grove, IL: InterVarsity Press, 2002.

McComiskey, Thomas. "The Seventy 'Weeks' of Daniel against the Background of Ancient Near Eastern Literature." *WTJ* 47, no. 1 (1985): 18–45.

Miller, Stephen R. *Daniel*. NAC 18. Nashville: Broadman, 1994.

Newsom, Carol A. *Daniel*. OTL. Louisville: Westminster John Knox, 2014.

Parry, Jason T. "Desolation of the Temple and Messianic Enthronement in Daniel 11:36–12:3." *JETS* 54, no. 3 (2011): 485–526.

Poythress, Vern S. "Hermeneutical Factors in Determining the Beginning of the Seventy Weeks (Daniel 9:25)." *TJ*, n.s. 6, no. 2 (1985): 131–49.

Robertson, O. Palmer. *The Christ of the Prophets*. Phillipsburg, NJ: P&R, 2004.

Steinmann, Andrew E. *Daniel*. ConcC. St. Louis, MO: Concordia, 2008.

Walvoord, John F. *Daniel: The Key to Prophetic Revelation*. Chicago: Moody Press, 1971.

Young, Edward J. *The Prophecy of Daniel: A Commentary*. Grand Rapids, MI: Eerdmans, 1949.

23

Ezra–Nehemiah

Mark D. Futato

INTRODUCTION

In ancient tradition, Ezra–Nehemiah was treated as a single book. The Masoretic text includes no final Masorah (text note) for the book of Ezra, and the final Masorah that follows Nehemiah gives a total number of verses and a midpoint that presume that Ezra–Nehemiah is one book. In addition, the oldest manuscripts of the Septuagint (the ancient Greek translations of the Hebrew Bible), Josephus (ca. AD 37–100), and the Babylonian Talmud (ca. AD 500) all treat Ezra–Nehemiah as one book. Origen (ca. AD 185–253) is the earliest church father on record to divide the two, and Jerome followed Origen, separating the two in the influential Latin Vulgate (ca. AD 382–405). The earliest Hebrew manuscript to separate the two dates to AD 1448. As a result of this trajectory, all modern translations read Ezra–Nehemiah as two books. However, the literary structure for the book argues for following the ancient tradition of reading Ezra–Nehemiah as a single literary work (see "Structure and Outline" on p. 518).

The book of Ezra–Nehemiah is the next to last book in the third division of the Hebrew canon, the Writings. The purpose of this third division of the Hebrew canon is to instruct God's people in how to live out the covenant established in the first division, the Torah.[1] Or to put it another way, the purpose of this third division is to instruct God's people in how to experience once again the ideals set forth in the first division, the Torah, but not achieved in the second division, the Prophets.[2] The

---

[1] Miles V. Van Pelt, "Biblical Theology: Old Testament: Structure of the Christian Bible," BiblicalTraining.org, accessed September 22, 2015, https://www.biblicaltraining.org/library/structure-christian-bible/biblical-theology/van-pelt-blomberg-schreiner.
[2] Marvin A. Sweeney, "Tanak versus Old Testament: Concerning the Foundation for a Jewish Theology of the Bible," in *Problems in Biblical Theology: Essays in Honor of Rolf Knierim*, ed. Henry T. C. Sun and Keith L. Eades (Grand Rapids, MI: Eerdmans, 1997), 370–71; Sweeney, *Tanak: A Theological and Critical Introduction to the Jewish Bible* (Minneapolis: Fortress, 2011), 24.

focus of Ezra–Nehemiah is the restoration of the temple of God and the city of God along with the reformation of the people of God, all in keeping with the Torah, that is, "the Law of Moses" or "the Law of the LORD" (Ezra 3:2; 7:6, 10; Neh. 8:1; 9:3).

Modern scholarship has tended to read Ezra–Nehemiah together with Chronicles as a literary and theological unit, referred to as the Chronicler's History. The first question in this regard concerns authorship (discussed in more detail under "Background Issues"). Numerous arguments have been made for the single authorship of this unified work.[3] Though some maintain unity of authorship,[4] the modern consensus is that independent authors wrote Ezra–Nehemiah and Chronicles with independent theological concerns.[5]

Even so, despite the likelihood of different authors for these books, Ezra–Nehemiah and Chronicles have much in common.[6] Both works share the key themes of the temple, the celebration of Passover, and the priority of the written Word of God. In addition to these themes, the parallel material in Ezra 1:1–4 and in 2 Chronicles 36:22–23 invites the reading of these two books as one literary and theological unit. So regardless of authorship, it seems best to read Ezra–Nehemiah as part of what could still be loosely referred to as the Chronicler's History.

In the Chronicler's History, the order of Chronicles and Ezra–Nehemiah is the opposite of that found in the English canon. In the Hebrew Bible, Ezra–Nehemiah precedes Chronicles. The English canon is much more interested in chronological order than is the Hebrew canon. This is evident, for example, in the moving of the book of Ruth from its ancient position in the Writings to its more familiar position just after the book of Judges. Since the book of Ruth opens with, "In the days when the judges ruled," chronological interests naturally position Ruth after Judges. The same criterion was operative in moving Ezra–Nehemiah from its ancient position before the book of Chronicles in the Hebrew canon to after the book of Chronicles in the English canon.

The Hebrew ordering, however, is more interested in theology than in chronology. The lead theme in the book of Ezra–Nehemiah is rebuilding the house of God, whereas the lead theme in the book of Chronicles is experiencing restoration in the house of God. Obviously, the house must be rebuilt before one can experience restoration within it. The Hebrew canon ends with Chronicles, a book that is obviously an idealization of Israel's history—as the Chronicler's treatment of a David without a Bathsheba and a Solomon without multiple wives and concubines makes clear. This book is a most appropriate ending to the third division of the Hebrew canon, which focuses on ideal life in the covenant community. From this theological point of view, Ezra–Nehemiah, with its ending that focuses on life far from the ideal, simply could

---

[3] In both Ezra–Nehemiah and Chronicles, (1) the preparations for building the First and Second Temples are similar; (2) the altar is erected before the temple is built; (3) heads of houses endow the temple; (4) there is an interest in sacred vessels; (5) the order of sacrifices is nearly identical; and (6) the temple liturgy is described similarly. For details, see Joseph Blenkinsopp, *Ezra–Nehemiah*, OTL (Philadelphia: Westminster, 1988), 53.

[4] See, for example, Blenkinsopp, *Ezra–Nehemiah*, 47–54.

[5] Tremper Longman III and Raymond B. Dillard, *An Introduction to the Old Testament*, 2nd ed. (Grand Rapids, MI: Zondervan, 2006), 205; Sweeney, *Tanak*, 460.

[6] John J. Collins, *Introduction to the Hebrew Bible* (Minneapolis: Fortress, 2004), 428.

not follow the book of Chronicles. Ezra–Nehemiah most appropriately comes before Chronicles with its emphasis on rebuilding the house of God in which ideal life will be experienced à la the book of Chronicles.

BACKGROUND ISSUES

Authorship

The authorship of Ezra–Nehemiah is difficult to determine with any certainty. On the one hand, Ezra 7–10 and Nehemiah 8 (and perhaps Nehemiah 9–10) contain memoirs[7] written by Ezra. On the other hand, Nehemiah 1–7 and some of Nehemiah 11–13 contain memoirs written by Nehemiah. In addition, materials written by other people have also been included in the book (see "Sources" below). But none of this addresses the question of who compiled all of this material into the book we know as Ezra–Nehemiah. The book itself is anonymous, as is typically the case with Old Testament books. Jewish tradition holds that Ezra is the final author of Ezra–Nehemiah, and this tradition may be correct, given Ezra's literary skills, as evidenced in his memoirs and by the note in Ezra 7:6, which says that Ezra was a "skillful scribe" (my trans.).[8]

Sources

The author of Ezra–Nehemiah drew upon and included a wide variety of sources in the final composition of the book. In addition to the memoirs by Ezra and Nehemiah, these sources include but are not limited to Cyrus's decree (Ezra 1:2–4), lists of returnees (Ezra 2:1–67; Neh. 7:6–68), Rehum's letter and Artaxerxes's reply (Ezra 4:7–22), Tattenai's letter and Darius's reply (Ezra 5:6–17; 6:6–12), lists of families who journeyed to Jerusalem (Ezra 8:1–14), and lists of families who intermarried (Ezra 10:18–43).[9]

A number of these source documents were originally written in Aramaic, the language of diplomacy in the fifth century BC, and were not translated into Hebrew but were incorporated into the biblical text in the original Aramaic (Ezra 4:7–6:18; 7:12–26). We cannot be sure why the author left these documents untranslated, but their incorporation into the text in the original Aramaic language does add a personal feel to the book.[10]

Date

The earliest datable event in the book of Ezra–Nehemiah is the decree of Cyrus (Ezra 1:2–4), which was issued in 538 BC. Ezra's return (Ezra 7:1–7) can be dated to

---

[7] "A memoir is a first-person writing that is distinguished from autobiography in that 'the memoirist writes of great events that he or she has observed or in which he or she has participated, whereas the autobiographer writes of the self who has observed and participated in the events.'" Longman and Dillard, *Introduction*, 209.

[8] For the Hebrew סֹפֵר מָהִיר as "skilled scribe," see *HALOT*, 2:767, 5:552.

[9] For more details, see Adele Berlin and Marc Zvi Brettler, eds., *The Jewish Study Bible: Jewish Publication Society Tanakh Translation* (Oxford: Oxford University Press, 2004), 1668–69.

[10] For the other places where the Old Testament contains Aramaic, see Gen. 31:47 (two words); Jer. 10:11; and Dan. 2:4b–7:28. Note also that the New Testament leaves Jesus's words untranslated and in their original Aramaic in Matt. 27:46 and Mark 5:41, two very personal texts.

458 BC[11] and that of Nehemiah to 445 BC. The latest events in the book took place sometime after 433 BC and before the death of Artaxerxes in 423 BC (see Neh. 13:6). The book of Ezra–Nehemiah may have reached its final form as early as 400 BC.[12]

Genre

As mentioned previously (see "Sources" on p. 517), Ezra–Nehemiah contains a number of genres. But the genre of the book as a whole is history writing.[13] This is not to say that the book is a bare chronicling of events. It is history with a purpose, and this purpose has been communicated through literary artistry.[14]

STRUCTURE AND OUTLINE

The decree of Cyrus sets the agenda for the book of Ezra–Nehemiah, when Cyrus says that the God of heaven "has charged me to build him a house at Jerusalem" (Ezra 1:2). The fulfillment of this charge is celebrated at the dedication of the wall "with gladness, with thanksgivings and with singing, with cymbals, harps, and lyres" (Neh. 12:27). Rebuilding the house of God requires a return from exile, so we are not surprised that the book of Ezra–Nehemiah uses the verb עָלָה ("go up") eleven times in reference to someone returning from captivity in Babylon to Jerusalem (Ezra 1:3, 5; 2:1, 59; 7:6, 28; 8:1; Neh. 7:5, 6, 61; 12:1). Returning and rebuilding are thus key concepts in the overall shape of Ezra–Nehemiah.

There are four movements in the book of Ezra–Nehemiah. The first is the return of a group of exiles and the rebuilding of the temple of God (Ezra 1–6). The second is the return of Ezra and the rebuilding of the people of God (Ezra 7–10). The third is the return of Nehemiah and the rebuilding of the walls surrounding the city of God (Neh. 1:1–7:3). The fourth is the return of another group of exiles and the rebuilding of the people of God (Neh. 7:4–13:31).

One insight gained from the shape of the book is the emphasis on the rebuilding of the people of God. While the rebuilding of the temple of God and the city of God are certainly important themes, the author spends more time on the rebuilding of the people of God than on anything else.

Outline

    I. Return of the Exiles and Rebuilding of the Temple (Ezra 1:1–6:22)
       A. Return of the exiles (1:1–2:70)
          1. The decree of Cyrus (1:1–4)

---

[11] While the date of Ezra's return has been debated, the best evidence supports the traditional date of 458 BC. See H. G. M. Williamson, *Ezra and Nehemiah*, OTG (Sheffield: Sheffield Academic Press, 1987), 55–68; Kyung-Jin Min, *The Levitical Authorship of Ezra–Nehemiah*, JSOTSup 409 (New York: T&T Clark, 2004), 31–35; Longman and Dillard, *Introduction*, 206.

[12] Min, *Levitical Authorship*, 35.

[13] Longman and Dillard, *Introduction*, 209. David M. Howard observes, "The books' [*sic*] immediate purpose is to present the life of God's people as it unfolded in the postexilic period, both immediately and after the exile and many years later." *An Introduction to the Old Testament Historical Books* (Chicago: Moody Publishers, 2007), 274.

[14] Tamara Cohn Eskenazi, *In an Age of Prose: A Literary Approach to Ezra–Nehemiah*, SBLMS 36 (Atlanta: Scholars Press, 1988); Douglas A. Green, "Ezra–Nehemiah," in *A Complete Literary Guide to the Bible*, ed. Leland Ryken and Tremper Longman (Grand Rapids, MI: Zondervan, 1993), 206–15; V. Philips Long, *The Art of Biblical History*, FCI 5 (Grand Rapids, MI: Zondervan, 1994).

1. The need to repopulate Jerusalem (7:4–5)
2. Record of returnees (7:6–73a)
  B. Rebuilding of the community (7:73b–13:31)
   1. Renewing the covenant (7:73b–10:39)
     a. Reading of the law (7:73b–8:18)
     b. Confession of sin (9:1–37)
     c. Ratification of the oath (9:38–10:39)
   2. Dedication of the wall (11:1–12:47)
     a. Listing of residents (11:1–36)
     b. Listing of priests and Levites (12:1–26)
     c. The dedication proper (12:27–43)
     d. Temple arrangements (12:44–47)
   3. Reformation of the people (13:1–31)
     a. Exclusion of foreigners (13:1–3)
     b. Dealing with Tobiah (13:4–9)
     c. The portion of the Levites (13:10–14)
     d. Observance of the Sabbath (13:15–22)
     e. The problem of intermarriage (13:23–31)

There are any number of ways to preach from the book of Ezra–Nehemiah. If one chooses to preach a series straight through the book, one might chose the second level in the above outline for preaching texts (e.g., "Return of the exiles [1:1–2:70]").[15]

MESSAGE AND THEOLOGY

The decree of Cyrus not only sets the agenda for the book of Ezra–Nehemiah but also contains the three major themes of the book: (1) rebuilding the "house" of God, (2) the importance of the people of God, and (3) the primacy of the written Word of God.[16]

Rebuilding the "House" of God

King Cyrus says that he has been commissioned to build a בַּיִת in Jerusalem for the God of heaven (Ezra 1:2). The Hebrew term בַּיִת can be translated "house," "palace," or "temple," depending on who inhabits the בַּיִת; this word can also be translated "household" or "family," in reference to those who inhabit the בַּיִת. While Cyrus no doubt had a temple in mind, the larger context makes clear that בַּיִת carries an expanded sense in Ezra–Nehemiah.[17] In context, the word בַּיִת includes not only the temple but also the city and the people who inhabit the city and worship at the temple.

As noted, the first and most obvious reference for בַּיִת is the temple that was rebuilt soon after the first wave of exiles returned home (Ezra 3). Of interest is the fact that the temple was completed in the sixth year of the reign of King Darius (Ezra 6:15), which we can date to 515 BC. Yet the text says that the people finished building

---

[15] "Return of the Exiles" is certainly not the language I would recommend for a sermon title on this text. For more on this issue, see my discussion of language in Mark D. Futato, *Interpreting the Psalms: An Exegetical Handbook*, HOTE (Grand Rapids, MI: Kregel, 2007), 202–4.

[16] Eskenazi, *In an Age of Prose*, 2.

[17] Eskenazi, *In an Age of Prose*, 2.

the בַּיִת "by decree of Cyrus and Darius and Artaxerxes king of Persia" (Ezra 6:14). Artaxerxes was the king who facilitated the return of Nehemiah to rebuild the city and to reform the people, but he ruled from 464 to 424 BC—starting his reign fifty years after the temple was completed in 515 BC. How could the text say the בַּיִת was finished by his decree? One helpful solution to this conundrum is to affirm an expanded sense of the word בַּיִת that includes the temple, the city, and the people.

At this point in the history of redemption, God's objective is to rebuild his בַּיִת, and this rebuilding is the focus of Ezra–Nehemiah: rebuilding the temple (Ezra 3), rebuilding the city (Neh. 12:27–47), and rebuilding the people (Ezra 10; Nehemiah 13). Nehemiah 12 would be a great ending to the book with a holy people living in a holy city and worshiping in a holy temple. It seems as if God's objective has been realized. But it is Nehemiah 13 that brings the book to a close with its litany of the people's failures and Nehemiah's reforms. The book thus ends with a certain ambiguity or uncertainty about the complete success of the rebuilding of the בַּיִת: "It is as if 'To be continued' has been written at the end of the work."[18] With its emphasis on the בַּיִת as the people of God, Ezra–Nehemiah anticipates the New Testament, which continues the themes of the book in terms of the people of God being fashioned into the temple of God (Eph. 2:14–22; 1 Pet. 2:4–5).

Ordinary People

Ezra–Nehemiah also emphasizes how God uses not only great and well-known leaders but also ordinary people to accomplish his objective in the history of rebuilding his "house." Cyrus commissions not nobles or military commanders but ordinary people to return to Jerusalem (Ezra 1:3). The long list of unknown people in Ezra 2 that is repeated in Nehemiah 7 also underscores how God used ordinary and unknown people to rebuild his "house." Here again Ezra–Nehemiah anticipates the New Testament, which teaches that leaders have as one of their tasks equipping ordinary people to do the work of ministry until God's objective is fully reached and the "house" attains "to the measure of the stature of the fullness of Christ" (Eph. 4:11–13).

The Written Word

All this rebuilding took place according to the *written* Torah of God (see Ezra 3:2; 7:6, 10; 10:3; Neh. 8:1–3, 7–9, 14, 18; 9:3; 10:29, 30, 35, 37; 12:44; 13:3). Soon after the days of Ezra and Nehemiah, God's people entered into four hundred years of silence, when there was no prophetic word from God but only the written Word to guide and govern them as they continued rebuilding God's "house." The book of Ezra–Nehemiah anticipates this era with its emphasis on the power of the written Word.

The text is careful to tell us, for example, that the decree of Cyrus, which is the initial force in the rebuilding of God's "house," was put in writing (Ezra 1:1). One of the reasons why copies of letters were included in the book was to show the power

---

[18] Green, "Ezra–Nehemiah," 213–15.

of a written word both to start the work of rebuilding God's "house" (Ezra 4:24) and to stop that rebuilding (Ezra 6:6–7). A written letter also gave Ezra the authority he needed to rebuild the "house" (Ezra 7:25–26). But it is the written Word of God that ultimately moves the narrative of redemptive history at this point. In its own way, Ezra–Nehemiah teaches that "the word of God is living and active" (Heb. 4:12) and is all that the people of God need for "life and godliness" (2 Pet. 1:3).

Sovereignty and Responsibility

Running underneath these three themes is the theme of divine sovereignty and human responsibility, particularly how God works sovereignly through responsible human beings to accomplish his objective of having his "house" rebuilt.

Cyrus issued his decree because God had moved his heart (Ezra 1:1). While some of God's people chose to remain in Babylon, others decided to return to rebuild God's "house" because God had moved their hearts (Ezra 1:5). Ezra was successful in his ministry because of his devotion and because the gracious hand of God was on him (Ezra 7:9–10). Artaxerxes granted Nehemiah's request because the graciousness of God was on Nehemiah (Neh. 2:8). Nehemiah made plans, and yet God put those plans in his heart (Neh. 2:12; 7:5).

As with other places in Scripture, the philosophical or theological interface between divine sovereignty and human responsibility is neither analyzed nor explained. The text simply teaches that God is sovereign and that humans are responsible, and that God sovereignly uses responsible human beings to accomplish his objective in history: the rebuilding of his "house."

APPROACHING THE NEW TESTAMENT

As the next to the last book in the Hebrew Bible, Ezra–Nehemiah expands the theological theme of holy space. As we have seen, the concept of the "house" of God includes the rebuilt temple but is expanded to include the rebuilt city of God and the reformed community of God's people. In Nehemiah 12:27–47 we read about the celebration of a holy people in a holy city at a holy temple.

Why then that "awkward"[19] concluding chapter (Nehemiah 13) that lines out a number of ongoing problems in the community? It seems that "the book of Ezra–Nehemiah concludes with an open question and a look to the future."[20]

That open question is answered and that look to the future is found in Christ. The apostle John tells us clearly that Jesus is the reality of holy space. Jesus is the true tabernacle of God (John 1:14), and Jesus is the true temple of God (John 2:18–22). The holy space in the old covenant was designed for the end that God would dwell among his people, and that dwelling *par excellence* is found in Christ. Jesus is the "house" of God—but not alone.

The apostle Paul tells us that Jesus is the "cornerstone" of the structure that is

---

[19] Tremper Longman III and Raymond B. Dillard, *An Introduction to the Old Testament*, 2nd ed. (Grand Rapids, MI: Zondervan, 2006), 212.
[20] Longman and Dillard, *An Introduction to the Old Testament*, 212.

becoming a "holy temple" and that the people of God who have been united to Christ are part of that "dwelling place for God by the Spirit" (Eph. 2:20–22). Elsewhere the apostle Paul says that the church of Christ is God's holy temple indwelt by God's Holy Spirit (1 Cor. 3:16–17). The apostle Peter also identifies the church in Christ as the true "spiritual house" of God, when he says,

> As you come to him, a living stone rejected by men but in the sight of God chosen and precious, you yourselves like living stones are being built up as a spiritual house, to be a holy priesthood, to offer spiritual sacrifices acceptable to God through Jesus Christ. (1 Pet. 2:4–5)

The foundation for Paul and Peter's teaching was laid in Ezra–Nehemiah.

But we must admit that at times the church in Christ looks more like Nehemiah 13 than it looks like a holy people in a holy city at a holy temple. Just as Ezra–Nehemiah forced us to look to the future, so does the reality of the church today. And it is with great hope that we look to the future because of that loud voice from the throne that the apostle John heard saying,

> Behold, the dwelling place of God is with man. He will dwell with them, and they will be his people, and God himself will be with them as their God. He will wipe away every tear from their eyes, and death shall be no more, neither shall there be mourning, nor crying, nor pain anymore, for the former things have passed away. (Rev. 21:3–4)

Unlike God's people in the days of Ezra–Nehemiah, we live without an open question, for God has revealed the answer in Christ. And like the people in the days of Ezra–Nehemiah, we live with a look to the future when a holy people in a holy city at a holy temple will become reality, just as John foresaw:

> And he carried me away in the Spirit to a great, high mountain, and showed me the holy city Jerusalem coming down out of heaven from God. . . . And I saw no temple in the city, for its temple is the Lord God the Almighty and the Lamb. And the city has no need of sun or moon to shine on it, for the glory of God gives it light, and its lamp is the Lamb. By its light will the nations walk, and the kings of the earth will bring their glory into it, and its gates will never be shut by day— and there will be no night there. They will bring into it the glory and the honor of the nations. But nothing unclean will ever enter it, nor anyone who does what is detestable or false, but only those who are written in the Lamb's book of life. (Rev. 21:10, 22–27)

Select Bibliography

Blenkinsopp, Joseph. *Ezra–Nehemiah*. OTL. Philadelphia: Westminster, 1988.
Breneman, Mervin. *Ezra, Nehemiah, Esther*. NAC 10. Nashville: Broadman, 1993.

Collins, John J. *Introduction to the Hebrew Bible*. Minneapolis: Fortress, 2004.

Davies, Gordon F. *Ezra and Nehemiah*. Berit Olam: Studies in Hebrew Narrative and Poetry, edited by David W. Cotter. Collegeville, MN: Liturgical Press, 1999.

Eskenazi, Tamara Cohn. *In an Age of Prose: A Literary Approach to Ezra–Nehemiah*. SBLMS 36. Atlanta: Scholars Press, 1988.

Fensham, F. Charles. *The Books of Ezra and Nehemiah*. NICOT. Grand Rapids, MI: Eerdmans, 1982.

Green, Douglas A. "Ezra–Nehemiah." In *A Complete Literary Guide to the Bible*, edited by Leland Ryken and Tremper Longman, 206–15. Grand Rapids, MI: Zondervan, 1993.

Howard, David M., Jr. *An Introduction to the Old Testament Historical Books*. Chicago: Moody Publishers, 2007.

Kalimi, Isaac. *New Perspectives on Ezra–Nehemiah: History and Historiography, Text, Literature, and Interpretation*. Winona Lake, IN: Eisenbrauns, 2012.

Levering, Matthew. *Ezra & Nehemiah*. BTCB. Grand Rapids, MI: Brazos, 2007.

Long, V. Philips. *The Art of Biblical History*. FCI 5. Grand Rapids, MI: Zondervan, 1994.

Longman, Tremper, III, and Raymond B. Dillard. *An Introduction to the Old Testament*. 2nd ed. Grand Rapids, MI: Zondervan, 2006.

Min, Kyung-Jin. *The Levitical Authorship of Ezra–Nehemiah*. JSOTSup 409. New York: T&T Clark, 2004.

Rata, Tiberius. *Ezra & Nehemiah*. A Mentor Commentary. Fearn, Ross-Shire, Scotland: Mentor, 2010.

Steinmann, Andrew E. *Ezra and Nehemiah*. ConcC. St. Louis, MO: Concordia, 2010.

Sweeney, Marvin A. *Tanak: A Theological and Critical Introduction to the Jewish Bible*. Minneapolis: Fortress, 2011.

———. "Tanak versus Old Testament: Concerning the Foundation for a Jewish Theology of the Bible." In *Problems in Biblical Theology: Essays in Honor of Rolf Knierim*, edited by Henry T. C. Sun and Keith L. Eades, 353–72. Grand Rapids, MI: Eerdmans, 1997.

Throntveit, Mark A. *Ezra–Nehemiah*. IBC. Louisville: John Knox, 1992.

Yamauchi, Edwin M. "Ezra and Nehemiah, Books of." In *Dictionary of the Old Testament: Historical Books: A Compendium of Contemporary Biblical Scholarship*, edited by Bill T. Arnold and H. G. M. Williamson, 284–95. IVP Bible Dictionary Series 2. Downers Grove, IL: InterVarsity Press, 2005.

Williamson, H. G. M. *Ezra and Nehemiah*. OTG. Sheffield: Sheffield Academic Press, 1987.

———. *Ezra/Nehemiah*. WBC 16. Waco, TX: Word, 1985.

24

1–2 Chronicles

Richard L. Pratt Jr.

INTRODUCTION[1]

It would be difficult to deny that Reformed theologians have given relatively little attention to the book of Chronicles (1–2 Chronicles). Traditional systematic theologians, creeds, and catechisms seldom directly refer to it. In biblical studies, the popularity of redemptive-historical hermeneutics has led many interpreters in this branch of the church to treat Chronicles as little more than a supplement to the historical information already available in Samuel and Kings.[2] Even so, shifts in Old Testament interpretation near the end of the twentieth century have made it possible to treat Chronicles as a much more significant part of the canon. I have in mind here shifts toward literary analysis, reading Chronicles with an emphasis on the integrality of its form, content, and historical context.[3]

As interpreters have increasingly viewed Chronicles with these sensitivities, it has become apparent that it presents many valuable theological perspectives. It highlights a number of doctrines that have been emphasized in Reformed theology: kingdom of God, covenant, divine retribution, providence, sin, the condition of the human heart, and the like. As a book written after the exile and preserved as the last book of the Hebrew canon, it also provides unique opportunities for evaluating Reformed teaching on the continuity of Old and New Testament faith. Especially important

---

[1] Adapted from Richard L. Pratt Jr., *1 and 2 Chronicles*, A Mentor Commentary (Fearn, Ross-shire, Scotland: Mentor, 1998), by permission of the publisher.
[2] Treating Chronicles as supplemental history can be traced back as far as the traditional Septuagintal (Codex Alexandrinus) title, ΠΑΡΑΛΕΙΠΟΜΕΝΩΝ, "the things left over." This title stands in contrast to the traditional Hebrew title דברי הימים, "the events of the days." Although Jerome himself titled the book *Prætermissorum* ("the things omitted"), some early editions of the Vulgate titled it *Chronica* or *Chronicorum Liber*, the title later adopted by Luther.
[3] For a comparison of redemptive-historical and literary approaches to Old Testament narratives, see my discussion in Richard L. Pratt Jr., *He Gave Us Stories: The Bible Student's Guide to Interpreting Old Testament Narratives* (Phillipsburg, NJ: P&R, 1993), 92–103.

for our day, differences between Chronicles on the one hand and Samuel and Kings on the other have much to say about our understanding of the historical inerrancy and theological consistency of Scripture. These and similar features of Chronicles make it a book to which Reformed theologians should give a great deal of attention.

Our purpose in this chapter is to point toward several introductory items that should provide opportunities for interpreters to discern more clearly many of the benefits of Chronicles.[4]

BACKGROUND ISSUES

As with all sacred Scripture, the Holy Spirit inspired the book of Chronicles. Yet he spoke through the experiences, personality, and purposes of a human writer commonly called "the Chronicler." Chronicles does not explicitly identify this human author, but a number of clues help us narrow the possibilities.

Authorship

Jewish tradition designates Ezra as the primary author of Chronicles, as well as the book of Ezra–Nehemiah. At least three considerations have been used to support this view. First, the book was composed after Israel's return from exile to Babylon. Second, many passages in Chronicles have theological affinities with the focus of Ezra's ministry. Third, the closing of Chronicles (2 Chron. 36:22–23) is very similar to the opening of Ezra (Ezra 1:1–4).

As late as Rudolph (1995),[5] it was generally accepted that one man or group of men was responsible for the books of Chronicles and Ezra–Nehemiah. In more recent history, this consensus has all but vanished. For instance, Cross refers to three major stages in the redactional history of Chronicles and Ezra–Nehemiah: Chr_1 (shortly after 520 BC), Chr_2 (after 458 BC) and Chr_3 (ca. 400 BC).[6] Williamson, Japhet, McKenzie, and Knoppers have been less extreme in their assessments of the redaction of Chronicles, but these approaches have yielded enough evidence to lead most contemporary interpreters to hold to separate authorship for Chronicles and Ezra–Nehemiah.[7] Two decisive pieces of evidence stand in favor of separate authorship. First, kingship and temple are conjoined in Chronicles in ways that do not appear in the book of Ezra–Nehemiah. Secondly, Chronicles largely avoids the issue of intermarriage that was so controversial in Ezra–Nehemiah (Ezra 9:10–12; Neh. 10:30; 13:23–31).

Although we cannot identify the Chronicler by name, we can infer at least two

---

[4] For more information on the material covered in this chapter, see my commentary, *1 and 2 Chronicles*.

[5] Wilhelm Rudolph, *Chronikbücher*, HAT 21 (Tübingen: J. C. B. Mohr, 1955).

[6] Cross brings together evidence from a number of sources and proposes three major redactions for Chronicles and Ezra–Nehemiah. He identifies 1 Chronicles 10–2 Chronicles 34, 1 Esdras 1:1–5:65[=Ezra 3:13], and much of the genealogical material found in 1 Chronicles 1–9 as composing the first redaction (Chr_1). His reconstruction of the second redaction (Chr_2) includes the *voltage* (original text) of 1 Esdras. He also argues for a third redaction (Chr_3), which consists of 1 Chron. 1:1–2 Chron. 36:23. Frank Moore Cross, "A Reconstruction of the Judean Restoration," *JBL* 94, no. 1 (1975): 4–18.

[7] H. G. M. Williamson, *1 and 2 Chronicles*, NCB (Grand Rapids, MI: Eerdmans, 1982); Sara Japhet, *I and II Chronicles*, OTL (Louisville: Westminster John Knox, 1993); Steven L. McKenzie, "The Chronicler as Redactor," in *The Chronicler as Author: Studies in Text and Texture*, ed. M. Patrick Graham and Steven L. McKenzie, JSOTSup 263 (Sheffield: Sheffield Academic Press, 1999), 70–90; Gary N. Knoppers, *I Chronicles 1–9: A New Translation with Introduction and Commentary*, AB 12 (New York: Doubleday, 2003); Gary N. Knoppers, *I Chronicles 10–29: A New Translation with Introduction and Commentary*, AB 12A (New York: Doubleday, 2004).

features of his life. First, we can be confident that he was among the leaders of Israel because he had access to Samuel and Kings, to noncanonical prophetic books (e.g., 1 Chron. 29:29; 2 Chron. 9:29), and to various royal annals of Israel and Judah (e.g., 1 Chron. 9:1; 2 Chron. 27:7; 36:8). Second, the Chronicler was probably from the tribe of Levi and perhaps from the high priestly family of Zadok. He had a keen interest in the priesthood and took time to focus on sacrifices, Levitical services, and the temple much more than Samuel, Kings, or Ezra–Nehemiah (1 Chron. 15:11–26; 16:4; 28:21; 2 Chron. 8:14; 30:15–27). This second factor connects the theological emphasis on the centrality of the temple and its Levitical orders in Chronicles with that found in the priestly book of Ezekiel.

Audience

As with many other biblical books, Chronicles certainly had implications for the general population of Israel as its secondary audience. Yet the Chronicler's primary audience was other religious and political leaders in postexilic Israel. We know this is true because he expected his primary audience to be at least knowledgeable of Samuel and Kings, of noncanonical prophetic books, and of the royal annals (e.g., 1 Chron. 21:17; 2 Chron. 33:20).

Date

The final verses of Chronicles provide us with the earliest possible date for final composition (2 Chron. 36:21–23). These verses record the edict of Cyrus in 539/38 BC that ordered the return of Israelite exiles from Babylon. The latest possible date for Chronicles is less certain. One important clue is that the style of Hebrew in the book gives no indication of influence from the Greek language. This evidence suggests that the book was written before Alexander the Great took control of Palestine around 330 BC.[8]

Within this range, recent commentators favor one of two orientations toward the date of Chronicles's final composition. First, some interpreters have proposed that the Chronicler wrote as early as the ministries of Haggai and Zechariah (ca. 520–515 BC). At least three points support this view: (1) The book consistently presents the temple and its personnel in close partnership with the royal line of David. This dual emphasis on king and temple suggests that the final composition took place near the days of Zerubbabel when expectations of Davidic and priestly partnership were still high (see Hag. 1:14–2:10, 20–23; Zech. 3:1–4:14). (2) The Chronicler gave much attention to the details of priestly and Levitical duties. This focus also suggests a date of composition during the time when Zerubbabel and his priestly partner Joshua (Jeshua) were establishing the new temple order (Zech. 3:1–4:14). (3) The striking omission of Solomon's downfall due to intermarriage (compare 1 Kings 11:1–40 and 2 Chron. 9:29–31) stands in sharp contrast to Nehemiah's reminder of the terrible

---

[8] The use of אֲדַרְכֹּן in 1 Chron. 29:7 is problematic since it can be translated either "daric" or "drachma." It is possible, however, that this rare word is anachronistic, representing a later editorial updating of the currency.

results of Solomon's foreign marriages (Neh. 13:26). This omission suggests that the Chronicler may have written in the generation before intermarriage had become a major problem in the postexilic community.

Second, the majority of recent interpreters have argued that the final composition of Chronicles took place during or just after the ministries of the men Ezra and Nehemiah (ca. 450–390 BC). The main evidence in favor of this view appears in the genealogy of 1 Chronicles 3:17–24. This genealogy extends to a number of generations after Zerubbabel. Some difficulties with interpretation make this evidence less than conclusive, but it would appear certain that the genealogy extends to at least two generations after Zerubbabel.

In light of the ambiguity of the evidence, it seems best to remain satisfied with a range of possibilities. This range extends from sometime near the days of Zerubbabel to sometime soon after the ministries of Ezra and Nehemiah (ca. 515–390 BC).

Is Chronicles History or Theology?

In Chronicles, history and theology are so thoroughly interdependent that it is impossible to justify suggesting that one had priority over the other for the author. Modern readers are often inclined to highlight the historical dimensions of the book because it is largely written in narrative. Even so, from the Chronicler's point of view, history was thoroughly theological, and his expression of theology was thoroughly historical.

On the one side, the Chronicler devoted himself to building his theological reflections on a reliable historical record of Israel's past. The Chronicler's careful handling of numerous written sources points to his concern for historical veracity:

1. He relied most heavily on Samuel and Kings.
2. He also drew from other biblical books.
3. He cited several royal annals: "the chronicles of King David" (1 Chron. 27:24), "the Book of the Kings" (2 Chron. 24:27), "the Book of the Kings of Israel" (1 Chron. 9:1; 2 Chron. 20:34), "the Book of the Kings of Judah and Israel" (2 Chron. 16:11; 25:26; 28:26; 32:32), and "the Book of the Kings of Israel and Judah" (2 Chron. 27:7; 35:27; 36:8).
4. He referred to prophetic writings that have since disappeared: the writings of Samuel (1 Chron. 29:29), Nathan (1 Chron. 29:29; 2 Chron. 9:29), Gad (1 Chron. 29:29), Ahijah (2 Chron. 9:29), Iddo (2 Chron. 9:29; 12:15; 13:22), Shemaiah (2 Chron. 12:15), and anonymous "seers" (2 Chron. 33:19).
5. The content and style of many passages also suggest that the Chronicler used other unidentifiable sources (see 2 Chron. 9:29–31; 12:15–16; 16:11–17:1; 21:18–20; 24:23–27; 26:22–23; 28:26–27; 32:32–33; 35:20–27; 36:8).

The Chronicler's use of these many sources indicates that he did not fabricate his reports but strongly desired to convey a true account of Israel's past.

On the other side, the Chronicler also wrote his history to convey theological perspectives. His theological outlooks can be inferred in at least five main ways:

1. He reported God's evaluative words and actions in his narratives (e.g., 1 Chron. 13:10; 14:10; 21:7; 2 Chron. 25:15).
2. He referred to prophetic speeches (e.g., 1 Chron. 17:1–15; 2 Chron. 15:1–7; 18:18–22; 21:12–15; 28:9–11).
3. The Chronicler made his own authorial comments (e.g., 2 Chron. 32:32; 33:9; 35:26).
4. Events are either implicitly or explicitly evaluated in terms of divine revelations given to Moses (e.g., 1 Chron. 15:15; 2 Chron. 8:13; 23:18; 25:4) and David (e.g., 2 Chron. 23:3, 18; 28:1; 29:2, 25; 34:2).
5. The Chronicler intentionally diverged from the records of Samuel and Kings to reveal his theological perspectives.[9]

STRUCTURE AND OUTLINE

Chronicles presents history and theology in the form of a literary work designed to lead its original audience step-by-step through a process of reasoning. The Chronicler reported events with implicit and explicit theological assessments that are entirely true and authoritative, but he did not write simply to tell the truth. He ordered his presentation to persuade his audience to endorse certain beliefs, attitudes, and actions.

The rhetorical structure of Chronicles is often overlooked because modern readers mistakenly treat chronology as the nearly exclusive organizing principle of the book. Despite the fact that we call this book "Chronicles," it is only roughly chronological. To be sure, the book follows historical sequencing in a variety of ways. It begins with Adam (1 Chron. 1:1) and ends with Cyrus's edict (2 Chron. 36:21–23). It reports the reigns of kings in chronological order: Saul, David, Solomon, Rehoboam, Abijah, and so forth. Even within the record of each king's reign, events are often in chronological order.

Still, the Chronicler's theological interests often marginalized his interest in chronology. For instance, the first chapter consists of genealogies that follow historical order, but the genealogies of the sons of Israel (1 Chron. 2:1–9:1a) recapitulate the same period again and again. In a similar way, the genealogies end with lists of those who had returned from exile with Zerubbabel (1 Chron. 9:1–34), but the main body of the book regresses chronologically to Saul's ancestry and the day of his death (1 Chron. 9:35–10:14). On many occasions the Chronicler set aside chronological organization in favor of theological organization.

This observation is important for understanding the literary arrangement of Chronicles. The book did not by any means simply give its original audience a record of how events unfolded. It gave them a record that served as a logical or theological

---

[9] Research in the second half of the last century has demonstrated that the interconnections between the Hebrew and Septuagint texts of Samuel, Kings, and Chronicles are complex. More specifically, 4QSam$_a$ and especially 4QSam$_b$ have indicated that the Masoretic text of Chronicles reflects dependence on a Hebrew textual tradition attested in certain (primarily proto-Lucianic) versions of the Septuagint. Every comparison of Samuel and Chronicles must take these complexities into account. In effect, most minor differences between the Masoretic texts of Samuel and Chronicles do not reflect the Chronicler's intentional divergence from Samuel. Rather, they resulted from the version of Samuel that the Chronicler followed. In the case of Kings, however, the Chronicler apparently followed a proto-Rabbinical (proto-Masoretic) Hebrew text, making differences between Kings and Chronicles easier to handle. See Steven L. McKenzie, *The Chronicler's Use of the Deuteronomistic History*, HSM 33 (Atlanta: Scholars Press, 1985).

path down which the Chronicler led his audience. So rather than simply thinking of the book as historical chronology, we should also view it as representing an underlying logical argument, a step-by-step effort at persuasion. The Chronicler's theological argument appears at every level of the text, from the smallest units to the largest. The following outline highlights some of the main ways he designed large literary divisions of the book to persuade the audience:

I. Part One: The Identity, Privileges, and Responsibilities of God's People (1 Chron. 1:1–9:34)

These chapters serve as much more than genealogical background to Israel's history. Time and again, the genealogies reach far beyond the initial narratives of the book. Rather, these chapters introduce the basic contours of the Chronicler's persuasive strategy, which he unfolds in more detail later in his book. He drew his audience's attention to genealogies that identified who should be counted among the people of Israel and what privileges and responsibilities God had ordained for them. The genealogies demonstrated that all the tribes of Israel were to be counted among God's people. They indicated that the royal family of David culminated in Zerubbabel's family. They also emphasized the critical service provided by the tribe of Levi, especially the high priestly family of Zadok. The Chronicler closed these genealogies with a representative list of those who had returned from exile (1 Chron. 9:1–34) to point to the relevance of his genealogies for his audience. As such, the genealogies set the stage for the theological outlooks that unfold throughout the book.

It would be possible to infer that the genealogies also focus on two tribes: Judah and Levi. This focal point in the postexilic community stemmed from a concern for kingship and temple—that is, the search for a true king and a true priest to lead and intercede for God's people in the restoration period. Of course, this search does not cease until we come to the genealogies of Matthew, when we discover that Jesus is both the King and the Priest anticipated by these lists.

II. Part Two: The Ideal United Kingdom (1 Chron. 9:35–2 Chron. 9:31)

These chapters deal primarily with the reigns of David and Solomon and explain how they received God's blessings as they unified the nation and devoted themselves to the temple. The Chronicler omitted most of the well-known failures of these kings that were recorded in Samuel and Kings because he sought to persuade his audience to seek God's blessings in their day by following the positive features of the reigns of David and Solomon.

III. Part Three: Judah during the Divided Kingdom (2 Chron. 10:1–28:27)

Rather than alternating between the northern and southern kingdoms like the book of Kings, this section of Chronicles concentrates on events in Judah from the days of Rehoboam to the days of Ahaz (ca. 931–715 BC). In so doing, the Chronicler led his audience to consider how the blessings and curses of God depended both on the rule of David's house and on the observance of the temple and its services. He rehearsed different scenarios of blessings and curses so that his audience could evaluate similar patterns in their own day.

IV. Part Four: The Reunited Kingdom (2 Chron. 29:1–36:23)

This portion of Chronicles extends from Hezekiah to the decree of Cyrus (ca. 729–538 BC). The most remarkable feature of this division is how the Chronicler represented Hezekiah as one who reunited the northern and southern kingdoms under the house of David and in observance of the temple and its services (2 Chron. 30:1–27). From this perspective, the successes and failures of Judah's kings in this section affected all the tribes of Israel. In this view, all the tribes of Israel symbolically endured exile to Babylon, but the edict of Cyrus called all the tribes to return to the Land of Promise under the leadership of David's house and in devotion to the temple and its services.

MESSAGE AND THEOLOGY

It is not difficult to discern the major themes of Chronicles if we examine this history with three questions in mind: How is Chronicles similar to and different from Samuel and Kings? What topics are repeated in his book? How do these factors correlate with the circumstances he and his audience faced?

As we consider the Chronicler's chief theological emphases, with an eye to these three questions, we also have to keep in mind that the early returnees had good reason to expect an outpouring of God's blessings in their day. Moses (Deut. 30:1–10) and the prophets (e.g., Ezek. 34:26; Joel 3:18–21; Amos 9:11–15) had predicted that return from exile would be a time of unparalleled blessings for Israel. Yet as the books of Haggai, Zechariah, and Ezra–Nehemiah indicate, the postexilic community failed to experience these blessings because of their unfaithfulness. As a result, they had some successes, but they also endured discouraging economic hardship, significant foreign opposition, and domestic division. The Chronicler found these disappointments intolerable as they failed to meet with prophetic expectation.

It is nearly impossible to summarize the main theological concerns of a book as complex as Chronicles in a sentence or two, but it may be helpful to think of his overarching purpose along the following lines: *The Chronicler wrote his historical record to direct his audience to reconsider what they believed about the people of God, about the king and the temple, and about God's blessings and curses.*

What Did the Chronicler Believe about the People of God?

When Chronicles was written, there was much confusion about who qualified as the people of God. Decades of exile had scattered the tribes of Israel and left them in disarray. Following the predictions of Old Testament prophets, the Chronicler longed for the people of God to be reunited in large numbers in the Promised Land. His emphasis on this desire appears in at least three main ways.

All Israel

The Chronicler believed that God's people included more than the small population of the postexilic community. The restoration of the kingdom was incomplete unless Israelites returned to the Promised Land in large numbers. As such, one of the

Chronicler's favorite expressions was "all Israel" (כָּל־יִשְׂרָאֵל) and other closely related phrases. He copied it from Samuel and Kings (1 Chron. 18:14; 19:17; 2 Chron. 7:8–9; 10:16; 18:16), modified Samuel and Kings to read "all Israel" in his version (1 Chron. 11:1; 14:8; 15:28; 2 Chron. 10:3), and included the expression nineteen times in material that was unique to himself (1 Chron. 11:10; 12:38; 15:3; 21:5; 28:4, 8; 29:21, 23, 25, 26; 2 Chron. 1:2; 12:1; 13:4, 15; 24:5; 28:23; 29:24; 30:1; 35:3).

Northern Israel

Chronicles gives special attention to northern Israelites because they presented a complex problem in his day. Most northerners remained where the Assyrians had exiled them. Others stayed in their traditional territories but were mixed with exiles from other nations (see 2 Kings 17). At the same time, on several occasions, groups of northerners joined themselves to Judah (2 Chron. 11:17; 15:4, 8; 30:11, 18, 21). Some descendants of these defectors had gone into exile in Babylon and joined the early returnees (1 Chron. 9:3–9).

The book of Chronicles offers a balanced assessment of this complex situation. On the one hand, it sees the southern kingdom as the center of God's work, and so the account focuses on Judah during the divided kingdom. With only one exception (2 Chron. 13:1; parallel to 1 Kings 15:1–2), the Chronicler omitted all North-South synchronizations from the book of Kings. Beyond this, the Chronicler gave strongly negative assessments of certain aspects of life in the North. He acknowledged the legitimacy of Israel's initial political separation from Judah (2 Chron. 10:1–11:4), but he condemned northern worship practices and other forms of wickedness (2 Chron. 13:4–12; 19:2; 21:6, 12–15; 22:3; 22:10–23:21; 24:7; 25:7; 30:6–9). Judah was not to make political alliances with the wicked from northern Israel. To form such agreements was to reject reliance on God (2 Chron. 19:1–2; 20:35–37; 21:5–6, 12–15; 22:3–6; 25:7–10). He lamented that Judahite (southern) kings behaved like Israelite (northern) kings (2 Chron. 21:6, 13; 22:4; 28:2–4).

On the other hand, the Chronicler knew that it was God's plan to include the northern tribes in Israel's restoration after exile. So northern tribes appear in genealogies and lists (1 Chron. 4:24–5:26; 7:1–40; 9:3). At least twenty-three times the Chronicler's inclusive terminology "all Israel" refers to the northern tribes. He noted that God had planned the division of Israel and Judah (2 Chron. 11:1–4). He also noted defections from the North to the South (2 Chron. 11:17; 15:4, 8; 30:11, 18, 21). He highlighted that on at least one occasion northerners obeyed God's prophet when Judah was rebelling against God (2 Chron. 28:6–15). He equated the moral conditions of Judah and Israel in the days of Hezekiah (2 Chron. 29:8–9). The Chronicler observed that the religious reforms of three Judahite kings extended into the northern territories (2 Chron. 19:4; 31:1; 34:6–7), and he condemned Asa's failure to reform the North (2 Chron. 15:17). He also underscored Hezekiah's symbolic reunion of the North and South at his Passover celebration (2 Chron. 30:1–31:1). These features of Chronicles were designed to show that the postexilic community should earnestly desire the inclusion of northern tribes in their restoration of the kingdom.

International Relations

The Chronicler also focused on relations between Israel and other nations in order to guide interactions with the nations after the exile. Once again, the Chronicler offered a balanced outlook. On one side, the book is open toward foreigners: (1) The opening genealogies and lists include Kenites (1 Chron. 2:55), Ishmaelites (1 Chron. 4:25), and foreign "temple servants" (see Num. 31:30; Ezra 8:20) among the returnees (1 Chron. 9:1–34). (2) David and Solomon had economic ties with foreigners whom God blessed (1 Chron. 22:2; 2 Chron. 8:17–9:26). And (3) Solomon even prayed that foreigners would come to the temple (2 Chron. 6:32–33).

On the other side, a strong warning balanced these positive outlooks. Dire consequences followed for those who relied on foreign powers rather than God (2 Chron. 16:1–9; 28:16–21). Even David did not help the Philistines when he was in their company (1 Chron. 12:19). Conversely, when God's people relied on God, the foreign nations feared and ceased aggression against them (1 Chron. 14:17; 2 Chron. 9:1–12; 17:10; 20:29; 26:8). These passages reminded the postexilic community to avoid depending on foreign human powers to sustain their newly restored nation; only divine power could secure the kingdom.

What Did the Chronicler Believe about Israel's King and Temple?

His emphases on David's dynasty and on the temple appear in the amount of space he allotted to the two tribes of Judah and Levi in the opening genealogies and in the special attention he gave to at least five motifs.

Royal and Levitical Families

The Chronicler highlighted the lines of David and Levi beyond what we find in Samuel and Kings. The genealogies give more attention to David's lineage (1 Chron. 2:10–17; 3:1–24) and the families of the priests and Levites (1 Chron. 6:1–81) than any others. He described David's permanent dynasty over the nation (1 Chronicles 17; 2 Chron. 13:5; 21:7; 23:3b) as a benefit, not a burden, for Israel (1 Chron. 11:4–8, 10–11a, 18–19; 14:2; 18:14; 22:18; 2 Chron. 2:11; 7:10; 9:8). The duties of priestly and Levitical families are also delineated (1 Chron. 15:2; 23:28; 26:20; 2 Chron. 19:8, 23:7; 30:27; 31:2; 34:13). The Chronicler indicated on a number of occasions that he expected the postexilic community to follow these God-ordained arrangements (see 1 Chron. 6:48–53; 9:10–13; 16:39–42; 23:13; 29:22; 2 Chron. 29:34; 34:10).

Religious Assemblies

The Chronicler emphasized that the king and temple were to be mutually supportive in his record of Judah's monarchs calling for religious gatherings. These assemblies occurred in the united monarchy (1 Chron. 13:2, 4–5; 15:3; 28:1, 8; 29:1, 10, 20; 2 Chron. 1:3, 5; 5:2–3; 6:3, 12–13; 7:8–9), the divided kingdom (2 Chron. 11:1–4; 20:5, 14, 26; 23:3; 24:6), and the reunited kingdom (2 Chron. 29:23, 28, 31–32; 30:2, 4, 13, 23–25; 31:18). The leaders of the postexilic community were to do the same in their day.

Royal Worship

The Chronicler also highlighted David's (1 Chronicles 13–29) and Solomon's (2 Chronicles 2–8) devotion to worship and the temple. He focused on renovations and reforms of temple worship in the divided and reunited periods (2 Chron. 17:3–6; 19:11; 15:8–15; 24:4–11; 29:1–31:1; 33:16–17; 34:3b–35:19). Chronicles also notes the failure of some kings to attend to the temple (2 Chron. 15:17; 16:2; 20:33; 21:11; 26:16–21; 28:4; 33:3). This devotion to worship was to be imitated in the Chronicler's day.

Music

The Chronicler took many opportunities to focus on which families of priests and Levites were to play instruments and sing (1 Chron. 6:33; 15:16, 19, 22, 27; 16:4, 7, 42; 25:1–31; 2 Chron. 5:12; 7:6; 23:18; 29:25, 26, 27, 30; 30:21, 25; 31:2; 34:12; 35:15). He noted how lots were cast for particular duties (1 Chron. 25:9). He emphasized practical matters like the training of Levitical musicians (1 Chron. 15:22; 25:7; 2 Chron. 34:12) and the rotation of duties (1 Chron. 25:9–31). He specified what musical instruments were used (e.g., 1 Chron. 13:8; 15:16) and when and how music occurred (2 Chron. 5:11–14; 7:6; 23:18; 29:27–28; 30:21), including in association with battle (1 Chron. 25:1; 2 Chron. 13:12, 14; 20:21–28). On a number of occasions, the Chronicler stressed that Israel rejoiced enthusiastically over the blessings of God, and these celebrations nearly always involved music. At times, the magnificence of the scenes overwhelm even modern readers (1 Chron. 15:16; 2 Chron. 5:12; 29:25–30; 30:21; 35:15). These depictions were designed to guide and inspire the original audience in the joy of worship.

Temple Contributions

One of the practical matters facing the postexilic period was the need to fund the temple and its services. Although Cyrus had supplied the early returnees (Ezra 1:7–11), the prophecies of Haggai indicate that the people failed to contribute to the temple (Haggai 1). Malachi later rebuked the people for not fulfilling their tithes (Mal. 3:8–12). As a result of this neglect, the Chronicler taught his readers the importance of supporting the temple by negative and positive examples from Israel's history. In times of judgment, temple treasuries were robbed by Judah's kings (e.g., 2 Chron. 16:2) and their enemies (e.g., 2 Chron. 12:9). By contrast, in times of blessing, the kings of Judah devoted much money to the temple (1 Chron. 29:2–5; 2 Chron. 2:1–5:1; 24:5; 31:3–21; 34:9).

What Did the Chronicler Believe about Divine Blessings and Curses?

A third major pillar in the book of Chronicles is the dynamic of divine blessing and judgment. The book of Kings dealt with God's curses primarily to explain that the exile to Babylon was God's just judgment against his people for covenant disloyalty. As a result, the author of Kings frequently pointed to the accumulation of divine wrath against Israel as the cause of the captivity (e.g., 2 Kings 17:1–41; 21:10–15). To meet the needs of his postexilic audience, the Chronicler emphasized what is often called *immediate retribution*, the notion that God's blessings and curses often, though not always, came within the generation of those who obeyed or disobeyed God. We will elaborate on this theme of immediate retribution in eleven ways.

Covenant

Immediate retribution rested on the fact that Israel was bound to God by covenant. On several occasions, the Chronicler used the term *covenant* to describe an agreement among humans (1 Chron. 11:3; 2 Chron. 23:1, 3, 11), but he concentrated on Israel's covenant with God, especially the covenant with Moses (1 Chron. 15:25, 26, 28, 29; 16:6, 37; 17:1; 22:19; 28:2, 18; 2 Chron. 5:2, 7, 10; 6:11). The Chronicler mentioned divine covenants from the past to affirm their continuing significance for his readers. God partially fulfilled the covenant he made with the patriarchs in blessings that came to David (1 Chron. 16:15–17). Similarly, David commanded Solomon to keep covenant with God (1 Chron. 28:9), and Abijah appealed to David's dynastic covenant ("a covenant of salt") to establish the legitimacy of his own throne (2 Chron. 13:5). In much the same way, the Chronicler himself explained that the continuation of David's line in the days of Jehoram resulted from divine faithfulness to the covenant God made with David (2 Chron. 21:7). These passages demonstrate that the Abrahamic, Mosaic, and Davidic covenants were valid for the people of God even after the exile. The Chronicler also stressed the importance of covenant renewal (2 Chron. 6:14; 15:12; 23:16; 29:10; 34:32), especially after the exile.

Mosaic Law

The Chronicler relied heavily on the standard of the Mosaic law. In many cases, he appealed to Moses's regulations for worship (1 Chron. 6:49; 15:15; 16:40; 21:29; 22:13; 2 Chron. 8:13; 23:18; 24:6, 9; 30:16; 31:4, 21; 34:14, 19; 35:6, 12). He touched on other matters from the law as well (1 Chron. 22:12, 13; 2 Chron. 6:16; 12:1; 17:9; 19:8, 10; 25:4; 33:8; 35:26). Even so, the Chronicler recognized that the Mosaic law had to be applied in creative ways in challenging circumstances (see 1 Chron. 21:28–22:1; 2 Chron. 5:11–12; 30:2).

David and Solomon

Chronicles also points out that Israel was to observe standards established by David and Solomon. The book often describes obedience as conformity to both Moses and David together (1 Chron. 15:15; 22:13; 2 Chron. 8:13–14; 23:18; 33:7–8; 35:4, 6).

It upholds specific practices established by David and Solomon for worship (1 Chron. 28:19; 2 Chron. 8:14; 23:18; 29:25, 27; 34:2; 35:4, 15), and it occasionally presents David as a model for more general patterns of life (2 Chron. 17:3; 28:1; 29:2; 34:2). These emphases indicate how important it was for the postexilic community to build on what God had revealed through David and Solomon.

Prophetic Instruction

The Chronicler also presented prophetic revelation as a standard for Israel. He referred his readers to a number of written prophetic records (e.g., 1 Chron. 29:29; 2 Chron. 9:29; 12:15; 13:22; 20:34; 21:12; 26:22; 32:32). On a number of occasions he designated Levites as "prophets" and "seers" (1 Chron. 25:1–5; 2 Chron. 20:14; 24:20; 29:30; 35:15). Moreover, Chronicles reports how the fate of Israel and Judah was often determined by their reactions to the prophetic word (1 Chron. 17:1–15; 21:9–19; 2 Chron. 11:1–23; 12:1–12; 15:8; 16:7–10; 18:1–34; 19:2; 21:12; 25:15; 28:9; 36:12). These many prophetic scenarios were designed to encourage the postexilic audience of Chronicles to pay heed to the prophets in their day.

The Heart

The Chronicler was a theologian of the heart. As elsewhere in the Scriptures, in Chronicles the terms translated "heart," "soul," and "mind" refer to the thoughts and motivations of people. These terms do not designate particular psychological faculties. All the deeper dynamics of the inner person may be summed up as the heart, soul, or mind. Above all, the Chronicler held before his postexilic readers the Mosaic ideal of obedience to God with one's whole heart. For instance, such obedience is closely associated with being "willing" to serve God (1 Chron. 28:9), giving money "freely" (1 Chron. 29:9), "performing all" required for completing the temple (1 Chron. 29:19), seeking God "with their whole desire" (2 Chron. 15:15), judging "in faithfulness" in the fear of God (2 Chron. 19:9), and performing well in "every work" (2 Chron. 31:21). The Chronicler often pointed out that certain kings did or did not serve God with their hearts. Zedekiah hardened his heart (2 Chron. 36:13). Pride is acknowledged as a condition of the heart (literally, "proud of heart," 2 Chron. 25:19; 26:16; 32:25, 26, my trans.). Repentance is said to involve the heart (2 Chron. 6:37). Seeking God should also stem from the heart (1 Chron. 22:19; 2 Chron. 11:16; 15:12; 19:3; 22:9).

It is important to note that the Chronicler explicitly distinguished between external behavior and the condition of the heart. Asa failed to destroy all "the high places" in Israel, but "the heart of Asa was wholly true all his days" (2 Chron. 15:17). Conversely, Amaziah "did what was right in the eyes of the LORD, yet not with a whole heart" (2 Chron. 25:2). In this case, the Chronicler distinguished between doing what was right and doing it sincerely and enthusiastically. These various examples revealed the Chronicler's ideals for Israel as well as a realistic awareness of the complexities of inner motivations and behaviors.

Prayer

The Chronicler exhibited a deep concern for prayer. The fullest expression of this concern appears in Solomon's temple prayer (2 Chron. 6:3–42; parallel to 1 Kings 8:22–53) and God's response (2 Chron. 7:13–15; parallel to 1 Kings 9:3–9). In Chronicles, God answers prayers on many occasions. In the opening genealogies and lists, the Chronicler mentioned the prayer of Jabez (1 Chron. 4:10) and the prayer of the Transjordanian tribes (1 Chron. 5:20). In the united kingdom, God heard the prayers of David (1 Chron. 16:7–36; 17:16–27; 29:10–20) and Solomon (2 Chron. 6:3–42). In the divided kingdom, the record of the first four kings of Judah includes answered prayers (2 Chron. 12:6; 13:14; 14:11; 18:31; 20:6–12). Answered prayers also appear in the reunited monarchy (2 Chron. 30:18; 32:20–21; 32:24; 33:12–13, 18). These examples of prayer in Chronicles demonstrate the importance of prayer for the Chronicler's postexilic readers. God's consistently gracious response to sincere prayers offered the returnees hope that God would answer their cries as well.

Humility

Humbling oneself before God is another important responsibility that the Chronicler associated with divine blessing and judgment. The Chronicler used the verb "to humble" (כָּנַע) eighteen times. The ESV translates this term "subdue[d]" (1 Chron. 17:10; 18:1; 20:4; 2 Chron. 13:18) and "humble[d]" (2 Chron. 7:14; 12:6, 7 [twice], 12; 28:19; 30:11; 32:26; 33:12, 19, 23; 34:27 [twice]; 36:12).

On three occasions in the united kingdom (1 Chron. 17:10; 18:1; 20:4) and twice in the divided kingdom (2 Chron. 13:18; 28:19), the term is employed in the more ordinary sense of being humbled through military defeat. The Chronicler took this concept and employed it as a theological metaphor. He described a number of situations in which people humbled (or did not humble) themselves before God. On a number of occasions, the Chronicler placed humility in a four-step scenario: (1) Israel was in rebellion against God; (2) they were confronted with the need for change; (3) they responded to the confrontation by surrendering themselves to God and submitting to his supremacy over them; and (4) this humility led to blessing from God. Humility before God brought dramatic blessings on no less than four occasions (2 Chron. 12:6, 7, 12; 30:11; 32:26; 33:12, 19). The Chronicler's repeated emphasis on this theme was designed to lead his postexilic readers toward humility. If they hoped to see more of God's blessings in their day, they had to surrender themselves to God in humility.

Seeking

Seeking God is another crucial responsibility of God's people in Chronicles. Two Hebrew verbs express this idea: דָּרַשׁ (forty-three times) and בִּקֵּשׁ (thirteen times). On one occasion the Chronicler indicated that these terms were closely related by using them together (1 Chron. 16:11). The ESV usually translates both terms as "seek," but "search," "require," "inquire," "avenge," and "question" also appear.

The Chronicler wrote of "seeking" in a theological sense with several specific objects: "all the commandments" (1 Chron. 28:8), "the word of the LORD" (2 Chron. 18:4), direction from a prophet (2 Chron. 18:6), and God himself (e.g., דָּרַשׁ: 1 Chron. 10:14; 13:3; 15:13; 16:11; 21:30; 22:19; 28:9; 2 Chron. 1:5; 12:14; 14:4, 7 [twice]; 15:2, 12, 13; 16:12; 17:3, 4; 18:7; 19:3; 20:3; 22:9; 26:5 [twice]; 30:19; 31:21; 34:3, 21, 26; בָּקַשׁ: 1 Chron. 16:10, 11; 2 Chron. 11:16; 15:4, 15; 20:4 [twice]). In these passages, seeking is an expression of loyalty and devotion to God. For this reason, in two cases (1 Chron. 16:11; 2 Chron. 7:14) the object of seeking is the very "face" of God (i.e., his favor [see Num. 6:26]). Similarly, seeking God is the opposite of forsaking him or abandoning the covenant relationship with God (2 Chron. 15:2).

The repetition of this motif throughout Chronicles called the postexilic community to seek God in their own day. As troubles and disappointments mounted against those who had returned to the land, the way of divine blessing was made clear. Those who sought God could expect his blessing. To fail to seek him was to ensure the failure of the postexilic restoration.

Abandoning and Forsaking

Chronicles also stresses that the people of God must not "abandon" or "forsake" (עָזַב) God. The ESV translates this Hebrew term as "abandon," "forsake," and "leave." Throughout his history, the Chronicler used the concept of abandonment to describe Israel's disowning, deserting, and leaving God behind. No less than eight times, Israel's abandonment is stated in personal terms—Israel abandoned God himself (2 Chron. 7:22; 12:5; 13:10; 21:10; 24:20, 24; 28:6; 29:6; 34:25). In 2 Chronicles 34:25 the personal character of Israel's abandonment of God becomes evident in that they left him "for other gods." For this reason, abandoning God is set in opposition to seeking him (1 Chron. 28:9; 2 Chron. 15:2).

Despite this personal dimension, Chronicles is clear that to forsake God is to violate the objective law of God. Israel abandoned God in two main ways: they flagrantly violated the law of Moses in general matters (2 Chron. 7:19; 12:1; 24:20), and they also neglected divine regulations specifically governing worship (2 Chron. 13:10–11; 15:2–3; 21:10–12; 34:25).

The doctrine of immediate retribution becomes evident in the way that the Chronicler connected Israel's abandonment of God and his abandonment of the nation (1 Chron. 28:9, 20; 2 Chron. 15:5; 20:37; 24:20; 26:18–20). Abandonment frequently resulted in some kind of military trouble or defeat (2 Chron. 12:5; 21:10; 24:24; 32:21; 34:25). Exile was the most severe form of God's desertion (2 Chron. 7:19–20). The Chronicler emphasized the theme of abandoning God to explain both why his audience suffered in their day and how they could reverse their circumstances.

Unfaithfulness

On fourteen occasions, the Chronicler noted that the people of God had been "unfaithful" (מָעַל). Frequently, he explicitly identified the object of Israel's unfaithfulness as God himself (1 Chron. 10:13; 2 Chron. 6:16; 12:2; 28:19, 22; 30:7). This infidelity was a direct and personal affront against God. The Chronicler also linked unfaithfulness with acts of turning away from the law of Moses, especially the laws regarding worship (1 Chron. 2:7; 10:13; 2 Chron. 12:2; 26:16, 18; 28:22–23; 29:6, 19; 33:19; 36:14). In every case of unfaithfulness, the Chronicler pointed to the severe consequences of divine judgment (1 Chron. 2:7; 5:25; 9:1; 10:13; 2 Chron. 12:2; 26:16, 18; 28:19, 22; 33:19; 36:14).

This correlation between infidelity and severe punishment reminded the original audience that the troubles they had experienced resulted from their own failure to remain faithful to God. It also warned that further infidelity would bring about severe consequences.

Repentance

On nine occasions Chronicles explicitly mentions the theme of repentance (שׁוּב). The ESV translates the Hebrew term reflecting this concept as "turn again" (2 Chron. 6:24), "turn" (2 Chron. 6:26; 7:14; 15:4; 36:13), "return" (2 Chron. 30:6, 9), "bring back" (2 Chron. 24:19) and "repent" (2 Chron. 6:37). The theme of repentance is not unique to Chronicles, but six of these nine occurrences appear in the Chronicler's additions to the book of Kings (2 Chron. 7:14; 15:4; 24:19; 30:6, 9; 36:13). The motif was an important dimension of his concept regarding Israel's responsibility before God.

The Chronicler's concept of repentance was twofold. On the one hand, repentance meant to turn away from evil. Solomon described it as turning "from their sin" (2 Chron. 6:26). Similarly, God spoke of Israel turning "from their wicked ways" (2 Chron. 7:14). On the other hand, repentance was an act of turning toward someone. Azariah the prophet referred to a time when Israel "turned to the LORD" (2 Chron. 15:4). Prophets spoke to "bring them back to the LORD" (2 Chron. 24:19). Hezekiah called northern Israel to "return to the LORD" (2 Chron. 30:6) and offered compassion from God if they would "return to him" (2 Chron. 30:9). Finally, Zedekiah is condemned for not "turning to the LORD" (2 Chron. 36:13). These expressions indicate the personal dimension of repentance. It did not amount simply to changing behaviors to match a set of regulations more thoroughly. Repentance was to approach God himself. The results of repentance are also explicitly noted in Chronicles. Those who refused to turn back to God would suffer his judgment (2 Chron. 36:13, 17), while those who repented would enjoy God's blessings (2 Chron. 6:24, 26; 7:14; 30:9).

The failures of the postexilic community had brought them to the point that the Chronicler called them to repentance. If his readers heeded this call, they would receive the mercy of God. If they refused, they could only expect further judgment from God.

APPROACHING THE NEW TESTAMENT

As one of the last Old Testament books to be written and as the final book in the Hebrew Bible, Chronicles presents theological emphases that fit easily within New

Testament theology. The Chronicler lived at a time when Jeremiah's prediction of seventy years of exile had partially been fulfilled (2 Chron. 36:22), but he sought to further the renewal that had been promised for God's people after the exile had ended. Sadly, Israel's continuing rebellion after the days of the Chronicler postponed any further blessings of renewal until the time of Christ. The problem of Israel's sin, their disobedience, and their hard-heartedness had not been solved in this particular return from exile.

The New Testament authors lived hundreds of years after the Chronicler had recorded this history, but they knew that Jesus had inaugurated the fulfillment of Jeremiah's prophecy of a new covenant after Israel's exile had ended (Jer. 31:31). Like the Chronicler, they sought to further the blessings of God on his people as they wrote their books. For this reason, many of the major themes of Chronicles have rather direct correlations with the theology of the New Testament, such as the heart, humility, seeking God, unfaithfulness, and repentance.

In general terms, however, we must keep in mind that New Testament theology teaches that Christ did not fulfill any of these themes completely in his first advent. Instead, the restoration of the kingdom of God in Christ comes in three stages. First, the *inauguration* of the kingdom came through Christ's earthly ministry and the work of his apostles and prophets (see Mark 1:14–15; Luke 4:43; 10:11; Acts 1:3; Eph. 2:19–20). Second, after the ministry of the apostles, the *continuation* of the kingdom of God extends throughout the world through the history of the church (Matt. 28:18–20). Third, in the future, Jesus will bring the kingdom to its *consummation* in the new heavens and new earth (see Rev. 21:1–22:21). If Christian interpreters keep these factors in mind, the book of Chronicles can speak forcefully to life in the New Testament age.

Select Bibliography

Ackroyd, Peter R. *I and II Chronicles, Ezra, Nehemiah: Introduction and Commentary.* TBC. London: SCM Press, 1973.

Braun, Roddy L. *1 Chronicles.* WBC 14. Waco, TX: Word, 1986.

Coggins, R. J. *The First and Second Book of the Chronicles.* CBC. New York: Cambridge University Press, 1973.

Curtis, Edward Lewis, and Albert Alonzo Madsen. *A Critical and Exegetical Commentary on the Books of Chronicles.* ICC. Edinburgh: T&T Clark, 1910.

Dillard, Raymond B. *2 Chronicles.* WBC 15. Waco, TX: Word, 1987.

Japhet, Sara. *I and II Chronicles.* OTL. Louisville: Westminster John Knox, 1993.

Klein, Ralph W. *1 Chronicles.* Hermeneia: A Critical and Historical Commentary on the Bible. Minneapolis: Fortress, 2006.

———. *2 Chronicles.* Hermeneia: A Critical and Historical Commentary on the Bible. Minneapolis: Fortress, 2012.

Knoppers, Gary N. *I Chronicles 1–9: A New Translation with Introduction and Commentary*. AB 12. New York: Doubleday, 2003.

———. *I Chronicles 10–29: A New Translation with Introduction and Commentary*. AB 12A. New York: Doubleday, 2004.

Mabie, Frederick J. *1–2 Chronicles*. In *The Expositor's Bible Commentary, Revised Edition*, edited by Tremper Longman III and David E. Garland, 4:23–336. Grand Rapids, MI: Zondervan, 2010.

McKenzie, Steven L. *1–2 Chronicles*. AOTC. Nashville: Abingdon, 2004.

Merrill, Eugene H. *1, 2 Chronicles*. Bible Study Commentary. Grand Rapids, MI: Lamplighter, 1988.

Myers, Jacob M. *I Chronicles: A New Translation with Introduction and Commentary*. AB 12. New York: Doubleday, 1965.

———. *II Chronicles: A New Translation with Introduction and Commentary*. 2nd ed. AB 13. New York: Doubleday, 1981.

Pratt, Richard L. *1 & 2 Chronicles*. A Mentor Commentary. Fearn, Ross-shire, Scotland: Mentor, 1998.

———. "Royal Prayer and the Chronicler's Program." ThD diss., Harvard Divinity School, 1987.

Rudolph, Wilhelm. *Chronikbücher*. HAT 21. Tübingen: J. C. B. Mohr, 1955.

Thompson, J. A. *1, 2 Chronicles*. NAC 9. Nashville: Broadman, 1994.

Tuell, Steven S. *First and Second Chronicles*. IBC. Louisville: John Knox, 2001.

Williamson, H. G. M. *1 and 2 Chronicles*. NCB. Grand Rapids, MI: Eerdmans, 1982.

Appendix A

The Seventy Weeks
of Daniel 9

Richard P. Belcher Jr.

I. NONMESSIANIC VIEWS OF THE SEVENTY WEEKS
A. Antiochus IV Epiphanes

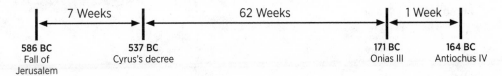

Cyrus is the anointed prince after seven weeks, although some identify the prince with Joshua or Zerubbabel. Onias III is the last legitimate high priest of the Jews who was deposed by Antiochus IV. The last week describes events related to the period of 168–165 BC.[1]

B. Antichrist

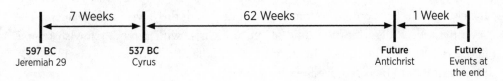

---

[1] John E. Goldingay, *Daniel*, WBC 30 (Dallas: Word, 1989), 260–63; Carol A. Newsom, *Daniel*, OTL (Louisville: Westminster John Knox, 2014), 303–9. Not all those listed as representatives for the various positions in this appendix will always agree exactly with the chart, and they will even vary to some degree among themselves. Yet they will fall into the general viewpoint under which they are listed.

The seventy weeks begin with the prediction of Jeremiah 29, a word about the restoration of Jerusalem. The sixty-two weeks span from Cyrus to the Antichrist, with the last week describing events at the end. The cutting off of the Antichrist will end the desolations.[2]

C. Antichrist

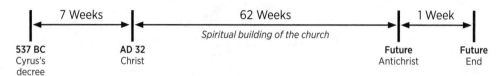

The first seven weeks span from Cyrus to Christ, the anointed prince. The sixty-two weeks describe the building of the spiritual Jerusalem, which ends with the Antichrist. The last week describes the church as losing its influence because the cause of Christ will seem to have failed due to the work of the Antichrist. The Antichrist will carry on his destructive rule until the decreed judgment upon him.[3]

II. Messianic Views of the Seventy Weeks

A. Dispensational Literal 445

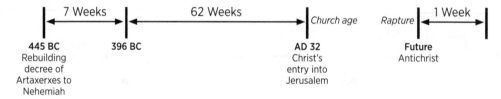

The seven weeks start with the decree of Artaxerxes to Nehemiah and end forty-nine years later. The sixty-two weeks end with the triumphal entry of Christ. For these periods to work, one must use a prophetic year of 360 days. The sixty-nine weeks bring one to the time of Christ (Dan. 9:25). The death of the Messiah and the destruction of Jerusalem take place after the sixty-nine weeks and before the seventieth week (Dan. 9:26). When the Jewish people reject their Messiah, the prophetic clock stops, which marks the beginning of the church age. At the end of the church age, the church will be raptured so that God can deal with the Jewish people again. The seventieth week describes the time of the Antichrist with a rebuilt Jewish temple and sacrifices that the Antichrist stops in the middle of the week, followed by great persecution until he is removed by divine judgment.[4]

---

[2] Thomas McComiskey, "The Seventy 'Weeks' of Daniel against the Background of Ancient Near Eastern Literature," *WTJ* 47, no. 1 (1985): 18–45; Allan M. Harmon, *Daniel*, EP Study Commentary (Darlington, UK: Evangelical Press, 2007), 236–46.
[3] Carl Friedrich Keil and Franz Delitzsch, *Daniel*, in *Commentary on the Old Testament*, vol. 9, *Ezekiel, Daniel* (Grand Rapids, MI: Eerdmans, 1978), 373–77; H. C. Leupold, *Exposition of Daniel* (Columbus, OH: Wartburg, 1949), 416–35.
[4] Robert Anderson, *The Coming Prince*, 14th ed. (Grand Rapids, MI: Kregel, 1954); John F. Walvoord, *Daniel: The Key to Prophetic Revelation* (Chicago: Moody Press, 1971), 228.

B. Dispensational Literal 458

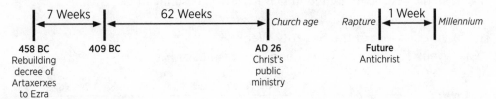

This view is similar to the previous view except that it begins with the decree of Artaxerxes to Ezra with the sixty-nine weeks culminating at the public ministry of Christ. This view uses a solar year to calculate the years. For a discussion of the meaning of the last week, see the "Dispensational Literal 445" view above.[5]

C. Nondispensational Literal View of the Seventy Weeks

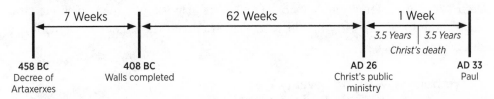

This view understands the seventy weeks as 490 literal years. The seventy weeks begin with the decree of 458 BC. Seven weeks (i.e., forty-nine years) later, the walls are completed. The sixty-two weeks end with the beginning of Christ's public ministry and three and a half years later (one-half of the final one week) Christ dies. The final week ends with the introduction of Saul/Paul at the stoning of Stephen.[6]

D. Nondispensational Chronological/Symbolic View of the Seventy Weeks

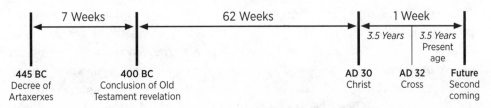

This view understands the sixty-nine weeks to have chronological significance. The seven weeks begin with the decree of Artaxerxes in 445 BC and end with the old covenant revelation coming to a close around 400 BC. The sixty-two weeks end with Christ. The last week is divided into two halves. The first three and a half years take

[5] Gleason L. Archer Jr., *Daniel*, in *The Expositor's Bible Commentary*, ed. Frank E. Gaebelein (Grand Rapids, MI: Zondervan, 1985), 7:113–18; Stephen R. Miller, *Daniel*, NAC 18 (Nashville: Broadman, 1994), 262–73.
[6] Jay E. Adams and Milton C. Fisher, *The Time of the End: Daniel's Prophecy Reclaimed* (Woodruff, SC: Timeless Texts, 2000), 84–88.

one to the death of Christ, and the second three and a half years describe the present age until the destruction of the Antichrist at the consummation.[7]

E. Symbolic View of the Seventy Weeks
(Last Week Focuses on Christ and the Results of His Work)

This view understands the seventy weeks in a symbolic way beginning with the decree of Cyrus in 538 BC. The seven weeks end with the completion of the building of the temple and the city under Ezra and Nehemiah. The sixty-two weeks bring one to Christ, with the final week describing the ministry of Christ. Although the destruction of the temple and city in AD 70 takes place outside the final week, they are a result of the ministry of Christ so they are described in connection with the death of Christ.[8]

F. Symbolic View of the Seventy Weeks
(Last Week Symbolic of the New Covenant Era)

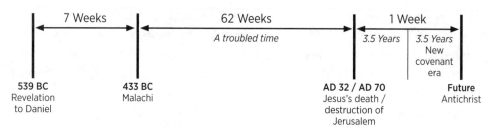

This view understands the seventy weeks in a symbolic way, beginning with the revelation of these events to Daniel. The seven weeks end with the conclusion of Malachi's ministry. The sixty-two weeks describe a troubled time marked by the absence of prophetic guidance and by intrigue surrounding the leadership of Israel in the person of the high priest. The final week is divided into two parts. The first half of the final week describes the death of Christ and the destruction of Jerusalem and the temple in AD 70. The second half of the final week covers the remainder of the new covenant era to the appearance of the Antichrist.[9]

---

[7] O. Palmer Robertson, *The Christ of the Prophets* (Phillipsburg, NJ: P&R, 2004), 338–46.
[8] Edward J. Young, *The Prophecy of Daniel: A Commentary* (Grand Rapids, MI: Eerdmans, 1949), 202–20; Andrew E. Steinmann, *Daniel*, ConcC (St. Louis, MO: Concordia, 2008), 468–76; Peter J. Gentry and Stephen J. Wellum, *Kingdom through Covenant: A Biblical-Theological Understanding of the Covenants* (Wheaton, IL: Crossway, 2012), 550–64.
[9] James M. Hamilton Jr., *With the Clouds of Heaven: The Book of Daniel in Biblical Theology*, NSBT 32 (Downers Grove, IL: InterVarsity Press, 2014), 131–33. Meredith G. Kline takes a similar view of the final week. "The Covenant of the Seventieth Week," in *The Law and the Prophets: Old Testament Studies Prepared in Honor of Oswald Thompson Allis*, ed. John H. Skilton (Nutley, NJ: Presbyterian and Reformed, 1974), 468.

The Role of Heavenly Beings in Daniel

Richard P. Belcher Jr.

The role of angels in Daniel fits with the teaching of Hebrews 1:14. Their chief role is to be "ministering spirits sent out to serve for the sake of those who are to inherit salvation." The angels assist in carrying out the purposes of God, and they primarily serve the people of God. Angels make proclamations to kings, as in Daniel 4:13, where the angel proclaims to Nebuchadnezzar that the tree should be chopped down. This angel is called "a watcher" and "a holy one" who comes down from heaven. The origin of the term "watcher" is uncertain,[1] but this angel functions as a herald to the king. The watcher's proclamation in 4:13 is called a "sentence . . . by the decree of the watchers" with the purpose that the living may know that the Most High rules over the kingdom of men. The plural "watchers" may reflect the idea of a divine council with angels surrounding the throne of God to carry out his purposes. In fact, in 4:24 the utterance of the watchers is also called "a decree of the Most High." What the watchers proclaim is what God has decreed.

Angels also impart understanding. In 7:16 Daniel approaches "one of those who stood there and ask[s] him the truth concerning all this." Daniel seeks out a member of the heavenly council to inquire about the meaning of the vision. This angel makes known the interpretation of the vision. The angel Gabriel also helps Daniel comprehend his visions. In 8:15–16 someone having the appearance of a man stands before Daniel, calling out to Gabriel that he should make Daniel understand the vision.[2]

---

[1] Carol A. Newsom, *Daniel*, OTL (Louisville: Westminster John Knox, 2014), 139.
[2] Most take the one who has the appearance of a man as an angel. It is interesting that Calvin takes this as a reference to Christ but does not understand Dan. 10:5–6 as referring to Christ. John Calvin, *Commentaries on the Prophet Daniel*, trans. Thomas Myers, in vol. 13 of *Calvin's Commentaries* (Grand Rapids, MI: Baker, 1996), 112.

Again in 9:21–22 Gabriel is sent to Daniel in response to his prayer of confession in order to give him insight. He then reveals to Daniel the vision of the seventy weeks.

Michael is another angel named in the book of Daniel. The role of Michael differs from that of Gabriel. Michael is called one of the chief princes (10:13). The word for "prince" (שַׂר) can refer to the leader of a military group (e.g., 1 Sam. 17:18), which fits the picture of Michael's role in Daniel 10. The book gives remarkable insight about the spiritual conflict taking place in the heavenly realms. The one sent to Daniel in chapter 10 was opposed by the "prince of Persia" (10:20), so that he was delayed for twenty-one days. The prince of Persia is an angel in charge of the kingdom of Persia. This idea goes back to Deuteronomy 32:8–9, where God divided the nations according to the sons of God, assigning each nation an angel. Michael is said to be in charge of the people of Israel (12:1). Apparently, not all these angels are on God's side, because there is evidence of conflict. The title "prince of Persia" indicates the military function of the angel who tried to prevent the mission of the one speaking to Daniel (11:13). These texts give a glimpse of the spiritual battles taking place in the heavenly realm that affect what takes place on earth.

Interpreters also debate whether some of these angelic appearances could be understood as manifestations of the preincarnate Christ. Three appearances deserve special attention: the fourth figure in the fiery furnace called "a son of the gods" (3:25, 28), the "one like a son of man" who is given an eternal kingdom (7:13–14), and the man clothed in linen (10:5–6).

The "son of man" in Daniel 7:13 has been identified by many as the angel Michael and by others as a collective symbol for the people of God based on 7:27.[3] However, the New Testament identifies the "son of man" in Daniel 7 with Jesus (Matt. 26:64).[4] Concerning the other two texts, there seems to be less certainty. Hamilton uses the description of the "son of man" in Daniel 7 as the standard by which to judge whether 3:25 or 10:5–6 are referring to the second person of the Trinity. He states, "If any of the other heavenly beings in Daniel can be identified with the son of man, we have reason to believe that Daniel intended those passages to describe the same figure."[5] However, Hamilton is shutting out other important Old Testament evidence when he restricts himself to the description of the "son of man" in Daniel 7 as the standard.

Several issues need to be addressed concerning the fourth figure appearing in the furnace in 3:25. The Aramaic phrase בַּר־אֱלָהִין is translated differently by different versions. The KJV renders it "the Son of God," whereas many modern translations have "a son of the gods" (ESV, NASB). The Aramaic plural אֱלָהִין should always be translated "gods."[6] This translation would also fit the perspective of Nebuchadnezzar, who sees a figure like a son of the gods—that is, a divine being. In Daniel 3:28 Nebuchadnezzar blesses the God of Shadrach, Meshach, and Abednego because he

---

[3] For a discussion of these options, see John J. Collins, *A Commentary on the Book of Daniel*, Hermeneia: A Critical and Historical Commentary on the Bible (Minneapolis: Fortress, 1993), 308–10.

[4] James M. Hamilton Jr., *With the Clouds of Heaven: The Book of Daniel in Biblical Theology*, NSBT 32 (Downers Grove, IL: InterVarsity Press, 2014), 136.

[5] Hamilton, *Daniel in Biblical Theology*, 136.

[6] John E. Goldingay, *Daniel*, WBC 30 (Dallas: Word, 1989), 67. It is possible that the Aramaic plural אֱלָהִין could be a Hebraism (cf. Dan. 4:5).

sent his angel to deliver his servants. From the perspective of the Old Testament, it would be natural to identify this angel with the angel of Yahweh, a prominent figure in the Old Testament. The king saw four men walking in the furnace, and the angel of Yahweh appears at times as a man (Gen. 32:22–32; Num. 22:22–35; Josh. 5:13–15; Judg. 6:11–23; 13:3–23).[7] This figure protected the three Jewish men from the fire. His role of delivering and protecting God's people is highlighted by Nebuchadnezzar when he states, "there is no other god who is able to rescue in this way" (Dan. 3:29). And this activity also fits with the role of the angel of Yahweh.

Who, then, is the man in linen in Daniel 10? On the one hand, some statements in the text lead one to think that this man is a preincarnate appearance of Christ. On the other hand, other statements call this identification into question. In the first line of thought, during a three-week period of mourning, Daniel sees a man clothed in linen. The description of this man is dazzling. He has a belt of fine gold, a body like beryl, a face like the appearance of lightning, eyes like flaming torches, and arms and legs like the gleam of burnished bronze. Even the sound of his words are like the sound of a multitude. This description seems to depict someone who is more than an angel. In fact, it resembles the description of the theophany of God in Ezekiel 1,[8] as well as the description of "one like a son of man" in Revelation 1:13–15. Table 23 illustrates the parallels between the Daniel and Revelation texts.

Daniel 10:5–6	Revelation 1:13–16
clothed in linen	clothed with a long robe
a belt of fine gold	a golden sash
face like the appearance of lightning	face like the sun shining in full strength
eyes like flaming torches	eyes were like a flame of fire
legs like burnished bronze	feet like burnished bronze
voice like the sound of a multitude	voice like the roar of many waters

Table 23

The parallels between the description of the man in Daniel 10 and the descriptions in Ezekiel 1 and Revelation 1 appear to justify the identification of the man in Daniel 10 as someone who is more than an angel. In fact, the parallels between Daniel 10 and Revelation 1 justify, at least indirectly, identifying the man in linen in Daniel 10 with the "son of man" in Daniel 7.

Not everyone agrees on this matter. Hamilton argues that if Daniel wanted us to connect the figure in Daniel 10 with the "son of man" in Daniel 7, he would make an explicit literary connection. Also, the book of Revelation describes the appearance

---

[7] These texts that indicate human form are noted by James A. Borland, *Christ in the Old Testament*, rev. ed. (Fearn, Ross-shire, Scotland: Mentor, 1999), 67.

[8] Both Newsom and Steinmann have a chart that compares the descriptions in Ezekiel chapters 1 and 8–9 with the man clothed in linen of Daniel 10:5–6. Newsom understands the man as an angel and Steinmann as a preincarnate appearance of Christ. Newsom, *Daniel*, 331; Andrew E. Steinmann, *Daniel*, ConcC (St. Louis, MO: Concordia, 2008), 499.

of some angels as glorious and dazzling (e.g., Rev. 1:16, where the angel's face is like the sun).[9] Additionally, when the man of Daniel 10 is sent to Daniel, he is opposed by the prince of Persia for twenty-one days. It seems unlikely that the second person of the Trinity would experience this type of opposition from one of the angels.

And yet, in the mystery of how the Old Testament foreshadows the work of Christ, there is good reason to consider that the man in Daniel 10 might be a preincarnate appearance of Christ. The associations between Daniel 10, Ezekiel 1, and Revelation 1 are striking. The use of the phrase "one like a son of man" in Revelation 1:13–15 establishes an indirect connection between Daniel 10 and the "one like a son of man" in Daniel 7. Additionally, the man in linen is mentioned again in Daniel 12:7, where he is above two other angels who are stationed on the bank of the stream. Thus he is positioned above the waters of the stream when he answers how long it will be until the end of these wonders. His position above the others parallels the "son of man" in Daniel 7, who is presented to the Ancient of Days. When Daniel seeks an interpretation of the vision, he asks "one of those who stood there," probably a reference to one of the angels of the divine council. The "son of man" and the man in linen both seem to have a higher position.

The greatest obstacle in identifying the man in linen in Daniel 10 with Christ is that he is delayed by the prince of Persia for twenty-one days. However, such opposition to a divine figure is not unprecedented in the biblical witness. For example, Genesis 32:24–30 records an incident where Jacob wrestles with a "man" identified as God. In that wrestling match, when the man does not prevail against Jacob, he touches his socket to put it out of joint. It is difficult to conceive that God would have trouble in a wrestling match with any human being, unless God purposely limited his power. Could the incident in Daniel 10, where the man in linen is contested by the prince of Persia, be a foreshadowing of the work of Christ, whose victory over the enemies of God will entail a great struggle? The second person of the Trinity will have to enter fully into the way of salvation where his weakness will become the avenue to save his people.

In conclusion, the heavenly messengers in Daniel play an important role. They make proclamations to kings and impart understanding to Daniel so he can interpret the visions. They also fight spiritual battles in heavenly places that impact events on earth. If one accepts the New Testament evidence, then there is no doubt that the "son of man" in Daniel 7 is the second person of the Trinity. The evidence is slightly weaker in the case of the man clothed in linen and not as strong for identifying the fourth figure in the furnace as a preincarnate appearance of Christ. Either way, it is remarkable to understand that the God we worship is able to deliver his people from any earthly trial. No matter how much the forces of evil seek to destroy God's people or how intense the persecution becomes, we have the assurance of victory because God and his heavenly beings are directly involved in human affairs. Of this fact, there should be no doubt.

---

[9] Hamilton, *Daniel in Biblical Theology*, 146.

Contributors

Richard P. Belcher Jr. (PhD, Westminster Theological Seminary) is the John D. and Frances M. Gwin Professor of Old Testament and academic dean at RTS-Charlotte. Dr. Belcher has taught at RTS since 1995, and his research interests include the Psalms and Wisdom Literature. He is author of *Messiah and the Psalms: Preaching Christ from All the Psalms* (Christian Focus, 2006), *Genesis: The Beginning of God's Plan of Salvation* (Christian Focus, 2012), and *A Study Commentary on Ecclesiastes* (Evangelical Press, 2014).

John D. Currid (PhD, University of Chicago) is the Carl McMurray Professor of Old Testament at RTS-Charlotte, where he has taught since 1993. Dr. Currid's interests are in archaeology, ancient Near Eastern literature, and the Pentateuch. He is the author of *Against the Gods: The Polemical Theology of the Old Testament* (Crossway, 2013) and *Ancient Egypt and the Old Testament* (Baker, 1997).

William B. Fullilove (PhD, The Catholic University of America) is assistant professor of Old Testament at RTS-Atlanta, where he has taught since 2013. Dr. Fullilove's current research interests include the Dead Sea Scrolls and Christian origins as well as the contemporary faith and work movement. He is the author of academic and pastoral articles in the fields of both Old and New Testament.

Mark D. Futato (PhD, The Catholic University of America) is the Robert L. Maclellan Professor of Old Testament at RTS-Orlando (1999–present). Dr. Futato's research interests are in online learning, the poetry of the Old Testament, and the book of Psalms. He is the author of *The Book of Psalms* (Tyndale, 2009), *Interpreting the Psalms: An Exegetical Handbook* (Kregel, 2007), *Joy Comes in the Morning: Psalms for All Seasons* (P&R, 2004), *Beginning Biblical Hebrew* (Eisenbrauns, 2003), *Transformed by Praise: The Purpose and Message of the Psalms* (P&R, 2002), and *Creation: A Witness to the Wonder of God* (P&R, 2000).

Michael J. Glodo (PhD Cand., Westminster Theological Seminary) is associate professor of biblical studies at RTS-Orlando, where he has taught since 2007. He also taught previously at RTS from 1990 to 2000. Between those RTS stints, Rev. Glodo served as stated clerk (chief administrative officer) of the Evangelical Presbyterian

Church, and he has also filled pastoral roles at churches in the St. Louis, Missouri, region. Professor Glodo is passionate about biblical studies and ministry philosophy, particularly regarding worship and liturgy. He teaches courses in Old Testament, New Testament, and practical theology, and he serves as dean of chapel.

Peter Y. Lee (PhD, The Catholic University of America) is associate professor of Old Testament at RTS-Washington, DC (2007–present), and adjunct professor at Redeemer Seminary. His research interests are in ancient Hebrew and Aramaic dialects, Second Temple Jewish literature, Jewish apocalypticism, and biblical messianism. He is the author of *Aramaic Poetry in Qumran* (Scholars Press, 2015).

Michael G. McKelvey (PhD, University of Aberdeen) is assistant professor of Old Testament at RTS-Jackson (2014–present). Dr. McKelvey's research interests are the Psalms, the Prophets, Hebrew poetry, and biblical theology. He is the author of *Moses, David, and the High Kingship of Yahweh: A Canonical Study of Book IV of the Psalter* (Gorgias, 2010).

Richard L. Pratt Jr. (ThD, Harvard University) is the president of Third Millennium Ministries Inc. in Casselberry, Florida. Dr. Pratt taught at RTS-Jackson and RTS-Orlando for a combined twenty-one years (1985–2006) and chaired the Old Testament Department in Orlando. Dr. Pratt's research interests are in Old Testament theology and integrating biblical and theological studies with practical Christian living. He served as general editor of the *NIV Spirit of the Reformation Study Bible* (Zondervan, 2003), and he is the author of *Pray with Your Eyes Open: Looking at God, Ourselves, and Our Prayers* (P&R, 1987), and *He Gave Us Stories: The Bible Student's Guide to Interpreting Old Testament Narratives* (P&R, 1993), to name a couple of books; of commentaries on both 1–2 Chronicles (Mentor, 2002) and 1–2 Corinthians (B&H, 2000); and of numerous articles.

John Scott Redd (PhD, The Catholic University of America) is associate professor of Old Testament and president at RTS-Washington, DC. Dr. Redd has taught at RTS since 2009, and his interests include literary approaches to the Scriptures and the implications of biblical theology for the public square. He is the author of *Constituent Postponement in Biblical Hebrew Verse* (Harrassowitz, 2014).

Daniel C. Timmer (PhD, Trinity International University), was associate professor of Old Testament at RTS-Jackson from 2009 to 2012 and is currently associate professor of Old Testament at the Faculté de théologie évangélique–Acadia University (Montreal). His research interests are in biblical theology, the Prophetic Literature, the wisdom tradition, and the Dead Sea Scrolls. He is the author of *Creation, Tabernacle, and Sabbath: The Sabbath Frame of Exodus 31:12–17; 35:1–3 in Exegetical and Theological Perspective* (Vandenhoeck & Ruprecht, 2009) and *"A Gracious and Compassionate God": Mission, Salvation, and Spirituality in Jonah* (InterVarsity Press, 2011).

Willem A. VanGemeren (PhD, University of Wisconsin–Madison) was professor of Old Testament at RTS-Jackson from 1978 to 1992 and is professor emeritus of Trinity Evangelical Divinity School, where he taught from 1992 to 2014. Dr. VanGemeren's research interests are in Isaiah, the Psalms, and Israel's ancient wisdom tradition. He is the author of numerous volumes—including *The Progress of Redemption: The Story of Salvation from Creation to the New Jerusalem* (Academie Books, 1988), *Interpreting the Prophetic Word* (Academie, 1990), and a commentary on the Psalms in *The Expositor's Bible Commentary* series (Zondervan, 2008)—and he has contributed to many volumes and journals and served as general editor of the award-winning *New International Dictionary of Theology and Exegesis* (Zondervan, 1997).

Miles V. Van Pelt (PhD, The Southern Baptist Theological Seminary) is the Alan Hayes Belcher Jr. Professor of Old Testament and Biblical Languages, director of the Summer Institute for Biblical Languages, and the academic dean at RTS-Jackson. Dr. Van Pelt has taught at RTS since 2003, and his research interests include Hebrew and Aramaic grammar, biblical theology, Old Testament canon, and the books of Judges and the Song of Songs. He is the coauthor of *Basics of Biblical Hebrew* (Zondervan, 2001, 2006) and numerous other Hebrew-language resources, and the author of *Basics of Biblical Aramaic: Complete Grammar, Lexicon, and Annotated Text* (Zondervan, 2011).

John J. Yeo (PhD, University of St. Michael's College in the University of Toronto) is assistant professor of Old Testament at Southwestern Baptist Theological Seminary in Fort Worth, Texas, and he served as academic dean and assistant professor of Old Testament at RTS-Atlanta from 2007 to 2012. Dr. Yeo's interests include the Pentateuch–Historical Books, biblical theology, and evangelical appropriations of historical criticism. He is the author of *Plundering the Egyptians: The Old Testament and Historical Criticism at Westminster Theological Seminary (1929–1998)* (University Press of America, 2009).

General Index

Scripture Index

With the exception of chapter 13 ("The Twelve"), indexed references to whole books of the Bible are limited to books other than the main focus of each chapter.

Teach the New Testament from a Reformed, covenantal, and redemptive-historical perspective

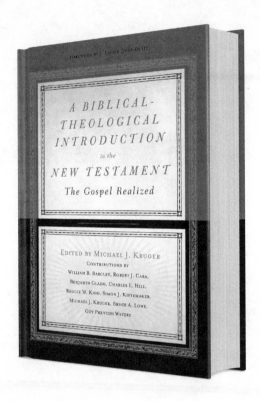

With an emphasis on the theology, key themes, and overall message of each book, this collaborative effort of nine biblical scholars will equip you to study and teach the New Testament with clarity and insight.

CONTRIBUTIONS BY:

- William B. Barcley
- Robert J. Cara
- Benjamin Gladd
- Charles E. Hill
- Reggie M. Kidd
- Simon J. Kistemaker
- Michael J. Kruger
- Bruce A. Lowe
- Guy Prentiss Waters

Available now